LOVE LETTERS FROM A WIDOWER

THE MYSTERY OF SOUL MATES IN LIGHT OF ANCIENT WISDOM

XAVIER PEREZ-PONS

Love Letters from a Widower

The mystery of soul mates
in light of ancient wisdom

Xavier Perez-Pons

bubok
EDITORIAL

Translation: João Duarte Silva

ISBN paperback: 9788468521510

Edited by Bubok Publishing S.L.

INDEX

ANNOUNCEMENT AND DISCLAIMER

On a spring afternoon in the year two thousand, I happened to wander into a bookshop in the old *Barri Gòtic* in Barcelona.

The owner was busy taking books from two large wooden boxes. I was curious, so I asked him if I could have a look. The books were in Catalan, Spanish, French, and English, some of them illustrated, most of them filled with underlinings and pencil notes on the margin; there were also a couple in Portuguese and some other in Italian. They were of all sorts of literary genres, although I could spot a common subject. I asked the owner where he had gotten these boxes. They had belonged to a man that had recently died; that is all he knew. He had bought them at an auction, along with other private libraries and lots from all over the place. I asked him to give me a price, and I took the whole lot home.

Actually, that is not true. There was more to the lot than those two boxes. There was a third one. A third box, which the owner let me have for free since it came from the same place as the other two. These books, though, did not seem to have any connection with the other ones. These were immaculate, bound in blue shades of Moroccan leather, without a single note written on the margins, and they were mostly novels of different genres. So, I declined the offer, which later I regretted, for reasons that soon I will make clear. When

I tried to go back for them, however, it was too late: the blue books were in the hands of an interior decorator. It pains me to picture them turned into an *atrezzo*, into furniture accessories.

For several weeks, I left the books in their boxes, forgotten in a room, as my job prevented me from going through them. When I finally found the time to exhume them, I found, scattered among several volumes, a manuscript in the form of correspondence: ten long letters, written in tight, minuscule handwriting on double-sided paper (the same handwriting responsible for the notes in the book margins). The last of these letters dated from just three months before my casual visit to the old man's bookshop, so the author must have written it right before he passed away. (He'd still have time, however, for a mysterious trip abroad. But we'll talk more about that later on.) Regarding his identity, my inquiries proved fruitless (the signature at the end of each letter was unreadable). The only biographical information we have, then, is what the author tells us throughout the manuscript: not much beyond his marital status as a widower, and his wife's, who is the recipient and *leitmotif* of the letters, first name: Blanca. The letters' private nature, how personal they were, had kept me from publishing them. Then I noticed a detail in the manuscript to which I had not given much thought: the crossed-out notes on the margins, which were evidently made at some later time, as they didn't come from the same fountain pen but from a thick marker. These cross-outs, which first appear on the second letter, were made in a hurry, as if its terminally ill author, guessing the future of his manuscript, had felt the need to cross out the notes he had made while writing the letters. In any case, the rushed approach to the blackouts allowed me to glean fragments of paragraphs and loose words from every note, which I thought appropriate to include in here, inserting them at approximately the same point they appear in the manuscript.

I have to say in advance that, from the tenor of three enigmatic allusions in the letters, it seems that all the notes have some connection with the aforementioned blue books. It also suggests something shocking, which I do not even dare to judge; I will let the reader do that. It implies that, through the blue books, the author believes he is receiving messages from his late wife. Not posthumous messages, but actual communications, as if she were still alive. In those books, that he frequently read, he finds – or believes he finds – luminous signs, faint phosphorescences that stand out to him and highlight a paragraph or a sentence, to which he confers a personal meaning and attributes to his dead wife. We can assume these messages usually come to him during a break in his writing (which appears to have been a nocturnal activity), and that he jots them down on the margins, maybe with the intention of coming back to them later.

Anyway, I have gone on for too long about this minor subject of the crossed-out notes. The thing is, instead of doing what he did, instead of taking the time to censure the annotations haphazardly, he could have thrown the whole manuscript away. He did not, though, and that convinces me he would not oppose its posthumous publication. Perhaps, and this is my primary motivation for publishing them, he thought these letters would offer a glimmer of hope to people in a similar situation as his. Maybe even spare some reader the same tortuous search for answers he undertook. Be it as it may, it is my duty to warn you that the content of these letters is as controversial as its circumstances. The author does not stop at scouring through ancient wisdom for the concept of twin souls: he uses it as a basis to draft – with a more or less steady hand, depending on which part – a metaphysical structure. Such structure, naturally (or other people would have already figured it out), though it finds support in the opinions of ancient sages (though not all of them), was not framed by them as such. Therefore, it is inappropriate to credit them as the author does.

That said, I have to add that nothing is invented. Moreover, while the author does generalise, he makes it work, connecting everything in his way and putting forward his own conclusions. With this, he draws a personal synthesis of ancient wisdom. It would be understandable for us to label this synthesis – along with the supernatural phenomenology I just mentioned – as something belonging to the fantasy genre. We should not, then, place too much faith on the results of his painstaking investigation work being the elusive Truth so eagerly sought by wise men across time and space. We could imagine the author – in one of those metaphorical exercises he seemed to enjoy – diving into the sea of ancient knowledge, resurfacing with a fist full of pearls, and then proceeding to thread them on the silk string of ancient belief in twin souls. The ancient sages are responsible for the beads, but the necklace is the author's work.

The pearls are, nonetheless, genuine. If we take for example what, from the modern perspective, appears to be the most unacceptable item in his structure: the devaluation of sensual love, which is, to a large extent, one of the pearls he salvages from ancient wisdom; all he does is thread it into the necklace, next to the other pearls. Beyond his excessive tendency to generalise, though, he also tends to oversimplify, perhaps with the intention of making more accessible, both to himself and to his wife, those "pearls", those old notions that, given the opportunity, he will not hesitate in clarifying as it suits him. All this leads to a subjective interpretation of the old wisdom: an analysis by a man in love.

In his defence, however, we can quote one of the books he handled (*The Burnt Book*, by Marc–Alain Ouaknin; an essay on the *Talmud*, the central text of Judaism). It goes like this: "Is it really necessary to go into a debate on interpretation? Did the authors referred to really have the intentions we ascribe to them? Who can tell? The only criterion for judging an interpretation is its richness, its fruitfulness. Anything that gives matter of thought honours the person who proffers it." This quote conveys what appears to be one of the main ideas in the *Talmud*, a book with origins in oral tradition; the idea that the old wisdom is not something settled, static; it is not a snapshot of the past, like a still life, but something alive and ever evolving. Old wisdom grows and blooms with each new interpretation, including –why not?– the one proposed by the author of these letters.

Besides, we never know, the world is so beautiful and mysterious that it could very well have hidden its structure from the wisest of sages, only to reveal it to a dilatant. In any case, if you are solely interested in ancient accounts of twin souls, the first two letters will be enough to satisfy your curiosity. However, if you are tempted to dive deep into the metaphysics of love, then do not be intimidated by the length of the text and do not give up reading until the very end – where a surprise awaits you.

Finally, I numbered the letters, gave them titles and divided them into sections for their publication. I also attached bibliographic references corresponding to the abounding quotes, all of them taken from the books now in my possession, from which I also took ten illustrations, and ten epigraphs to head them. I felt I should split the collection into two large sections, so that is what I did. Lastly, I titled it.

Xavier Pérez i Pons
Puigcerdá, July 1st, 2011

FIRST PART:

SPIRITUAL KINSHIP

For love is as strong as death

Song of Solomon

FIRST LETTER

TWIN SOULS

(OR LOVE PREDESTINATION)

Very well, this world, with the whole
Of its symbols, is the outskirts of the
Otherworld and what it contains. That
Otherworld is the Spirit and the Life.
Who in this world acts only for this
World, without knowing the Otherworld,
Acts in ignorance.

Book of the wise man and his disciple
Ja'far bin Mansur al–Yaman,
Ismailist poet and theologian of the tenth century

Barcelona, May 22nd, 1999

Dear Blanca,

Today we would celebrate... Correction; today we celebrate fifty years of marriage. Our golden anniversary. To celebrate it, I took my pen (your pen, the one you gave me) and started writing to you. First, I want to apologise for not having done this before. Or, to be fair, for not being able to continue beyond the first line, because the fact is I tried, countless times, without success. It wasn't because I didn't have anything to say to you. It just so happens that sorrow is a great obstacle for words; it stops them from flowing out of your mouth or pen. Even the more pressing ones. One's life could be in grave danger, and it would still be a superhuman effort just to ask for help. This could easily sound like an excuse, but believe me: it's not an excuse, it's a good reason. Anyway, since this time I was able to go beyond the cursed threshold of the first line, you can deduce that I have found some consolation to my sorrow. And it's precisely about that, my love, about the foundations of this consolation, that I want to talk to you.

Since it could not have been in any other way (no other argument would have worked), this comfort of mine is based on the hope that you and I will be together again. I know, it sounds bizarre. After all, you are dead. Nevertheless, please allow me to explain myself. The good thing about this is that it's not an elusive dream, a mere exercise in voluntarism – like when you, in some summer nights in Palamós, would wish upon falling stars. Of course, there is no conclusive proof that we will be together again; at least I have not found it. However, I have found some things... hints that open the door for hope. I can see you smiling ironically at my detective talk. Laugh all you want, but the truth is that in last few years I have become a sort of modest emulator of Hercules Poirot, just to name your favourite detective. Except the mystery that I'm investigating has nothing in common with the kind of cases to which the famous sleuth applied his cunning. My research, conducted in the realm of ancient knowledge, takes a more intangible and elusive scope. The field of transcendence, of the hidden reality.

You know, while you were alive, I – unlike you – was never particularly interested in these kinds of mysteries. (See? You had to die so that nothing else would interest me as much.) As with most of my contemporaries, the word *mystery* would immediately take me back to crime novels and thriller films.

That is trivializing the word, though. Etymologically speaking, *mystery* means "hidden thing"; it applies to *Cat Among The Pigeons* and to *The Woman In White* (to name two mystery novels from the blue book collection) because in them things also tend to have a hidden dimension, a secret skein from which the protagonist pulls the thread. The word *mystery*, however, was coined in Ancient Greece to refer not to the crime novel dimension beyond things, but (like that other word: *mystic*, to which is related) to a sacred dimension; a subtle, hidden reality lying beneath the harsh visible reality.

I say *reality*, Blanca, because this mystery is not like the ones in crime novels or thrillers: it's not, as many people might think (as I would have thought, a few years ago), fiction. It's a reality that, though intangible, is present and decisive in our everyday lives.

Unfortunately, these days most of us have lost this perception. Today, the world is only mysterious in the eyes of children (the awe, the sense of wonder with which children discover the world!). To understand the mystery, I mean the real dimension of things, one has to look beyond its surface. Years ago, I might have claimed that scientists do look beyond the surface, that science examines reality to the core. Now I have changed my opinion. Now I say that even those investigating the DNA molecule and genes, the brain and sub-atomic particles are not looking beyond the epidermis of reality; all they are doing is examining that epidermis to its core. Because an atom or a gene, Blanca, is not any less material than the physical body to which it belongs or which it defines. And Matter – the physical world – is, for the ancient sages, the crust of things, the epidermis of what is real.

To look beyond the surface, then, means to look beyond Matter. And how does one look beyond Matter? The secret, the ancient sages tell us, is in silencing the mind. Our mind is seething with noise; it's filled with ideas, plans, fears, prejudices; it oozes with worries, hopes, and dreams. All that needs to be silenced. Only when all mental activity stops, are we in a position to perceive the "other side", the spiritual side of reality, its mystery... Look, you are a big art lover. We used to attend exhibitions together. I remember that time we visited a tapestry studio. We could see then that the reverse side of a tapestry is highly complex; not just a replica of the front: it's where all the loose ends lead you. In a tapestry, we have the mystery of the "reverse side", which a painting lacks. There are no secrets behind a painting; everything is right there in front of our eyes. That is how, Blanca – like if it's a painting – that we, in modern days, tend to look at the Universe. The ancient sages saw it more like a tapestry – except that, unlike what happens with tapestries, the "reverse side" of the Universe is infinitely more valuable than the "front". They *knew* that underneath the surface of the Universe – that is, beyond the physical world – lie wonders and hidden treasures of incalculable value...

THE SECOND SIGHT

To the ancient sages, Blanca, the Universe is mysterious. Existence, in general, is mysterious, and so is its every aspect. Including that fundamental aspect of human existence, the "reverse side" of which we are going to investigate in this letter and the ones following it – the subject is too complex, and one letter will not be enough. I am talking, of course, about erotic love. The love between man and woman (though, of course, this kind of love can also happen between two people of the same gender). With a detective–like spirit, we will delve into erotic love. Although we will not do so like biologists and neurologists, who like watchmakers trying to understand the inner workings of a watch, would disassemble it and study its parts. Don't worry; I will not talk to you about hormones, cerebral areas and processes, or about dopamine releases or other such things that are the latest fashion in scientific discoveries. The point of view we will adopt is that of the old sage, who, to better understand the watch, undertakes a reflection on Time.

Existence is mysterious, I was saying, and so is every aspect of existence. Each particular life, Blanca, is mysterious. Everything holds a mystery for the ancient sages. Hence them not being satisfied with disassembling the watch, with scrutinising the surface of things. They were curious about what was on the other side, on the hidden side of the tapestry, and consequently, they strove to look behind it. This action – which you can take even with your eyes closed – of looking beyond appearances, has a name, my dear: it's called "to intuit". Intuitions sprout from the unconscious, and recent studies have shown that on that level you can find cognitive processes on a much larger scale than on the conscious level. Our ancestors knew this, Blanca, and that is why intuition, mystical intuition, is the quintessential ancient organ of perception. The ancient sages depended on it to unravel the world; that is to say, to analyse the other world. Let me clarify that when I talk about ancient sages, I am thinking in particular about those old wise people that today we would categorise under labels such as *esoterica*, or *occultism*, which is actually the field of knowledge, and this includes the area behind the religions of the Book – Judaism, Christianity, and Islamism –, on which we'll focus here. It will be mainly the authority of these ancient sages (always outlawed by the pontifical representatives of orthodoxy), to which we will take heed of in these letters. And, by the way, I should tell you that almost every ancient sage passing through these pages (except for some contemplative mystics) will be male. But don't complain: is it my fault that the history of philosophy and religion – on both their sides, the front and the reverse, the exoteric and the esoteric – feature so few women? This fact, though, is misleading; there is no doubt that women contributed decisively to ancient wisdom, even if men received all the credit. There is a reason why women are considered to have much more developed intuitive capabilities.

Anyway, Blanca, these days neither men nor women use this tool, this mystic intuition. We prefer reason and empiric experimentation. Essential tools, no doubt, but why must we cast aside like an old trinket a tool – the one ancient sages symbolised with the so-called "third eye", "inner eye", or "eye of fire" – which allows us to see the essence, the spiritual dimension of things? Why limit ourselves to the tip of the iceberg when reality is unfathomably deeper? The problem, as I was telling you, Blanca, is that, in general, the modern man no longer believes in the occult dimension. We are much more inclined to see the world as a painting instead of as a tapestry. Which does not mean – since almost every rule has its exception – that no modern sages has approached existence with their "back eyes". With their *second sight*, to use the term coined by one of them, one of the most remarkable modern sages: Carl Gustav Young[1]. And, if you allow me, I will quote the French philosopher Henri Bergson, who brought back to modern philosophy this ancient idea of re-

1. C.G. Jung, *Memories, Dreams, Reflections*, p. 62

ality as something too dense to be perceived by intelligence. Intelligence, said Bergson, shows us the exterior of things; intuition shows us the interior; how things really are on the inside. Modern sages with an "an ancient perspective" will count among our sages.

There is no doubt, my dear, that mystic intuition is an organ of perception of extreme efficiency. This inner vision, however, captures the other world – the "reverse side" of the world – *in fragments*. That being the case, there are occasions on which two mystic intuitions say contradictory things. We tend to assume, then, that one of them is wrong. That is not necessarily the case, though. Take, as one of the most striking examples of that disparity, the religious beliefs in the West and the East. It's true that there are considerable differences between them. However, that does not mean that they are mutually exclusive; what happens is that each of them focuses on a *different aspect* of transcendence. I remind you of that famous Indian parable about the blind men and the elephant: A group of blind people approaches an elephant from different sides. They had never heard of such an animal, so they try to conceptualise it by touching it. Since they are all touching different sides of the elephant, their versions differ. The one examining the trunk ("it's long and flexible, like a snake") has nothing in common with the one studying one of the legs ("it's like a pillar"), or with the one touching the belly or the tail of the animal. None of them is wrong, though. They all hold a *part* of a truth that has many sides.

Intuition, then, captures the "reverse side" of the world in fragments. But it does so, Blanca, in *broad outlines*; meaning it lacks detail. It perceives everything as if it were all shrouded in a grey mist, like the one obscuring the scenery on your hometown. I don't know if there is an etymological reason, or if it's just a happy coincidence, but in the English word *mist* is the Greek root of the words *mystery* and *mystic*: *mys*, which means "hidden". Within the mist, things appear blurred; they are, for all purposes, "hidden things", things enveloped in uncertainty. They are, therefore, open to interpretations, allowing for different readings. Since we were talking in zoological metaphors, Blanca, suppose you see an animal in the mist. You can distinguish its proportions; almost two meters wide, one and a half meters tall; it has four long and bony legs, and at the top of a strong, large neck, a thin snout-shaped head. With this basic information, would it not still be difficult to tell me what animal you are seeing? We can have at least three different interpretations. Anyway, it's something along those lines that happens with the descriptions of the Afterlife offered by the ancient sages. There are several pretty much unanimous perceptions, but the details vary from sage to sage. Almost all of them see, say, a four-legged animal, tall, large, with a snout. Except some of them believe they are looking at a horse, while others a zebra, and others yet a donkey...

One practically unanimous perception of the ancient sages concerns what lies behind the human being. If everything in this world, my dear, is much more than meets the eye, then the same must apply to us humans. If we are to believe the ancient sages, then you were right and I was wrong; we are not rational animals, we have a reverse side; and it's immaterial, spiritual, and, therefore, immortal and eternal. Ancient sages called this reverse side of the human being its *soul*. To say, though, that we have a "reverse side", "we have a soul", is not accurate: we *are* a soul. This is because the "reverse side", Blanca, is the *essence* of things, what things really *are*. We have a body, age, a name, intelligence, a temper, some skills or talents, even a personality. We *have* all that; the soul, in contrast, is what we *are*. Mystic intuition is specifically an ability of the soul: the "third eye" is the eye of the spirit (the "eye of the heart" like some ancient sages called it, because the heart – remember this every time I mention it – was seen as the headquarters of the soul and, therefore, its embodiment).

Being the existence of the soul the foundation of the theory we will be unfolding in these letters, it would be important to give some consistency to that premise. I will not bring up the rational demonstrations by the philosophers, but an empiric fact documented by the medical community, which, if I am not wrong Blanca, you were well aware of in life: I am talking about what they call Near Death Experiences. Modern CPR techniques have made it possible to bring someone who was clinically dead "back to life". And many of these people return with something to tell us about their experience. Since the 70's, when Dr Raymond Moody dedicated himself to collecting some of these accounts, all around the world there have been more doctors and scientists interested in listening to them. These stories deserve the attention, Blanca, because they all seem to follow the same pattern. A pattern that tears down the main objection science imposes on the idea of the soul. This common template (of which there are plenty ancient accounts, like the famous painting by Hieronymous Bosch, *Ascent of The Blessed*), talks about a journey through a tunnel with a white light at the end, where a glorious, shining figure awaits the traveller, radiating an absolute love. The thing is, my dear, this traveller travels without the equipment science considers indispensable for travelling: without a physical support, without being biologically alive. This astral traveller defies the scientific dogma that says consciousness, the *self*, does not survive death. And is in itself, I think, a very consistent evidence supporting the existence of the soul.

I mentioned the figure in white light on the other side of the tunnel of death. The astral traveller identifies this warm, loving character who welcomes him from the Afterlife as God. This indirectly grants a certain credibility to another idea – the idea of God. An idea strictly associated with the concept of the soul, and which will be equally fundamental in our letters, my love... There are many arguments in favour of the existence of God, I am sure you know them better than I do –, but I think one of the most convincing ones is also one of the simplest. It's the argument put forward by theologians according to which Man has felt, since the beginning, bound to a being that transcends him, and that this feeling, by itself, is proof of the existence of God. If in the dark, we call for a light that we know should be there, is that not a sign that one day we saw it with our own eyes? If we are thirsty, it's because water exists; you cannot crave something that does not exist... Thus, the existence of God is another unanimous perception of the ancient sages. Another one is that the soul – the soul that, in essence, each human being is – is, so to speak, "lame"; it's imperfect, it's incomplete. It's actually half a soul, instead of a whole one. And it's here, my dear, where the mist starts blurring the edges, and where the unanimity among the ancient sages gives way to controversy. It arises when they try to figure out what happened to this "missing" half, and how, then, we can restore it back to the original shape of the human soul. We can classify the different opinions into two main groups. On one side, we have the sages who claim the missing half of the soul is not external to itself, meaning it's not missing but inhibited: the case would be, then, about making it blossom, awakening it. We will call this interpretation "psychological hypothesis". Then we have those who believe the missing half really is absent from the soul, and that we have to search for it outside. This second group also splits into two separate opinions: one says the missing half is God (or can be found in God and therefore is an angelic, transcendent doppelgänger of each human being: the "angelic hypothesis", we'll call it); and the other who believes the lost half of the soul is nothing but a similar human soul, or rather, a *soul mate*.

Of these three possible interpretations, four if we are counting the angelic hypothesis, all of them equally indemonstrable, I choose the last one, Blanca. And I do it for a personal reason, though that is as valid as any other (maybe even more if we think, like the philosopher Kierkegaard, that "the conclusions of passion are the only trustworthy ones"). I need to believe in it, because it's what offers me the strongest grip on hope: the hope that you and I will one day be together again... Maybe the ancient sages who favoured this hypothesis did so for the same reason I do: maybe they were widowers or aware that one day either they or their wives would become widowers and be forced to part ways. Whichever the case, it was them –the ancient sages who supported this interpretation– the ones who preferred to look behind this fundamental aspect of human existence: erotic love. It's what they saw there, Blanca, what we, without further ado, will look into next.

A SECRET BEAUTY

Think about how we met. It was by chance that on that day you had a job interview and that, because it was raining, I had to take the tram instead of walking as I usually did; had it happened any other way, and we would not have met. Without thinking, I used the word "chance". But have you ever asked yourself if chance really had anything to do with it? If it was just a coincidence? Yes, one cannot deny that, in appearance, our meeting was purely incidental. Yet the ancient sages did not trust appearances; they found them deceptive. They believed the avatars of chance did not explain every encounter. Or, in other words, that in many cases chance "didn't know what it was doing". Chance was only apparent: what they called *Fate*, which would be some kind of supernatural force, or invisible hand pulling the strings of luck. (It's impossible to think of the notion of "necessary chance" or "chance as Fate" without imagining an infinite Intelligence behind it, capable of pulling those countless strings.)

If we had told the story of our first encounter to an ancient sage, he would have absolved chance of any responsibility. "Chance had nothing to do it with it – he would have said – it was Fate. You were predestined to meet." A poet would say something like that but in verse. I forgot to tell you that intuition is also essential to the poets (and that is why we will count them among the ancient sages): it's through intuition that they capture the poetry of life; its *mystery*...The nineteenth century English poet Coventry Patmore must have been inspired by an encounter like ours to write these verses:

> He meets, by heavenly chance express,
> The destined maid; some hidden hand
> Unveils to him that loveliness
> Which others cannot understand.[2]

2. Conventry Patmore, *The Angel In The House*, The Poems, p.77

"By heavenly chance express", Blanca. Meaning that encounter, while coincidental in appearance, was actually arranged. Heaven scheduled an appointment, so to say, and put them both in that place at that exact time so they could meet. You know, the last two verses also make me think about your beauty. Because before and after that afternoon – the one we met –, I had seen women who were more beautiful than you. Yet, it's strange; none of them looked so to me. Those two verses – "Unveils to him that loveliness / Which others cannot understand" – suggest an idea that I posit as the starting point to these letters: the idea that beyond objective beauty exists a subjective hidden beauty; a mysterious beauty that reveals itself only to its predestined eyes. (One must not confuse this subjective beauty with the set of spiritual qualities a person might possess, qualities we call "inner beauty": while inner beauty, my dear, is certainly superior to outer beauty, it's just as objective.) Moreover, unlike what happens with objective beauty, everyone possesses this other "encrypted" beauty, which is – regarding the twin souls theory – true beauty.

In other words, Blanca, we are all beautiful to the right set of eyes. Your beauty, your secret beauty, was for my eyes only because only I – my second sight, my intuitive eyes – had the key to untangle it. The key is the predestination of love.

The belief in the predestination of love had many supporters in ancient times. It explained a phenomenon that is otherwise quite difficult to explain. A phenomenon we could articulate in the following manner: "There are secret links of affection, that no reason can be rendered of."[3] This

3. Thomas Gataker, *A Good Wife God's Gift*, quoted by Laurence Lerner in *Love and Marriage*, p. 121

quote comes from an essay on matrimony written by a representative of seventeenth century Protestant Puritanism, the Englishman Thomas Gataker. Six hundred years before, a distinguished Andalusian poet and philosopher called Ibn Hazm of Cordoba, had expressed the same thing with these words: "If the cause of Love were physical beauty, the consequence would be that nobody defective in any shape or form would attract admiration; yet we know of many a man actually preferring the inferior article, though well aware that another is superior, and quite unable to turn his heart away from it. Again, if Love were due to a harmony of characters, no man would love a person who was not of like purpose and in concord with him. We, therefore, conclude that Love is something within the soul itself."[4] You might find that last sentence enigmatic now, but later you will understand what Ibn Hazm meant by it... We will wrap up the testimonies with a passage from an ancient sage I am sure you know. The sixteenth century Swiss doctor and alchemist, Paracelsus, who wrote: "when two beings search for each other and, without apparent explanation, unite in burning love, one must think their affection is neither born in, or a resident of the body, but that it comes from the spirit of both bodies, united by mutual links and superior affinities... To these, we call twin souls."

These three passages, my dear, express a common realisation among the ancient sages: the fact that love, when real, does not obey objectively measurable criteria. You and I can think of some examples – I believe anyone could – that illustrate this postulate. I have this memory of a family reunion at aunt Magda's place, where there was a heated discussion

---

4. *Ibn Hazm, The Ring of the Dove*, translation by A.J. Arberry

about cousin Inés' engagement with Marcel, her current husband. No one understood why she was with him. They did not understand how she could favour him instead of another suitor who was, in their opinion, far more handsome and charming, not to mention more successful. Only you defended Marcel. I cannot remember your argument. Gataker's, Ibn Hazm's and Paracelsus' argument, though, would have been this:

Love, true love, often looks incomprehensible to its witnesses. I am confident aunt Magda and the others would understand what Inés saw in Marcel if they could have seen it *with their own eyes*. Except their eyes were the eyes of a witness, and those are *objective* eyes, Blanca, eyes that know nothing about secret beauty. The protagonist of love, in contrast –the true lover–, sees their beloved with the "subjective" second sight. The witness to love judges the loved one based on measurable criteria; by the standards of objective beauty. The true lover does so by these other mysterious standards – those of subjective beauty. A beauty that –invisible to the impersonal eyes of objectivity– only they are capable of deciphering... The standards of objective beauty are revealed then to be ineffectual when it comes to account for love; to explain why the true lover loves. The more perceptive witnesses will, therefore, conclude that love operates under its own beauty standards, its own eminently subjective criteria; while everyone else will assume there are no rules whatsoever in love, and so will reach the conclusion that love is blind. Only when they fall on its web, will they be ready to see the truth; to understand that, from the moment they were incapable of seeing the personal, nontransferable beauty beyond objective beauty, the blind ones were them.

THE ORIGIN THAT IS ALSO THE DESTINATION

This subjective beauty, the one that really matters, Blanca, is encrypted, waiting for someone to decipher it. But who? The only holder of the key: the twin soul, the predestined partner... What does the notion of predestination of love we are addressing here says? It says that each individual is, at an ontological level, essentially connected to another by bonds of love. In other words, that every person is tailor-made to fit one other person, which they are destined to love. This idea is ingrained in countless romantic clichés. Like that old commonplace: "we're made for each other." Or those mundane lines – too tacky for my taste – from romance novels or romantic comedies: "I didn't know I was looking for you until I found you," "It's like we knew each other our whole lives"... Those banalities only assume their full significance when the ancient sages say it. Couples repeat it barely thinking about their meaning. But they have one, Blanca; it reflects an idea so widespread that it could not have been a mere invention, but a personal experience – obscure, but no less intense – common to everyone.

I remember once, a long time after we met, asking you what it was you saw in me that afternoon to accept my bold invitation to meet up the next day. "I saw the perfect excuse", you said laughing. Our first date coincided with your aunt Magda's monthly visit, so you thought if you went out with me, you could skip it. Not only you ended up not skipping it, though, but you also dragged me along to her place too. But besides an excuse, you saw something else in me, because you immediately added that you found me kind and trustworthy. "Like a feeling of familiarity", you said. And to tell you the truth, I was surprised to hear that, because I felt the same thing. The thing is, Blanca, we were both circling another big romance novel tacky cliché: the one where certain amorous encounters have the sweet aftertaste of a "homecoming". Of course, this idea of home not as a place but as another person that somehow completes us comes from antiquity. Did you know that aphorisms such as "*A man's home is his wife*"5, are plentiful in the *Talmud*, a central text of Judaism? The theme of "homecoming" attempts to reflect that ineffable feeling of *deja vu* we experience before our predestined partner: a feeling linked to the revelation of their subjective beauty. The mysterious synchronicity, the "chemistry", as we would say now, or –more in line with the tone of these letters– the "alchemy" that sometimes forms between a man and a woman hitherto unknown to each other, is, according to the ancient sages, due to mutual recognition. It's not a very distinct phenomenon from the one raised by those olfactory and gustatory perceptions to which you were so susceptible, Blanca: those feelings connected to smell or taste –like Proust's madeleine– that suddenly emerge from childhood, awakening faded memories.

Recognition may be immediate; love at first sight... Speaking of which, not long ago I witnessed quite a spectacular example; a textbook case of love at first sight, we could say. Writing it here will provide me with the opportunity I was seeking to tell you about an extraordinary trip, of which my legs have not yet recovered: the pilgrimage on the Road to Santiago. When we were young, you and I often planned to go on this trip together, but there was always a setback or another preventing us from going. Well, a few months ago

---

5. Yoma 1,1

I decided to go by myself. In spirit, though, it was as if you had been there with me, you know? Because when you spend a whole morning alone, walking through wheat fields and sunflowers under the enormous dome of the sky, or struggling to climb a hill carrying a heavy rucksack on your back, it's normal to find yourself talking to yourself; which in my case, is the same as talking to you. It was that continuous exercise in introspection, I suspect, that paved the way to these letters... As I was saying, I witnessed a case of love at first sight. Yes, because in the month and a few days it took me to go to Santiago de Compostela and back, I was not always by myself. Occasionally, for a stretch of the way, one or more pilgrims would accompany me. At one point, I had to slow down to hike along a young man who walked with a limp. His name was Alfons. He was a brooding man of few words, yet, when I asked him, he told me he came from Valencia, from where his pilgrimage started, and had set off on the Road because he had "heard the call". I assumed he meant the call of Christ. I thought he was considering becoming a monk or a priest and, though he did not confirm or deny it, I don't think I was very far off, judging by his displays of piety each time we entered one of the many churches on the way (ah, Blanca, the Romanic architecture along the Road, wonderful!). However, his call ended up being another. We were crossing Astorga, and we had just gotten supplies for the next stage. It was early in the morning, and the first rays of light echoed in the crystal clean air. To tell you the truth, I had not even noticed her: just a girl, like so many others with whom we had crossed paths in towns all over the Road. But Alfons adjusted his pace, and so did she. They greeted each other and talked for a few minutes. I kept my distance, waiting for him to introduce me, as I thought they knew each other from way back: that is the impression they gave. But then, to my surprise, I heard them exchanging names... Well, that was the end of the trip for Alfons; we agreed to meet on my return from Santiago. That is when he introduced her to me: "I'd like you to meet my girlfriend...", he said.

You see, my dear, next to that one, our love at first sight moment pales. And paler it will seem next to the cases I want to remind you of now, as those are the flagship instances of love at first sight in Western literature, consigned by two of its greatest poets. I am talking, of course, about Dante, smitten by the sight of Beatrice, and Romeo by that of Juliet. The former one is a true story. Dante Alighieri was only nine years old – same age as her – when he saw Beatrice. It was the year 1274. Dante tells it in his *New Life*: At that moment I say truly that the vital spirit, that which lives in the most secret chamber of the heart began to tremble so violently that I felt it fiercely in the least pulsation, and, trembling, it uttered these words: Behold a god more powerful than I (meaning Love), who, coming, will rule over me.' At that moment the animal spirit, that which lives in the high chamber (the brain) to which all the spirits of the senses carry their perceptions, began to wonder deeply at it, and, speaking especially to the spirit of sight, spoke these words: Now your blessedness appears."[6]

It's almost, my love, as if Dante had been struck by a revelation: the revelation of Beatrice's blessedness. Given that her blessedness was mainly recognised by the spirit of sight, I assume that one could easily replace that word by the word *beauty*. It would then read "Now your beauty appears". The apparition of Beatrice's beauty overwhelms Dante, and

6. Dante, *Vita Nuova*, II

nothing stops us from thinking, Blanca, that this beauty is the subjective beauty; that the eyes to which the poet alludes are the spirit's eyes of fire. And that, further along in the same book (and again in the *Divine Comedy*, where Beatrice turns into the poet's guide on his journeys through celestial regions) when Dante exalts Beatrice's beauty, he is maybe referencing, besides her objective beauty, that other beauty visible only to his eyes, to the eyes of Dante's soul.

Then we have the famous example out of *Romeo and Juliet*, a book that, along with other bilingual Shakespeare editions, takes a proud place in your library. Now that I mention your library ("the blue library", we used to call it, because you bound all your books in shades of blue), allow me to make a small confession within the larger confession that forms these letters: you know, one of the things I miss the most about us living together (there are many things I miss, but this one especially) is reading with you. Those evenings when, after dinner, we would sit down, facing each other at the same table from where I am writing to you. The balcony doors wide open in the summer, as they are now, and closed in the winter, though always with open shutters and pulled curtains, so that the filtered glare of the street lamps created the dreamlike atmosphere so conducive to our reading sessions... I close my eyes, and it's as if I can see you again. Yes, there you are, adjusting your reading glasses in your poised allure, unlocking the old glass-paned cabinet doors, taking, from the one hundred and fifty-seven blue volumes, the one we had put on hold the night before, and sitting across from me, opening it by the bookmark, asking: "Are you ready?". I say yes, and you begin reading aloud, while I listen to you or, sometimes, just watch you, or I focus on the sound of your voice, the graceful shifts in inflection you breathed into the dialogue as the characters changed...

That is how I like to remember you, Blanca, sitting at this table reading aloud for both of us. Also at your little studio down the corridor, using scraps of cloth and watercolours, seashells, newspaper clippings, and old music scores to compose small collages on starry backgrounds, which your friend Irene would then sell. I also like to remember you sleeping by my side, with an angelic expression on your face, while I tried to guess what you were dreaming, and how I could surreptitiously insert myself into it... I will stop now because, without realising it, I am beginning to slide down the path of sentimentality and (no matter how much you reproached me for it, and saw it as a manifestation of self-loathing) you know I cannot stand that. Besides, we have had enough rambling. Let me just add that I was very happy with you, happy twice over: because you made me happy, but also because I could tell I made you happy, which for me was the greatest joy. And we're done: period. Let's proceed with the example above.

Young Romeo is recovering from a broken heart; his friends drag him to a party – he does not want to go, he is swamped in grief. There, he meets a girl, and, like Dante, he is struck by a revelation: Juliet's beauty.

> ¡Oh, she doth teach the torches to burn bright!
> It seems she hangs upon the cheek of night
> Like a rich jewel in an Ethiope's ear,
> Beauty too rich for use, for earth too dear.
> So shows a snowy dove trooping with crows
> As yonder lady o'er her fellows shows.
> The measure done, I'll watch her place of stand,

And, touching hers, make blessèd my rude hand.
Did my heart love till now? Forswear it, sight!
For I ne'er saw true beauty till this night.[7]

Indeed, Blanca, Romeo had met, before that night, other beauties like the one for which he yearned. However, those were objective beauties. Standing before Juliet, he faces for the first time that other mysterious beauty that is for his eyes only. All others were, in a way, false; Juliet's is the true beauty: "For I ne'er saw true beauty till this night." Consequently, the love he felt for those other women was somehow false as well: "Did my heart love till now? Forswear it, sight!". We could say those other loves were similar to mirages. Like how, generations later, the romantic poets would say, "you only love once"[8], "love is an infinite repetition" ("you are an eternity to me: love is an infinite repetition"[9], Novalis would write). The beauty Romeo's eyes - not his physical eyes: his second sight - perceive in Juliet, signals his recognition of his predestined partner, his twin soul. In the case of Romeo, Blanca, as in Dante's, this recognition is immediate. There is room for another possibility, though: that this recognition may emerge little by little, throughout the course of an entire life. Whatever the case, being immediate or gradual, one who experiences this feeling, rarely identifies it. When it happens, recognition is usually intangible, as if in the dark ("the person doesn't see it, but his star does", I read it embellished in the Talmud). It happens under the threshold of consciousness. One is only touched by the powerful attrac-

7. Romeo and Juliet, I, V
8. Friedrich Schlegel, *Literary Notebooks*, 1297
9. Novalis, *Friedrich von Hardenberg*

tion exercised by the other person and, maybe, by a vague feeling of familiarity too, as in our case. The ancient sages teach us to see, beyond that attraction and familiarity –thus explaining them–, recognition.

They would say that on that afternoon on the tram, you and I recognised each other... Yes, I know: recognition implies a previous acquaintance, and we had never seen each other before. However, we had never seen each other *in this life*. And what is a life, my love? A life, for the ancient sages, is no more than an instant, a link on a long chain... And with this, we arrive at the idea of reincarnation, a belief that is widespread in the East, as it used to be in the West, and as it has always been among the ancient sages. According to them, a person's "before" goes back very far in Time. It spills over the narrow boundaries of a lifetime and extends back through a multitude of reincarnated shapes until it reaches a point beyond Time. This point beyond Time, Blanca, is the true home of the soul. Following the ancient sages' footsteps, we will call it *The Origin*. But we will leave this mysterious starting point (which doubles –and this is what's most important to us– as a finishing line, a destination) for later. Now I want to cite other examples of instant recognition, of which we can find so many in Literature.

THE THUNDERBOLT

Out of all the examples I know, the loveliest one, in my opinion, was imagined by the English writer D.H. Lawrence in the dawn of this century of ours. Lawrence created the character of Tom Brangwen to head the three generations that are the focal point of his novel-saga *The Rainbow*. He then had to find a wife for him. He chose Lydia, a Polish immigrant before whom Tom Brangwen experienced a feeling of familiarity so overwhelming that it produced –so tells us Lawrence– the irruption of a transcendent flash in his grey life. Tom Brangwen was returning from Nottingham, one day, to his home in Cossethay with the cart packed with sacks of seed. He was walking alongside the horse when he saw a woman on the road, coming his way...

> She had heard the cart, and looked up. Her face was pale and clear, she had thick dark eyebrows and a wide mouth, curiously held. He saw her face clearly, as if by a light in the air. He saw her face so distinctly, that he ceased to coil on himself, and was suspended.
>
> "That's her," he said involuntarily. As the cart passed by, splashing through the thin mud, she stood back against the bank. Then, as he walked still beside his britching horse, his eyes met hers. He looked quickly away, pressing back his head, a pain of joy running through him. He could not bear to think of anything.
>
> He turned round at the last moment. He saw her bonnet, her shape in the black cloak, the movement as she walked. Then she was gone round the bend.
>
> She had passed by. He felt as if he were walking again in a far world, not Cossethay, a far world, the fragile reality. He went on, quiet, suspended, rarefied. He could not bear to think or to speak, nor make any sound or sign, nor change his fixed motion. He could scarcely bear to think of her face. He moved within the knowledge of her, in the world that was beyond reality.
>
> The feeling that they had exchanged recognition possessed him like a madness, like a torment. How could he be sure,

> what confirmation had he? The doubt was like a sense of infinite space, a nothingness, annihilating. He kept within his breast the will to surety. They had exchanged recognition.
>
> He walked about in this state for the next few days. And then again like a mist it began to break to let through the common, barren world.[10]

After this first encounter, Tom Brangwen went around town gathering information about this stranger. He felt "a curious certainty about her, as if she were destined to him... It was coming, he knew, his fate. The world was submitting to its transformation. He made no move: it would come, what would come."[11] Lydia was not exactly a beautiful woman, you noticed: "Her face was pale and clear, she had thick dark eyebrows and a wide mouth, curiously held." How to explain that sudden infatuation, then? An infatuation that, maybe for the first time in his life, made Tom Brangwen aware of the existence of a secret order, of a hidden reality concealed behind the visible reality. How to explain it, Blanca, if not referring to the concept of subjective beauty?

The next example is taken from a short story by to one of the great masters of the genre, and a great master of the theatre too: I only need to mention *The Cherry Orchard* for you to know whom I'm talking about. That's it: Anton Chekhov... Two hunters are staying overnight at a country house. There, they hold a conversation that quickly drifts towards the subject of love (*On Love* is the name of the story). Then the host, to illustrate the theme, proceeds to tell them his own story, which is a story about adulterous love, Blanca. Not one of

---

10. D.H. Lawrence, *The Rainbow*, p. 22
11. Ibid p. 24-25

those tragic adultery stories to which Literature has accustomed us: it's not *Anna Karenina*, to cite another illustrious Russian text from the blue library. It's a much more modest story, a minimal story where nothing happens. It's about a man and a woman who fall deeply in love for each other, but out of loyalty to their friend and husband, they repress that love. That is it. Ah, but while the story is slim, it's stuffed with inner things. What kind of things? Well, look: the feeling that comes over the protagonist when he sees, for the first time, the woman who will be the love of his life: "I felt her at once some one close and already familiar, as though that face, those cordial, intelligent eyes, I had seen somewhere in my childhood, in the album which lay on my mother's chest of drawers."... A few months go by after that first encounter, since that revelation of familiarity on the face of a stranger. But Aliohin does not forget: "I did not think of her, but it was as though her light shadow were lying on my heart." One night, at the theatre, he sees her again, "and again the same irresistible, thrilling impression of beauty and sweet, caressing eyes, and again the same feeling of nearness."

If we had time to read the Chekhov's short story anthology you bought a few months before your death (and I am certain you would have loved it), this scene that I just told you would have reminded you of another famous story by the brilliant Russian writer: "*The Lady with the Dog*". The protagonist has also fallen in love with a married woman, whom, after some time, he sees again in the middle of the audience at the theatre: "Anna Sergeyevna, too, came in. She sat down in the third row, and when Gurov looked at her his heart contracted, and he understood clearly that for him there was in the whole world no creature so near, so precious, and so important to him; she, this little woman, in no way remarkable, lost in a provincial crowd, with a vulgar lorgnette in her hand, filled his whole life now, was his sorrow and his joy, the one happiness that he now desired for himself, and to the sounds of the inferior orchestra, of the wretched provincial violins, he thought how lovely she was. He thought and dreamed." Gurov is a Don Juan, or so he was up until that point. He is a lover of feminine beauty. And this is where he all of a sudden feels subjugated by this rather plain woman, from whom he'll never again want to be apart. "Anna Sergeyevna and he loved each other like people very close and akin, like husband and wife, like tender friends; it seemed to them that fate itself had meant them for one another, and they could not understand why he had a wife and she a husband; and it was as though they were a pair of birds of passage, caught and forced to live in different cages."

For you to see that similar experiences are not just literary inventions, but are instead based in the immediate reality, we will momentarily leave literary fiction and will look at several personal testimonies. The first corresponds to that nineteenth century Danish philosopher I quoted at the beginning. There are not many philosophers whose work was so clearly influenced by a woman as is the case of Soren Kierkegaard. It's not that this woman consciously helped to shape his thinking. It's that their love at first sight was so intense and disturbing for both sides, that their lives could never escape its influence. And with Kierkegaard, life and work were inextricably linked. In the diaries he kept all his life, this is how he described the impression produced in him by his first encounter with Regina Olsen:

> You, sovereign queen of my heart, "Regina", hidden in the deepest secrecy of my breast, in the fullness of my life-idea.

> There where it is just as far to heaven as to hell – unknown divinity! O, can I really believe the poets when they say that the first time one sees the beloved object he thinks he has seen her long before... Everywhere, in the face of every girl, I see features of your beauty, but I think I would have to possess the beauty of all the girls in the world to extract your beauty, that I would have to sail around the world to find the portion of the world I want and toward which the deepest secret of my self polarically points – and in the next moment you are so close to me, so present, so overwhelmingly filling my spirit that I am transfigured to myself and feel that here it is good to be.[12]

Later she would also speak about the powerful attraction she felt towards him the first time they saw each other. When Kierkegaard got his posthumous fame, many were the curious people who wanted to know and research the woman who moved about through most of his books like filigree. Kierkegaard had made a commitment with her in his youth, but he was a man of unhealthy melancholy, and he feared his character would make her unhappy. With great pain in his heart, he decided to break their engagement and, in light of her dismay, pretended not to love her so she could forget him and rebuild her life. However, he sunk into despair when she took him for his word and married another man. But although they lived apart, Kierkegaard and Regina were forever in each other's hearts, and their love was unconditional until the end of their lives.

The second personal testimony I want to show you comes from a modern day sage, Ken Wilber, and his wife, Treya.

---

12. Alexander Dru, *The Journals of Soren Kierkegaard*, Oxford University Press, 1938

Wilber is an authority in transpersonal psychology and in the investigation of consciousness. Apart from numerous essays on those subjects, he published a book a few years ago where he recounted a painful experience he lived through. As it happens, Blanca, this experience is the same one I went through: the illness and death of his wife. The book alternates between the story and the author's reflections, and the diary entries her wife had written. In the first pages, they both describe their first meeting, and how do you think they do it? Well, how else? In terms of recognition: "When Treya and I first met, we had the strangest feeling that we had been looking for each other for lifetimes, but I don't know if that is literally true... / ...But when I put my arm around her, I felt all separation and distance dissolve; there was some sort of merging, it seemed. It was as if Treya and I had been together for lifetimes."[13] Treya, in turn, reminiscing in her diary about that first hug, says she felt "...something indescribable then. A warmth, a kind of merging, a sense of fitting together, of blending, of being completely one... What had just happened? Some kind of recognition, a recognition beyond this present world. It had nothing to do with how many words we'd shared."[14]

The last personal testimony we will visit before returning to the bountiful fields of literary fiction is by a modern poet of "ancient perspective". It's not by chance, my love, that this poet born at the turn of century, the French André Bréton, was a key figure of Surrealism, a movement that called for the primordial role of intuition in art in general, and in poetry

---

13. Ken Wilber, *Grace and Grit: Spirituality and Healing in the Life and Death of Treya*, p. 3 and 9
14. Ibid, p. 8

in particular. Having studied esoteric tradition in depth, Bréton was a profound connoisseur of ancient knowledge. Well, then, it's in the autobiographical *Arcane 17*, where he writes to his beloved Elisa, with whom he married almost immediately after meeting: "Before I met you, but what am I saying, these words make no sense. You know that the first time I saw you, there is no doubt I recognised you."[15] This, Blanca, is love at first sight, what in French is known as *coup de foudre*, "thunderbolt". That is to say, a sudden love that sweeps you off your feet, which Bréton himself baptised as *amour fou*, "mad love". "Naturally –he points out– I'm talking about a love that holds absolute power, that is connected for an entire lifetime, that refuses to see as its object anyone other than that one being. In this respect, this experience, as distressing as it has been (it's relevant to point out here that Breton and Elisa ended up getting a divorce), has taught me nothing: so powerful is this aspiration for me, that I am aware I could not renounce it without sacrificing everything I live for. I am still bound to one of the most powerful myths, to which no apparent setback in the context of my adventure would prevail."[16] The myth he is referring to, my dear, is none other than love predestination, the myth of twin souls. A myth he subsequently articulates: "Every human being has been thrown into this life in search of that one other being of a different sex which, from every perspective, is its counterpart, to the point that one without the other appears as the result of a dissociation, of a dislocation of a single block of light."[17]

---

15. Andre Breton, *Arcane 17*, p. 24
16. Ibid, p. 24
17. Ibid, p. 28

There is an Arabic legend (though many defend it as historical fact) that portrays an extreme example of *mad love.* It originated in Arabia during the second half of the seventh century and, in the following centuries, spread to the entire Islamic East, spawning innumerable different versions. (This, Blanca, is the East appropriated by the fables: the multitudinous East of the one thousand and one nights, embodied in Arabia, in Andalusia, and in Egypt, in Turkey, in Iraq and in Persia, and even in India.) The hero of this legend is known by his nickname, Majnun, meaning "Madman". His story is very simple. It's the story of a man who loses his mind due to the impossibility of being with the young woman he loves. She loves him back, but her father forces her to marry another man. Since then, Majnun lives obsessed with the love of Layla. His love makes him a target of people's scorn. It leads him to wander semi-naked through deserts and mountains, living in the company of wild animals. In an attempt to dissuade him from this "mad love", his father takes him on a pilgrimage to Mecca. But it's pointless, for Majnun's Mecca is Layla. The legend concludes with the death of the "mad lover" near the tomb of his beloved and, in one of its most famous versions – by the twelfth century Persian poet Nizami Ganjavi – with the corollary of the lovers' reunion in Paradise. Majnun and Layla met each other in childhood; they shepherded the same herd together, according to some versions. Their first encounter had the character of a revelation to Majnun, who was immediately struck by Layla's beauty. But look at this, Blanca: the legend requires Layla to not be particularly beautiful, to be ugly, even. In one of the episodes, the caliph tries to bring the foolish man to reason, showing him countless far more beautiful women. But Majnun doesn't listen to reason: he is under the spell of his twin soul's subjective beauty. Layla is to Majnun (as Dulcinea is to that other egregious fool, Don Quixote, willing to die rather than denying it) the most beautiful woman in the world. And so he shouts it from the rooftops in poems of passionate lyricism he composes. As time passed, those poems proliferated across Arabic literature because there were many poets who, moved by this drama, attributed their love poems to "Layla's madman".

In this other book I'm holding now (no, it's not bound in blue, it's not one of the books from your library), the protagonist does not need anyone to point out there are more attractive men than her beloved: "About six years ago I saw you for the first time; You were young, handsome, amiable; Other young men appeared to me more beautiful and dashing than you; None gave me the slightest emotion, and my heart was yours at first sight. I thought I could see on your face the features of the soul that were missing from mine... It hasn't been two months since I thought I had not been mistaken; Blind love, I said to myself, was right; We were made for each other; I would have been his if the human order had not disturbed the ways of Nature; And if anyone were allowed to be happy, we would have been happy together."[18]... See? Just like Majnun and Layla, this young couple is also not allowed to be happy together. That means –writes the protagonist to her beloved– there has been a change in Nature's plans. Nature, however, does not give up, Blanca, and throughout the book, it conspires to fulfil that destiny. The book is *The New Heloise*, by the French philosopher of Enlightenment Jean-Jacques Rousseau, and it's a love affair told through letters.

18. Jean-Jacques Rousseau, *Julie ou la Nouvelle Heloïse*, p. 250, troisième partie, lettre XVIII

If you want my opinion, it's one of the most beautiful romance novels in Western literature. It's a pity it was not part of your library so we could have had the pleasure of reading it together. No, I will not summarise it here, I prefer you read it if you have the chance (I am sure you have access to the best libraries). In this novel, furthermore, what is essential is not the plot, but the characters' feelings. Hence, the epistolary format, because letters, Blanca –and here you have the one I am writing–, are the ideal vehicle for the expression of feelings. Like the ones expressed by Julie in the previous passage. Or like those articulated by her lover when trying to convince her to run away with him in spite of her strict sense of duty: "No, know this once and for all, my Julie, an eternal judgement of Heaven has destined us one for the other; This is the first law to be listened to, it is the main task in life; to unite with who makes it sweet... / ... Come, O my soul! Reunite in your friend's arms the two halves of our being."[19]

Rousseau found inspiration in a seventeenth century pastoral novel, which I'll only mention due to your fondness for fairy tales and the colour blue. Along with the recounting of these kinds of stories, and intellectual and charming conversations, the live reading of this novel – *L'Astrée,* by Honoré d'Urfé – was among the *Chambre Bleue*'s select members' favourite amusements... You have never heard about the "blue chamber" at the Hôtel de Rambouillet? That palace no longer exists, but in its day, it was neighbours with the Louvre. Since it's Paris we are talking about... And here, my love, a vivid memory emerges from my mind: the two trips we took together to *Ville Lumière*, especially the second one, our tenth-anniversary celebration. Although you were already

19. *Ibid*, p. 56, première partie, lettre XXVI

feeling the first symptoms of your long illness –or precisely because of that–, it was the most intense of the two, the one we lived life to the fullest, eclipsing even the memory of the first trip.

Well then, place yourself in Paris during the *Grand Siécle*, the Paris of the Three Musketeers and Cyrano de Bergerac, and imagine a palatial bedroom completely lined with blue velvet, in a social environment where, in matters of interior decoration, the only acceptable colours were red and light brown. At the back of the candle lit alcove, a magnificent canopy bed from where the marquise of Rambouillet, reclined on her mattress, presiding over the most famous of Parisian salons. A salon frequented by the flower and cream of the contemporary intellectual circle, including the first literary women, the notorious *précieuses*, also known as *bas–bleues*, or "bluestockings", this garment being the club hallmark worn by the women who were regulars at the *Chambre Bleue*'s gatherings. Among them, Blanca, we could certainly find an "old acquaintance" of yours: Madame d'Aulnoy, who with the title of one of her books –*Contes de fées*– would name for posterity those popular stories which, conveniently adapted to aristocratic tastes, caused a sensation in the salons of the day. Like *L'Astrée*, a forgotten novel today, but probably one of the most widely read in its century. A book that shares with *The New Eloise* the same inspiration: both could be defined as a glorifying ode to spiritual and platonic love; both have the theory of twin souls ingrained in them like a watermark; and in both, Fate's actions are evident, conspiring to reunite the two halves.

Yet, we can find another even more ruthless conspiracy by Fate to impose its design in an old legend, Blanca. One that is possibly (if Romeo and Juliet, and Abelardo and Eloise don't mind), the most famous love story in the West: the legend of Tristan and Isolde. Although we know its origin dates much further back, the oldest surviving written versions of *The Romance of Tristan* – the French versions by Béroul and Thomas – come from the twelfth century. In the story, the fulminant flash of love caused by mutual recognition is illustrated through the ingestion of a love potion. Before this episode, though, you already have a glimpse of the hand of Fate –disguised as chance– pulling the strings. Let's take a look.

Tristan is the nephew of King Mark of Cornwall, where an Irish warrior arrives one day, demanding young maidens as a tribute. Tristan challenges and kills Morholt the Giant in single combat. When his dead body is returned to Ireland, the giant's sister, the queen, extracts from his fatal wound a broken piece of the sword that killed him; a shard princess Isolde stores in a chest, swearing to use it to identify and seek revenge on the man who killed her uncle. Meanwhile, Tristan finds himself forced to leave the kingdom because, during the fight, he was stabbed with a poisoned spear, and the wound was getting infected. Its smell was so rotten no one wanted him nearby. One day he decides to set sail aboard a rickety boat. He arrives in Ireland having been adrift, without sails, rudder or oars (which shows Fate was guiding him). At the Irish court, he disguises himself as a troubadour who was wounded in a clash with pirates. The queen, who is also a sorcerer skilled in magic potions, cures his fetid wound, and princess Isolde dresses it and takes care of Tristan while he convalesces.

Once recovered, Tristan, fearing being recognised by Morholt's henchmen, returns to Cornwall. There, he receives a warm welcome from everyone but his uncle's barons, who believe him to be the heir to the crown. They believe it because

King Mark has no wife and no descendants. The barons, then, compel the King to get married. He eventually gives in and announces he will be marrying the owner of a golden hair, dropped in his window by a swallow. The barons feel mocked, but Tristan remembers Isolde the Fair and offers to go find her. (Obviously, at this point, he had not been struck by the recognition of Isolde yet, otherwise he would have never thought of her as a wife for his uncle.) There goes Tristan, then, sailing back to Ireland; this time with a specific mission: to find a wife for his uncle. According to some variants, it will once again be chance, in the form of a storm, what, for a second time, leads Tristan to Ireland (and therefore to Isolde; meaning that once again the hand of Fate is revealed to be pulling the strings).

Always in disguise, Tristan kills a dragon who was terrorising the capital, but he is not able to stop it from injecting him with his venom. Taken to the court, the queen cures him once more, and Isolde looks after him. But the young lady (whose hand in marriage is the reward promised for slaying the dragon: Fate is looking to unite this couple anyway it can!) finds a nick in Tristan's blade. She compares it to the broken blade piece she kept in a chest and confirms they fit together, so she prepares to have her sworn revenge. But then she does not follow through with her plan. According to some versions, as she is about to kill him, she finds herself strangely moved by the young man's beauty, and this changes her mind. Thomas' version has this moment, not when they drink the love potion, be the instant in which they fall in love. That is to say, the instant of mutual recognition. (Predictably, Blanca, it's not Tristan's apparent beauty what moves Isolde. It's his secret beauty, the one destined for the eyes of his twin soul only, the beauty that reveals itself to her – to both, according to Thomas – in that magic moment.)

However, Tristan is now an ambassador on a mission. When he announces this to the kings of Ireland, they consent in marrying their daughter Isolde to King Mark, but she adamantly refuses. The queen, then, before Isolde boards, prepares a love potion and tasks her handmaiden with serving it to her and King Mark as soon as they reach Cornwall. Ah, but did you expect Fate to sit back and do nothing? Again, it interferes. And so, during the journey, Tristan and Isolde drink the magic liquid thinking it's wine and instantly fall desperately in love with each other... We will stop here. The story continues, Blanca, but I will tell you the rest in another letter. What I wanted to show you is how Fate seems determined to unite Tristan and Isolde. It tries it by all means possible and fails. Until it finally, as a last resort, makes use of the love potion.

The potion symbolises, at the same time, the intuitive recognition provoked by love predestination. This recognition is, Blanca, to a much larger extent than in the West, a recurring theme in Eastern literature. We will analyse in some detail now, three examples taken from Eastern literature, one from China, another from Japan, and one from India. Each of them is the classic work most representative of its respective country's literary history. It's no coincidence, then, that the subject of love predestination features substantially in all three of them: it shows us how deeply rooted this topic is in Eastern thought... But before I tackle these three eminent examples, I can't resist quoting a modest one. First, because it classifies a type of love stories – ubiquitous in the East – that finds a fundamental element in the concept of reincarnation. And second, my dear, because I know it will please you since it's an example of that traditional genre you enjoy so much.

Once upon a time, a young princess lived tormented by a terrible sorrow, the cause of which no one knew, that prevented her from speaking. (See how sorrow really is a formidable obstacle for words? How the reason I gave you for having postponed writing to you was not just an excuse?) The king promulgates an edict offering her hand in marriage to the man capable of taking her out of her desolation and making her speak. Many suitors of noble lineage parade through the palace. They all fail. Finally, it's up to a beggar; everyone thinks does not have the slightest possibility. But as it happens, the story had previously shown us a fairy who revealed to the beggar all his previous lives and, in all of them, he had been prematurely separated from his twin soul. Therefore, when we find him among the suitors, we can already imagine the ending: "You are the one I have been waiting for all this time", says the princess upon seeing him, recovering her speech and her joy.[20]

THE STORY OF THE STONE AND THE FLOWER

Let's now leave that indefinite past, the vague "once upon a time" from the fairy tales, and transport ourselves to a specific time in History: halfway through the eighteenth century. This was when China's most popular classic novel was written, and when it takes place. Two titles contend for the cover: *The Story of the Stone*, and *Dream of the Red Chamber*.

20. Compiled by Henri Gougaud in *L'arbres à soleils*

I can use both to introduce you to the novel. We will begin with the second one's red colour: in ancient China, red was a sign of social class; only members of the upper classes could wear and decorate their houses with that colour. The "red chambers" are, then, the rooms in old Chinese feudal noblemen's residences where the novel unfolds. It produces the effect of a great altarpiece (three thousand words!) about the day-to-day life of a family. But it's eminently the story of the predestined love between two of the younger members of the family. Their twin kinship is already insinuated through their names (Bao-yu and Dai-yu) because both feature the same word: yu, "jade". It's the Stone mentioned in the first title.

The Stone mostly identifies Bao-yu, because a little prodigy marked his birth. Upon bursting into tears, a little piece of jade came out of his mouth. Bao-yu would forever keep this stone as an amulet. In the figurative language the author, Cao Xueqin, employs to talk about things from the Afterlife, the Stone is Bao-yu's celestial symbol; Dai-yu's is the Flower. Stone and Flower represent the masculine and feminine poles respectively *(ying and yang,* in the Chinese tradition), upon which, according to the ancient sages, everything is assembled. Before descending into this world, meaning before reincarnating, Bao-yu and Dai-yu were pure spirits: he was a "Stone-spirit", she was a "Flower-spirit". In their higher home world, Flower and Stone were intimately connected, as it's told at the start of the novel... It begins with a provincial civil servant who falls asleep and enters a strange dream, where he travels to the Afterlife. There, he meets two immortals: two clergymen who tell him they hold the "secret to the mechanism of destinies". In Taoism, the religious/philosophical background to this novel, the "immortals" are the souls that have been set free from material shackles, souls who have reached enlightenment and, with it, divine status. The two clergymen tell the story of the Stone to the civil servant – and through him, they tell us readers. First, they start by placing the story in their upper home world, the "Paradise of Love", where Stone works as a gardener. Except his garden is metaphorical, Blanca; it's a garden consisting solely of one Flower (a detail I am sure will remind you of another dear literary gardener: the Little Prince, also devoted to looking after a lone flower on a distant planet). When Stone is forced to descend upon our world, their close relationship prompts Flower to do the same. However, they don't come down by themselves: according to the two immortals, along with Stone and the Flower comes an enormous number of souls. These souls are arranged in couples; since it's mainly the relationship with their respective *yuan–ci*, their "predestined enemy" (that is how peculiar the notion of twin souls was in ancient China), what the souls come to our world to work on. In his figurative language, Xueqin tells us of a "debt of tears" that each soul has to its counterpart. It's the payment of that debt what justifies the recurring reincarnation of souls into our "lower world".

Stone and Flower reincarnate two years apart. The former in the bosom of a noble family, the Jia; the latter, in a more modest one. It turns out, though, that the families are related, so when Dai–yu becomes an orphan, the Jia take her in. And so it happens, Blanca, the famous recognition scene. The meeting of the two cousins raises in them the distant reminiscence of their old relationship in Heaven: "'How strange', she thought in the depths of her heart. 'I am almost certain I have seen him somewhere else: so familiar is his face!"[21] And he, surprised, says: "This little cousin... but I have seen her before!", and faced with the objection of grandmother Jia –the clan's matriarch who has just introduced them: "Even if I haven't, her face really is familiar, and in the bottom of my heart I feel as if I had found an old friend after a long time apart."[22] From the moment of mutual recognition onwards, the two children become inseparable. They sleep on the same bed and eat at the same table: in short, they grow up together. Reaching adolescence, they each move to a pagoda in the garden or, more accurately, in the immense park surrounding Jia's palace. It's there, in the paradisiacal "Grand View Garden", where, aided by handmaidens of the same age who act more like playmates and confidants, Bao-yu and Dai-yu live their pure and innocent love, a love contrasting with the lecherous atmosphere that fills the palace. Thus, in between poetry pageants, tender conversations, and innocent childish games, their existence happily passes by. Until they reach marrying age. That is when a vague threat starts looming over them.

That threat, Blanca, is the threat of separation. You see, the decision about their marriage does not depend on them; it's Grandmother Jia's responsibility. And even though no one doubts they are predestined to become husband and wife, the official announcement of their engagement is delayed, which opens the way for speculations, and sows anxiety in the cousins' hearts. Hence one night, Dai-yu, after

21. Cao Xueqin, *Le Reve dans le pavillon rouge*, Ed. Gallimard, two volume edition by Li Tche-Houa and Jacqueline Alézaïs, vol. I, p. 77 (This title, though traditionally accepted, is not accurate. The correct translation of the Chinese title is "Dream of the Red Chamber".)

22. *Ibid*, p. 81

complaining her parents did not have the foresight of arranging her marriage to Bao-yu before they died, has a nightmare in which she finds herself forced to marry a widower. In her dream, she runs away to find her cousin, who denies their marriage was not agreed in advance: "You were originally promised to me". Accodring to him, it was due to that agreement that Dai-yu ended up at the Jia's mansion as a child. "Suddenly, she thinks she vaguely remembers having, indeed, been promised to Bao-yu in the past; and thus her mourning gives way to joy."[23] But then -absurdly, but obeying the secret logic of dreams- Bao-yu cuts his chest open with a knife so Dai-yu can read in his heart the truth of what he told her. As he collapses, bleeding to death, she holds him and weeps. At that point, she wakes up. Through her cousin's handmaiden, she will later discover Bao-yu also had a nightmare that night, and that his nightmare (he moaned and exclaimed his chest was being ripped open with a knife) strangely agrees with hers- which is evidence of a kind of spiritual communion between the cousins.

The threat of separation seems to be the origin of a strange illness that, around that time, starts to afflict them both. This illness will accompany them throughout the rest of their short lives, it will keep them bed-ridden for long stretches of time, and it will even take them, on several occasions, to the verge of death or madness. One of these occasions is involuntarily brought about by Dai-yu's handmaiden when, faced with the uncertainty of her lady's future -and therefore her own-, decides to test Bao-yu's love by falsely announcing his cousin intends to abandon him. Dai-yu falls victim to a similar misunderstanding when she

23. *Ibid*, vol. II, p. 592

hears rumours claiming her cousin is to be married to a high-ranking official. In both cases, only the denial of the unfortunate news proves to be the cure. In short, Blanca, the rumours spread and fuel gossip. So, consequently to this episode, two handmaidens are chatting: "I believe young Bao-iu and Dai-yu's destinies are connected by a tight affinity. Those who repeat the old saying *True love's path is never easy* are correct. But those who say: *Nothing can be done against true affinities,* are also speaking the truth. Judging by their mutual feelings, and by how Heaven revealed its will (this referring to Dai-yu's miraculous recovery upon discovering the awful rumour to be false), it's most certainly due to this very will, that both form a couple destined to come together in matrimony. It's evident they are one of those couples of which the old proverb says *The two have been destined to each other since the Origin*"[24]

Eventually, the fateful day in which the threat of separation finally becomes real arrives. Grandmother Jia, faithful to the ancestral Chinese disapproval of marriages of love (which do nothing but weaken parental authority) reaches a decision, and it's not the one everyone expected: as a wife for her grandson she selects not Dai-yu, but another one of his cousins. Aware of the tight bond between them, she gives instructions for Dai-yu not to be informed until the day of the ceremony. She also takes advantage of the nuptial convention forbidding all contact between spouses-to-be, to deceive Bai-yu into thinking he is about to marry his beloved. Alas, no precaution is enough to prevent the truth from finding its way to Dai-yu, who decides to take her own life. She refuses food, burns all her poems, and dies the same instant

---

24. *Ibid*, vol. II, pp. 788-789

Bao-yu gets married. When he becomes aware of the ruse, it's already too late (during the ceremony, his bride's face had been hidden behind her bridal veil), and, upon learning of the death of his love, he once again falls ill, which this time takes him through the doors of the Afterlife.

An immortal approaches him there. Every human being, he tells him, has a predetermined time of death, and his has not yet come. Bao-yu refuses to return without Dai-yu (there you have it, Blanca, a classic theme of ancient literature: the faithful lover travelling to the Afterlife in search of his deceased beloved). The immortal, though, does not budge. He warns him: "If you truly wish to reunite with her, you should henceforth dedicate yourself, with all your heart, to cultivating knowledge and virtue. Then, the time you can once again stand before each other will arrive in a natural way. If instead, you are not able to accept continuing your peaceful existence, you will be guilty of your premature death; confined to the depths of Hell... and doomed to never again see the departed Dai-yu."[25] The warning is effective: Bao-yu recovers, and from this point onwards - nearly up until the end- the course of the novel shifts. The Taoist system, which up until now had been more of a discreet backdrop - jumps to the foreground. Bai-yu adopts an indifferent attitude towards the world and ends up handing over the jade with which he was born to a mysterious clergyman, who is none other than one of the immortals who are telling the story. Then he vanishes. No one knows what happened to him, but the cession of the jade to the immortals is most eloquent: the Stone has returned to its native home. And it's like the narrator tells us: "Once the immor-

25. *Ibid*, vol. II, p. 1000

tal Flower, temporarily reincarnated on Earth, has returned to its original shape, what reason would the Stone have to not return as well to its origin?"[26]

And that's it, Blanca, the romance of the Stone and the Flower. It's true that, towards the end, the Taoist backdrop imprints a nihilistic turn on the story: Bao-yu and Dai-yu's love fades away along with them into the absolute void. But that does not deny the novel's fundamental fact, which is also, as I aspire to show you through these letters, one of the fundamental facts of ancient knowledge. The ancient sages valued this fact -the existence of a predestined love between souls- in different ways, according to the religious or philosophical ideology they followed. Among the Taoists, it was deemed irrelevant. However, although open to interpretation, the fact is there, my love, and that is all that matters.

EVENING FACES

I will tell you now another love story that is only a moment within a much larger story. But that moment is, in my understanding, the central episode of the main narrative, a book titled *The Tale of Genji*. This is Japanese literature's classic novel par excellence. Its author, Murasaki Shikibu, was a lady with close ties to the imperial court of the eleventh century. This courtier, the lady-in-waiting to the young empress, created a prince of a sumptuous court; Prince Genji, son of the Emperor and his dearest concubine. Genji, who is in a marriage of convenience, is seeking love outside of wedlock, but he finds nothing beyond fickle sexual adventures, to the

26. *Ibid.*, vol. II, p. 1581

point that he convinces himself that is what love is. Besides the occasional lovers, he also keeps a stable relationship with a court lady, Lady Rokujo, who will turn out to be, as we will see, the source of his misfortune. The episode in question is entitled Yugao, which means “evening faces” and is the name of a delicate white flower that only blooms at night. As in Xueqin’s novel, here we also have a flower as an allegory for a woman.

Prince Genji first notices this flower’s beauty when he is incognito, one night, walking through a humble neighbourhood in the capital, on the way to visit his old nursemaid. It’s an unexpected visit, and while they don’t open the front gate, his carriage waits on the street. While waiting, an ivy-like creeper with white flowers next door catches his attention. The delicateness of the flowers overwhelm him, and he asks one of his servants to pick some for him. We can see here, Blanca, subtly disguised –transferred into someone’s emotion when faced with a flower’s beauty– the mystery of recognition. The prince feels he is being watched from inside the house, and his suspicions are confirmed when a little girl opens the door and offers him, on behalf of her lady, a fan to place the flowers on. Genji has no time to ask her anything: the front gate before which he awaits is opened. But, following the visit, he again focuses on the flowers, gracefully resting over the fan. Examining the fan, he discovers some scrawled verses with the ink still fresh: “The flower that puzzled you was but the Yugao, strange beyond knowing in its dress of shining dew”. Such words awaken his curiosity; they have on him, one could say, the effect of a secret password only he understands.

His loyal servant, Koremitsu, arranges for him an evening date with the mysterious lady. After this date, others will follow; always at night (Yugao is a nocturnal flower), to elude not only his father's spies but also the jealous Lady Rokujo. Soon, Genji is spending every night in the company of Yugao at her humble home. During the day, though, being apart proves to be unbearable. The lady exerts an unexplainable and irresistible attraction over him. One night, they hear a chant coming from the street: "Glory be to the Saviour that shall come". They look out the window and see an old man on his knees under the moonlight. Yugao's house is located near a sacred mountain regularly visited by pilgrims. The sight of this old man, who prays while waiting for dawn to break, arises in Genji's memory these verses, which he recites for Yugao: "Do not prove false this omen of the pilgrim's chant: that even in lives to come our love shall last unchanged."[27]... I want to stop here for a moment, my dear. Behind these verses breathes a true story, one of the greatest love stories in the East. Its author attributed them to eighth century Chinese Emperor Hsuan–tsung, famous for having thousands of concubines at his disposal, yet unable to see beauty in any but one of them, one who wasn't even among the prettiest. The tragic love story between the Emperor Hsuan–tsung and Lady Yang Kuei–fei has inspired, throughout the years, countless of poems in the East. One of the most celebrated comes from the Chinese poet Po Chu–i, and it concludes with the emperor's sad return to his palace after the rebellion that cost him the life of his beloved. In those verses, we see him wandering the long corridors and enormous deserted halls like a ghost, prey to an unspeakable nostalgia that is as death in life. Finally, he resorts to a

---

27. Murasaki Shikibu, *The tale of Genji*, as translated by Arthur Waley, p. 64

necromancer to establish contact with the disembodied soul of Yang Kuei-fei who, through the seer, sends him a message requesting what -as we are about to see, Blanca- is her final wish, the twin souls' desideratum. Taking for granted their future re-encounters in other lives, she asks for them to make a pact; to on Earth "vow to be as two intertwined branches of a tree.", and in Heaven: "to be as two birds flying wingtip to wingtip"[28]

Going back to *The Tale of Genji*, it now transforms into a ghost story. Urged by the pilgrim's chant, Genji and Yugao decide to run away together that very night. They give out the appropriate orders and set out on their journey through the deserted streets. Sleep, however, gets the better of them and Genji orders the carriage to stop in front of an empty house. His servants set up one of the dilapidated rooms, and the young lovers go to sleep. But in the middle of the night, Genji jumps out of bed in terror. Standing before him is a majestic feminine figure. He does not recognise her, but the reader knows it's Lady Rokujo, or rather her disembodied spirit, chasing Genji in his dreams. The ghost berates him, moving as if she wants to drag Yugao away from him. Genji unsheathes his sword and strikes at the spectre, but the sword cannot touch it. He believes he is suffering from a hallucination or from a nightmare of which he cannot get out, and when he tries to wake up Yugao he finds, to his horror, that she is cold: the ghost had taken her life.

Koremitsu and the other servants, then, have to rush to carry out all the funeral rites in secrecy (they move her body to a monastery in the mountains). Rush to bury what was – in their eyes – just a fleeting and insignificant affair in their

---

28. Po Chü-i, *Song of Everlasting Sorrow*

master's life. To Genji, though, it was not a fleeting and insignificant affair at all, Blanca. And to prove it, we have the nervous illness (as with the protagonist of *Story of the Stone* and many other characters from countless novels) that besets him over the death of his beloved, which will take him to the brink of death. The reflections on this episode Genji makes some time later, when he's recovered, are also significant: it was an episode that "affected me strangely and I went to very great trouble to see her. There must have been a bond between us. A love doomed from the start to be fleeting – why should it have taken such complete possession of me and made me find her so precious?"[29]

A LOST RINGAND THREE DROPS OF BLOOD IN THE SNOW

There is, Blanca, a text that is a classic not just of Eastern, but also of universal Literature. A play that, when it was translated from Sanskrit into English at the end of the eighteenth century, repeated in the West the same success it had enjoyed in the East for fourteen centuries. It's the masterpiece of one of the most notable Sanskirt language poets, Kalidasa, who lived in India -around the fourth century- a life today haloed by legend. There are several variants of the title, depending on different transcriptions: "The Recognition of Shakuntala", "The Token-for-Recognition of Shakuntala", "Of Shakuntala Who Is Recognised". Some versions omit the word *recognition*, but allude to the symbol that triggers

29. Here, the letter's author follows the translation by Edward G. Seidensticker. Ed. Alfred A. Knopf, New York, 1985, p. 79

it: "Shakuntala's Ring", "Shakuntala or the Lost Ring". The play is popularly known by the name of its hero.

Shakuntala is the young daughter of a hermit and a nymph. She lives with her father in a cabin in the woods. One day, Dushyanta, the king of India, happens to walk through these woods and falls madly in love with her. This love at first sight is mutual. Although in the beginning they are both afraid of not being loved back, soon they confess their love for each other and get married in secret. But Duyshanta is the king and, as such, he has obligations that call for his return to the court. Before leaving, he gives his signet ring to Shakuntala, as a proof of their marriage and his swift return. Shakuntala loses the ring: it falls in a lake during her ablutions. Months go by without her having any news of her husband. Finally, she decides to set off in search of him. She shows up at the palace. The king does not recognise her, denies they are married, and she does not have the ring to prove it. Suddenly, Blanca, one of those miracles typical of Eastern stories happens: a great wind rises and sweeps Shakuntala off into Heaven. Duyshanta stays on Earth, immersed in thoughts, trying in vain to remember. Because it's not that he rejects the wedding, he just does not remember it: "With a hermit-wife I had no part,/ All memories evade me;/And yet my sad and stricken heart/Would more than half persuade me." One day, some soldiers find the royal ring on a fisherman. They accuse him of stealing it and take him to the palace. He claims he found the ring in a fish's innards. And this is where the sight of the ring brings the king out of his state of forgetfulness. He immediately remembers having given it to Shakuntala as a sign of their secret marriage and curses himself for not having remembered sooner.

The king despairs, he neglects his obligations; all he can think of is Shakuntala and their secret wedding. From Heaven, she shares his despair, powerless to do anything about it, unable to understand as well "that such powerful love would need a symbol to be remembered". What does Duyshanta do, then? I tell you this with emotion, Blanca, he does the same thing you used to do when you were upset: he paints. He paints a portrait of his lost wife, based on his newfound memory. His counsellors think he has gone mad, for he spends all his free time with the painting, talking to it as if it were the real Shakuntala. Thus arrives at the palace a messenger from the gods. As you know, in ancient literature gods are participant characters in human dramas. They ask Duyshanta for a favour: they ask him to fight the demons that are threatening peace in Paradise. Skilled in the use of the bow, Duyshanta provides that service and, as a reward, they make his eagerly awaited re-encounter with his secret wife possible. They also clear up the mystery of his memory loss, the reason why "such powerful love would need a symbol to be remembered". It was, they tell him, the effect of a curse: only upon seeing the ring would it break.

This is, Blanca, in short, the story of Shakuntala. When I learned about it a few years ago, I was already familiar with the literary cycle from the medieval West that revolves around a mysterious sacred object fallen from Heaven, sought by many, found by very few: The Holy Grail. I was surprised to find parallels between the plot of *Shakuntala* and the matrix story of the Grail cycle. It has for a protagonist a wandering knight named Perceval, who at the beginning of the story lives in a cabin in the middle of the woods, like Shakuntala. Both happen to live away from society, in the company of a parent of the opposite sex: she with her father, he with his widowed mother. Despite all that, their roles are reversed: Perceval's role in the Grail cycle corresponds, in the Indian play, not to Shakuntala's but to king Duyshanta's. Because it's Perceval who, like the king, forsakes and forgets his twin soul after marrying her (both in Gerbet de Montreuil's and Wolfram von Eschenbach's versions) and spending time in her company. Apart from that, if Duyshanta recovers the memory of his original wife upon seeing the ring, Perceval gets his memory back in more subtle and surprising circumstances: the sight of three drops of blood in a snowy meadow. The mix of red and white invokes in him the rosy complexion of his wife, Blanchefleur. The knight atop his steed, engrossed in the contemplation of a rose-coloured stain in the snow that reminds him of his lover, is, Blanca, one of the most beautiful literary images I can remember. Let's see if you think the same:

> That night, out in a field, they slept alongside a wood. And as they slept snow fell, and the country was cold; Perceval had arisen early, as he always did, wanting to hunt for adventure and the chance to prove how brave he could be. And riding across the fields, beneath the frigid sun, he came to the king's camp but saw, before he reached the tents, a flock of wild geese, dazzled by the heavy snow, fleeing as fast as birds can fly from a diving falcon dropping out of the sky. It struck at a single goose, lagging behind the others, and hit it so hard that it fell to the earth. But the hawk didn't follow it down, not hungry enough to take the trouble, Too lazy to chase it. So the falcon flew off. But Perceval rode to where the goose had fallen. The bird's neck had been wounded, And three drops of blood had come rolling out on the snow, dying it vivid red. The bird had not been badly hurt, just knocked to the earth, and before

the knight could reach it it had flown away in the sky. But its body's oval shape was printed in the snow, the blood dyed colour suffused inside it, And Perceval, leaning on his lance, sat staring at the sight. Blood and snow so mixed together created a fresh colour, Just like his beloved's face, and as he stared he forgot what he was doing and where he was. The red stain against the white snow seemed just like her complexion. The more he looked, the happier he grew, seeing once again the exact colour of her beautiful face. The morning slowly passed away, and still he sat there musing, Until at last squires and pages emerged from the tents and saw him, and thought him asleep.[30]

THE PERFECT UNION

The subject of forgetfulness of one's twin soul, present in the stories of Shakuntala and Perceval, is a typical subject of those popular tales you loved so much, Blanca: fairy tales. Let's consider two parallel examples taken from that sky-blue bound book, *Grimm's Fairy Tales*. Both the heroes from *The Drummer* and *Sweetheart Roland*, before getting married, feel the need to say goodbye to their parents. After parting with their fiancées, they forget them. In the first case, he ignores her warnings about kissing her on the right cheek at the risk of forgetting her. Bewildered, he consents to marry the girl his parents chose for him instead. Roland too will fall for the ploy of the "fake bride" (another typical motif in fairy tales, associated to the forgetting of one's twin soul). While

30. Chrétien de Troyes, *Perceval or the Story of the Grail*, as translated by de Burton Raffel, p. 132–133

in the first tale, the real bride will not stop until she brings her beloved out of his state of amnesia, on the second one she gives up and loses him. But in that vague fairy tale country, tradition demands of every young lady to sing in front of their groom on the day of the wedding. Roland's real bride tries to wriggle out of this, but the other girls drag her to the church. And when he hears her sing, Roland recognises her voice, at which point he recovers his memory and returns to his former self.

These examples would be ideal, Blanca, if, before being prisoners of oblivion, the heroes of these stories were married instead of merely engaged. That is why I think the stories of Shakuntala and Perceval are more appropriate to illustrate the subject of recognition of your promised mate. Because in the secret marriage of Shakuntala and Duyshanta, as with Perceval and Blanchefleur, one can perceive the original matrimony of twin souls: a matrimony celebrated in Heaven – in the Origin – which, once on Earth, is forgotten by the spouses, or they keep only the slightest reminiscence of it. This original matrimony is the cornerstone on which our theory rests, my love, the theory of twin souls; the "twin" part coming precisely from the fact that the souls had been, once, *married.* I mean a marriage that is not a mere adhesion, a simple sum of factors but on the contrary, a *perfect union*, without cracks, a state of absolute non-separation, of non-Duality. In the rich metaphysical vocabulary, coined by the most ancient languages, there is a specific word for it, since it's one of the key concepts of Metaphysics. That word is *adjava* or *advaita* in Sanskrit, yehud in Hebrew, *tawhid* in Arabic...

You can picture the twin souls' journey, Blanca, by imagining them as biological twins (to which our ancient sages often compared them) in their mother's womb. Identical, or monozygotic, twins are, at the beginning of reproduction, one thing only, a single zygote; it's in the course of gestation when that one thing splits, dividing into two embryos. According to our sages, the single Original soul's split into two separate souls is the root of sexual differentiation, so, in that case, another way of showing the twin souls' journey is as Perceval's teacher does when, initiating him into the code of chivalry, he says: "Man and woman grow from the same seed, never forget that."[31] The *Zohar* explains in a similar way... But before I transcribe that passage, my dear, let me tell you about this enigmatic book to which we will frequently refer in these letters: *Sefer Ha-Zohar*, the "Book of Splendor", or "*The Kabbalistic Bible*", as some people call it.

I should start by saying that Kabbalah is Judaism's esoteric knowledge. *Kabbalah* means "tradition" in Hebrew. An oral tradition born from mystic intuition and which seed dates back to the Babylonian exile (sixth century BC), or even more: to the time of Moses, according to the Kabbalists. But it would not be until the thirteenth century that Kabbalists from Provence and the Iberian Peninsula would begin writing down, in numerous books, all this vast oral tradition... Let me just say, while we are on this subject, Blanca, that the Kabbalists were like you in their near religious respect towards books. The cult of the book is, in fact, one of the constants in Jewish tradition, where books are not destroyed; when they become unusable, they are buried in a cemetery, following the required ritual. A medieval rabbi[32] recommends his students, when they knock over the inkwell

31. Wolfram von Eschenbach, *Parzival*, p. 99
32. Rabbí Yeuda-el Hassid, *Sefer Jasidim*, quoted by Marcos Ricardo Barnatán, *La Kábala*, p. 63

while writing, to first clean the stain from their books and only then from their clothes. After the *Torah*, or Pentateuch (which for the Kabbalists was a kind of autobiographical book, since they believed it to have been dictated by God), the most sacred Jewish book is the *Talmud*. But another book would, in time, reach its importance; to the point that the *hassidim*, the pious, would in their prayers thank God for having been born after it came out, thus being able to benefit from its profound wisdom. That book, Kabbalah's canonical text, is the *Zohar*.

A dense halo of mystery has always surrounded the *Zohar*. Not only for its highly esoteric content, but also for its authorship. The wisdom it contains are the grounds resulting from a long process of sedimentation. But the identity of the person, or people, who converted all that millenary knowledge into a book, has been a regular subject of controversy. The legend, which quickly took over the subject, presents opinions to suit everyone's tastes. Some date the book back to the patriarch Abraham; others claim it comes directly from Heaven, through the prophet Elias; others yet attribute its authorship to Solomon – considered one of the first great Kabbalists. There are even those who conjecture angels brought it to Earth. But the most widespread opinion, Blanca, is the one supported by the book itself, which points to a notable second century Tannaitic sage, Simeon bar Yochai, and his disciple, Rabbi Abba. That theory implies the book had been kept hidden for a long stretch of time, waiting for the right moment for its dissemination. It's told that a Kabbalist from Safed discovered the first page of the *Zohar* being used as fish wrapping paper. He rushed to rescue the rest from the hands of the Arab fishermen who sold it to him, who had found it in a cave. But leaving legends aside, my dear, the fact is that the *Zohar* became known to the public at the end of the thirteenth century. The man responsible for this was a renowned Castilian Kabbalist, who today is considered by most scholars as its true author. However, he – Rabbi Moses ben Shem-Tov from Leon – has eluded the honour, claiming he only copied from an ancient manuscript that had miraculously reached his hands and attributed it to the aforementioned Simeon bar Yochai, who is also the central figure of the book.

It was Simeon bar Yochai's answer to one of his disciples what I intended to cite to you a moment ago. It goes like this: "Before coming to this Earth, each soul and each spirit is composed of one man and one woman united in one single being. Descending to Earth, these two halves are separated and sent to incarnate two different bodies. When it's time for marriage, God unites them as before."[33]

This last sentence, Blanca, subscribes to a belief also widely shared among our sages, echoed in the maxim *Marriages are made in Heaven*. It's the belief that Fate tends to reunite on Earth those who had been mates in the Origin. Of course, this tendency not always follows through to success. Sometimes it's interrupted. Such is the case with the main characters from *The Story of the Stone*, for example. But in that admirable Chinese novel, there is also an example of accomplished matrimonial predestination, Blanca. We can find it towards the end of the book. It's as if, to finish, the author -Xueqin- had wished to make up for the earlier failure of his main characters' matrimonial predestination. To achieve this, he used Aroma -Bao-yu's maid, but also his friend and confidant- and the amateur actor Bijou. Aroma

33. *Sefer ha-Zohar*

and Bijou never appear together throughout the book, but they had exchanged a proof of love without even realising it. How is that possible?, you ask. It's possible, Blanca, because on a certain occasion Bijou had offered a red silk belt to his friend Bao-yu, who in turn borrowed from Aroma a green belt to return the favour, while giving her the red one. The years go by and we arrive at that terrible day (or fortunate day, according to the Taoist perspective) in which Bao-yu vanishes. Consequently, Aroma becomes unemployed, and so her family arranges a marriage for her. In the morning after the wedding, her husband is helping her unpack when, among her dresses, he finds the red silk belt. Surprised, he fetches the green belt and shows it to her. "Upon seeing the belt Bao-yu had received from her, Aroma understood that her new husband was none other than the amateur actor Bijou, and began to believe in the predetermination of conjugal unions."[34] "Aroma's married life -ends Xueqin- is the first chapter of another story."

So then, Blanca, even though Fate tends to reunite twin souls here on Earth, there are multiple interfering factors capable of ruining it. Let's go back to that *Zohar* passage. After saying that, when the time for marriage has arrived, God reunites the Original mates (the souls who had been one in the Origin), it concludes "But this union depends on man's life, on how he has lived it. If he has lived a pure and pious life, he will enjoy such union as the one preceding his birth, which was the *perfect union*. This way, the man and his mate will belong to each other forever"[35] Meaning the *Zohar* makes the union with one's twin soul on Earth conditional

34. Cao Xueqin, *Le Reve dans le pavillon rouge*, vol. II, p. 1577
35. *Ibid.* (Italics by the letter's author)

on one living a virtuous life. This determining factor, along with others, led its author to annotate his statement saying "the Holy One, blessed be He... brings couples together"[36] with "It's difficult for the Holy One to bring couples together".[37] (Are you shocked by the soubriquet? It's only one of the many methods employed in Jewish tradition to refer to God without naming Him, as is prescribed.)

Joseph Gikatilla, another great man of the Jewish Kabbalah, agrees with his contemporary, Moses of Leon, about the meeting of the twin souls depending on whether they are worthy or not. In his opuscule *The Secret of the Marriage of David and Bathsheba*, Gikatilla supports the idea that King David did not find his twin soul at first due to his "evil inclination", which in Jewish tradition is also a euphemism for lust. "In that sense, know and understand that David, peace be upon him, had an evil inclination. For that reason he was not worthy of Bathsheba from the beginning, even though she had been destined to him since the six days of Genesis (since Creation, Blanca, which took six days, according to the Genesis), from where emanated the soul of David and that of Bathsheba, the female half of the couple."[38]

A LOVE STORYLINE

If we believe the ancient sages, my dear, it's not enough to perform good deeds in this life, or in previous ones, to

36. *Sefer ha–Zóhar* I 89a, 90b, 91b, 137a, 229a
37. v.353
38. Joseph Gikatilla, translated from *El secreto de la unión de David y Betsabé*, p. 58

reunite with your twin soul on Earth. There are other reasons explaining why said reunion does not happen in every link along the chain of reincarnated shapes that is human life. That it does not always happen, at least, in propitious circumstances to delve into erotic love, the specific love between twin souls. Our twin soul may have elected to embody not our Earthly spouse, but someone else close to ourselves, maybe a brother, or a friend. In those cases, the affinity will still shine through, except it will do so through its corresponding bond – fraternal, friendship... Our twin soul may have even chosen not to coincide with us in this life at all, Blanca. We could compare it to what happens in those long romance novels, of which you have so many in your library: The protagonist's beloved is not always present in every chapter there either, or not always with the same prominence. The love story may sometimes be put aside for a moment in favour of other episodic storylines. The novel begins and ends with its protagonist couple and its main storyline; but in-between, side plots and other characters intertwine. In addition, that seems to be what also happens with the vital cycle of a soul, with the cycle formed by all its reincarnations. The main storyline is a love story: the relationship of the soul with its twin. Those are the protagonists. But sometimes, in certain chapters, certain existences, a side plot or secondary character develops a momentary relevance. Maybe in past lives the soul had contracted with that character what Xueqin metaphorically called a "debt of tears" – a karmic debt, in Eastern metaphysical jargon – and now the time has come to settle that debt. (What is peculiar about a "debt of tears" connecting a soul to its twin, is that the debt was contracted in previous lives, and not in the Origin.) Alternatively, perhaps that character or side story can provide the soul with something, teach it an important lesson. Or maybe such lesson must be learned in solitude, without the help of the twin soul. In any case, once the debt is settled, once the lesson is learned, the main storyline comes to the fore again, and the twin soul recovers its corresponding importance.

And if finding our twin soul on Earth isn't guaranteed, Blanca, neither is recognising it in case we find it. Recognition may require a certain degree of maturity, a certain refinement or *evolution* of the soul (we will clarify this concept in future letters) that allows us to keep our "eye of the heart" open; the heart being the metaphorical organ of recognition since, as an Arabic adage says, *the heart sees what the eye can't.* It may happen that only one of the twin souls has reached that evolutionary stage; then, recognition will not be mutual, but unilateral. It's a rare case, no doubt. But so thorough was the study performed by that Andalusian sage I mentioned at the beginning, that such possibility did not evade him.

> It may be objected, that if Love were as I have described, it would be exactly equal in both the parties concerned, since the two parts would be partners in the act of union and the share of each would be the same. To this I reply, that the objection is indeed well-founded; but the soul of the man who loves not one who loves him is beset on all sides by various accidents which occlude, and veils that encompass it about, those earthy temperaments which now overlay it, so that his soul does not sense that part which was united with it before it came to occupy its present lodging-place. Had his soul been liberated from these restrictions, the two would have been equal in their experience of union and love. As for the lover, his soul is indeed free and aware of where that other is that shared with it in ancient proximity; his soul is ever seeking for the other, striving

> after it, searching it out, yearning to encounter it again, drawing it to itself if might be as a magnet draws the iron.[39]

I should insist, however, Blanca, on emphasising how exceptional cases such as the one Ibn Hazm contemplates above are. From what I could gather from my readings (among them Hazm's book, *The Ring of the Dove*), twin souls usually evolve in unison. When recognition is unilateral, without reciprocation, or with passing reciprocation, then the odds are we are dealing with a mistake. Unrequited loves tend to be misguided loves, errors of perception, since recognition, as we will see, is fallible. In any event, if one is the exception (though there is no human way of telling), if there is, indeed, a certain obfuscation preventing recognition on the part our twin soul, then the best thing to do is to leave it alone, to give it time. If it does not recognises us in this life, it will in the next; forcing recognition will only result in further obfuscation. That rainy afternoon on the tram, Blanca, if you had changed seats instead of laughing at my jokes, would you have liked it if I, not taking the hint, sat again next to you? You would not have liked that, would you? Have no doubt, the best advice for a spurned lover is to accept it, turn the page, and search for love in other arms. (On my part, I am sure that I would have found it, you know? Remember that girl from my neighbourhood, the one I had my eye on when I met you? I am positive that I could had been happy by her side too. It's just that, had she been in your place, it's quite possible that now I would not be here playing detective, nor writing this letter.)

Speaking of meeting your twin soul on Earth, and its difficulty, it reminds me now of a film I watched some years ago.

39. Ibn Hazm op. Cit.

(It's so strange, how difficult it is to go to the cinema without you!) I hesitate writing the title here because, in this context, it sounds quite inappropriate. It's titled *Don't Die Without Telling Me Where You're Going*[40] and it's by one of the last remaining cinematographic poets. I know you would have loved this film. In spite of its fair share of humour, the plot is serious, sometimes even moving. It tells us about a man who is visited by the ghost of a woman. This woman had been his partner in numerous past lives, and she would have been so too in this one except, somewhere between lives, they lost track of each other. He reincarnated as a new person, but she did not want to start a new mortal life without him. So, from Heaven, she pulls some strings to find him and appear to him as a ghost.

A noted fourteenth century Italian poetry book brings us another ghost of a woman – another ghost in love: *Il Canzoniere* written by Petrarch. In those melodic, wonderful verses, Petrarch, filled with emotion, tells us how his dear Laura (for whom he fell in a powerful case of love at first sight, like his compatriot and contemporary Dante, when he saw her coming out of mass at the Saint-Claire d'Avignon convent, one Good Friday) appears to him, from beyond the grave, to console him. Sometimes he can only hear her voice inside his head. However, most frequently she would appear to him fully visible. She appears at night, sitting at the foot of his bed, and starts a conversation with him, in a most "sweet, soft and quiet" tone. What do they talk about? Well, you can imagine; they talk about their love and of whatever is happening in his life. In these nocturnal dates between life

---

40. Argentinian film written and directed by Eliseo Subiela, original title: *No te mueras sin decirme adonde vas* (1995)

and death, both reach a stage of spiritual intimacy such as they had never experienced in her lifetime. They never experienced it, Blanca, because their lives took different paths; Laura was married to another man. Despite that, when referring to their lives, Laura's ghost employs the singular "*our* life", as if between her life and Petrarch's existed a secret bond. As if their lives, separated only in appearance, had been, deep down, lived together.

CHILDREN'S LOVE

Petrarch's *Il Canzioniere* is not a blue book, my love, it cannot be found in your library. Many other excellent books can, though, among them several novels by the English sisters Brontë, of which one portraits a similar situation to that of Petrarch's in *Il Canzioniere*. In it, a couple is also deeply in love, but the circumstances of live separate them. Then, she dies and he is left sad and alone. But what appeared to be a permanent separation turned into a renewed proximity, for she comes back from the dead. Returns to the world –or to her lover's imagination– as a ghost. And to see her again, to talk to her again, brings him great comfort... As you may have guessed, I'm talking about *Wuthering Heights*, the great romance novel written in mid-nineteenth century by Emily Brontë (that sky-blue book we read together one summer, not in the intimate domestic soirées I reminisced about earlier, but outside, sitting in the shade of a pine tree or walking through the vineyards in the afternoon).

The main characters were children when Catherine's father took Heathcliff off the streets and adopted him. The two kids soon grow close because, regardless of the social chasm between them, they recognise a secret affinity between them. Later, Catherine will reflect aloud about that affinity, saying: "...so he shall never know how I love him: and that, not because he's handsome, but because he's more myself than I am. Whatever our souls are made of, his and mine are the same" Do you see, Blanca? Catherine recognises in Heathcliff her twin soul. *Wuthering Height*'s approach is similar to that of *The Story of the Stone*, only in a different frame: while in the Chinese novel we had an idyllic garden, in here we have lonely moors and pastures. Apart from that, the similarities are considerable. There are also children in love. Two children -one adopted- raised as brother and sister, who are traumatically separated upon reaching adulthood. We have the theme of love sickness: for several weeks, Catherine falls in a grave "state of delirium" after Heathcliff's sudden departure. We have the theme of the "false bride" -groom, in this case. And the theme of dying out of love, and love after death.

In fact, both stories fit the mould of a very old story template. This template, Blanca, is reproduced in many love stories not only in the West but also in the East, as it's a universal template. I am sure you will find the main couple of this type of stories to your liking since they are not only a couple in love but, usually (and I know one of your great sorrows in life was not having children), a couple of children in love. The reason behind my choice lies in the nature of children's love, that of early adolescence, which is also, besides a pure and innocent love, an extremely intense love -as intense as it is pure, the two seem to be correlated. An intensity that is, furthermore, constant: a love that is forever riding high on the crest of a wave that will never break on the seashore. Adult love, on the other hand, will eventually cool down, settle over time and become a habit. Though I have to add something that you and I know from experience, Blanca: this cooling down of love is not inevitable. It's not true that love, after its initial voluptuousness, can do no other thing besides declining. There's one other way, and that way is up: it's *transformation*.

But I'm getting ahead of myself: such is my eagerness to share my findings with you! So, there is a template that repeats itself in romantic literature across time. A boy and a girl raised together in intimate harmony. These two children are often described as twin brothers, though such condition is often circumvented (as Brontë and Xueqin do) by using adoption as a subterfuge. Nevertheless, it's still apparent in the fact that the kids are inseparable, that they do everything together, and that there exists between them a great physical similarity, as well as a kind of affinity, a secret bond, as is the case with twin brothers. Their childhood together is often described in paradisiacal terms. But tragedy is near, with the coming of adulthood. And what does that tragedy consist of? Of mutual separation, which banishes the children from the private Paradise that is their life together. The two young lovers are cast off into the world, like Adam and Eve in the biblical Genesis, and spend the rest of their lives searching for each other as they yearn for that lost Paradise of infancy. Here it's, Blanca, the pattern in which a great number of classic, and modern, love stories are cut. We will have occasion to see more examples, but that will be in later letters, now I should wrap up this one. Rereading it, I noticed the inappropriate recurrence of the subject of *post–mortem* appearances, and I hasten to clarify that there is no hidden intention behind it. Don't get me wrong, I am not deliberately insisting on that subject to incite you to follow suit. But I am sorry, it's no laughing matter. In fact, I confess that because of my inquiries, I have been more alert, more receptive. Maybe that is why I am noticing details now that before would have passed me by. Or they would have looked incidental to me, like when one night a navy blue book came off the shelf when I opened the glass-paned door, and from it fell a little flower you had left between the pages to dry. I cannot be sure, of course, but it might have been a flower from the first bouquet I bought you over fifty years ago. Then there is –like now, while I am writing to you– that indomitable feeling of you being here with me. It's so strong that sometimes I cannot avoid turning around suddenly, hoping to catch you there *in fraganti* (Don't tell anyone, but I feel like you are receiving this letter as I am writing it, as if you were reading it over my shoulder.) Lately, I seem to smell your perfume...

Ah, and speak of the devil: your perfume. What was it called? I have been trying to remember it for a long time. It's a shame there is no opened bottle on your dresser. I wish I had kept one, to open it once in a while, you know, like you used to do with the collection of smells from your childhood, to be transported back through the tunnel of time to those happy days. Your friends could not tell me, and at the perfume shops, they tell me there is no linden blossom perfume. However, yours always reminded me (yes, I know you thought it was absurd) of the sweet aroma of linden. Now look... the opposite happens: it's linden that stirs in me memories of your perfume. That is why I have become so fond of infusions and –in Spring afternoons– of strolling up and down the fragrant Linden Tree Avenue at the Parc de la Ciutadella, which, on top of that, brings up so many memories of when we were young and used to go there... But let me tell you, all that has become superfluous: because now your perfume follows me. It surrounds me as I write to you, like a ghostly scent. I cannot help but speculate you are really present, even if not physically. Or maybe it's your absence what I perceive, as they say of the amputees, who are awaken in the middle of the night by a stinging sensation in their absent limb... It's a pertinent comparison, for I feel like they have amputated the better half of me. And it's curious, my love, because, in some way, this feeling supports the theory of twin souls, the one I wanted to introduce you to in these letters.

Yours

SECOND LETTER

THE HEAVENLY MARRIAGE

(OR THE ANDROGYNE)

For this reason, a man will leave his
father and mother and be united
to his wife and the two will become
flesh. This mystery is profound.

St. Paul, Ephesians 5:31–32

Barcelona, June 17th, 1999

Dear Blanca:

From time to time, you talked to me about God. Fortunatly, it was very sporadically, really: because hearing about a supreme being that, back then, did not exist for me, would get on my nerves, to tell you the truth. On the other hand, I could hear you talk about Jesus for hours. In fact, you know the Gospels were, and still are, one of my favourite reads. For me, Jesus existed on an extraordinary level: he existed, most of all, in his message of love for everyone, in his predilection for the humble and the afflicted, in his unconditional love for humanity, and in his sacrifice. But God, that invisible God to whom Jesus, hanging from the cross, screamed in agony "Why have you forsaken me?" That God did not exist to me. So, hearing you talk about Him bothered me, I'm sorry; it riled me up, no matter how much I tried to hide it.

However... no, look, now I'm thinking that what really upset me was not that; maybe I was aware that, even though reason denied it, my heart agreed with it. Do you know what I mean? Ah, but the heart always stands on the losing side: since to know about such matters, reason always appeared to be the most reliable approach. Theologians are probably right when they claim all of us harbour a feeling of God, it's just that sometimes we ignore it. But note, though, how theologians go even further: they maintain that the mere presence of a feeling of God in Man's heart is in itself a proof of His existence. Since –as they assure us- that feeling is innate, it's actually a reminiscence. Well, if it's as they say, Blanca, then along with a feeling of God (and, as I hope to demonstrate during the course of these letters, closely bound to it), there exists in Man's heart another innate feeling of no less power. The feeling of the twin soul, of the one creature who, out of every other, is destined to us, for it's the other half that will complete us.

Yes, you're right: To be fair, we have to recognise that, in this world, it's very rare to have those two feelings validated by our immediate reality. It often seems like reality is actively intent on denying them. One only has to turn on the news, open the newspapers, look around, or look to oneself. If we are talking about God, we have the countless adversities and injustices overshadowing the world; if we are talking about twin souls, the proliferation of divorces, disagreements and loneliness... One thing makes you think, though, Blanca: those feelings seem to possess a strange tenacity. How many people continue to believe in God after a tragedy? And how many drag behind them a long list of heartbreaks and failed love affairs, and still refuse to give up the search for their other half?... And then we have the exceptions; the rare cases where those feelings do find some kind of validation –even if subjective– in our immediate reality. And so, speaking of the feeling of God, I am reminded of these words by C.G. Jung, the modern sage with an "ancient perspective" I mentioned before. While preparing his memoirs, Jung confided in his collaborator, Aniela Jaffé, something quite surprising for a psychologist: He told her that, for him, God had always been "one of the most immediate experiences"[41].

But let's continue with the feeling we were discussing: that of the twin soul. As far as we know, the first westerner to give it a theoretical shape was the Greek philosopher Plato, who, in the fifth century BC, told the following wonderful story, as if being told by his contemporary Aristophanes: Formerly –he explains– human beings were dual... "the primeval man was round, his back and sides forming a circle; and he had four hands and the same number of feet, one head with two faces, looking opposite ways, set on a round neck and precisely alike; also four ears, two privy members, and the remainder to correspond."[42] That made Man extremely powerful. However, since such power defied the Gods, Zeus broke them in half. Since then, each half is looking for the other half that completes it: "Each of us when separated, having one side only, like a flat fish, is but the tally-half of a man, and he is always looking for his other half."[43]

There are those who, to discredit this speech, Blanca (people are very fussy), would point out that Aristophanes was a comic playwright. But that would be missing Plato's intended effect; he used a comic mask to hide from the majority what

41. CG Jung, *Memories, Dreams, Reflections*, p.xi
42. Plato, *Symposium*
43. *Ibid*

was for him -from what we can gather from the testimonies of his disciple, Aristotle- one of his most valuable theories, the core of Plato's so-called "unwritten doctrines". In another of his *Dialogues*, Plato clearly said that the philosopher never writes down what for him holds the "highest value"[44]. Others, to depreciate the testimony, would object to the fact that Aristophanes differentiates three separate bi-units: one male/female, one male/male, and one female/female when scholars agree to see it as Plato's attempt to justify homosexuality, which was rather widespread in his homeland. Referring to the passage in question, interpreters often translate into "tally-half" the Greek word *symbolon*. A *symbolon*, Blanca, was a wooden tally stick split into two that allowed two people who had never met to recognise each other by joining both halves of the stick. In ancient China, they had a similar practice, only it was for a different purpose. Chinese couples who got along well, if they were to be apart for a long time, would break a hand mirror in two, each keeping one-half. This way, by looking into their split mirrors, they would have their feelings confirmed: the current absence of their other half. In China, the mirror was a symbol of conjugal happiness and, universally (due to it duplicating individuals), a traditional symbol of kinship..., for which reason a broken mirror certainly becomes an ideal tally-half between twin souls, my dear. For us, on the other hand, the wooden tally will also work as a metaphor.

Doesn't the definition of the Greek *symbolon* remind you of that idea we spoke of last time? The concept of a beauty subjective to each individual, that sort of encrypted message decipherable only to the holder of the key? Your subjective

---

44. Plato, *Phaedrus*, 278 D

beauty, Blanca –that hidden beauty made for my eyes only– would be the counterpart to my half of the *symbolon*. In the story of *Shakuntala* that I told you in my previous letter, that tally–half would be symbolised by the ring, thanks to which King Duyshanta recognises his secret wife. In another famous Eastern book (a book that, with its six volumes bound in a midnight blue that matches its title, stands out from all the other tomes in your library), in *One Thousand and One Nights* I mean, there is a delightful story in which rings also seem to play the part of *symbolon*, of a tally–half for recognition. Even though we read that story in one of those dearly missed domestic soirees, it's been many years (*One Thousand and One Nights*, you'll remember, was one of the first books we read together), and there are so many *Nights*, so many stories, that maybe you don't remember the one I'm about to tell you:

In two kingdoms very far apart, lived a prince and a princess unknown to each other; yet they were so alike one could take them for twins (again and again, narrators resorts to this metaphorical kinship). One morning, the young princes wake up wearing each other's rings, remembering and missing each other. What happened? Something very odd happened, my dear. You see, that night they had the attention of a couple of genies –the invisible and improbable beings that populate *One Thousand and One Nights*. The female genie discovered the prince, the male genie the princess, and both argued over who was the most beautiful. To compare them, they moved the sleeping princess across the skies, and placed her next to the prince in his bed. Lying next to each other, their kinship became so evident; it delighted the mischievous genies, who decided to wake them up one at a time to observe their reaction. Obviously, the young couple immediately fell in love; it was a case of mutual love at first sight. As proof of their love, they each took the other's ring before falling asleep again at the hands of the genies, who quickly returned the princess back to her bed in the faraway kingdom. This exchange of rings, though, will later serve for them to, sight unseen, mutually recognise each other as their "lost love."[45]

Going back to Plato's story, there are similar tales concerning the double nature of the Primordial Man in several spiritual traditions. Thus, one of the key pieces of Hermetic tradition (about which we will have the opportunity to talk at length in a future letter), a treaty called *Poemander*, recounts the excision God inflicted upon the original Men, the ones considered to have been dual, simultaneously male and female. It says, "...the bond that bound them all was loosened by God's Will... and some became male, some in like fashion female..." We can also find stories of the same tenor in Jewish tradition. According to a rabbinic commentary on the book of Genesis, written towards the end of the fifth century, "Adam and Eve were made back to back and united by the shoulders; afterwards, God separated them with one blow, splitting them into two". Following this, he mentions a variation of this theory: "There is another opinion: the first Man was half male on his right side, half female on his left side"[46]. Further down in the same text, we can also read "Rabbi Jeremiah b. Leazar said: When the Holy One, blessed be He, created Adam, He created him a hermaphrodite, for it's said, *Male and female created He them and called their name Adam* (Genesis 5, 2). Rabbi Samuel b. Nahman said: When

---

45. *One Thousand and One Nights, "The story of Kamar Azzaman, son of King Xahraman"*
46. Midrash Genesis Rabah 1:1

the Lord created Adam He created him double-faced, then He split him and made him of two backs, one back on this side and one back on the other side. To this it is objected: But it is written, and He took one of his ribs, etc. (Genesis 11, 21) *Mi-zalothaw* (means one of his ribs), replied he, as you read: *And for the second side (zela') of the tabernacle, etc.* (Ex. xxvi, 20)"[47]

Elémire Zolla adds to this type of stories another frequent mythological motif: the decapitation of the primordial half-man, half-female being by a supreme God. In this case, Blanca, the male, represented by the head, is separated from its body -the woman-, either to destroy a power that could rival God's own, or to create the world and all that came about from that sacrifice. As an example, he quotes from the Hindu myth of *Namuci*, who, having snatched *soma* -the drink of the Gods- from Indra, the God of the Sky, was decapitated by Indra's *vajra*, his diamond thunderbolt. And since I mentioned a Hindu myth: the primordial Man of Hinduism, Purusha, contains in himself both man and woman. "The wise man knows that woman resides on the left side of the male", one can read in a Hindu sacred text, the *Tripura Samhita.*

To the old exegetes, the attentive annotators of the Scriptures, Eve was contained in Adam. That is how God was able to extract her from his body: "The Lord God caused a deep sleep to fall upon the man, and while he slept closed up his ribs and closed its place with flesh, and the rib that the Lord God had taken from the man he made into a woman..." (Genesis 2: 21:23) As we have seen above, the Hebrew word for "rib" (sela') can also be translated as "side", which led Jewish exegetes to the idea (though they had already thought

47. Midrash Genesis Rabbah 8:1

of it, Blanca, the Scriptures only corroborated it) that Eve was originally one of Adam's sides -the left one, to be precise. Meaning Adam, the first Man, was, in the moment of his creation, a dual being.

TWO IN ONE

The Primordial Man, my dear, this half-man, half-woman human being (the time has come for me to introduce you to the protagonist of these letters), is the *Androgyne*. Anthropologists and religion historians have pointed out the coincidence in so many different cultures characterising the first man, the Original Man, as an androgynous being -from *Andros-gyne*, "man-woman" in Greek. The Androgyne is a recurring figure in ancient thought and art. Artists would sometimes paint it as a single human individual in possession of both sexes, or as a man and a woman joined at the back. More often, though, it was represented by the shape of a double human, either with two heads on one body, or two halves of a face on one head: The left head or face, and its corresponding half body, unequivocally female; everything on the right side, distinctively male. (Finding this enigmatic figure, with its double pair of eyes, staring at me from the cover of an Alchemy book on display on a bookshop's widow, was what, shortly after your death, put me back on your track, Blanca. To be honest, that was the first of a series of coincidences, usually book related, that have marked my way up to this point: to this hope I have of being with you again in a more or less near future.)

In the illustrations, the Androgyne usually appears wearing a crown and dressed in regal finery. Its both halves are often accompanied by symbols reinforcing their complementarity by contrast: the male half may be shown with a rising sun on its back or wielding a sword (a phallic symbol), and the female half may be seen alongside the moon or holding a cup (symbolising the vagina). The ancient artists bestowed on the Androgyne all sorts of symbolic objects. Thus, it's common to find it holding in its hands an open compass, or a letter Y, both symbols of the androgynous essence, which consists of their dual nature, of them being two in one (the branching of the compass and the letter Y, evokes a united Duality, or a dual Unity). Or, with identical symbolism, the Androgyne can be shown holding a rod with two intertwined serpents –the caduceus, or rod of Hermes. It may also appear haloed by a rainbow, or an iridescent peacock tail, both symbols of the union of all colours, meaning diversity in unity. Or (as I saw it on that bookshop window) backed by an eagle, or holding a blue flower in its hand (yes, my love, a flower of this specific colour). And do you know how it's depicted sometimes? Flaunting a pair of wings and crushing a dragon beneath its feet: this serves to indicate its otherworldly nature.

Because the Androgyne's nature is not from this world, did you know, Blanca? It's true that the illustrations (such as those that often appear in Alchemy books) portrayed them with a corporeal form, carnal, and that is also how the ancient sages described them to us. We have already observed that Plato portrayed the Original androgynous Men as having arms, legs, ears and even genitals. Nonetheless, it would be a mistake to interpret these portraits literally. The corporeal holds for them a symbolic value: it refers to an immaterial reality –that of the soul– impossible to describe if not symbolically. In Plato's description, the spherical human body with eight limbs -four arms and four legs- represents the perfect union of two *souls*. That is how, for example, a ninth century Arab writer -Ibn Dawud al-Isfahani- sees it when, concerning the famous passage from the Platonic *Symposium*, he writes: "Certain philosophy followers have believed God, praised be His glory, created every spirit as a round shape, like a sphere, and then split it into two halves, placing each half in a different body. For that reason, the body that finds the other body in which its other half soul is contained will fall in love with it due to that primitive affinity, and so human characters will associate according to the needs of their nature."[48]

The Androgyne awakes secret reverberations in the soul. They come -as it has been shown in our century by C.G. Jung- from the deepest recesses of human memory. Hence its universality, hence the Androgyne being a recurring motif in Art and universal Literature, and us being able to find it in every culture's imaginary. This universality, my dear, matches the universality of the love predestination concept, for the simple reason that a common origin determines a common destination. As Plato claims through Aristophanes, the primordial Androgyne explains love predestination and its cause. Twin souls are predestined, they are made for one another because they share the same origin, because both together formed one entity in the Origin; their calling is to restore the Androgynous being. Thus, Androgyny takes place not only in the origin of erotic love, Blanca, but also in its destination. It's not relegated solely to the distant past, but (and this is what matters the most to us, my dear) it projects itself into the future.

---

48. Ibn Dawud al-Fahani *The Book of the Flower*

As old and universal as the Androgyne, is the Origin myth that usually accompanies it: the myth of the *dual man* who is split into two halves. We can find traces of this myth, in its innumerable versions, as far back as prehistoric times. Most of them describe the excision in terms of punishment and tragedy. That is the case with the Platonic version. Nevertheless, there are variants in which the split does not have a negative connotation. This favourable interpretation is the predominant one in Eastern texts. Take, for example, a famous passage from *Brihadaranyaka Upanishad*... Forgive me, I mentioned this text as if it was one of the blue library books. What are the Upanishads? Originally, they were secret teachings the ancient Hindu sages imparted on their disciples during gatherings in the woods, away from worldly noises. Their purpose was the induction to the knowledge of the Vedas, Hinduism Sacred Scriptures. These "secret teachings" (that is what the Sanskrit word *upanishad* means), these inspired comments on the Scriptures, would then be compiled in a large series of texts, which later on became the last section of the Vedas.

Well, one of these sacred texts, Blanca, one of the greatest ones, is the *Brihadaranyaka Upanishad* which I was about to quote. There, we can read: "In the beginning, this universe was but the self of a human form *(Purusha)*... He was not at all happy. Therefore, people (still) are not happy when alone. He desired a mate. He became as big as man and wife embracing each other. He parted this very body into two. From that came husband and wife. Therefore, said Yãjñavalkya (to whom the teachings in *Brihadaranyaka Upanishad* are attributed), this body is one–half of oneself, like one of the two halves of a split pea."[49]... But let's look at another fa-

49. *Brihadaranyaka Upanishad,* 1.4.1–1.4.3

vourable version of the excision of the Primordial Man into two halves, this time a Western one. It's brought to us by Renaissance wise man Judah Abravanel, otherwise known as Leo the Hebrew, in his *Dialogues of Love*. It's based, as you'll see, in two Creation stories from the Book of Genesis:

> Adam, the first man, created by God on the sixth day of Creation, being one sole human individual, contained in himself both male and female without distinction, and it says (in the Scripture) that "God created Adam in His own image, male and female He created them". He employs the singular form first –Adam, a man– (the Hebrew word *adam*, Blanca, refers not to the male gender but to the generic "man", to the human being independent of its gender) and the plural form next – "man and female He created them" – thus indicating that even when Adam was one individual only, he contained male and female simultaneously. A note on this passage, made in the Chaldean language by ancient Hebrew scholars, says "Adam was made of two people: on one part male, on the other, female". This is specified towards the end of the text, when it says God created Adam, male and female, and named them Adam, clarifying that Adam alone contained both genders and that an individual formed by both genders was called Adam, for the female, Eve, is never mentioned until she's separated from the male, Adam. This is from where Plato and the Greeks took the primitive Androgyne, half-male and half-female. Then, God proceeds "It's not good that man should be alone; I will make a helper suitable for him", meaning it did not appear as Adam, male and female, were happy sharing a body, united by the back, with faces on opposite sides. It would be better if the female was separated and standing before him, face to face, so she could be of help. To prove it, He brought before Adam

all the animals from land and sky, to see if he would be satisfied with having one of the female animals as his companion; and he named the animals according to their nature, yet found none that would be a suitable helper and consort. So God caused Adam to fall into a sleep, and He took one of his sides (*sela'*), which in Hebrew is a misleading word, also meaning *ribs*, although in this passage, and others, it's used as *side*: that is to say, He took the side, or feminine person, which stood behind Adam, on his back, and separated it from him, and He closed its space with flesh, and from that side He made woman, separate. After being separated she was named Eve, but not before, for then she was part of Adam. Once having created her, God brought her to Adam, recently awakened from his slumber, who said: "This is now bone of my bone, flesh of my flesh; and she shall be called 'woman' for she was taken out of man". And he continues, saying "That is why a man will leave his father and mother and be united with his wife, and the two will become one flesh.", in other words, since they derive from the division of an individual, man and woman are joined back together, through the means of marriage and coitus, as one single carnal individual. From here, Plato took the division of the Androgyne into two separate halves, male and female, and the birth of love, which is the inclination each half feels towards reuniting with the other, thus forming one flesh only.[50]

O MY AMERICA! MY NEWFOUND-LAND!

Even without mentioning us by name, Blanca all these testimonies could still very well be talking about us. They could

50. Leon the Hebrew, translated from *Diálogos de Amor*, p.333-334

be referring to the root of our mutual recognition and, thereby, our mutual love, which then would date back to a time before Time, to a distant Origin in which you and I were not only together, but also *perfectly united*, in such a way that we both formed one single being. If we consider those testimonies, along with others by the ancient sages, the mysterious phenomenon of falling in love (I'm talking about genuine love, that which comes from "deciphering" the subjective beauty) would be nothing but the more or less conscious – and, unfortunately, more or less fallible– recognition of our other half; that other part with whom we formed one whole being in the Origin. Thus, Plato said "And when one of them meets with his other half, the actual half of himself... the pair are lost in an amazement of love and friendship and intimacy, and would not be out of the other's sight, as I may say, even for a moment."[51]

Up until the discovery of America, Earth had also been as a *symbolon*, with its two halves lost to each other. This is a metaphor employed by a great baroque poet, Blanca, for whom I confess my predilection, the English John Donne, when he wrote about his beloved as "my newfound America": *O my America, my newfound–land*"*52*. Except it's not always easy to find, or recognise, the other half of the *symbolon*. Not everyone has our luck, my love. (Or John Donne's luck –though we had agreed luck is not the correct word– who also quickly found, recognised, and secretly married his twin soul. However, this would later result in him losing his job, his social standing, and even his freedom, which some obtuse spirit would surely call *bad* luck!)

---

51. Plato, *Symposium*
52. John Donne, *Elegy 19, To His Mistress Going To Bed*

Nevertheless, I insist: Not everyone has our luck. The discovery of America, to wrap up the metaphor, took many centuries. And that's not all: remember Columbus died convinced he had reached India, he did not recognise the new continent; the same thing can happen with one's twin soul. Besides, sometimes love is wrong, as the song goes, (Attention, though, this is only casually speaking, as even when love is wrong, it's still right, for love is in itself right.) However, love being occasionally wrong seems to me (since I am already speaking casually) undeniable. Actually, it's a fact that you and I loved other people before we fell for each other. And maybe, when we met them, we even experienced the same feeling of familiarity we felt towards one another the first time we met. There is no doubt, though, that in those cases love "was wrong", in the sense that it got the wrong person, like when we believe we recognise someone from afar, only to then approach them and realise our mistake. Or maybe it was objective beauty what we recognised in the other person. And I say recognition here deliberately, my love: because objective beauty is also an old acquaintance of the soul.

To when and where can we trace back this recognition? I'll tell you: to the same time and place as subjective beauty. I mean, it does not really date back (otherwise, such beauty would not attract us since, according to our sages, the soul is only attracted to what reminds it of home) to a "time" and "place" but to that point beyond Time and Space we have called "the Origin". This is something generally accepted among the ancient sages. We can see it in Plato's writings, where instead of recognition, another equivalent word is used: *anamnesis*, that is "reminiscence". In the Origin, says Plato, we lived in perpetual mystic contemplation of Beauty, of absolute Beauty, of Beauty in itself. And even if we forgot it by coming down into Time and Space, any glimpse of beauty still provokes in us that obscure reminiscence. Hence the powerful attraction we feel towards all that is objectively beautiful; particularly (because beauty in people is not the same as beauty in objects) towards beautiful people of the opposite sex.

Of course, the ancient sages were aware of this powerful attraction, this bedazzlement. But notice they were equally aware of the need to resist it. For the beauty that really matters is the one I talked about before: subjective, encrypted beauty, which is a sign from Destiny; a beauty "for your eyes only", for the eyes of the twin soul. Well, as much as objective beauty makes for a powerful stimulus for love, Blanca, "it is not love itself, which resides instead in the identity of the souls who were united in a higher world and that, under our Sun, frantically search for each other once they overcome the material obstacles disfiguring and restraining them."[53] These words are by a prominent Islamicist commenting on a famous eleventh century Arabic treatise on love and lovers. I quoted from this text in my previous letter: *The Ring of the Dove*, do you remember? The title will not sound as cryptic if I tell you that it refers to the good or bad deeds the dove of the soul uses to build the ring of its destiny. Well, in *The Ring of the Dove,* Ibn Hazm of Cordoba writes a discourse on "the Nature of Love", where he says "For my part I consider Love as a conjunction between scattered parts of souls that have become divided in this physical universe, a union effected within the substance of their original sublime element...

53. Translated from Emilio García Gómez', introduction to Ibn Hazm's *The Ring of the Dove*

an affinity of their vital forces in the supernal world, which is their everlasting home, and a close approximation in the manner of their constitution."[54]

Al-Mas'udi, another Arabic wise man, contemporary of Ibn Hazm, regales us with yet another example of the same belief when, alluding to his beloved, he proclaims: "My soul was bound to hers before we were created."[55] And a Sufi sage (a sage who adheres to Sufism, the biggest strand on the "reverse side" of Islam), the Persian Ruzbihan Baqli of Shiraz will, one century later, express an identical conviction in his treatise on mystical love *The Jasmine of the Fedeli d'Amore* (The Jasmine of the Love's Faithful)... But first, what are The Love's Faithful? "Love's Faithful" is what numerous ancient sages and poets of mystical temperament, both in the East and the West, often called themselves. These ancient sages, Blanca, were protectors of a belief essential to the theory of twin souls: the belief that erotic love has its ontological roots in Divinity. The Love's Faithful served as a secular religion: a religion without temples, or Scriptures, priests, or dogmas. A secret religion where they worshipped God under the name of *Love* (which is the most appropriate name for Him, my dear, for, as A. Afifi explains, to these mystics "love is not an abstract quality superadded to [God's] Essence", but rather "the reality of love is identical to the Essence")[56] and access to God wasn't achieved through meditation, but through human love.

---

54. Ibn Hazm, *The Ring of the Dove*, translation by A.J. Arberry
55. Mas'udi, translated from *El banquete en casa de Yahya la Barmécida*. Cf. Emile Dermenghem, *Les plus beaux textes arabes*, La Colombe, París, 1951. (Quoted by R. Nelli, *L'érotique des troubadours*, p. 53)
56. Abu'l-Ala Afifi, *The Mystical Philosophy of Muhyid'Din Ibnul-Arabí*, Cambridge, 1936

Well, then, Ruzbihan Baqli of Shiraz, the Persian Love's Faithful, writes "The holy spirits, in their homeland, in the highest of divine cities, contemplated each other... In this mutual contemplation, they saw the divine traces imbued in their being. Under the spell of this beauty, they united in matrimony, each couple associating according to their degree of affinity. When they came to this world, again they saw each other with the same eyes (the second sight, Blanca), in proportion... to the closeness of one soul with another. Under the light of physiognomy, they recognised each other, and mutually experienced love."[57]

THE SECRET OF THE MARRIAGE OF DAVID AND BATHSHEBA

I just cited from three Muslim examples. The belief in amorous predestination of souls can also be found among sages from the other great religions of the Book. In the previous letter, we talked about Rabbi Joseph Gikatilla, who lived in Castille in the thirteenth century and was one of the great masters of Jewish mysticism, that is, the Kabbalah. Among other treatises on mystic subjects, Gikatilla authored *The Secret of the Marriage of David and Bathsheba*, a text that, as stated in its first lines, he wrote at the request of a friend who had consulted him about the meaning of the Talmudic saying "Bathsheba was destined for *David from the Six Days of Genesis.*[58] The secret revealed in this treatise, Blanca, can be summarised by saying that worldly love cannot always be

57. Ruzbehan Baqli Shirazi, *Jasmine of the Lovers*
58. *Talmud*, Sanhedrín 107a

explained by worldly circumstances: sometimes they obey a celestial circumstance. What is this celestial circumstance? It's that lovers' souls may fortuitously be the split halves of a unique, celestial Soul.

This simultaneously unique and dual Soul, this soul composed of two halves, is none other than the Androgyne, my dear, upon which (akin to most of our sages) Rabbi Gikatilla builds his theory of love predestination. "...in the moment of his creation -he writes- Man was created androgynous by the soul. That is to say, two faces, a form that is both male and female"[59] Gikatilla, then, sets out to shed light on other sayings from the *Talmud*, for example: "*...a Divine Voice emerges and states: 'The daughter of so–and–so shall be the wife of so–and–so'*"[60]. Or this other one, about the inappropriateness of letting certain criteria guide you when it comes to choosing a spouse: *anyone who marries a woman for the sake of money or beauty... will come in a month, and go in a month,61* meaning that such marriage is doomed to fail. One must be guided by the heart, he tells us, we must wait for our twin soul. But we have seen before that to Gikatilla, discovering one's twin soul depended on one's worthiness. This is why, according to the Kabbalists, King David's union with Bathsheba was delayed because of his early penchant for lust. For this reason, she was already married when David met her... I'll remind you of the episode, told in the Second Book of Samuel:

David, King of Israel, while taking a stroll in his palace's terrace one day, sees a woman bathing in a neighbouring

59. Joseph Gikatilla, translated from *El secreto de la unión de David y Betsabé*, p.46
60. *Talmud*, Sanhedrin, 22a
61. *Talmud*, Kiddushin, 70a

house and he falls in love with her. But this woman is married to an army officer stationed at the border. Taking advantage of his absence, David has an adulterous affair with Bathsheba. He wishes to make her his wife, though, so he does a horrible thing, an act that will unleash upon him and his people a divine punishment. He sends a missive to his army's general ordering him to send Uriah, the deceived husband, to the front line. His death opens the way for David and Bathsheba's marriage. But this despicable conduct offends Yahweh, who causes a devastating drought over Israel, and sends a messenger –the prophet Nathan– to rebuke the King. David confesses his sin and repents, but he cannot escape the punishment. The punishment is the death of his son with Bathsheba. Yahweh, however, will give them another son: Solomon, heir to the throne of Israel. Although that, as they say, is another story.

The first crossed-out note on the manuscript's margin. The fact that both surviving words (mon envie) are in French, just like in a subsequent crossed-out note I managed to identify as belonging to *The Magic Mountain* by Thomas Mann, allows me to attribute this quote to the same source, and complete it: (in French, from the German original) "*Je t'aime* -he babbled-, *je t'ai aimée de tout temps, car tu es le Toi de ma vie, mon rêve, mon sort, mon envie, mon éternel désir...*"

When he meets Bathsheba, King David is still controlled by the weakness that, according to Rabbi Gikatilla, has kept them apart up until that point. This weakness, Blanca, this flaw which in the ancient Rabbinic literature is euphemistically referred to as the "evil inclination" *(yatzer hara)*, is lust.

It's this flaw that leads him to murder Uriah, his rival, and to keep countless wives, even after meeting his true love, his original spouse, the one destined to complete his soul. Gikatilla goes as far as detecting, in a verse from the Psalms attributed to David, the King's own acknowledgement of the dilemma standing before him: "I confess my iniquity, and my sin troubles me." (Psalm 38: 18) The Rabbi's interpretation might seem far-fetched, Blanca, but keep in mind that, in general, Kabbalistic interpretations are based on its author's belief system. Taking as interpretative key the postulate that says every human being's true spouse was originally lodged on his side, to Gikatilla the verse's meaning is clear: David was predestined to love Bathsheba, but his evil inclination kept getting in the way.[62]

MARITAL STATUS IN THE ORIGIN

Many Christian sages also professed their belief in the love predestination of souls, the belief that crystallised into the concept of the twin souls. Such concept used to cover the marital form: the twin soul was each individual's true and original *spouse*. It's through this perspective, Blanca, that we will now examine the idea of matrimony as held by the ancient Christian sages and, in particular, some of the Early Church Fathers; I should start by saying that not every opinion held by the Father's, the immediate successors of the Apostles, would be adopted by the Church and incorporated into the dogma. One example is the doctrine of the

62. Cf.: Charles Mopsik in his notes on *El secreto de la unión de David y Betsabé.*

pre-existence of the soul and reincarnation, in which some Fathers believed; we can find another example, in part, in the theory of matrimony that I will now present to you.

To the ancient Christian sages, marriage is not a mere social convention; it's the work of God Himself. The idea is that God had established a heavenly union or marriage in the Origin, and then created humankind from that template, based on that mould. In other words, Blanca: he created it in couples, in marital couples. Love predestination lies, then, in God's act of creation, in which He did not create man and woman separately but simultaneously, in one single act: he created them *united*. Although the Christian sages reached this conclusion through an intuitive process, this intuition was supported by a deep examination of the Book of Genesis. Specifically, the two stories it tells us about the creation of Man –the same stories mentioned by Leo the Hebrew in a passage I quoted above. Let's remember them.

The first one says: "So God created man in His own image, in the image of God He created him, male and female He created them" (Genesis 1: 27–28). As Hebrew points out, single and plural are mixed here. The Bible was seen as a book inspired, if not actually dictated, by God, therefore an editorial mistake was unthinkable. So, if in this verse they first employ the singular and then the plural, there must have been a good reason to do so. The old exegetes, who –like a Hercules Poirot of the Holy Scriptures– dedicated themselves to figuring out those hidden reasons, interpreted said verse in this sense: God had created man and woman *united*, in such a way that, albeit being two, they could be referred to as one, for they were merged into a single being. They found support for their interpretation further down the Book of Genesis: "In the day that God created man, in the likeness of

God made He him; male and female created He them; and blessed them, *and called their name Adam.*" (Genesis 5: 1–3) He gave them a collective name, Blanca, one name for both.

What conclusion did our sages take from all this? Most of all, they concluded that, with the creation of Adam and Eve, God had also created the institution of marriage. God had not just created the first man and the first woman, he created them united, paired, *twined*. He created them together as a superior Unit, in other words, *a married couple*. With Adam and Eve, God created the first marriage, the first husband and wife, justifying how some Aramaic versions of the Genesis translate that verse as: "...male and *his spouse*, created He them".

Let's now consider the second story, according to which God created Man out of clay (that being the literal meaning of the word *adam*), and the woman out of the man's rib, or side. "And the Lord God formed man out of clay, and breathed into his nostrils the breath of life; and man became a living soul", we read in Genesis 2:7. Further down: "The Lord God caused a deep sleep to fall upon the man, and while he slept closed up his ribs and closed its place with flesh, and the rib that the Lord God had taken from the man he made into a woman..." (Genesis 2:21–23)

The simultaneous creation of Adam and Eve is not so clear here, is it, my dear? At first glance, it seems as if woman was created afterwards. But, if we analyse this second story carefully (as carefully as Leo the Hebrew did), we will reach the same conclusion as in the first one. In fact, according to this second version, God does not create Eve out of nothingness, out of a pile of clay, as He previously created Adam. He creates her out of a fragment –a rib, a side– of Adam's body. Actually, according to the exegetes, He does not create her:

He *extracts* her from Adam. From which they inferred that Eve already existed, she had already been created simultaneously with Adam, of whom she was a part, with whom she originally formed one single being. Eve's apparently delayed creation is but the chronicle of that unitary being's subsequent traumatic split. (The unitary being is, of course, the Androgyne, Blanca, considering this is not the only instance, given the male bias of most ancient sages, in which the Androgyne was seen, overall, as a male, the female form being encompassed by the male.)

Adam and Eve, my dear, represent and foreshadow all humanity. Therefore, saying God created them simultaneously (or together) and that, consequently, with this act of creation established the institution of marriage, is comparable to saying God created the original mankind in pairs, as married couples. The exegetes will find in Genesis 2: 24 a confirmation of this: "That is why a man will leave his father and mother and be united with his wife, and the two will become one flesh." Note it does not say man will unite to *a* wife but to *his* wife: meaning the one with whom he was created. This specific allocation of each woman to her man –and, inversely, of each man to his woman– is also announced in the previous verse, where Adam recognises Eve as *his* wife. "This is now bone of *my* bones, flesh of *my* flesh."

So, these are the arguments the ancient Christian sages searched for –and found– in the Old Testament to justify their intuition: that the human being is, in its origin, one–half of a couple. They could also find the same class of arguments in the New Testament. In this respect, Origen of Alexandria, a Greek Early Church Father, considered the following words by Jesus to be relevant: "So then, they are no longer two but one flesh. Therefore what God has joined together, let not man separate" (Matthew 19: 4–7). Origen (who prescribed mystic intuition for the perception of suprasensible realities, and was deemed a heretic due to some of his intuitions) saw in the words "what God has joined together" evidence that worldly marriages were predestined from the beginning, given that even though they are split, God has created them *joined together*. St. Augustine of Hippo, another prominent theologian and Father of the Latin Church, confirms it: "Nor did God create these each by himself, and join them together as alien by birth: but He created the one out of the other"[63] In one word, Blanca: he created them *united*, forming between the two "one flesh", one unitary being, one *couple*.

To St. Augustine, then, marriage, in its pure form, dates back to a time before the Fall, before sin. He reasserts this at the beginning of one his treatises vindicating this sacrament: "Our purpose, therefore, in this book, so far as the Lord vouchsafes us in His help, is to distinguish between the evil of carnal concupiscence from which man, who is born from it born, contracts original sin, and the good of marriage. For there would have been none of this shame-producing concupiscence... if man had not previously sinned; *while as to marriage, it would still have existed even if no man had sinned.*"[64] Incidentally, in this passage we learn that in St. Augustine's intuition (as in that of other Early Church Fathers', and of philosophers such as our friend Kierkegaard's and as we will see, in the intuition of most our sages), the fallen state of humankind is linked to the appearance of sex. To our sages,

---

63. St. Augustine, *Of the Good of Marriage*, 1,1
64. St. Augustine, *On Marriage and Concupiscence*, 1, 1, 1 (Italics by the author)

Blanca, marriage in the Origin was a purely spiritual union. This perfect, divine and spiritual model of marriage, was unconsciously adapted by Man to the imperfect, human and sexual reality in which we live in. We could say that Earthly marriage is loosely inspired in the original matrimony, in the heavenly archetype established by God in the Origin. "When husband and wife are united in marriage they no longer seem like something earthly, but rather like the image of God Himself", says St. John Chrysostom, another Early Church Father who, like St. Augustine, dedicated much of his time to thinking about marriage. In the beginning, due to their dual creation, human souls were participants in the Original heavenly marriage. Then came the Fall: we lost our heavenly condition and, with it, its inherent marital status. Now we vaguely yearn for that privileged status we once enjoyed, which, through the institution of marriage, we try to restore here on Earth.

A MATCHMAKER GOD

It's not just according to the ancient Christian sages, Blanca. The idea that every human being – having been created by God not as individuals but as *couples* (though one could argue that the individual, the elemental unit, is the couple)– is originally a spouse, had also been established by ancient sages of the two other religions of the Book. In fact, the marital status is specifically mentioned in the first page of the Quran: "O mankind, fear your Lord, who created you from one soul and created from it *its* mate and dispersed from both of them many men and women." (4:1) Notice how here too God creates the first man's wife *from him*. From which we can infer (as in the Judeo–Christian Book) that she had been created at the same time as her husband, by the same act of creation, and that her subsequent "creation" was really just the split of the androgynous being.

Ibn Hazm, whom we cited above, cites a similar verse from the Quran in the "Of the Nature of Love" speech from his *The Ring of the Dove*; one that says: "It is He who created you from one soul and created from it its mate that he might dwell in security with her." (7:189) He quotes it in support of his thesis –the same thesis as our sages– in which he argues that couples who get together in this world, are often compelled to do so by a cosmic law: the law that determines all things tend to pair up with what is similar to themselves. A similarity that, in the case of human couples, corresponds to their souls' common descent from the superior soul they formed before being split in half. Finding support in this Quranic verse, then, Ibn Hazm would say the reason we lived together for over forty years, Blanca, is that you and I are two halves of the same soul. "Be it noted that the reason God assigns for man's reposing in woman (and, by extension, you and I, and every other paired twin couples) is that she was made out of him."[65]

Crossed–out note on the margin. The fast marker pen missed the entire note: *I was sending modulated messages*. Surely it's a quote taken from one of the blue books, as is the case with the other notes, and the author must have seen in it a communication from his deceased wife.

---

65. Ibn Hazm, *The Ring of the Dove*, translation by A.J. Arberry

In Jewish tradition, my dear, they also think of marriage as the work of God for having created our first parents united. In the *Zohar*, they comment on the biblical verse "The man said, "The woman you put here with me--she gave me some fruit from the tree, and I ate it." (Genesis 3: 12) in the following manner: "The expression 'with me' suggests Adam and Eve were created together in one single body." In one word, they were created *married*. Imagine that Adam and Eve's wedding ceremony, with God serving as officiant and master of ceremonies, is even described in the *Talmud*: "The wedding of the first couple was celebrated with pomp never repeated in the whole course of history since. God Himself, before presenting her to Adam, attired and adorned Eve as a bride. Yea, he appealed to the angels, saying 'Come, let's perform services of friendship for Adam and his helpmate'... The angels accordingly surrounded the marriage canopy, and God pronounced the blessings upon the bridal couple... The angels then danced and played upon musical instruments before Adam and Eve in their ten bridal chambers of gold, pearls, and precious stones, which God had prepared for them."[66]

Adam and Eve, let me remind you, are the image of every male and female souls created by God in the Origin. When God created the souls, so the rabbis teach, He paired each soul with its *zug*, that is, with its "spouse", with its counterpart of the opposite sex (its *bat zug* in the case of male souls, its *ben zug* in the case of female souls)... So then, we can see that in Judaism as well, God had arranged all marriages in Heaven, Blanca. From here comes the old Jewish saying: *a*

66. Louis Ginzberg, *The Legends of the Jews*, quoted by Alan Watts, *The Two Hands of God*

match made in heaven... There is a *Yiddish* word to refer to the soul with which one was created: it's the word *bashert*, which means "destined". The Kabbalists, the ancient Jewish sages, talk to us about that destined companion, who will ensure our soul is complete. In *The Secret of the Marriage of David and Bathsheba*, Rabbi Joseph Gikatilla explains that "when a being of the male sex is created, his female sex spouse is necessarily created at the same time, because a half form is never created in the Higher World, but a single, whole form."[67] And in the Zohar, we can read: "All the world's souls, who are the fruit of the labour of God Almighty, are mystically one, but when they descend upon the World they are separated into male and female. They are together throughout the first creation, and then they are separated, one towards the right (the male), the other towards the left (the female), and then God joins them in couples; God, and only God, for only He knows the appropriate spouse for each soul. Happy is the man who is righteous in his work and follows the path of the truth so that his soul can re-encounter his original spouse, and he can become effectively perfect, and through his perfection, the whole world is blessed."[68] (Note, Blanca, that by alluding to a "first creation" of the human being and, implicitly, to a second, the author of the Zohar is abiding by the words in the book of Genesis: the two successive creations correspond to the two stories about the creation of Man therein.)

Did you know that the bridal language in the Old Testament could have been interpreted –in a second esoteric

---

67. Joseph Gikatilla, *translated from El secreto de la unión de David y Betsabé, p.46*
68. *Sefer ha-Zóhar* I, 90b

reading of the Scriptures– as referring to that conjugal model instituted by God in the Origin? As referring, then, to a love predestination established by virtue of the previously mentioned joined, or dual, creation? Expressions from the Book of Malachi such as "the wife of your youth" and "the wife of your covenant", lend themselves to be read in the context of the couple's Original Unity. In this case, youth would refer to the soul's most distant past (in the Origin, in that "time before Time"); the covenant –marriage covenant– would be the result of the double creation... Around the time the Book of Malachi was written, Israelis were enduring severe punishments, and they asked themselves why God had turned their back on them. The prophet Malachi answered: "You ask 'Why?' It is because the Lord is the witness between you and the wife of your youth. You have been unfaithful to her, though she is your partner, the wife of your marriage covenant. Has not the one God made you? You belong to him in body and spirit. And what does the one God seek? Godly offspring. So be on your guard, and do not be unfaithful to the wife of your youth." (Malachi 2: 14–16)

According to these verses, Blanca, God turned His back on the Israelis because they had rejected their original wives, Israelis like them, to marry foreign women. In that case, if we were to look –along with the Kabbalists– for the hidden meaning of this passage, we could interpret it as saying that, with "the Israelis' original wives", he was actually alluding to their "twins", to the women with whom they were created. This interpretation also suits the legend, recorded in the *Talmud*, in which the first Israelis were all born duplicates, each in the company of a "twin sister". This thought is expressed in an aphorism relating to the sons of the patriarch Jacob (baptised *Israel* by Yahweh and genealogical father of the Israelis), that appears in several rabbinic texts: *Each of the twelve tribes was born with its twin.*69 Here, the noun *tribe* designates its eponymous, that is to say, the twelve sons of Israel. Therefore, the untangled aphorism would say: "Each son of Jacob would be born with his twin sister". The twelve couples contracted matrimony, as it was their fate, and from those twelve marriages descended the twelve tribes of Israel, and, from them, the Jewish people. The ancient Jewish sages extended the double birth of the patriarchs to their descendants and to the whole of mankind, Blanca, and thus, according to them, every soul had come into this world accompanied by a twin sister with whom he was destined to marry. If this destiny were fulfilled, it would be the source of many blessings: "For it has been written in the secret doctrine of the Mishnah (the oldest, most essential part of the *Talmud*) that if a man takes his sister, it will be the source of benignity."[70] But if for whatever reason, the predestined marriage does not take place, or if it falls apart (an event to which the above quote from the Book of Malachi could be interpreted as referring), then we could expect from God nothing but calamities.

As it's to be expected, Blanca, the exaggerated value placed on the matrimonial union with the twin soul in this world, has given the issue of the choice of mate an extraordinary relevance. Charles Mopsik, in his erudite introduction to Gikatilla's treatise, informs us that entire generations of Kabbalists (as fond as they were of imagining esoteric methods to question the hidden reality) immersed themselves in thinking up "means and strategies to find their unknown true companion".

---

69. Midrash Genesis Rabbah 82: 8
70. Zohar

In the Old Testament, we can find several examples of predestined love. There is the story of Isaac and Rebecca: Abraham sends a trustworthy man to the land of his ancestors in search of a bride for his son Isaac. He should look for her not only among his master's compatriots but also –in agreement with a Mosaic Law– among his relatives. In other words, a needle in a haystack. The man prays to God for His help and improvises a strategy not very different –I imagine– from what the Kabbalists later devised to find their *bat zug*. He convenes a signal with God: he will take up position near a well in the outskirts of a city; in the afternoon, when the women come up to the well for water, he will ask them for a cup of water, and she who also offers water to his camel will be the one predestined by God. He had not even finished formulating the plan in his head when Rebecca, the girl who will meet all requirements and pass the test, approaches the well carrying a jug on her shoulder.

The Book of Tobit features another clear example. I am sure you know the episode, but I will refresh your memory... Tobit is responsible for claiming a cash deposit in a city several days away by foot. He is looking for a travelling companion knowledgeable of the region, and he finds a young man whom he can trust. What Tobit does not know is that this young man is actually an angel sent by God. They take off and, halfway through, they reach the gates of a city. The angel informs his fellow traveller that in that city lives a girl named Sarah, with whom –in accordance with that same Mosaic Law mentioned above– Tobit has the right to marry. Thereupon he cites a deeper motive: "she has been assigned to you before the world came into being." (Tobit 6: 18) Hearing this, Tobit shudders; he feels the touch of Fate and decides to ask for Sarah's hand in marriage. Her father confirms the angel's assertion: "Heaven itself decrees she shall be yours. I, therefore, entrust your sister to you. From now on you are her brother and she is your sister." (Tobit 7: 12)

Let's consider this last sentence, Blanca. Fraternal symbolism, along with matrimonial, are the two ways the concept of "twin souls" was represented in Antiquity. They would often get confused for one another, hence there being so many old stories (in the Old Testament you have the paradigmatic case of the Song of Songs) in which married couples call each by brother and sister, and are referred to as such by the narrator. Apart from the implicit reference to their common origin, meaning their kinship, the fraternal form of address also suggests the type of love that ideally should join these couples: a chaste, spiritual love, like that of a brother and sister. That is why Tobit, before consummating his marriage to Sarah, says to God: "And so I take my sister, not for any lustful motive, but I do it in singleness of heart." (Tobit 8: 7)The holy text tells us Tobit was Sarah's eighth husband. The other seven died suddenly and mysteriously in the nuptial chamber before consummating the marriage. Though they called it the machinations of a demon who was in love with Sarah, some exegetes interpreted it as God (displaying the severity that characterises Him in the Old Testament) punishing them for loving her with lust whereas Tobit loved her with true love. However, there is room for yet another reading, Blanca, a Kabbalistic reading of those mysterious deaths: Sarah's seven dead husbands were not predestined to her, none of them was her *ben zug*, her twin soul. With the marriage of Sarah and Tobit, the Destiny decreed by God is finally fulfilled, making good, from then on, of that aphorism from the *Mishnah*: "if a man takes his sister, it will be the source of benignity."

UNMATCHABLE NATURES

If you allow me, dear, I would like to tell you now –since I expounded on worldly marriage and its Heavenly model– a few words about divorce... We were talking before about the Early Church Fathers. About how some of them interpreted worldly marriage as a restoration of the true marriage, the one which had taken place in Heaven, under divine auspices. These Christian sages supposed that worldly marriages would be infallible, in the sense that they would reunite the original spouses. Hence, they considered divorce inadmissible. They did not count on the mistakes one would predictably make when recognising their predestined spouse among the crowd of potential candidates. John Milton, the great English poet, coming after Shakespeare and Donne, did count on those factors, Blanca. This led to the curious incident where if some Early Church Fathers put forward the concept of love predestination as an argument against divorce, Milton, in the seventeenth century, did it in favour.

Milton wrote four treatises in defence of divorce. Although it sounds paradoxical, he advocated in its favour precisely for having such a high regard for the concept of matrimony: which derived from the belief –he professed– in what we have called "heavenly marriages". He believed that every human being has already been married in the Origin. Married neither by the Church nor State but by God Himself. And that this marriage is the one that truly matters because, though it fell apart as a consequence of the Fall, the bond still remains. The bond is unbreakable. Milton is of the opinion that worldly marriage is important, it should not be taken lightly, but it must come second to that primary heavenly bond. The ideal would be that all of us on

Earth could marry our heavenly spouse, our true spouse. But Milton knew by experience that such ideal not always corresponded to reality. Worldly marriage is fallible, it's subject to mistakes; society must provide a way to fix those mistakes, and that way is divorce.

In Milton's days, as in ours, the Church considered certain reasons for which a marriage could be annulled. For example, if it turned out that one of the spouses was already married. Or if blood ties between the couple were uncovered. Or if intercourse between them proved to be unviable. All those reasons seemed inconsistent to Milton. In his mind, the only good reason was an incompatibility between the spouses; an incompatibility based on the theory of twin souls, Blanca, since it's not a question of character, but of *nature.* Two spouses, said Milton, are incompatible when they do not share the same nature, which for him meant that they are not made for each other. They are not two halves of the same *symbolon*. Well, just as a *symbolon* share the same piece of wood in exclusive, only the souls who are twins share the same nature. When a worldly marriage does not match with the heavenly marriage arranged by God in the Origin, then those spouses fall, according to Milton, into an incompatibility of natures and, in such cases, divorce is not only admissible, it's advisable. Thanks to divorce, we can avoid the tension of grudgingly sharing a life with someone, just as we can remove the temptation of adultery.

Milton thought and proclaimed this in the seventeenth century, Blanca. However, because ideas (especially those that spring from mystic intuition) are timeless and cannot be ruled by chronology, Theophrastus Paracelsus had, one century before, made a comment in advance of Milton's thought, writing: "When it happens that the two who belong together and are ordained to do so do come together, no adultery can occur. The reason for this is *that the anatomy and concordance are as one and do not break*. But if they do not come together [properly], there is no affirmed love at hand, but rather a shaky one, like a reed in water. For a man who whores around in this way does not possess his true wife in accordance with the content of the anatomy; [and] a woman who whores around also does not have her true husband. For to each human being, the desire has been given by God, [but] not for the purpose of becoming an adulterer. For this reason, the commandment is directed to those who do not belong together: to adhere to it as though they did belong together. In consequence, there are two different unions: the one God joins, as stated above; and the human beings who join themselves together. The first adhere to one another without the commandment; the others do not do so, but are instead bound by the commandment."[71]

Getting back to Milton, though, he believed in "heavenly chance expressed", as Coventry Patmore put it in his verses (Patmore was not as great of a poet as Milton, but they had the same great intuitions about love). Milton believed chance was like a disguise worn by God (since God seems to prefer to go by unnoticed, albeit that does not mean we cannot intuit or read between the lines, so to speak) to intervene incognito in worldly affairs. To intervene, for example, in interpersonal relationships and in marriages, in particular. Milton shared with the Kabbalists the idea that "The Holy One, blessed be He, joins couples together". Under the guise of chance, God acts, one could say, as a matchmaker, trying

71. *Paracelsus, (Theophrastus Bombastus Von Hohenheim, 1493–1541): Essential Theoretical Writings*, p. 561

to get heavenly couples to come together in marriage here on Earth as well. Of course, He not always succeeds, Blanca, because human beings have free will: we can ignore our intuition's inner voice that pulls us in one direction, and go the opposite way instead. We can marry someone who is not our Original spouse. This might be considered a mistake. Milton, though, was even more drastic: he said that was perverting God's plan. In one of his treatises on divorce, he writes: "And when He forbids all unmatchable and un-mingling natures to consort...if they chance through misadventure to be miscoupl'd, he bids them part asunder, *as persons whom God never joyn'd*"[72]

> **Crossed–out note on the margin. What could be, on account of other crossed–out notes, another quote, was partially saved: *...the postman brought the letter that she (had been waiting) for so long.***

Of course, treatises on divorce are not Milton's main legacy, Blanca: his poetry is. Specifically *Paradise Lost*, a long poem he composed while blind: putting the verses together in his mind, memorising them, and dictating them to his close friends when they visited him. Throughout ten thousand verses, Milton narrates the Biblical story of Adam and Eve. However, he does so from his own perspective, and that is where its interest and charm lie. Milton's personal perspective converts the story of Adam and Eve into an ode to conjugal love, to heavenly marriage and to twin souls. He openly proclaims something that in the Genesis is hidden

---

72. *Doctrine and Discipline of Divorce*, as quoted by Anthony Low in *The Reinvention of Love*, p.195

beneath the surface: that Adam and Eve are the two halves of the same soul. He says, for example, when Adam describes Eve as his left side, "the side nearest [his] heart":

> His flesh, his bone; to give thee being I lent
> Out of my side to thee, nearest my heart,
> Substantial life, to have thee by my side
> Henceforth an individual solace dear:
> *Part of my soul I seek thee, and thee claim*
> *My other half.'*...[73]

He also explicitly states it further down, in the verses in which Adam describes Eve's subjective beauty:

> So much delights me as those graceful acts,
> Those thousand decencies that daily flow
> From all her words and actions mixt with Love
> And sweet compliance, *which declare unfeign'd*
> *Union of Mind, or in us both one Soule;*[74]

The couple formed by our first parents is the image of every couple of twin souls, Blanca. In such a way that the story of Adam and Eve is our own story. We will have the opportunity to come back to this, to cite more verses from *Paradise Lost*, but now we should take one step forward in our investigative quest. I'll remind you that when, a few years ago, I prepared to take this same step, I thought it would be advisable if I adopted a special frame of mind: the same I would recommend you if your disembodied state didn't

---

73. John Milton, *Paradise Lost, IV*, 483-488 (Italics by the author)
74. *Ibid, VIII*, 601-604 (Italics by the author)

make it unnecessary. A frame of mind similar to that of the bold travellers of yesteryear (and some contemporaries of ours too; I'm thinking of two explorers of what I believe is your favourite place on Earth: Alexandra David-Néel with her books on Tibet, and Peter Matthiessen, author of that other precious blue book, *The Snow Leopard*) who had the audacity to go deep into uncharted territories. For it was an unknown and secret territory that I was prepared to explore, my dear. By chance (I don't trust this word, you know that) I found in an old bookshop one of the few connoisseurs of that *terra incognita*. Following the example of Tobit with the angel, I immediately recruited him as cicerone and travelling companion. Now he shall be our guide too. No, it's not an angel... it's someone who, according to his own books, consorted with those celestial creatures.

OF LOVE IN THE AFTERLIFE

So far, we have been looking into the ancient sages' inquiries on love, the mysterious hidden details of love in Earthly life. Love does not stop there, on Earth, though, just as it does not stop at the individual: it continues through to the Afterlife. The ancient sages' inquiries don't stop at that point either: that is how we will be able to tackle this subject. Naturally, before doing it I had my doubts, because what am I going to tell you about the Afterlife that you don't already know? But because the Afterlife has several planes, apparently, and I don't know in which one you are, I don't think it would be too much if I offered you a vision of the whole ensemble. First, however, and in the way of a preamble, allow me once again to open the *Zorah*. In that all-encompassing book, we can read: "And each soul seeks its own mate in the Afterlife. The souls that have not found their true companions on earth, wander, after death, in search of the twin soul. And he who has not sought, or has not found his true mate on earth is, after death, like an atom tossed about by all the winds. He will not find peace until he comes together with his true mate. The sighs of those parting from their loved ones are echoed by the soul seeking its sister soul."...

I will not ask if you can hear my sighs echo on your soul as I can hear yours on mine, lest we go down a mawkish path: something against which I will be struggling constantly throughout these letters, I am afraid. Even so, it's a pertinent question, my love. Because you may be in the Afterlife, but at the same time, you have not moved from my side, you cannot deny it: especially now, that you have taken to manifest yourself through the blue books.[75] Anyway, in the eighteenth century, at the height of the Age of Enlightenment, going against the tide of contemporary thought, a Christian wise man proscribed by the Church, the Scandinavian Emmanuel Swedenborg, experimented with mystic travels to the Afterlife and mingled with the inhabitants of Heaven, the angels. If we accept his testimony, then Heaven is not the spirit world, to where souls go after the bodies die (where you have gone, my dear). Heaven is above the spirit world, though spirits can, under certain conditions, become angels and ascend to Heaven. The angelic state is the heavenly state. There is a beautiful sentence by Swedenborg that summarises the conditions to access Heaven. It says: "...a way stands plainly open into heaven; but none can enter the way

75. The first of three enigmatic allusions that support the hypothesis ventured in the preface.

but those who have heaven within them."[76] Spirits can go down into Hell too, according to Swedenborg; both ways are open. I am sure, though, that is not your case, so I will leave out that second way. Every angel in Heaven was previously a man. While still being a whole, Heaven has countless divisions and subdivisions, about which I will tell you later.

Swedenborg identifies several stages in the crossing over to the Other World after one's death. The first one, Blanca, is that the Other World is not external to the individuals but within him or her. It's a spiritual world too, since, for Swedenborg (as for our sages in general), the physical and material world is nothing but the outer appearance of true reality, which is spiritual and internal. The departure of the physical world through death supposes, then, the full immersion into the inner and true dimension of existence, a dimension within the individual himself. During the stage immediately after physical death, the individual keeps the same personality he had in life. By submerging deep inside himself, he enters the world of spirits, where his deceased friends and family welcome him. If his mate on Earth has passed away before him, he reunites with her and they resume their life together. Then, on the second stage, Swedenborg reveals what he calls the individual's "state of interiors". This is where the individual sheds his worldly personality, which is an external, adopted personality, and assumes his own –inner– personality, that is to say, he becomes his *true self*. By uncovering his "state of interiors", or his true self, it's revealed whether the people with whom he had a relationship in life are truly like him, and whether his mate in life is his true spouse, what

76. Emmanuel Swedenborg, *Conjugal Love*, 500, translation by Samuel M. Warren

to Swedenborg means: if the other soul is absolutely alike the individual's own. If it is, they stay together and enjoy true conjugal love, which is Heavenly love. If it's not, then they part ways, and, if their true spouses have already left the physical world too, they will reunite with them.

As the attentive reader you are, you surely noticed that twice I alluded to the notion of likeness, or similarity. That notion is one of the foundations of Swedenborgian anthropology and it implies, as we will see, the notion of twin souls. According to Swedenborg, the souls of men are alike each other in varying degrees and, in Heaven, they tend to group in accordance with that standard. That is to say, those that are similar tend to get together, while those that are different distance themselves naturally: "those who differ much being far apart, and those who differ but little being but little apart, and likeness causing them to be together."[77] What does Swedenborg understand by "likeness"? What is it that determines whether two souls are alike? What determines whether two souls are alike is their "state of interiors", or their "state of love", in another word, Blanca: the quality of the souls, their propensity for good or –as Swedenborg defines it– their "dominant love". This quality, this "state of interiors" of the souls, does not pre-exist their experience on Earth. In this aspect, Swedenborg differs from most of our sages, since he does not believe that similarity between souls is the result of their creation together. The way he sees it, two souls are more or less alike depending on their evolution on Earth. If they had a parallel evolution, if as a result of that evolution their "state of interiors" is alike, then they

77. Emmanuel Swedenborg, *Heaven and Hell*, 42, translation by John C. Ager

are alike and –it doesn't matter if they coincided on Earth or not– that likeness will determine their bond in Heaven; the strength of that bond depending on their degree of likeness.

Crossed–out note on the margin. The marker pen damaged the middle part of the annotation. We can only read the date (26–9–99) and what presumably is the ending of a long quote: ...*she had found that (way) of saying she loved him*.

Meaning, Swedenborg did not believe in the predestined love of twin souls, at least that is what one can assume from his writings. In his view, twin souls have not been twins since their creation: *they become twins* through their evolution on Earth. It's not ontological kinship, then. "How could it be that Swedenborg –I understand you would like to ask– did not believe in predestined love, an idea, according to you, so ingrained in ancient knowledge?" Well, I have two answers. First, it's that maybe that idea wasn't as widespread as I, in my enthusiasm, may have led you to believe. Second, Blanca, is that even the wisest of sages could make mistakes. Regardless of how much support they could find in mystic intuition, we have already talked about how intuition cannot be perfect: it's fragmented, like a vision through the mist... However, let's dive, without further ado, into the Swedenborgian doctrine of similarity and its associated bonds between souls.

TRUE CONJUGAL LOVE

According to Swedenborg, when two or more souls are alike, when they show a similar propensity towards good, they recognise each other in Heaven. They recognise their affinity –as if they belonged to the same family of souls– and their desire is to live together. In consequence, they naturally come together as a group and weave relationships more or less tight, in accordance with their degree of similarity. Thus, they integrate different societies. In each of these societies, there are several levels of association, according to the degree of likeness of its members. The home of a soul is its peers, the other souls related to it. "Like –writes Swedenborg– are drawn spontaneously as it were to their like; for with their like they are as if with their own and at home, but with others they are as if with strangers and abroad."[78] So much so, Blanca, that the souls with a propensity for evil feel as if at home when in Hell –where Swedenborg says they'll end up–, since that is where they will be in the company of similar souls.

Although we cannot find it openly expressed in Swedenborg, from his testimony –based on books such as *Heaven and Hell*, his most known work– it follows that there are several degrees of likeness between souls, from a distant similarity to one so tight they become identical, absolutely alike: in one word: twins. Each degree, in turn, determines the strength of the bond between similar souls. For example, Blanca, if, on a scale of one to ten, the degree of similarity between two souls is two, then their bond would be the equivalent, in our world, to that of two fellow countrymen –Swedenborg would say they belong to the same "society" of souls. If their likeness scored a four, we could say they came from the same city, if a six, then they would be neighbours. In the eighth degree, we already would be in family territory. The

78. *Ibid*, 44

ninth degree of similarity would mean a very tight bond, corresponding to that of close family. (According to the ancient sages, such close affinity between related souls determines a strong inclination towards reincarnating together.)

And the tenth degree? The tenth degree of similarity, or twins, is the most important of all, Blanca, since it creates Heaven's elemental unit, the *married couple.* The Swedenborgian Heaven is based on an eternal life as a couple. Swedenborg rejects the most obvious reading of that famous Evangelical episode in which Jesus, when questioned about which of a widow's seven successive husbands would be her husband for all Eternity, says that in eternity "people will neither marry nor be given in marriage; they will be like the angels in Heaven."[79] We must take into account –says Swedenborg– who asks that question: it's a Sadducee, a member of a materialistic sect that did not believe in eternal life. Jesus' answer, then, saying that in Heaven there is no marriage, refers to marriage as the Sadducees understood it: a marriage based on social conventions and the gratification of instincts.

So, when I classify marriage as the highest level of bonding between two souls, I am not drawing up a mere equivalence, Blanca –like I did when I spoke of fellow countrymen, neighbours, etcetera. It's not a metaphor: according to Swedenborg's testimony, the conjugal state is a real state in Heaven. Not every case comes to fruition because, as we will see, the heavenly couple has to deserve it. Naturally, the number of individuals or souls integrating the different groups –the groups corresponding to each degree of similarity– decline as we get near the tenth degree. Thus, "society" is the most

---

79. Matthew 22:30, Mark 12:25, Luke 20:34–36

populated group, while the most restricted one is the married couple: being twins is the couple's prerogative.

Detailed descriptions of the conjugal state in Heaven are abundant in the work of Swedenborg. It's the most desirable state in the Afterlife, -he assures us- and it consists of the "conjunction of two into one mind."[80] It's a state of *perfect union* with the other soul (with another alike soul because the union is only perfect when one comes together with another who is alike). And that *union* is *perfect* in virtue of "true marital love", which is what unites souls of absolute likeness, or twins. A soul incarnates in the physical world in order to reveal in itself true marital love. To Swedenborg, earthly marriage (today we would say: in general, couple's relationships on Earth) is the school preparing us for the real marriage waiting for us in Heaven. What do we learn from that school? We learn the lesson of true marital love: that is to say, we learn to love our spouse in an "innocent" way; in Swedenborg, this means an unconditional and altruist way, but also in a spiritual way (they are both connected).

You know, Blanca, in the course of his astral travels through the Otherworld, Swedenborg had the chance to admire couples of Heavenly married angels: and while at first, these angels seemed to be individuals, soon, when he got closer to them, they revealed themselves dual. However, he could not perceive them clearly, because their beauty was such that it overwhelmed him. He also explains how one gets to those marriages. He says: "I have also been permitted to see how marriages are contracted in the heavens. As everywhere in heaven those who are alike are united and those

80. *Emmanuel Swedenborg, Heaven and Hell*, 367, translation by John C. Ager

who are unlike are separated, so every society in heaven consists of those who are alike. Like are brought to like not by themselves but by the Lord and equally consort to consort whose minds can be joined into one are drawn together, and consequently, at first sight, they mostly love each other, and see themselves as consorts, and enter into marriage."[81]

The spouses whose minds are in conditions of uniting into one, my dear, are those which have learned the lesson of true marital love. In *Heaven and Hell*, Swedenborg says he heard an angel describe true marital love in these terms: "*...it is the Lord's Divine in the heavens*", which is Divine good and Divine truth so united in two persons, that they are not as two but as one... *the Divine is imaged in the two that are in true marriage love...*; and this is why all things of heaven are inscribed on marriage love with more blessings and delights than it is possible to number."[82] (I have highlighted two sentences from this quote: they will not be the only ones to which I will point your attention until the end of this letter. Let's put them all on the table and, like in that children's game, join the dots and see what drawing comes out.)

Swedenborg dedicates entire chapters of his books to describing marital love, which he characterises as "the fundamental love of every love in Heaven"[83], even comparing it to Heaven itself, and placing "true marital love" in the most intimate Heaven, which consists of supreme delight. It's clear this is a subject very dear to his heart, not only for the extent and for the thoroughness with which he handles it, but for the passion he puts in his descriptions. It's curi-

81. *Ibid, 383*
82. *Ibid 374*
83. *Apocalypsis Revealed*

ous then, that he never got married, nor do we know of any amorous adventures he might have had. However, Blanca, upon reading his work, preferably *Conjugal Love*, one gets the impression that this is a man with a great yearning for this type of love. Besides, in that book, he claims that everyone, married or single, who in their earthly life aspired to true marital love, will find their true spouse in the Afterlife; the celibates, though, those who never craved a partner, will find it difficult to find one. If celibacy was, in Swedenborg's view, wrong, is it not logical to presume he would not practice something against which he argued? We should not count him, then, as one of the celibates but as one of the single people who yearned for a mate. But then, why didn't he get married? Every sign, Blanca, points to him not getting married because (just as King David, but certainly for a different reason) when he found his twin soul it was already too late; she was married. This woman, whom Swedenborg secretly loved, and in whom he believed to have recognised his "true spouse", was a neighbour of his; a writer of devotional books, Countess Elizabeth Gyllenborg-Stjerncrona, with whom he maintained a close friendship. We know, due to certain documents, that Swedenborg hoped someday to recreate with her the heavenly marriage he witnessed in the Other World. And since by talking about Swedenborg's ideology of love we have drifted towards more personal grounds, I would like, then, to introduce you, in a little more detail, to this most singular man, born in Stockholm, Sweden, towards the end of the seventeenth century.

The fact is that it's hard not to have some respect for Swedenborg once you get to know his personality. His most remarkable quality was one that, all things considered (I know you will agree with me), is the most remarkable quality in anyone. That character trait that, when it's lacking, is also a person's deepest flaw. I am talking about kindness, of course. The kindness or viciousness of someone's heart tells us about their "state of love" or "state of interiors", to use Swedenborg's words, and it's how we can get to truly know someone beyond the temporary earthly personality that sheaths us all. Kindness, Blanca, kindness is the central quality of inner beauty; and inner beauty, though as objective as outer beauty, presents a distinguishing feature that makes it infinitely more precious. Let me illustrate this with an example: If I think about your physical beauty, am I really thinking about *you*? Your big, dark eyes, say, are they consubstantial to you? Or is there a possibility that you could have been born with green, almond-shaped eyes? It's true, isn't it? So, in that case, your eyes are not really yours, my dear: they are as yours, almost, as a pair of earrings your parents could have given you when you were born. On the other hand, no one gave you your kindness, it's yours by independent right; when I am thinking about your kindness, I am really thinking about *you*, in who you really are. And Swedenborg's kindness reminds me of yours. It showed itself in the same things: in the love for children, for example, in how he always remembered to carry sweets with him on their account. He had the same innocence, the same purity of heart as a child. A friend who was by his side on his deathbed him remembered him with these glowing words: "I do not recollect to have known any man of more uniformly virtuous character than Swedenborg; always contented, never fretful or morose... He was a true philosopher and lived like one. He laboured diligently, and lived frugally... He possessed a sound judgement upon all occasions... and expressed himself well on every subject... He was a model of sincerity, virtue and piety, and from what

I have seen, there is no one in my country possessing as a profound a knowledge as that of Swedenborg."[84]

His biography is as extraordinary as his personality. In the first half of his life, he built a fruitful scientific career, during which he laid the foundations for many modern discoveries. Then his life took an abrupt turn. The triggering events were the mystic ecstasies that began coming upon him and that would never leave him again. During those ecstasies, his soul would leave his body and, in a quick flight, it would travel to celestial regions, where it met the angels. So, you can see, halfway through his life, the eminent scientist –one of the most important of his day– turned his back on science and earthly matters and became a mystic, a visionary, devoting himself to the task of writing down everything the angels taught him. "I don't make it up, I only transmit", he claimed. He felt bound to passing on those teachings so, as there were so many, he wrote every day with barely any rest. Since there was no freedom of the press in Sweden back then, once each book was finished, he travelled to Amsterdam or London to publish it. He did not care about fame or money, so he published them anonymously, paying out of his own pocket.

He kept this incessant activity up until his death, at an advanced age, in London, as was his wish. It's as if he foretold the exact day. This clairvoyance had already manifested itself on other occasions, though he never boasted about it. This did not prevent the public from hearing about some of his most astonishing feats. One of these, in particular, my dear, marked an era: it was talked about not only in Sweden but all around Europe, leading to Swedenborg becoming famous

84. Quoted by D.T. Suzuki, *Swedenborg: Buddah of the North*, p.44

against his will, which ended up unmasking him in the eyes of his contemporaries as the author of those visionary books written in Latin that, for fifteen years, had been coming to light anonymously. It happened like this... Swedenborg had left Stockholm to spend a few days in Gothenburg. In the night in question he, and other guests were having dinner at a friends' house. We could think of it as a soiree not much different from our Friday nights at Esther and Enrique's, more crowded, maybe. In that case, Blanca, look, imagine I am telling you about those pleasant evenings at which you and I were regulars: here we are, in Esther and Enrique's spacious loft. Besides the usual guests, there is an old friend from Madrid. He loves Barcelona and drops by whenever he can. The night is cheerful, we are enjoying the conversation and the delicious meal (ah, that *suquet de peix* Esther cooks better than anyone!) But look: suddenly our friend leaves the table and, without saying a word, goes outside onto the balcony. "What happened?" We ask him when he comes back a few minutes later, "are you alright?" His face had turned pale. He looks at us and says that a tremendous fire has been reported in his city and that it's spreading fast.

Now realise that our friend had no human way of knowing this. We are in the middle of the eighteenth century: over one hundred years before the invention of the radio, the television, the telephone..., and, obviously, you cannot see Madrid from a balcony in Barcelona, no matter how high up it is. First, we would think the man is joking, but then we would see the look of horror on his face, so we would start doubting his mental health. Especially when he keeps going to the balcony and refuses to let go of this foolishness. Here is an old friend of ours whom, up until now, we thought of as a reasonable man, –a renowned scientist– filled with anxiety, telling us about all the new developments of a fire happening over three hundred miles away! Anyway, news of its extinguishing is still a couple of hours away. Meanwhile, the only thing that was put out was our evening –only him, you, the hosts and I remain–, and the alarming rumours have spread all over Barcelona. It even reached the mayor, who quickly summons the seer and asks him what joke is this. Yes, yes, a joke: two days later, the first horseback messengers from Madrid arrive, and confirm not just the news of the fire but Swedenborg's detailed report.

Fantastic, isn't it, my love? Indeed, but anecdotal. What is substantial for us is Swedenborg's body of work, his books. Travel books, we could say, for they are the account of an explorer of the Afterlife. But don't think his chronicles fell on deaf ears: they enlightened many later thinkers, including great thinkers from our century, like D.T. Suzuki, who introduced Buddhism to the West, and Henry Corbin, who did the same for Islamic mysticism. He also influenced a great number of poets and novelists. Two illustrious exponents of this influence, both in the nineteenth century, are the English novelist Wilkie Collins and the French Théophile Gautier, about whom I will talk below.

TWO FANTASY NOVELS

We owe Wilkie Collins some delightful reading nights, my dear. We owe him for two blue books from your library, *The Woman in White* and *Moonstone*: in many critics' opinion, two of the finest detective novels ever written. But, apart from the crime genre, Collins also developed melodramas, a genre to which *The Two Destinies* belongs, the novel I shall now tell you about. Although it's considered a melodrama, it could easily be labelled as a fantasy novel, because it features a supernatural element.

The destinies from the title belong to Mary and George, whose lives painfully drift apart after a childhood together. The plot is cut out from the same universal template I pointed out to you in my previous letter. So here, you can also find two children in love who spend their days together until they are traumatically separated. For the rest of their lives, they search for each other without even realising it. In the course of their adult life, their paths occasionally cross by providence. And although in those occasions none of them is aware of having rediscovered their childhood partner, recognition happens on another level: "It was as if, expecting to see a stranger, I had unexpectedly encountered a friend... Her eyes rested on my face with a strange look of inquiry in them."[85]

At the beginning, Collins delights himself in describing our heroes' idyllic childhood in a paradisiacal English lakeshore, where they live out their tender love hand in hand. When adult George –who is also the narrator– recalls those days, the image of Adam and Eve in the Garden of Eden will spring to his mind, and he will talk about his childhood alongside Mary as "our first paradise, before sin and sorrow lifted their flaming swords and drove us out into the world."[86] He draws his boyhood companion for us in the most delicate lines, and he confides in us that "we were mysteriously united by some kindred association of the spirit in her and the spirit in me, which not only defied discovery by

---

85. Wilkie Collins, *The Two Destinies*, chapter VII
86. *Ibid*, chapter I

our young selves, but which lay too deep for investigation by far older and far wiser heads than ours."[87]

However, it will be a far older and far wiser head –Mary's eccentric grandmother– that will unravel the mystery of that profound kindred association. George recalls this old lady sitting by a window with an open book by Swedenborg on her lap. Dame Dermody is sort of a distant disciple of the Swedish mystic; she is in contact with the angels and has the gift of clairvoyance. It's through her sixth sense that she recognises in Mary and George two souls whose "union [was] predestined in heaven"[88] and that they are "walking unconsciously on a heavenly path of their own, whose beginning was on earth, but whose bright end was among the angels in a better state of being."[89] The elderly lady predicts their traumatic separation, but also the predestined lovers' ultimate triumph, which comes towards the end of the novel when the titular destinies converge into one. Dame Dermody's prophecy is rooted in her system of beliefs, mixing –says Collins– "Swedenborg's teachings on angels and departed spirits, on love to one's neighbour and purity of life, with wild fancies, and kindred beliefs of her own."[90] Lady Dermody herself summarises it thus:

> "I hold the belief that all love that is true is foreordained and consecrated in heaven. Spirits destined to be united in the better world are divinely commissioned to discover each other and to begin their union in this world. The only happy

---

87. *Ibid,* chapter II
88. *Ibid,* chapter II
89. *Ibid,* chapter II
90. *Ibid,* chapter II

marriages are those in which the two destined spirits have succeeded in meeting one another in this sphere of life When the kindred spirits have once met, no human power can really part them. Sooner or later, they must, by divine law, find each other again and become united spirits once more. Worldly wisdom may force them into widely different ways of life; worldly wisdom may delude them, or may make them delude themselves, into contracting an earthly and a fallible union. It matters nothing. The time will certainly come when that union will manifest itself as earthly and fallible; and the two disunited spirits, finding each other again, will become united here for the world beyond this..."[91]

You see, my love, even if Swedenborg didn't believe in love predestination, his testimony gave rise to that belief, which was otherwise firmly entrenched and with clearly defined coordinates in ancient wisdom. A belief that also informs the literary legacy of Théophile Gautier, his novel, *Spirite*, pertaining to the fantasy genre.

Here we also have a sort of distant disciple of Swedenborg, a compatriot of him, on top of that, who is "like him, hanging over the abyss of mysticism".[92] Baron Féroë's role in *Spirite* is analogue to Dame Dermody's in *The Two Destinies*: the clairvoyant witness to an extraordinary love story. Whereas the background, Blanca, could not have been any more conventional... Paris! So, Guy de Malivert is a charming young man with an active social life in Paris, but, strangely, he remains a bachelor (halfway through the nineteenth century, when the novel takes place, that was still consid-

91. *Ibid*, chapter II
92. Theophile Gautier, *Stronger than Death, or Spirite*, p.37

ered strange). It's as if, we are told, a sixth sense had advised him to keep waiting. Malivert, however, ends up lowering his guard and becoming half-heartedly engaged to a young widow. Soon, strange things start happening to him: premonitions and unexplainable events about which he confides in Baron Féroë. With the young Baron's help, he manages to perceive around him an invisible and protective presence of a woman (just as I perceive your invisible and protective presence around me, Blanca!), a woman with whom he falls madly in love, despite merely having a sense of her.

Crossed–out note on the margin. The ending of the annotation is barely visible: *...that how was he to believe in ghosts.*" The inverted commas suggest this is indeed a quote. The presumed message from the Afterlife seems to relate here with the immediate context of the letter in which it is written (that being the case, it would be an ironic gesture). It is one of the few occasions where this coincidence takes place.

Over time, this ghostly presence manifests itself: it's the disembodied spirit of Lavinia, a young lady who was secretly in love with him when she was alive... Malivert is falling deeper and deeper in love with Lavinia, with Lavinia's spirit, her ghost. She tells him about her life, which –like Mary and George's lives in Collin's novel– crossed paths with his on several occasions (note the hand of Fate, as always, pulling the strings!), without Malivert ever noticing. For some time, Lavinia cherished the hope that someday he would eventually come to recognise her as what she really was: "the soul made for his soul". But then she heard the rumours of her beau's engagement and since she could not imagine herself with any other man ("any other union appeared to me a sort of crime"[93]), she opted to pronounce her vows in a convent.

She would not live much longer; sorrow would consume her in the end. As her disembodied soul crossed into the Otherworld, she confessed: "I knew then that my instinct had spoken truly. We were predestined, the one for the other. Our souls formed that celestial couple which, when united, makes an angel; *but the two halves of the supreme whole,* to be united in immortality, must have sought each other in life, have recognised one another under the veils of the flesh, and in spite of all trials, obstacles and distractions. I alone had felt the presence of the sister-soul, and, impelled by the instinct which never deceives, had attempted to join it. With you, the clearness of vision was much less acute, and served only to put you on your guard against ordinary ties and coarse attachments. You understood that you had not yet encountered the heart that was made for yours..."[94] (Keep in mind the sentence in italics, Blanca, the one that defines twin souls as the two halves of the supreme whole. And this one too, from the same novel: "What is even the happiest human union in comparison with the rapture two souls enjoy in the eternal embrace of divine love?"[95])

The ending? Oh, yes, of course: in the end, Malivert dies at the hands of some bandits, while on holidays in Greece. Ah, and a Swedenborgian colophon: right as he is passing over to the other side, Baron Féroë (whom we find reading that "strange, mysterious work of Swedenborg's, which

93. *Ibid*, p. 190
94. *Ibid*, p. 214
95. *Ibid*, p. 214-215

is entitled *Marriages of the Other Life*"[96]) is taken over by a vision. The walls of his house become transparent and, in the heavens, "not the Heaven which human eyes are wont to gaze upon, but the Heaven which is pervious to the eyes of faith alone"[97], he sees the souls of Lavinia and Malivert merge into one single "angel of love".

This angel of love, this double angel, is, of course, the Androgyne, Blanca... which brings us back to the main theme of this letter.

HUMAN INTEGRITY

In order to define Androgyny, my dear, one word would be enough: *Integrity*. This word defines, like no other, the fundamental quality of the Androgyne, which is *being whole*. Provided that to this definition we then add the formula "two in one", since the Androgyne's Integrity derives precisely from its dual character. This is key, Blanca: the essence of Androgyny does not consist so much in being simultaneously male and female, which are adjectival qualities, but in being *dual*, which is what is substantial: in being *two in one*, in being one single entity composed by the conjunction, by the union of two others. The male–female duality would not be anything more than the earthly expression of this essential Dualism. You know, the Androgyne, the "male–female", was for the ancient sages the complete and perfect human being. The idea is that we humans are (forgive the vulgar comparison) like shoes: we go in pairs. A loose shoe is an anomaly; and

96. *Ibid*, p. 292
97. *Ibid*, p. 293

so is a man without a woman, and vice-versa. This is expressed in the Genesis through that famous maxim "It's not good for man to be alone" (Genesis 2: 18). Apart, man and woman are an anomaly, Blanca, because the human unity is the couple. This intuition of the essential human "bi-unit" is common to the ancient sages, and Western and Eastern spiritual traditions. I have already cited some testimonies, to which now I will add a few more.

"The male without the female is looked upon as only half a body, nor can the female without the male be regarded as more complete... But if the two be conjugally united, there is a perfect body..."[98]: this was written by seventeenth century alchemist Basil Valentine. Neither male nor female –notes Paracelsus– "but the two put together make up a unity from which the human being is procreated."[99] And Swedenborg: "For the male person and the female person were so created that from two they may become as one person, or one flesh; and when they become one, then taken together they are a person [homo] in fullness; but without this conjunction they are two, and each as it were a divided or half person."[100] Otherwise, the Hebrew word *adam* did not refer only to the male, Blanca, it encompassed both genders; which helped the ancient sages justify their intuition of the androgynous, double, nature of the first created man (Adam before the Fall), the original model for all who followed. In a famous passage from the *Zohar*, a disciple asks Rabbi Simon bar Yochai whether "love between a man and a woman is a pro-

98. Basil Valentine, *The Twelve Keys*, The Sixth Key
99. *Paracelsus, (Theophrastus Bombastus Von Hohenheim, 1493–1541): Essential Theoretical Writings*, p. 833
100. Emmanuel Swedenborg, *Conjugal Love*, 37, translation by Samuel M. Warren

found and sublime experience", to which the Rabbi answers: "The world is based on the principle of the union between male and female. The form in which we find ourselves, the male form and the female form, is not a whole or superior form. *God will not establish His residence in a place where such union does not exist.* The name Adam was given to a man and a woman united in one single entity." (Attention: retain the italicised words.)

In other passages, the *Zohar* stresses the same idea: "*Adam* refers to the perfection a man attains through his union with the woman"; "The word *Adam* indicates finishing, fulfilment"; "The male does not deserve the name man until he is united with the female". And the *Talmud* agrees: "A man without a woman is half a man". Joseph Gikatilla, in a passage from *The Secret of the Marriage of David and* Bathsheba I partially quoted above, explains: "When a being of the male sex is created, his female sex spouse is necessarily created at the same time, because a half form is never created in the Higher World, but a single, whole form. And never a soul is produced which does not contain the male and the female... This way, in the moment of his creation, Man was created androgynous by the soul. That is to say, two faces, a form that is both male and female."[101] (The expression "two faces" alludes to the rabbinic motto "When the Lord created Adam He created him double-faced, and then He split him..."[102])

This Unity or human Integrity, Blanca, is what our ancestors hoped to restore through earthly marriage, thus the

101. Joseph Gikatilla, translated from *El secreto de la unión de David y Betsabé*, p.46
102. Midrash Genesis Rabbah 8: 1

great importance placed on this institution by the ancient and primitive societies.

When we talk about earthly marriage, we must begin by saying that it's a human institution, meaning that it had to be invented, it's not something natural to Man as sex is. In fact, that invention came to restrict Man's instinctive sexual freedom: getting married was equivalent to caging the bird of love, the gender of which you could not distinguish. Men needed to have powerful reasons, then, to implant matrimony. Of course, there were practical and social reasons. Above all was an ontological reason: deep down, on a subconscious level of perception, they believed that by reuniting a man and a woman, earthly marriage was, in a way (a truly crude and precarious way), restoring the heavenly couple or the Original Androgyne. It mended the primal Integrity, the integrity represented in the nuptial ceremony by an ancient symbol of completeness: the ring.

And in one way or another, my dear, marriage is a universal institution and it was, in the past (and still today, in some cultures), almost a duty. In Jewish tradition, getting married stands among the religious commandments. "Any man who has no wife –says the Talmud– lives without joy, without blessing, and without goodness", and it adds: "Any man who has no wife is no proper man."[103] There is an identical belief in Hindu tradition: "A man who is not married is only half a man, for his other half is the wife." It's a belief they have in common with primitive societies, where the social condition of celibacy or bachelorhood is so frowned upon, that there are practically no bachelors, and the few that exist are reviled, socially marginalised, and often have their lives

103. *Talmud*, Yeb 62b, 63a

made into a living hell until they marry. (Allow me to say in parenthesis, and in jest, that this attitude is quite common in advanced societies as well, where there are people, like dear Aunt Magda, with the same matchmaking obsession and methods just as efficient.) In her book *Male/Female*, the anthropologist François Héritier mentions numerous examples; she quotes B. Gutmann, who studied the East African Chaga tribe, where the few single men are despised by everyone and called "those who have no life in them". This epitaph is revealing because in most societies, as Héritier observes, celibacy is considered "the self-denial of the individual, given that [he] will only consider himself fulfilled in and through marriage"[104] At the height of their marital ambition, the Chaga even go as far as arranging posthumous marriages between deceased single people. They are doing them an invaluable favour, Blanca, because in their superstition they believe that when a young man dies without having married, he will lead a very unhappy life in the Otherworld.

Look, now that we are talking about marriage, our wedding, which turned 50 years old last month, comes to mind. The memory is fresh in my mind because just the other day I was leafing through the pages of the photo album. The truth is that I got nervous, I don't know why, but it always happens when I stumble across any picture of you other than the usual ones I keep around the house. I discovered that from that day, from the day of our wedding, (besides my granduncle's little scene, that is not easily forgotten) I can only recall small details. It was a very plain wedding, maybe that is why. What kind of details? Well, for example, the way you discreetly removed your uncomfortable shoes during the

104. François Héritier, translated from *Masculino/Femenino*, p. 246

wedding reception: how hard you were holding my hand as we left the church; the kindness and attention you showed towards my Aunt Elvira, who had come from so far away, suffering from the same illness that would later afflict you... Anyway, trivial things, the kind that normally ends up being our most cherished memories.

Crossed–out note on the margin. Underneath the quick pen marker lines, we can read a quote in Catalan. Thanks to my friend C.B.'s erudition, I was able to identify it. It is an extract taken from *In Search of Lost Time* by Marcel Proust: "Now the memories of love are no exception to the general laws of memory, which in turn are governed by the still more general laws of Habit. And as Habit weakens everything, what best reminds us of a person is precisely what we had forgotten."

NOSTALGIA FOR THE ORIGIN

Let's not veer off–track; we were talking about primitive beliefs regarding marriage. Such beliefs, Blanca, are related to those primitive societies' Origin myths; and several Origin myths are indigenous versions of the most ubiquitous Origin myth there is; the myth of the primordial "double–being" that is split into two halves. For example, the belief in an Original Androgyne that splits into a male individual –Soma– and female individual –Nyamba– is deeply rooted among the Mali tribes of Sub–Saharan Africa. Soma and Nyamba are seen as the progenitors of humanity, which is characterised by its division into men and women. And, you know, the primitive Man has obscure memories of the Origin. Not of his earthly origin, you see, when his African ancestors came down from the trees, standing on their hind legs, but the memory *of his heavenly Origin*, from that "time before Time", when there were no men and women, only androgynes. And among the androgynes, our mythical ancestors: double beings like Tuisto, the primordial Man from Germanic mythology, whose name shares its root with the Old Norwegian word *tvistr*, "two–part", and the Latin *bis*, "double". Since that "Golden Age", since the paradisiacal days of the "double–men", our mythical ancestors have come down –or, more accurately, have fallen– into prehistoric times because of their division into two halves. Thus began the human race.

Mircea Eliade –the highest authority on History of Religion– tells us that the Origin's "timeless Time" enjoyed a magical, sacred standing among primitive minds, while historical time was seen as profane and corrupted: a decadence of our ancestors' mythical time, for which man felt a deep longing. That longing (or *saudade*, as our Lisbon friends, Sara and João, would say. Oh, By the way, they came to see me last summer. We visited the Sant Pere de Rodes ruins together, and then we had dinner at Fonda Europa. We talked about you throughout the whole meal) that longing, Blanca, was what led him to refresh it periodically through rituals. The symbolic revival of the Origin served to renew, to regenerate a world worn out by the future, by the passing of history. Such rituals coincided, in general, with the New Year festivities: after a year functioning within Time, it was necessary for the world to leave that flow temporarily, in order to regenerate. It would then emerge from those rituals looking new, as though it had just been created.

The Origin to where they symbolically returned was not populated by men or women but by androgynes.

Consequently, the rituals of the renewal of the world included the symbolic androgynisation of the individual. Men and women swapped clothes so that men became women and vice-versa. This way, they mirrored their mythical ancestors, who were androgynes, "dual men". And, for the same reason, Blanca (because the Origin's Higher World was a world populated by androgynes, not men and woman), symbolic Androgyny was also one of the distinctive features of the intermediaries between the Lower World and the Higher World: the shamans. But, you know, it was not enough for the shaman to put on the clothing and adopt the manners of the opposite sex: they would, furthermore, reach for true Androgyny. How, you ask? According to Mircea Eliade (who is our guide for this stretch of the way) through the confluence with an imaginary spouse, with whom the shaman would marry in the course of an ecstatic voyage to the Higher World.

In case I have not made it clear for you yet, the historical Man and his mythical ancestor are not two different Men; they are the same, only with two different ontological status. In addition, do you know what marks that point of ontological inflexion, what draws the temporal border delimiting a before and an after in Man? The Fall. Before the Fall, Man was whole, dual, androgynous; after the fall he became a "half-man", fruit of the primordial whole Man's split into male and female. The Fall meant, in the primitive mentality, a terrible ontological loss, a loss that we could read as the transition from the sacred to the profane. And also as the passage *from reality to illusion*, my dear, because the time before the Fall -the Origin- was seen as real time, while after the Fall -historical time- was, to primitive mentalities, nothing but an illusory time, resulting from the degeneration of real time. It was also understood that the Origin's "inhabitants" -our dual mythical ancestors- were the real men, of whom historical and *individual* men, Blanca, were nothing but false versions, fallen and imperfect transcriptions.

To the primitive people, historical Men were only real when they emulated their mythical ancestors' whole, dual nature. One of their methods was symbolic androgynisation, another was earthly marriage, the latter being much more effective than the first. Primitive men sensed something that later ancient sages could rationalise. They sensed that, in historical time, nothing was as close to the timeless Androgyne as the sacralised union between male and female. Thus the extreme importance given to earthly marriages in traditional cultures. Marriage was seen as a sort of palliative to the split that, in time immemorial, separated man and woman. The nuptial ritual acted, so to speak, as glue: it joined two into one, restoring, in a way, the Primordial Androgyne. Among other things, Blanca, that explains why in Classical Greece the nuptial rituals resembled that of the *Sacred Mysteries.*

In case you did not know, that is the name used to refer to the doctrines and secret ceremonies from ancient religions intended for mystical initiations: that is to say, to the changing of ontological status, the transition between a profane "way of being" to a sacred one. And what was the sacred "way of being" by excellence? Lo and behold, it was Androgyny. So, the nuptial ritual, which granted access to Androgyny, was assimilated into mystical initiations and was often a part of them; it was considered a *rite of passage* from a *profane* "way of being" -bachelorhood, individuality- to a *sacred* one -the human being's complete form. Significantly, in Classical Greece -the same as in other ancient cultures- marriage called "consecration", *télos*. Although to be truthful, Blanca, I must say that marriage, in those cultures, was quite far from being the union based on love that, fortunately, it usually is today. The entire system of beliefs that surrounded marriage in Antiquity resulted from a correct intuition, the kernel, though, eluded them. The crux of the matter –the true marital love of which our friend Swedenborg spoke– was never within the reach but of a minority of lovers and sages of sharp intuition.

But let's proceed. Often, the meaning of androgynous restoration in the nuptial union was underscored by the symbolic androgynisation of the newlyweds, who would exchange clothes. And now, my love, I'm laughing (I apologise for the digressions but, given a little room, my mind easily takes me back in time) I'm laughing thinking about a funny episode from our youth, a youth that now figures so distant in the past (though, all things considered, maybe now you're back to being young!). I suppose that, at this point, it was inevitable to remember that time we went to a fancy dress party as each other. All you had to do was tie your hair up and put on my suit and tie, but your determination to turn me into your perfect doppelgänger made my characterisation much more laborious. I remember that to make our portrayals more believable, I would blurt out solemn words while you dragged your feet as if you were a prisoner in shackles... But wait, now that I think of it, wasn't that party in Amélie-Les-Bains? No, ah, I remember, it was in Toulouse, in that little getaway from Amélie-Les-Bains to Toulouse during our honeymoon... Look, then! What an extraordinary coincidence! Because, it turns out, back then we were unknowingly following an ancestral rite: the symbolic androgynisation of the newlyweds.

That rite implied that, through marriage, a kind of osmosis between the man and the woman took place: they would merge. He would become an integral part of her, and she of him, returning to their primordial Androgyny. From two beings, they would become one.

The intersexual disguise was not limited to the nuptial rites, as I have said before. It was also a tradition in sacred festivities, such as New Year's, when they would enact *Hieros Gamos*, Hierogamy, the "sacred marriage" of the God and the Goddess, about which we will talk on another occasion. Also, in the proper initiation ceremonies (initiations to adulthood, for example), men would often dress as women and women as men. This symbolic androgynisation was also transferred to legends and myths, where heroes learned how to disguise themselves and pretend to be heroines... It's in the nuptial rite, though, where the symbolism of intersexual disguise obtains its full significance. The religion historian Marie Delcourt, who has studied this practice in the context of Classical Greece, points out yet another motif usually associated with intersexual disguise and marriage: the feat of prowess. "Initiations –she explains–, the feat of prowess, the donning of the clothing of the other sex, and marriage are co–ordinated phases, in an order which escapes us, of a complex ceremony."[105] Meaning that access to matrimony, to Androgyny, requires a great feat: only through an act of heroism can the man merge with his lost half.

Just like that, a subject that I am saving for later quietly sneaks in; love heroism: the idea that, in short–term, the androgynous restoration is only possible by heroic means.

105. Marie Delcourt, *Hermaphrodite: Myths and Rites of the Bisexual Figure in Classical Antiquity*, p. 15

Even though I will elaborate on this in a future letter, I will remind you that one popular manifestation of this theme is the famous mythological and folkloric motif of "damsel in distress", also a recurring theme in your beloved fairy tales. Think about that universal story template (in which some scholars have detected traces of an ancient initiation rite) where, to reunite with his princess, a prince must climb an inaccessible tower where she is held captive. Aa tower surrounded by a forest of thorns in *Sleeping Beauty*, or a tower in the middle of the ocean in the Greek myth Hero and Leander, a tall tower with neither door nor stairs in *Rapunzel*...; there are infinite variants, as the prisoner in the tower is a universal romantic archetype. Naturally, the prince achieves his purpose because, it goes without saying, fairy tales always have a happy ending: usually this consists of the loving reunion between the prince and the princess. In some versions of this tale, in Brothers Grimm's, for example, a couple of twins are born from that reunion, a boy and a girl. It's quite normal, Blanca: there are man1y stories where the main couple begets twins of the opposite sex. What at this point in my letter will not surprise you is that this has been interpreted as a clear sign of bi–unity, of spiritual kinship.

UNILATERAL MEN

I mentioned the longing felt by the primitive Man. But that nostalgia for the Origin, for the Original Integrity, is shared by men across time –even if not with the same level of inhibition, of course. This nostalgia is inherent to Man, my love, because Integrity is the *real* Man's "way of being". And the most efficient way of alleviating that nostalgia, as we have said, is through marriage. In the past, then, earthly marriage was given that most important of purposes: to recreate Integrity, Androgyny, and the primordial Unity of the spouses. However, our sages were aware that, even in the case of original spouses, earthly marriage was still nothing more than a palliative. A clumsy imitation, a replacement for the real marriage. That is why, Blanca, that once reunited on Earth, the twin souls from the platonic *Symposium* are not satisfied with the pleasure of being together again, they aspire to something more:

> And when one of them meets with his other half, the actual half of himself... the pair are lost in an amazement of love and friendship and intimacy, and would not be out of the other's sight, as I may say, even for a moment: these are the people who pass their whole lives together; yet they could not explain what they desire of one another. For the intense yearning which each of them has towards the other does not appear to be the desire of lover's intercourse, but of something else which the soul of either evidently desires and cannot tell, and of which she has only a dark and doubtful presentiment. Suppose Hephaestus, with his instruments, to come to the pair who are lying side by side and to say to them, "What do you people want of one another?" they would be unable to explain. And suppose further, that when he saw their perplexity he said: "Do you desire to be wholly one; always day and night to be in one another's company? for if this is what you desire, I am ready to melt you into one and let you grow together, so that being two you shall become one, and while you live a common life as if you were a single man, and after your death in the world below still be one departed soul instead of two–I ask whether this is what you lovingly desire, and whether you are

satisfied to attain this?"–there is not a man of them who when he heard the proposal would deny or would not acknowledge that this meeting and melting into one another, this becoming one instead of two, was the very expression of his ancient need. And the reason is that human nature was originally one and we were a whole, and the desire and pursuit of the whole is called love. There was a time, I say, when we were one, but now because of the wickedness of mankind God has dispersed us...[106]

Expert welder as the Greek god of forge and fire, Hephaestus expresses the ultimate longing of platonic lovers: "meeting and melting into one another... becoming one instead of two". A longing akin to that of every true lover, Blanca, true lovers like (to quote from another example) Wamiq and Azra, a famous couple from Persian literature...

'What I wish,' answered Wamiq, 'is to flee all alone with Azra into a desert, is to seek my native country in solitude and to pitch my tent beside a spring, keeping far from friend and enemy alike, soul and body both in peace, safe from men. May I be able to walk more than two hundred parasangs in any direction without finding human footprints. And then may every hair of my head, every hair on my body, become so many eyes, and may the one object of my sight be my Azra, so that I may turn to her with thousands of eyes and contemplate her face forever. Ah! better yet, may my contemplative condition be abolished. What I seek is to be delivered from duality, is to become She. As long as duality remains, distance remains, the soul is branded with the iron of separation. When the

---

106. Plato, *op. cit.*, 192 B–E

lover enters the retreat of Union, it can contain but one alone. Peace!'[107]

Do you see, Blanca? Wamiq and Azra, like the platonic lovers, are not content with being together. Not even with being together by themselves, far away from everyone, with no other occupation but eternal mutual contemplation. Their joy will not be complete while they don't merge with one another and become one. The author of this passage –the Sufi poet Jami, who lived in fifteenth century Islamic Persia– shared with Plato a belief common among the ancient sages: that the current state of humanity is an anomalous state, defective, ill. He also shared the diagnose; that we are half forms and not complete forms. He also believed, along with Plato, that earthly marriage could not be called upon to heal that state, only to offer relief. A temporary relief at that, Blanca, as your death painfully demonstrated... In Christian tradition, when the Genesis establishes earthly marriage with the words "That is why a man will leave his father and mother and be united with his wife, and the two will become one flesh."[108], the latter part is metaphorical. The two will not *actually* become one flesh, it is only *as though* they were. A real abyss remains between two earthly married twin souls. This abyss opened upon the split of the primordial Androgyne into two halves. Now those two halves seek and yearn for each other, and maybe they will even find one another and marry. But being married down here on Earth, as you and I were, my love, is not the same as being married up there, in

107. Jami, *Salomon and Absal*, quoted by Henry Corbin in *Avicenna and the True Visionary Recital*, p. 215

108. Genesis 2: 24

Heaven. Down here, even if we are married (even if it is with our original spouse), we continue to be "half-forms".

Before the ancient sages, primitive societies had already felt the altered, fallen, infirm condition of the human being. They too intuited the diagnose: being a half-form instead of a full-form; being individual and not double; being a man or a woman instead of a one-man-and-one-woman. The primitive stories about the split of an Androgynous being into two halves are the proof of that ancestral intuition, Blanca. So is a curious, widespread phenomenon: the representations of vertically cut "half-men", that is to say, unilateral men, one-sided men -one eye, one arm, one leg. We can find similar descriptions and images in alchemical treatises (where these halves of men are given the name *monocolus*, "one eye only", or *uniped*, "one foot only"), but it's in primitive societies where this motif is particularly abundant. The cave paintings and carvings representing unilateral men date back, in many cases -according to François Héritier- to the second half of the Neolithic and their distribution is near universal. "The motif can be found in Australia, Tikopia, Marquesas Islands, New Guinea, Indonesia and China; among the Giliaks, Yakuts, Samoyeds and Buryats; in India, Ceylon, Europe -Romania, Greece, Germany, Ireland, in the Arabic world, Africa and Madagascar; among the Eskimos, the indigenous people of the Pacific and of the plains, the Iroquois, the Aztec and even among the extinct peoples of the Tierra del Fuego."[109]

These unilateral characters are present in the Origin myth I cited above: Some and Nyamba. According to descriptions collected by anthropologists, Soma and Nyamba are vertically

109. François Héritier, translated from *Masculino/Femenino*, p. 166

cut. "Soma is one being with one arm and one leg only; he's the right half of the body of which Nyamba was the left side and that he cut in two."[110] Héritier highlights a curious case documented in China: of these fabulous beings "twice unilateral, if we can put it that way: they possess one right arm and one left leg, or the other way around, and marry whoever has the missing pieces of the puzzle."[111] From this theme of the "half man" arises another group of motifs, such as the "one-legged hoppers" and the "barefoot", to which Héritier offers this explanation, out from many others: "the individual cannot be thought of in myth, only the couple, as is the case of the primordial human beings from Greek thought, who were cut in two, with each half seeking its complement. The unilateral figure represents, then, the unthinkable, the absolute monstrosity: the individual."[112]

Crossed–out note on the margin. Only a name remains: *Darcy*, from which we can infer that the note was a quote taken from Jane Austen's novel. *Pride and Prejudice*.

CINDERELLA'S SHOE

This group of motifs, my dear, is also present in folklore, I mean, in the popular oral tradition of many countries. I am

110. Translated from Viviana Pâques, *L'arbre cosmique dans la pensée populaire et dans la vie quotidienne du Nord–Ouest africain*, Institut d'Ethnologie, Paris, 1964. Quoted by Jean Libis, *Le mythe de l'androgyne*, p. 85.
111. François Héritier, translated from *Masculino/Femenino*, p. 169
112. *Ibid*, p. 167

going to show you an example you will enjoy: it's your favourite fairy tale and it illustrates the theme of the "barefoot".

The story of Cinderella is so old that you can only imagine how many versions of it there is; about five hundred in European folklore alone! (Though it appears that the story has its origins in the East). The most famous versions are the one compiled by Charles Perrault in France, towards the end of the seventeenth century, and the one written down by the Brothers Grimm in Germany, a century later. It may surprise you, as much as it did me, to find out that the stories compiled by the Brothers Grimm and other authors are not necessarily stories for children. I was also convinced that the fairy tales were conceived for the little ones, but according to studies by Jung and the so-called depth psychologists, that is not accurate. We cannot even say, with exactitude, that they were "conceived", imagine: it seems like they appeared, in part, spontaneously, like dreams when we are asleep. (There is a reason, perhaps, why night time, sleeping time, has traditionally been considered the appropriate time for fairy tales, Blanca. People in many places go as far as believing that telling them during the daytime is exposing oneself to death.) This common origin with dreams explains the universality of these stories' scope of dissemination, as well as the fact that its thematic patterns coincide in various cultures. Just like dreams, fairy tales would be, largely, products of the subconscious, which is where Man keeps the memory and the nostalgia for the Origin –therefore, the nostalgia for Integrity, for Androgyny. Let's interpret the story of *Cinderella* in these symbolic terms.

Cinderella dances with her prince. This palatial ball takes place in the Origin, where both spouses are united into one single androgynous, bilateral being, as dancing couples appear to be. Then, Cinderella runs away, and in her flight she loses a shoe (which reminds me, I'm sorry, of that time when I lost a shoe on the train and, facing my initial reaction of thinking someone had stolen it, you caustically noted that since we were dealing with a one-legged thief, it would not be too hard to catch him). The loss of the shoe is a symbol for the loss of her dancing partner –her "other side", her "other half"– as consequence of the separation, of the split of the Androgyne they formed together. Now Cinderella is a unilateral being, merely someone's half. The same applies for the prince, who goes all around the realm in search of his missing half. To recognise her, he uses the shoe she left behind. This shoe is the prince's half of the *symbolon*, which he places before any potential counterpart in hopes of finding his other half. Only upon trying it on Cinderella does the prince find someone on whom the shoe perfectly fits: the prince has finally found his twin soul. After getting married, they returns to the palace, to the Origin's eternal ball, where they reintegrate Original ball's couple, the Androgyne.

As you can see, my dear, behind this kind of esoteric x-ray of the Cinderella story, breathes the myth of the primordial Androgyne split into two halves. But, do you know what I really wanted you to notice here? How the prince does not recognise Cinderella as his former dancing partner until he tries the shoe on her. What happens is that, when the price appears at her doorstep, at the house where she lives with her stepmother and stepsisters, Cinderella is no longer the radiant young girl from the ball. Now she dresses in poor raggedy clothes and soot and ashes darken her face. If he had seen her with physical eyes, surely he would not have recognised her; he would not have perceived her subjective and secret beauty, that which was reserved for his eyes only.

However, he pays no mind to her appearance; he is only focused on whether the shoe fits her foot: meaning, on whether she corresponds to his tally-half, the tally-half of the soul, the heart, represented by the shoe. The prince looks at her with the eyes of the heart, and that is how he recognises her.

The benefits of looking with the eyes of the heart rather than the physical eyes, Blanca, is, as you know, one of the most repeated messages in fairy tales. It's also the central message of that modern fairy tale, *The Little Prince*. What's more, many stories echo Cinderella's plot, that of the lost and recovered Paradise, with the prince and princess' mutual search, the obstacles and challenges they must overcome before finally uniting (a union that is usually a reunion) and their wedding at the end. Here abides, as I was telling you, the same subconscious and nostalgic memory of the Origin that gave rise to the universal myth of the Androgyne. But in the story of Cinderella, there is yet another collateral theme also present in countless other fairy tales: superficial ugliness, the ugliness that enshrouds a great beauty.

Cinderella's true looks, my dear, are the ones shining in the ballroom: a radiant beauty. Her true condition is that of a princess: her rags are only a disguise; the ashes smudging her face, a mask. Surely you can remember other fairy tales in which the prince or princess, due to a spell or a curse, have a hideous appearance. Did you say *The Frog Prince*? Did you say *Beauty and the Beast*? Those are probably the most famous examples. Instead of contemplating their "repugnant partner" with the physical eyes, the heroes must learn to see them with the eyes of the heart. Only then will they be able to recognise the other as their twin soul and consent to unite in matrimony. In fairy tales, this union is often represented by the kiss. The moment the loving kiss restores the Origin's heavenly marriage, the curse breaks and the frog or the Beast recover their princely condition.

Allow me to make a brief aside to tell you that this theme of ugliness as a disguise and of the benefit of looking beyond it, with the eyes of the heart, seems to me like a reminder meant for a certain type of people. Those who, guided exclusively by the standards of objective beauty, embark on impossible loves, on loves that in no way whatsoever could be corresponded, instead of falling in love with someone within their reach –and, in general, no one is more within someone's reach than their twin soul, Blanca. Forgive me, but I am thinking of your cousin Jean–Paul, always falling in love with women far more attractive and younger than him who, of course, would never give him the time of day. We are all susceptible to such mistakes; I have already told you objective beauty is deceitful, capable of producing in us the emotion of recognition and making us falsely believe that we are in the presence of the other half of our *symbolon*.

Allow me to expand this aside a little bit. Following all this, my dear, another acquaintance of ours sprang to mind (don't see this as gossip, I'm only trying to illustrate the subject). Do you remember Alfredo? Of course you do! That seductive *bon vivant* and unrepentant bachelor, much younger than I, who ran an art gallery. You said he looked like Glenn Ford. Well, now every so often I stumble upon him. He moved into our neighbourhood. His old apartment turned out to be too small because, take a guess, he finally got married. He told me how one day he came across a "Titian's Venus" holding arms with a blind woman, which apparently moved him and further stirred in him the desire to meet her. Never before, he confessed to me (though I did not believe him), had he felt such an impulse to follow a woman down the street. He even mentioned the word Fate: something along the lines of Fate guiding his steps behind those two women. Anyway, he managed to find a way of starting a conversation with them, invited them out for a coffee and, with time, gained their trust. Today, I'm telling you, Alfredo is a happily married man. Ah, but not with Titian's Venus, imagine, but with the blind woman! So if someone, let's say you, asked me to interpret this event, I would tell you that the first woman may have had objective beauty on her side, but it was the second lady who held the subjective beauty that applied Alfredo.

All this, Blanca (the brief aside keeps getting longer, I'm sorry), makes me think of that film that always moved us every time we watched it at the cinema –several times when it came out– or on television. I'm talking about *Marty*, an unconventional love story, seeing as it doesn't star the most statuesque film stars of the day, but instead stars Ernest Borgnine, not bad at all, and Betsy Blair, who plays an ugly woman while, in my opinion, being anything but. Although, getting back to the subject at hand, I suspect that what is asked of us mere mortals is not as extreme a sacrifice as those of the heroes of *The Frog Prince* and *The Beauty and the Beast*. You know how fairy tales go: its characters are archetypes, its world is a world of extremes; the princess is always beautiful, the prince is always valiant, the witch is always the ugliest and meanest. In those stories, we effectively have two extreme characters, one is splendid, the other hideous. The message again is the same as in *The Little Prince*: "It is only with the heart that one can see rightly, what is essential is invisible to the eye.", or in other words, it is preferable to focus on subjective beauty rather than objective. However...

However, Blanca, I am afraid us humans are too conditioned by objective beauty to simply dispense with it completely. Would you have recognised me on the tram, that afternoon, if all my teeth were missing? Would I have recognised you if you had looked like a wicked witch out from some fairy tale? In its still low evolutionary level (in later letters I will be able to justify this expression), erotic love has some commercial transaction aspects to it. Just as when we buy a product we expect the best quality for our price range, so too when it's time to find a partner, we will not be satisfied with someone of a much inferior objective beauty; that only happens, I am afraid, in fairy tales... This is to tell you, my dear, that in real life, the Beast would be hard–pressed to be recognised by the Beauty as her twin soul. I think that the recognition of the subjective beauty concerning each one of us still requires –as long as we remain in the current evolutionary state– the additional presence in the twin soul of a level of objective beauty similar to the one's own. It's likely, then, that twin souls tend to reincarnate in accordance with that criteria.

OF BEAUTY

By restoring the Origin's heavenly matrimony, we were saying, the "frog" or the "Beast" recover their original beauty. This happens because heavenly marriage, Androgyny, beautifies the spouses. Yes, yes, you have read that correctly, Blanca; Androgyny beautifies. We would have to search for the explanation in the Androgyne's own nature as imagined by the ancient sages, to whom the Androgyne was the perfect human, and beauty nothing more than the splendour of that which is perfect. The essential requirement of beauty, as it has been recognised since yesteryear, is symmetry, and what is human symmetry? You are right: human symmetry is the Androgyne. If according to what we have seen, the unilateral man, the "half-man" who is the man without the woman and the woman without the man, is hideous in the eyes of the ancient sages' second sight, then that is precisely because of its asymmetry. So then, the prince and princess, when united in the Androgyne, were beautiful to the highest degree of Beauty. It was upon losing Androgyny, upon separating from each other, that they simultaneously lost that adorning quality. Thus, all beauty (including yours, my love, it pains me to write so) is circumstantial and temporary; it's but a pale reflection of the original Beauty, which is absolute Beauty, Beauty itself.

This loss is what in fairy tales is represented by the prince's enchantment, which converts him into a frog or Beast. The act of disguising oneself, the act of adopting a miserable condition that is not one's own: such as the king disguising himself as a pauper, the princess dressing in rags and smudging her face with ashes... Regarding this, a famous enchantment from the blue library comes to mind: that of Don Quixote's damsel, Dulcinea del Toboso, who, from a princess of unrivalled beauty, as she was in the mind of her enraptured knight, metamorphosed into a rustic and ugly wench. Don Quixote must now free her from that curse, just as fairy tale heroes must overcome a series of trials (and here we have the theme of loving heroism sneaking up on us again) before being allowed to come together with their princess, or prince, and recover their original Androgyny and, with it, their past beauty, the beauty inherent to Androgyny. In the story of Cinderella, this original beauty appears through the radiance of her ball gown, which in many variants is a cosmic radiance: it encompasses the sun, the moon and the stars. In the writings of the ancient sages, Blanca, references to this incomparable beauty abound. Swedenborg talks about the "beauty of the angels of Heaven", and he says they "have all their beauty from marriage love"[113] in Heaven, which is true conjugal love, a love that unites the spouses "into one single mind". One century earlier, another great Christian mystic, Jakob Boehme, painted the primordial human "dressed in supreme glory, neither man nor woman, but both."[114] And according to the *Zohar*, while Adam and Eve were merged into one, they irradiated a dazzling beauty: "Adam's beauty was like an emanation of a higher brilliance, and Eve's was such that no creature could look at her directly."

You will remember that in the previous letter we verified this self-evident fact: that we all feel powerfully attracted, dazzled even, when standing before an objectively beautiful person of the opposite sex. We were saying that this happens because, in a way, we recognise that beauty; and that if we recognise it, then that is because we have seen it somewhere else before; and that this "somewhere else" (a mystical, not physical place) is the Origin. Well, now the time has come to be more specific about those claims, to go into detail, to consider and answer the question: who, in the Origin, was vested in that Beauty? That Beauty of which Plato said we lived in perpetual mystic contemplation? Or rather: Whom were we contemplating? Do you know? I think I know: in light of the theory of the twin souls, the answer leaves no room for

113. Emmanuel Swedenborg, *Heaven and Hell*, 382a, translation by John C. Ager

114. J. Boehme, *Von der Gnadenwahl*, 5:35

doubts, my dear: We were contemplating (contemplation, in this case, is the natural consequence of love) our twin soul, with whom we formed one androgynous Whole. That Beauty before which we lived in perpetual mystic contemplation is none other than the Androgyne's Beauty, consubstantial then with our twin soul and ourselves –only we contemplated our Beauty as reflected in hers, as though we were looking in a mirror.

A few pages back I told about how, in his ecstatic voyages through the Otherworld, Swedenborg was able to see couples of heavenly married angels. In a chapter from *Conjugal Love* entitled *Marriages in Heaven* (the book Baron Féroë was reading when he caught Lavinia and Malivert merging into one single "angel of love") the Swedish mystic describes to us one of those androgynous angels. He cannot possibly do it justice, though, as its beauty, he tells us, blinds him: such is its splendour. The incomparable beauty ("Beauty itself") of the spouses was the result of their mutual love, of the loving way they contemplated each other. And it was only thanks to the wife's kindness, who partly turned away from her husband, that he, Swedenborg, could observe and later scarcely describe that beauty, for it was more intense "when they mutually turned towards each other, and less when they were partly turned from each other."[115]

The ineffable beauty that dazzled Swedenborg, the Androgyne's Beauty, was sometimes depicted, by the ancient sages, with the colours of the rainbow, a Natural element traditionally linked to Androgyny, Blanca... At this point, I cannot help but recall a magic moment you and I lived many

115. Emmanuel Swedenborg, *Conjugal Love,* 42, translation by Samuel M. Warren

years ago. You must remember it! One of those magic moments that life sometimes bestows upon twin souls –I bet you thought of it too. That rainy afternoon when we reached the summit of the Puigmal and saw the majestic spectacle awaiting for us there: the sight of a vibrant rainbow unfolding before us, as rainwater, or maybe blissful tears, ran down our eyes... Despite all that, despite the colourful splendour and the beauty so moving it brought us to tears, the view was still describable: It was within the reach of a great painter's brush or a great writer's pen. Whereas this other Beauty I am telling you about, Blanca, this Beauty embodied by our twin soul in the Origin, is impervious to description, it's beyond any representation; earthly beauty is but a footprint, a shadow, a pale reflection. Even then, the reflection abides by its model: that is why beautiful people of the opposite sex dazzle us. In a way, it's a recognition, a reminiscence, Plato would say... except it's not the person we are recognising, it's her *beauty*.

Unfortunately, as I was saying, this distinction is not always easy. Look, ever since you passed away (and sometimes before), I think I see you on the street, on the bus, or at the cinema. The other day it was at the supermarket: my heart skipped a beat, I rushed towards you, called you by your name but, obviously, you did not turn around, it was not you, it could not be you... I think it happens to all of us, believing we all of a sudden recognise someone. Someone who, by their way of talking or dressing, or by their countenance, or by the way they walk or turn the pages of a book, reminds us a loved one, a person whom, in one way or another, we have in our mind all the time. I believe this is the same type of mix–up we fall for when standing before a beautiful person of the opposite sex: we think we recognise them but, actually, it's *their beauty* what we recognise. That beauty seems familiar and dear to us because it vaguely reminds us of that other beauty which vested our twin soul back in the Origin, when we were one.

BASTARD GODS

I am afraid this letter turned out to be longer than I was expecting. But the nights have also been longer, my dear, I have been suffering from insomnia lately, it must be the heat. Ah, but before I finish, I bring up all the sentences I asked you to keep in mind before. There are five of them, in case you were not counting, the first two by our friend Swedenborg, the Swedish mystic: "[true marital love] is the Lord's Divine in the heavens" and "...the Divine is imaged in the two that are in true marriage love..." The third one is from the *Zohar*: "God will not establish His residence in a place where such union does not exist" (it refers to the union of male and female). And the other two from *Spirite*, the novel by Théophile Gautier: in that book, they allude to twin souls as "but the two halves of the supreme whole", and they pose the question "What is even the happiest human union in comparison with the rapture two souls enjoy in the eternal embrace of divine love?".

You noticed, I am sure, that all five sentences converge and point in the same direction. A delicate direction that will probably surprise you, my love, because even though you knew that "God is Love", as it's written in the Christians Scriptures, maybe you did not perceive such a tight bond between God and this specific type of love; erotic love. Because it's not just that erotic love –as the ancient sages intuited– is the fundamental love, the matrix from which branch out all other loves, love to thy neighbour, paternal love, friendship, brotherly love, even the reciprocal love between God and Man: it's that God revealed Himself, in the eyes of the ancient sages (to their second sight) as the fruit of an erotic love: as the fruit of heavenly marriage. He revealed Himself to them, then, *as identical to the Androgyne.*

This intuition of God and the Androgyne's identity, Blanca, appears to have already been suggested in that most fabulous platonic story with which we opened this letter, and with which we will now close it. In his retelling of the split of the androgynous Original Man into two halves, Plato said that the power of the double men, of the androgynous men of the Origin, was such that it threatened to emulate the Gods' own power: men were threatening to "scale heaven". Well, we can imagine that –maybe in the Eastern myth that, according to some scholars, inspired Plato– it was not just a threat, but also a done deed: that those Original men already rivalled, in fact, the Gods, meaning Men and Gods were alike. Well now, how do the "legitimate Gods" manage to dispossess those other "bastard Gods"? "They could not put them to death", tells us Plato – an unequivocal sign that Men were effectively Gods, Immortals. What do they do, then, to bring them down from the Divine pedestal? What they do, Blanca, is splitting each one of them into two halves. That is to say, they take their dual Unity away from them, their Androgyny.

The ploy is successful: the men–Gods lose their powers, they become simple men, simple mortals. From this, we can arrive at the conclusion that what gave them the power of the Gods, was precisely that one mysterious attribute: the one we thoroughly talked about in this letter, Androgyny.

Yours

THIRD LETTER

THE DOUBLE GODS

(or DIVINE BI-UNITY)

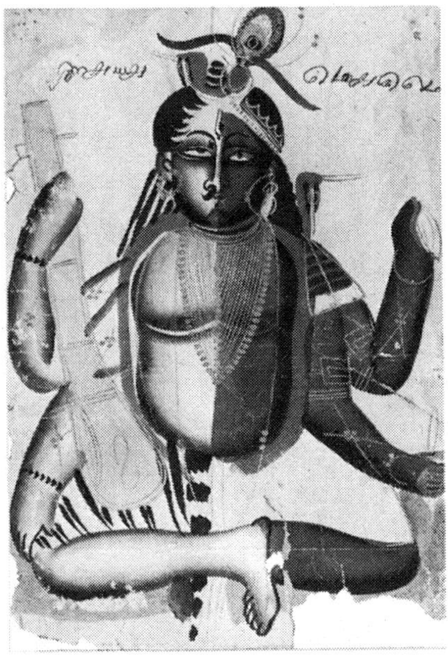

Within the secret of the relationship
Between man and woman, is God.

Letter on Holiness
Anonymous, thirteenth-century

Barcelona, July 20th, 1999

Dear Blanca,

Amélie-les-Bains has not changed much since our honeymoon. I have just spent a few days there. I go back every year around this time and I stay at the same hotel, in the same room (the one from where you said you could see a rock shaped like a lion's head), and I take the same walks. Do you remember our walks and bicycle rides, our talks in the cafes, the sunsets by the fireplace, of lying down on the prairies, contemplating those skies furnished with clouds...? What I want to remind you right now, more than anything, my dear, is of our trips to the mountain. That is because what I would like to propose to you at this moment, is a kind of trip. Not a recreational trip, of course, as those we took back then... but I hope you will enjoy it just the same. This will be more like an exploratory trip, like the one we undertook last time under the guidance of Emmanuel Swedenborg, through equally mysterious territories. Although while that other path had barely been trodden, this one to which I am inviting you now has been visited by theologians, philosophers and other detectives of the ethereal. If you agree to join me, then it will be our turn –for the good of our investigation and hand in hand with those more experienced detectives– to venture into the mysterious territory of Metaphysics, the field of realities and ultimate meanings.

Yes, you are right: we have already walked through this inhospitable place in the previous letters. However, we limited ourselves to the foothills of that mountain. Now we will climb higher. And at such heights, the landscape becomes more abstract, vaporous as the white clouds over the skies of Amélie-les-Bains, and thus harsher and harder. And so I will ask you the same question you asked me every time you were about to read a book aloud for the both of us: Are you ready? Yes? Then away we go...

At the end of the previous letter, we put forward the conclusion that God and the Androgyne were the same thing. Now we must take the trouble of explaining it. Let's begin with the definition of God often given by ancient sages. Alternatively, better yet, with the characteristic Divine attribute which, according to the ancient sages, defines God: *Unity*. In every spiritual tradition, Blanca, God is eminently *the One*. Unity is what, above all, characterises God, who's Divinity resides precisely in His unitary character to the point that if God were not One, if He stopped being One, then He would no longer be God. Ah, but Unity, what does it consist of? For the ancient sages, Unity is *the attribute of what is whole*, of what is perfect: that is to say, the attribute of everything that constitutes an Absolute, a Whole. Unity consists, then, of Integrity: of something that is whole, we say that it's One. In the previous letter, we saw that Integrity was the distinguishing attribute of the Androgyne, and we talked about it in relation to the human being. But Integrity is God's prerogative, Blanca: God is the only whole, perfect, total being, for He is the only One. Therefore, God is the Androgyne; the only Androgyne there is, so when in the other letter we talked about the Original human being as an androgynous being, we were actually talking about God.

Yes, you have read that correctly, that is precisely what I am saying: in the Origin, Man was no different from God. However, if you don't mind, we'll leave this delicate matter of the Original Man's involvement in the divine essence for the next letter. In this one, I will be talking not about Man but about God. About God, which is the same as the Androgyne, I mean; which finds in the Androgyne –for Androgyny is the defining symbol of Integrity– His symbol par excellence. More than that, Blanca. We could say that the Androgyne is also an "x–ray" of God since, in Him, we cannot see with "the naked eye" anything other than the One, while the Androgyne reveals an "x–ray" image of that One: an image of the two halves that merge into the One. That is because, as I have said before, Integrity, by itself, is not enough to define the Androgyne. Integrity is the result of a synthesis, of the fusion of two things into one: one single thing of which the other two are the two halves... The ancient sages could discern in Divinity those two sides: what is visible to the "naked eye", and the "x–ray". Therefore, the Jewish sages symbolised God (although it's a multipurpose symbol) with a six–pointed star, the star –or shield– of David, which upon closer inspection appears to consist of two superimposed and intertwined triangles. The Chinese sages also represented what they called *Tao* –which would be Divinity– with that dual appearance. The "naked eye" appearance of the *Tao* is the *Tai Kih*, the Great Essence, represented by an empty circle; the x–ray is the *yin–yang*, represented by that same circle helicoidally divided into two halves: a white half –*yin*– corresponding to the female principle, and a black half –*yang*–, the male principle. (To symbolise that both principles are also present in their opposite, the white zone has a black circle and vice–versa.)

The ancient sages, Blanca, saw in God an "empty circle", a neutral being, asexual, an entity that is neither male nor female, quite the opposite. But when they took an x–ray of God, they distinguished –in that One God– two halves, two separate Persons, one male and another female. Now, look, this Couple or Duality, that deep down is God, is a Couple or Duality *in love*, a Couple eternally immersed in the sublime emotion of love. Thus, we arrive, then, through this unexpected path, at the ancient sages' fundamental intuition, laconically proclaimed in the Gospel of John: that "God is Love" (I John 4: 16). If we applied the old scholastic distinction here, we would say that Unity is the *substantial form* of God, and Love (starting with erotic love, which is the root of all love) His *raw material*. Just as it says in the *Zohar*: "*Love holds the mystery of the Unity*". Well, just as the heart is a muscle that needs to be filled with blood in order to work, Blanca, Unity is a muscle that is fuelled by Love.

LOVE WITHIN GOD

A poet I quoted in the previous letter, Coventry Patmore, wrote the following verses:

Female and male God made the man,
His image is the whole not half;
And in our love we dimly scan
The love which is between himself.[116]

They allude to the first of two retellings of the creation of Man in the Genesis, and to its interpretation according to the ancient sages. I will remind you of the passage "Then God said, 'Let us make mankind in our image, in our likeness'... So God created man in His own image, in the image of God He created him, male and female He created them."[117] Several ancient sages, Blanca, Jewish and Christian, saw their fundamental intuition of God confirmed by this passage: the intuition of His Androgyny. First, they asked themselves: when God said "Let us make mankind in our image, in our likeness", with whom was He speaking? Was He talking to Himself? Why was He using the plural? They found these questions indirectly answered by interpreting the subsequent verses. According to their interpretation, of which I already talked at length in the previous letter, God had not created a man and a woman separately, but a couple of spouses: a united, married couple; hence the singular form being applicable to them ("He created him"). Or we could look at it from another angle: God created a man, singular; except this man was double, androgynous; he was composed of a couple, hence the plural form being applicable to him ("He created them"). Then it says God created Man (this double Man, this male–female Man) *in His own image*. From which the ancient sages logically con-

116. Quoted by Elémire Zolla, *The Invisible Lover*
117. Genesis 1: 26–27

cluded that God Himself was double, androgynous. God was a conjugal couple, which would explain the plural form in “Let us make mankind”.

So you see! The sagacity of the ancient sages could rival that of Hércules Poirot! But there is more. They also saw another secret insinuation of Androgyny in the duality of the expression “in our image, in our likeness”: the “image” would correspond to the male Person and the “likeness” to the female Person of God. The Kabbalists could discern God’s Androgyny even in His own Hebrew name –YHVH (Yahweh). They related the tetragram’s *Y* with the male half, the *H* with the feminine, and *VH* represented the union of both, the Divine Androgyne.

Let’s look at Patmore’s verses, though. The first one confirms Man’s past Androgyny: “Female and male God made the man”. The second one, God’s current, eternal Androgyny: “His image is the whole not half”. (By the way, Blanca, notice how these verses reveal that, for Patmore, Integrity comes from it being made of two, from being *two in one.*) From these two verses, we deduce a consequence substantiated by the following two: “And in our love we dimly scan / The love which is between himself”. Indeed, if God is a divine Couple in whose image He created the Original human couple, then, my dear, the love professed by the two fallen halves of the Original couple in this lower world, is the reflection of a higher love, of *the love within God*. Or, putting it another way: from the fact that human Duality is amorous and that such Duality was originally created in the Divine image, Patmore deduces the amorous character of God’s Duality. He infers that the relationship kept between God’s two implicit Personas is a relationship of conjugal love, of erotic love (and that erotic love has its roots in the essence, in the very nature of Divinity, in God). It's clear that the difference between the current human nature -split, "broken"- and divine nature -whole- determines that erotic love between man and woman is very different from the one between the Two Persons of God: the first, says Patmore, is "dim" when compared to the second one, which is implied to be radiant.

In sum, with these four verses, Coventry Patmore is echoing an ancient and universal intuition: that God consists of Two Persons, and that theirs is a relationship of erotic love. God would be what in the previous letter we called a "heavenly couple", that is to say, a *Couple of heavenly Spouses*. But all this while remaining, above all, One. Therefore, by being *perfectly united*, this Couple integrates one single Person, a third Person that transcends the Couple itself (and that is infinitely more important than the Couple itself is). Since this is the essence of the concept of Androgyny, my love: being *two in one*, being *two* while at the same time being -above everything else- *One*.

THE MARK OF THE DIVINE

Let's stop for a moment in God's Unity. Above, we were saying that Unity is (along with Love) the essence of God; that Unity is what Divinity consists of: And Unity stems from Integrity, from the idea of Perfection, in the sense of "finishing"; from the idea of Completeness, of Totality; from the Absolute, which is a word that comes from Latin, meaning perfect, complete, finished. That is to say, Blanca, that God is God because He is One, and He is One because He is whole, perfect because He is absolute and complete. He is God because He is total: That is why the ancient sages called

Him either *the One* or *the Whole*. That is why they depicted Him through a perfect shape: the circle.

Yes, Blanca, this idea of Perfection, of Totality, this idea of Integrity represented in mythology by the Androgyne and in numerology by the One, has, in geometry, a round shape. The shape of a sphere. Hence, out of all the symbols of His unity, perfection, and totality, out of every symbol of God, the sphere, or the circle, is what the ancient sages more often used. It should not come as a surprise, then, that the old Chinese symbol for *Tao* has a circular shape. Neither should we find it strange that said symbol is composed of two complementary halves of a dynamic shape similar to the blades of a propeller, seeing that Perfection, Completeness, the Integrity embodied by the sphere, is the result of the harmonisation of two elements of opposing signs: every sphere has two poles.

As I have said before, the ancient sages thought of this harmonisation as having an erotic nature. "A *yin* and a *yang* –claims the ancient Chinese sage Chuang Tzu– is called *Tao*: the passionate union of *yin* and *yang* and the copulation of husband and wife represent the eternal model of the Universe." So it's confirmed, Blanca, that within divine Unity underlies a Duality in love; that Unity, that God, is the fruit of an amorous interaction. It's in this light that certain ancient sayings, such as this Kabbalist aphorism, were understood: "Within the secret of (the relationship between) man and woman, is God."[118] Or this line from an old Hindu text: "There are the Moon and the Sun, and between them the Seed: This last is that Being, whose nature

118. Translated from *Lettre sur la Sainteté*, p. 35 (paraphrasing a phrase from the *Talmud*, Sotah 17a)

is Joy Supreme."[119] Or the first lines from this prayer from the first centuries of Christianity: ""From Thee, Father, and through Thee, Mother, the two immortal names, Parents of the divine being..."[120]

The idea of God as a Couple of Spouses (a couple in love) frequently appears in the history of religions. So does a concept deriving from that idea: the concept of *hierogamy*, the "sacred marriage". *Hierogamy* describes the loving union within Divinity, that is to say, the divine coupling –the union between God and Goddess– that becomes the One, the neutral God, a God that is neither male nor female but, so to speak, quite the opposite. Religion historians tell us that, in primitive religions, liturgical celebrations often revolved around the sacred matrimony between the priest and the priestess, or the priestess and the king. They also tell us, Blanca, that in primitive religious thought, Androgyny, the "two in one" conjugal attribute, was essential to Divinity. Mircea Eliade speaks of Androgyny as the identifying sign, or "the mark", of the Divine, and she claims that it was seen as a defining trait of the gods. Of *all* the Gods, including those typically male or female in appearance.

I am talking about gods, plural, my dear, and I am sure that by doing so I am probably using the world a little carelessly. That is because Unity requires Uniqueness: God is singular, there are no gods; there is only one God, a God unique in His nature. What happens is that the mythologies and primitive religions to which Eliade refers, and to which we are referring now as well, followed that contradiction. We

119. *Hevajra Tantra*

120. Hyppolotus of Rome, *Refutationis omnium haeresium*, V, 6 quoted by Elaine Pagel, *The Gnostic Gospels*, p.49

must not lose sight, though, that even in polytheist religions there is a God that rises above all others: the gods' diversity is ultimately subordinated to a supreme God; a God that is either androgynous or a divine couple.

Humanity has known countless examples of "double gods" –androgynous gods, or divine couples. Let's take a look at some of them.

Zeus, the Greek supreme God[121], despite his masculine reputation, in some archaic depictions he is an androgynous being. A statuette discovered in Labranda, in Caria, shows him beardless and with four rows of breasts on his chest. To the Orphic initiates, he was the "male–female god": "Zeus is born male; immortal Zeus comes forth a nýmphi (female)", so proclaims an Orphic hymn. Hercules, the quintessential virile hero, also presents certain dual–god connotations: there is an episode from his legend where he dresses in women's clothing, and there is evidence that –at least in some places of the ancient world where he was worshipped– his priests and initiates dressed as women as well, just as the god himself. The Phoenix, a bird symbolising immortality, was male and female at the same time. In Cyprus, they worshipped a bearded Aphrodite called Aphroditos; and her Roman equivalent, the goddess of Love, Venus, had an androgynous version as well: the bald Venus of ancient worship. Artists and poets conceived and depicted her son Eros (Cupid to the Romans) as an androgyne. The nuptial goddess Hera (wife and sister of Zeus) not only had an androgynous figure but she also conceived her sons by herself, which is a clear sign

121. For this chapter dedicated to the Gods of Grego–Latin classic Antiquity, the author has based himself on the second chapter of Marie Delcourt's book *Hermaphrodite*

of Androgyny, Blanca. Most deities of flora and fertility were androgynous; like Dionysus, god of the vine, who was the paradigmatic bisexual god: they refer to him as "man-woman" in a tragedy by Aeschylus. In another, by Euripides, he is "the woman-like stranger". (Although if in archaic times Dionysus was depicted in the full scope of his dual nature, in the Hellenistic era he would lapse into a graceful, effeminate adolescent.) The Romans knew numerous legendary characters- such as the Faun and Fauna, Ruminus and Rumina, Liber and Liberia- who would split into a male persona and a female persona. And this is only regarding the Greco-Roman civilisation[122]. Let's travel to India now.

In Hindu religion, there are many gods, my dear, but ultimately it all comes down to one divine couple: Mahadeva and Mahadevi, "Great God" and "Great Goddess". This uniform couple, popularly known as Shiva and Shakti (*Shakti* meaning "wife" in Sanscrit), is identified with the One, with the Absolute. Sometimes they are shown fused in a tight embrace, others, under the form of a single androgynous being. In the former's case, they have also been given the names Kameshvara and Kameshvari; in the latter's, Addhanarishvara (*Ardhanari*: "the Androgyne"), or simply Ishvara, "Lord", which is the supreme God's habitual title. The Buddha, who, while not being a God, is called upon like one ("Lord Buddha", he is called), is often represented tightly hugging his Shakti... Just as it happens with the Judeo-Christian God that C. Patmore was echoing in the verses quoted above, Blanca, erotic love also operates in the bosom of Hindu Divinity. And like the Judeo-Christian God, this love is not something adjacent or contingent but, on the

122. *Ibid*

contrary, something substantial and essential to the Divine. This is notable in the names of Kameshvara and Kameshvari, where –next to *Ishvara* or *Ishvara*, "lord" or "lady"– appears the word *kama*, "love". Even when the god Kama, equivalent to Cupid in Western mythology, has several types of arrows at his disposal, each corresponding to the type of erotic love he wishes to induce, the Sanskrit word "kama" tends to be generally associated with sex, with carnal love (think of the famous *Kamasutra*), which gives me room to make the following observation:

Ancient mythologies and religions usually described the love operating within God in sexual terms, in carnal love terms. However, don't let this language fool you; we must not interpret it literally. Look, my love, erotic love as we humans experience is tinted with sexuality; it's understandable, then, that we have traditionally attributed those same colours to every erotic love, be it human or divine; that we tend to see those colours as essential to erotic love. What if I told you, though, that those colours are actually accessories, like a dye colouring a colourless water? It's not me who says it, it's our ancient sages, and as a great sixteenth century French thinker observed: "To judge great, and high matters requires a suitable soul; otherwise we attribute the vice to them which is really our own."[123] Let's take heed, then, of the criteria of souls greater and higher than ours.

You will see, my dear, that the ancient sages too often resort to sexual language to allude to the love within God. However, they do so in the figurative sense. Our sages are aware –just as we should be– that every human being we believe to be simultaneously present within God, is also present

---

123. Michel de Montaigne, *Essays, Book I, XL*

in Him in a different way: with a different trait, more subtle and clear, in a purer state, or rather, more "naked". Remember how Patmore distinguished between the nature of the love within God from the one within human couples: the latter being, as he said, dimly scanned when compared to the former. Why is it dimmer? It's dimmer precisely because it's not naked, because it's not colourless. It's tinged with sexuality, with desire, and, as it's claimed in the most popular of all Hindu sacred texts, as it's written in that epitome of Vedic literature and the Upanishads, the *Bhagavad Gita*: "Just as a fire is covered by smoke, a mirror is masked by dust... Similarly, one's knowledge gets shrouded by desire."[124]

Now, let's be clear, Blanca: sex is a human phenomenon, not a divine one. The two poles around which revolves the heavenly couple, or the Androgyne, are not sexual, even if metaphorically we attribute such traits to them. The male–female duality is the expression, in Matter, of the essential Duality of the Androgyne, who is a purely spiritual being, a "virginal" entity as described by our sages, who, to indicate this, represented him flaunting wings and crushing a dragon underneath his feet. As we will see later on, the dragon is a symbol of Matter. The material nature of sex prevents its presence in the Androgyne, where a love of a different class operates: a love that does not submit to that yoke, to the intolerable bondage that is, for our sages, the carnal itch. Christians named this emancipated love *Agape*, the "virginal" love that is genuine love, of which sexuality is but a fallen version, love translated into the crude language of Matter.

But wait, wait! I am going too fast! Everything in due time. Anyway, you can see where I am going with this, can you not,

124. *Bahgavad–Gita*, 3: 38

my love? Like the trout, I am swimming against the current. By the way, I fished a huge one last month! You should have seen it, almost three kilos, as big as that one you caught that one time; you should have seen Enrique's face! With all his theories about fly–fishing, he came back empty–handed.

I apologise for how easily I get off–track. I was telling you I am swimming against the current (except it's not me: it's our sages!), against today's widespread tendency to glorify sex. Of course, my dear, I know this would sound outrageous even to jaded people such as Esther and Enrique. Surely the majority of people are not ready to hear what I am about to tell you in these letters –but as it happens, I am not writing to the majority of people, I am writing to you. People tend to think that sexual desire is no different from other appetites and that, consequently, there is no reason to treat it any differently. It would not occur to anyone to doubt his or her actions if, when faced with hunger or thirst, they took the necessary steps to satisfy that hunger or quench that thirst, as long as they are not hurting anyone. That is why they find it odd that, when it comes to sexual desire, so many traditions and ancient sages extol the virtues of abstinence. What happens, though, is that for the sages, my dear, sexual desire is not merely another appetite. In its scope, takes place a phenomenon that, although it can be explained by natural causes (a biologist would tell you of endorphins and neural discharges), widely transcends the material order and, by catapulting us beyond Matter, reveals to us the existence of another more subtle, crystalline dimension of the Universe. That mysterious phenomenon is love.

You know, the other day I heard a sexologist on the radio saying that love is like yoghurts: it has an expiry date, it lasts for approximately eighteen months and then it's over; or, in the best-case scenario, it's followed by something more resembling friendship. This theory may have the virtue of offering an answer to the question of why is it so easy to change partners these days: people are not resigning themselves, as they did before, to living with an expired love. But, in my opinion, this is supported by a false premise. Look, Blanca, occasionally I have lunch at Quimet's restaurant, which now is run by his son. You remember Quimet and Marta, may they rest in peace, right? Well, so his son, who is a fantastic young man and knows how close we were with his parents, sometimes joins me for dessert. And up until recently, he always ended up asking me the same question: "But why don't you get married again?" I always dodged the question, until one day I had enough and gave him the real reason. I told him that I loved you and that you being dead did not change a thing. As he appeared intent on objecting, I made the indiscretion of telling him about our theory. I had to explain myself. Have you noticed how interested people get every time the theory of twin souls come up? "Honestly –he told me when I was finished talking– if it is as you say, I rather not find my twin soul, if that implies being tied to one person forever, to close the door on new relationships". In vain, I objected that according to the theory I had just told him, he already was tied to someone forever and that diving into that relationship did not mean limiting himself, quite the contrary: Limitations come from not going beyond the surface of love, from jumping from one affair to another without ever delving deep into any of them. To love more, I concluded, does not consist of having more lovers, but of loving more deeply; and this entails exclusivity.

I mention this story, my dear, because Quimet's son's standing on this matter appears to be representative of that of a wide majority of people, to whom (as the radio sexologist) love is concentrated on the first stages of a relationship, on the effervescent voluptuousness of the first months. Few suspect that love has a "reverse side"; much less that complicity, that intimate friendship which, in the case of true love, follows passionate love, and which they interpret as the down-spiral of love, is, in reality, a higher state of love, a ripeness. Because true love does not grow old; it matures. You and I are a clear example of this. So was that old couple we would see walking hand in hand in our neighbourhood, do you remember? You said they reminded you of the old lovers from the Serrat song, who cradled each other at night like two little children, and who in the morning would ask "Are you ok? Nothing hurts today?" I bet that those tender twilight lovers, which we would have grown to be if you had not left so soon, knew much more about love than our young newlywed neighbours upstairs, who make passionate love all the time. Because, you know, I believe we could say that love, contrary to most people's opinion that it's a young man's game, is what is facetiously said about youth: it's wasted on the young.

We will expand on this in another letter. Now let's go back a few pages and pick up the thread of the "double gods" relationship:

The primitive Australian's primordial god was androgynous. So was feudal China's supreme god, which happens to be another typical example of splitting, for even though they called him *Sovereign on High and August Heaven*, this name split into two parts, Sovereign on High and August Heaven.[125] (It's, as you can see, two redundant designations,

125. Cf Marcel Granet, *Religion of the Chinese People*

twins.) The famous feathered serpent *Quetzalcoatl*, the pre-Columbian deity, was also androgynous. The belief in the supreme god's androgyny has also been observed in several Native-American pueblo peoples -pueblo peoples such as the Zuni, worshippers of a deity called "He-She" (*Awonawilona*). The native inhabitants of ancient Mexico called their god "Father-Mother" (*Ometecuhtli-Omecihuatl*), a prevalent name in mythology. Thus, on the Indonesian island of Kisar, in the Malukus Islands, the supreme deity was called "Our-mother-Our-father" (*Apna-Apha*).

What else? The old Baltic religion knew a God by the name of *Jumis*, a word that in the Baltic languages denotes "two things grown together into one unit."[126] Similarly, among the Scandinavian mythological gods (Odin, Frey, Loki, Nerthus...), there is no lack of a more or less veiled androgynous component. The Goddess Nerthus, for example, is the female version of Njörd, god of the wind and the sea. The fertility god Frey ("Lord" in Norwegian) has a twin sister, Freya ("Lady"). Legend says that Frey and Freya are Njörd's sons and, for a while, lived together as a married couple. On the other hemisphere, we have the bisexual gods of old Babylon. We have Zurvan, the archaic Iranian god, god of "Infinite Time", depicted in a bronze sculpture as a winged and androgynous god that gives birth to two twin gods, Ohrmuzd and Ahriman...

Certainly, you noticed that I have just mentioned two instances of divine twins. I have told you about twins, I have said it's a widely observed motif in primitive religions and mythologies. Twins, Blanca, account for the splitting of a

126. Marija Gimbutas, *The Encyclopedia of Religion* by Mircea Eliade (article "Doubleness"), MacMillan Publishing Company, New York.

single being (a religion historian talks about the "[127]the implicit matrimony in twin kinship") into the two powers or people that implicitly integrate it. Mythological twins are often of the opposite sex, but when that does not happen (Romulus and Remo, for example, or Castor and Pollux...), then one is usually characterised as solar, and the other lunar, the sun and the moon being symbols of masculinity and femininity. Many divine spouses from mythology are taken for twin brothers and, on occasion, are openly presented as such. In Japanese mythology, the supreme deity, the creator of all things, assumes the shape of a pair of brothers, Izanagi and Izanami. I have also mentioned before, that Zeus and Hera, besides being married, were also brother and sister, just like the Egyptian gods Isis and Osiris: hence the tradition of the pharaoh, regarded as the embodiment of God, marrying his sister. Almost every god from the Egyptian pantheon has his kin, his consort: Amon/Amonet, Noun/Nounet, Heh/Hehet, Bes/Beset..., and the older gods being, furthermore, bisexual. So, according to the linguists, the supreme god's name, Aton (later associated with the sun-god Ra), possibly means "the one who is whole". In such case, Aton justifies his name for, even though he male, he was, in reality, bisexual: in the writings on sarcophagi, he is referred to as "the great He-She", which certainly leaves little room for doubt. Maat, daughter of Ra, also had the power of splitting, a common power among the Egyptian gods... I will stop now, Blanca, I don't want to drown you in an interminable list of gods. It's better if we turn our attention to monotheism, which is

127. Ugo Bianchi, *The Encyclopedia of Religion* by Mircea Eliade (article "Twins")

simpler to enumerate. Let's focus on the God closer to you and me: the Judeo-Christian God.

MOTHER AND FATHER GOD

It's true that, in its exoteric or "front" side, both Judaism and Christianity gave us a male God. However, it proved to be quite difficult for them to impose that unilateral, sexist vision of Godhood. Both religions had to face a popular propensity to regard God as a Mother instead of as a Father. Christianity was not able to neutralise this tendency completely, so it had to partly compromise. Judaism was more successful in that enterprise, though it took centuries to take down the Canaanite goddess Asherah –or Atirat, or Asratum– from the throne next to Yahweh, of whom she was considered the spouse, as she had been of Baal. The book of Deutoronimous ordered the symbol of this goddess –a tree planted next to shrines dedicated to Yahweh– to be cut down and burned, but Hebrew inscriptions alluding to "Yahweh and his Asherah" date back to as recently as the eighth century.

It was mostly the esoteric side of these religions that conserved the intuition of the Divine as a Couple of Spouses or an Androgyne. Let's consider the Jewish God first: Yahweh Elohim, the protagonist of the *Torah*, a God that created Man in His own image, and created him "male and female", which, as we have seen, several Jewish exegetes interpreted it as a tacit revelation of His Androgyny. When in Genesis 1:26, God says –to what was assumed to be the Universe– "Let us make mankind...", the exegetes deduced that Father God was talking to His Wife.

First of all, I cannot resist transcribing here a beautiful passage from the *Zohar* referring to the power of the Wife of God, called *Shekinah* in Kabbalah -and also “the Mother”, “the Matron [Matronita]”, “the Queen”, “the Married Woman”. It goes like this:

> Above them, He has appointed *Matronita* to minister before Him in the palace... / ... Who is the way to the Tree of Life? *Matronita*, who is the way to that great and mighty tree, the Tree of Life (the symbol of divine immortality). When Matronita moves all the celestial armies move behind Her... Every mission that the King wishes issues from the house of Matronita; every mission from below to the King enters the house of Matronita first, and from there to the King. She is the perfect intermediary between Heaven and Earth. And although it doesn’t appear to be compatible with the glory of the Great King that He should trust every matter to the Matronita, including the affairs of his claws, it is, however, comparable to a King from our world coming together with a superior woman in possession of notable qualities. And because the King wants the people to know and appreciate the qualities of their Queen, He entrusts Her with all the great works in the Kingdom and asks the people to obey and respect her.

A king who loves his wife so much that he relinquishes all merit for the work done in his kingdom and, therefore, the recognition of his people. A very nice touch, isn’t it, Blanca? It reminds me of an equally charming story told about a royal couple you admired. It’s told that, whenever King Baudouin of Belgium went anywhere without his wife Fabiola, his fellow citizens would shout, “Long live the Queen!” as he passed through. Moreover, if a foreigner, puzzled by this incongruity, were to ask about it to any of the shouting people, they would tell him, "We cheer for the Queen because we know it pleases the King". Anyway, I was going to talk to you about the Kabbalah. Do you know those verses by C. Patmore I quoted at the beginning of this letter? They claim that, within God, operates the same love as in between two lovers. Well, then, my love, no other mystic tradition insists so much on the importance of that love within God, as the Kabbalah does. That love is the model of every intersexual love, the ideal background for every erotic love. Marriage is a sacred mystery for the Kabbalists, since every true matrimony symbolically reproduces the union of God and Shekinah. It's not for nothing, Blanca, that the most sacred text of all Holy Scriptures is, according to the Kabbalists, the Song of Songs, which is a love dialogue between two spouses. You are already familiar with this poem, you are aware of its beauty. There is not in the Scriptures, nor anywhere else, any other literary piece that has been the object of so many mystic commentaries. One of these commentaries, one of the most celebrated ones (a verse-by-verse commentary), is the one written at the beginning of the thirteenth century by a fellow compatriot of ours, Azriel ben Menahem of Girona.

This Catalan Kabbalist defines the Song as "the most sacred book of the Holy Scriptures", that "which contains all the most valuable mysteries and secrets". This is because even though the book tackles the passionate romance between King Solomon and Queen Sabah (you know the story, right? She had heard the merchants and traders crossing her kingdom speak so much and so highly of him, that she wanted to meet him in person), it has also been interpreted as alluding to God's interiority. Thus, where the wife is written as saying "Draw me after you, let us make haste. The king has brought me into his chambers. We will exult and rejoice in you" (Song 1:4) Azriel of Girona interprets "his chambers" as the intimate quarters of the Divine, and as the intimate places of the Garden of Eden. The Kabbalistic treatise *Sefer Bahim*, "Book of Clarity" follows along these lines, having also read "his chambers" as the home of God, "the last of His chambers". Naturally, this intimate chamber is a nuptial chamber, Blanca. Within God takes place an amorous exchange –the exegetes say– similar to that of the lovers from the Song (the lovers before their separation, since the Song goes through several stages: love, separation, adultery, and reconciliation). According to rabbinic tradition, God Himself recites from the Song of Songs every day; which is a metaphorical way of saying: each day of His Eternity, God consummates the mystic love mentioned in the Song; each day of His Eternity, God unites with Himself in an amorous embrace.

This union, Blanca –of God with Himself, that is, of God's two Persons–, constitutes the very *Unity* of God. This *Unity* (*Yehud*, in the Kabbalistic jargon) is precisely what God is, that of which Divinity consists. From which follows that God is only God while He is united to His Wife. That is, that *the divine status is eminently a conjugal status.* Although it has been traditionally interpreted in a variety of ways, the Kabbalists saw the Hebrew ideogram Seal of Solomon, or Star of David, as a symbol of Divinity's conjugal status. The superimposed and intertwined triangles would have represented the "holy union" of the divine Spouses. The Kabbalah describes that union in sexual terms, but I have already cautioned you against a textual reading of this type of descriptions –although it's true that many Kabbalists tried, in the words of Gershom Scholem, "to uncover the mystery of sex in God Himself". "The mystery of sex, as it appears to the Kabbalist -writes Scholem, the highest authority on Jewish mysticism-, has a terribly deep significance. This mystery of human existence is for him nothing but the symbol of love between the divine 'I' and the divine 'You', the Holy One, blessed be He and his Shekinah."[128] This union of the two Persons of God -male and female- is, to the Kabbalah, the cornerstone of the Universe, my dear. It's a fruitful union not only above but below too. It not only spawns divine Unity: it spawns Creation.

And the Creation of the Universe is precisely the subject on which we will focus now.

TWO EMBRACED CHERUBS

What is the Universe? First, Blanca, the Universe is not merely the vast domain of the stars, the nebulas, and the galaxies; it's not just the physical Universe. For the ancient sages, the physical Universe is only the lower step of a tall pyramid. The Kabbalists describe this tiered pyramid more in terms of Manifestation rather than divine Creation. God does not *create* the Universe: *He manifests Himself* through the Universe. Or -we could say- God creates the Universe from nothing (the famous *ex nihilo* Creation) but Himself. In the third century, the neo-Platonic philosopher Plotinus said that the One, wishing to know Himself, produced an *emanation*. The ninth century Christian theologian John Scotus Eriugena talks about the process of *unfolding* of the divine Unity. The Kabbalah also deals with the concept of

128. Gershom Scholem, *Major Trends in Jewish Mysticism*, p. 227

emanation: the Universe emanates God in a large chain or descending series of emanations or divine manifestations.

The root of this chain is known as the Primordial Point or the Hidden Point. This Point is the Origin, Blanca, *the point beyond Time and Space* to which we alluded in previous letters. And I mean Point here, in the strictest sense of the word. Among the ancient sages, *the point* (the philosophers' monad: from the Greek *monos*, "unit") enjoyed a sacred prestige, for it symbolised the Centre, and the Centre of the Universe is the very essence of the sacred (the Centre of the Universe is God, as we will see). The sphere was considered a perfect geometric shape precisely for being modelled based on the point. Due to its lack of extension, it's not difficult to imagine the point as dwelling outside of Space and –every time both coordinates are linked– outside of Time. From this Primordial Point, then, from this sacred fountainhead, emanates the Light of the Spirit –Life, Being, the divine substance–, light that flows down like a torrent (we could compare the Hidden Point to a heart pumping blood to the entire organism). This torrent creates in its path the different emanations, known to Kabbalists as *Sefirot* (the *Sefirot* are divided into couples starting from the double forces, masculine and feminine, which constitute Divinity). As the torrent goes down, as it moves away from the Fountain of Life, its waters gradually grow darker and its Light dimmer. The *Zohar* conceives the paradoxical metaphor of the veils: as He manifests Himself, God hangs successive veils before His Face. Due to these overlapping veils, divine manifestations become more and more opaque, more "profane"; the Light filtered through the veils becomes dimmer...

This cosmic pyramid, Blanca, can be divided into three sections, three overlapping levels or "worlds": the lower or material world, the middle or spirit world (which is the world you inhabit now), and, at the apex, the Hidden Point, also known as the "Root of all roots". This Higher World, the sacred and divine headquarters, the source of all Creation or, better yet, of all divine Manifestations, is known in the Kabbalah by the Hebrew word *Mahshabah*, which means "Divine Thought", and it's a word filled with secret connections, on which we will linger for a moment.

Given as they were to observe the "reverse side of the tapestry" of reality, the Kabbalists conceived a curious method of esoteric research. They attributed a numeric value to the letters of the Hebrew alphabet, which allowed them to discover secret equivalencies between concepts. Through this deductive procedure called gematria, these Hércules Poirots of Metaphysics sought (and, surprisingly, found!) confirmation for their own intuitions. Well, so by applying this technique to the word *mahshabah*, they obtained suprising results: *Mahshabah*, "God's Thought", adds up to thirteen, the same number as *Ahabah*,"Love", and as *Echad*, "One".

Going back to the cosmic pyramid, the Higher World or Hidden Point was compared by the Kabbalists to the *Sancta Sanctorum*, the "Holy of Holies" (*Qodes Qodasim*, in Hebrew). This was the holiest sanctuary of the holiest place in Israel: the Tabernacle in the desert, later the Temple in Jerusalem built by King Solomon, which counted with three enclosures, emulating the structure of the Universe. Separated from the second enclosure by a veil, the "Holy", or "Holy of Holies" was the innermost sanctuary of the three and the most sacred one. It housed the Ark of the Covenant, where the Divine Presence resided (meaning, the Shekinah, which the Kabbalists later personified and to whom they gave the role of God's Wife... but let's not complicate this any more than we need). Over the Ark's mercy seat rose the *Kerubim*, two gold chiselled "Cherubim" whose presence was not accidental, it was part of God's instructions for Moses to build the Ark: "And you shall make two cherubim of gold; of hammered work shall you make them" (Exodus 25:18). And because God does not do anything, or orders anything to be done without having a good reason, Blanca, the exegetes asked themselves, when it comes to the Cherubim, what could that good reason be?

You remember that sentence from the *Zohar* relating to the conjugal union: *God will not establish His residence in a place where such union does not exist.* That being the case, and from the moment that God had established His residence in the Ark of the Covenant, the conjugal union had to manifest itself on the Ark. The two Cherubim represented, then, the divine Spouses. The Scripture says that they contemplated the sacred Ark, but also each other, "their faces one to another; toward the mercy seat shall the faces of the cherubim be" (Exodus 25:20). The tradition of depicting God and His Wife face to face, looking into each other's eyes, came from Antiquity, dated back to the pagan religions, as archaeological findings can attest. In fact, Blanca, it's the posture in which spouses, and lovers in general, have always been portrayed (remember the heavenly couple described by Swedenborg, of how they extracted their Beauty from mutual contemplation), and it denotes their own intimate union.

Even though it's not specified in the instructions for the Ark's construction, some exegetes ruled that the Cherubim were of the opposite sex. They based this idea on a grammatical circumstance, which is that to say "two", the Exodus does not use the word *shene* but *shenayim*, which, contrary to the former, expresses not a mere Duality but a Duality of *opposites*. Others went even further and, in spite of each Cherub standing on one end of the Ark, they deduced from their face-to-face position, that they were *embracing* each other, being that embrace the very image of the *perfect union*, of the *Yehud*, of God's Unity for the ancient Jewish sages. The famous eleventh century French Rabbi Schlomo Yitzchaki, better known by the acronym Rashi, compared the *Kerubim*'s embrace to the mutual relationship between the yolk and the white of an egg; just as the egg is the result of the perfect union between the yolk and the egg white, so God is the fruit of the embrace of His Two Persons.

Crossed–out note on the margin. From loose words, we can reconstruct the quote: "The alarm clock didn't ring at the scheduled time: Now time was short." If we are to admit the hypothesis that the author's wife was communicating with him through the blue books, then we have to assume this is a personal allusion, the meaning of which eludes us.

Presided this way by the two embraced Cherubim, the *Sancta Sanctorum* of the Temple appeared as an earthly replica, symbolic of another *Sancta Sanctorum*, that of the Universe: that is, the Hidden Point, where Kabbalah says the sacred union of the divine Spouses takes place. The constant amorous interaction between them generates the torrent of Light generously flowing downwards, disseminating Life on its path. As far as the Cherubim are concerned, Kabbalist literature provides their references. In the *Zohar*, Rabbi Simon bar Yochai, commenting to his disciples the verse from the Psalms that says *How good and how pleasant it is for brothers to dwell together in unity*, points out that "the expression 'in unity' refers to the Cherubim. When their faces looked upon each other, (that is to say when they were 'together in unity') that was favourable to the world: 'how good and how pleasant'. But when the male turns his face away from the female, that was bad for the world." And an anonymous thirteenth century opuscule on marriage (a kind of instruction manual for newlyweds entitled *Letter on Holiness*, but also known by the title of *The Bridal Bed* and *The Relationship of Man and his Wife*) tells us of the Ark's Cherubim as bearers of a great "secret".

What is this secret, my dear? Well, nothing less than the secret of Divinity, of which a modern-day Kabbalist writes: "the secret is locked with two locks, male and female"[129]. Well then, with this secret under lock and key, we will also close this chapter -though we will throw away the key, as we will sporadically return to the Hebrew God. Now, before turning our attention to the Christian God, we will stop for a second to embark on an exercise of the imagination about a heterodoxic, esoteric branch of Christianity, and its ideas relative to the "heavenly marriage". This long gone branch of Christianity is the Gnostics.

GNOSTIC MYSTERIES

What do we understand by *gnosis*? It's a Greek word and it means "knowledge". But in religion, Blanca, the word *gnosis* alludes to a specific class of knowledge: the one operated by the fire in the dark that is mystic intuition. That is the reason the qualifier "gnostic" is applied to describe many ancient

---

129. Mario Satz, *Umbría lumbre*

sages that did not belong to what is known as the Gnostic movement in the strictest sense. Meaning, the Christian movement of a mysterious character (mysterious in the sense of *sacred mysteries*) that flourished in the first centuries of our era, though its roots go back to pre–Christianity doctrines, and which influence transverses the history of Western thought (C.G. Jung, for example, was regarded as an intellectual heir to the Gnostics) up until the modern day.

Although Gnosticism has one foot in Judaism and the other in Christianity, it clearly distances itself from both religions' official line. The resurrection of bodies, for example, Blanca, is not among the Gnostic beliefs. Jesus did not resurrect; he did not die on the cross: who died was the "substitute" (his body, that is), the Gnostics said. The spiritual person, the soul, Jesus' and everyone else's could not die because it was a divine and eternal spark. Albeit the Gnostic movement itself did not enjoy a long lifespan, its philosophical system endured and experienced a new peak between the tenth and twelfth centuries. As its name indicates, the Gnostic system (if indeed we can talk about one single system, given the variety of sects and doctrines), claimed to be based on the *gnosis*. The Gnostics held the "eye of the heart", the mystic intuition, as the sole organ of knowledge capable of unravelling the reality of the Universe. They equally rejected knowledge acquired through reason, as it did not delve deep into reality, and through faith, as it was imperfect. Perhaps to embed into Christianity their mystic intuitions about God and the essence and destiny of Man, the Gnostics claimed they were the keepers of a secret knowledge that Jesus (not only while he was alive, but afterwards as well, through visions) would have passed on to a few select disciples. This esoteric knowledge was recorded in several manuscripts, many of them apocryphally attributed to prominent personalities of the Holy Scriptures.

We owe our knowledge of Gnostic thought, Blanca, in good measure, to an event that will seem to you taken right out from the pages of the *One Thousand and One Nights*. The year was 1945; the end of World War II was in sight. A farmer from Nag Hammadi, an Egyptian village, saddled his horse one afternoon and went up the mountain, hoping to collect a certain type of soft soil to fertilise his lands. He began digging at the base of a crag when his hoe hit something hard. The farmer himself would tell this story many years later, once his findings had proven to be one of the most important discoveries in religious historiography. He kept digging until he found a sealed jar, about one metre tall, made of red clay. He hesitated before breaking the seal because he had heard those typical *One Thousand and One Nights* stories: stories about genies trapped in jars, who are just as likely to reward their liberator generously, as they are to cause him great misfortune. When he finally decided to open it, the jar turned out to enclose not an enchanted genie, but thirteen ancient and harmless leather-bound papyrus codices.

In the past, however, these books had not been so harmless, judging by the Early Church's determination to destroy them. It was in order to avoid this threat that, around the fourth century, its owners (who probably were monks from a nearby monastery) hid them in a jar, and buried it in the mountain. The fact is, my love, that thanks to this monastic indiscipline, today we are able to learn the keys of Gnostic thought since the books were compilations of around fifty Gnostic texts. They are translations of Greek originals into Coptic –ancient Egyptian–, among which figured a collection of Gospels that differed from the canonicals, in some cases even surpassing these. Besides sayings and proclamations by Jesus already present in the New Testament, these Gospels included others that no one had ever seen before. For example, it referred to Mary Magdalene as Jesus' faithful companion, whom "the saviour loved more than any other woman."[130] And so, in the *Gospel of Philip* (one of most prominent ones, along with the *Gospel of Thomas*) you can read: "Three Marys walked with the lord: His mother, his sister, and Mary of Magdalene, his companion."[131] And also: "The companion is Mary of Magdalene. Jesus loved her more than his students. He kissed her often on her face, more than all his students, and they said, 'Why do you love her more than us?' The saviour answered, saying to them, 'Why do I not love you like her? If a blind man and one who sees are together in darkness, they are the same. When light comes, the one who sees will see light. The blind man stays in darkness.'"[132]

Like in the Kabbalah, the subject of conjugal love abounds in Gnosticism. "Great is the mystery of marriage!" claims the *Gospel of Philip*. In the text, there are plenty allusions to the bride and the bridegroom, as there are to the Bridal Bed or Chamber where both must unite in matrimony to restore the heavenly Husband and Wife, the Androgyne. Another of the Gnostics favourite metaphors is one of which the Kabbalists were also quite fond, Blanca: the Temple of Solomon as an image of the Universe, a cosmic Temple. It was precisely the *Sancta Sanctorum* of this sanctuary (the Hidden Point of the Kabbalists) what the Gnostics meant by the metaphor of the

130. *Gospel of Mary*, Chapter V, 5
131. *Gospel of Philip*, Three Marys
132. *Ibid*, Wisdom, Mother of the Angels

Bridal Bed or Chamber. "The holy of the holies is the bridal chamber"[133], we read in the *Gospel of Philip*. And: "Now the woman and man are one in the [bridal] chamber"[134]. And more: "the bridal chamber is part of something superior to it and the others (meaning the sanctuaries, the other cosmic levels) because you will find nothing like it."[135] This is the high Chamber where the Original spouses, divorced because of the Fall, are to marry again, because "Redemption happens in the bridal chamber."[136]

Based on this symbol, the Valentinian Gnostics (the followers of Valentinus, the most notable of Gnostic masters) even developed a ritual. "Chrism in the Bridal Chamber", some texts call it. In case you don't remember, in Christianism, chrism is the ointment oil used in sacraments and consecrations. This Gnostic ritual, then, was possibly a kind of sacrament similar to marriage. Even though the exact procedure is unknown, from the texts we can infer it was a ceremony to symbolically recreate the bridal couple's Original Androgyny. The original union between Jesus and Mary Magdalene also served as a model. Be it as it may, my love, don't forget that we are not talking about an earthly marriage here. The symbol and Gnostic ritual of the Bridal Chamber –where "two become one"– refers to the heavenly marriage. The union of the bridegroom and the bride mentioned in Gnostic texts is not a carnal union but a mystic one, a sacred union.

Carnal union –the foundation of earthly marriages– was seen by the Gnostics as impure, corrupted. "Therefore,

133. *Ibid*, Three buildings in Jerusalem
134. *Ibid*, Reunion in the Bedroom
135. *Ibid*, Three buildings in Jerusalem
136. *Ibid*, Three buildings in Jerusalem

contemplate Pure Mating –instructs the *Gospel of Philip*– for it has great power!"[137] Nevertheless, Blanca, earthly marriage achieved among the Gnostics its just respect as a substitute, as a shadow or simulation of the heavenly marriage and, because of that, not all of it was considered contemptible: "Marriage in the world is a mystery for those who are married. If there is a hidden defilement in the marriage, how much greater is the true mystery of the undefiled marriage! It is not fleshly but pure. It belongs not to desire (of the bodies) but to the will (of the heart). It belongs not to the darkness of the night but to the day and the light."[138] For the Gnostics, the true marriage is not the one taking place in the lower world; it's the one happening in Heaven. It's not the one occurring in front of everyone ("If a marriage is open to the public, it has become prostitution." [139]), but the one happening within the secret, innermost sanctuary of the Cosmic Temple.

This sanctuary is the Place to which brides and bridegrooms truly belong: "Bridegrooms and brides belong to the bridal chamber. No one shall be able to see the bridegroom or bride unless one becomes a bridegroom or bride."[140] No one can see them, Blanca, because the *Sancta Sanctorum* lies beyond the reach of "profane" eyes. These can only imagine it: they can only picture it through images and symbols; preferably, the symbol of marriage. Only the "sacred eyes", the eyes of the second sight, can penetrate the veil covering the *Sancta Sanctorum*: eyes such as those of the Gnostics, the Kab-

137. *Ibid,* Marriage
138. *Ibid,* Mystery of Undefiled Marriage
139. *Ibid,* Mystery of Undefiled Marriage
140. *Ibid,* Mystery of Undefile Marriage

balists, of Swedenborg or as those of his literary disciples: Dame Dermody or Baron Féroë...

As I have said, the heavenly marriage to which the Gnostics aspired aimed to restore the Primordial Androgyne through the reunification of the two halves that were split apart following the Fall. According to Gnostic belief, my love, "humanity, which was formed according to the image and likeness of God (Father and Mother) was masculo-feminine"[141]. We read in the *Gospel of Philip*: "Those who are separated will be joined and filled (completed)." And following that: "If you become an attendant of the bridal chamber, you will receive the light."[142] Here is a motif –the light– already present in a previous quote, one that said uncontaminated marriage aligned with the light, opposing darkness. We see now that also aligning itself with the light is heavenly marriage, the Divine Unit. That is why the Origin's androgynous Adam –the Adam that contained Eve– is described in the Gnostic texts as a figure of a radiant light; a light that eclipsed the sun's and that faded upon the Fall. Hence the saying from the *Gospel of Thomas* as well: "I say, if you are whole, you will be filled with light, but if divided, you will be filled with darkness"[143].

It's not only among the Gnostics, Blanca: in the majority of spiritual traditions, darkness is a symbol of this lower world; the light –colourless light, light in a pure state, white light–, icon par excellence of the Higher World, of the Original world, of the world of Divinity. (But it's not just an icon: think about the white light at the end of the

141. Ireneaus, *Adversus Haereses*, quoted by Elaine Pagels, *Gnostic Gospels*, p.56

142. *Gospel of Philip*, The Perfect Light

143. *Gospel of Thomas*, 61

tunnel in Near-Death Experiences.) "Everyone who enters the bridal chamber will kindle the light..."[144], so declares the *Gospel of Philip*. Everyone whose time has come, my love: the time to kindle the light of the Bridal Chamber. That is to say, the moment of merging with our twin soul. It's a *restoration*, as we had been unified before, "when Eve was in Adam (when their souls were merged, that is) there was no death. When she was cut from him, death came into being. If he enters what he was and takes her in him fully, death will disappear."[145] And, underneath, the same Gospel adds: "If the woman and man had not come apart, they would not know death. Christ came to repair the split, there from the beginning, and join the two and give them life who had died because of separation."[146] The idea is clear: the Original heavenly marriage, despite having been contracted for all Eternity, fell apart; the spouses got divorced, and now it's time to correct that divorce. For the majority of us, it will take thousands of years to achieve this goal (because reincarnation is also a Gnostic belief), but the Gnostics aspired to shorten that time. I insist, Blanca, that this is a restoration, a second wedding *with the same mate*. The soul is not compelled to get heavenly married to just anyone, no, it has to be to the same soul that had already been its celestial spouse in the Origin: that is, its twin.

This idea of love predestination seemingly appears in the following saying from the *Gospel of Philip*: "Every sexual act between unlike persons is adultery."[147] Does the expression

---

144. *Gospel of Philip*, The Perfect Light
145. *Ibid*, Eve in Adam
146. *Ibid*, Reunion in the Bedroom
147. *Ibid*, Cain

"unlike persons" not remind you of the Swedenborgian concept of likeness and the Miltonian concept of incompatibility of souls? Some of the sayings attributed to Jesus in the *Gospel of Thomas*, urge the androgynous restoration: "When you make the two one... when you make the male and the female one and the same, so that the male not be male nor the female female... then will you enter the kingdom."[148] Saying the Kingdom (of Heaven), my dear, is the same as saying the Hidden Point, the Bridal Chamber... Another example: "If two make peace with each other (meaning if the two come together and become One) in this one house, they will say to the mountain, 'Move Away,' and it will move away."[149]

There is another saying in the *Gospel of Thomas* that deserves our attention, Blanca. The one in which "Jesus said, "When you disrobe without being ashamed and take up your garments and place them under your feet like little children and tread on them, then will you see the son of the living one, and you will not be afraid."[150] You will have recognised the allusion to the passage from the Genesis in which, immediately after the Fall, Adam and Eve feel ashamed of their naked bodies and thus cover them with fig leaves sewn together. When you are capable of once again standing naked without shame, Gnostic Jesus tells them, it will mean that you have corrected the mistake that caused the Fall. Then you will return to the Kingdom. Well, the *Gospel of the Egyptians* incorporates this idea with that of androgynous restoration. According to this Gnostic text, when asked when his followers would have the answers to their questions, Jesus replied:

---

148. *Gospel of Thomas*, 22
149. *Ibid*, 48
150. *Ibid*, 37

"When you trample on the robe of shame, and when the two shall be one, and the male with the female, and there is neither male nor female."[151] By connecting both ideas, Jesus is making an association that is prevalent in Gnostic texts: he is linking Adam and Eve's Fall with their divorce. Beneath all these Gnostic sayings, my love, lies the androgynous nature of the Primordial Man, the Higher World's Perfect Man. A world in which -the Gnostics assure us- "there is neither male nor female but a new creature, a new man that is androgynous."[152]

"I AM THE FATHER, I AM THE MOTHER, I AM THE SON"

With the Gnostics -who had, as I said, one foot on each religion- we have crossed from Judaism into Christianity, so now we will be talking about the Christian God. And we will do so without moving away from the Gnostics, Blanca, because if in exoteric Christianity the intrinsic Androgyny or Bi-Unity of God was often silenced, that was not the case with esoteric Christianity, starting with its earliest form: the esoteric Christianity of the Gnostics. For them, God was a divine couple of Spouses. He was the Father and the Mother at the same time and was called upon as such in the prayers and texts. The *Apocryphon of John* refers to Him as *matro-pater* ("mother-father"). Another text, entitled *Great Annunciation*, addresses "both sides" of God, male and female, of which it says they "are separable one from one another and

151. Quoted by Clement of Alexandria, *Stratomata, III*
152. Hippolytus of Rome, *Philosophoumena* (V, 7, 13-15)

yet are one."[153] And for the first known Gnostic, Simon the Sorcerer -who had elevated his twin soul, Helen of Tire, to a high mystic rank-, God was *Arsénothélys*, the "male-female".

Crossed–out note on the margin. I was only able to salvage the ending of the original phrase or paragraph, albeit quite mutilated: *... the lieutenant (frowned) his lips.../... and if there was anything I didn't believe, it was precisely in coincidences."* It is almost certainly a quote taken from a crime novel.

In tune with this conception, sexual symbolism is usually present in the Gnostic descriptions of God -as it is in Kabbalist theology. Thus, the text entitled *Trimorphic Protennoia* puts the following unusual self-portrait in the mouth of God: "I am androgynous. [I am both Mother and] Father, since [I copulate] with myself."[154] Valentine said that God has a dual nature, male and female, and refers to the feminine nature of God -the Mother- as the receiver of the Father's seed. That seed bears fruit and gives origin to every androgynous couple (described by him with the Greek word *Eones*, "Eternities") which according to Valentine integrate the divine "Plenitude", which the Gnostics called *Pleroma*... But I will tell you about these couples now; that belongs to the next letter. I will tell you, instead, about another of the ancient sage's opinions: that from the loving intercourse between the Father and the Mother, comes the eternal Son, a third Person who is the One itself. The opening of that Gnostic prayer I cited a few pages back ("From Thee, Fa-

---

153. Quoted by Elaine Pagels, *op. cit*, p.89
154. *Trimorphic Protennoia*, quoted by Elaine Pagels in *op. cit.*, p.55

ther, and through Thee, Mother, the two immortal names, *Parents of the divine being...*") is a formulation of this idea. An idea that encapsulates the Holy Trinity mystery, Blanca, the "three in one", which is but a variant of another mystery: the binary or "two in one". Effectively, the Trinity (Tri–unit, Three in one) is simply a different wording for the concept of Androgyny... Does it surprise you? Actually, the Holy Trinity is not a Christian patrimony, my dear; it's older than Christianity. In fact, it's a typically pagan notion, in which the three Trinity Persons usually present themselves as a Father God, a Mother Goddess and a Son God. Meaning they identify with the three Persons coexisting in the Androgyne: namely, the Two and the One, fruit of the fusion of both.

Yes, Blanca: it's in love, in erotic love, where the mystery of the Holy Trinity rests, a mystery so inscrutable that it would be easier, for St. Augustine, to empty the ocean using only a shell than to ever understand it through intellect alone. Divinity revealed itself to the ancient sages' eyes of the second sight as a Trinity, a ternary system: one God encompassing three Persons. The ternary system has been defined as the deep structure or the *inner life* of the Unit, and that is the reason, my dear, why in religions and mythologies, the ternary system is nearly as frequent as the binary and, in fact, overlaps it. Therefore, the *Tao* is a ternary system: the Father and the Mother are the *yang* and the *yin*, and their Son is the *Tai Kih*, the empty circle. The Christian notion of Trinity (Father, Son and the Holy Ghost) would be a disfigured reformulation –adapted to the theological needs of the young religion– of that same Universal androgynous scheme. A scheme to which the Gnostics remained faithful nonetheless, as evidenced by the fact that the Holy Ghost –who is of the feminine gender in the Semitic languages– was identified as the feminine Person of God, which they named *Sophia*, "wisdom" in Greek. (Without getting into details, I will mention that, in the Middle Ages, the Eastern, Orthodox or Greco-Russian Church would adopt this Gnostic notion, a notion that later on would pave the way for an important theological speculation known as *Sophiology*.)

The Gnostic *Apocryphon of John* describes a mystical vision of the Trinity that appeared to St. John following the crucifixion of Christ: St. John saw a light, and in the light "a figure with three forms". And this figure introduced itself by saying: "I am the Father; I am the Mother; I am the Son". This primeval conception of Trinity would be distorted in the Christian Trinity dogma by the removal of the Mother, the feminine Person of God, His Wife. It would live on, though, in the sages' mystic intuition, my dear. Even as late as the eighteenth century, a Christian mystic of Pietistic tendencies (a mystic who subscribed to a German Lutheran movement that placed mystic intuition before religious dogma), Count von Zinzendorf, referred to the Holy Trinity in terms of Husband, Wife, and Son. On the other hand, Blanca, even if the Mother was removed from the dogma, she remained in the hearts of the believers, who promptly turned their attention to two female evangelical characters. I am referring to Mary Magdalene and, especially, the sublime Virgin Mary.

Even though the ecclesiastic hierarchy has unreasonably dedicated itself to stigmatise Magdalene as a prostitute (and I believe I am interpreting your thoughts here, my love, if I add in parenthesis, and in an indignant tone, that prostitutes are not usually so by vocation, thus the stigma should not be on them but on society), the Fathers and Christians of the early centuries placed a great deal of importance on her. We have seen before how the Gnostics saw Magdalene as the companion of Jesus, but don't think that this was an exclusively Gnostic perception. The average Christians, ignoring the Church leaders, did not see this woman as a mere repentant sinner, they recognised in her relationship with Jesus something that went beyond a simple teacher–student relationship. They recognised it because, in the Gospels, Magdalene heads the list of women who accompanied Jesus; as well as on her presence by the cross, a privilege reserved to the closest and most intimate. In addition, they recognised it, on the scenes at the house of Lazarus of Bethany, when his sister, Mary (who is Mary Magdalene, for the exegetes), is enraptured by the words of Jesus, pours perfume on his feet and wipes them with her hair. But most of all, Blanca, do you know where they recognised it? In that passage from the Gospel of St. John: John 20, 1–18, which for the Christians is, if you ask me, the most important passage from the Scriptures because it justifies the hope for Resurrection. It's the passage in which following the crucifixion, after the prescriptive day of rest, Mary Magdalene, without even waiting for dawn, unable to bear Jesus' absence, returns to the garden where he was buried. She finds his tomb empty and rushes back to warn Peter and John, who simply observe the fact and leave. She stays there alone, breaks out crying, and at that moment she sees two angels on the tomb. "Why do you cry?" they ask her. A character who she believes to be the gardener asks her the same question: "Why do you cry? Whom is it that you seek?" Thinking he was the one responsible for moving the body, she asks him to return it, that if it was a nuisance she would take care of it herself. And that is when, surprisingly, the gardener calls her by her name: "Mary!" She is filled with emotion upon recognising Jesus resurrected, embraces him, and calls him by a term of endearment: *Rabuni*, "my teacher"...

Look, Blanca, I have read many romance novels, many of them we read together, but I cannot recall a more moving and tender love scene. And without it even being a traditional love scene: there are no kisses, there is no sexual passion. But there is another type of passion, a passion that is familiar to you and me, my love, a passion I intend to explore in the course of these letters, for it's precisely the type of passion that –in the words of our sages– stirred the twin souls in the Origin. This passion transcends sexual passion, though it's just as intense, more thrilling, more intimate, and more profoundly satisfying. Many Christians would be scandalised (I know that you will not) by me seeing this episode as a love scene. But I am not the only one, you know? The Gnostics saw it the same way and, after them, many normal Christians did so too, as did the artists who, especially in the Middle Ages, depicted it in their canvases. Not forgetting the countless preachers that, throughout the centuries, adopted Magdalene as the prototype of the "wife" from the Song of Songs –which had in Christ the "husband", according to allegorical interpretation.

If in the Middle Ages the devotion to Mary Magdalene spread through all of Christianity, Blanca, that is because in the medieval imaginary Magdalene was regarded as the wife of Jesus. There is even a tradition, not without its arguments, that claims Jesus had descendants: Christ's lineage would have been perpetuated in the South of what is France today, to where Magdalene could have fled following the crucifixion... Be it as it may, Mary Magdalene was the wife of Jesus *the man*, not Jesus *the God*, not Jesus as a divine hypostasis. For the role of "God's Wife", popular devotion discovered in the Scriptures a more suitable figure: the Virgin Mary.

The first prayer to the Virgin Mary (whose colour is blue, as you know, just as, for the artists, Magdalene's colour is red, the colour of passion), the first known prayer to the Virgin Mary dates back to the fourth century. One hundred years later, pressured by the believers, the Church found itself forced to find room in the dogma for the feminine Person of God. This event took place at the council of Ephesus, where they bestowed upon the Virgin the title of *Theotokos*, or "Mother of God". From there to seeing her as the Mother Goddess, the Wife of the Father God, was only a step. Little by little, the Mother took her place in popular devotion and worship, her place next to the Father, where she justly belonged. To the point that (in the eleventh and twelfth centuries) Marian devotion emerged all over Christendom. Cathedrals dedicated to "Our Lady" flourished all over the place, the *Hail Mary* became the Mother's hymn, just as the *Our Father* was the Father's, and mystics such as the Bernard of Claravall began making Virgin Mary the object of their contemplation. Still today, the Virgin is, for us Catholics, beloved (as *Shekinah* is for the Kabbalists), the privileged intermediary between God and men...

Well, and that is it. The Christian God is the final touch closing our long list of "double gods". A somewhat exhaustive list, my love, but one that I hope it worked as a demonstration of the androgynous trait attributed to God in Antiquity. We already know that this trait is a divine prerogative: it's not that God is androgynous; He is the Androgyne, the only one that exists. Ah, but Androgyny is not only a characteristic *specific* to God, you know? Next, we are interested in exploring the reason why the ancient sages said that it was also His trait *par excellence.*

Androgyny is God's trait par excellence because the mystery of God's Unity resides in His Androgyny, given that

God is, by definition, the One. We can reduce this mystery to a simple formula: "two in one". In other words, Blanca, Unity is intrinsically double. Not only that but, remember, *Unity emanates from its inner Duality*... You will see it clearer with the help of a metaphor. But before that, my dear, a little personal anecdote related to this subject that I am sure will make you laugh. Although I am writing these words under the light of an office lamp, on the corner of the desk –as you can undoubtedly see– burns a few of candles, like those you used to create an ambience in the flat. So lately, I have decided to put the large supply of candles you kept in a drawer to good use too. Well, one night, when the streetlamp outside was broken and this lamp and the kitchen lights were off, Luis showed up unannounced. You know him: Paula's husband, soon to be *ex*–husband because they are in the process of getting a divorce. Ah, yes, you did not know? The thing is I don't know why he chose me as a confidant and shoulder to cry on, but that is why he was there with two pizzas that night. I had just lit your candles and when he showed up, he caught me immersed in this pale blue light, with your portrait on the table. And he thought: Look at him, lost in some kind of dark spiritist stunt to communicate with his wife. He confessed so, still suspicious, while we were taking good care of the pizzas. And do you want to know what I thought, Blanca? I thought: Ah, my friend, if you only knew that I don't need that, that the dead also find ways to communicate with the living...[155]

Anyway, as I was saying, having no electric lamps, the ancient sages often lit their way with candles much like these

155. The second allusion that supports the strange theory put forth in the preface.

ones burning now on the corner of my desk. Like these ones? Well, not exactly, I imagine theirs were not blue. Each time I light one of these candles, Blanca (I am so sorry for going off on another tangent), I remember what you always thought about when you lit them, as you once confessed: I remember the "little match girl". And, you know, in my memory, that charming Hans Christian Andersen character is inseparable from what you once told me when we finished reading that story. You said –in that enigmatic, sententious way you sometimes said things– something that sounded to me then, and still does today, if I am being honest, like the cheesiest thing, my dear. Something like how you wanted us to always carry the little match girl in our hearts, for us to continuously rescue her from the cold streets and bring her home, to the warm home the light of the matches reminded her of and which, according to you, was our home... Anyway, just as the flame's tremulous light held for the little girl a tremendous evocative power, so it did for the ancient sages, Blanca. The flame's heat producing, cleansing, and illuminating action, its ascendant vocation suggested to them beautiful mystical metaphors. The one that I am about to propose to you was imagined by a great seventeenth century Christian mystic called Jakob Boehme, and it refers to a golden light...

Boehme draws from the premise that the light, which is one, is generated by the combination of two principles: brightness and radiance. By itself, brightness (meaning, whiteness) is not light; it does not have the radiance of light. Neither is light radiance by itself, since that –according to Boehme– radiance by itself is black, it lacks brightness; the conjunction of both principles, brightness and radiance, is required to generate light. Its golden colour is the result of the combination of brightness' natural white with radiance's innate red... Well, then, so it goes with Unity: it's the fruit of the harmonious combination of two principles. There is no Unity without Duality. For the ancient sages, Blanca, Duality is *the element* of Unity, the clay from which Unity is sculpted. Duality would be to Unity what cement is to a house. (Except these two types of cement –and this will sound like pedantic nit–picking to you, but it's important– *are not ontological*: if we are talking ontologically, then we must invert the terms and say that Unity is the foundation of Duality, its permanent support.)

You can also compare Unity with a puzzle with all its pieces in place. Pon, that giant the puzzle that took us months to finish and then hung over the entrance hall of our first home... I am sure you remember it. It depicted the arrival of an evening train to a little station in the mountains. It's as if I could see it now; I squint and there it is, the Alpine scenery... The stars gravitating over the snowy mountains, the windows on the train splitting the dark with their intense yellow, the nuanced lights of a lantern projected over the platform, and a few passengers carrying their luggage rush towards the side, where a brick building stands tall with its typical train station clock and its huge black hands... Ah, can you see it now? It was not our first puzzle, though it was the first worthy of the honour of being framed and hung on the wall. It deserved such an honour because its picture reminded us of a novel we had just finished reading, one we had particularly enjoyed, do you remember? We imagined that train station in the mountains to be Dorf station, end of the line for the clientele of Berghof International Sanatorium, where the protagonist of Thomas Mann's *The Magic Mountain* arrives with the intention of spending a few days that, inadvertently, end up becoming a few years... Well then: let us say that the pieces of that puzzle are Duality. The pieces, which in the lower world are scattered and disorganised, fit together in the Higher World to compose the picture, to reveal Unity. In the ensembled puzzle, two levels coexist: the simple level (the station in Dorf), and the complex level (the pieces that form it). We could say the same thing of Divinity: its mystery resides in the harmonious coexistence between the simple and the complex, between Unity and Duality. A mystery that is embodied by the notion of Androgyny, my dear: hence its conception as the secret key of God and as its attribute *par excellence.*

THE MAGIC CIRCLE

The importance Duality holds for Unity is revealed in the ancient sages' cosmogony, in their way of explaining the formation of the Universe. First, Blanca, what was the ancient sages' vision of the Universe?

I have already given you a preview of their cosmovision by mentioning the Creation according to the Kabbalists. We know that for the ancient sages, the Universe was comparable not to a painting but to a tapestry. In a painting, everything is in plain sight, nothing is hidden; a tapestry, on the other hand, has a "reverse side". The "reverse side" of the Universe is called the *Higher World,* and the series of levels -often set in seven and grouped under the label of the *intermediary world-* situated between that and the *lower world.* Thus, we have three cosmic worlds. Frequently, the ancient sages depicted this system by drawing concentric circles surrounding a central point, from which the circles irradiated. This is the famous "magic circle" or *mandala.* The circumference –the bigger outer circle– represents the lower world. The central point, internal, embodies the Higher World or Hidden Point, headquarters of Unity. The ancient sages identified Unity with Centrality, Blanca: the One is the mystical, sacred, centre of the Universe. This centre is sentient and it has been defined as the "eye of the Universe". "He has the power of seeing the Universe within His own being", notes Moses Azriel, thirteenth century Kabbalist...

You can visualise the cosmic mandala in the different areas of light and shadow surrounding the flames from the candles on this desk: in how light gradually dims from the centre outwards until it fades out in darkness. You can picture it too in the concentric waves on a pond or a mountain lake after you have thrown a pebble in: in how the waves expand from that central point. You can also think of the Universe as a Chinese box, or a Russian doll, nesting one inside another. Or you can take that image to which we turned when talking about the Creation according to the Kabbalists: the image of the torrent or river. This image, my dear, is ideal to express the notion of the Universe as a Divine emanation, just as many ancient sages understood it. Ancient Egyptian sages imagined it as the River Nile, flowing from the tears spilt by the sun god Ra. The Genesis makes use of the same metaphor by making a divine river that splits into four branches, corresponding to the four cardinal directions, rise from the base of the Tree of Life –in the very centre of Paradise. In its headwaters, the river is narrow: the Higher World is only a dot. It's in the course of its descent that the River grows, widening its bed until it flows into the sea. A dark sea, Blanca, for the sea has typified the lower world since Antiquity and –compared to the Higher World, which they saw as radiant– it appeared dark to the ancient sages. Its darkness, though, did not make it any less beautiful: a silver sea as the one underneath the moonlit nights of Palamós, where the heat was such that we could not sleep so we would go out onto the balcony to breathe in the fresh air...

Of course, as you can see, it has a pyramidal structure (the pyramid is another classic metaphor for the Universe): wide at the base, the top just a dot. It could be said, my dear, that, unlike the lower world, the Higher World lacks extension. If the lower world is large, the Higher one is *intense*: it's compressed, flowing inwards. The ancient sages explain that nothing exists in the Origin other than the Hidden Point. But, for some reason (a transgression, according to some, the need God had to manifest Himself, according to others), part of the essence of this inwards-flowing point inverted its flow, projecting itself outwards, spilling as if a River. A River that flows downwards, creating the different worlds in its path... There is no fracture between one world and the next. It's more like a spectrum coming down from the essence of the Higher World. This essence, Blanca, is Divinity..., and Divinity and Unity are homologous, according to what we have seen. We have, then, the divine essence of the Higher World, Unity, sliding downwards, fading out as it further descends.

What does Unity fading out means? It means it's gradually splitting into the two halves that form it. The ancient sages called this fading, divine, unitary essence by several names: they called it Life, Light, Being, Holiness...

As it descends, the River loses its "divine essence". Unity slowly gives way to its opposite, Duality, as the day gives way to the night. Unity splits into Two, originating on its path increasingly dual, less unitary, worlds. Gradually, it also originates the coordinates of those divided worlds: Time and

Space. When Unity is fully broken, two separate, opposite halves remain. That is the moment the lower world comes into existence, the world of Time and Space, which is the quintessential world of Duality, a world in which everything comes together in couples of opposites. We can read about this world in the *Zohar*: "One tradition teaches us that everything produced in the lower world is divided, there being no unity beyond the Higher World... there is no *perfect union* here, only division." To exemplify this cosmogony, I will also quote a few lines from a key work of Christianity's "reverse side", a work nonetheless proscribed by the Church: *De Divisione Naturae*, by the aforementioned ninth century Irish monk, John Scotus Eriugena. However, before the quote, I cannot resist telling you another personal anecdote. Another. Yes, except this one will not make you laugh, Blanca. At least it did not make me laugh, though maybe it will split your sides, you have always been unpredictable in that sense. I want you to know the bizarre way –mysterious, even– in which this venerable book came to be in my possession:

As it happened, one night, when I was visiting Enrique and Esther, our good friend found herself a little under the weather and, while Enrique took care of dinner, I volunteered to go down to the pharmacy to get her some aspirin. The pharmacy was closed, so I walked a few blocks more to the "on-duty" pharmacy. But, on the corner of Muntaner, I was witness to what I think the police calls a "smash-and-grab raid": a car deliberately crashed against a shop window and, after its occupants snatched everything they could, sped away. I managed to write down the license plate and called the police, who immediately appeared and invited me to accompany them to the police station to give evidence. When I left the station, Enrique was waiting for me in the car. I had him stop by the pharmacy, where an old man asked me to help him hail a taxi. While I was helping him get into one, I found a book on the backseat. I took it. I did not have time to warn the driver because the old man had already closed the door and they were already speeding down the street. I stood there with the book in my hands. But look, Blanca, it was not the kind of book one expects to find forgotten on the backseat of a taxi. It was not a *bestseller* or a typical novel to pass the time, nor it was a travel guide, but an old bilingual and annotated edition (just going by the smell of old printed paper, you would have loved it) of a very old theological treatise. And look at this, when later on I decided to read it, it turned out to be, to my astonishment, a key piece of the puzzle I was then composing in my head – this puzzle which now, with every piece in its place, I am submitting for your consideration, my dear. And a shiver went down my spine; I had the ineffable feeling that while it could not be older than fifty years, this book had been paving its way through the centuries, from the ninth century until now, to be with me. Like those bottles with a message that, riding the waves, cross the ocean until beaching on a remote shore where a curious hand uncorks it.

Well, this time that curious hand was mine; the book was the *De Divisione Naturae*, and these are the lines which I was about to transcribe: "The division of substances –writes Scotus Eriugena– begins in God, and, descending by degrees– ends in the division of man into male and female. The reunification of the same substances must begin in man and go up by the same degrees until it reaches God Himself, in whom... there is no division, for He is One."[156]

---

156. *De Divisione Naturae*, II

THE SUPREME MYSTERY

Look at this illustration now –if you can read my letters, you can see it too. It's a reproduction of a drawing by a fourteenth century Italian member of the Love's Faithful, the poet Francesco de Barberino. The six men and women lined up at the left and right of the central figure, respectively, form six married couples. The central figure is also a married couple, though a heavenly matrimony, a couple in which the spouses are merged into one flesh only. This androgynous couple –named "Husband and Wife"– is a divine figure: Above it floats "God Love", the God of the Love's Faithful. To denote its purity and spiritual nature, Francesco de Barberino paints it rising on the back of a white, winged horse. Underneath, the caption reads "From us two, Love made one, thanks to the heavenly virtue of matrimony." Notice how the symmetric disposition of the couples evokes a mandala. Two characters –male and female–, inhabit each one of the six concentric circles symmetrically arranged in relation to the seventh and central circle; in such a way that the farther apart the circle is from the Centre, the more divorced its inhabitant spouses appear to be.

Seeing it this way, Blanca, one could say that Francesco de Barberino's drawing reproduces the ancient sages' cosmogony, except specifically alluding to couples of twin souls: to their descent or fall from Divinity. See? Is not as if the Original union is breaking up as they –by the Centre's irradiation– descend towards the periphery? Therefore, this is the same couple in seven different phases of its fall. Obviously, my dear, this hierarchy of couples, this sequential representation of the Fall, could also be read the other way around: then, we would be seeing in it the twin souls' gradual return to their primeval Unity. The fact that the Centre spouses are unified into one single flesh, aligns this mandala's imagery with mandalas from medieval Europe and the East. In its inner circle the mandalas usually display an Androgyne or a divine couple of spouses; in the Eastern mandalas, it's a couple fused in the unified embrace Rashi mentioned.

The ancient sages conceived the cosmic mandala's inner circle, Blanca, the inner essence or Centre of the Universe, as an intrinsically dual Unit. There is a medieval novel about which you might have heard –the *Romance of the Rose*– that regales us with a beautiful illustration of this subject. It tells us about a young man interested in initiating himself in the mysteries of Love –which are also those of the Universe. One night, this young man dreams that he is walking down a road that ends before a wall. He knows he must pass to the other side of this wall, but in order to locate the door, he finds himself having to go all around its border. What is on the other side? On the other side of this circular wall, the dreamer finds a secret garden –the "Garden of Love" from medieval and renaissance iconography–, where, in the centre, a circular fountain stands. And the dream continues until it reveals that this fountain contains two pristine crystals, on which the surprised dreamer discovers the entire garden (the Universe) is reflected. And these two crystals floating in the fountain become one single flower, but not just any flower: the perfect flower, the rose, ancient symbol of the Centre, where the dreamer understands the ultimate mystery of the Love to be...

Do you see, Blanca? Two crystals but only one flower: in the centre of this medieval mandala operates the "two in one". And that is what happens in almost every mandala, my dear, because the ancient sages conceived the Centre of the Universe (and also the Centre of the soul, which, as we will see, deep down is the same thing, for there is only one Centre) with the shape of a dual Unit, that is to say, a couple. That is how one of the most ancient Chinese classic texts, the *I Ching* or *Book of Changes*, can talk about marriage as the realisation of the "heart of the Universe"... The case is that such conception of the Centre of the Universe as a dual Unit or couple did not lack arguments, you know? If the Unit fragmented into two in the course of its descent, that means that the Two were present in the Unit. Of course, that was a potential or implicit presence: because in the Unit, the Two were married, they were unified in a *perfect union*. But there was yet another reason to postulate the implicit presence of Duality in the One. Perhaps it's a less consistent reason, but surely a more charming one for you: There is a reason why the literal meaning of the word *Eden* is "happiness", "joy"; Eden is Paradise, it's the spatial embodiment of the Hidden Point; and the ancient sages placed absolute happiness within the Hidden Point –since the One, the Supreme Being, could only enjoy supreme happiness. Now, what is the height of happiness? According to the ancient sages, our friend Swedenborg for example (though for what our testimony is worth, we don't need to call upon the teachings of the sages), the greatest happiness of all is none other than conjugal happiness, the joy lovers find in one another. How could God's own supreme happiness, then, be defined in any terms other than Lover and Beloved, Husband and Wife?

Ah, but these are all rationalisations, my love! And we already know that the ancient sages arrived at their convictions not so much through reason but rather through mystic intuition. All reason ever did was to support intuition. It was through a stroke of intuition that they learned about how the lower world does not have the monopoly on Duality, that Duality crosses the entire Universe and is present in the Hidden Point, except that it's present There in a different manner. There, the Two are not opposed, they are not separated as they are in the lower world. In the Hidden Point, the Two are harmonised, understanding each other; they are, to use a Gnostic formula, "in peace with one another in the same house"...

That house is the one to which the Queen of Sheba alludes when, in the Song, she says to her husband: "How handsome you are, my beloved! Oh, how charming! And our bed is verdant. The beams of our house are cedars; our rafters are firs." (Song 1:16–17) This house, if you want to know, Blanca, cannot be compared to our little house in Palamós, it cannot even be compared to the houses that appear in publications such as *House and Garden*, where your friend Irene works. That house, infinitely more beautiful, is the Unit, it's the house of the One.

In the Hidden Point, then, the Two are perfectly unified, integrated; and that Integrity is the original state of Duality –since, you know, what happens to Duality is similar to what happens to water, which can appear in a different state rather than its original liquid state. If we go by the words of the ancient sages, Duality is implicit in the Unit (in the Unit of the Hidden Point, there is no other!), because the One is formed through its inner Duality: the Two's *perfect union* begets the One. This does not conflict with the requirement that says the One is of spontaneous origin (the One is the *primus agens*, the first cause, and therefore it must itself have been uncaused). There is no conflict, my dear, because His cause is internal, *intrinsic to Himself*. The integrated Two, the Two whose integration gives birth to the One, are not external to Him –hence we being able to refer to the One as a Trinity. Therefore, it's not strictly a cause, then. A cause is, by definition, external, outside its effect; when the cause is internal, it's more appropriate to refer to it as a *mechanism* or inner *dynamic.* If for the ancient sages, Duality is the Unit's implicit substrate, then that is because another idea comes from the idea of Unity: Integrity, Totality, the idea of Perfection. And the whole, the total, the perfect implies the conciliation of two opposites. Our Kabbalist friends saw this as why, in the Song, the husband calls his wife by *thamathi*, "my perfect one". According to a passage from the *Zohar* commented by the wise man Abbot Busson[157], he calls her by that word precisely when she adheres herself to his side, that is to say, in the moment she makes him whole. The *Zohar* also reminds us that *thamathi* can also be read (in virtue of the Hebrew language's lack of vowels) as *thamuthi*, "my twin"[158].

A thing is only total, whole and perfect when it integrates or synthesises in itself the two opposites/complementaries in which that thing conjugates. It's a cosmic law that everything must conjugate in couples. In the Higher World, these couples are integrated, they are complementary spouses; in the lower world, though, by being divorced, they are couples of opposites. The tension between opposites inherent in all Matter, Blanca, leads the ancient Chinese sages to classifying the twin souls of this world under the metaphorical condition of enemies; and it also justifies God, in the Quran, attributing such condition to Adam and Even upon their

157. Abad Busson, *L'Origine égyptienne de la Kabbale*, quoted by Elémire Zolla in *The Androgyne*

158. *Sefer ha–Zohar*, cap. 713

banishment from the Garden of Eden: "Come down from the Garden. You are now enemies", 2:34.

Crossed–out note on the margin. Headed by the date (31–7–99), the original note was the stanza of a poem. I have managed to identify it from the surviving first verse. It is a poem by Emily Dickinson, an author mentioned in the letters in relation to the blue books. The erased stanza goes like this: *Our journey had advanced / Our feet were almost come / To that odd Fork in Being's Road / Eternity by Term —*

You should know that, among the ancient sages, the implicit presence of Duality in the Unit was not a firmly established conviction: it was a great mystery for them. As such, it was not part of their public teachings but part of the esoterica they passed on to select disciples. Disciples such as Jesus had in Mary Magdalene and the apostles Thomas and Philip, if we are to believe the gnostic gospels. Or as Plato had in Aristotle, who said in his *Metaphysics* that his master placed at the top of the cosmic chain not only the "monad" (the One) but also the "Dyad" (the Two), and so did his predecessor, Pythagoras. For Plato and the Pythagoreans, the Dyad has no birth; it does not derive from the Monad: it is as eternal as the One, from which it constitutes the substrate, the *raw material* –the Monad is, then, the *substantial form.* And if the Monad is the cause of all that is good, the Dyad, in its split version, is the cause of all evil. These teachings form the bulk of Plato's secret teachings known as "unwritten doctrines", of which the story of the Androgyne featured in the *Symposium* is but a glossy version tailored for a wider audience.

We can find a modern exponent of this ancient intuition, my love, in a nineteenth century Christian scholar, the main theoretician of that theological speculation that I mentioned in passing a few pages back, which, as with so many other mystic reflections, failed to escape the anathematising zeal of orthodoxy. I am referring to Sophiology and the Russian Vladimir S. Solovyov, whose heterodoxic ideas we will study in detail on another occasion. Solovyov, who did not observe the ancient sages' secrecy, had no doubts about proclaiming Duality as the foundation of the Unit. Duality, he claimed, is consubstantial with Unity just as the two sides of a coin are consubstantial with its Unity. Is a single-sided coin conceivable? Well, a One that is not composed by two spouses is even less. The union of the two sides produces the coin just as, Solovyov thought, the union of two spouses produces the One.

THE UNITY OF OPPOSITES

Do you remember how I began this letter? I started by saying that God was by definition *the One*. But since then, we have seen that Unity by itself is not enough to define God. This definition will be completed by the addition of that element that accounts for the intimate essence of God (that is, of Love): the *two in one* attribute. In the lower world, such attribute shines due to its absence: the physical Universe is made of opposites; it's the quintessential kingdom of Duality. However, it's a split Duality: a kingdom in which the fraction of Integration or Unity between the Two equals zero. Because, when the Unity River (to use an old metaphor) ends in the sea, there is no more Unity left in it: Unity has split into two halves; the complementaries have become opposites. "Who are we?" I recall you asking me once in a transcendental mood. Well, here is your answer, my love: you and I are one of those divorced Dualities, one of those bastard Gods banished from Heaven I mentioned at the end of the previous letter; we are a drop from the divine River that, spilling from the Hidden Point, ended up in the physical Universe. Together with every other human soul, we compose the diminishing portion of God, and due to that diminishing, we assume several bodies and are no longer One. The *Zohar* is talking about us when it says that "before coming to this earth (before the Fall), each soul and each spirit is composed of a man and a woman united in one single being" and "on coming down to Earth these two halves are separated and sent to animate two different bodies"[159].

That separation supposed for us the loss of Paradise. Since Paradise is not an actual place, you know: it is a transcendent state, resulting from (such is the definition proposed by Scotus Eriugena) the "reunion of the human being, meaning, of the two sexes, in the Primordial Unit"[160]. By reunion of the two sexes, we should read the heavenly marriage between the two *Original spouses*, Blanca, since for our theory, the theory of twin souls, sexual differentiation counts only as the earthly manifestation of the primordial rupture. Hence, Paradise is Unity, it's the heavenly marriage of the Two, as suggested by Gnostic sayings such as: "When you make the two one, and when you make the inside like the outside and the outside like the inside, and the above like the below, and when you make the male and the female one and the same, so that

---

159. *Sefer ha-Zohar*
160. *De Divisione Naturae*, II

the male is not male nor the female female... then you will enter the Kingdom!"[161] Then you will enter Paradise, Integrity, you will enter the Uni–Totality of the Hidden Point.

In other words, my dear, while you and I remain, so to speak, "heavenly divorced", while we don't restore our Original heavenly marriage, we will be deprived of that transcendent state. The German sage Nicholas of Cusa, in the fifteenth century (although the concept was Universal and much older), defined that state with the formula *coicidentia oppositorum*, "unity of opposites", of which he said it was the most thorough definition of God. Nicholas of Cusa believed that, although God's reality was outside the grasp of human intelligence, it could be glimpsed through mystic intuition. And his intuition told him (that intuition, as I said, was widely shared by the ancient sages: the Kabbalists had already named the Hidden Point, *Ha–achdut Ha–shawah*, "a unity of opposites") that was the closest to Divinity: the "unity of opposites", the unification of the opposites in a synthesis that transcends them... If you look carefully, you will see that this is nothing more than a broader formulation of the notion of Androgyny, the idea of "two in one" or "integrated Duality". If the lower world is composed of couples of *opposites* –light and darkness, black and white, tall and short...–, in the Hidden Point the opposites "agree", they reconcile, they unite; they become *complementaries* and, in a way, equals. This "unity" paves the way for a third thing. A third thing that (as unthinkable as it may appear to our dualist intellect) is unitary: both light and darkness, black and white, tall and short...

There are innumerable couples of opposites, there is nothing in this lower world without its opposite. But ultimately,

161. *The Gospel of Thomas*, 22

they all go back to a single one: the male–female couple, which is the prototypical synthesis, the quintessential pair of opposites. This is what allows the ancient sages to say that the mutual love between a man and a woman is the pattern for universal love, for the love that, as Dante had written, "moves the sun and the other stars" (*l'amor che move il sole e l'atre stelle*). Note, my dear, that just as the notion of divorce implies a previous marriage, the notion of "couple of opposites" supposes a past time where those couples were combined. Finally, if all other couples of opposites are adjectival and only describe the male–female couple, then that is because the male–female couple is the ultimate earthly expression of the conjugal polarity within the Hidden Point; the twin souls...

Are you following me? It weighs on my consciousness to bombard you so many disquisitions, but I did warn you, I told you the terrain would be rough and difficult. Anyway, if you find my letters tedious, please say so, and I will write you a conventional love letter... like those I used to write to you when we were dating, do you remember? Some time ago, I inadvertently found the hiding place where you kept them and I took the liberty of reading a couple. "My sweet love: These days that you are far away, I walk through the fields every afternoon after work and, lying on the grass, I contemplate the passing clouds, with the secret hope that they may continue on their voyage until you can see them and read the messages of love that I mentally place in them..." Did I really write you such cheesy letters? And yet, look: that emotion was no different from this intense emotion with which I am writing to you now. You will say that I am not showing it as much, maybe you miss maudlin passages as the one transcribed above. But, surely, you can already read the emotion in my soul, my dear, as you have always done, while the conclusions I have reached through my detective work will not be clear to you unless I write it down in black and white, which is what I, with your permission, will proceed to do right now.

If the lower world does not hold the monopoly on Duality, if it's also present in the very bosom of the Higher World, in the One, althought There we have an *integrated* Duality, then, by being present at every cosmic level –from the lowest to the highest–, Duality reveals itself to be the backbone, the warp on which the Universe is woven. Duality is effectively the frame of the Universe, the cosmic foundation (except that foundation *is not ontological*, if you allow me the pedantic, though noteworthy, distinction: the ontological foundation of the Universe, the engine that brings the Universe into existence, is the Unit). And as a common substrate or guiding thread of the three worlds, Duality prevents discontinuity between them; it determines that the three worlds are, deep down, one single, whole Universe. The difference is in the degree of "unity", that is, the degree of *amorous integration* of the Duality common to the three worlds: grading goes from Duality's absolute split in the lower world to its perfect, seamless integration in the Hidden Point. (A good system to memorise this, is visualising cosmic Duality as an inverted "V", where the two points appear very far apart on the base and then come together in one single point at the top.)

There is a kinship between the lower and the Higher World, Blanca. This kinship is comparable to the one we can find in a sculptor's studio (I am thinking of the lovely sculptor we met in Toledo), between a sculpture and a block of stone. Both have the stone in common, just as both worlds have Duality in common. Duality is the carving stone of the Universe. In the lower world, that stone is a shapeless block

–a split Duality. In the Higher world, it's a proper sculpture, a Unit. The Unit is much more than integrated Duality, Blanca, just as the sculpture is more than a mere chiselled block of stone. The block of stone and split Duality are also alike in another way: in the fact that when they achieve what we could call their intimate vocation, they both transform into *something else.*

Their intimate vocation, I said. And it was well said, Blanca, because, for the ancient sages, Unity is, in a way, already present in the split Duality. It's potentially present, as if it were a secret identity, a desideratum, an intimate vocation. Similarly, the sculpture is already present in the block of stone. At least that is what our sculptor friend from Toledo told us... What was his name? Wait, I don't remember... Bah, I forgot his name, but not our conversation. With that insatiable curiosity of yours for the ins and outs of art, you asked about the material he used for his work: it could be marble, granite, sandstone, and the size of the block varied too. Then he added something that surprised us: he said that variety was not in function of the sculpture but the other way around. Meaning he did not plan the sculpture first; before even thinking about the sculpture, he chose the stone. But "thinking" is not the word, what he did was sit back on his armchair and from there he contemplated the block for a long time. He contemplated it for hours until –through what we could effectively call the "artistic intuition"– it revealed its true identity to him: a naked torso, perhaps, or maybe a Pieta, or an abstract figure. "The sculpture is hidden in the stone –he declared– and my job as a sculptor is to bring it to light."

We will return to the subject of the durability –in the form of a secret identity– of Unity within the split Duality on another occasion, Blanca. What I want to emphasise now is the inverse circumstance: the durability of Duality within Unity, symbolised by this obvious, albeit relevant for the purposes of our metaphor, detail, which is that *the stone endures within the sculpture*. In a different shape, in a different form, but it endures. Yet another way in which Duality and the sculpture are alike. Because does the fact that the Two from the Hidden Point compose a perfect matrimony means that they stop being *two*, they stop being a couple? Putting it another way: does the disappearance of opposition between the Two in the Hidden Point imply their own disappearance? The answer is absolutely not, my dear. As long as we don't omit this very important caveat: Duality's survival within the Unit is implicit, hidden, secret.

We can say, then, that two dimensions coexist in God, one is explicit, which is the One's, the other is implicit, underlying. That is the dimension of the Two. Thus, God is explicitly *One* though implicitly *double*, my dear, so much so that traditionally God could have been defined as a dual Unit or a Bi–Unit, that is to say, as a Unit structured in two poles. It's upon uniting, upon mutually neutralising, that the Eternal Male and the Eternal Female –as the poles were described by the ancient sages– give room to God's explicit dimension, Unity, which (just like how white light comes from the synthesis of every colour, while itself being colourless) is neither male nor female, it belongs to a third gender, a neutral, unitary gender that is the divine gender itself: the *androgynous gender*.

Now, Blanca, this word coined by the ancient sages to describe the divine gender, this word composed of *andros*, "male", and *gyne*, "female", shows by itself that, for the ancient sages, the male and female live on in the Unit (they endure not only in an implicit manner but in a sublimated way as well, with no sexual connotations). Let us recall, in this regard, the Hindu version of the myth of the Primordial Androgyne and its split into two halves brought to us by the *Brihadaranyaka Upanishad*: the Original world is referred there as "a single Soul in the shape of a Purusha". The Purusha, Blanca, the Primordial Man, was considered to have a purely spiritual nature, he was "soul" or "consciousness" or "inner self" (*atman*), as opposed to *prakrti* or "Matter". Due to his pure spiritual essence, the Purusha was not confined to the limitations of a body, he was boundless. In one word, Blanca, the Primordial Man was also a cosmic Man, he encompassed the entire Universe and the ancient Hindu sages considered him essentially identical to God, to Ishvara. Well, then, Blanca, you remember that single Soul identical to God, the Purusha, was "as big as a man and wife embracing each other"... Can you clearly discern here two dimensions of God? The single dimension (the "single Soul") and the dual ("a man and wife embracing each other")? For the ancient Hindu sages responsible for the *Brihadaranyaka Upanishad*, the unitary dimension of God implicitly embraces the dual, as it is corroborated in the following lines of the text. In order to alleviate his loneliness, it tells us, the Original Purusha, knowing that within himself slept, so to speak, an embraced man and woman, proceeded to awaken them; meaning, to separate them. He made explicit the male and female that heretofore had been implicit within him, thus "he parted this very body into two. From that came husband and wife."[162]

162. *Brhadaranyaka Upanishad*

A PROPELLER IN PERPETUAL ROTATION

The very existence of the One, Blanca, is unequivocal proof of the Two's implicit continuity, since that it's the *constant* agreement or amorous integration between these what produces the One... Above, I mentioned the two dimensions of God as the "naked eye" dimension and the "x-rayed" dimension, which the ancient ideograms of Divinity often combine; and I will mention the Hebrew Seal of Solomon, or Star of David, and the Chinese *Tao* symbol. Well, then, notice that, in both examples, the implicit aspect generates the explicit. In the seal of Solomon, the overlap of the two equilateral triangles produces the six-pointed star. In the *Tao*, the amorous interaction between the *yin* and the *yang* gives birth to the *Tai Kih*, the empty circle. This interaction is suggested by the helicoidal shape (the shape of a helix or an S) of the line delimiting the two halves of the circle, black and white, *yin* and *yang*. The helicoidal shape gives us the idea of movement, of interactive rotation between the two halves; such rotation is what generates the empty circle. If you look at a resting propeller, you will see the two halves that compose it, but if the propeller is spinning at great speed, you will not see anything but a white -empty- and uniform circle. Due to their perpetual rotational movement (to their constant amorous interaction), the two halves of the circle are imperceptible to the naked eye; only the effect of their interaction is visible: the white, uniform, complete circle, that is, the One. The cause, the Two's active love (an internal cause, let's not forget), is not perceptible by itself in the *Tao*; only implicitly in its effect: in the One.

Because Unity *implies* Duality, Blanca. Unity requires the constant interaction between the Two implicit in Itself.

Unity is inherently dual, the same way a coin intrinsically has two sides. The effect supposes a cause or, in its absence, an internal mechanism; and Unity is the effect, the fruit, of the constant amorous interaction between the Two. Thus, even if *yin* and *yang* apparently dissolve in the *Tai Kih* or empty circle, we can rest assured that they remain there. They disappear, certainly, but in the literal sense of the word: they cease to be apparent, they become invisible, they move out of the way... And so it is, my love: the Two must "disappear" into the One. Because the One is not merely a juxtaposition of the Two (in which case they wouldn't "disappear"), but its *synthesis*, a third thing, different from the sum of both parts. A metallurgist would tell you how the amalgamation of two metals would result in a third one, a third metal with its own properties, more perfect than the two alloyed metals. The two become a third thing –the One–, same as, under the sculptor's chisel, the block of stone becomes a sculpture, and, in their fast rotation, the two halves of a propeller transform into a white, uniform circle. The Two "die," in a sense, to reborn in the shape of the One (this image will be endlessly explored by the alchemists, as we will see). But, just as the stone remains present in the sculpture under a different shape–its true and original shape–; and the white circle tells us about the secret, implicit presence of the propeller; so does Duality endures within Unity, my dear: its death, its dissolution within the One, is only apparent.

Thus, we reach the end of this letter. In it, we tackled God and how the ancient sages intuited a hidden, implicit and secret dimension within Him. A dimension that is, we could say, like God's kitchen, where Divine reality is cooking. Picking up the old scholastic definition: the explicit dimension would correspond, in God, to the *substantial form*, to the

Unit; the implicit, to the *raw material*, to Love. God is both things, Unity and Love, inseparably, since Love, the love that operates within God –I mean the love between Its Two Persons–, is the Unit's *internal mechanism*. Hence the ancient sages placing such emphasis in God's implicit dimension, Blanca. As I did in this letter, since it's in this dimension where we are referring to the notion of twin souls, which is the notion that fuels my hope, the hope that you and I will one day be together again.

Yours

FOURTH LETTER

THE FALL

(OR EXILE)

What liberates us is the knowledge
(the gnosis) of who we were,
what we became;
where we were,
whereunto we have been thrown;
whereunto we speed,
wherefrom we are redeemed;

Theodotus, second-century Gnostic teacher

Barcelona, August 17th, 1999

Dear Blanca:

I don't think the languid barking we hear in the distance comes from same dog we could hear moaning on hot nights such as this. No, it cannot be. You will make fun of me, but do you know of what it reminds me? It reminds me of the pilgrim's chant from the *Tale of Genji*, that book I told you about a few letters ago. In the story, the chant was a good omen, I hope that is also the case here: "Do not prove false this omen of the pilgrim's chant: that even in lives to come our love shall last unchanged"... The night is at a standstill. As if enchanted by a witch from your fairy tales. Only the dog and the indefatigable mosquitoes seem to have escaped the witch's spell, whose instrument appears to be a vague linden blossom ambience (yes, yes, don't laugh) that comes to me as I am about to begin this letter.

In the previous one, you had the courage to accompany me –you and I, hand in hand, like a pair of explorers– through a wild and rough territory that was rather useful for our purposes. I have let a few days go by to replenish our strength, as our journey across the land of Metaphysics is not over yet. We still need to finish the profile of God's implicit dimension, taking into account His secret Multiplicity. That is what we will do in this letter. Although this time we will not focus on God, we will focus on man. Or, better yet: on the transition from one to the other. On the ontological decline of God –of a portion of God– to the rank of man, and the reasons behind it.

This decline begins with man, in the past, being part of divine nature... Yes, I understand that such premise may sound bold to you, even blasphemous if you think about men like Genghis Khan or Hitler or Jack the Ripper. However, wait until you see these monsters once they have purged their guilt at the end of a particularly long and painful cycle of reincarnations. Remember what we heard someone say... who was it? My memory fails me. Don't be fooled by the references to names and dates in these letters: I constantly need to check my books and notes; hence, the mess you see around me, which you would have never allowed. Anyway, we heard someone say at a conference: "Wise is the one who is capable of seeing in an acorn an oak, in a chrysalis a butterfly, in a sinner a saint", the saint whom the sinner will one day become... Our anonymous conference speaker was echoing a doctrine that enjoyed a widespread consensus among the ancient sages, Blanca. A doctrine that Early Church Fathers such as Origen of Alexandria supported –even if it meant being suspected of heresy–, and that Scotus Eriugena justified saying that the opposite would be the same as accepting the definite victory of sin. It's the doctrine of *apokatastasis* or of "reconstitution", a name taken from Greek astrology. *Apokatastasis* was the word that referred to the star's return to its starting point, the state it found itself at birth. That is a good metaphor for a doctrine that claims "every creature, without exception, is destined to be saved at the end of times".

So let's forget Genghis Khan, Hitler, and Jack the Ripper. Let's forego the sinners and focus on the saints. People such as Gandhi, Abbé Pierre, Mother Theresa... The truth is, my dear, that the "reverse" side, the "inner" side of every religion has unambiguously proclaimed man's divine filiation. It's possible that the "outer" side had similar suspicions, although they never dared to say so. Claiming, in the Genesis, that man had been created in *God's image* (or that, in the Origin, he was in a position to contemplate God's face, His essence), it stopped at placing man in God's immediate surroundings, while never identifying him with Him; it had the same reservations about taking that step as you. That is why it clung to the *ex nihilo* concept of Creation, the idea of Creation from nothing. For the ancient sages, however, the origin of man is not in a creation *ex nihilo*, Blanca. I have mentioned they preferred talking about "emanation": God emanates man. In any case, when they talked about "creation", they did not mean a creation from nothing; they meant that God created man *from His own essence.*

Man being of divine filiation means that in his origin –in the Origin– man was, in the words of twelfth century theologian Guillermo of Saint-Thierry, "what God is". Deep down, for our sages, Mankind and Divinity are not separate realities –as they would be if the latter had created the former from nothing. They are the same reality in two different states, just as water's solid and liquid states are two different states of the same substance, do you see? Just as liquidity is water's original state, then, so the solid state –ice– is its adulterated state. Thus, as strange as it may sound to us, Blanca, the human state is anomalous, it's a fall from Divinity, which is the proper, original state of this single essential reality of which we speak.

Indeed, this single essence cannot mask the abysmal dissimilarity between the human and the Divine. But, is not ice very different from water, even though their reality is not essentially different? I mean, man is not "what God is" but if we take the word of our sages, my dear, he was so in the past. When? If you paid the slightest attention to my letters, you will be able to answer this. Man was "what God is" when he possessed the quintessential divine attribute, Androgyny: which happened, as we have seen, in the Origin. It was the Original Androgyne's split into two halves what –just as the lowering of the temperature determines the transition of water into ice– what marked the passage of divine status into human status.

If each human being, when they were one with their twin soul, was whole, androgynous, and thus formed a particle indistinguishable from God, then that explains a common tendency among the ancient sages, Blanca. I am referring to the tendency of depicting human androgynous couples within circles or spheres –the circle being, as I told you, the symbol par excellence of Divinity. In fact, the androgynous Original Men portrayed in Plato's *Symposium*, are round: "The primeval man was round, his back and sides forming a circle". The pearls in which the ancient Muslim sages placed the blessed ones, those who had gained access to Paradise, were also round. Beyond its spherical shape, the pearl is, as we will see, an ancient symbol of androgynous Unity, of Paradise, and in this Paradise, the blessed one was not alone: he was accompanied by his predestined *huri*, his "spouse in Paradise", as *huries* are defined in the Quran. (Even if the prophet predicts a tremendous number of them for each man, it appears that the ancient Muslim sages spoke of only one.) Although, as an example of a depiction of lovers inscribed in spheres, Blanca, the one closest to us is that extraordinary fifteenth century painting before which we planted ourselves every time we visited the Prado Museum, while we were in Madrid. I mean –I am sure you guessed it– *The Garden of Earthly Delights* by Hieronymus Bosch, whose motley Paradise in the central panel, appears to be populated by androgynous couples of lovers, each couple lodged within a transparent sphere.

THE WALTZ OF THE UNIT

So, when the soul came together with its twin in "one [spiritual] flesh only", both enjoyed, in their mutual *perfect union,* of supreme Unity. Man, then, was not man in the strictest sense of the word: he was "what God is". But you are right when you ask me—or when I think you ask me: "If each whole or androgynous man, if each Original double man was 'what God is', how is it possible that God, being One, could have been, at the same time, so numerous? Did we not agree that the plural applied to God was a contradiction?"... It's not that God had been numerous *in the past*, Blanca: God *is* numerous, He is so eternally, and that is part of His nature. *Of his implicit nature*: this is the key. God's Plurality is secret, implicit, underlying, the same as His Duality. The

Couple of Spouses implicit in God, –I spoke about it in the previous letter– is not only one; they are many.

For the ancient sages of Greek culture, that multiplicity of Divine couples were called *Syzygias*, which in Greek means "unions of two". Note the *Syzygias* don't identify varied Units but always the same one, God's Unit, which is, by definition, unique. The Unit's diversity is adjectival, Blanca, not substantive. Perhaps to make this concept more easily understandable, the greatest Sufi theosophist, the Love's Faithful Ibn Arabi of Murcia, increased the number of God's Names given by the Quran. God –announces Ibn Arabi– has infinite Names. One for each soul, he says. One for each couple of twin souls, we may venture to say so ourselves. One for each *Syzygia*. That is to say, the Plurality of God is nominal and does not affect His essence. It's similar to what happens with God concerning the different religions. In each religion, God receives a different name –Allah, Yahweh, Brahma, Christ...–, but that does not mean that there are as many Gods as religions; God is universal, it's the same One for all of them; only His Name and His circumstances change.

We could find other metaphors to help us picture God's implicit Plurality that are just as valid, my dear, albeit more trivial. We could imagine, for example, a beach. The Castell beach in Palamós, for example, so full of memories for us. The beach is one, but it consists of an infinity of grains of sand, and while each one of them, by itself, *is* beach, it is not *the* beach. Well, I understand that in this same context one could say that each one of the Original human Souls, that each one of the double or androgynous souls from the Origin, was God. Each one of the infinite integrated Dualities, each one of the infinite *Syzygias* eternally existing within the One *is* God –in the present indicative... Or we could think of a book (in which case we would not be that original, as the metaphor of Divinity as a book was already a commonplace among the medieval sages). A blue book, if you would like. A blue book with infinite pages; the *One Thousand and One Nights*, for example, which, as Jorge Luis Borges pointed out, could give one that impression of infinity. Upon opening that immeasurable book, a certain number of pages would come off and fall on the floor, just as it actually happens with some volumes from the blue library... Or we could invoke a metaphor that is even more common among the ancient sages: that of Divinity as a Fire. The fire appears to us as a compact whole, a single unit: the flame is one. Only when sparks come out of the single flame that this uniformity proves to be composed of an infinite number of small particles. So, similarly, a myriad of beings is within God in a unitary, uniform way, without Plurality. Or, more precisely, God's Plurality is underlying, secret, explicit only when it falls. This reasoning, through which, if you can remember, we deduced the implicit presence of Duality within God, will also serve us now to affirm the presence of the Multiple within God: if the Multiple could come out of the One, that is because, in a way –in an implicit, underlying way– it was already there.

When we talk about fire, Blanca, I imagine that the picture that comes up in your head is of fire on the hearth, the wood crackling, smoke going up the chimney, and the smell of soot permeating everything. The ancient sages imagined it more as an inextinguishable Fire, an archetypal Fire of which the most famous example is that of the supreme Egyptian Divinity, represented by an enormous ball of fire, the Sun-God Ra. The icons show it in the shape of a red disk with yellow borders, two colours that for the Egyptians symbolised the male and the female respectively, according to an illustrious

Egyptologist, who adds "The inward essence of divinity was considered by the Egyptians as male and female. The heat of the fire represented the universal male principle. The light of the fire was the female principle."[163] Does this not make you think about that metaphor I told you the other day? Of the brightness and radiance of light? Well, that androgynous Fire with which the ancient sages represented Divinity, Blanca, that single Fire, is composed of an infinite number of *sparks*, each one of them androgynous and carrying their own Unity's "grain of sand", their own small fraction of brightness for that infinite Fire. In the Origin, there was nothing but the endless Fire. But then, something happened; something necessary, according to some, an unfortunate accident, according to most. Upon losing their Androgyny, upon the split into two halves, a certain number of divine sparks (a great, although limited, number; an insignificant number, next to divine Infinity) stopped carrying their contribution of Unity towards the One. At that very moment, those divided sparks broke out of the Original Fire. They fell. And as they fell, they created the different worlds on their path: the middle worlds and, lastly, the world of division or Duality: the lower world, where they finally ran aground.

Another metaphor that suddenly came to me, and which I know you will like, brings up the palatial ball from the story of *Cinderella*. Imagine that the palace is the Unit, which is embodied by the dancing couples. And suppose that when the fateful clock strikes twelve, many couples come undone instead of just the one. These broken couples rush out of the palace to venture into the cold darkness of the night, and

163. Frédéric du Portal, *A comparison of Egyptian symbols with those of the Hebrews*, p. 65

leave the illuminated warm halls behind. In a trance, men and women lose their shoes and swap their immaculate garments for ashes. And during all this, the band keeps playing inside the palace of Unity, the dance continues, for there are infinitely more couples who remained than those who left... To what are these couples dancing? Ah, I knew you were going to ask that! Perhaps I should tell you that they are dancing to the sound of the music from the spheres, the music of the cosmic ocean, which, judging by the old paintings, is played by the angels and, I imagine, one must dance to it as though it were a waltz. But look, maybe you prefer to imagine them, and why not, dancing to the sound of our song: *Que reste–t–il de nos amours, que reste–t–il de ces beaux jours, une photo, vieille photo de ma jeunesse...*

Crossed–out note on the margin. The erased sentence is only visible in bits and pieces, but the name *Hans Castorp* gives away its origin (*The Magic Mountain* by Thomas Mann) and allows us to complete it: "*Hans Castorp... As always whenever he set eyes on that heedless creature, the likeness reasserted itself which had puzzled him for a while and then been revealed in a dream.*"

The ancient sages, Blanca (and, especially here, you should keep in mind that we are talking mostly about the esoteric ones, those from the backrooms of knowledge, we could say), had that intuition: that of Multiplicity inherent to Unity. The intuition that God is not composed of one single Couple of Divine Spouses, but of a multitude of them: an infinite number of *Syzygias*. For the ancient sages, the Multiple was not something that the Universe had pulled out of its sleeve following the Fall; on the contrary, it was something eternal, ever–present within the One. In fact, my dear, if we accept the Duality implicit in God, we must also accept without hesitation His implicit Multiplicity, as both notions are correlated, inseparable from one another. The "ten thousand beings", as the ancient sages described the Multiple, the myriad of beings, are consubstantial with the Dual. There is no Duality without Multiplicity and vice–versa: both categories are mutually implied.

Up until now, we had characterised the lower world, the physical world, as dual: a world in which everything is conjugated by couples of opposites. Ah, it's obvious, though, that the lower world is also characterised by Multiplicity: a world in which the couples of opposites are "ten thousand", where they are multiple. If we take the only substantive couple of opposites, we will see that there is not (as is the case with Adam and Eve in Paradise) a single man and a single woman, there are multiple men and multiple women. Duality is always multiple, Blanca: wherever it exists, so does Multiplicity. Now, as we have seen, Duality also exists in God. Therefore, this divine Duality must necessarily be multiple. But I repeat: this must not lead us to think of multiple Gods, because –as with His Duality– God's Multiplicity is *implied*; that Multiplicity is, so to speak, comprised within the single One.

Getting back to Cinderella's palace (except there, she does not answer to the name "Cinderella", since that name denotes the fallen state), getting back to the dazzling palace of Unity, where an infinite number of *Syzygias*, of dancing couples, dance the eternal dance of the One: Do you know what each of those couples is? Each one of those couples is a *Monad*, a particle of "Unity". But, again, I insist: these multiple

Monads are not, as much as this sounds paradoxical, different Units. In every single case, it's the same single Unit multiplied to infinity, because, as the knowledgeable voice of Henry Corbin explains, this is not an arithmetic Unit, it's an ontological Unit: the One –the One that invests each one of the infinite divine Monads with its Unity– is always the same... We are then talking about one single One, my dear. But a single One that, because of Its implied Multiplicity, has the effect (a metaphor by Haydar Amoli, a disciple of Ibn Arabi, which will also be to your liking) of a candle surrounded by mirrors. Although it appears that there are multiple candles, in reality, there is only one; what is actually multiple, is not the candle but the mirrors.

What is multiple in God is not His Unity; it's the *implicit Duality in His Unity*. We could outline this fundamental intuition of our sages by using that popular image of the twin souls, the one involving an orange: The orange is one; the couple of half oranges that integrate it is multiple. Or rather, my love, that the union of any couple of half oranges –you and I, for example– gives place not to a specific orange, particular to that one couple, but to *the* orange. The orange is itself universal, common to every couple of half oranges. It is particular only in the sense that one accesses it in a particular way: through the union of a couple of specific half oranges, different from all the others...

ONE SINGLE GOD WITH INFINITE NAMES

We can find traces of this intuition of the implicit presence of the Multiple within the One, Blanca, in the ancient sages' systems, as well as in different esoteric movements. The Sufi master Ibn Arabi of Murcia and his disciples expressed it through the aforementioned metaphor of the Names, the infinite Names of God, one for each spark of the infinite Fire. Plato had already hinted at it much earlier, in his "theory of Ideas". His followers, led by Plotinus, would later formulate it by specifically placing these eternal Ideas, these heavenly models of earthly shapes from which they emanate, in a Supreme Mind: the mind of *Theos*, the mind of "God". Proclus speaks of *Henads* (synonymous of *Monads*: "Units") to refer to the multiplicity implicit in the One. There is in the One a plurality of *Henads*, claims Proclus; though this plurality, he adds, should be seen as unitary. In the East, several myths tell us how the One felt the need of being Many, and, consequently, how It proceeded to multiply Itself or to make Its implicit Multiplicity explicit, which is the same. In the Hindu *Bhagavad–Gita*, we can read about how a "portion" of the Ishvara condescended to embody the multiple human souls. Another Indo–European doctrine of ascendency, Druidism, the mystic Celtic doctrine, was seemingly based (although there is little factual evidence to establish it with certainty) on a *multiple monism:* in the belief in a Unity of Being; a Unit that nonetheless carries an intrinsic Multiplicity within. Unity is hidden underneath the Multiple now, although, presumably, there was a time in which it was the Multiple what lied beneath the Unit. This conception is also part of the doctrinal core of Taoism.

If we focus now on Judaism, Blanca, we will realise that the name *Elohim*, which is the name given to Yahweh in the Scriptures, is a plural name, the plural form of *Eloah*; it means "Gods, Angels". The Kabbalists found it significant that, to refer to the one God, the Scriptures employed a word used to allude to numerous pagan Gods. This was not the only sign they used to defend the One's implicit Multiplicity. They also found that the myth of the Tree of Life rising in the centre of Paradise, according to the Genesis, supported this idea. They observed that the top of this Tree, a Tree that is a symbol of the One, was composed of countless leaves. Among the Kabbalists, Blanca, the Tree of Life is also the "Tree of Souls", because each leaf of that luxuriant crown (every leaf is composed of two symmetrical sides) represents one of the Original androgynous souls. Some of which fall, as dead leaves do, ending up in the lower world.

Crossed–out note on the margin. We can read a clipped quote: "*Together (they had) faced so many (hardships?)…/… face together the maximum (hardship?): (that of) separation.*" It seems to be an obvious allusion to the author and his wife's forced separation, imposed on them by her death.

To this symbol of the Tree, we can add the Spring, since it's at the foot of the Tree of Life where the cosmic River is born, the River of the worlds of which I told you about in the previous letter. This representation of the cosmic Centre as a Tree, or a Spring, is not exclusive to Judeo–Christian tradition, it's universal. We can find a testimony referencing the Spring in a twelfth century Arabic–Persian text titled *The Story of Western Exile*. In this text, the Spring of Life is described as a natural spring in which a multitude of fish swims. Marvelled by the presence of this implicit Multiplicity within the One, the astral traveller (a kind of Persian Swedenborg) inquires: "But who are these fish?" The answer: "They are many other images of yourself. You are sons of the same Father."[164] That is to say, Blanca, those fish are the equivalent of the divine sparks immersed in the ever-lasting Fire.

In another Arabic-Persian from the same period, it's not fish but birds. The mystic epic poem *The Conference of the Birds*, by the Sufi poet Attar of Nishapur, narrates the odyssey of a flock of thirty birds (this number stands for Many) as they ascend to the Heavens. The title alludes to a passage from the Quran that says that the soul, in order to be "filled with good", must learn the "language of the birds" (or of the angels: the language of the Spirit), which is the soul's native language. The thirty birds aspire to reach the highest of Heavens, in which their King resides, the Simorgh, whom they vaguely remember and miss. The Simorgh embodies the divine Unit, the Fire from which came the flying sparks. To reach their destiny, the flock must cross seven valleys or seas. (Seven is another symbolic number that is often featured in the ancient sages speculations, signifying a cycle, a complete sequence.) Once in Simorgh's celestial Palace, the birds make an unexpected discovery. They are dumbfounded to discover that their king is not just another *one of their own* (the Persian term *si-morgh* means "thirty-birds") but themselves at the culmination of their trip. Upon contemplating Simorgh, they see themselves as though in a mirror:

> In that moment, in the reflection of their faces, these thirty birds (si-morgh) saw the face of the spiritual Simorgh. Then, the astonishment caused them vertigo, and they did not know if they were still themselves or if they were Simorgh, for they saw that it was Simorgh who stood there, in that place; and

164. Quoted by Henry Corbin, *ibid*, p. 39

when they gazed upon themselves, they saw that they were Simorgh. And when they looked to both sides at the same time, they saw that themselves and Simorgh were one single being. That single being was Simorgh and Simorgh was that being. No one else in the world heard such a thing.[165]

The Simorgh is one single being, Blanca. But this single bird implicitly encompasses many: this is what the amazed earthly birds who reach Him discover, those who become Him while implicitly remaining themselves. A Hermeticist like Idries Shah expresses it thus: "This is how the Seeker understands the mystery, the paradox, of how an individual drop can be merged with an ocean and still remain meaningful".[166] According to Attar, this is "the great Mystery". This great Mystery, Blanca, is the existence of an implicit dimension in God, one that englobes Multiplicity as well as Duality; the *One* that at the same time is the Many and the *Two*. Attar speaks about "the enigma of the reality-of-us (of the Many) and the reality-of-the-you (of the Two)". Because the Many and the Two possess "reality" in God; except that, unlike the One's, theirs is an implicit reality.

This Persian Simorgh is identified as a fabulous bird from Islamic mythology, the *Anka*. The tenth century Arab historian Al-Masudi mentions it in *The Meadows of Gold*: "The prophet (Mohammed) told us one day: 'In the first ages of the world, God created a bird of astonishing beauty and bestowed upon her every perfection: a face like that of Man, a radiant plumage of the richest colours... God created a female on the likeness of the male and named the

165. Attar of Nishpur, *The Conference of the Birds*
166. Idries Shah, *The Sufis*

couple *Anka*'."[167] Note how that is the couple's name; it is, then, a double, androgynous bird, a bird that embodies the mystery of the "two in one". Among the ancient Muslim sages, the Anka became a symbol of Divinity equivalent to the Simorgh, to which it eventually became similar. Its radiant plumage, says Masudi, is "of the richest colours", which leads us to imagine it to be similar to the peacock, covered in the colours of the rainbow, that androgynous symbol. Yet, it would not be ridiculous to imagine it as a blue bird... No, Blanca, I am not thinking about Madame d'Aulnoy's story[168] when I say this, I am thinking about another fairy tale of the same name written as a theatre play by a Belgian poet and playwright from the *Belle Epoque*. A play that I am sure you would have loved to know and would have certainly made it a tenant of your library.

I am talking about Maurice Maeterlinck, an author that reclaimed intuition as the organ of knowledge par excellence, even claiming that "everything that does not come from the most unknown and secret depths of man, does not come from his only legitimate source"[169]. His play *The Blue Bird* tells the story of a couple of small children, Tyltyl and Mytyl, brother and sister (twins, if we consider the similarity of their names), who go on a trip to Heaven, in their dreams, in search of a blue coloured bird. A fairy told them of the existence of this mysterious bird in which, she said, "the great secret of things and happiness" resided. Tyltyl and Mytyl arrive in Heaven, and that is where, among other wonders, they

---

167. Al-Masudi, *The Meadows of Gold*, 4, 19 s.
168. A reference to *L'Oiseau Bleu*, "The Blue Bird", one of the *contes de fees* French aristocrat that made fairy tales fashionable in the seventeenth-century.
169. *Confession de poète*

find an enormous door. Upon opening, it reveals the most "unreal, infinite, ineffable, the most unexpected garden of dreams and night light, in which, among stars and planets, illuminating everything they touch, flying endlessly from rhinestone to rhinestone, from moonbeam to moonbeam, magical blue birds perpetually and harmoniously evolve to the confines of the horizon, so innumerable that they seem to be the breath, the celestial atmosphere, the very substance of the wonderful garden". In other words, Blanca, the divine Blue Bird is one but multiple.

The flying, therefore aerial, "spiritual", condition of the birds, makes them ideal symbols for the "Many", the inhabitants of the Higher World, just as, for the same reason, the angels also are. In fact, for the ancient sages, talking about Multiplicity implicit in God was often equivalent to talking about Angels. So it is, for example, for the Gnostics, for the Muslim theologian Avicenna, for the Neo-Platonic Proclus, and for many others. Significantly, the Angels from Abrahamic tradition -Michael, Gabriel, Raphael, Seraphiel, Uriel, etc- all carry the suffix *el*, which in the Semitic languages (as it can be seen in the etymology of the word Allah) means "God". The names of these Angels with a capital A, of these Androgynous Angels, would be, then, the Names of God, the Infinite Names of the one only Divinity. This agrees with Proclus' terminology, which, besides the aforementioned *Henads*, talks about *Dii Angeli*, the "God Angels", with whom he identifies the Platonic "Ideas".

An esoteric sect of Islam, a very ancient sect that is known in the West thanks to Henry Corbin: the sect of the Ismailist theosophists conceives the Higher World, which in this case is given the name of "world of *'Aql'*", "pure Intelligence", as a purely spiritual world integrated by beings of that same nature, that is, the Angels. The Ismailist Angels form a *Pleroma*, a Greek term, meaning "Plenitude", that has its origin in Hellenistic philosophy, and which we have already seen when discussing the Gnostics. The *Pleroma* is the Higher World, or the world of the Divine, *in its plenitude*, in its infinite richness. It connotes, then, Multiplicity, Blanca; it evokes a *One* that is, simultaneously and free of contradiction, *Many*. Certainly, for the Ismailist theosophists, the Pleroma or world of revealed Divinity (there is yet another instance: the hidden Divinity, although we will leave this one for another occasion) is a hierarchised world: there is an entire hierarchy of Angels. But, to my understanding, this is an adjectival and arguable datum that does not overshadow the base fact. The base fact is that of the intrinsic Multiplicity of the divine world.

These theosophists go as far as detecting, in said angelic hierarchy, the exact point where the rupture which caused the Fall was produced: it was, they assure us, at the level of the third Angel of the Pleroma. This level corresponds to the Original heavenly Mankind, Blanca, since for the Ismailist theosophists, we human beings, before the Fall, were Angels, we were an integral part of the divine Pleroma.

A Gnostic master –Theodotus– also talks of the "Angels of which we are a fallen portion."[170] At this point, let's also remember that Biblical origin myth as reformulated by the ancient sages: the myth of the fallen Angels led by Luzbel or Lucifer, whom some of our sages stripped of demonic connotations to turn him into an unhappy symbol of the human race. Finally, I will mention an old Biblical exegesis

170. *Extracts from Theodotus*, quoted por H. Corbin, *The Paradox of Monotheism*

brought up by Henry Corbin -whom I found to be a great help when it came to writing about Angelology. It's an exegesis written by a Greek Priest of the Early Church, Methodius of Olympus, of an old Evangelical parable: "What do you think? If a shepherd has a hundred sheep, and one of them has gone astray, does he not leave the ninety-nine on the mountains and go in search of the one that went astray?" (Matthew 18:12). Methodius sees the mountain as the Higher World, the hundred sheep as the infinite Angels that inhabit it, and the stray sheep as the human soul that has left the mountain to come down to the plain, to the lower world.

ONE GOD ONLY... THOUGH NOT ONE LONE GOD

Theodotus and Methodius are not the only Christian sages for whom Multiplicity and Unity, far from being incompatible, co-exist harmoniously in God, my dear. I told you about the Swedenborgian Heaven, populated by angels, married angels grouped in countless societies. Valentine and other Gnostic masters spoke of the *Eones* or "Eternities" that, yoked in the *Syzygyas* or spiritual Couples, integrate the divine Pleroma. (As the Ismailists', the Gnostic Pleroma is hierarchised, although I insist that this piece of information seems dubious to me.) Another example is Gregory of Niza, in the fourth century. According to this Father of the Church, although God has been and always will be One, before the Fall this One was inhabited by multiple spiritual and androgynous Men. Divine Men, then. Such Men integrated a Whole or a Pleroma: the *Anthropines Pleroma*, the "Human Pleroma". Gregory likens those Men implicit in God with the Angels, and says that they sinned and caused their exit from God: the Fall. For Gregory, the Fall consisted, on one hand, of a Multiplicity hitherto implicit in the Unit becoming explicit; and, on the other hand, on sexual division: on the split of each androgynous Angel into one male and one female, which meant the beginning of the material and divided man, man with a small "m".

In the ninth-century, John Scotus Eriugena referred (in the work where he reveals the process that runs downwards from God towards the creatures and upwards from these back to God) to the *caelestium numerositas* or *spiritualis numerositas*, "celestial or spiritual numerosity" of Men potentially contained, in an implicit form, in the bosom of God before the Fall. (Scotus Eriugena was influenced –just as he influenced many later medieval mystics– by Gregory of Niza, but I reiterate my opinion that quoting the influences of an ancient sage does not make much sense, for we never know if those influences actually shaped their ideas or if they just confirmed their intuitions.) These heavenly Men were androgynous, they were not men in the strictest sense but gods, since that for this great sage as well, Blanca, Androgyny is the original condition of the human being, and a condition he lost because of sin. "If man had not sinned, he would not have suffered the split of his simplicity into two sexes"[171], writes Eriugena, for whom the blossoming of the Multiple was nothing but the actualisation of a "Numerosity" latent in God.

Anyway, my love. I think I have cited enough examples of the ancient intuition of the Multiplicity implicit in the One, indissoluble of His implicit Duality. As you can see, if in

171. John Scottus Eriugena , *De Divisione Naturae* IV, 799 A

previous letter we were able to define God as a dual Unit or a bi-Unit, now we can dare to define Him as a plural Unit or a multi-Unit as well. But we dare to do so always with the understanding that His Plurality and His Duality are implicit, that it's God's Unity what defines Him as such. God's Duality and Multiplicity are eclipsed by His Unity (just as the stars disappear in the light of the noon sun without it meaning that they have ceased to shine). In short: as paradoxical as it may appear to us, God is not a simple Unit, He is a compound one; He is *One*, but *implicitly* He is *many*, and those *many* are *double*. *Implicitly, God is a Multiplicity of Couples.*

Now, what is the difference between those infinite Couples of twin souls that are God (that are God in the same way that the grains of sand of the Castell beach are the beach) and those that, as you and I, are subject to the cycle of reincarnation? One substantial difference, my dear: unlike us, the Couples of twin souls of the Higher World have not lost their androgynous condition. They form a heavenly matrimony, and every other difference derives from this basic difference; one of them is related to the feeling in which I have been tangled up lately. I mean solitude; a feeling inherent to fallen twin souls, but completely foreign to the twin souls implicit in God. Because there is no room in God for solitude, Blanca. The amorous union of the multiple Couples existing in His bosom dispel the solitude to which His Unity could be expected to condemn Him. "That union –asserts Henry Corbin (Corbin is one of the supporters of the "angelic hypothesis" as an explanation for the mystery of the lost half of the soul; although this assertion is also valid from the point of view of our hypothesis)– that union –asserts Corbin– governs an ontology where the individuation (ie, where the unification of the Two that become one single individual) fulfils not the solitudes of the One, but the mystery of the One that is Two, of the Two that is One."[172]

Because did we not agree that Love was the *raw material* of God? And if in the Origin there was nothing but God, if in the Origin God was alone in the Universe, then that loneliness –that Unity– could not be absolute; on the contrary, if God was absolutely alone, who would He love? With whom would He practice the Love that He is? The ancient sages understood this very well. They realised that, given the dual essence of Love, the Oneness of God gathered, for example, in the profession of Jewish faith ("Hear, O Israel, the Lord our God is One") and Muslim faith ("There is no God but God"), could not be but relative. They also understood that while it is true that God is One, He is so on the outside; inside, God is "inhabited" by Couples, by *Syzygias*.

In that case, solitude does not affect Hidden Point, Blanca, the *whole* nature, that of the Androgyne, the nature of God. Solitude is limited to the divided and human nature of the lower world. However, our solitude is not essential; it's not an ontological solitude. It's accidental because, in the words of the ancient sages, the Fall is something transitory and surmountable, an insignificant parenthesis in the midst of Eternity. (In Infinity, every parenthesis, as tragic and dilated as it may be, becomes insignificant.) To close this subject of solitude, we could turn to the *Zohar* again, which is much more than a book, my dear, it's more like an encyclopaedia of the human condition: there is no subject of importance to man that is not thoroughly discussed in it. In the *Zohar*, a disciple of Simon bar Yochai, reflecting on the verse from the Genesis: "Yahweh Elohim said: it is not good for the

---

172. Henry Corbin, *op. cit.*, p. 50

man to be alone" (Genesis 2: 18), asks himself whether man is essentially alone. He concludes that no, and appeals to the authority of the Genesis and rabbinic tradition: "Is it not written 'man and female He created them', and have we not learned that man was created with 'two faces'?"

Thus, man is not alone because, in essence, ontologically speaking, every human being is half of a unitary couple, of a couple that in a paradoxical way constitutes a Unit. And his intimate vocation –as well as his destiny– is to restore that original, divine couple, from which he comes.

GOD'S EXILE

We have now reached the main subject of this letter: the Fall.

Practically every esoteric version of the Fall shares the same conclusions. To begin, the Fall is conceived as a *drama occurring within God Himself*. This cosmic drama would have consisted of two simultaneous and correlated events. On one side, the atomisation of the primordial One –of a portion of the primordial One– into the myriad of beings. On the other, of the division of each of those beings into two differentiated halves. In short, Blanca, the Fall would have consisted of what was implicit in God becoming explicit: His Multiplicity and His Duality. As I told you, we can think of it as a supreme Fire, from which many sparks rise, each splitting into two halves - a distinction which, as we have seen, presupposed the very genesis of the Fall, since it represented, for a portion of the One, the loss of His Integrity, His Unity, of His Divinity. We can define the Fall as a weakening of God, as the loss of a portion of God; and man as the result of that weakening. God dethroned and lowered to the human rank.

According to this, the ancient sages saw man (the human soul) as a fallen God; Mankind, as a portion of God in exile. The idea of Exile supports that of the Fall; it alludes to a portion of God that alienates and exits Himself –the Unit– and ends up in the world of division or Duality. It stops being One to become Two. Or rather, it stops being *Two in One*, which is integrated Duality, to become "*Two outside the One*", split Duality.

Because –one more time, my dear– the Two already existed in the One. Since this is a fundamental belief of ours, this co-existence of Duality (and Multiplicity) with the Unit in the Higher World, I cannot resist quoting yet more testimonies. As the one by first century philosopher and exegete Philo of Alexandria. For him, when God made Man male and female, according to the Genesis, Man still had not been divided into male and female, *but these two were implicitly present in the whole Man*; hence the sacred text mentioning it before their separation –ie, before making it explicit, which happened much later. And so –concludes Philo–, now when man and woman find each other, "love supervenes, brings together and fits into one the divided halves, as it were, of a single living creature, and sets up in each of them a desire for fellowship with the other with a view to the production of their like."[173]

Another testimony comes from an Irish monk that has already appeared quite often in these letters. For that reason, he deserves that we pause for a moment and focus on him. John Scotus Eriugena was one of the greatest theologians of the Middle Ages, and was recognised as such by his contemporaries. Among them, was the grandson of Charlemagne,

173. Philo of Alexandria, *De Opificio Mundi* 152, 1.37, LIII

Charles the Bald, who received Eriugena in his court when, due to a foreign invasion, he had to seek exile abroad and abandon the monastery in which he had received his education. Charles, to whom, upon the partition of his grandfather's empire, corresponded the territory of what is now known as France, entrusted Eriugena with the running of the Palatine Academy, the most renowned school of its day. There, our sage found the peace of mind necessary to elaborate the first original philosophical system of the Western Middle Ages, expressed in that text to which I referred before, the *De Divisione Naturae*, "The Division of Nature".

In that book, Eriugena writes about the necessary return of the fallen sparks back to the original Fire: "Inferior things (Duality and Multiplicity) are naturally attracted and integrated by superior ones (Unity), *not in a way that they cease to exist*, but so they preserve and subsist within them and become one."[174]

Jakob Boehme -do you remember the Lutheran mystic from whom we borrowed the metaphor of the candle's brightness and radiance?-, he also believed that both sexes were implicit and prefigured in the Original Androgyne. Given that he is another one of our reference sages, we will take the liberty of sketching a portrait of him... Jakob Boehme, in essence, is similar to that other later Christian sage, Swedenborg. Both had mystic intuitions that were a little more than that: they were visions, direct experiences of the "reverse side" of the Universe, and they felt the obligation of passing these on. His personal circumstances, however, were quite different. Born in the German town of Görlitz, in the state of Saxony, in the last third of the sixteenth century, Boehme was a shoemaker

174. John Scottus Eriugena, *De Divisione Naturae* V, 879 A

-he is known, in the history of theosophy, as "the Görlitz cobbler". We know he was not a particularly cultured man (which goes to show that wisdom has little to do with erudition, a far different thing, although they are often mistaken for one another). Several generations of thinkers and poets found inspiration in his books *Aurora* and *Mysterium Magnum*, making him one of the most influential theosophists of all time. But, as it usually happens (as it also happened with Swedenborg and the Swedish Lutheran Church), his mystic intuitions were not well received by the clergy of his time, who forbid him to disseminate them; a prohibition which at first he followed but later defied. Like Swedenborg, he strongly defended the authenticity of his visions, presented in his books in a style that was arcane, though fascinating for the strength of its imagery -the metaphor of the brightness and radiance of light is a good example of it.

Above, I told you about Unity as the distinctive characteristic of God, and the lack of it -fragmentation- as the characteristic trait of the physical world. Well, that, my dear, is one of Boehme's visions, one of his foundational intuitions. Another one, is the one that points to fragmentation as the existence of evil in this world. Yet another one (and this is the one of most interest to us) is that of the Original Androgynous Man, whom Boehme identifies as Adam, from whom his wife Eve had not yet been separated. "Adam was a complete image of God, male and female -we read in the *Mysterium Magnum*-, and nevertheless, neither of them separately... Adam was man and wife in one individuality."[175] The

175. Jakob Boehme, *Mysterium Magnum*, I, 103, quoted by Diane Long Hoeveler, *Romantic Androgyny*, The Pennsylvania State University Press, U.S.A. pág. 43

Fall came to play havoc with this privileged state of things. For Boehme, the banishment from Paradise is merely the culmination of the Fall, which instead he perceives in the Biblical episode of Adam's sleep, during which he splits into two. Adam's sleep would symbolise the Original Androgynous Man's estrangement from Divinity: as he falls deeper in his slumber, both genders implicit in him become explicit, they become objective, giving rise to the separated man and woman. Adam inaugurates, then, a new existential status: the human being. He goes to sleep being "what God is", a man with a capital M, and wakes up as a simple mortal man; he falls asleep *whole* and he wakes up split into two halves. For a fervent Christian such as Boehme, this split supposed a tragedy comparable only to the crucifixion of Christ.

Another Christian sage, three centuries after the Görlitz cobbler although very much influenced by him, was Leopold Ziegler, another German, who also saw in the Fall an ontological diminishing or degradation that caused Man to lose his original androgynous Integrity, and with it his divine nature. Ziegler conceives God as a bi–Unit, as one single entity with two sides, the "paternal side" and the "maternal side". But if the ancient sages frequently symbolised God through the geometric shape of the circle, he considered the ellipsis to be a more suitable representation. This is because, with its oval shape, the ellipsis does not have only one centre, it has two: "The living God –notes Ziegler– is not a circle around one centre, but an ellipsis from two points, ambivalent in itself, bicentric, bipolar."[176] And since the original Man was

176. Leopold Ziegler, *Menschwerdung*, quoted by Sophie Latour in her article *L'archétype de l'androgyne chez Leopold Ziegler* (*L'Androgyne*, p. 198)

of a divine nature, Ziegler defends that this linked polarity also operated in him until the Fall disconnected it: in other words, the divorce of the Spouses, the Androgyne's split into a separate man and woman. It meant, then, the Unit's sinking, the deterioration of God, of that portion of God called Man, to the status of man with a lower case "m".

A STONE THROWN INTO A POND

For the Greek philosopher Empedocles, man is a "vagabond exiled from the divine mansion"[177]. The definition of man as "God in exile" abounds in texts written by the ancient sages, Blanca. But not just there: we can find it under disguise in popular tradition as well; particularly in your dear fairy tales. In those stories, protagonists with royal ancestry, princes, are quite common. Frequently, these princes find themselves stripped of their dignity and exiled from their kingdom. Thus, they become beggars, vagabonds, and must overcome a series of trials before restoring their original condition. *Royalty*, in ancient symbolism, is synonymous with *Divinity* (I told you about how the Androgyne was almost always depicted wearing a crown and dressed in royal finery). Said tales could be interpreted, then, as allusive to the Fall or Exile, to the descent of God –of a portion of God– to the rank of man.

Given the premise that divine Unity is, implicitly, *integrated* Duality, the Fall would have consisted of the disintegration, the split of that Duality into a portion of God. Since before the Fall, all Duality was integrated (there was nothing

177. Empedocles, *Purifications*, fr. 117

besides God), the Fall would have entailed the emergence of the split Duality and, therefore, the emergence of the worlds where it exists in a larger or smaller scale: the inferior world and the ones in the middle. In the Origin, only the Hidden Point, only the Unit existed. God filled everything. There was nothing outside of Him because there was no "outside of Him": everything was Him, everything was "inside", there were no divisions or degrees of reality. Returning to that metaphor –of the concentric waves– we used in the previous letter to visualise the cosmic mandala, we will say that in the Origin everything was like the calm surface of water right before the impact of a stone.

I just wrote "outside of God" concerning the middle and lower worlds. But this expression is deceitful and requires an immediate clarification on my part. When you hear me talking about an "outside of God", my dear, please note that it's for us to better understand each other, you should not take it at face value: in the strictest sense, there is no such thing. What exists are decreasing degrees of Divinity as we go down the range of worlds. But even the last of worlds, even the one furthest apart from God, which is this one from where I am writing to you, is within the divine scope. Therefore, to refer to this world, it would be more accurate (but less clear, I believe) to say the outskirts of God, as if it were a city we were talking about, where even the outer–most neighbourhoods are part of it no matter how far away from the centre they are.

With this reservation in mind, then, the Fall could be described as the exit of a portion of God outside Himself. Thus came into existence the "outside" that some sages named the "wrapper" of God –which like any wrapper, vaguely preserves the shape of what it covers. "The Universe is the wrapping, the cladding of God"[178], the Jews read in the *Zohar*. And the Hindus, in the *Isa Upanishad*: "All this, whatsoever it exists in the Universe, should be covered by the Lord." We could compare the Fall to a gas leak (including the explosion: the Big Bang that science tells us), except that instead of gas, we would talk of Unity, of the divine essence. As Unity escaped, as it moved further away from the One, it would split into two, originating Duality –split Duality. One spark and this world came into existence, the world of Matter, the lower world of Space–Time. When, in the previous letters, we mentioned the Kabbalist cosmovision, we defined this "leak", this departure of God outside Himself as a voluntary descent through which God manifested Himself. But according to a more pervasive opinion, Blanca, it was not a voluntary descent at all, it was, in reality, *a Fall*. God would not be manifesting Himself, He would be Falling. Always in the understanding that what fell was not the totality of God, but a portion.

In this respect, the Kabbalah, as I told you, differs from most esoteric schools of thought. Generally, the Kabbalists did not believe that the unfolding of worlds from the Hidden Point consisted of a fall in the strictest sense. We should talk about it more in terms of a process of divine manifestation; of a theophany consubstantial to Divinity, that it would need to eternally manifest Itself, reveal Itself through that unfolding of worlds. This approach that also postulates the appropriateness of the primordial split of the Androgyne into two separate halves. The fifteenth century Spanish Kabbalist, Ibn Gabbay, claimed that human perfection could only have been achieved once Adam and Eve were separated

178. *Zóhar*, I, 19b

and, therefore, were able to find one another and love each other face to face (the very posture of conjugal love, as we have seen). This opinion was shared, as we know, by Leo the Hebrew, who reflecting on the verse from the Genesis: "Yahweh Elohim said: it is not good for the man to be alone; I will make a helper suitable for him", reached the following conclusion: "It did not appear that Adam, male and female, was well in one single body, united by the back and with opposing faces; it would be better if the female was separated and facing him, face to face, to be able to help him."[179] In Sufi tradition, we can also find this point of view, supported here in the idea that God felt the need to be known and, with that aim, Love, which is Him, split into two halves: the one who knows -the Lover- and the one who is known -the Beloved-. *I was a hidden treasure and I longed to be known*, says a famous *hadith*, a famous saying by the prophet Mohammed.

Many Hindu cosmologies (because in Hinduism, my dear, instead of a single cosmology, there is a mosaic of sometimes-contradictory systems) also agree about the voluntary nature of the Fall. And since we are here, we should go a little deeper into Hindu mystic philosophy...

The Hindu Divinity, Ishvara (or Prajapati or Brahma, which are His other names), presents two potential aspects: one male and another female. These two aspects, or these two Persons (Shiva and Shakti), are implicitly contained in Ishvara, they are *perfectly unified*. Therefore, they are immersed in the glorious state of *Advaita*, the state of Unity, of Plenitude, of Integrity, that characterises Divinity. However, at some point, Ishavara feels the need for making His implicit Duality explicit. Remember the *Brhadaranyaka Upanishad*,

179. Leo the Hebrew, *Dialogues of Love*

according to which God, feeling lonesome in his Unity, decides to make His potential Duality explicit. Ishvara feels the need to actualise what is within him in potential, and decides then to sacrifice a portion of Himself to produce the Universe. This self-sacrificing portion of God is the Purusha, the primordial, or cosmic, Man, who in mystic Hinduism is not essentially different from Ishvara. Thus, the Purusha, or more accurately, the Purushas, equivalent to the "sparks" or divine particles from the Western model, exile themselves from Unity, from God, their true homeland. They split into two halves and, from that sacrifice, rise the different dual worlds, the worlds where Duality is, in a larger or smaller measure, explicit.

Some Hindu systems resort (as is the case of the Hebrew Kabbalah and the Neo-Platonic philosophers) to the concept of "emanation". Divinity, they say, cannot stop manifesting Itself continuously. Here, the split of Shiva and Shakti is not responsible for Creation; it's the eternal copulation, or amorous union of this divine couple that generates a continuous process of emanation, or unfolding, due to which all the worlds or cosmic levels come to be, ending with the physical world. Obviously, Divinity will lose its properties throughout Its path... starting with what for Hindu thought is the most important of all divine properties, my dear: *reality*, the property of being, of really existing. In such a way that this world –the last link on that large chain of emanations– appears in Hinduism as something illusory.

Don't let this fool you, though: the Hindu sages who defend this point of view are also trying as hard as everyone else to return to the Origin; they also consider themselves to be "half halves" until they are once again able to access the plenitude of the Unit, the original Integrity of the One.

They think that the cosmic process of divine manifestation responsible for the re-immersion of the Self or the Spirit (*Purusha*) in the cycle of reincarnations, is a process of coming and going; that everything that comes off from the One, will sooner or later return to Him; and they aim to expedite that return. But, at the same time, they don't perceive that continuous manifestation cycle and reabsorption as something negative. It is more like some kind of game; a cosmic game eternally played by Divinity.

Ibn Arabi and other ancient sages put forward a similar conception. In any case, Blanca, I insist: this idea of the Fall as a voluntary descent from Divinity was not the hegemonic one in ancient wisdom. Even Hindu and Buddhist sages could not reach a consensus on it, as two classic texts of Eastern mystic philosophy show: the *Chandogya Upanishad* and the *Dîghanikaya*. In the former, the Fall is compared to the kidnapping of a man by some bandits: they take him from his hometown, blindfold him, and abandon him in a faraway field.[180] In the latter, the Buddha talks about an undetermined number of gods whose memory was fading and, consequently, of how they fell from Heaven and assumed the bodies of men.[181] Even the Kabbalah has opinions regarding this... But I want to stop here for a moment. I would like to open a parenthesis to mention an episode, from a few years back, that will shed light on this tendency of mine to quote from the Kabbalah and to call upon Jewish tradition at any given opportunity. You must admit this intrigues you, and that you even thought I might have gotten myself circumcised, and that I swapped my suit and tie for a black frock

180. *Chandogya Upanishad*, VI, 14, 1-2.
181. *Dîghanikaya*, I, 19-22.

coat and phylacteries, and grew my beard and my sideburns in a curl.

Besides, this episode will take us back to a story from my childhood that I think I never told you, and that you will enjoy because it has a hint of mystery. It turns out that a few years ago I met an Israeli anthropologist who was visiting Spain. Ariel Gershman was staying in Gerona then, but before that, he had been to Toledo and Cordoba, three cities with a rich Kabbalist past. I met him at a small bookshop in the Jewish Quarter of Gerona. We both wanted the same book, but there was only one copy left, so Ariel suggested we split the costs and take turns to read it, which we did. He took a lot more from it than I did, as he was a Kabbalah scholar whereas that was the first book on the subject that I had ever read in my life, and it was not exactly a primer for beginners. The thing is when he passed the book on to me, he had the courtesy of explaining some of the more obscure concepts, and that is how, on a rainy afternoon, chatting at a café in Gerona, we became friends.

At the first chance I had, I talked about you and my detective work; I told him I wanted to study Kabbalah to see if I could find in it some clue that could strengthen my hope of getting back together with you. And lo and behold, he told me that yes, Kabbalah could give me that hope. For a few weeks, Ariel became my tutor in matters of Kabbalah and Jewish tradition, and I turned out to be a diligent student because I was passionate about the subject. And when we got to the subject of *gilgul*, which is the Kabbalistic term for reincarnation, Ariel let slip that he would not be surprised at all if in a past life I had been a Jew. This means that you would have been one as well, my dear, since, back then, Jewish people tended to marry their own, and I cannot conceive a past life in which you were not my wife). And so I remembered that once, when I was a child, to fight the boredom of another calculus class, I invented a name. Not just any name, but a name with which, without it being my own, I could identify. I did not need to think for very long because one quickly sprung to mind. It was a strange name for me, I had never heard it before, it was "Abecassis", with all those letters, including the two s's. From then on, whenever I was tired of being myself (which sometimes still happens), I played at being Professor Abecassis, who was myself while, at the same time, being somebody else. The mysterious part is that, a few years later, I came about that name in print by chance. I found it in the acknowledgements section of a book from my father's library that I had taken with no intention of reading –what I was looking for was an Emilio Salgari novel, imagine that– but still flipped through the pages just to have something to do. That book was about the *Talmud*. This strange path led me to discover the name I thought I had made up as a child. In reality, it was made-up name; it was a Jewish name.

But I was going to tell you about Kabbalah –Kabbalah with a capital "K", as my friend Ariel writes it, as Kabbalists write it. You know, with Kabbalah, it is a little bit like with Hinduism: it is not a unified expression of thought; it is a compendium of different, sometimes even contradictory, mystic speculations and intuitions collected during the course of many generations. One of these speculations is the one laid out in the sixteenth century, and later, by the school of one of the last great Kabbalah masters: Isaac Luria, from Jerusalem.

Luria's dictum about the world and the human being can be summarised by this single word: *Galut*, which is Hebrew for "Exile". Luria (who, as so many other Kabbalists, lived an exemplary life, a *tzadik*, a "righteous" life, the life of a holy man) talked about an initial cosmic drama, of a Fall which had a portion of God as a protagonist. In the words of an authority in Jewish mysticism: "Lurianic Kabbalah presupposes that the process of creation was bound up with a divine crisis, termed 'the breaking of the vessels.' This crisis caused the divine sparks to fall within the 'world of the making' or the 'world of the *Qliphoth*' or demonic shells."[182] The Kabbalist imagines the divine Light stored in a series of heavenly vessels. The rupture of these Vessels entails the transition of primordial Unity to Multiplicity, it entails the disintegration of divine Light into multiple particles or "sparks" that fall into the lower world, where they remain buried under Matter, which covers each one of them as though it were a "shell". Man's mission, Luria says, is to restore the original Unity of the Vessels through the liberation of the captive sparks. (The "shell" that imprisons the spark is Duality, my love, it is Matter's own split Duality –since, besides being scattered, each spark is also split into two halves.)

This version of the Exile or the Fall is based on an ancient Kabbalist theory known as the theory of "contraction" (*Tsimtsum*), which is the replica or counterpoint to that other Kabbalist theory we saw in the previous letter; the "emanation". In this case, what takes place is not an "unfolding", but a "withdrawal" of God over Himself. We have said that, before the Fall, God encompassed everything. Well then, the *Tsimtsum* theory defends that, at some point, God –the Unit– contracted inwards, concentrating at one point. A hole was left outside, an emptiness that was immediately

182. Moshe Idel, *Messianic Mystics*, p. 171

invaded by His opposite –Duality–, thus originating the lower world and the middle worlds too, Blanca, because it was a tiered contraction. Remember all the sunsets we witnessed together from the Palamós Casino square, or from the lighthouse (those sumptuous pink twilights, a little too corny for my taste if I may say so) and you will understand what I mean. For just as there is no sudden jump between the day that is ending and the night that is falling, but rather a gradation, a chiaroscuro escalation, similarly, other worlds remained between the Higher World and the lower world –the former filled with God, the latter "empty". These were intermediate worlds, hybrids of Unity and Duality. Worlds in which God's retreat consisted more of a diminishing, of a fading of His Light.

"The Lord took His powerful Light from a part of Himself", we can read in the *Zohar*, where we can also find a curious metaphor to explain the *Tsimtsum* doctrine. It compares God to a man who finds himself forced to use a tourniquet to interrupt the blood flow in one of his arms. The blood would be the Light (or Life, or the divine Being). The blood would be Unity. The arm in which it would have stopped flowing would then be at the mercy of Duality. It would continue to be part of God's "body", Blanca, as what happened was not an amputation –since, as I told you, there is no "outside of God". Although it would become, so to speak, an orphan of Unity, an orphan of the divine essence.

Such representation of the Universe under the anatomic shape of a man –a divine, androgynous man– is not new in the Kabbalah; one of the most regular symbols is the Cosmic Man *Adam Qadmon*, the primordial Man, the androgynous Adam from the Origin. The *Adam Qadman* is shown wearing a crown, and his different sections are connected to every world. The Higher World is situated above the crown (which many Kabbalists assimilate), and the inferior world corresponds to the feet. If we applied the *Tsimtsum* theory to this anatomical metaphor of the Universe, we could talk about Unity as the flesh that, emanating from the crown, originally covered *Adam Qadmon*'s skeleton –Duality. And we would say that at some point the flesh contracted, it retreated step by step back to its origin in the Crown in such a way that only bones remained of the Cosmic Man's feet. The result, for the ancient sages, is clear: the lower world is a "fleshless" world and –standing before the absence of "flesh" – *a world in exile.*

THE STRAY PEARL

The subject of Exile, as we have said, supports the Fall.

In the twelfth century, a Muslim sage of Persian descent called Shihaboddin Yahya Sohrawardi uncovered the rich esoteric tradition of ancient Persia (a tradition crystallised around the prophet Zarathustra) and, drinking from that venerable fountain, composed several stories about the Fall in the form of parables. Among these stories, Blanca, is the text I mentioned above: the *Story of Western Exile*, which, written in the first person, begins like this: "When, along with my brother Asim, I set out on a trip from the region beyond the river to the Western country, while attempting to hunt a flock of birds on the shore of the Green Sea, we suddenly found ourselves in 'the city inhabited by oppressors', the city of Kairouan. When its residents realised that we had just approached them and that we were the sons of the famous sage al-Hadi ibn al-Khair the Yemenite, they surrounded us, made us prisoners by shackling us with iron chains and they threw us down a well of infinite depth."[183]...

The cardinal points play a prominent role in this story. But first, you must be aware that in ancient symbolism, East and West are thought of vertically rather than horizontally. The East, the horizon's cardinal point from where light ascends –light being a universal symbol of the divine– figured in the Higher World, therefore, in the book of Genesis, the Garden of Eden is located in "the East". We can also think of the mythical East of the German Romantic poets, the *Morgenland* or "land of tomorrow", as they also called it in the Golden Age of classic tradition, the human being's lost Paradise. The West, on the other hand, where the light declines, embodied the inferior world. The middle world, for Sohrawardi, was the "Middle East".

Crossed–out note on the margin. A long quote was erased, only the beginning remains with no dates: *On the northern slope of the Jungfrau...* Looking ahead for other references in later notes on the margin. Let us remember, though, that the Jungfrau is a peak of the Bernese Alps, in Switzerland.

Very well, from the East, from "the region beyond the river", the narrator embarks on a trip towards the West following the sun's itinerary. And he does so in the company of his brother, which –in light of what we've seen so far, my dear– will not seem like a gratuitous circumstance to you. In fact, the myths that narrate how the lower world came to be –the myths of the Fall– often have a couple of twin brothers

183. Quoted by Henry Corbin in, *El hombre y su ángel*, p. 32

as protagonists. These couples represent, as we said, the unfolding of the Original Androgyne into the two persons that integrate it. Now, take this the paragraph of the *Zohar* that says that in the Origin, each soul was composed of a man and a woman united into one single being, and that only upon coming down to Earth did the two halves separate. Or this other one that explains how God created the souls with his breath: "It should be observed that each one of the breaths (the souls) of the world is created male and female; and when they come out (of God's mouth) into the world, they come out male and female and that is when they separate."[184] If we consider both these paragraphs, and other lines of the same nature written by the ancient sages, Blanca, we can presume that the narrator of the *Story of Western Exile* and his brother unfold and become two upon setting out towards the West.

That is to say, that in the East, in the Origin symbolised by the East, the two brothers were *a single one*. They were the primordial Androgyne, as their familiarity with the "famous sage al-Hadi ibn al-Khair" confirms it. Because do you know who the Hermeticists found disguised as this mysterious character? The One, God, because he is the "Yemenite", and Yemen, Blanca, is a geographical symbol of the Hidden Point: the prophet Mohammed felt the "breath of the Merciful One" coming from Yemen. (In Islam, they call the knowledge achieved not through reason but through mystic intuition, "Yemenite wisdom".) The close relationship between the two brothers and this important character suggests, then, that in the Origin they were the Yemenite, they participated in the divine, unitary essence of the Yemenite. And it was

---

184. *Sefer ha-Zóhar*

upon distancing themselves from Him that they lost that unitary essence, splitting into two individuals. (Although in this split we see the primordial divorce of the twin souls, the *Story of Western Exile* has frequently been interpreted based on the "angelic hypothesis".)

The brothers distance themselves from the Yemenite to embark on a trip towards the West, towards the kingdom of Duality embodied here by the city of Kairouan (in modern day Tunisia, which is quite far west for a person like Sohrawardi), the "city inhabited by oppressors". In Kairouan, the Unit, the divine spark that fell from the East, has been held captive, in suspense. This is, Blanca the exile of God in the lower world, the exile of the Unit in the kingdom of Duality. Now, the two brothers are no longer One other than in potential. For them, the Yemenite has become a nostalgia; a celestial reference too: their Father who art in Heaven. Above all, He has become a hope: the hope of one day returning to Him.

There is a Gnostic story –known as the *Song of the Pearl*– written at least ten centuries before Sohrawardi's story, but possibly based on the same ancient Persian parable (although, as I told you, that does not detract from the testimony) as both stories have many points in common. As it happens with most Gnostic writings, its author is unknown; it did not matter who the author was, what mattered was the message. The text in which it is included –*Acts of Thomas*– dates back approximately to the second century. The first thing you should know, Blanca, is that the pearl, the symbolism of the pearl, is comparable to that of the spark: it tells us about the Unity of God in its concretion in each individual. Meaning, it alludes to the whole soul, to the original androgynous soul of the human being. Although there are many pearls, in reality, it is just one *single* pearl. As Ibn Arabi would say: one single pearl under many Names.

Well then, this priceless pearl sunk to the bottom of the deepest sea. From the luminous kingdom of the East, a young prince travels to the antipodean country, the country of the West, this time represented by Egypt (where the Gnostics' ancestors, the Israelites, were enslaved), on a mission to retrieve it. On a mission to retrieve "the one pearl that is in the middle of the sea surrounded by the hissing snake". The sea, a traditional metaphor for the lower world, plays here the same role as Egypt, the symbolic country where (as the ancient Israelites) the prince is imprisoned: its inhabitants gorge him with food in order to plunge him into a deep sleep. "I forgot that I was a son of kings, and I served their king. And I forgot the pearl, on account of which my parents had sent me. Because of the burden of their exhortations, I fell into a deep sleep."[185]... This sleep is allegorical, Blanca, as is everything else in the *Song of the Pearl*: what appears to be an adventure tale, in reality, hides a metaphysical text. It tells us the adventure of the human soul, which due to the Fall lost its Unity, Divinity, Androgyny. It lost it in the world of the split, to where it returns over and over again, in successive reincarnations, with the mission of retrieving it. But, once in this world, the earthly pleasures and ambitions alienate the soul in such a way, that it forgets its true identity and the mission that brought it here...

Naturally, the story continues. But we will stop here. We will have the occasion of picking up the thread in another letter. Because what I want to do now, my love, is to describe the Fall or the Exile to you, from the perspective that seems

---

185. Quoted by Mircea Eliade, *History of religious ideas*

to me the most appropriate: from the perspective of the two aspects or dimensions of God.

AN INSIDE OUT SOCK

Saying that a portion of the One split into two and originated Duality, would be over-simplifying. That is because Duality already existed prior to the split, it existed in the very core of the Unit, except it existed there in an implicit manner. It would be more accurate to say that, with the rupture of the Unit in two, the Duality implicit in the Unit became explicit. Or -even more accurately- that within a portion of God, the genuine order was reversed, the original order of the two divine dimensions, the explicit and the implicit. From the perspective of God's two dimensions, the chronicle of the Fall would be, then, more or less as it follows:

When God "[dwelled] alone, in silence . . . since, after all, [he was] a Monad, and no one was before Him..."[186] (This is not my preamble, I borrowed it from a Valentinian Gnostic. I shall say it now in my own words:) When God was everything that existed, when the skeleton of *Qadmon* was covered in the flesh of divine essence, across the entire Universe the Unit was the explicit and Duality the implicit. Now then, due to the departure of a portion of God from Himself (or, if you prefer, because of the contraction of a part of God), this primordial order was disrupted. There was an exchange of planes: in that portion of God, Unity became implicit, Duality explicit. I will make it visual for you: it was

186. A *Valentinian Exposition,* quoted by Elaine Pagels, *The Gnostic Gospels,* p. 31

like turning a sock inside out. When we turn a sock inside out, what is inside comes outside and what is outside goes inside, does it not? Well, then in a similar way, in that portion of God, the implicit Duality within the Unit became explicit. The Two jumped into the foreground and the One went out of focus and blended with the background. And, because Duality always goes hand in hand with Multiplicity, its jump to the foreground entailed the blossoming of Multiplicity, which up to that point was also implicit in the One...

Right: in practice, this inversion of the original divine order came to mean, for the Two, its divorce. With one exception: Unity became implicit in Duality. Which means, Blanca, that even after our fall, our divorce, the Two remained connected by a bond. This bond is our spiritual kinship, an exclusive and unbreakable bond that prevents the fallen Two from restoring the lost Unit until they come together. Now, from the following words by Plato, uttered through Aristophanes in the *Symposium*: "...so ancient is the desire of one another which is implanted in us, reuniting our original nature, making one of two, and healing the state of man", from these words, we could infer that if the multiple divorce that took place in the bosom of the One was the origin of love, then heavenly marriage will be its end. But no, Blanca, that is certainly not what Plato meant to say. Because for the ancient sages –for Plato as well–, love, far from being something accidental, constitutes an essential and eternal category. Before falling, before its divorce, the Two –the multiple Twos– already loved each other. And will continue to love each other after the final redemption in Paradise because, as it is so beautifully declared in the *One Thousand and One Nights*: "When nothing existed, love existed: and when nothing remains, love will remain; it is the first and the last."

What Plato surely meant was that this multiple divorce was the origin of love *such as we human know it*, the origin of this loving desire, longing, of the nostalgia-tinged love that characterises couples' relationships in the lower world. Ah, but this is not proper love, Blanca! This is more like the love jetsam, the debris of a shipwreck. Love from the Origin, love with a capital L, is the love that eternally operates within the One, it is not a longing or unsatisfied love; on the contrary, it is, by definition, fulfilled. It is consummated, and therefore satisfied, love. It is not thirsty but satiated. "Thirst" is not, as some opine, essential to love; it is a component of fallen love. When the "thirst" is satiated (and this thirst can only be satiated in the One), the "thirst" disappears. That is not so with love: love endures, my dear. And there is a crystal clear reason for that: love is consubstantial to the Two; and we already know that within the One, the Two endures.

In effect, wherever Duality exists, you can say without any doubt that love exists there. In addition, we have already seen that, as the framework of the Universe, Duality exists at all cosmic levels, including at the highest level, at the level of the One. There, love also exists. (but we knew this, did we not?). And more, love exists there in a perfect way, because, this being the type of Duality existent in the One –integrated Duality– the perfect form of Duality, its love constitutes the perfect form of love –and, as a consequence, its model, its paradigm... Note that it is not just that the love of the Two exists in the One. And it is not just that it exists there in its perfect form. It is that this love of the Two shapes the One. *It is the One*, Blanca: that is why it is not madness to say that love, besides being consubstantial to the Two, is what makes it precious, just as what makes an oyster precious is its pearl and not its shell. "There is no God other than Love," said the Sufi Fakhr-al-Din Iraqi in the thirteenth century, paraphrasing the profession of the Muslim faith. He referred to love in general, but preferably to this specific class of love: the love of the Two, erotic love, which is the quintessential class of love, Blanca, the first class of love, in which, in the Origin, the Love that is God was concentrated. It was following the Fall, upon the Two and the Multiple becoming explicit, that this quintessential love opened up to reveal a whole variety of loves, as the petals of a blooming rose-, beginning with the love of God for His fallen portion.

THE MILLION-DOLLAR QUESTION

Tyltyl and Mytyl's oniric trip aside, we have alluded to sleep twice in this letter. The first time concerning Adam, who found himself split into two halves after falling asleep. The second one, relating to the Eastern prince that came down into this world in search of "the pearl" of Unity and fell asleep, trapped in Duality. The act of falling asleep as a metaphor for the Fall from the Original world into this dual world, and sleep itself as the metaphor for staying in it, are commonplaces in mythologies and in the ancient sages' discourse. In fairy tales too, Blanca. The *Sleeping Beauty* template, for example. You know it by heart, so I will just write a quick summary: A young princess lived in a castle in the middle of the woods. One day, while spinning, she pricks herself on a finger, and immediately falls into a deep sleep, for the puncture was subject to a curse. Only the kiss of her predestined prince can awake her. No other kiss can, although many will try in vain.

We must use a symbolic key to interpret this episode, Blanca, a symbolic key provided to us by the theory of twin souls. It is an easy task if we look at its biblical predecessor: the story of Adam's sleep. We can suppose that, just as Adam prior to falling asleep, the insomniac princess symbolises the primordial androgynous soul, that which encompasses the princess and the prince. The act of falling asleep represents the Fall into the world of Duality through the split of the Androgyne into two halves. The prince splits from the princess as she falls asleep, just as Eve separates from Adam when he is defeated by sleep. From then on, every effort will be focused on restoring the primordial Unity of the couple through the reunification of the prince and princess. Such reunification, such marriage, is signified by the kiss; which is an ancient symbol for the union of two lovers (Even today, the first thing newlyweds do to sanction their union, is to kiss). In this tale's primitive versions, it seems that the unification of the prince and the princess was described in a cruder fashion, through a symbol of unification even older than the kiss: coitus. The prince raped the sleeping princess, who then would wake up...

If sleep is equivalent to the fallen and dual state, my dear, then in religious symbolism, *awakening* corresponds to the return to Unity; the restoring of the primordial Androgyne. Allow me to add that a somewhat different version of the *Sleeping Beauty* –a version chronicled by the German poet Heinrich Heine in his *Travel Pictures*–, includes another classic motif of fairy tales: the predestined couple's recognition. In this supposedly more genuine version, when the prince finds the sleeping princess, he is not yet willing to wake her up, so he takes the precaution of cutting a piece of the precious veil that covers her. Thus, after a whole series of heroic tests, the prince's valour finally breaks the curse, and he rushes to be at her side again. And when he asks her "Beautiful princess of mine, do you know me?" she answers: "Valiant knight of mine, I do not know you.", and so he shows her the little piece of cloth she was missing from her veil, which fulfils the power of the *symbolon*: "they both tenderly embrace, and the trumpets sound, and the wedding is celebrated!"[187]

The *Sleeping Beauty* example, my dear, remits us to another case of symbolic sleep: one from the erotic poem of mystical resonances attributed to King Solomon: The Song of Songs. Here too, the soul drowns in sleep, in the sleep of Duality, and is awakened in Unity by the spouse, through amorous union: "Under the apple tree I awakened you; there your mother *conceived you*; there she who was in labour gave birth to you." (Song 8: 5) The reference to the mother (I speak now as an expert Kabbalist would) is not by accident. It is repeated in other parts of the Song where the home or the maternal bedroom is to where the bride leads the groom to consummate their union: "...when I found him whom my soul loves. I held him, and would not let him go until I brought him into my mother's house, and into the chamber of her that conceived me." (Song 3:4) "I would lead you *and* bring you into the house of my mother, who used to instruct me; I would give you spiced wine to drink from the juice of my pomegranates." (Song 8: 2–3) The references to the mother and the house or bed where she conceived point to the place where the spouses separated, there is where the split Duality was conceived. They point to the Hidden Point, Blanca: which at the same time is the soul's bridal bed, for

187. Heinrich Heine, *The Harz Journey*

the original Union of the spouses could only be formally restored in the same place it broke.

Very well, to ascend that high, one must climb back up from the Fall, one must retrace its steps. If I tell you that is what the wife seems to say to her husband when she urges him to "be like a gazelle or a young stag upon the jagged Beter mountains" (Song 2: 17) you will have a big sceptic grin on your face, I can see it now. But if you and I, young and good climbers as we were, would be interested in climbing those mountains, my dear, we would be sorely disappointed. As the Kabbalists observed, the Beter Mountains only exist on a symbolic level: the name *Beter* comes from a Greek root word that means "split into two", "separate". Therefore, the wife from the Song would be urging her husband to overcome the split Duality to reunite with her, to restore their original Unity... Now here is the million-dollar question: How do we achieve this? How can we cross the jagged Beter Mountains?

Actually, no one would pay us one million dollars to answer this question. That is because the answer could not be simpler, Blanca; we don't need to resort to mystic intuition, logic will be enough. Logically, there is only one way to invert the effects of the Fall, to abolish the primordial Unit's split into two, and that is to annul its cause... Let's look, then, at what caused the Fall. Let's answer the question that the novelist Herman Melville put in the following poetic terms: "What Cosmic jest or Anarch blunder / The human integral clove asunder / And shied the fractions through life's gate?"[188] (Imagine this unfortunate blundering Anarchist as one of those bastard Gods whom I told you about towards

188. Herman Melville, *After the Pleasure–party*

the end of the first letter.) Let's then pass this question over to the ancient sages. Their opinion will provide us with the key to answering this other question, which, putting it this way, becomes the million-dollar question: What is the way back to the Origin?

We shall begin by referring to my previous letter, where we described the Universe as seen by the ancient sages. They saw it –we said– as a succession of concentric circles. They named the central point the Higher World or Hidden Point; the following circles were the middle world, and the outermost circle was the lower world. This last one –characterised by Duality, by split Duality– is the circle in which human beings live while they remain embodied. The middle world is the world of the soul, and it is a transition world inhabited by angels and disembodied human beings (you are one of them now, my love). At the centre, in the Hidden Point, lives God. Although it is not as He inhabits it: the Hidden Point *is* God, and His defining trait is Unity, that is, integrated Duality.

When I revealed this cosmovision to you, though, I deliberately omitted one fundamental point, even if I have already alluded to it in the course of these four letters. Now the moment has come for me to openly address it: What is the nature of the lower world? And of the Higher World? (We will leave out the middle world, as it is a gradation between both.) In other words, Blanca: Yes, the lower world is defined by split Duality, and the Higher World by integrated Duality, by Unity. Ah, but what is Unity made of? What is split Duality made of?

Well, then, the ancient sages' verdict is clear and decisive: split Duality is made of *Matter*, therefore it is corporeal. Whereas Unity is immaterial and incorporeal, it is made of *Spirit*.

"That which pervades the entire body, know it to be indestructible. No one can cause the destruction of the imperishable soul... The soul is neither born, nor does it ever die; nor having once existed, does it ever cease to be. The soul is without birth, eternal, immortal, and ageless. It is not destroyed when the body is destroyed... The soul is spoken of as invisible, inconceivable, and unchangeable..."[189] It is with these amazing words that they talk about the Spirit in the Bhagavad Gita, Blanca, in the "Song of God", written over two thousand years ago. Throughout the centuries, the concept has kept the same halo of mystery..., a prestige that has started to fade these days. You know, today the Spirit does not get good press, it has become an outdated concept; people furrow their brow when they hear someone talk about the Spirit. The same circumstances that used to fuel its mystery –that it is beyond thought and that it cannot be seen by mortal eyes– have turned people against it. Now, the world is seen more as a painting rather than a tapestry. The fact that during the course of history, it has been manipulated in favour of spurious interests does not help it. They even wanted to impose it: man should renounce Matter in favour of the Spirit. But isn't incongruous to impose freedom onto someone? Well, this is the same: you cannot impose the Spirit; you cannot impose the Spirit on other people, for that matter: it is conquered within the heart of each person. We will see it in the next letter. We will also see that the progressive conquest of the Spirit is also the progressive conquest of Unity. For the Spirit is what Unity is made of, Blanca. That is why Plato, considering the incorporeal nature of ideas, defined the world of Unity, the Higher World, as a "world of

189. Bhagavad-Gita, 2: 17, 20, 25

Ideas". Each thing in our material world has, according to Plato, its origin in that superior world; everything in this material world is a trace of a spiritual model, of an Idea.

The ancient sages even went as far as abstracting, in Matter, the separative principle responsible for the split. This principle, my dear, is none other than selfishness. And they recognised the opposite principle within the Spirit: altruism; a unifying principle that opens the door for the perfect union of the Two in the Hidden Point. The Spirit is copulative; Matter is disjunctive. Vladimir Solovyov explained this contrast using a famous Physics law: the law of impenetrability of Matter, and the opposite property of the Spirit. Two material objects, Solovyov reminds us, are, unlike two spirits, impenetrable for each other; this makes them mutually exclude each other; they can never occupy the same space at the same time; therefore, they can never merge into one single being.

Described in this manner, Blanca, Matter and Spirit could seem like two essentially different substances, two antagonistic substances separated by an insurmountable abyss. And well, I will not tell you that that was not the belief of certain ancient systems –such as Zorasthrism, Maniquism, and the gnostic systems, for all of whom two different, irreconcilable substances coexisted in this Universe. However, generally, it was more common to believe in the existence of one single substance, one substance that would have adopted, so to speak, two opposing states. We could think of two places antipodes from each other but placed in the same orbit. This orbit or common substrate, this unique elemental substance, the ancient sages called it, among other names, the Being, in allusion to the irreducible essence of everything that exists.

Crossed–out note on the margin. The black marker ink smudges out a large portion of the page's margin, covering what presumably was a quote. However, along with the date (28–8–99) and loose words, we can still read: "...school trip to the museum of.../... an old pocket watch in a shop window... //// Look, this is from my time!" In view of subsequent notes, we can probably date these words to the eighteenth century.

Now let's turn to that image that we already used at the beginning. Suppose that the Being, that this unique substance I am talking about, was water. Suppose that this water is collected in a reservoir at the peak of a mountain and that a catastrophe is afoot: the overflow basin cracks and a certain amount of reservoir water flows down the mountainside as a river. Now, Blanca, suppose that at the peak of this mountain, a constant temperature kept the reservoir water in its original liquid state and that as we plummet down the slope, the temperature progressively goes down too. (I know this is not plausible, but we are only supposing.) We would see that the water from the river would change state as it plunged down the mountain, right? It would gradually go from the liquid state to the solid state. And, when it reached the lower part, the valley, it would have completely solidified, it would have become ice. What does ice do? Ice leaves everything in suspense; it distorts things, it strips their properties of effect... (Instead of Being, we could have also said Light, and then we would be talking about an eclipse, an obscured Light.)

Well, if we can imagine that the water is Being, the only substance in the Universe, then its liquid state corresponds, in our metaphor, to the Spirit and the solid state to Matter.

The Spirit is the Being's true state, the state in which it is itself, its state in the Origin before the Fall, just as the liquid is the original state of water, the state of water in its reservoir. And if the Spirit is Being in its natural state, Blanca, then what is Matter? Obviously, it is an unnatural and anomalous state, the state resulting from the degenerative process in which Being is distorted and temporarily put in suspense, with its potential and dignity plummeting. (In this subject, my dear, I am closely following one of the greatest sages of all time and, if we attend to one of his contemporaries' testimony, one of the holiest too: the Neo-Platonic philosopher Plotinus.) So, Spirit being what Unity is made of, and Matter being what Duality is made of, the aforementioned process in which a portion of spiritual Being from the Origin lost its nature or changed states, is the exact reflection of the process that we described a few pages back: that in which Unity –integrated Duality– transformed into split Duality by falling through the worlds.

That is to say, Blanca, that at the very moment spiritual Unity splits into two, its two halves begin to "materialise", to become corporeal; they become heavy and, thus, they fall. The subtle substance from the Origin condensates and turns into the dense, crude substance that composes the lower world. The lower world is the kingdom of the split Duality, and it is made of Matter. But –and this is an important detail, my dear– Matter does not reside in Duality but in the split: when it is integrated into the One, Duality is as spiritual as the One Itself (if that was not the case, then it could not integrate It). The Two implicit in the One is, then, spiritual. And most of all, their *mutual love* is spiritual, for the fact that it is the mutual love of the Two, upon consummating in *perfect union*, that which conceives the One. It is precisely the innocent, spiritual nature of the love of the Two implicit in the One that -due to the previously mentioned unifying property of the Spirit- holds them in cohesion, merged in *perfect union.*

Very well, I think that now with these clues, it will be easy for you to guess what caused the Fall; what was it that, according to our sages, triggered the "divorce" of the Two and the following degradation of God -of a portion of God- to the rank of man... You guessed it: the cause is a change in the nature of the mutual love of the Two: *in the loss of its innocence*, its spirituality. Or, another way of putting it, my dear: in the intrusion of materiality in its mutual love... What do I mean by "materiality in its mutual love"? You know what I mean, don't play dumb. Materiality in love is sexual desire, which, if you want to know, is an eminently selfish desire and, as such, it is foreign to divine nature, completely alien to the Unit. Sex implies separation and division; the very word gives it away. You know, etymology is a priceless source of clues for detectives in my field, and the word *sex* means "to cut", "to separate"; it comes from the Latin root *sec*, which also originated the verb "section". How could sex, then, have a place in *the One*? As a homage to one of your favourite Agatha Christie books: it would be like placing a *cat among the pigeons*. Which I would not recommend, but, after all, according to our sages, that is what happened. They did not use these words, of course. But this was their idea: sex is love's original sin; Matter, is the Spirit's original sin.

But hey, let me guess, are you grimacing now? For your peace of mind I can tell you that I have not thrown myself into the arms of an Anti-Vice League, nor have I embraced the puritanical ideology of John Calvin, nor am I now a member of a strange cult. This is not the babbling of an old man either, and I have not pulled these ideas out of my sleeve like a vulgar conman: I arrived at these ideas following long years of inquiries in the literary world of ancient knowledge. For years, I have been researching and investigating (entire libraries have been combed for clues), I have been tracking (because often a book would lead me to another and this one to a third one) and exhaustively interrogating the ancient sages in search of answers to my questions. And I have many questions, Blanca, but they all lead to a single one: will I ever see you again? Now I am bringing you the answers I found, so that you, who always reproached me for being a sceptic, know exactly what I believe in.

So, as I was telling you, it was the intrusion of that "foreign body", of sexual desire, into the One that caused a portion of Unity to stop honouring its name and *section* into two. What caused a portion of Unity to plunge into the world of division and Matter. Except this world of division and Matter, Blanca, did not exist before the Fall: it came into existence simultaneously with it. In fact, the rupture of Unity lead to the emergence of the split Duality and, with it, the "split" worlds, which are the middle worlds and the quintessential split world, the lower world. Hence the ancient sages seeing a correlation between the Fall and creation (the almost instantaneous creation described in the Bible) of the physical Universe.

This correlation holds an implication that deserves to be addressed, as it is connected to mythological and early religious postulates. As a result of the infiltration of sex in the love between the two Persons of God, the physical Universe appears to us as the fruit of the sexual intercourse between those two Persons. This matches the primitive descriptions of the creator gods: bisexual gods that created the Universe by copulating with "themselves", that is to say, with their divine couple. These gods, my dear, would embody the two Persons of God corresponding to His fallen portion. In other words, they are no longer One. Or rather, they are the One at the very moment He falls, the One at the precise moment in which the Two implicit in Him desecrate love by swapping spirituality by the sexuality of intercourse.

There is yet another exception we should point out. It is regarding the idea of infiltration or intrusion of a foreign body in the One. It is like when I told you about an "outside of God": it is only a manner of speaking, a rhetoric expression that is useful for us to understand each other, but that it turns out to be false if we take it literally. In fact, taking the concept of infiltration literally here would prove false because it presupposes the existence of two different and independent substances, one of which ingests the other. And I already told you that although that opinion has its supporters, they were not the majority among the ancient sages, who instead believed in the existence of one single universal substance. It is not as if the love from the Origin found itself invaded by an alien love. It would be more precise to explain it by saying that this high love became distorted, emptied of content, by losing its innocence, its original and defining spirituality. It is not as though a strange liquid infiltrated a water bottle: it is more like the water spilt from the bottle.

THE SLEEP OF MATTER

You will remember that the cause of the Fall is typified in the Genesis by the ingestion of the forbidden fruit from the Tree of the Science of Good and Evil. As its name indicates, Blanca, it is the tree of Duality, of split Duality, that is, the tree of opposites. Also known as the Tree of Death, it is opposed by the Tree of Life, the tree that is characterised by Unity and which fruit fed Adam and Eve in Paradise before they were tempted by the insidious serpent. The fact that the instigator of the transgression was a serpent is equally revealing, as –like dragons and reptiles in general, who live at ground level– the serpent has been, since antiquity, a symbol of Matter. And that is even without mentioning its phallic and sexual symbolism: I read in an anthropology article that, among the peoples of the Middle East, circulated the superstition that snakes instructed men in the performance of intercourse. And, you know, the mere act of plucking the fruit from the tree is indicative of the kind of transgression in question. Because "plucking fruit" was a common euphemism for the sexual act. In addition, tradition says that the forbidden fruit was specifically an apple, an old symbol of earthly desires and sexuality in particular. I don't need to remind you that what caused a famous fairy tale character to fall into a deep sleep (or into a fallen, dual state, which is the same), was the ingestion of an apple.

And since I mentioned *Snow White*, my dear, if we go ahead and extract the "reverse side", the original symbolism of this tale (as we did before with *Cinderella* and *The Sleeping Beauty*), you will see that it will appear to us as a kind of *naif* recreation of the Fall. Just like the sleeping beauty, the still awakened Snow White represented the original state of the soul, its divine and androgynous status before falling. A status characterised by spirituality, which –with its connotations of innocence and purity– is also evidenced by the name

"Snow White", the name of the soul before the Fall -just as Cinderella[190], with its insinuation of grey and darkness, would be the name of the soul after the fall. The carrier of the apple, in this case, is a witch instead of a serpent, but it is the same thing. When Snow White eats the apple, she loses her "whiteness", her innocence, and, as a result, she falls into a deep slumber. Only the kiss of her prince, of her twin soul, can rescue her from this sleep, which is the same as that of *Sleeping Beauty*, the sleep of split Duality.

I have already talked about how the kiss is the ancient symbol for the *perfect union* of two lovers. Now, I will add that this union is a union of souls and not of bodies for, in a kiss, breaths come together, and the breath was the quintessential stereotype of the soul, the spirit. *Pneuma*, *ruach* and *ruch*, respectively the Greek, Hebrew, and Arabic words for *soul*, literally mean "breath", which in Abrahamic tradition, is what God blows on Adam to bring him to life.

More clues. Numerous esoteric traditions point to the appearance of concupiscence, that is to say, of selfish and material desires, of sexual desire, as the triggering factor for the Fall. There are many Gnostic systems that talk about the Fall as the result of a voluptuous falling in love of a god: following that sexual act, the dual and material world would have come into being. Hermeticism also germinated the idea of an amorous slip as an explanation for the Fall. "and he that knew himself -states the *Poemander*- (meaning, he who recognises himself for what he is: a spiritual being of divine filiation), came at length to the Superstantial of every way substantial good. But he that through *the Error of Love*, loved the Body, abideth wandering in darkness,

190. Cinderella, as in "little cinder girl".

sensible, suffering the things of death."[191] Because, for the old Hermetic sages, Blanca, carnal desire goes together with death, it is in the origin of the loss of divine immortality. In the same Hermetic masterpiece, we can read: "And let Him that is endued with Mind, know Himself to be Immortal; *and that the cause of Death is the Love of the Body...*"[192] "O ye People, Men, born and made of the Earth, which have given Yourselves over to Drunkenness, and Sleep, and to the Ignorance of God, be Sober, and Cease your Surfeit, whereto you are allured, and invited by Brutish and Unreasonable Sleep!" [193]

An old Indian parable in the vein of the Persian *Story of Western Exile* and the Gnostic *Song of the Pearl*, regales us with an Eastern example. Once upon a time, an old Yogi Master called Matsyendranâth, who, blinded by curiosity about physical love, managed to get his spirit into the body of a young man who had just died, bringing him back to life. In this borrowed body, Matsyendranâth satisfies his curiosity, but at that very moment, he falls into a state of amnesia. Having forgotten his true identity, he is imprisoned by the women of Kadali, a country that in this story symbolises Matter and the lower world. It falls upon his disciple, Gorakhnâth, to save him and bring him out of his amnesia. And just look at the original scheme he comes up with: to attract the attention of his master, he adopts the suggestive shape of a dancer. But his dance contains an encrypted message, it is loaded with symbols; symbols that restore the master's memory once he deciphers them.

---

191. Corpus Hermeticum, *Poemander*, 39–40 (italics by the autor)
192. *Ibid*, 38 (italics by the author)
193. *Ibid*, 75

Another Eastern example, my dear, is from same Buddhist doctrine. In fact, Buddhism identifies concupiscence –*lobha*– as one of the three causes (the other two are wrath and ignorance) of this diminished life that is human life. Considering that the source of *lobha* is selfishness, the Buddha says that the most efficient way of fighting it is through altruistic thought: it is by thinking of others, of your neighbour's physical and spiritual well-being, before your own. According to the Tibetan Book of the Dead or *Bardo Thodol*, of all the attractions with which Matter tempts the soul of the deceased to prevent its liberation and compel it to remain stuck in the cycle of reincarnations, the union of the flesh is, by far, the most successful. Hence the Lamas who watch over the dying trying to persuade them to pass away with only the thought of pure love in mind. This means, Blanca, that for the Buddhists, sexual desire would have been not only the cause of the soul's initial Fall but also the main responsible for the successive and repeated reincarnations of the soul in this lower world.

The rise of sexual desire as the responsible factor of the Fall is also –now back in the West– one of the key aspects of Pietism. And as I believe your knowledge of this religious movement is probably limited to a mention in a violet-blue book (the young Vanenka from *Anna Karenina*, "that angel of kindness" as Tolstoy defines her, counts among its followers), I will tell you that the Pietistic movement was born in the bosom of the German Lutheran Church in the eighteenth century. In line with our sages, the Pietists emphasised their followers' mystic intuition and inner experience over religious dogmatism; and they had an evolutionary vision of the world in consonance with that of our sages (I will expound on this vision of the world in my next letter). Besides, for these mystics, the goal of the human being was none other than androgynous perfection: i.e. the return to the Origin, since another central point of Pietist thought is that God would have created Adam as an androgyne. And this androgynous perfection, Blanca, can only be reached, according to them, through a predetermined love, and that is how conjugal love, for Pietists such as the Count of Zinzendorf, plays the role of saviour.

I have warned you that I am not much in favour of citing influences. But mentioning here that Jakob Boehme was a source of inspiration for the Pietists will allow me to once again bring up this seventeenth century Christian theosophist and, specifically, his interpretation of Adam's sleep...

Boehme suggests that when Adam fell asleep (the androgynous Adam, ergo an Adam indistinguishable from God), "he imagined himself in Nature (*Physis*, in Greek)". That is to say, he imagined himself in the physical world. He dreamed of himself in material form, split into two halves. Matter –and split Duality– slipped into the androgynous and spiritual Adam from the Origin as he slept. Disciples of Boehme, such as J.J. Wirz and Gottfried Arnold, would specify Adam's "material fantasy" by saying that he had imagined himself mating "like the animals" with his "hidden wife": that is the reason why Eve separated from him. The German theosophist Michael Hahn shared the same opinion. For him, Adam's mistake (and, inversely, Eve's mistake, although Hahn does not say so) was to feel a carnal desire towards his wife Eve, whom he would have tried to sexually possess. "If Adam had always possessed his wife spiritually –he writes–, she would never have separated from him." (This aggressive act, if you allow me the hindsight, would be in the origin of the "debt of tears" that, according to the *Story of the*

Stone I mentioned in my first letter, the soul contracts in the Origin with its twin.)

Around the same time, our friend John Milton wrote the Archangel Michael saying following words, regarding Adam and Eve:

> Their Maker's image, answered Michael, then
> Forsook them, when themselves they vilified
> To serve ungoverned Appetite; and took
> His image whom they served, a brutish vice.[194]

In other words, Blanca, according to Milton's Paradise Lost, Adam and Eve lost the "Maker's image" within them (so, Divinity and Unity) due to the intrusion of "brutish vice", meaning concupiscence, in their mutual love.

AN AMOROUS INFIDELITY

The idea of a material deviation in the purely spiritual love from the Origin, the love of the Two implicit in the One, is also suggested –as I have said– by the recreation of the Fall offered by the *Poemander*. But before we attend to this treatise again, Blanca, I should provide you with some context for it.

To talk about the *Poemander* is to talk about a philosophical current that has its roots deep in Western esoterica: Hermeticism. And if we are talking about Hermeticism, then, first, we must talk about its cradle, the Hellenised Alexandria from the dawn of our era. You will see that some of the ancient sages that parade through our letters –I am thinking

194. John Milton, *Paradise Lost*, XI, 515–518

of Origen, of Philo, of Clement of Alexandria- have this city's name added to their own. But there are many others -such as Plotinus and Proclus, the Gnostic master Valentin and the astrologer Ptolemy- whose name could be linked to this Egyptian city by the use of an epithet. All of them lived there during a fertile period in its history: the early years of Christianity. We could claim, without exaggeration, that for those first centuries, with a few parenthesis, for almost a millennium, Alexandria stood as the mecca of ancient knowledge and, for that very reason Blanca, of ideological tolerance. In that cosmopolitan city, all the philosophical currents and scientific schools of the time, all the mystical tendencies of the West and the East and all the religious denominations, including a wide range of sects, coexisted in harmony. And the thing about harmonious coexistence is that it promotes fusion: the blending of influences and mutual enrichment. It was here, then, in this sort of Noah's Ark of ancient wisdom, in this fertile field of ideas, where Hermeticism was born -and Neo-Platonism as well, and Gnosticism, and Christianity as practised by the Greek Fathers of the Church, and Alchemy...

Hermeticism owes its name to a legendary Egyptian sage who was a contemporary of Moses: Hermes Trismegistus, meaning Hermes the "Thrice Great". The prodigious corpus of Hermetic literature was lost for the entirety of the Middle Ages. It was during the Renaissance, in Italy, when some texts, the *Poemander* among them, were salvaged based on Byzantine copies. These copies were compiled in what today is known as the *Corpus Hermeticum.* You know, Blanca, the discovery of a lost spiritual text, is one of those things that, according to the sages, does not happen by chance. It is said that books such as the *Poemander*, the *Zohar* or the Gnostic

Gospels were waiting for the right moment to come to light so that their wisdom would not be wasted. Actually, there is a beautiful old story about how the *Corpus Hermeticum* finally saw the light of the day; I know you will like it. They say that in a house in Alexandria, a stone statue stood atop a wooden column. People worshipped it as an image of a great wise man of Antiquity and often looked below his feet, for an inscription compelled them to do so if they wished to "know the secret of the creation of beings and how Nature was formed". No one ever could find anything below the statue's feet, but one day a little boy moved into the house, and when he grew to be able to read the inscription, he understood its true meaning and looked not below the statue's feet, but underneath the wooden column. Thus he found an underground chamber, and in the chamber, a tomb presided by the imposing statue of a sitting man. The man held an emerald tablet with carved hieroglyphs saying: "Here is the formation of Nature"; and in a luminous book by his side: "Here is the secret of the creation of beings and the science of the cause of all things."[195] That tablet, Blanca, was none other than the *Smaragdine Table*, the famous founding text of Alchemy; the book was the *Corpus Hermeticum*, and the statue and tomb were that of Hermes Trismegistus.

We cannot say whether this great wise man really existed, but if so, his legend surpassed him when it identified him with Thoth, the god of knowledge in ancient Egypt, assimilated by the Greeks into their Hermes. Real or apocryphal, Blanca, Hermes Trismegistus has been traditionally been given the role of patron of esoteric and hidden wisdom (hence the adjective *hermetic* being used to describe anything secret);

195. Balînûs (Apolonio de Tiana), *Kitâb sirr al–Halîka*

so we can assume that some of our sages would resort to him at the time of scrutinising, with the eyes of the second sight, the "reverse side" of the Universe. Furthermore, it is no wonder that such an honour fell on a sage from Pharaonic Egypt, a mythical civilisation, if there ever was one, for the ancient sages of the West who gave it the reputation of the cradle of ancient wisdom. And even if this mysterious character turned out to be a sage of flesh and blood, Blanca, he could not possibly be the author of most of the books from Antiquity that were attributed to him: Only in Alexandria, there were about twenty–five thousand! Which justifies, or is justified by his reputation as protector of libraries and inventor of writing. The name "Hermes Trismegistus" was a catchall name to which everything of uncertain authorship in esoteric wisdom was attributed. Books, aphorisms, symbols, even the foundation of Alchemy, Hermetic art par excellence, are spuriously attributed to him. There were many ancient sages, though, that opting for anonymity, credited their own work to a legendary sage: that is what the author of the *Zohar* did and, certainly, what the authors of the Greek texts attributed to Hermes Trismegistus and compiled in the *Corpus Hermeticum*, of which the *Poemander* is the first book and cornerstone, did as well.

Do you know how I imagine the author of the *Poemander*, Blanca?

Maybe it is because of the superhero comics from our childhood, but I imagine him living a double life. In the morning, he works, say, as an artisan, or maybe he manages a pharmacy (like Attar, the Sufi poet) in a bustling street of Alexandria. But then, in the afternoon, he dedicates himself to the laborious task of writing that sort of pagan Genesis –as his book has been described. In the afternoon, he turns into Hermes Trismegistus just as the shy reporter from the Daily Planet transformed into Superman when the occasion required it. I squint and it is as if I can see him: there he is, sitting at a table by the candlelight, in the great hall of the Library of Alexandria, which according to records housed up to one million manuscripts (how insignificant is the blue library next to it!). Thoughtful, with the quill in his hand, he shuffles through the Greek dictionary in search of the right words to describe the Fall. To narrate it exactly as his mystic intuition presented it to him, which was a little something like this: The primordial Man, whose nature was "male and female at the same time", lived happily in the Heavenly Kingdom since his essence was no different from that of God. But he had the imprudence of looking downwards, instantly falling in love with Nature –with *Physis*. In one word, he fell in material love, which caused his fall into the lower world, "and Nature... imprisoned him in its hand"[196]. Now, split into two (because, as a consequence of the Fall, "the bond that united all things broke...; all living creatures, having been up to that point bisexuals, became split into two... and thus they became male and female"[197]), now, I say, "it is dominated by carnal desires and by forgetfulness". By a forgetfulness of the same type as that which afflicted the protagonist of the *Song of the Pearl*, my dear; it is not for nothing that the central myth of Gnostic tradition is related to that of Hermeticism.

In fact, the Gnostic myth also tells us of a drama within Divinity: in summary, it says that blinded by a desire for knowledge of the flesh, a portion of the *Eones*, or the incorporeal *Syzygias* that eternally integrate the luminous sphere

196. Corpus Hermeticum, *Poemander*, 39–40 (italics by the autor)
197. *Ibid*, 18

of Divinity –the divine Pleroma–, turned towards Matter and was immediately engulfed by it.

Among the spiritual traditions that interpreted the Fall as the perverse effect of a deviation in the love of the Origin (in the love of the Two implicit in the One), there is one that I cannot help but mention: The legend of the Holy Grail. There is a lot to say about this legend, Blanca, and, although I will do so mainly in another letter, I can start by saying that the Grail symbolises the original state of the human being, his lost Integrity. It appears in an enchanted castle, a castle of uncertain location and difficult access, inhabited by a King who has lost his Integrity as well as his Kingdom. The scenography of these apparitions has the magic, supernatural quality of dreams. And maybe that is precisely it, you know? The expressing of the dream, the expressing of the diminished King's nostalgia, the Fisher King who dreams of restoring his lost Integrity.

In the story of the Holy Grail, there are two explanations for the Fisher King (he is fishing enthusiast, like me) and his Kingdom's fall from grace. One of them is the so-called *Elucidation*. It describes the original state of the Kingdom as a paradisiacal state in which the blessed knights enjoyed the chaste companion of supernatural women: beautiful virgins that served them plentiful food and drink in cups of gold: a way of saying that they enjoyed perfect bliss. This, Blanca, is a description very similar to Valhalla's in Norwegian mythology, where the virgin Valkyries look after those who fell in combat. Or to how the ancient Celts described their Paradise, located on a white and secret island, the island of Avalon, later converted into the Land of Faeries from the tales. It also has a hint of familiarity with the Muslim Heaven, which is a Heaven populated by beautiful and always virginal *huries*, instruments of the blessed one's bliss, whom the ancient Muslim sages imagined, as I mentioned, living in the centre of pearls (a symbol of Unity, of *Tawhid*, as they say in Arabic), each one of them in the company of his predestined *huri*. It is not inconceivable that the anonymous author of *Elucidation* was inspired by one of these Heavens when it came to characterise the Kingdom of the Grail before the Fall. In any case, for him, the loss of this paradisiacal state would have been due to the blessed knights' breaking the sacred law upheld in that kingdom: chastity.

Another Grailic explanation for the Fall is the one offered by Wolfram von Eschenbach in *Parzival*, the German version of the legend. To write his version, Eschenbach claims he based himself not on the first known version, the *Story of the Grail* by Chrétien de Troyes, but on an earlier text, also written in Old French, and itself based on another Arabic text. Wolfram stresses that only knights who are "chaste and pure" can perform the service of the Grail.[198] And he specifies that the Fisher King's malady (the King is called Anfortas here, from the Old French *enfertez*, "infirmity") was because the King -whose motto was the word Love- "yearned for love outside chastity"[199], a behaviour incompatible with the Grail, according to Wolfram. The author applies this judgement to another interpretation; one that claims the Grail King "fell" for having turned his eyes towards a woman who was not his. That is to say, towards a woman who was not the one the Grail had assigned to him, as we can count among the Grail's innumerable virtues the power of magically arranging the marriages of all those who are affiliated to its lineage.

---

198. Wolfram von Eschenbach, *Parzival*
199. *Ibid*

The Grail King fell, then, for having been unfaithful to his wife. But Wolfram insinuates that there is another way of looking at this infidelity, Blanca. For him, to look at one's own wife with inappropriate eyes, with lascivious eyes, is in itself a kind of conjugal infidelity. This detail provides us with the key to understanding an enigmatic reflection made by Parzival when he marries Blanchefleur or –as Wolfram calls her– Kondwiramurs, "She who leads to love". In fact, at least in the German version, this marriage holds a symbolic character, it is a nuptial rite similar to those practised by the Gnostics, and it consists of them lying down on the same bed together without any kind of sexual contact, because –Parzival reflects– "if now I craved carnal love, infidelity would act instead of me."[200]

This notion of the Fall as a result of an act of conjugal infidelity, Blanca, pointedly agrees with an old Hindu legend relating to the god Shiva and his Shakti, his "wife", embodied by the goddess Parvati. In general, in the Hindu Origin myths, Shiva, compelled by the creator god Brahma, expels his feminine side away from himself with the intent of creating the physical Universe, and she strives to reunite with him. But this legend I am telling you –recorded in a mythological text called *Skanda Purana*– inverts the rules: Parvati, furious because of Shiva's flirtations with another woman, decides to break off their marriage and separate from him. Shiva then goes to her and implores: "You are the offering and I am the fire (the fire that receives the offering), I am the sun and you are the moon. So you must not cause a separation between us as if we were two separate persons."[201] Such

200. *Ibid*
201. *Skand Purana*, 1.3.2, 18–21

words disarm the goddess, who once again agrees to contract matrimony with Shiva, and thus he incorporates her in his own body –in the left side of his body–, restoring the primordial Unit.

THE HIDDEN WIFE

Now let's return to seventeenth century Germany, to Jakob Boehme and his disciples. In these Christian theosophists' texts, Blanca, Adam's original "hidden wife" is called Sophia. They borrowed this name; if you paid attention to my letters, you will know from whom (it was from the Gnostics: that is what they called God's feminine person.) The Boehminists reserved the name Eve for the earthly, "fallen" wife; the manifested wife, the wife after divorcing her husband. For them, "Sophia" was not a woman's name like "Eve", it was a Goddess name and in their texts, they referred to her as such. "Celestial Virgin" or "divine Virgin", they called her. And they insisted that it is this Woman for whom men feel true longing: she is the secret object of their quest for the twin soul. And any man who believes he has quenched his thirst for love by marrying Eve on Earth is merely fooling himself with a pale imitation, because, deep down, it is with Sophia he aspires to marry. With Sophia, who had been his wife in the past, in the Origin. You will notice that I am talking from a male perspective –I am following the theosophists in this–; but evidently, my love, this subject has two sides. If we were to stand on the opposite side, we would talk about Eve's original "hidden husband", whom we would not call Adam but some other name, so we could distinguish the "hidden husband" from the manifested one.

Yet besides this sexist omission, my dear, the Boehminists, in my view, committed a far graver mistake. They placed such emphasis on the "celestial Woman", that they lost sight of a basic fact: they forgot that Sophia is Eve, except she is Eve in her true and original form. That is it, Blanca: Eve and Sophia are the same person; just as in the story of *The Frog Prince*, the frog and the prince are one and the same: the frog is but a lesser version of the prince, he is the prince having fallen from grace. To take another variant of that same tale: this beggar we see today is none other than the Queen from yesteryear, now divorced, for whom her ex feels nostalgia, and about whom he still dreams in secret. "It is always the lost woman who sings in the imagination of man", wrote André Breton, the French surrealist poet, "But she must also be –he added–, at the end of their trials, the rediscovered woman."[202] Given Breton's great interest in esoteric tradition, it is safe to assume that among the subjects of his studies, we could find Tarot. I know that I am not saying anything new by saying that Tarot cards are the prototype for the modern playing cards, but did you know that, unlike these, the Tarot cards enclose hidden meanings? Meanings encrypted in them by their creators, probably members of some medieval underground society, who wanted to secretly disseminate through those cards their esoteric knowledge. I am talking about Tarot, my dear, because there is a card of this mysterious deck that appears to illustrate the dilemma to which I was referring, the false quandary between the Queen and the beggar, between the "celestial Woman" and the "earthly woman". In *The Lovers*, Tarot's sixth Major Arcana, we can see a man who, at some point in his path, arrives at a

---

202. Andre Breton, *Arcane 17*, p. 56

crossroad. This crossroad is personified by two women; one is wearing a crown, the other is not (in some versions, the other one is wearing a crown made of grape leafs). One represents the heavenly Woman, the other the earthly or "fallen" woman. Both women have also been seen as embodiments of spiritual and carnal love respectively, but I will not go into that now. In one of the oldest versions of this card, from the Marseille Tarot, a winged archer –Cupid– hovers above the man and, given where his arrow seems to be pointing, appears to be favouring the earthly woman. Apparently, the man is attracted to both women, but he must choose one and so his heart is torn.

This Marseilles card is rich in meaningful details. For one, the earthly woman is so similar to the man –the illustration's central character– that one could say they are twins: the same facial traits, the same expression, the same blonde hair, the same simple clothing. Whereas the woman wearing a crown looks nothing like him. In fact, he and the blonde woman seem to form a couple: they are facing each other, one next to the other, in a sort of embrace (the brunette and crowned woman is standing in the foreground, in profile). Everything points to the man having arrived at that place in the company of the blonde woman; that is when the other one appeared to him, and now there he is, torn between the two... We could suppose, Blanca, that the card's author was aware (and that would be the card's hidden message) of what you and I already know: the correct answer in *The Lovers* is not to choose one of the two women, because, deep down, they are one and the same at two different points in time. The celestial Woman or Queen corresponds to a distant past (and a distant future); the earthly woman or the beggar is the woman of today. The beggar is the dethroned Queen: this is what Boehme and his disciples seem to forget when, arriving at this fork in the road, they favour one over the other. They also seem to forget (although here the forgetfulness may be only apparent) that the man is also a beggar, a dethroned King; that both of them –man and woman– are on equal footing. They fell together and now they must rise together. It is up to both of them to get rid of their rags –of their materiality, of their selfishness– and to cover themselves in the dignity of Royalty: that is, spirituality, *virginity* in the jargon of these theosophists.

My eyes are getting heavy with sleep, my dear, I am forced to finish this letter. But before, let me just add that these inner and correlated processes of shedding and covering are quite slow: the beggar couple will not recover its royal dignity, Adam and Eve will not look at each as they did in the Origin –with pure eyes, with "virginal eyes"– before they go through a long process of learning. In the following letter, we will deal with this arduous learning process in which we, whether we want to or not, are immersed. Now, I would like to close this one with that mysterious, sacred object that fell from Heaven, the Holy Grail, of which we said it appeared in dreams (maybe the weight on my eyelids is the accumulation of dreams brought up by this letter) in a castle of a dethroned and fallen king; a king who strayed from Royalty by losing his original Integrity, which is precisely what the Grail reminds him of. Ah, but look: in those apparitions, the Grail is inseparable from the beautiful maiden who carries it. This maiden is the Queen of the Grail and her splendour is as great as that of the holy object she holds: "So fair her face that they thought it was the morning's dawn."[203] Wolfram insists on

203. Wolfram von Eschenbach, *op. cit.*

this Queen's "virginity", on her purity (the Grail itself is, as she says, "all purity"). How can we not see in this Virgin Queen, bearer of the Grail, the Fisher King's "Sophia"? His original wife from whom he was painfully separated when he intended to love her "outside chastity"? The King lost his Integrity because of that traumatic separation. In the story, this is symbolised by his failing health following a "painful wound" that left him crippled. Now the King dreams of the lost Integrity that is embodied by the Grail. But Integrity is, in his dreams, inseparable from his other half. Hence, the Grail always appearing before him carried by the same beautiful maiden... and this maiden being a *Virgin Queen*: because that is the image the Fisher King has of her. That is how he remembers his twin soul from the Origin.

Yours

FIFTH LETTER

EVOLUTION

(OR THE RETURN TO THE ORIGIN)

...we know what we are,
But not what we may be.

William Shakespeare

Barcelona, September 12th, 1999

Dear Blanca,

Can you see how, little by little, letter by letter, my hope of us being together again is beginning to take shape? Because if you and I are two halves of the same thing, if you and I share the same essence, then we can only hope to share the same destiny as well. That destiny, Blanca, can only be the restoration of our tiny fraction of Unity. Because our Origin is in Unity, my dear, and it's a law of the Universe that everything must return to its original state. According to the ancient sages, the Fall is reversible: us Two are called upon to return to the One from which we fell, to once again make our essential Unity explicit. The process is underway. You and I are now on our way home, on the long path back to the Origin, a path of improvement ("Each one travels towards his perfection", says Attar in the *Conference of the Birds*). And that trip, my love, involves you in my case, and vice versa. It involves each person's twin soul. A progressive amorous approach to the twin soul that culminates in the fusion with it. Only this fusion can bring us Unity.

So, the soul can only reach Perfection by interacting with its twin, therefore the twin becomes the key to return to the Origin, to the return to the soul's Home. This Home is a duplex, a house for two, and it's the same house for every couple of twin souls, Blanca. Because there are no multiple Ones: each couple of twin souls that merged into "one [spiritual] flesh only" is fulfilling God, the only One. This consummation of erotic love in God should not surprise us if we think –along with the ancient sages– that the reality in which we are immersed is a cyclical process where the goal was also, in the past, the starting point. If erotic love has its roots in God, wouldn't it be natural that its finishing line would also be in Him?

We'll call the spring that launches us in this Homecoming, this return to the Origin, *Evolution*, which is a synonym of maturation and growth. "Each blade of grass has its angel hanging over it, whispering '*grow, grow*'", you can read in the *Talmud*, suggesting that the entire Universe conspires in favour of our growth... Look, Blanca, us human beings often ask ourselves what is the meaning of our existence. We mainly ask it at times such as those I was going through when I started this research: when we are unhappy. In those moments, we like to think that our afflictions are not sterile, that there is a good reason for us having bothered to appear in this world. As a rule, when we are happy we don't pose these questions, and if we do, we say that the meaning of life is to enjoy it. The ancient sages were convinced that there is, in fact, a good reason for being in this world. But this reason is not just to be happy, or, better yet: the goal is to be happy, yes, but that's not a short-term objective but a long-term one. The objective is the *supreme bliss* of the Origin, the happiness of the One; not the limited, fragile, and often-paltry happiness we can enjoy in this world...

Don't get me wrong: I'm not saying happiness is not a desirable bonus in life. What I'm saying is that it's not its purpose; the meaning of life is something else. We're not here to be happy, we're here to *grow*. And growth usually goes hand in hand with suffering, that's just how it is. In fairy tales, if you remember, the hero's trials and tribulations are necessary for his evolution. Because what truly matters in life, Blanca, are not the external vicissitudes, pleasurable or irritating, that happen to us, but the internal ones, the movements of our soul. And the soul is tempered in hardships, it's how it matures and lives up to its potential... I could quote from many ancient sages to support this claim. From the great Athenian tragic poet Aeschylus, who wrote, "It is a law: he who learns must suffer", to C.G. Jung, or the thirteenth century Christian mystic Hadewijch of Antwerp, who stated: "If one does not suffer, one does not grow". Even a person as sensual and hedonistic as the Irish poet and playwright Oscar Wilde. In times of suffering, he recognised that pain is the nourishment of the soul, writing, " love of some kind is the only possible explanation of the extraordinary amount of suffering that there is in the world... because in no other way could the soul of man, for whom the world was made, reach the full stature of its perfection."[204] Well, we could find the same idea in the East, dressed as the concept of *karma* or the cosmic law of the fair retribution of actions.

As harsh as it may sound, my dear, a misfortune in life may be providential to help us react and correct the mistakes

---

204. Oscar Wilde, *De Profundis*

made in previous lives. We grow by correcting mistakes and, as people learn better what they discovers by themselves, suffering is often the only way to becoming aware of our mistakes. So, even if sometimes the contingencies of our lives may appear adverse, in reality, they are favourable. Favourable for our growth, which is, in the ancient sages' opinion, the only criterion to consider when assessing a life: if it helped us grow and mature, then it was a rewarding life... Now I'm thinking about a funny scene I saw in a film some time ago and I'm smiling. The film was called *The Tiger and the Snow*, and in this scene, a literature professor is lecturing his students about the conditions propitious to write good poetry. He's exhorting them to never waste a good opportunity to suffer: "suffer, suffer everything you can", he tells them, remembering that most great poets forged their soul in the anvil of suffering.

Given your current circumstances, my dear, what I'm about to say will probably sound obvious to you, but I'll say it anyway: there is a form of happiness independent from the avatars of existence. I'm referring to a happiness that does not exclude pain because it's not the opposite of pain, it's its integration, the overcoming of suffering. This type of happiness, reputed by the ancient sages as genuine happiness, depends on the extinction of material attachments and selfish desires, and the Buddhists, mainly, have pointed out how to achieve it. They call it the "Noble Eightfold Path": right view, right resolve, right speech, right conduct, right livelihood, right effort, right mindfulness, and right meditation. Of course that, to honour such righteousness, one would have to be quite ahead in the Evolution path (or maybe one would have to be as you are now: disembodied). To walk this path here on Earth means, in Buddhist doctrine, to definitely escape *karma* and suffering, and to put an end to the cycle of reincarnations: that is, to reach the peak of Evolution.

Evolution is a slow growth. Therefore, it's connected to becoming, to Time; it began with Time and with Time it will end, once it has completed its mission, which is to bring the fallen souls back to their Origin. Because it's the *soul* that grows, it's the soul that evolves in the course of Time through successive reincarnations. As the great Indian sage, Sri Ghose Aurobindo proclaimed, "The true foundation of reincarnation is the Evolution of the soul." Reincarnation and Evolution: two inseparable concepts. You know, we could apply Greek philosopher Heraclitus' principle to the soul; the principle that says that everything changes, that we can't bathe twice in the same river because the water flowing in it is always different. The soul is always different as well because it flows, it's in continuous evolution.

Of course, the soul's physical support, its "rack", has also evolved parallel to it, until it ended up at the very complex rack that is the human body. That's how our soul, Blanca, before embodying a human being, has climbed up the ladder of beings: it has embodied bacteria, fish, reptiles and mammals. But –and this is the important point– the rack's evolution has always been subject to the needs of the soul. When the rack is needed to support a –let's say– a meagre loincloth, a simple hook does the job. But now, if what we need is to hang an elaborate evening dress or a tuxedo with top hat included, then what we need is a complex contraption with many arms. Naturally, from the mechanistic perspective that characterises science, this conception is unacceptable: the spirit –they say– is nothing more than a by-product, an appendix, an extension of its rack. For the orthodox scientists, Blanca, you could not be reading this letter, given that you don't have a rack made of atoms and molecules to support you. For science, the spirit follows the evolution of the rack and not the other way around. The ancient sages, on the other hand, believed that not only is the spirit independent from its rack, it generates and adapts it as it sees fit. The physical support (starting with the consciousness's elaborate rack: the brain) is nothing more than a vehicle for the soul. The body is to the soul what the conducting wire is to electricity: electricity comes from the wire, it needs the wire to manifest itself, but it's not generated by the wire. The soul is not generated by the body, it exists prior to it and –in the case of human beings– comes "from above". Every time the human soul descends upon the physical world, it adopts a "rack" made of atoms and molecules to conduct itself through.

A TRANSITIONAL BEING

Evolution began a long time ago, long before man burst onto the cosmic landscape. In the previous letter, we saw that the ancient sages interpreted the Fall as a reduction of God; as the degradation of a portion of God (a minute portion: what are a few sparks compared to a great Fire?) to the rank of man. It's not a bad definition, Blanca, but it's reductive, it's a rough description; things are not that simple. Thanks to the research performed in the nineteenth century by that great Hércules Poirot of Nature, Charles Darwin, today we can refine that definition and claim that, in the beginning, the Fall was much sharper. In reality, its extent was enormous since, having started from Absolute Consciousness, it would have led to the opposite extreme: to unconsciousness, pure nothingness. Only after a great and eventful *Evolution*, could the divine particles or "sparks" embody man.

Anyway, my love, this was not a big secret for the ancient sages. They, our compatriot Ramón Llull for example (the great thirteenth century Catalan mystic and philosopher), perceived the ladder of beings, from the simplest to the most complex: from the plants to the animals and from the animals to man, and from men to the Angels and finally God. They also perceived a certain continuity between the different rungs. They even intuited the soul's slow progression up the ladder. Thus, long before Darwin laid bare the evolutionary ancestors of the human being, the ancient sages had already spoken of man's previous existences as animals. "I was a bird and I was a darting fish in the sea", reminisces the Greek philosopher Empedocles, around five centuries before Christ.[205] And a great Muslim mystic poet, a contemporary of Lull, Jalal ad-Din Rumi, wrote verses as striking as these:

> I died as a mineral and became a plant,
> I died as plant and rose to animal,
> I died as animal and I was Man.
> Why should I fear? When was I less by dying?
> Yet once more I shall die as Man, to soar
> With angels blest; but even from angelhood
> I must pass on: all except God doth perish.
> When I have sacrificed my angel-soul,
> I shall become what no mind e'er conceived.[206]

---

205. Empedocles, *On Purifications*, fragment 117
206. Rumi, *The Masvani*

The ancient sages, then, intuited the evolution of species, Blanca. What happens is that, unlike scientists, they seem to have not given it much importance. They considered that what really mattered began only when Evolution made itself present in the human being. The years, they probably said, only make sense if man is here to count them. For them, the cosmic drama fluctuated between two poles: a higher one, God, and a lower one, man. From this point of view, the billion–year process from the *Big Bang* to the appearance of man would have only been a long prelude, a long labour to give birth to the second pole of the cosmic drama. The actual cosmic drama would only begin with the appearance of man (with the flowering of the consciousness and free will of man): the human adventure of the *return to the Origin*.

You know, there's an old myth that I have come across several times during my research, that shows how the ancient sages had the intuition of the extreme depth of the Fall. It's the myth according to which the sparks that came off the original Fire would have plunged into the Abyss of Nothingness forever if God had not interfered. Meaning, my dear, that according to this myth God did not stand idly by as a portion of Himself fell, he did something about it. What God did to stop the Fall, to make the sparks run aground before hitting the bottom, was to create the world, to place it in their path and to create the fruit of the world: man (don't confuse this mortal man created by God with the immortal Man, the uncreated resident of Paradise)... I find it likely that the ancient sages who devised this myth vaguely intuited the truth: that, at the first, the Fall had reached the bottom of Nothingness, the Non–Being or Chaos. But God rushed in aid of his fallen portion and from Chaos He extracted Order: the lower world, this world that would become the uterus for the birth of man as well as the custom-made background for the human adventure.

The divine creation of man would have consisted, then, of a rescue. Before elevating them to the human level, God would have rescued his fallen sparks from Nothingness, from the unconscious abyss where they fell and from where they could not escape by themselves (again, be good and don't confuse, as many have, this state of absolute unconsciousness with the Origin and the Home of the soul)... So, Blanca, it turns out the Genesis was right when it insinuated that God extracted man and the world from Nothingness. Although creation, this rescue, would have taken a lot longer than seven symbolic days, as it's written. The creation of the world and man would have taken God billions of years. Let's say God planted the seed where, after a long germination, the world (the world as we know it: the world made to human measure) and man would sprout.

Now then, go ask a farmer if he plants only one seed to get the fruit he wants; you know what he'll tell you, right? He'll tell you that in the beginning, crops require a lot of care. If the ancient sages could have seen the history of the physical Universe in perspective –as the astrophysicists of today can–, from the formation of the first stars until the eclosion of consciousness, they would not have failed to notice the hand of God everywhere, hidden under the silken glove of chance: there are so many coincidences that had to happen in the course of that long cosmic process, Blanca. It's true that they too, like the astrophysicists, would have felt some kind of vertigo at first, a feeling of waste when confronted by the enormity of space-time magnitudes (The number of galaxies in the Universe is estimated at about two hundred billion, and the age of the Universe in thirteen thousand seven hundred million years!). But perhaps they soon reflected about something that the astrophysicists are now only beginning to realise, my dear: that, given the improbability of the development of consciousness, such enormity of magnitudes was also an indispensable condition. When a farmer is committed to introducing a specific type of fruit in his fields, he doesn't care about how many hectares he has to sow just to reap one sprout, or how much time it takes for it to germinate.

I could even cite you some eminent scientists (starting with Jean–Batiste Lamarck, a predecessor of Darwinism, who at the beginning of the nineteenth century already conceived Evolution as "a natural process guided by an impulse for perfection"). Some eminent scientists who recognised in this long process of evolution a certain direction, a secret tendency towards conscious life, that is, towards man. Of course, Blanca, those same scientists avoid invoking a transcendent cause, an invisible hand behind Evolution. But if we open our mind, is a kind God that unthinkable? A God that –just as a rich man would rescue his suddenly bankrupt family members from misery– would extend a helping hand to His fallen portion to bring it back up to the light of consciousness?

Crossed–out note on the margin: Once again, I credit my friend C.B. for recognising, based on two single words, this poem by Emily Dickinson: *"Alone / I cannot be / for ghosts / do visit me / recordless company"*

Well then: what's most astonishing about this subject is that Evolution doesn't stop at the appearance of consciousness and man. "Man is a transitional being", declares Sri

Aurobindo. The apparition of man marks a milestone, but that's not Evolution's endgame, it's only the end of its first phase. While the fallen sparks embody man, a second phase begins, and this still incipient second phase, which will culminate with the ascension of man to the divine rank, is to what the ancient sages paid most attention, Blanca. They were not interested in the sparks' slow elevation from Nothingness to the human level. Why bother with something that had already played its part, they probably thought, with something that belonged in the past, over which we had no control? We attained some control in the second phase, when our free will came into play. Each one of us is actively involved in this phase of Evolution, my dear. If during the first phase's billions of years, Evolution had worked, let's say, in auto-pilot (a pilot activated by God immediately following the Fall), then from hominization forwards, each spark took control. Before that, we had already been the protagonists of a film we could call *Return to the Origin*; but after that, we also became the directors.

The second phase of Evolution is consciousness and it's associated, as I told you, to the concept of reincarnation. Only consciousness reincarnates. Therefore, Blanca, when Empedocles says, "I was a bird and I was a darting fish in the sea", he's not strictly speaking about reincarnation. Whereas he's doing so when he says of his master, Pythagoras: "When in fact he tensed all the powers of his mind, he easily saw all the things that is, in ten or twenty human generations."[207] To reincarnate, there needs to be something that reincarnates, and that something, that flame that (to employ a traditional metaphor you'll enjoy) that moves on to another

207. Empedocles, *On Purifications*, fragment 129

candle when the first one is consumed, is consciousness. Consciousness, as the German Romantic Novalis wrote, "is the peculiar essence of man fully glorified, the divine archetypal man."[208] That which has not yet reached consciousness is likely to become, after death, immanent to the physical world; it dilutes in the physical world as sugar in coffee, so that it can then reorganise into a new, slightly more evolved shape. This is how, my dear, since the dawn of time, we've been climbing the steps of the evolutionary ladder until we arrived at the landing of consciousness.

And it's precisely here where we can find another discrepancy between the two phases of Evolution: the first one is a progressive conquest of new, gradually more complex organic shapes. The amino acid turns into a fish, the fish becomes an amphibian, the amphibian turns into a reptile, the reptile into a mammal, and the mammal into a man. These are, let's say, "external" conquests. On the second phase, on the other hand, these are "interior" conquests: to evolve, man does not need to go beyond the confines of the human form; he grows on the inside –in his soul, in his consciousness– while always remaining a man on the outside. The human rack is complex enough to support even the most elaborate clothes. Only at the conclusion of Evolution (with the heavenly marriage of the twin souls, if our theory is on the right track) will the human form evolve into a divine form. At the end, the human form must also be replaced, Blanca, because –as Goethe suggested– everything that exists in this world, exists in function of its process of becoming something else: "Everything perfect in its kind has to transcend its own kind, it must become something different and incomparable."

208. Novalis, *Henry von Ofterdingem: A Romance*, p. 125

The second phase of Evolution culminates, then, with the restoration of the original Divinity of man. It's the preparatory road that leads to that restoration and, of course, it consists of going back the same path, the one that once went from God to man. Only by correcting, by annulling the cause of the Fall, will man be able to rise up to his true and original condition. Towards the end of the previous letter, we saw what this cause might have been, in the opinion of our sages: we talked then about the infiltration of matter in the mutual love of the Two, do you remember? Well, Blanca, if that is so, then the return to the Origin must be the result of the "dematerialisation" of that love. The Two took the path of desire to come down to humankind; now it's the human Two who is climbing back up that path in the opposite direction, to recover its Divinity.

Very well. Doesn't it sound obvious that to dematerialise our mutual love, us twin souls are called upon to dematerialise ourselves? Of course, I don't mean the kind of dematerialisation that you, unfortunately for me, are enjoying now, my love; I'm not talking about the physical body. We've already said that the physical body was but a vessel for our development through the outer circles of the cosmic mandala. When I say that we're called upon to dematerialise, I don't mean so much the vessel but the *pilot*: I'm talking about the soul, Blanca, the human soul can also be material –in fact, it is so to a greater or lesser extent. It's material in the sense that it's anchored to Matter, stuck to Matter, in the sense that it's dominated by its instincts and material desires, in the sense that its focus is turned "downwards" instead of "upwards", in the sense that it's selfish.

According to this, we'd have to differentiate (as Plotinus does, for example, when he says that that the human soul has a double nature, it's heavenly on the higher end, terrestrial on the lower) two aspects in the human soul or in the Self. Or, if you prefer, my dear, we'd have to differentiate (as the Sufis do) two souls within the human being; one is material, the other spiritual. Both are present in each human in different proportions, depending on the soul's evolutionary stage. The spiritual Self is the true face of the soul, its true Self. The other one is, so to speak, a mask, a blanket of matter in which the soul covered itself when it fell into this world, and thus it's a false self. (The ancient Jewish and Christian sages, who also believed in this kind of "material clothing" of the soul, hermeneutically justified their belief by invoking the verse from the Genesis in which, immediately after being banished from Paradise, Adam and Eve are covered in "garments of skin": "And the Lord God made garments of skins for the man and for his wife, and clothed them.", Genesis 3:21)

This false self is so vain that it sees itself as the navel of the Universe. The Sufis compared it to the Egyptian Pharaoh, who considered himself the centre of everything. This false and egocentric self inherent to every human being, this "carnal" or material soul that is the source of instincts and concupiscence is known by the Sufis as *naf*. In the West, we call it *ego*. Both words describe the same thing: a sort of material clothing that is not the physical body but still covers the human soul, preventing it from realising its full potential. Evolution consists of the gradual stripping of these clothes, the progressive release of the soul's material ballast so that it can soar back to the homeland from where it fell. Thus, the soul could be compared with a hot air balloon (like the one we rode that one time in Granada, remember?): like the balloon, the soul naturally tends to go upwards, but it finds itself attracted to the ground by all the ballast it carries, all the negative impulses derived from selfishness and Matter. To rise, to liberate its original heavenly nature, the soul must make an effort to sublimate itself, to become lighter and more volatile: let's say that the soul must grow wings.

In support of this fundamental postulate of our theory, Blanca, I will begin not by quoting from a religious figure, that would be too easy, but from a literary one: from one of the French literature greats, Victor Hugo, who in his *Intellectual Autobiography* notes: "All Creation is a perpetual ascent from beast to man, from man to God. The law consists of stripping us more and more of Matter, and covering us more and more in Spirit." The genius Catalan philosopher, Francesc Pujols said that the Spirit tends, through an indefatigable natural process of Evolution, to progressively distance itself from Matter. This sage (beautifully nicknamed "Clock Tower Sage", after the place where he lived) takes the ladder of beings described by the medieval mystic Ramón Llull, which goes from inert Matter to God, and imagines the Spirit gradually climbing that ladder. Pujols was a fellow compatriot and a contemporary of ours, Blanca, that's why I mention him here. But he wasn't the only (we have those verses by Rumi I transcribed above) nor the most meticulous annotator of the Spirit's slow crystallization, of the soul's process of growth or decantation. The most meticulous annotator was another modern sage of "ancient perspective": the French Pierre Teilhard de Chardin, who will be our guide for this next part.

A SWERVING CAR

Teilhard de Chardin was a Jesuit. But, as with so many other former clergy members (such as Origen and Clement of

Alexandria and John Scotus Eriugena...), his heterodox opinions earned him the reprobation of the Church. In addition to his religious studies, Teilhard had a solid scientific background, excelling as a palaeontologist, a subject to which he devoted many years of research in China. Science gave him a description, in evolutionary terms, of the formation of the Universe. But, you know, Teilhard wasn't one to be satisfied with merely observing the front side of the "tapestry", so he took the trouble of looking at the other side. There, he descried something that gave meaning to the physical Universe. He descried a *purpose*. He saw the Universe evolving in a predetermined direction with a specific goal.

Of course, this wasn't anything new: many ancient sages before him had approached the hidden side of the Universe's development and had seen that secret purpose. We owe the next example to Henry Corbin, who salvaged the Ismailist text containing it from oblivion. The text is called *Book of the wise man and the disciple* and although we can't be sure when it was written, it dates at least as far back as the tenth century. It's structured, as its name suggests, as a dialogue between a wise man and his disciple. The former tells the latter: "The ignorant man's lie when he compliments the world is obvious, for he ignores the hidden meaning ('the inner reality' adds Corbin), that which God wanted for the world. Their opinion is that God has created the world without it having any meaning at all. Now, God's creation of the world was not a mere game. If the world was in itself its own purpose, there would be no way out; this creation would be absurd, for every creation that leads to nothing is ridiculous, and all discourse that lacks meaning is nonsense."[209]

209. Translated from Henry Corbin, *El hombre y su ángel*, pp. 114–115

Crossed–out note on the margin. A few fragments were saved from which –thanks to a reference made further down– I managed to identify three verses by Rabindranath Tagore, taken from his *Later Poems*: "*We two shall build a bridge for ever / Between two beings, each to the other unknown, / This eager wonder is at the heart of things*."

The idea that there is a meaning to this physical world, Blanca, that there is a secret purpose for the Evolution of the Universe, is something that even today most scientists –accustomed to only seeing the front side of the tapestry– have a hard time accepting. Albert Einstein's famous opinion that "God does not play dice with the Universe" has received little recognition from his colleagues. Science's most widespread opinion is that Evolution is like a boat adrift, guided by chance –not by "necessary chance", but by the kind of chance that does not obey the secret order of things– and that as such, the Universe is not predestined: it's not being pulled towards a goal, towards a destiny that has been fixed beforehand. Science makes only the following caveat: While life in the universe arises fortuitously, once it emerges, it adopts what we might call an immediate purpose, a short–term objective: survival. Life –they say– only thinks about perpetuating itself, about guaranteeing its continuity through reproduction. For science, then, Evolution would be like a moving car going nowhere, a car that its only purpose would be to go on for miles. Whereas for Teilhard, the car didn't hit the road for no reason, without having an exact idea of where it wanted to go and how it could get there. Of course, unexpected things may happen on the way; eventually, the car might even take a wrong turn; but it always comes back to the programmed route. Teilhard intuited a goal for Evolution, a long-term objective. Do you know where he intuited this goal to be? In the long process that led to the appearance of erotic love on Earth, as well as the following maturation and sublimation process in which, according to him, erotic love has been immersed ever since.

Let's quickly examine the evolutionary path that led to the emergence of erotic love on Earth, Blanca; you'll see that this examination will reveal a curious fact.

In the dawn of life (life was the result of one of those "random" concatenations of events to which I referred earlier) reproduction was asexual. The organisms, which were then no more than bacteria, reproduced by simple division: they split into other identical organisms, that is, they duplicated themselves. Then (and this "then" means after one billion years: just so that you have an idea of how difficult and improbable these changes are), this reproduction system fell in disuse, being replaced by the current system: sexual reproduction imposed itself quickly. The thing is, my dear, that if this change appears convenient from an evolutionary point of view, from an individual perspective it's an inexplicable extravagance. What caused organisms to all of a sudden come up with a new reproduction system out of nowhere, when everything was in favour of keeping the old system, which was more practical and efficient? With this new system, reproduction didn't depend on one single individual anymore, now it required the interaction of two individuals. Moreover, these two individuals had no need to be different from each other, they each could have incorporated both sexes (as it already happens with certain species), which would be a lot more reasonable, in terms of survival of the species, by ensuring a greater reproductive capability. But this is where, against every prognosis, a clear differentiation between those two individuals emerged: one of them became a male and the other a female, thus establishing the foundations of erotic love.

The cherry on top of Nature's approach to love was the human species' adoption of the "face to face" sexual position –which is, as we've seen, the spouses' emblematic position.

In view of all this, Blanca –and of the lack of a convincing scientific explanation–, this detective can only subscribe to the words of the Romantic author Friedrich Schlegel, when he defined love as "Nature's greatest sacred miracle"[210]. The greatest, but not the one and only. Another example of a "miracle" is the emergence of free will, which, as one of the most conspicuous tenants of your library (G.K. Chesterton) said, is the "valour and dignity of the soul"[211]. That's because, from the individual's point of view, my dear, the old decision–making system –genetic programming– was the perfect system. For an individual accustomed to blindly following the rules of nature because he's programmed to do so, to evolve towards another system that, by granting him freedom of choice, entails the difficulty of discerning between good and evil, is to complicate his life for no reason.

Now this is the curious part: the car of Evolution suddenly swerves, rejecting easy paths in lieu of venturing along uncertain roads. Would we say that the purpose of the car is simply to move along? To move along at all costs, no matter where? Teilhard doesn't think so, Blanca. For him, it's evident that the car of Evolution is moving towards a specific and predetermined finishing line. He calls this line the "Omega Point". The Omega Point is the Kabbalists' Hidden

210. Friedrich Schlegel, *Kritische Ausgabe*, V, 67
211. G. K. Chesterton, *Heretics*, cap. VII

Point expressed in evolutionary terms: being the last letter of the Greek alphabet, the *omega* gives the idea of the last link on a long chain. Just like the ancient sages, Teilhard imagines the Universe in the shape of a mandala, in the shape of concentric circles around a central point. This Point is the Universe's goal. It's hidden because it's *inside* the Universe. Evolution goes inwards from the outside, from the visible to the invisible (being, in each case, *one's self* the very door to the "inside"). It's a slow process of interiorisation, it's the Universe diving in itself (*inside* also means *above*, and *outside, below*: Evolution is also an ascension). So, for Teilhard –and for the ancient sages–, the goal of the Universe, then, is within the Universe itself. It's the Centre of the Universe. This Centre, this Omega Point towards which everything will end up converging is, besides interior, *spiritual, conscious* and *personal.* And simultaneously with its progressive interiorisation, the Universe, then, tends to a progressive spiritualisation, a growing consciousness... and an increasing personalisation as well.

"The Universe is in the process of personalisation"[212] declares Teilhard... There's an idea here that may surprise you, my dear. It's the idea that the personal goes far beyond the human category, the idea that the human condition is nothing more than a milestone (a key milestone, yes) in the transit of the Universe towards absolute personalisation, which is an attribute of the Hidden Point. Considering that the Hidden or Omega Point, in spite of not being human, is of a personal nature, Blanca: it's the supreme Person –as it's also the supreme Consciousness and Spirit. Now, then, this supreme Person is incomparable to the human person. Be-

212. Teilhard de Chardin, *op. cit.*

cause, you know, among the ancient sages (and now we're getting into a rough and narrow road that we should leave as soon as possible, lest we go astray), it was a commonly accepted principle that, in reality, the supreme or absolute Person *transcends the personal*. In other words, because He is personal, God surpasses this category, so He is beyond reach, and not just for intelligence now: for mystic intuition itself. Beyond a certain point, where there are no more footholds, intuition loses its footing and it has no choice but to stop there, on the threshold of where revealed Divinity becomes hidden (*Deus absconditus*, "Hidden God", in Latin), where the personal God becomes an unknown and unknowable God. There are no references to this God, nor can there be: it's an absolute unknown. Nothing is known about Him, and therefore nothing can be said... except this, maybe: that He is a suprapersonal God, a God that transcends the personal (and not an impersonal God, as many believe). That's why the ancient sages stayed one step below the *Deus absconditus* and talked about God as a personal being. Same as we do –following their example– in these letters.

There's a very common false impression in the West, Blanca. Generally, people tend to believe that this idea of God as a personal being is an eminently Western idea, when in reality almost every religion identifies the Hidden Point with a personal being. We've already said that Hindu belief systems –and Eastern belief systems in general– are innumerable. Of course, then, we can find the belief in an impersonal God: Brahman. But the opposite belief, as well, which is just as widespread or more. In fact, numerous Upanishad schools present Brahman itself as a personal God. The Hindu Ishavara ("Lord") is a personal god. In the "Upanishad of Upanishads", as they call the *Bhagavad Gita*, he's referred to as "the highest Person", the supreme Self. In other Hindu sacred texts, when they avoid talking about God as a person, that is because they are alluding to the *Deus absconditus*, to the "hidden God", about whom nothing is known and nothing can be said. In the Vedas, the two conceptions of God –personal and impersonal– co-exist: in some texts, they refer to Brahman, "the Absolute Person", in others Brahman, "the Absolute". We can even find (certainly because of interpolations and edits made over time) both notions appearing mixed in the same text. That's what happens in the Upanishad we cited before, the one where they talk about the original split of the One into two: first, it's said that the One is a Person –*Purusha*– ("In the Origin, this world was one Soul in the shape of a Person"[213]), but further down, when they're reiterating that first verse, they swap *Purusha* for *Brahman* ("In the beginning this [world] was indeed Brahman, one only"[214]).

Since we've moved to India for now, the great Indian poet, Rabindranath Tagore (author of that beautiful sapphire-blue book, *Later Poems*) often told a curious parable, whenever someone talked to him about the One, the Absolute, as something impersonal. He imagined a record player and an alien (yes, you've read that correctly.) Let's suppose, he said, that while exploring the planet Earth, an alien happened to hear a human voice coming from a record player. If he only went by appearances, we would think that the music, the voice he heard, was the product of something as impersonal as the spinning of a disc on a metal box. He would have to make an abstraction effort to find the truth, to realise that,

213. *Brhadaranyaka Upanishad*, 1.4.1
214. *Ibid*, 1.4.11

beyond the record player, there was a person, a person who gave it its voice.

THE HUMAN MOLECULE

Teilhard de Chardin conceives God in *personal* terms. He writes, "I cannot conceive an evolution towards spirit which does not culminate in a supreme personality. The cosmos cannot, as a result of its convergence, be knit together in *something*; it must, as already happens in a partial and elementary way in the case of man, end upon *someone*.[215]" The path to overcoming the Fall, what we call Evolution, has to necessarily go from *Something* to *Someone*, Blanca, since the Fall consisted of the inverse transition (although actually, the starting point, as we believe we know, dates much further back to Nothingness or Non–Being). From the numerous versions of the Fall offered to us by the Kabbalah (except we're not talking about a Fall in the strictest sense here, but more of a voluntary descent), the most succinct one says that the *What* split off or emanated from the *Who* (in Hebrew: *He* split off or emanated from *Me*). The *What* or the *Something* is Matter, the unconscious, the impersonal; it's located in the outer circles of the cosmic mandala. The *Who* or *Someone* is the Spirit, consciousness, the *person*, and it lives in the Centre, in the Hidden Point.

Do you see, my dear? Matter is the quality of the impersonal, of objects, while the Spirit is personal. Human beings are in the middle of those two characteristics, between the *Something* and the *Someone*. We already are "someone", but

215. Teilhard de Chardin, *How I Believe*

we're still "something" too; our soul is still connected to an *ego*, it's still a carnal soul. The next evolutionary step consists of letting go of our *ego*, or our "something". The ancient sages saw this step (which, in its second phase, is the responsibility of each one of us) as an internal process of purification, of *undressing*. "Some people are afraid that they may arise from the dead naked, and so they want to arise in flesh. They do not know that it is those who wear the [flesh] who are naked. Those who are [able] to take it off are not naked."[216] As you have probably guessed from the cryptic and categorical style, that is a fragment of the Gnostic Gospel of Philip. Out of all the ancient sages, Blanca, the Gnostics were perhaps the ones who more often used the metaphor of internal stripping as man's essential task. Thus, in the *Saviour's Dialogue*, Matthew asks Jesus for "the place in Life... where there is no darkness, but a pure a light", to which Jesus responds, "While you carry that flesh, you will not see it." Another example is a saying that we already cited here, although in a different context (the vague symbolism of the Gnostic sayings is not limited to one meaning only), "When you disrobe without being ashamed and take up your garments and place them under your feet like little children and tread on them, then will you see the son of the living one, and you will not be afraid."

So, the individual's soul is called upon to undress, to gradually strip itself from *ego* in the course of Evolution. But Teilhard, Blanca, does not lose sight of the idea that the Evolution's protagonist is not the individual, it's the couple, or the individual as a member of a couple: i.e., the individual as a spouse. For Teilhard, Evolution is, above anything else,

216. *Gospel of Philip*, 56

the Two's return trip to the One. "The mutual attraction between sexes is such an essential fact -he writes- that any biological, religious, or philosophical explanation in the world that does not find a place for it, would be virtually condemned to fail[217]". And he adds: Evolution "forces the simple personal elements to complete themselves in a couple .../... it's not limited to the individual, it goes beyond it, towards a perfect concentration"[218]. It moves towards what Teilhard calls "the complete human molecule... a more synthetic and spiritualised element than the individual-person to begin with. The human molecule is a Duality that carries the male and the female at the same time."[219]

This spiritualised human molecule composed of two atoms, male and female, is none other than... can you guess it? The Androgyne, of course. The Androgyne, whom we know lives at the centre of the cosmic mandala, and who is a third Person, separate from the two whose mutual union conceives it. "Elementary personalities -confirms Teilhard- can, and can only affirm themselves by acceding to a psychic unity or higher soul. But this always on one condition: that the higher centre to which they come to join without mingling together has its own autonomous reality. Since there is no fusion or dissolution of the elementary personalities, the centre in which they join must necessarily be distinct from them, that is to say, have its own personality."[220] (The claim that in the One there is no fusion nor dissolution of the primary persons -meaning the Two, but also the Many-, would

217. Teilhard de Chardin, *Sketch of a Personalistic Universe*
218. *Ibid*
219. *Ibid*
220. Teilhard de Chardin, *Human Energy*

have to be understood in the sense that the Two will remain implicit in the One resulting from its union.)

Let's agree, then, that the protagonist of Evolution is not so much the individual soul but the soul *as a spouse*. The protagonist is the soul inasmuch as it's another soul's twin, and this is because the goal of Evolution –Unity– is fulfilled, for each soul, upon the restoration of their own original Unity, this being, if we agree with our theory, the Unity they composed with their twin in the Origin. That is why, my love, Evolution has always worked so hard to pave the way for the emergence of the intersexual relationship and, through it, of what our old friend Swedenborg called the "conjugal state": the face to face relationship between two twin souls. Because that relationship is the crucible for the refinement of erotic love, which is the glue that holds the couples of twin souls together in Unity. And look, Blanca, love on its own is not enough: for its gluing effect to work, it must be free of impurities, it must be naked. Hence, Evolution's determination to not only implement erotic love in this fallen world, but to exalt it to its very quintessence, to the highest degree of purity and nudity inherent to the One. The undressing of erotic love thus stands at the junction of Evolution, just as Teilhard emphasises:

The most expressive and profoundly authentic way of counting the universal Evolution, would no doubt be by following the footsteps of the evolution of love.

> The most telling and profound way of describing the evolution of the universe would undoubtedly be to trace the evolution of love. In its most primitive forms, when life was scarcely individualised, love is hard to distinguish from molecular forces; one might think of it as a matter of chemistry or tactisms.

Then little by little, it becomes distinct, though still confused for a very long time with the simple function of reproduction. Not until hominization does it, at last, reveal the secret and manifold virtues of its violence. 'Hominised' love is different from all other loves, because the 'spectrum' of its warm and penetrating light is marvellously enriched. No longer only a unique and periodic attraction for purposes of material fertility; but an unbounded and continuous possibility of contact between minds rather than bodies; the play of countless subtle antennae seeking one another in the light and darkness of the soul; the pull towards mutual sensibility and completion, in which preoccupation with preserving the species gradually dissolves in the greater intoxication of two people creating a world.[221]

"ULTRAVIOLET" LOVE

If you paid attention to this paragraph, you noticed that Teilhard mentions the "spectrum of light" regarding hominised love. What we'll do now, Blanca, is elaborate on that metaphor. We'll draw the profile of erotic love's Evolution, the Evolution of the mutual love of the Two, and we'll do it with the same images handled by Teilhard de Chardin in his writings. But before we start, let me remind you that when we talk about the Evolution of love, it's implied that we are referring to Evolution in its second phase, that is to say, to human Evolution, since that it's with man that an indispensable condition for love appears: free will.

Teilhard borrows the spectrum of electromagnetic vibrations of light and uses it to build a metaphor. The light

221. Teilhard de Chardin, *The Spirit of the Earth*

spectrum is the whole range of colours, all the variety of colours existing in Nature. A part of this spectrum is invisible to the human eye and that's why this metaphor is suitable, as we'll see. Teilhard imagines a "love spectrum" comparable to that of light and says that, at the beginning of love's Evolution, the range of colours visible to the human eye (to love) was minimal. Only the colours on the lower end of the spectrum were visible to us, Blanca: meaning pure sex, without the soul's involvement. The Evolution of love, says Teilhard, is the on-going history of the human being's slow and gradual conquest of the colours on the higher end of the spectrum. We have now reached the point where we can have a still-precarious glimpse of a colour with high vibrations: a love in which sex is secondary and dependent on spiritual love. This vision is still very frail, but it should settle down little by little. Maybe we still have a few thousands of years to go, who knows? Even then, we still won't have reached the top of the spectrum; there will still be heights and colours above it to discover. Human love will not stop evolving, Teilhard says, until it reaches the highest colour of all: *ultraviolet*; in other words, purely spiritual love, a love independent from sex. "Love is the threshold of another Universe. Above the known vibrations, the iris of its shades is still growing. But despite the fascination the low-end colours hold over us, the creation of light will only move towards the ultraviolet. It's in these invisible and immaterial zones where the authentic initiations into Unity await us."[222]

Let's go over this last sentence for a moment. According to it, love's slow turn towards the "ultraviolet colour" supposed the lovers' initiation into Unity. Meaning, Blanca,

222. Teilhard de Chardin, *The Evolution of Chastity*

that the Evolution of love towards the Spirit constitutes, for Teilhard, an initiation, an indispensable preparation for the unification of the Two, for their return to the Origin. And this is because (as I've said) *the Spirit is, in essence, unitive*; it tends to unite, to make opposites coincide, to make them complementaries in virtue of that fundamental property of the Spirit: altruism. Because opposites oppose one another the same way each one looks towards itself rather than the other: selfishness isolates, altruism brings together. There is a sentence by Teilhard that you'll love, a very beautiful definition of true love: "Love –he says– means to place one's own happiness in someone else's happiness." Only a love of this kind, an altruist and purely spiritual love –a completely evolved love, an "ultraviolet" love–, can unify the Two in such a perfect way that it results in a third Person (God, the One) different from the mere sum of both parts.

> **Crossed–out note on the margin. I was able to save two short fragments from the long erased paragraph: *...who fought a duel...* and: *...stopped the carriage on the side of the road.* Duels and carriages are two typical eighteenth century elements, a recurring period in these notes on the margin.**

Our Universe, the physical Universe that finds its conscious embodiment in humankind, is evolving, and this is the same as saying (knowing, as Teilhard de Chardin knew, that love is the core, the very heart of the Universe) that human love is evolving. As I said, this is a very long road and we've just turned the first corner. We still have many "colours" to discover before being able to say we've reached the summit of love. Colours that lead to a territory unknown to most people: "Beyond a certain degree of sublimation, spiritualised love, by the boundless possibilities of intuition and communication it contains, penetrates the unknown."[223] We know the abysses of Matter; we come from the depths of those chasms. But we still don't know the heights of the Spirit: we have only begun climbing them. There is still a long way to the top, because "the depths we assign to Matter are but the reflection of the heights of the Spirit."[224]

Note that Teilhard spoke of heights, of summits, of higher vibrations. In this context, my dear, *above* is equivalent to *inside*. Ascension is a progression *towards inside*, towards the essence, which is always internal. The law of the unfolding of love –the colour range of its spectrum– goes outwards from inside, to culminate in the highest and innermost colour: ultraviolet, the colour that corresponds to the Centre.

Teilhard divides the Evolution of love, i.e. the second phase of Evolution, into two different stages:

> I have come to the point where, it seems to me, two phases in the creative transformation of human love are emerging for me. During a first phase of humanity, man and woman concentrate upon the physical act of giving and the concern for reproduction: at the same time, a growing nimbus of spiritual exchanges is gradually being built up around this fundamental act. At first, this nimbus was no more than an imperceptible fringe; slowly, and yet ever more clearly, there is a shift, and the fruitfulness and mystery of union move into that zone: and it is on that side that the balance finally gives way and comes to rest. At that very moment, however, the centre of physical

223. Teilhard de Chardin, *Human Energy*
224. Teilhard de Chardin, *The Evolution of Chastity*

union from which the light was radiating is found to be incapable of accepting any further intensification. The focus of attraction suddenly shifts further and further endlessly, indeed ahead. If the lovers are to be able to continue to increase their mutual possession in spirit, they have to turn away from the body and look for one another in God. Virginity rests upon chastity as thought rests upon life: each is arrived at through a reversal of direction, or by passing through one unique point. Such a transformation, of course, cannot be effected instantaneously on the surface of the earth: time is essential. When you heat water, the whole volume does not turn into steam at once the "liquid phase" and the "gaseous phase" are found together for some time, and this must necessarily be so. Nevertheless, that duality covers but one single developing event the direction and "dignity" of which are shared by the whole. Thus, at the present moment, physical union still retains its value and necessity for the human race; but its spiritual quality is now defined by the higher type of union to which it has served as the preliminary and which it now fosters. Within the noosphere, love is now undergoing a "change of state"[225]

Let me summarise this dense paragraph. Teilhard imagines a centre of gravity in love, a point of attraction between men and women. And this point of attraction is not fixed and immutable, it moves as a result of Evolution, it advances along what we called the "love spectrum". Progress is extremely slow, it's imperceptible. And, even today, that centre is still based on the lower end of the spectrum, anchored to sexual act, to reproduction, to the propagation of the species. Ah, but in the course of Evolution, another attraction

225. *Ibid*

of a different class has gathered around sexual attraction, a spiritual attraction that is slowly gaining weight. The day will come –predicts Teilhard– when the spiritual component overthrows the sexual in the mutual attraction between man and woman, the day when love's centre of gravity moves towards the higher end of the spectrum. But Evolution will not stop there: it will keep pushing in the direction of the Spirit.

In the love spectrum, the lower end's point of reference, the pole around which material love turns, is the sexual act; and God is the spiritual pole, the higher end's point of reference. Evolution happens between those two poles. This polarity, this tension of Matter in pursuit of the Spirit had already been observed by a predecessor of Teilhard, our friend Swedenborg: "There is implanted in every man from creation, and consequently from birth, an internal conjugal principle, and an external conjugal principle; man comes first into the latter, and as he becomes spiritual he comes into the former."[226] Teilhard's vision is more like a scale, the typical scale with two identical dishes: the sexual act would be the left dish; God would be the right. At the beginning, there would be nothing other than material love: the left dish would be full and the scales would completely tip to that side. But, with the passing of time, spiritual love would begin settling in the right dish. That's how today, Blanca, generally, when people think about erotic love, they don't think exclusively about a sexual exchange anymore: there is also a spiritual component involved. We can predict, along with Teilhard, that the day will come (although that day is still many centuries away) when both dishes will be balanced. And, since the inexorable tendency is for love to become in-

226. Emmanuel Swedenborg, *Conjugal Love*

dependent from sexuality, the balance will end up tipping in favour of the right dish. Only when the right dish is full and the left dish empty, will Evolution be able to say, "mission accomplished".

A LOVE TRIANGLE

Teilhard's intuition is not unique, Blanca, not even close. I have just quoted Swedenborg, but many other sages envisioned the same truth from the vantage point of mystic intuition. From our modern and distant perspective, the evolutionary horizon that they contemplated can appear bland. But I guess it's like when they made us read classic books in school and we found them terribly boring: if you read those books now, after all these years, they will reveal their essence to you. We could describe that distant horizon with a quotation from an ancient sage, and another from a modern sage. The first one comes from a pseudo-Clementine homily from the second century (I mean from a homily perhaps erroneously attributed to the Greek Father of the Church, Clement of Alexandria, who was something of a Gnostic sympathiser, to the point of even being accused of heresy). Clement -or whoever was hiding behind that name- analyses the Gnostic formula of "...and the male with the female, neither male nor female", and interprets it in the following manner, "... that a brother seeing a sister should have no thought of her as a female, and that a sister seeing a brother should not have any thought of him as a male. These things if ye do, saith He, the kingdom of my father shall come."[227] The second one

227. *Second Epistle of Clement,* 12: 5-6

may sound familiar to you, I took it from your library, from one of the *Letters to a young poet* by Rainer María Rilke. It says "... and the great renewal of the world will perhaps consist in one phenomenon: that man and woman, freed from all mistaken feelings and aversions, will seek each other not as opposites but as brother and sister, as neighbours, and will unite as human beings".

Rilke, like the ancient sages, held the same opinion that I told you before: that the *person* condition transcends the human scope, and if the human condition entails the differentiation between both sexes, that's not the case with the person condition. The person goes beyond the difference between the sexes, it belongs to a neutral gender, a third gender of a spiritual nature which we could call the androgynous gender (and this way, we would find support in our theory for the "psychological hypothesis", detailed in my first letter regarding the debate about the lost half of the soul).

Compelled by Evolution, the physical Universe has led to the appearance of the human being, but, predictably, it won't stop there, Blanca; it will continue its climb. And, as it progresses, the role of sex in the relationship between the two poles –male and female– will decrease. The spotlight will increasingly fall on another kind of complementarity other than sexual. A complementarity of a personal and spiritual order, which constitutes the "reverse side" of sexual complementarity, its "naked" version. And this slow, imperceptible drift won't stop until it achieves absolute personalisation: such is the purpose of Evolution. According to Teilhard, we human beings are urged to eventually carry our *person* condition to the full extent of its consequences. This implies stripping ourselves of our sexual covers and, as a result, unknowingly crossing the border that divides the human from the divine.

How chimeric this sounds, doesn't it, my love? Teilhard was the first to admit it: "From the practical point of view -he writes-, I must confess that the suggestion presents such difficulty that what I have written here would be dismissed by nine people out of ten as overly ingenious or even wildly extravagant. Does not universal experience show conclusively that spiritual loves have always come to a sordid end? Man is made to keep his feet firmly on the ground and flight has always been beyond our dreams... I am quite sure about my answer; yes, there have been madmen with such a dream, and that is why we have now conquered the air."[228] It's true, Blanca. Today the skies belong to us. However, in the fifteenth century, when the great Leonardo Da Vinci prophesied that one day man would fly, few believed him; the prediction sounded as unbelievable for his contemporaries as the evolutive future conjectured by Teilhard does to us. But let's go back to the passage where he conjectures it...

Tagging the sexual act (and its natural consequence, reproduction) as a referent of material love, and God as a referent of spiritual love is not new. One of the keys of the ancient sages' love theory is the postulate that while material love seeks to be fertile down below -it seeks to produce descendants-, spiritual love looks up above: it seeks to produce God. When Plato describes spiritual lovers (the humanist Marsilio Ficino will call them "platonic lovers" in his honour) as being unhappy with their split condition, yearning to merge with one another to become one, the Unity to which they aspire is the divine Unity. We knew this, right? There's a multitude of Dualities, but only one absolute Unit in which they all converge. So when each couple of twin souls, in a more or

228. Teilhard de Chardin, *The Evolution of Chastity*

less conscious manner, aspires to merge "into one [spiritual] flesh only", what they are really aspiring is to become is God (to become "God in God", as the famous thirteenth century Christian mystic, Master Eckhart, put it). And thus, God emerges in the hidden goal, in the secret and undeniable objective of spiritual lovers, in the upper pole towards which they converge.

In a previous letter, we alluded to the centre panel of the masterpiece that is the *Garden of Earthly Delights*. Let's take a look now to the left side of the tryptic, where the biblical Garden of Eden is depicted. In the middle ground, presiding over the composition, stands the slender Fountain of Life. As we've seen, the exegetes identified the Fountain with the Tree of Life, for that's where it stood, located at the centre of Paradise, from where the River that split into four streams and irrigated the whole Universe rose. Below, in the foreground, are the main characters of this drama: Adam and Eve before the Fall, when their mutual love still had not been desecrated by Matter; God is in their midst, wearing a tunic of the same pink colour of the Fountain above Him. Adam is sitting down, Eve is on her knees and both their faces are in a half-profile. God, majestic, stands between them, looking back at the viewer.

There is a detail in this painting, Blanca, that appears to be insignificant, but Bosch, through it, seems to have intended to show God not as oblivious to the mutual amorous relationship between Adam and Eve, but as an intrinsic and essential part of that relationship. I'm referring to how God is in intimate contact with them both: His right foot is placed on Adam's left foot, His left hand is holding Eve's right hand. It's as if Bosch had wanted to present God as connecting factor between the primordial Couple, as if God appeared as the referent of Adam and Eve's intimacy as a couple; of the embodiment –and fruit– of their union... (I know what you're thinking. But let me tell you that hunting for symbolic references in paintings by artists such as Bosch is not a gratuitous task typical of idle detectives. We could define Bosch as an esoteric painter. We know he belonged to a secret Gnostic society known as the Brethren of the Free Spirit; we know he was a visionary and that his paintings are filled with hidden clues.) Seeing that Adam and Eve's love in Paradise, before the Fall, was purely spiritual, without a hint of Matter (as we've said before, Matter has no place in the Higher World), Bosch's Garden of Eden can be interpreted as the portrait of spiritual love in its highest form: in the immaculate purity of Paradise. And there stands God, between the two lovers, in intimate contact with them. As though suggesting that spiritual love entails God –which converts it into a *divine love*. As though suggesting that the more spiritual a love is, the more God makes Himself present between the lovers, up until we reach Paradise, where His Presence between the couple becomes Absolute. A Presence that, in a way, absorbs them.

In short, my dear, we can imagine spiritual love as a triangle: two of its three vertices maintain a relationship at the same level, and then, above them, rises a third vertex in which they come together. Referring to marriage based on spiritual love, Teilhard writes that, "the pair will find its equilibrium only in a third being ahead of it. What name must we give to this mysterious 'intruder'?"[229] For Teilhard –and for the ancient sages–, that name is "God", Blanca. The twin souls' bond is, then, for the French Jesuit, a kind of three–

229. Teilhard de Chardin, *Sketch of a Personalistic Universe*

way dialogue with three participants: "Love is a three–term function: man, woman, and God. Its whole perfection and success are bound up with the harmonious balance of these three elements."[230]

Very well, these pages were dedicated to the foresight or, better yet, the inner vision, the mystic intuition Pierre Teilhard de Chardin had of the evolutive future of humankind. From what we've seen, erotic love plays a key role in that future. And if you're thinking about asking me whether erotic love also played a key role in Teilhard's present (in this specific present in which his soul reincarnated into the body of a Jesuit priest), I can tell you that, as surprising as it may sound, given that he was a celibate man of the cloth, the answer is yes. Take a look at what he wrote at thirty years old –shortly after being ordained priest– regarding his reencounter with his cousin Marguerite Teillard–Chambon, to whom he had always been very close (they were born only a few months apart and would die only a few years apart too): "Through the sharp tips of the three arrows which had pierced me, the world itself had invaded my being and had drawn me back into itself... And, under the glance that fell upon me, the shell in which my heart slumbered, burst open. With pure and generous love, a new energy penetrated into me –or emerged from me, which, I cannot say– that made me feel that I was as vast and as loaded with richness as the Universe."[231] Let me quickly clarify that this was always a purely spiritual and platonic love (besides being faithful to his vows, Teilhard saw the sexual act as a "crude union"). Naturally, Blanca, it's always risky for someone on the

230. *Ibid*
231. Teilhard de Chardin, *Writings in Time of War*

outside, for a witness with no access to subjective beauty, to point out someone's possible twin soul. Especially when that someone is a celibate priest. But we've said before that twin souls don't always reincarnate as lovers and that their essential affinity is clear independently of the nature of their relationship. Teilhard and Marguerite exchanged letters throughout their whole lives, but the most remarkable ones were written during the years of the Great War. In them, Marguerite witnessed the awakening of her cousin's mystic intuition. Those letters have been published, my dear (hers, although lost, are reflected in his), and, unless my detective instinct deceives me, they are compromising letters: they reveal their souls' essential affinity.

THE INTERNAL MEANING OF LOVE

Teilhard is not the only one, Blanca. Other modern sages of "ancient perspective" have spiritualised the strictly naturalist and Darwinian notion of Evolution. These sages, for whom biological evolution is only the first phase of a long process tending to the emerging and perfecting of the Spirit, have been dubbed "metaphysical Evolutionists". For them, Evolution is not random; or if you prefer, the luck that rules over Evolution is not random: it obeys a kind of divine determinism. I've already talked about the Indian mystic Sri Ghose Aurobindo. And if we're talking about metaphysical Evolutionism, we must mention the French philosopher Henri Bergson and his notion of "vital impulse": an impulse that "is God or of God" and that, through a daring struggle with Matter, leads Evolution towards increasingly higher levels of consciousness and spirituality. We also could not leave Madame Blavatsky and Rudolf Steiner out of this list; they were the founders of the so-called Theosophical Society. Or the esoterics Gurdjieff and Ouspensky. Or the North American philosopher, John Fiske, who wrote in his *Through Nature to God* "that spiritual perfection is the true goal of evolution, the divine end that was involved in the beginning." We should even include Swedenborg, who wrote things like "With those who are made spiritual by the Lord, conjugal love is more and more purified and rendered chaste."[232]

But, out of all the metaphysical Evolutionists, Blanca, the one who most profusely dealt with love and the Evolution of love in his writings (therefore the one who deserves a higher share of our attention) is a sage that has already appeared in these pages: Vladimir S. Solovyov.

If you think you don't know this brilliant Russian theologian and poet, think of Alyosha, the more spiritual and compassionate of the *Brothers Karamazov*. It seems that Dostoyevsky was inspired by his friend Solovyov to create that character (the twin soul of *Anna Karenina*'s Vanenka, if you'll allow me to keep matching spiritual kinships, even between fictional characters). It's not as risky to conjecture about Solovyov's twin soul as it was about Teilhard's: all his biographers agree in pointing out Sophia Chitrovo as the only love of his life. The impossibility of marrying her motivated him to renounce marriage, and encouraged the obsessive dedication to theology that would undermine his health and eventually lead him to an early grave. Is it a coincidence that Solovyov's theology prominently features the mystical speculation of Gnostic inspiration –Sophiology, the doctrine of

232. Emmanuel Swedenborg, *Conjugal Love*

divine *Sophia* or "Wisdom"–, which also carries the same name as his beloved?

Solovyov's ideas are, in their essence, in alignment with those of the ancient sages that I have presented to you in these letters. He also thought that, in its current fallen state, man was one-half of a true Man: an imperfect and incomplete being. He was also convinced that man was destined to overcome that state; destined to restore his original state of Perfection and Integrity: "The human being can... to accommodate absolute content in his own proper form, become an absolute personality. But in order to be filled with absolute content (which in the language of religion is termed eternal life or the Kingdom of God), that same human form must be restored in its entirety (integrated). In the empirical reality of the human being, as such, this is by no means so– he exists only in a specific onesidedness and finiteness, as a male or a female individuality... However, a true human in the fullness of his ideal personality, obviously, cannot be merely male or merely female, but must be the higher unity of both. To realise this unity, to create the true human being as a free unity of the male and female principles, preserving their formal individualisation but having surmounted their essential separateness and divergence – this is the proper immediate task of love."[233]

The purpose of love's Evolution is this, Blanca: to enable the advent of the "true man", who is the androgynous man. To issue man's passport to Paradise, to Unity, and to "create out of two infinite and perishable natures one absolute and immortal individuality."[234] To achieve this, it's necessary to

233. Vladimir Solovyov, *The Meaning of Love*, p.55
234. *Ibid*, p. 61

take love to the limit, to make it reach its zenith, the summit of its Evolution, meaning, *true love* – the "ultraviolet colour" of Teilhard's metaphor. Only then will the Two's divorce be rectifiable. Only true love will make the "true man" possible, a "true man" who is no different from the "Uni-totality", which is how Solovyov calls God. And it's true that such summit is still so far away that it's invisible to us. But should we deny the existence of the ultraviolet colour just because our eyes are not capable of seeing it?

> It would be completely unjust to deny the possibility of realising love (true love) merely on the basis that hitherto it never has been realised... Even rational consciousness itself, before becoming a fact in humans, was only a perplexed and unsuccessful aspiration in the world of animals. How many geological and biological epochs passed away in unsuccessful attempts to create a brain qualified to become the organ for the embodiment of rational thought? Love (true love) is as yet for humans what reason was for the animal world: it exists in its beginnings, or as an earnest of what it will be, but not yet in actual fact.[235]

Solovyov then points out a substantial discrepancy between both evolutive processes –that which thousands of years ago lead to the appearance of human reason, and that in a distant future will result in the blossoming of pure and true love. The difference is that the first process, corresponding to the first phase of Evolution, was unconscious, whereas the second one, associated with the second phase, is conscious: it's in our hands, Blanca, in the hands of the twin souls. "It follows only that it is well to remember that if the reality of

---

235. *Ibid*, p. 54

rational consciousness has manifested itself in humans but not through humans, the realisation of love (of true love), as the highest stage towards the true life of that same humanity, must issue not only *in humanity* but *through it.*"[236]

Solovyov draws a rough sketch of Evolution, and he does so in the following terms: Evolution, he says, is the "contradiction and antagonism between the species and the individual."[237] The battle is long and arduous, but it's destined to lean in favour of the individual. Throughout Evolution, he will cut a path through the homogenisation of the species. He will crystallise and stand out from the dark background of Nature, where he had hitherto been, let's say, diluted... To illustrate it, my dear, you could recall a spectacle of which you were a great fan, even though you had to get out of bed early to watch it. I mean the morning twilight: do you remember how the diffuse outlines of the landscape at night would gradually become sharper under the rising morning sun? Well, the same happens with the individual under the light of Evolution. Since the *individual* belongs to the spiritual category and the *species* to the material category, we could also put it this way: In the course of Evolution, *the Spirit will make its way through Matter*. Slowly, the individual –each half of a fallen spark, buried underneath a pile of debris– will crawl of out that tomb. Matter belongs to the species: therefore, it strips itself of what does not belong to it as an individual. Since that, as Solovyov points out: "The fullness of life's powers bubbling over in the individual being is not its own life, but an alien life, the life of a species..."[238]

236. *Ibid*, p. 54–55
237. *Ibid*, p. 72
238. *Ibid*, p. 71

Crossed–out note on the margin. I was able to salvage, although very fragmented, the following quotation: ... *upon leaving the museum (along with?) the other children .../... the inexplicable feeling .../... he, in another (time,) had been someone else."* Maybe its source is the same as that quotation dated from 28–8–99.

In animals, the life of the species is absolute, all-embracing. Animals are not free; they have no initiative of their own: everything they do is dictated by their species' instinct. Human beings are freer, although, to a lesser extent, we also obey the instincts of our species. Many of the things we do, we do them because we are compelled to them by those material life powers. It's what Solovyov calls the "tyranny of the species over the individual"[239]. Evolution's task consists precisely of our gradual liberation from those material determinations. Through Evolution, we will become -in Solovyov's words- "capable of internal freedom from the demands of the species"[240]. And as this happens, Blanca, we will liberate our own life, the life of the individual, the life of the Spirit. Given that, apart from the biological, corporeal and material life, there exists a secret and invisible life, a Life with a capital L, a life in the religious sense of the word, a spiritual life, that of the soul, which (unlike the biological, an immortal life) is each person's "proper life". (Being a result of the Fall, the other one happened to us and, therefore, it is alien to oneself.)

In the course of Evolution, the proper life -the life of the soul, the individual's life- will then become independent from that other alien life, the life of the body, the "life of the

239. *Ibid*, p. 72
240. *Ibid*, p. 72

species". And love follows a parallel evolution, Blanca. Just as there is a "life of the species", there is also a "love of the species". This love revolves around sex. This is the love that determines that we should come together in carnal union for the reproduction of the species, for that is, my dear, the purpose of this love that happened to us because of the Fall, a love which is, then, alien to the individual. There exists, buried under the alien love, a self-love, a "love of the individual". This is genuine love, love as it was before falling: a love that does not pull towards carnal intimacy but towards the spiritual one, not towards the union of the bodies, but to that of the souls. This type of love will cut its way open through Matter in the course of Evolution. Matter will give birth to it as in a long labour.

The "love of the species'" slow drift over to the "love of the individual" is a transition towards the *interiority of love*, towards what Solovyov called the "internal meaning of love". Like Teilhard -like the ancient sages, Blanca- Solovyov thought that Evolution took place from inside out. According to him, everything had an internal meaning, an ultimate "reverse side" towards which they were secretly inclined. (In a similar way, the Gnostics referred to the unfathomable "depths" of every being, and for the Kabbalists, "nothing exists without a great depth"[241].) The internal meaning of all things is written in the language of the Spirit, and, in our mandala-shaped diagram of the Universe, it would be located in the Centre. The Centre would be like a magnet attracting everything from the outer circles of the cosmic mandala towards itself. This tension *towards the inside* is what defines Evolution and Life. "All that is external and incidental -claims Solovyov- is subordinated

241. Gershom Scholem, *On the Kabbalah and Its Symbolism*

to the internal meaning of life."[242] Naturally, this tension towards the inside is counterbalanced by forces of the opposite nature; material forces that place on it a tension towards the outside: "The True Being, or the idea of unity-of-the-all, is opposed in our world by material existence, which, with its senseless stubbornness stifles even our love, and does not allow its meaning to be realised."[243] So, Evolution is about resisting that external counterbalance –that song of the Siren that pulls us towards the outside–, and allowing ourselves to be pulled by our internal "magnet".

Sexual union has its own "internal meaning", Blanca, as everything in this world has. "Love is only something –opines Solovyov– thanks to its meaning or idea as the restoration of the unity or integrity of the human personality, as the creation of an absolute individuality."[244] The "reverse side" or internal meaning of sexual union is, then, for Solovyov, the *perfect union* or heavenly marriage of twin souls. Since that –in his own words– the internal meaning of love "demands the reunion of that which is wrongfully separated"[245]... Which means that the Evolution of love happens from the "outside" or sexual union, towards the "inside" or heavenly marriage.

AN IMPERFECT METAPHOR

For Solovyov, that man that is separated from his woman (the soul that is separated from its twin) is an imperfect and

242. Vladimir Solovyov, *op. cit.* p. 99
243. *Ibid*, p. 106
244. *Ibid*, p. 64
245. *Ibid*, p. 102

insufficient being: "The relation between husband and wife is a relation between two differently acting, yet equally imperfect potentialities, which attain perfection only in the process of reciprocity."[246] Everything tends towards its own perfection, its own internal meaning. That is why the soul tends towards its twin with all its strength and seeks to unite with it. First, it seeks to unite through sexual union. But later, this proves to be a "false union", incapable of *perfecting* (of truly uniting) the twin souls. Hence the need for sexual union to step aside, in the course of Evolution, in favour of another type of union:

> Death, generally speaking, is the disintegration of a being, the falling apart of its constituent factors. But it is the separation of the sexes –not eliminated by their external and transient union in the act of generation– it is this separation between male and female elements of the human being which is already in itself a state of disintegration and the beginning of death. To remain divided into sexes means to remain on the path to death, and whoever will not or cannot abandon this path is bound in accordance with natural necessity to follow it to the end... Only the human being in its entirety can be immortal, and if physical union cannot really restore the integrity of the human being, then this means that the spurious union must be replaced by a true one...[247]

This Integrity, Blanca, this perfection consisting of the true union of twin souls, finds its total complement solely in God. ("This perfection, which for us is still only being

246. *Ibid*, p. 85
247. *Ibid*, p. 73

realised, is for God, i.e., in the truth, already real."[248]) So, in the end, the twin souls are destined to exchange their human condition for the divine, which is their original and true condition. And halfway through releasing such ballast, to turn their back on Matter and face the Spirit. Their mutual love is destined to become independent from the material pretexts –reproduction and sensual pleasure– that were useful for them to take the first steps, just as a child becomes independent from the baby walker when she learns to walk by herself. In Solovyov's voice:

> Within the limits of animals which propagate exclusively in the sexual mode (the division of vertebrates), the higher we ascend in the hierarchy of organisms, the weaker the power of propagation becomes, but, on the other hand, the greater the power of sexual attraction becomes. In the lowest class of this division –among fish– propagation takes place on an enormous scale: the embryos produced every year by each female are vaunted in millions; these embryos are fertilised by the male *outside* the body of the female, and the method by which this is done does not admit of the supposition of any powerful sexual impulse. Of all the vertebrate animals this cold-blooded class undoubtedly propagates most of all and exhibits the passion of love least of all. In the next stage –that of amphibians and reptiles– the power of propagation is far less significant than among fish... together with a smaller rate of propagation, we already find in these animals more intimate sexual relations... Among birds, the power of propagation is far weaker, not only in comparison with fishes, but also in comparison, for instance, with frogs, yet the sexual attraction

248. *Ibid*, p. 91

and the mutual attachment between male and female attain a development unheard of in the two lower classes. Among mammals -which are already viviparous- the power of propagation is significantly weaker than among birds, and sexual attraction among the majority, at any rate, is less constant; but, to balance that, it is far more intense. Lastly, in humans, in comparison with the whole animal kingdom, propagation is effected on the smallest scale. But sexual love attains its utmost significance and its highest power, uniting in the superlative degree, both constancy in the relation (as in birds) and intensity of passion (as in mammals). So then, sexual love and propagation of the species are found to be *in inverse ratio* to each other: the more powerful the one, the weaker the other. Speaking generally about the aspect which is being examined, the whole animal kingdom develops in the following order: At the bottom, there is an enormous power of propagation with a complete absence of anything resembling sexual love (owing to the absence even of division into sexes). Farther on, among the more perfect organisms, sexual differentiation, together with its corresponding sexual attraction, makes its appearance. At first the attraction is extremely weak, but later it gradually increases in further stages of organic development, as the power of propagation diminishes (i.e., attraction is in direct ration to the perfection of the organisation and in inverse ratio to the power of propagation), until finally, at the very peak -in humans- the most powerful possible sexual love makes its appearance, even to the complete exclusion of propagation. So, if in this way, at the two extremes of animal existence we find on the one hand propagation without any sexual love, and on the other hand sexual love without any propagation, then it is perfectly clear that these two phenomena cannot be bonded indissolubly with one another. It is clear that each of them possesses its own independent significance, and that the meaning of the one cannot consist in its being a means to the other. The result is the same if we examine sexual love exclusively in the human world, where it is incomparably greater than in the animal world, and where it assumes that individual character by power of which just *this* person of the other sex possesses for the lover absolute significance, as unique and irreplaceable, as a very end in itself.[249]

It's quite moving to think that when Solovyov wrote these things, he had this Sophia Chitrovo in mind... By the way, have you noticed the parallels between Solovyov's portrayal of the Evolution of love and the one Teilhard de Chardin describes a few pages back? According to the Russian man, in the course of Evolution, erotic love increasingly becomes more independent from the reproductive function –later it will also distance itself from sexuality, the Frenchman added. But let's stop for a moment on that last sentence in Solovyov's explanation, where he emphasises that the erotic love's process of independence is accompanied by its own progressive individualisation; which is the same as its *personalisation*.

Crossed–out note on the margin. Besides a few loose words (*wheel, mountain, water...*), we can read the Roman numeral XVIII.

Let's begin by saying that, when it comes to Evolution, the concepts of "Person", "Consciousness" and "Spirit" are equivalents. Evolution is a leap from the impersonal, the unconscious, from Matter, to the Person, Consciousness,

249. *Ibid*, p. 20–22

to the Spirit. It moves from chaos to order; from the indistinguishable (hence the sea as an obstinate symbol of the material world) to the differentiated; from the species to the individual. From the *raw material* to the *substantial shape*. In another letter, we used the metaphor of the sculpture and the block of stone; we can use that metaphor in this case as well, at least partially. We can visualise God as a sculptor who, through the chisel of Evolution, smooths down and *shapes* a block of stone. The block of stone is Matter; the *shape*, that which is defined by the blows of the chisel, that which following each blow emerges more and more from the undifferentiated depths of Matter, is the individual, *the Person*, the Spirit. The human soul, before being revealed by the sculptor's chisel, is intrinsic to the block of stone (Evolution is also a leap from the intrinsic to the transcendent). It's already there, Blanca, but diffuse, undefined, as if asleep. The sculptor's chisel pulls it out of its slumber, it liberates it, it gives it life, and it progressively lifts the veil that made it invisible: it forces it to crystallise, to become an individual. Very slowly, the sculptor extracts from a shapeless block of stone the sculpture with a face and eyes: *the Person*, the Spirit.

This metaphor, though, has a flaw –hence me saying that it is only partially useful in this context. It's that a sculptor, to shape the block of stone –to reveal the stone's hidden sculpture, as our sculptor friend from Toledo would say–, needs only to remove the excess if stone. In this case, though, the whole stone is in excess. The same circumstance that made the metaphor ideal to talk about the Two and the One, makes it now unfit to talk about Matter and the Spirit. That's because the stone remains in a sculpture; whereas in the evolutive process endgame –that is, in the absolute Personality, in the absolute Spirit– there should be no trace of Matter. Matter and Spirit are inversely related: to become totally spiritualised, the soul most totally "dematerialise".

If in the course of Evolution, the soul becomes spiritualised and personalised, then so does the mutual love of the Two, Blanca. Because the love of the Two evolves along with them. This seems unquestionable to me: the evolution of the love between twin souls is the faithful reflection of the souls' own evolution. The more spiritualised a soul is, the more spiritualised its love is. And *the more it becomes personalised...* We thus reach an important point stressed by Teilhard and Solovyov: the fact that the Evolution of love runs in the direction of progressive personalisation and individualisation. That is to say, that in virtue of its Evolution, erotic love stops being indiscriminate and becomes individualised: it increasingly tends to limit itself to a determined individual to the exclusion of all others. (With this, it reveals its contrast with generic love, the love for one's neighbour, the perfection of which lies precisely in the opposite: in its indiscriminate character.)

Such personalisation is directly proportional to the love's level of spirituality. In the lower level of its Evolution, erotic love –which here is one hundred percent carnal– is indiscriminate, fickle, and promiscuous. It's not, in Solovyov's terminology, the love of the "individual" but of the species. As we go up the evolutive ladder, we find ourselves with a gradually more spiritual and exclusive love, a love that is progressively more of the "individual". In fact, Blanca, both the carnal love of the lower levels and the spiritual love of the higher ones, apparently seek the same thing: an individual belonging to a generic group, to a "species", individuals of the opposite sex (or of the same sex, in the case of homosexuality). The difference is in where they place the emphasis:

carnal love places it on the species, spiritual love on the individual. While "love of the species" is the foundation of carnal love, spiritual love is based on the "love of the individual".

The point is, Blanca, that, deep down, the object of carnal love is not a specific individual of another sex, it's every individual of another sex in general. What it seeks is less an individual than the "species" it embodies. And, since every individual of the same species fits that requirement, carnal love is eminently indiscriminate: its preference may fall on any individual belonging to that "species". And it's promiscuous as well: it tends to not settle with only one individual. Naturally, the carnal lover will have its own preferences: from among the individuals of the opposite sex, it will prefer those who are beautiful (I mean objective and apparent beauty here, the only one within the carnal lovers' reach). And even from the beautiful individuals of the opposite sex, it will be more attracted, for example, to the brunettes rather than the blondes, the tall ones instead of the short ones... equally generic preferences that will hardly be specific to a single individual.

In any case, the carnal lover's individual preferences are only adjacent to its love. The only substantial element is belonging to the "species", which is to what the carnal lover is really attracted. That is to say: the carnal lover does not love an individual for what it might have that is specific to itself –and the most specific thing about an individual is its *personal* essence–, but for the generic elements that the individual shares with the rest of its "species". On the contrary, for the spiritual lover, Blanca, the individual preference –the preference for a specific individual over all the others from the same "species"– is substantial. That preference (which obeys to subjective criteria rather than objective ones) is not an accessory to its love: it's its constitutive element. This is demonstrated by the fact that if for any reason the beloved person were to disappear, it would be very difficult to replace him/her, it could even prove to be impossible. Whereas for the carnal lover, nothing would be easier.

So it is, then, that the evolutive tendency of erotic love towards an ever higher spiritualisation, determines a corresponding tendency towards an increasingly higher personalisation. If you notice, Blanca, this tendency is consistent with the ultimate purpose of the Evolution of love: the soul's return to the One –to its original Unity– through the reunification with its twin. Because, to reunite with its twin, the soul must, first single it out, "isolate" it from all the others. And finally, this singling out process culminates in the attitude stressed by Solovyov: the attribution of "an absolute importance" to the twin soul that makes it "unique and irreplaceable", that turns it into a purpose in on itself for the soul.

LOVE CLASSIFICATIONS

I've just reread what I wrote in this letter so far, and do you know what my first impression is? "My God, how hard I try to make my exposition flow in the easiest way possible, and how little success I have in my endeavour!" I wish I had a more subtle understanding and a finer and more eloquent pen to lay it all down in a clear and pleasant manner. But my pen and my understanding are what they are and one must accept it. Furthermore, add my limited skills to the intrinsic difficulties already embroiled in this subject.... In any case, I promise to keep trying hard.

So far, I've told you about Teilhard de Chardin and Vladimir Solovyov, and I've also named a few metaphysical Evolutionists. But much older sages had already intuited the Evolution of erotic love, that which was depicted as an amorous ladder or hierarchy where the "floor" or lower level corresponded to carnal love, and the "ceiling" to a pure or spiritual love with no trace of Matter. In the characterisation they made of this hierarchy, carnal love entailed the separation or disagreement between the lovers –for which Matter was understood to be of a selfish and divisive nature. Whereas spiritual love entailed –in virtue of the Spirit's unifying property– the union or communion between them (in the lower world, this union was intangible, *virtual*, but it was regarded as the precursor to the *real* union, for which one would have to wait until after death). Said amorous hierarchy was often crystallised in three levels. The two aforementioned levels were joined by an intermediate level corresponding to mixed love, a blend of carnal and spiritual love, resulting thus in a ternary or tripartite classification of love that corresponded to the division of the Universe into three worlds.

The illustrious medievalist René Nelli observes, "The first ternary divisions that simultaneously account for the unity and internal movement (Evolution) of Love from the lowest level to the highest, appeared in the Islamic world much earlier than in the Latin West."[250] The medieval Muslims had borrowed from Aristotle and the Eastern and Greek astrologers of Antiquity. One of the latter was Claudius Ptolemy, whose astrological data served as a base for Al-Masoudi, in the tenth century, to elaborate the following ternary classifi-

250. Translated from R. Nelli, *L'érotique des troubadours*, p. 251. The author took the ternary classifications from this book.

cation of amorous union: "First level (the higher level): *The Union* –or pure love–, that is explained by the reencounter of two souls on the same planet at the moment of embodiment. Second level: *Union of friendship or usefulness*: the two lovers are useful for one another because the same planet was in exaltation when they were born. Third level (the lower level): *the disagreement–love*, which reflects the existence of the same planetary opposition in the birth chart of the two lovers."[251]

Such classification, Blanca, is supported by an ancient science –astrology, the science of the stars– that many followers in Antiquity regarded as the key to interpreting the world in general, and human relations in particular, the mysterious details of which were sometimes attributed to the astral bodies. This way, the failure of an earthly marriage could be blamed on the incompatibility of the spouses' zodiac signs... which, if you look at it carefully, suggests the idea of love predestination (astrology was, in fact, another one of the channels that found the intuition of spiritual kinship).

The first ternary classification of love known in the West dates back to the twelfth century. It was established by Andreas Capellanus, chaplain of the Countess Mary of Champagne, on her request, in his treatise *Ars honeste amandi*, "The Art of loving honestly". In this treatise, known as the *De Amore*, Cappellanus discerns three levels of love and advocates in favour of the highest one: the *amor purus*, consisting, he says, of "the contemplation of the spirit and affection of the heart", a unifying love, a love that brings the lovers' souls together. Capellanus is indulgent with the next level –*amor mixtus*–, an intermediate and hybrid level. Although

251. Al-Masoudi, *op. cit.* (quoted by R. Nelli, *L'érotique des troubadours*, p. 251

he condemns the lower level, the *amor per pecuniam acquisitus* ("the love based on interests"), which is a love that seeks to profit from the beloved, be it in a sensual sense, economic, social or whatever else.

Many other ternary classifications of love would follow this first one, Blanca, all of them cut from the same cloth. We have classifications made by the troubadours, great experts in the matter of erotic love (to the point that, with obvious exaggeration, they are said to have invented it). The Occitan troubadour known by the nickname "the monk of Montaudon" distinguishes three classes of erotic love: the highest one is pure love; the lowest one is useful or venal love; and between them stands mixed love, a blend of the two extremes. Another troubadour, Guiraut de Calanson, attributes to the first level of love, which he calls *heavenly* or *divine love*, "such potency that it elevates its kingdom above Heaven."[252] Matfre Ermengaut, in his *Breviari d'Amor*, places his Dame in the first level of the ternary, crushing a dragon underneath her feet... the dragon, of course, is standing in for the third level or carnal love. Certainly, not every troubadour shared Ermengaut's idealised vision of love, Blanca; although many held an unfavourable opinion of love. This was not, mind you, a question of prudery but of strict objective worth. In general, troubadours subscribed to the words of an illustrious successor of theirs, the symbolist French poet Mallarmeé, when he said that the flesh was sad: "*la chair est triste, hélas.*"[253]

This disregard for carnal love, considered to be a fraud, a profanation of real love, is quite common among the ancient sages. In the first (along with the already mentioned

252. *Ibid*, p. 254

253. Mallarmé, *Brise marine*

Dialogues of Love by Leo The Hebrew) and most prominent of all treatises that flooded Italy between the fifteenth and the seventeenth century, Marsilio Ficino's *De Amore* addresses the following acerbic commentary to "vulgar love": "The anxious restlessness that torments the vulgar lovers day and night, is a kind of madness. While love remains, afflicted first by a fire in the bile, and then by the burning of black bile, they throw themselves into the fury and the fire and, like blind people, ignore where they are plunging into. How pestilent is this false love both for the lovers and for the beloved... for man, through this fury, becomes a beast."[254] And, following the same line of thought, another contemporary great Esoteric sage, the travelling philosopher Theophrastus Paracelsus, wrote: "Just as there is love between beasts, who group in couples, male and female, so there is among men a love of an animalistic nature and heritage. From this heritage, we can achieve nothing but animal greed, interest, and love; this love is perishable, inconsistent, and is only of use for the man who is dominated by his instincts. It knows no higher purpose."[255] The nineteenth century American philosopher, Henry David Thoreau (who, by the way, was a part of the Transcendentalist school of thought, a movement that advocated mystic intuition as a way of getting closer to the "reverse side" of the Universe), pointed out that "the generative energy, which when we are loose, dissipates and makes us unclean, when we are continent invigorates and inspires us. Chastity is the flowering of man; and what are called

---

254. Marsilio Ficino, *De Amor*, chapter XII
255. Translated from Paracelsus, *Textos esenciales*, p. 92

Genius, Heroism, Holiness, and the like, are but various fruits which succeed it."[256]

We could quote from other secular authors. Those from the ancient Stoic tradition, for example, who always emphasised the nullification of material passions in lieu of the purity of soul. But I don't want to continue before adding a testimony from the most prolific field in this respect: religion.

Maybe you are familiar with the story that St. Augustine writes in his *Confesiones* about his abjuration of carnal love, and of how he nevertheless resisted abiding by the decision that he had already taken in his heart. The anguish that such discordance caused him, led him one day to a paroxysm of desperation, in the middle of which he claims to have heard a sweet voice compelling him to read the book he had by his side. The book was the Epistles of St. Paul, from where he read the first paragraph he saw: "Let us behave properly as in the day, not in carousing and drunkenness, not in sexual promiscuity and sensuality, not in strife and jealousy. But put on the Lord Jesus Christ, and make no provision for the flesh in regard to its lusts." From that moment on, he abided by his heart's desire..., as his coetaneous Gregory of Nyssa had once done, "But the grosser mind looks down; it bends its energies to bodily pleasures as surely as the sheep stoop to their pasture; it lives for gorging and still lower pleasures; it is alienated from the life of God, and a stranger to the promise of the Covenants."[257]

We could find as many testimonies of this ilk as we wanted, my dear. But even among the ancient religious sages, there are those who did not lose sight of the fundamental role

---

256. H. D. Thoreau, "Higher Laws", *Walden*
257. Gregory of Nissa, *On Virginity*, IV

that flesh plays in the journey of love towards the centre of itself, towards its "internal meaning". Thus, the great twelfth century mystic Bernard of Clairvaux (who had refuted the scholastic theologians by replacing knowledge with love as the path to Divinity) finds it inevitable that, given that we are made of flesh, our love begins *in the flesh.*[258] What these sages are telling us is that before we walk we must first learn how to crawl. And after all, my love, if sexual attraction did not exist, how could spiritual attraction gather around it –according to Teilhard's metaphor– until it takes over? *One must rise by that by which one falls*, prays an old Tantric saying (a saying from the esoteric variant of Hinduism and Buddhism, Tantra). For our sages, sex triggered the Fall, yes. But it's also the starting point for the return, it's the base camp from where we tackle the highest peak of the Spirit, from where love and the souls fell. If we're willing to come up with sports metaphors, we could think of the pole the jumper uses to go over the bar. Or of the first runners in a relay race. And, searching for a simile outside sports, a certain space mission comes to mind, the one that millions of viewers all over the world, you and I included, followed with excitement in the distant year of 1969... You'll remember that, in the Apollo 11 mission to the moon, what landed on the moon was not the entire rocket that departed from Earth. Only a small part landed, the essential part. The rest was released in successive phases along the way. But those discarded parts, Blanca, played a decisive role in the early stages of the trip. The lower parts held the engines that propelled the spaceship into orbit. Without them, man would not have set foot on the moon that early. Of course, he would not have done so either if he had in-

258. Bernard of Clairvaux, *On Loving God*

tended to make the whole trip with the entire spaceship: the lower parts had to be gradually discarded; otherwise, they would become a hindrance, an impediment for the final approach to the moon. Well then, we talk about the approach to Love in the same terms: in the beginning of Evolution, sex is an indispensable factor; then it becomes more like garnish, let's say; then finally –in the last stage of its trip to the Centre– it becomes a dead weight, a useless obstacle that must be cast aside. In any case, my dear, the key concept is this: love, Love with a capital L, ascends from and through the lower loves. Note that such an ascending and evolutive conception of love also implies the idea of its unitary nature. Meaning: it demonstrates that the three loves are, in the end, only one. This continuity or community of essence is what enables love to Evolve from one level to the next or, in other words, it's what enables the progressive refinement of a lower level of love until it liberates its winged substance, its "soul". This soul is *spiritual* or *divine love*, and it's the only love; love in its purest essence, except this essence, in the lower levels, is brutalised and covered in impurities.

Carnal love then, deep down, shares the same essence with pure love, Blanca. This idea that I pointed out to you in the previous letter, if I remember correctly, also enjoyed a wide consensus among the ancient sages. Again, a metaphor will help us visualise it. Let's take a book from the blue library; a classic; let's say *The Treasure Island* by R.L. Stevenson. Although it was originally written in English, this moralising adventure novel has been translated into several languages, Catalan being one of them, which is the language of the copy in your library. However, if an English reader of *The Treasure Island* who did not know a word of Catalan were to flip through the pages of your book, he probably would not realise that it was the same novel: that's how different translations are from the original. The translation can completely differ from the original in many ways, not just the arrangement of the letters: the letters themselves might be different, if it's a different alphabet. But because it would still remain the same text, the conclusion we can reach is that, no matter how different they are in appearance, translation shares the same essence with the original. We could apply same lesson to love if we think that carnal love is like the material and fallen translation of the Original love.

This unitary notion of love, mind you, is a further reflection of the unitary notion of the Universe according to which the three worlds are, in the end, one and the same. We talked about it two letters ago, do you remember? We saw then that the common denominator of the three worlds was Duality, and what differentiated them was the degree of *integration* of that Duality in each one of them. But, if we are to imagine the cosmic Duality as a tree, then the sap flowing in the entrails of that tree is the mutual love of the Two; This is also a factor common to the three worlds. And this common sap factor is presented in each one of the three worlds in a different way, with a different degree of spirituality. If the love of the split Two of the lower world is characterised by a fraction of spirituality close to zero, then absolute spirituality is what defines the love of the integrated Two of the Hidden Point. (We've already seen that *spirituality* and *integration* are correlated concepts, now we see of what that correlation consists: spirituality is to integration what the mutual love of the Two is to Duality, its "sap".)

I've just made a reference to the role played by carnal love in the Evolution of love towards its pure essence. Well, this role, my dear, could be extended to that of Matter in universal

Evolution. A Tantric saying (a variant from that other saying I transcribed above) tells us that *When we fall to the ground, the ground will help us rise again*, meaning, we need the ground to support our hands, the ground helps us stand up, so to speak. And that is the function of Matter for the soul: to be the support it needs to rise (which is precisely the function that, according to the Creation myth I described before, God predicted for the world when he placed it between Him and Nothingness). Matter can be seen as a mother in labour, giving birth to the Spirit (by an etymological whim, "Matter" and "mother", *mater* in Latin, are related words). In the course of the first phase of Evolution, the Spirit would have been gestating in Matter's womb. Matter was pregnant with the Spirit and, when the moment came, its waters broke. The appearance of man and consciousness represented the Matter going into labour. The birth, Blanca, would correspond to the second phase of Evolution, the one in which we are immersed now. It's a laborious birth, a painful and extremely slow birth, but regardless of whether the child is facing the right way, she will end up leaving her mother's womb. Then she will remain connected to her for a minute: the time it takes to cut the umbilical cord (because souls will never be totally free as long as they remain embodied). Nevertheless, Evolution will be complete; it will have reached its goal: the spiritualisation of the Two, meaning of you and me, Blanca, but also, and above all, of our mutual love; because the birth of the Spirit from Matter –we've just seen it– also applies to erotic love. Once our mutual love is completely sublimated, the Two of us will have repaired the cause of our divorce. We can get married again just as we had already been in the Origin: in heaven, in *perfect union*. This union, as we said, is ascendant, it bears fruit towards above and not below ("the true union is upward: in the Spirit"[259], notes Teilhard); its fruit is God, the One. The sparks would have returned, then, to the original Fire from which they fell, consummating with it the secret plan of life in the Universe: the reintegration in God of His lost portion, of His exiled portion. God will once again be one whole, as our friend Eriugena had predicted: "*You will be whole when nothing remains but You.*"[260]

The appearance of man, my dear, constitutes a fundamental milestone in that long way up that is Evolution. Up to that moment, the soul had evolved as though it was in autopilot; from that moment onwards, it begins to take control. Evolution continues, but through other means. It starts taking place under the light of consciousness. With the transition from the subhuman to the human, the Universe begins to feel self-aware; it begins to personalise, to spiritualise. The soul has already released enough ballast to ascend. So that, when the body dies, the soul does not remain here, immanent to this physical world; it rises to the middle world, which is the human being's true headquarters, just like the lower world is the subhuman's, and the higher the Divine's. The ascent is, at the same time, an interiorisation; each man is, so to speak, a door to the inside of the Universe, and that door opens when he dies, so that the soul can pass through it. We project our next reincarnation from the middle world, since that for as long as there are traces of *ego* in us, we must return to the physical world: except here, we can shake off the material bonds that weigh down our soul.

Now, with the transition from the subhuman to the human, we produced the transition from animal love –purely

259. Teilhard de Chardin, *Human Energy*

260. John Scottus Eriugena, *De Divisione Naturae*

physical and sexual– to human love per se, which is *mixed love*, Blanca, the second level of love's ternary division. But we have already said that the Evolution of love does not stop there, at the human level: it moves beyond it, towards the first and highest level. If God is Evolution's terminal station, my dear, then it must tend to the establishment of that perfect love, of that purely spiritual love that operates within God... Yes, all right, let's face it again: this class of love, today, sounds like a chimaera. The "ultraviolet" love is yet to be discovered, it vibrates at a frequency that is much too high (even though all of us might have caught a glimpse of it, maybe in our adolescence) for it to be perceived by the human eye. But in a remote future, the human eye will conquer that colour, it will make it his. In fact, Blanca, in the modern age there already are (and there were even more of them in the old days) people that are capable of seeing that colour which is invisible to most. They described it to us in every detail, but since most of us are blind to that strange colour, we did not pay them any attention and took them for madmen.

Do you know who could see that colour? Your dear Emily Dickinson:

I see thee better
in the dark
I do not need a light
the love of thee
a prism be
excelling violet

"THESE MIRACLES WE MADE"

I can hear... I think I can hear your ethereal voice asking me when is humanity supposed to cross the threshold of the Hidden Point. But I don't have an answer to that question, Blanca, no one does. First, because, as you understand, there are no deadlines for this. Then, because we can't talk about humanity here as a whole, we must talk and consider men individually. Since what is at play here is not a collective redemption but an individual one. Each human soul will take as long to return to the Hidden Point as the time it takes it to surmount –the number of lives it takes it to surmount– the spiritualisation process that we just mentioned. Each person progresses at his or her own rhythm. The important thing is to know that we are on our way... Now, while it's true that, generally, the rhythm is slow, it has been observed throughout human history a flowering of a number of souls that intensify the process to such a degree, that they notoriously stand out from most others. It would be appropriate, then, to classify souls in two generic levels, attending to the rhythm of their evolution: the vast majority's level and that of a small advanced minority.

As far as the vast majority is concerned, the Hidden Point is a distant evolutive horizon. How distant? No one can say, my dear. But, judging by the current temporal unbalance between the two phases of Evolution (it has been calculated that the time we've been in the second phase, in relation to the first one, would correspond to the last eight minutes in the life of an eighty-year-old individual), the majority still has a long way ahead of them. However, an aware minority anticipates that distant horizon. For this minority, all that long process of reincarnating hundreds of times is compressed into a handful of lives. The ancient sages decidedly bet on this type of souls, among whom many of them could be counted. There have always been souls who could not wait to go back "home", Blanca. Souls that didn't settle for floating along a slow current like pieces of cork, and instead decided to swim with verve.

In the following letters, I want to tell you about those who are nostalgic for the Origin, the souls that rather than marching along with everyone else, walk ahead and set the pace. By acting like this, they collaborate with God for the cause of Evolution, of which they are the advance party, the spearhead. Using the well-trodden metaphor of the shortcuts, we could say that this select minority is diverting from the main path– filled with twists and turns since it goes around a mountain– to take a shortcut up a climbing route. As the shortcut is steeper and rougher than the normal path (although don't go around thinking that the main evolutive path is a walk in the park), the ancient sages called it the *warrior* or *hero's* way. Because stripping the soul supposes a sacrifice similar to that which is expected from a warrior who goes off to war. Except that this is a bloodless combat, my dear, an initiation, an interior fight; a fight against oneself; or better yet, against a part of oneself –the *ego*, the carnal soul– a part that in reality does not belong to oneself, because it's accidental, it's something that suddenly happened to oneself.

Crossed–out note on the margin. Only the ending of the quotation is readable: *...jumped lightly down into the Looking–Glass room.* I am almost certain that the sentence the author had written down had been a quotation from the extremely famous Lewis Carroll book,

***Through the Looking-Glass*: "*In another moment, Alice was through the glass, and jumped lightly down into the Looking-glass room.*" We could consider that the author saw in this line an allusion to the parallel world from where his wife was supposedly communicating with him.**

This heroism consisting of the stripping of the soul, implies, first of all, an amorous heroism. That is to say, the struggle to strip love of all its materiality, all its sexuality. The heroic lovers' feat lies in this: in loving each other in a spiritual and platonic way, voluntarily renouncing sex. It's important that you understand, Blanca, that this is not a celibate's renunciation, it does not mean that one must renounce love at all, on the contrary: it means one must refine it and embrace genuine, naked love. Because there's an apparent paradox implied here, you know? It's that the hero renounces sex *for the sake of love*. And given that this supposes the hero must overcome no one but himself (it's a secret heroism, a heroism which deeds operate in the intimacy of hearts), the amorous heroism is incomparably superior to the warrior's heroism. As sages from all over the world have emphasised throughout the ages, the true merit is in overcoming oneself. If you remember my childhood stories as well as I remember yours, you know that I, personally, didn't learn this postulate from any sage or book: my mother used to tell it to me whenever I got into a fight with another boy. When I was eleven years old, I was a physically strong but emotionally weak boy, given to boasting and bragging. My willpower left much to be desired, and I knew that this was what my mother meant with her advice... But I'm getting side-tracked. Besides, I've already told you this God knows how many times. What I never told you before is that there was a spurious etymology among the ancient sages: it claimed that the word *hero* derived from the Greek term *eros*. It was an attempt to justify their intuition that supreme heroism lies in this internal struggle to refine love. Before these letters, I also had never read you passages from the *Bhagavad Gita*, where we can find this verse, where Krishna -the *Gita's* personal God- exhorts young Arjun: "O mighty armed Arjun, subdue the self (senses, mind, and intellect) by the self (strength of the soul), and kill this formidable enemy called lust."[261]

Arjun has the makings of a hero, Blanca; he'll do well in following Krishna's advice. But we should keep in mind that not everyone is made of the same stuff, and so such advice - "kill this formidable enemy called lust"-, as peremptory it is, cannot be extrapolated to the common man.

Consider this beautiful poem by John Donne, entitled "The Undertaking"[262]:

I have done one braver thing
Than all the Worthies did,
And yet a braver thence doth spring,
Which is, to keep that hid.

It were but madness now t'impart
The skill of specular stone,
When he which can have learn'd the art
To cut it, can find none.

261. *Bhagavad-Gita*, 3:43
262. John Donne, *Songs and Sonnets*, "The Undertaking"

So, if I now should utter this,
Others (because no more
Such stuff to work upon, there is,)
Would love but as before.

But he who loveliness within
Hath found, all outward loathes,
For he who colour loves, and skin,
Loves but their oldest clothes.

If, as I have, you also do
Virtue attir'd in woman see,
And dare love that, and say so too,
And forget the He and She;

And if this love, though placed so,
From profane men you hide,
Which will no faith on this bestow,
Or, if they do, deride:

Then you have done a braver thing
Than all the Worthies did;
And a braver thence will spring,
Which is, to keep that hid.

The undertaking to which Donne alludes –an undertaking that converts its maker into the greatest of heroes– is to love not the spouse's sexual condition: not the gender but the *person*. To love her spirit, not her flesh. According to the ancient sages, this undertaking has the power to bring lovers closer together and, proportionally, closer to Unity, to God. The intersexual heroic love, my dear, is tightly connected to mysticism, to religion; they are, as we'll see, closely associated phenomena. It's not by chance that heroic love -which has been called "courteous" love- and mystic love were born at the same time. The heroic lover is the *sacred* lover. In another poem, Donne will describe it as "Love's clergy"[263]. To elude the incomprehension or the jokes of profane lovers, who are the vast majority, he will advise the hero to keep his undertaking a secret: "'Twere profanation of our joys / to tell the laity our love."[264] So great was the effort required, that he does not hesitate in calling it a miracle: "What miracles we harmless lovers wrought..."

> First we loved well and faithfully,
> Yet knew not what we loved, nor why ;
> Difference of sex we never knew,
> No more than guardian angels do ;
> Coming and going we
> Perchance might kiss, but not between those meals ;
> Our hands ne'er touch'd the seals,
> Which nature, injured by late law, sets free.
> These miracles we did; but now alas!
> All measure, and all language, I should pass,
> Should I tell what a miracle she was.[265]

From the moment that even caresses and kisses are off-limits, these lovers' spirituality strikes me as exaggerated, my love (what a torture to have you next to me, as you seem to be now, and not being able to caress or kiss you!). The

---

263. *Ibid*, "Valediction of the book", v. 22
264. *Ibid*, "Valediction Forbidding Mourning" v. 7-8
265. *Ibid*, "The Relic"

lovers' bodies remain sealed off, "Our hands ne'er touch'd the seals". But it's not to the communion of bodies that they aspire, it's to the communion of souls. Their souls who remain embraced in intimate contact. Their love transcends sexual differentiation: "Difference of sex we never knew"... If the poet was writing from experience (as it's believed to be the case with most of Donne's poems), this "never" should nevertheless be called into question: the poems from his youth show us a womanising Donne. However, later in life, Donne changed. And do you know what the scholastics think was the turning point for this change? He found his twin soul: Anne More, a young lady whose aunt was married to a high-ranking court member where Donne was a secretary (this was the trick Destiny devised to bring them together). It seems like from the moment they met, they knew they were made for one another. And what happened was that the amorous cynicism that he had shown until then, gave way to an increasingly higher and deeper conception of love. A conception that was intertwined with the idea of God, Blanca, as evidenced by the proliferation of religious references in his later works... In one of those poems, Donne warns Anne More about the likely event of one of them dying before the other. There is no need for despair, he tells her, because it will not be an actual separation: it will be like when spouses turn around in bed, after kissing goodnight ("Are but turn'd aside to sleep").[266] In their sleep, they go their separate ways; but there they remain, lying next to each other, maybe dreaming of one another; knowing that night will be followed by morning, and the morning will awake them.

266. *Ibid*, "Song", v.32

Providence gave Anne More and John Donne seventeen years to be together before succumbing to "sleep". That does not seem to be enough time to ascend the three levels of the hierarchy of love observed by the ancient sages. But it was enough for them, apparently. At the end of their life together, John Donne and Anne More would come to be a part of that heroic minority that succeeds in inhabiting the very core of love, where it is most sacred; while the majority of people –the profane and the clueless– develop on its outskirts, where this kind of love is incomprehensible. It's incomprehensible because it's inhuman, Blanca, because sex is a basic ingredient of erotic love between human beings. The one hundred percent spiritual love, pure spiritual love, does not belong to the human world but to the divine world. What happens, then? The strangest thing happens, my love: the heroes find themselves embarking on that transition. Knowing that love is a current that flows both ways, generating men as it goes down, and gods as it goes up, they choose the second option. In their effort to unload their *ego*, their carnal soul, they are breaking down human limitations and crossing the threshold into divinity. The reason for their effort could be summarised by a famous speech by Jakob Boehme that could also very well be their motto: "God asks for gods!". On top of it, his contemporary Angelus Silesius added, "Man, be not ever man! The summit must be gained! In God's house, Gods and Gods alone are entertained."[267]

Yet, Blanca, as incomprehensible it is for the majority of people, the heroes' love foreshadows tomorrow's erotic love, given that in virtue of Evolution, the scope of human love is widening, its nature is changing... Can you hear the booming

267. Angelus Silesius, *Cherubinic Wanderer*

brass voice of the pendulum? It's warning us that it's time for us to separate, for us to turn aside to sleep, as John Donne would say, although in this case, it's in the literal sense: time to go to bed. But I don't want to finish this letter without first refuting an impression that I may very well have given you... Admit it that, reading this letter, you had the impression that your husband, bewildered by extravagant readings like a revived Don Quixote, reached the point of thinking that sex, a basic ingredient of human love, was something perverse... You'll see: if you and I were One, if we were the two Persons implicit in God, then I would have no doubt in proclaiming that, in fact, yes, sex is something perverse from which we must abstain. But we are human beings. And as such, you and I enjoyed sex together for a few years. We could have sworn that it was a fundamental part of our love. Afterwards, we discovered that no, we didn't need it, our love didn't depend on sex. But we lived with that false idea for years. And I'm sure it was true for a while: indeed, sex was a fundamental part of our love back then. But our love "grew", it matured in a few years, as John Donne and Anne More's, except in our case it wasn't due to some heroic will (I suspect that it was harder on me than on you, I must confess that in the first years I was tempted by the idea of infidelity), it was forced on us by the circumstances: your illness, which first restricted, and then denied us the enjoyment of sex. The point is that now is not exactly the same love as it was then. Was the old love perverse, and this one pure? No. More like: that love was in its infancy, today's love has evolved, it's an adult love. "When I was a child –wrote St. Paul–, I talked like a child, thought like a child, reasoned like a child; when I became a man, I put aside childish things." (I Corinthians 13:11–12) That's what happened to us: without realising, we put aside the childish things of love. But for us, those childish things had their moments. And we would not have thought about labelling them as childish back then –that's an adult description. A child's interests are very different from those of an adult person. The adult thinks that the child's interests are futile, and maybe they are. But what for an adult is a childish thing, for a child is the most important thing in his life and he would not know how to live without it. And if someone told him that, with the passing of the years, the interests that today he believes will last forever, will appear futile and be replaced by new pleasures that, up until then, he could not have predicted, he would not believe you. That is what the growing up process in which the soul has embarked does, Blanca: it makes so that many things are right... until they're not.

Yours

Second Part:

Love Heroism

Perhaps the inebriation of the senses
belongs to man as sleep belongs to life.
That is not the noblest aspect, and
man will always prefer to stay awake
rather than to sleep.

Novalis

SIXTH LETTER

LOVE HEROISM

(OR THE QUEST FOR THE GRAIL)

If thou askest me:
'Dost thou prefer Paradise or Ramin?'
By thy sun, I prefer Ramin.
For the sight of him seems
Paradise to me.

Gurgani, *Vis and Ramin*,
Twelfth century Persian novel

Barcelona, October 6th, 1999

Dear Blanca

After a few days' rest, I resume our correspondence with the confidence, almost certainty, that you're receiving my letters on time. In the last one, we tackled the path of Evolution, along which the fallen souls ascend back to the Origin, to the Unit. It's an extremely slow path, where often a little progress can only be achieved by taking a bigger step back. Evolution does not advance in a straight line: it's more like a spiral stairway. Nevertheless, my love, despite being intertwined with regressions, the evolutive and ascending baseline eventually prevails. In my opinion, this is an unappealable realisation. All we have to do is look back on History. Not only has humanity collectively progressed as a whole, I would venture to say that we've even advanced on an individual level: in general, today we're better persons than our ancestors were. Compassion, social and ecological awareness, respect towards animals... these are all eminently modern traits, traits that would have made the ancient man laugh.

Regarding our subject, Blanca, we need only to compare the modern average man's notion of erotic love to the one held by the average man of two thousand years ago. Today, this notion includes a spiritual component –the falling in love or romance– that was absent back then. This progress is reflected in the sexual act itself, where the brutality of yesteryear –women being raped by men– has been losing ground to mutual tenderness. What I feel for you, the sublime emotion of falling in love, was unknown to the majority of our ancestors; it underscores a relatively recent evolution. Scholars usually place around the twelfth century our inflexion towards the Spirit, which, little by little, opened the door to erotic love as we know it. Today, Blanca, it's obvious that erotic love is not an exclusively sexual matter: it's more than that. If in practice that does not appear to be as evident, at least it is so in people's imagination. Keep in mind that the evolutive conquests of "the second phase" take shape in our imagination long before they become reality: to accomplish something, we must first imagine it.

You just have to look at the concept of love emerging from countless songs, novels, and films. It's a romantic conception of love, a concept with which the public identifies. I'm sure you could name heaps of songs that talk about a love of this nature. And your library is swarming with romantic novels that were best-sellers. And what can we say about the cinema? The box-office success of films such as *City Lights* or *An Affair to Remember*, to name two of your favourites, would have been unthinkable two thousand years ago. Back then, romantic films would have been relegated to a small audience, just as it happens today with avant-garde cinema. And this spiritual component that love conquered, Blanca, defines a degree of "personalisation" of love that was unknown two thousand years ago.

In fact, these days we feel that it's almost impossible to love –to erotically love, I mean– two people at the same time. While it lasts, love is prone to fidelity, to exclusivity. That is due to the spiritual component that, albeit still in an incipient form, love has conquered. Two thousand years ago, love did not include that component, or if it did, it did so on a much smaller scale. It was an indiscriminate and promiscuous love. Of course, I'm talking about love as it relates to the average person, the most common notion of love at any given time. The subject of Evolution is the average person, the majority; in evolutive terms, the advanced minority does not count. The Universe only takes one step forward in Evolution when the number of individuals that support it reaches what a scientist would call "critical mass": that is to say, when the exception becomes the rule. We Catalans have a saying: *Una flor no fa estiu ni dues primavera*. We can welcome Spring when there are many flowers, but not before.

Very well. Although it's true that the heroic minority by itself does not represent any kind of evolutive progress, it's also true that it *foreshadows that progress*. In the future, we will all be those men and women, hence our interest in knowing the characteristics of this rarefied channel: love heroism. That is why we will dedicate this letter and the following ones to exploring this subject. We will investigate love as experienced by ancient heroes, thus getting a glimpse into the love of the future, the love of future average people... However, before

I begin telling you about that minority, Blanca, I would like to make a few comments on my previous letters. From what I said then, you could erroneously infer that, unlike what happens in the heroic path, to follow the Evolutionary path we would only have to let ourselves be carried away; that we could sit idly by because Evolution would take place anyway. This was only the case in the first phase of Evolution: we have already seen that in its second phase –the one that began with the human being– we are in the driving seat. God granted us control of Evolution by bestowing *free will* on us: meaning, by allowing us to be free to advance, retreat, or remain stationary. From then on, Evolution became our business.

This freedom is necessary, Blanca. A father takes care of his son while he is a child. But, when the boy grows up, the father should step aside and let him take the helm of his life, otherwise, he would be restricting his growth: because we only grow when we are free. Free will implies the power to choose, therefore the possibility of making a mistake. Nevertheless, we learn from our mistakes, and those are the lessons that make us grow and evolve. God cannot, then –or should not, lest he obstructs it– force Evolution beyond a certain point. His mission is over with the exhumation of consciousness, meaning, with the appearance of man. In another letter, we compared the Unit, human being's original Divinity, to a house, do you remember? Well, then, this house has collapsed and now is in ruins. God will take care of pulling its residents from under the debris; but once they are free, they are responsible for rebuilding the house. God can guide them, he can bring them the bricks, and show them the blueprints, but he cannot rebuild the house for them. If He did, it would not belong to them, they would only be borrowing it, and it seems like that is not what God wants. God wants us to have our own property.

Crossed–out note on the margin. Besides the date (7–10–99), the words "*...the candle's glow in the mirror*" are all that remains from the original paragraph or sentence. Despite its apparent relation to the previous quotation, *Through the Looking–Glass* is not its source. In any case, in view of previous revelations, the two quotations allow us to imagine the author compelled to observe the moon through a candlelit mirror.

With the data science provides us these days, we can venture to draw a profile of the cosmic process of Evolution. It would be more or less like this:

Before the appearance of man, the soul was immanent to Matter; it lied immersed in Matter, buried underneath its rubble. This means the soul was subjugated by genetic determinism, which is Matter's biological mechanism. But God, God's "chance", guided genetic determinism towards the path of self–destruction, that is, towards the path that led to the appearance of man. Because saying "appearance of man", Blanca, is equivalent to saying the emergence of consciousness, of the Spirit, and, with it, free will. And free will is the mortal enemy of genetic determinism. (Matter is determinism and slavery; the Spirit is freedom.) The emergence of free will meant, then, the relativisation of biological determinism, which ceased to be inexorable. It signified the end of the soul's submission to the empire of Matter. From that moment, we acquired the ability of choice regarding the evolution of our soul. However, in every other aspect, we remain conditioned, subject to that servitude: to Matter's dictatorship, to genetic determinism. The genes determine, for example, our physical aspect and our intelligence; they also determine, along with the environmental factor, our frontal or external personality (hence the need to look through the eyes of the heart to recognise our twin soul). However, they do not determine our moral attitude towards the world. In that aspect, the choice is ours. It's in our hands to choose between good and evil, to choose between altruism and selfishness, between spirituality and materialism. The concept of free will refers to this type of freedoms, to the kind of choices of which the ascendant movement of our soul's evolution depends. We do not have the freedom to choose to be more intelligent, but we are free to use our intelligence –the one determined by our genes– to do good or evil, to pursue altruist of selfish, spiritual or material goals.

Genes are not impartial in that choice, my dear. Genes are selfish by nature. In the lower, material levels of Evolution, where genetic determinism leaves no room whatsoever for free will, selfishness is the standard behaviour. Altruism is an evolutive conquest of the second phase: the Spirit speaks through that vital posture. In fact, Blanca, altruism is the clearest proof of humanity's victory over animality, the triumph of the individual over the species. The genes' attention is focused on the species (which is a material magnitude), not on the individual. The spiritual magnitude that is the individual is of no interest to generic determinism beyond its small contribution to the perpetuation of the species. That is the only law genes know, and selfishness and materialism are their greatest allies. Our genes force us to compete with each other, to move exclusively through that class of interests; in short, they pull us "down" or –which is the same thing, Blanca– "out". But we have free will, which means that we can resist that pull, we can choose to act against our material and selfish natural inclinations –against our instinct, our genetic determinism– and behave in accordance to our conscience. Our conscience pulls us in the opposite direction, towards altruism and spirituality: it pulls us "up"/"in". To summarise, we are free to remain under the yoke of Matter or to break free of that yoke. That choice is our responsibility.

A MAGIC LETTER

I don't need to tell you that the ancient sages knew nothing about Matter's biological mechanism, that is, about genetic determinism. However, even without the knowledge of that mechanism, they knew that Matter tends to determine human behaviour, including when it comes to moral choices. At first, it fully determines it and the human soul is its prisoner, it's enslaved by Matter. Then, little by little, through a progressive and increasing awareness, the soul becomes free. Or rather, this awareness suddenly awakes and thus liberation occurs abruptly. That's what happens with the protagonist of the *Song of the Pearl*. Because the story does not end where we left it in the other letter: I mean with the Eastern prince's imprisonment and the following forgetfulness of his origin and the mission that brought him to that Western country. The story continues, then, with the Eastern kings (a royal couple: remember the symbolic value of Royalty) sending their son, the captive prince, a missive in which they remind him of his origin and, therefore, his identity. In some kind of magic mail, the kind I would need to send you this letter, the missive descends on the prince and it becomes Speech. In the *Story of Western Exile* –which is possibly a retelling of the same story–, a hoopoe brings the letter to the captive brothers. The voice from the letter says, "Awake and rise from your sleep and hear the words of our letter! Remember that you are a son of kings and see the slavery of your life. Remember the pearl for which you were sent into Egypt!"

The effect it has over the prince is immediate, "I awoke and rose from my sleep. I took it, kissed it, broke its seal, and read. And the words written on my heart were in the letter for me to read. I remembered that I was the son of kings and my free soul longed for its own kind. I remembered the pearl for which I was sent down into Egypt, and I began to enchant the terrible and snorting serpent. I charmed him into sleep by calling the Name of my Father over him and of my mother, the queen of the East. I seized the pearl and turned to carry it to my father."[268] Let's analyse the symbolism in these enigmatic words.

We've already discussed how the pearl, how the perfection of the pearl's spherical shape, symbolised Unity, the prince's original Integrity; meaning, his androgynous soul in the Origin. But we should also interpret it in another way: as the prince's soul *in its original nudity*. Due to the Fall, the soul covered itself with Matter. This is symbolised here by the pearl sinking to the bottom of the ocean, where it's held captive, "surrounded by the hissing serpent". It's the same symbolism as in many fairy tales, my dear: stories that tell us about a buried or submerged treasure, guarded by a serpent, or a dragon, or a demon. From the middle world, the prince comes down into the lower world to liberate the pearl from its captivity... But what's keeping it captive? The soul cannot be fettered to the bottom of the ocean: it is kept there by the

268. Mircea Eliade, *History of religious Ideas*

hissing of a serpent (serpents and reptiles in general, as we said, symbolise Matter). The captivity of the human soul, its enslavement, is voluntary, in the sense that its liberation is in its own hands; it depends exclusively on itself. There are no shackles, it can leave its prison whenever it wants; all it has to do is ignore the Siren's song, the hisses of the serpent.

The hisses represent the temptations of Matter, instinct seducing the still "dressed" and embodied soul, the material and selfish motivations determined by genes. The prince from the *Song of the Pearl* is a hero. He has an intuition or reminiscence of his remote origin and, goaded by nostalgia, finds the courage to return home. In the first letter, I told you about Perceval, the quintessential hero of the Grail legend. He also starts immersed in absolute amnesia or ignorance, which in this case is the same. He cannot remember his own name; he does not know who he is. (For the ancient sages, the name symbolised the essence of the thing; the most profound self, in the case of a person; hence why in many religions it's forbidden to utter God's name.) His mother, the Widowed Lady, has kept him away from society, isolated in a cabin in the woods. But one day he has an unexpected and providential encounter. Hunting in the woods, he crosses the path of five errant knights who are chasing after the kidnappers of some maidens. He finds himself standing before the knights and, ignorant of what knighthood is, having never seen one in his life, he is in awe of the vision of these gallant horsemen in shining armour.

The effect such vision has over Perceval is the same that the magic letter has over the prince from the *Song of the Pearl*: it's a reminder. The knights bring the confusing memory of his own knightly origin to his mind, they remind him of his lineage, which is a lineage of kings. In a way, the message from the letter in the *Song of the Pearl* echoes in young Perceval's ears (the reminder's message is always the same): "Awake and rise from your sleep and hear the words of our letter! Remember that you are a son of kings and see the slavery of your life. Remember the pearl (in Perceval's case, it's the Grail) for which you were sent into Egypt!" And after this, the ignorant young man cannot linger in ignorance any longer. He says goodbye to his mother and leaves to join King Arthur, of whom the knights spoke with great praise. He is knighted by the king and sets off in search of adventures, in the course of which he regains his memory. He quickly remembers his name, when a maiden who later turns out to be his cousin asks him, "'My friend: tell me your name.' And then, not knowing his name, he somehow he still knew, and said he was Perceval from Wales..."[269] Following the vision I cited last time –the three drops of blood on the fresh snow–, he also remembers Blanchefleur, his twin soul. But most importantly, towards the end, he remembers the Grail; he remembers to ask the pertinent question in its presence. Others, less pure, less mature heroes, such as Gawain, will waste their opportunity to do so, when they visit the Fisher King's castle, by succumbing to fatigue and sleep –the sleep of Matter and forgetfulness.

THE HISSING SERPENT

Just like Perceval, Blanca, after suddenly regaining his consciousness, the protagonist of the *Song of the Pearl* returns to his mission. "And I began [then] to charm it, the terrible

269. Chrétien de Troyes, *Perceval, The Story of the Grail*

loud-breathing Serpent", he says, until it fell asleep. This probably took him many years, perhaps even many lives. When he finally succeeded, he conquered his much-desired freedom, which here is equivalent to the soul's nakedness. His soul stripped itself from the Matter that restrained it like a straightjacket. Now, with his soul naked, with the pearl in his power, the prince is ready to join his twin soul -who predictably followed an identical process- and thus cross, the two of them together, the threshold of Unity, the threshold of his parents' house, which is his own house.

Well, Evolution follows the same path, except much slower and without abrupt leaps, without sudden awakenings of consciousness. The awakening of the evolutive majority's consciousness is slow, gradual, like a wine's decantation process. It comes about progressively in the course of many lives. And like every gradual process, Blanca, it's imperceptible to the individual experiencing it. Similarly, a boy is not aware of his crossing into adolescence, and an adolescent does not notice his transition into a young man, and the young man is unaware he has reached adulthood. It's only upon looking back that we can see the path we unknowingly walked: the transitions sneak up on us. Evolution is related to natural growth processes (like those of children, trees, or grass), which are carried out imperceptibly, as if walking on tiptoes.

Evolution is a slow and progressive charming of the "hissing snake", of Matter. Naturally, only God knows the details of the evolutive machinery, we can only speculate and imagine its intricacies. We could apply here the metaphor suggested by the Kabbalist Isaac Luria: the metaphor of the "rupture of the Vessels". I'm sure you remember the divine Vessels that shattered, letting the Spirit, or Light of God, escape and scatter as a multitude of holy sparks, each one of them divided into two halves. Well then, according to Luria, each fallen half-spark had been buried underneath a thick layer of Matter –"the shell" or "slag", as he calls it. Evolution's aim would be to redeem the fallen sparks, to liberate them from the shell that covers them, so that they could return to the Origin from where they fell.

Now suppose, Blanca (let's see if you buy this metaphor), that this "shell" was an eggshell. At the beginning, the soul is inside the shell, like yolk; it lacks shape. Because of the Fall, we had become diluted in the bosom of Matter, which completely defined us. Then, this yolk seeks to define itself, to reveal a shape: this is the individual opening way through the species. This does not happen by itself: the egg needs to be incubated. In Evolution, this necessary external intervention is the responsibility of God. But this intervention stops the moment the chick is formed, the moment man appears. From then on, man is the protagonist. Man is in charge of breaking the shell –which in this metaphor represents genetic determinism– and liberating himself. The evolutive majority has not broken the shell yet, they have not even cracked it. But the chick has begun to betray the confinement of its prison and to deliver it its first blows. One only has to pay attention to hear the first signs coming from behind the shell in the form of confused mutterings.

Those "confused mutterings", my dear, correspond to every behaviour that is not guided by selfishness nor materialism. Because this kind of behaviour cannot be attributed to genetic determinism. The inclination towards altruism and spirituality is the exclusive responsibility of the soul, and it indicates an equivalent degree of liberation. Although it's still to a limited extent, we can find such inclinations in the average man: in his amorous behaviour, for example. This is not operated, as it was in the past, exclusively by selfishness and sexual instinct. The spiritual component that has infiltrated love cannot be explained by genetic determinism. From the genetic point of view, it's an anomaly, since genes pull the individual precisely in the opposite direction: their purpose is the conservation of the species. Genes are interested in a high rate of reproduction for individuals, which does not particularly contribute to spiritual love, which furthermore entails exclusivity, another drastic limitation of reproductive possibilities. Another sign of the chick's uprising is the emergence of pacifism in the world, Blanca, considering the species' natural predisposition for wrath and aggression. I mention it because I know how much you admire Gandhi, Martin Luther King and, most of all, Jesus Christ, who told us to forgive those who offend us and talked about turning the other cheek. To repress one's anger is a heroic attitude comparable to our heroes' repression of desire: in both cases, they are overcoming our human condition and broadening our horizon. It's not in vain that in Buddhism, wrath and desire –or concupiscence–, along with ignorance, are the three main burdens that drag the human soul down to the lower world over and over again. According to Buddhist doctrine, only our victory over these three natural attributes –wrath, desire, and ignorance– will allow us to embrace our original divine nature.

Do you know how else you can imagine the soul's gradual liberation from the yoke of Matter or biological determinism? You could recall that spectacle you and I watched together in Pálamos so many times: the sunrise, the sun's slow liberation from its nocturnal prison. Slowly, our spiritual essence –the Self– detaches itself from its material circumstances, from the *ego*, rising in "sky-blue freedom" (to put it in the words of a poet), which in this lower world translates into letting go of the genetic and social conditioning that determines our behaviour. I insist, my love, the soul's process of self-determination is not, in its second phase, something that happens spontaneously. Evolution is connected to becoming, to Time. And what is Time, can you tell me? Henry David Thoreau said that Time was nothing more than the river where he went fishing. Fishing, not for trout as we used to do, of course, but for opportunities for growth and maturing. It's up to each one of us to cast our line and reel in those opportunities, do you understand? Time is the path towards Eternity, towards "timeless Time", if that makes sense; but from the moment that we have legs to walk, we are walkers. If we remain stationary, if we take too long to get there, we will come to a standstill halfway to our destiny, on the outskirts of the second phase of Evolution. Since this phase is a conscious process architected by each one of us, its protagonists, it cannot come to fruition without our active intervention. Hence, the ancient sages proposing the pilgrim as a role model to be followed by everyone. Human existence, they claimed, should be seen as a pilgrimage. We must not stay in the comfort of our homes; we must hit the road. "Leave -exhorts the Sufi poet Farid al-Din Attar-, leave this ocean like rain and travel, for without travel you will never become a pearl!"[270] In the quest for the Grail, about which we will talk later, there is a law in effect that says one must not spend the night at the same castle for two consecutive nights. Certainly, travelling along the evolutive road of the majority is not the same as taking the heroic path; the first one is much less steep, much easier -much slower too. But to

---

270. Farid al-Din Attar, *Diwan-i qasa'id wa ghazaliyat*

advance, both ways require the motivation to walk. In both situations, the individual is in control of his progress. This, above all, means making choices.

Given your situation, my dear, I'm sure you are aware that we don't have to make choices only while we are embodied. In the period between lives, we choose the next reincarnation and its main guidelines. In–between lives, the *ego* remains suspended and the soul temporarily recovers the Spirit's inherent lucidity; so that those choices we make are always in the pursuit of progress. This amnesia is part of the rules of the game: we are not allowed to play with an advantage. Thus, there are many souls that despite carefully planning each new existence with their evolutive progress in mind, at the decisive moment they veer off track. Life after life, they waste every opportunity to grow that is offered to them, and so they lag behind. They find themselves, then, caught in a truly difficult reincarnation (remember that the most bitter drinks are often medicinal) through which they can recover lost time. Because as we said, growth and suffering walk hand in hand. Unfortunately, it seems like that's how it is: difficult lives offer the greatest opportunities for growth. That's why they are the ones favoured by those souls who have chosen (since that's also our choice) to follow the heroic path. We see it, Blanca –in chivalric romances, for example–, when the hero is at a crossroads; he always chooses the most difficult path, the apparently impracticable one bristling with bushes and thorns. Is it masochism? No: it's longing for improvement.

Crossed–out note on the margin. I can only read, *I take up my pen in the year of grace 17…* As short as it is fragmented –it corresponds to the opening line of a famous

book already mentioned in the letters–, it was not difficult to identify its source: *Treasure Island* by R.L. Stevenson. Once again, we see the eighteenth century become the benchmark for quotations written down by the author on the margin of his manuscript.

Well, my dear, this is, broadly speaking and translated into modern terms (such as genes, about which the ancient sages knew nothing, starting with their very existence), what we can learn from the ancient sages about the dynamics of Evolution. Most of all, remember the idea that Evolution is not, in its second phase, something that happens apart from us, but rather something that happens *thanks* to us, with our assistance. We are in charge; we are at the helm of the process. Evolution is no longer the one that acts on us: we are the ones who act on it; we make it move forward, move backwards, or cause it to stagnate. And the key is in free will, which we finally possess.

Free will entails that each soul's degree of evolution is different. Nevertheless, Blanca, and as I said, we can place souls in two asymmetrical groups, according to their evolutive level. There is the majority, the average person, the thick of Evolution. Then, there is a small advanced minority –a scanty minority, let's not fool ourselves. In addition, there is also, way behind, a great number of stragglers, but we'll disregard these for now. The ancient sages metaphorically applied the idea of "age" to the souls: the souls are not all of the same age; they are older or younger, depending on their degree of evolution. The more evolved ones are old souls; the less evolved are younger souls. In this case, old age is preferable to youth.

A STAIRWAY TO HEAVEN

The advanced minority has always been misunderstood by the majority, Blanca. However, all they do is anticipate future evolutionary conquests. They are ahead of their time, of the evolutive level achieved by the contemporary average person. Evidently, such anticipation supposes they will have access to Evolution's finishing line before the end of times, that is to say, before the majority does. That which for the majority will take tens of thousands of years –hundreds of reincarnations–, for the minority, will take only a few lives. But they will be extremely busy lives, similar to the hard journey of a mountain climber intent on conquering the summit. The active attitude required to venture through this evolutionary shortcut is different from the one demanded by the majority's path: it's more committed, more striving. That's why the ancient sages used heroic or warrior symbolism to embody it. And to depict the hero's progression through that shortcut, they conceived a literary storyline typical of your dear fairy tales: the adventurous voyage of discovery.

We can find numerous Eastern examples of this among the night-time stories that saved princess Scheherazade in *One Thousand and One Nights*. Sinbad's trip –his seven trips, actually– are very famous. But there is another adventurous voyage on which the narrator of the *Nights* places greater importance, since it is, she tells us, one of the most extraordinary stories ever told, "worthy of being copied in golden letters and displayed in a prominent place in the libraries of the royal palace" (and in blue libraries, if I may add). That's why I will transcribe it here.

In the magical universe of the *Arabian Nights*, stories –as you know– are worth their weight in gold. Well, this is about a king who has that passion, the passion for listening to stories. But he is growing old, and he knows that he is yet to hear the greatest story of all. So he summons the best storyteller in his kingdom and he gives him a year to find this story. The storyteller sends emissaries all over the East to find the story of Saif-ul-Malook and Badr-ul-Jamal, which he knows is the most extraordinary of all. It's also the most secret one. It's so secret that only one of his emissaries, right when time is running out, succeeds in his mission. In Damascus, an old storyteller agrees to tell this story, but only on the condition that he is not to tell it to anyone. (this secrecy denotes a high level of symbolism destined only to the enlightened). The story –maybe you remember when we read it together– begins with a pagan king who, distraught by his lack of descendants, sends his vizier to Solomon's court. Solomon agrees to intercede with God on the king's behalf and hands the vizier two gifts for the future son of the king, for he is certain of being worthy of God's favour. And so, when prince Saif-ul-Malook comes of age, he receives from his father, along with the royal crown, Solomon's two gifts: a ring and a tunic.

Sewn in the lining of the tunic, Saif-al-Malook discovers the picture of a young woman with whom he falls in love. He also discovers an inscription with her name and the country where she was born, a country that no one knows for sure where it is. Even so, he sets sail in search of Badr-ul-Jamal, the young woman from the picture in Solomon's tunic. Shipwrecked on an archipelago of the China seas, he goes through a real ordeal. Hopping from island to island, he escapes evil genies, and the jaws of an ogre, he escapes a cannibal tribe, a giant crocodile, and he becomes a slave to a harpy... After many years of hardship, he docks on an island where a genie holds a damsel in captivity. This damsel turns out to be Badr-ul-Jamal's foster sister, and she tells him that only the owner of Solomon's ring can kill the genie. Saif-al-Malook shows her the ring, kills the genie, and with the help of the freed damsel, finds his beloved.

We can feel the same halo of prestige and mystery that enshrouds the preamble of this story around other stories from the *Nights*, such as the one about Hassan of Basra, the goldsmith. Here, too, they go specifically in search of the story as it's "one of the most extraordinary stories of all time". Only one storyteller in the world knows it, so the search is difficult. A (Sufi) dervish told it to him before dying, as he had heard it from another holy man. The seeker finds himself forced to swear that he will not reveal the story to ignorant ears. It's about a young goldsmith that, intent on initiating himself into the secrets of Alchemy, embarks on a perilous adventure where he falls in love with a gorgeous winged woman. To keep her by his side, he tears off her wings and hides them, but she finds them and escapes to her faraway country -the island of Uak- to where she summons her beloved for the final reunion. In her pursuit, Hassan will cross "seven mountain ranges without summits, seven seas without banks and seven deserts without limits", in another long and dangerous voyage of discovery with a happy ending.

There are great similarities, Blanca, between these Eastern journeys and that epic Greek poem dated from eight centuries before Christ and attributed to the blind poet, Homer: the *Odyssey*. This chronicle of the eventful homecoming of a Trojan War hero fits the template of the exiled king who is forced to overcome trials and tribulations before being able to return home. For the ancient Western sages, Odysseus or Ulysses became the quintessential initiatory hero; and the country he longs for –the island of Ithaca–, the prototype for man's lost Paradise. But look: our sages didn't overlook that what Ulysses missed the most, what made Ithaca his lost Paradise, was ... you know what? His beloved wife, Penelope. In a way, she was his country. Just as he was hers, and so Penelope (akin to Scheherazade, who spun tales night after night, postponing the time of her death) kept her suitors at bay by unravelling, at night, the veil she wove during the day... But we won't go into Ulysses' adventures now, my dear. Nor into Perseus', that other Greek hero known for his fantastic journeys. From all the Western adventures symbolising the *return to the Origin*, we'll choose one from the European Middle Ages. Perhaps the most famous one. It's a multiple example –sprawling over numerous books–, where Celtic, Christian, and Eastern elements converge, and which enjoyed a tremendous success in its time. I'm referring to the legend of the *Queste*, the legend of the "Quest" for the Grail.

It's a shame that there are no volumes from this literary cycle in the blue library because, as the fairy tale enthusiast that you are, the *Story of the Grail* and its numerous sequels would have certainly delighted you... Since I'm not sure if you are familiarised with the myth, I will quickly set the scene: The Holy Grail appears for the first time as a literary subject in the context of medieval chivalric novels, and it does so in the hand of a legendary sixth century Breton king. According to the legend, King Arthur summoned the bravest errant knights to his Camelot court, and he gathered them around a round table (like this one from where I'm writing to you), thus the chivalric Order they founded came to be known as the "Round Table". Said Order, like every self-respecting chivalric Order, was devoted to protecting the weak from the powerful. However, with time, the Knights of the Round

Table began feeling that such noble mission had become too small for them, and so they decided to aim higher: earthly chivalry drifted towards the spiritual one. This was triggered by rumours that had been going around the court, rumours about an enigmatic object: the Holy Grail.

What is this object? Maybe you understood it to be a sacred cup, a golden chalice, or, according to other stories, a precious stone. But it does not matter, Blanca. The physical object is of no importance. What's relevant is what it symbolises, and that is Divinity, Unity, Integrity, and Androgyny. The Grail symbolises man's lost Paradise. Wolfram von Eschenbach defines it in his *Parzival* as "*Wunsch von Pardîs*"[271], which is Old German and can be translated as "the Consummation of the yearning for Paradise" or "the ideal of Heaven". That is what the Knights of the Round Table are chasing! Now then, this had belonged to them before. The Grail is nothing new for man, who had enjoyed its bliss in the past –hence he keeping its reminiscence more or less buried in his memory. "No one shall know the Grail if he has not yet seen it in Heaven", as it's sentenced in one of these stories. This reminiscence and nostalgia have become a constant for the hero. He feels an unspeakable yearning for the Grail and so he goes off in search of it. In search of the glorious title it confers: *Mystic Royalty*.

Mystic Royalty, Blanca, is like saying true nature, man's original condition. Once again, a beggar becomes Grail *King*; or, in other words, returns to the Origin, to the primordial Fire, to the *Kingdom* of Heaven: such is the goal of our heroes. In short, the quest is about unravelling the thread that lowered God to the rank of human. This descent –as we

---

271. Wolfram von Eschenbach, *Parzival*, p. 128

believe we know– had consisted of the loss of divine Unity in favour of human Duality. In light of our theory: Of the "divorce" of the two spouses, whose heavenly marriage conceived God in the Origin. The way back, then, was clear: one would have to remarry the two unduly divorced spouses. I don't mean marrying them on Earth! That is not what the hero aspires to! Earthly marriage is incapable of restoring the primordial Androgyne, my dear, even if humans unconsciously invented it for that purpose. Have you ever stopped to think why, when a couple divorces after a few years –let's say after thirty years of marriage– people say that the marriage failed, even if most of those years were happy? Well, it's because a couple who gets married aspires to be united forever. Earthly marriage is drawn to eternity, Blanca, which denotes man's obscure –and, of course, futile– ambition to re-establish the Original Unity on Earth... This ambition is futile because, in earthly marriage, the spouses' Unity is merely formal, therefore it's fictitious. It's not a true fusion of two beings into a single one; it's not a *perfect union* with no cracks. Only the *perfect union* of the Two forms the One, and only heavenly marriage forms the *perfect union*. Although there were some ancient sages for whom earthly marriage re-established the Original heavenly marriage and recreated its fruit: God or the One. I cannot resist citing you an example taken from the *Zohar*... In a praise of the conjugal act, Rabbi Abba, after proclaiming God as the One, asks himself:

> When can man be called One? When he is male and female (...) When a man finds himself in intimate and unbreakable union –male and female– with the pure intention of becoming holy, then he is labelled as perfect, he is One, he is flawless (...) Thus united, the two form the Unit, one single soul, one single

body; "one single soul" because they are merged with each other; they are linked to each other with the same will; "one single body" because we know that, as a tradition, the man who has not taken a woman to wife, who is not married, is, so to speak, one half of a body. It is when the male and the female unite in the carnal intimacy of matrimony that their two unified bodies form one only, and their souls becomes one and the same; they are then referred to by the word One, and that is when the Holy One, blessed be He, resides in the One and entrusts a Holy Spirit to that One. They are worthy of being called *the sons of the Holy One, blessed be He.*[272]

However, we will side with the more widespread opinion that the twin soul depends on *heavenly marriage* to restore its androgyny, to return to the Centre of the cosmic mandala. By the way, do you know how the ancient sages often imagined this mandala? They imagined it as a labyrinth. Certainly, that's the reason behind the proliferation of designs and construction of this ilk throughout History. And speaking of labyrinths, do you know the myth of the Minotaur? So there we are, in Ancient Greece; Minos, the king of Crete has the city of Athens under his rule, and he demands from them an annual tribute of young men and women destined to be fed to the Minotaur, a half-man, half-bull monster who is confined to a no less monstrous labyrinth the king had the architect Daedalus purposely build. Athens endures this bondage for years until the hero Theseus volunteers for the sacrifice. And, according to the legend, this is what happens: Theseus arrives at Crete along with the other doomed young men and women. While they parade before the local

---

272. *Zohar*

population, the king's daughter, Ariadne, instantly falls in love with Theseus and secretly summons Daedalus and coaxes him into revealing the secret to overcoming the labyrinth, to find the way out. Theseus enters the maze and, as he advances, he unravels a thread provided by Ariadne. When he reaches the centre, he finds the monster asleep. He slays it. Then, he gathers his companions and, following the loving thread, traces his steps back until he finds the exit. There's a ship at the dock waiting to take them back to Athens, where Theseus and Ariadne plan to get married... But this legend does not have a happy ending. According to the most reliable version, while on high seas, they are hit by a violent storm and Theseus drops Ariadne in an island to keep her safe, with the intention of coming back for her. But the storm does not abate and hopelessly drags his ship away.

This myth's focal point for us, my dear, is the symbolic value of Theseus needing a woman's intervention to successfully overcome the labyrinth. Because we could say that what links Theseus to Ariadne is the same thing that connects the human soul to its twin. We can only hope to find our way to the Centre of the cosmic mandala with the help of the loving thread provided by our twin soul. The twin soul thus stands as the means by which the soul reaches its own goal, which is God. It's in this context that the article of faith of the Love's Faithful and the Eastern and Western heroic lovers could be interpreted by this beautiful metaphor by Ruzbihan Baqli of Shiraz: "The soul flies towards the world of divine love on the wings of human love."[273]

Another classic metaphor, well worn by our sages, is that of the stairway. A stairway made of human love, leading to

---

273. Ruzbehan Baqli Shirazi, *Jasmine of the Lovers*

Mystic Royalty, to Immortality ("Immortality" is the secret meaning that the Occitan Love's Faithful, Jacques de Baisieux, attributed to the Latin word for love, *amor*, a meaning derived from its breakdown into syllables: "a", a negation prefix, "mor", the Provencal word for *death*). Every soul has in its twin its own stairway to God. Adam's stairway was Eve (the love for Eve "is the scale by which to heavenly love thou mayest ascend...",[274] says an angel to Adam in *Paradise Lost*). Dante's was Beatrice ("*quella che imparadisa la mia mente*", as he defined her, "after the lady that emparadises my mind"). Petrarch's was Laura; Isolde was Tristan's; Juliet, Romeo's...; every soul has, in its twin, its stairway to God. The evolutive majority goes up one step at a time; the heroic lovers, four at a time; other than that, there is no difference. Because there is only one way up this stairway, my love, and that is by spiritualizing love. That is the purpose of Evolution and the hero's mission.

PRIVATE PARADISES

If the restoration of Unity, of the soul's lost Androgyny, depends on its reintegration with its other half, it follows then that the hero's Quest entails the Quest for his twin soul. But, you know, in this heroic context, my love, a curious phenomenon takes place. And it's that the line separating the goal from the means through which that goal is achieved becomes blurred for the hero. I mean that for the hero, on an emotional level, the twin soul itself becomes the goal. "Woman is the purpose of man", said the German Romantic Novalis, a

---

274. John Milton, *Paradise Lost*, viii, 591–592

generalisation that (always assuming our theory is correct) is true at a particular level: the purpose of *each* man is *a* woman. One specific woman, to the exclusion of all others.

Crossed–out note on the margin. The annotation's date is still readable, *12–19–99*, as well as the first two words of a long message in the form of a quotation: "*Your pain*... It is impossible to determine its source with certainty. However, in the following letter, the author mentions Khalil Gibran's *The Prophet* as part of the blue library. There is a poem, in that book, that begins with those words, so the quotation could be, "*Your pain is the breaking of the shell that encloses your understanding. Even as the stone of the fruit must break, that its heart may stand in the sun, so must you know pain.*"

So it is, Blanca: in the heart of the hero, the nostalgia for the Grail (for God, for the Origin) is confused with the nostalgia for the twin soul. If we were to ask the heroic lover what his goal was, he would be as likely to answer "the Grail" as to mutter the name of his beloved. For him, both go hand in hand. Because he will only gain access to God through his twin soul, through the *perfect union* with the other half that completes him, that makes him One. "I am what I am only through thee", so says Novalis' Heinrich Ofterdingen to his dear Matilda. And, as the knowledgeable poetry reader that you are, you know there are plenty testimonies in the vein of that verse by Petrarch, the one where he confesses that, in Heaven, he aspires to "see [his] Lord and that lady of [his]" (*veggia il mio Signore e la mia donna*275). Or that other verse

275. Petrarch, *Canzoniere*, 349

by the troubadour Arnaut Daniel, where he proclaims, also alluding to God and his lady, that his "soul's joy in Paradise will be doubled". We can find testimonies such as these in romantic literature all across time, and they would support this assertion: emotionally, each hero –and each man, at a subconscious level– has two goals, two Grails, two lost Paradises. Two Paradises that, deep down, are the same, Blanca. There is a Paradise common to every man, a collective Paradise, we could say, the One, God, the Androgyne. Then there is another private and exclusive Paradise, which is the specific way through which each individual gains access to the collective Paradise. This individual Paradise, specific to each soul, is the twin soul.

A good example of this confusion, or duplicity, of goals is that of the great Sufi master from whom we borrowed the Name metaphor. Ibn Arabi of Murcia had left his hometown to embark on a long trip. Not an adventurous trip like Sinbad's or Ulysses', but a journey for knowledge. This was quite common back then: many restless individuals travelled back and forth not like a tourist, but more like a bee: tasting the honey of knowledge from the local sages of each place where they passed through. Well then, in the city of Mecca, Arabi became the disciple of a sage of Persian background who had a daughter called Nizam, herself gifted of great wisdom and sensitivity towards spiritual matters. These days, no Islamic mysticism scholar would doubt that Ibn Arabi saw Divinity as his life's goal. Yet, Blanca, look: he himself would later confess that the object of his Quest was, at the same time, that young lady with whom he consorted during his stay in Mecca. What, one century later, Beatrice would be to Dante, Laura to Petrarch: that is what Nizam was to Ibn Arabi. Inspired by her, he composed the brilliant verses that were compiled in a book, *The Interpreter of Desires*, from which I have to, at least, quote these lines from the prologue: "And I took her as a model for the inspiration of the poems contained in the present book, which are love poems... although I was unable to express so much as a part of the emotion which my soul experienced and which the company of this young girl awakened in my heart, or of the generous love I felt, or of the memory which her unwavering friendship left in my memory, or of the grace of her mind or the modesty of her bearing, since *she is the object of my Quest and my hope*, the Virgin Most Pure."[276]

In one word, Blanca, she is Ibn Arabi's "Sophia". Do you remember the divine Virgin that, according to Jakob Boehme, is the true object of every man's love? She is his Original heavenly wife, who he already recognises, thanks to his mystical insight, under the disguise of the mortal Nizam. The re-reading that the forty-year-old Andalusian sage makes of his own earlier writings, in light of his love for this young woman, troubled some Sufist scholars. They failed to comprehend how a sage whose exclusive dedication to divine love had earned him the title of *Sheij al-Akbar*, "the greatest of all masters", could open his heart, with the same passion, to the love of a woman. But these scholars, my dear, leave much to be desired as detectives. They do not realise that these two apparently contradictory loves, in reality, are but two different aspects of the same love. They have not accepted the fundamental postulate of amorous heroism; a postulate that, prosaically, can be stated thus: Although there is only one Unit, each one accesses that unique Unit *from its own Duality*.

276. Henry Corbin, *Creative Imagination in the Sufism of Ibn Arabi*, p. 137

In fact, if we take several famous couples –Romeo and Juliet, Tristan and Isolde, Abelard and Heloise, for example– the *perfect union* of Romeo and Juliet's heavenly marriage does not lead to a different "place" than Abelard and Heloise's, and Tristan and Isolde's, and that of every other couple of twin souls, you and I included. This "place", my love, is God. Well now: although the God resulting of each couple's *perfect union* is, in every instance, the same, the couple differs in each case. It's in this sense that one could say, along with Ibn Arabi, that God possesses infinite Names. I should add that this couple's composition is not random; it does not depend on the circumstances. Remember the Greek wooden sticks broken in half: if the *symbolon* allowed two people unknown to each other to recognise one another, that was because only the union of the two halves of the same wooden stick could restore its perfect union; only the sectioned corner of the one perfectly fit the other. Likewise, Blanca, only the soul's union with its twin (with the other half of itself, separated from it by the Fall) could be perfect and thus lead to God. Because as the *Talmud* says, "Only when one joins their like, is the union indissoluble."

Therefore, Romeo –to illustrate it in one of those famous couples– will never end up in God through, let's say, Isolde. Romeo will never end up in God except through his *perfect union* with Juliet. "It is impossible to cross the torrent of Unity (of Unification: *Tawahid*) without crossing the bridge of your love"[277], declares Ruzbihan Baqli of Shiraz to his beloved. For Romeo, his love for Juliet figures, then, as his passport to Heaven, his bridge to Paradise. And if Romeo cannot aspire to access God other than through Juliet, my dear, isn't

277. Ruzbehan Baqli Shirazi, *Jasmine of the Lovers*

it somewhat understandable that, in his heart of hearts, one could be mistaken for the other? That in some way, Juliet becomes Romeo's God, Heaven, his own particular Paradise?

"THE PARADISE OF THEIR MUTUAL EMBRACE"

Poetry books –and again, your fondness for poetry won't let me lie– are overflowing with testimonies identifying the twin soul as the poet's Paradise. In fact, poems describing Paradise as a state of Unity, of Totality, of beatific Perfection based on the union with the loved one, are plentiful. Hell is to be separated from your lover. Let's take a look at some examples from one of the highest peaks of poetry: Milton's *Paradise Lost* and Dante's *Divine Comedy.*

When Dante refers to Beatrice –in that famous verse transcribed above– as "*quella che imparadise la mia mente*", he uses a made–up verb, which will also occur to Milton. Milton paints Adam and Eve's *perfect union* before the Fall as their fusion in a mutual embrace, and beautifully suggests that their arms are each other's Paradise: "*these two, imparadis't in one anothers arms*"... In his retelling of the Fall, Milton shows us that Eve, disregarding Adam's warnings, separates from him. The devil was waiting for that moment. Because the devil cannot do anything while they remain embraced. The Fall is only possible when they come apart. Milton emphasises this, as if suggesting the correlation between the Fall and the separation of the twin souls, as intuited by the ancient sages (we already know that Adam and Eve embody all those couples, they're their prototype). As if, in Adam and Eve's initial separation, Milton had foreseen the beginning of the Fall, or the Fall itself, of which the forbidden fruit episode would be but the symbolic climax. Other readers of the Genesis –I'm thinking Boehme and his disciples– trace the separation of Adam and Eve, the Fall, even further back: to Adam's sleep. But it's in the forbidden fruit episode where the Genesis places all the weight of the Fall, Blanca, so that's the episode we'll tackle now...

You know the story: tempted by the devil, Eve defies God's prohibition and takes a bite out of the forbidden fruit; then she offers it to her companion, who eats it too. In the Genesis, Adam agrees to eat the forbidden fruit without thinking. But, in Milton's version, Adam is fully aware of the implications of this action. He knows that eating the fruit implies falling, separating from God. Yet he eats it anyway because he does not want to leave Eve's side. He wants to share the same fate as her, even if it's a terrible one. Deep down, he knows that their destinies are indissolubly linked. When Eve approaches and offers him the fruit ("Thou therefore also taste, that equal lot / May join us, equal joy, as equal love", she tells him, as she also cannot conceive a destiny apart from him), Milton puts the following touching words on his lips:

Holy, divine, good, amiable, or sweet!
How art thou lost! how on a sudden lost,
Defaced, deflowered, and now to death devote!
Rather, how hast thou yielded to transgress
The strict forbiddance, how to violate
The sacred fruit forbidden! Some cursed fraud
Of enemy hath beguiled thee, yet unknown,
And me with thee hath ruined; for with thee
Certain my resolution is to die:
.../...

Should God create another Eve, and I
Another rib afford, yet loss of thee
Would never from my heart: no, no! I feel
The link of Nature draw me: flesh of flesh,
Bone of my bone thou art, and from thy state
Mine never shall be parted, bliss or woe.[278]

As you can see, Blanca, it's clear from Adam and Eve's words that they are each other's Paradise. Adam and Eve share a private Paradise, which is to be together, even in disgrace. In the *Divine Comedy*, we can find the same idea in reference to a couple sentenced to hell. Take note of his astral trips through Heaven, purgatory, and hell (as Swedenborg will do centuries later, except, unlike the Swede, the Florentine poet's trips are, as far as we know, solely literary). In hell, he strikes a conversation with a couple of adulterous lovers, Paolo and Francesca, whose declarations he transcribes. They tell him how they fell in love (it happened precisely when they were reading an Arthurian novel, one of those which we'll go over next), and that's when Francesca refers to Paolo as "*questi, che mai da me non fia diviso*", "this one, who shall never be parted from me". They will never be parted, Blanca, because they were sentenced to hell together for all Eternity. Dante is moved by their story. But what's most moving for us, is what a detective much sharper than me (because I would have never noticed that detail by myself[279]) pointed out: it's that Dante appears to envy this couple's fate, which is to never be parted. Dante, thinking of Beatrice, must have seen this fate as a form of Paradise, even if in hell.

278. John Milton, *Paradise Lost*, IX, 900–915
279. J.L. Borges, *Seven Nights*

Because –for the umpteenth time, my dear– Paradise consists of being together. And hell? Naturally, hell consists of being apart. Hell is the deprivation of the state of Unity with the twin soul that the soul enjoyed in the past, in the Origin. In that sense, we could say that human existence is hell. But the worst hell of all is that to which the devil himself has been cast, as we can read in Milton's verses.

> Aside the Devil turned
> For envy; yet with jealous leer malign
> Eyed them askance, and to himself thus plained.
> Sight hateful, sight tormenting! thus these two,
> Imparadised in one another's arms,
> The happier Eden, shall enjoy their fill
> Of bliss on bliss; while I to Hell am thrust,
> Where neither joy nor love, but fierce desire,
> Among our other torments not the least,
> Still unfulfilled with pain of longing pines.[280]

Meaning, the devil's hell consists of the absence of a twin soul. Another great English poet about whom we'll have the chance to talk about, the Romantic William Blake, will later define the devil as a "male without a female double"[281]. In another letter, I told you about loneliness and about how the human being's loneliness is not essential and ontological. Well then: the devil's is. It's a terrible loneliness, my love, because it's for all Eternity. Adam and Eve, although separated by the Fall, at least have the hope of one day being together again. (There's a Gnostic scripture called *The Apocalypse*

---

280. John Milton, *Paradise Lost*, IV, 501–510
281. William Blake, *The Four Zoas*, VIII, E, 377; K, 347

of Moses, in which their hope is fulfilled when God attends to Eve's pleas to reunite with Adam in Resurrection.) Ah, but the devil does not even have that hope. His loneliness is not accidental: it's ontological. Unlike the human being, the devil lacks a twin soul; he is ontologically alone.

I know, I know, this subject sends a shiver down my spine. But given that we have gotten into it without realising, and since that it's for the benefit of our investigation, let's stop for a moment to consider that mythological character: the devil.

First, we should say that's all he is, a myth: the devil does not exist. He does not exist, my dear, because if we believe in the presence of one single elemental substance in the Universe, then that substance is good, since it necessarily comes from God. The devil only exists within religious mythology, where he is conceived as God's antagonist. Each divine attribute corresponds to an opposing satanic one. If God is Unity, the devil is split Duality; if He is of a spiritual nature, then the devil embodies Matter; if He is free of sexuality, then the devil is characterised by lust. (To some extent, then, we all have a devil hidden in our soul: the *ego*.) You'll remember that metaphor I told you last time: the Fall as a River that, in its descent towards the sea, gradually loses its "divine essence". This deteriorating essence is Unity, Androgyny. Now, my dear, Unity is associated with every kind of perfection: Truth, Good, Beauty..., which also suffer that deterioration. When the River flows into the sea, representing the lower world, Unity has transformed into Duality. But, furthermore, this Duality –this split Duality– is accompanied by the opposites of every divine perfection: Lies, Evil, Ugliness, etcetera; these imperfections are personified as the devil...

Except that this personification is fictional, Blanca. Unity is personal; it's legitimate, then, to characterise it as the Supreme *Person*, gifted with all kinds of positive attributes. But we cannot say the same of split Duality: its characterisation as a personal being is metaphorical. Split Duality is impersonal; therefore, the devil does not exist as such. By not existing, what he metaphorically personifies does not exist either: meaning, split Duality, Matter, and its attributes –Evil, Ugliness, Lies... Ontologically speaking, none of that exists, since they are (and I'm following the Neo–Platonics, and St. Augustine, and Scotus Eriugena on this) negative magnitudes, negations of the corresponding positive properties and principles attributable to God.

So we have, for example, the problem of pain and suffering. And, by the way... everything I wrote in the other letter about growth going hand in hand with suffering, and that oftentimes bad things happen for a greater good, I believe that all that is true. But that does not stop this problem from being, I think, the biggest pebble in a believer's shoe. You said so yourself, that there is nothing as devastating for one's faith in God as watching a child suffer. (But I remember you immediately added: "However, you look in that same child's eyes and you see faith coming back with double the strength. Because God is in those eyes, in that tender and sad look.") Some ancient systems (Zoroastrianism, Manichaeism, Gnosticism, and Catharism) solved the problem of Evil by resorting to an evil God that rules the world, as opposed to the kind and true God in Heaven. However, I believe that there is no need for that. Suffering can be explained by the simple *absence* of God, by the absence of God's Light in this world. Remember that phrase I quoted from the *Zohar*: "The Lord took his powerful Light from a part of Himself", and the metaphor of the man that applies a tourniquet to his arm...

Even clergymen and women observe this absence of God in our world. Or have you forgotten about when Sister Clara, your childhood friend, and the atheist I was back then, argued about the wars and the famines, the diseases and calamities of all kinds that afflict humanity, she understood my point and told us, ruefully, about the "Silence of God"? Of course, then she immediately followed it with what the theologians usually do, with what I'll also tell you now, my love: and it's that, even though human beings feel the Silence of God, we are like the blind man who, living in darkness, still feels the presence of light. Like the blind man, we intuit that the darkness that characterises this world (this darkness, apart from that, is relative: it's not, if we look carefully, total darkness, and that's thanks to those imperceptible golden beams that are constantly filtering down, which are the strings of "necessary chance" that God pulls) that this world's "darkness", I say, is not its own entity, it's merely the negation of something; it's only absence: the absence of Light. If we are talking about Evil, there are evil people, certainly, but we cannot say that Evil exists as such. "If you did no Evil, Evil would not exist", said Leo Tolstoy. But Good would still exist even if no one practiced it, my love, because Good itself exists within God...

Crossed–out note on the margin. The smudge of black ink has left the following words unscathed: *...books, a pile of books from the – century...* The Roman numeral is unreadable. But we can venture a guess based on other quotations...

You see the difference, right? Evil is nothing but the absence of Good, Ugliness is the absence of Beauty, Lie of Truth, split Duality of Integration, Matter (we would have to side with Eastern sages when they claim that, despite its overwhelming appearance of reality, Matter is *maya*, it's an illusion) is nothing more than the absence of Spirit... The devil is the absence of God, Blanca, a fiction, then. Good for him, because if he were to exist, he would be miserable, a poor devil if you allow me such easy wordplay. Because if the devil is the personification of split Duality, then he also personifies the main consequence of that split: loneliness. Loneliness is inherent to the devil, as I told you: it's part of his nature. And the devil's loneliness is not the same as the one that afflicts us humans, it's not the loneliness that affects you and I at the moment, just to use an example with which you might be familiar. You and I *are* alone, we *are* separated; whereas the devil *is* loneliness, *is* separation; his is an ontological loneliness... Surely, you've heard that the ancient sages *demonised* sex. In many cases, that's literally correct: they linked it to the devil. But they did so for a reason, my love: because split Duality is in the essence of both sex and the devil. I already told you that, etymologically, *sex* means "to cut", "to separate": well, etymology also says that the *devil* is "he who tears apart", "the separator". And he's the separator, Blanca, because he himself is a separated being: he has never met, nor will he ever meet his twin soul, which in practice, is the same as not having one. It's the ontological deficiency that afflicts this myth, this fictitious personification of split Duality and Matters that we call the devil.

Such deficiency didn't go by unnoticed by the primitive myth creators. Among the Dogons of Sub-Saharan Africa, to give you a classic example featured in anthropology textbooks, there is a mythological diabolical figure called Yurugu. As evil and unhappy as the devil from *Paradise Lost*, Yurugu is depicted in the form of a jackal. And his sinister and sad figure is opposed by that of Nummu, humankind's "mythical ancestor", the primordial Man before the Fall, who was a kind and happy entity. These figures' contrasting characters are explained, according to the Dogons, by their distinct ontological condition. Nuumu is ontologically perfect; and he is so precisely in virtue of his *double* character: he is characterised either as a pair of perfectly joined twins of the opposite sex, or as a married couple (the icons depict them in a funny way: as a man with two little people, male and female, coming out of his head like horns). Yurugu, on the contrary, is described as being single. Yurugu suffers from that serious ontological deficiency consisting of being one single individual, of lacking a twin soul. His mythological figure is equivalent to that of the devil; he's another personification of split Duality, characterised by loneliness, by an individual existence rather than a double one. (Another paradigmatic example would be that of Seth in Egyptian mythology: a lone, sombre and evil figure, contrasted by the luminous and benevolent Osiris, who is gifted with a feminine double, his wife and sister, Isis.)

THE KNIGHTS OF THE ROUND TABLE

You know what day it is today, right? Really? Have you already forgotten your birthday? I guess you don't follow our calendar there. But even so... You weren't so indifferent when I forgot about it! Anyway, you can see that I've remembered this time; even without having your friends calling to congratulate you early in the morning to remind me... But let's get to the subject at hand because I'm worried that this letter is already quite a few pages long and I haven't even gotten to the main theme. So, let's go! Let's dive head first into the Quest for the Holy Grail. But let's do it right, that is, guided by legendary heroes of the *Queste*. I'll show you how, for all of them, the Quest involves the exclusivisation of erotic love. That is to say, how there are two Quests intertwined here: the Quest for the Grail and the Quest for the predestined woman, the twin soul; and how oftentimes those two Quests can be confused.

The importance of the maiden for the hero of the Quest in the Grail stories is quite evident. No scholar will dispute it, on the contrary: they insist on the maiden's role as the initiator, as the mediator between the hero and the Grail. And more: they recognise that the maiden often takes the place of the Grail itself as the object of the hero's aspirations. To the point that many scholars detect two purposes for the Quest, two distinct objectives: the Grail and the "one lady". But in reality, both those objectives are linked, Blanca, deep down they are one and the same. Because if the hero fights for his lady's loving reward, this reward is none other than the Integrity that comes with their union –an Integrity of which the Grail is the symbol. All this will become clearer to you after we break down the most representative heroes of the Quest. Let's start with Galahad, or Galath, who, while being the last one to sit at the Round Table, is, along with Perceval, the quintessential hero of this enterprise: only he and Perceval succeed on their Quest, only they end up discovering the Grail and conquering Mystic Royalty.

Galahad's Quest was chronicled in the twelfth century (although the attribution is not reliable at all) by the Welsh

Walter Map in the *Quest for the Holy Grail.* The main episode involves a maiden whose name is omitted; this does not take any importance away from her character for, independently of what significance is attributed to this adventure, one thing is certain, and that is that Galahad and the anonymous maiden are together in it, they form a couple, they are connected by mysterious bonds. Their first encounter is not exactly accidental: One afternoon, Galahad receives the unexpected visit of this unknown maiden, whom he invites to follow him on an endeavour that he describes as the "greatest adventure a knight has ever lived". She gladly accepts it and they both depart. They stop by the maiden's castle so that she can pick up a mysterious coffer, then they set sail. It's a long boat trip, but they finally arrive at a desert island where a ship got stranded after being adrift at sea for two thousand years with no one aboard. This ship is God's ship, Blanca, and, according to what the maiden tells him, it's his destination. Built out of wood from the Tree of Life, it was launched by King Solomon and it contains three symbolic objects: a "big and rich" bed, a golden crown, and an equally magnificent sword. When it comes to the bed, I don't think you'll be surprised by its symbolism at this stage: the bed is the bridal bed where the twin souls are to join in *perfect union* to conceive the Androgyne, to whom the golden crown and the sword belong. Both those objects are symbols of sacred, mystic, and transcendent Royalty (meaning Divinity), having both been previously owned by sacred kings: the golden crown was worn by Solomon, the sword belonged to his father, King David. This way, Map ties this story together with Jewish tradition, where the crown's symbolism, Blanca, is particularly rich.

In fact, in the Kabbalah, God's highest manifestation or emanation is characterised as *Kéter,* the "Crown", which many Kabbalists recognise as the Hidden Point itself. Now: in the Kabbalah, Royalty, the Crown, depends on the union of the King -the Holy One, blessed be He- with his wife, the Queen, the Matrona; and according to an important Kabbalist school, the King and Queen are separated due to the Fall, that is to say, they are in Exile. About this Exile, we can read in the *Zohar*: "The King without his Matrona is not in possession of his crown as before", for "(while) He is not by her side... He is not One."[282] But I've told you enough about the Kabbalah in previous letters. We had just climbed aboard Solomon's ship in the company of Galahad and the maiden... Out of the three eminent objects contained in this boat, the most significant one in Grail literature is not the crown. Nor the bed. The most significant object is the sword because it's the "Sword with the Strange Belt", a symbol equivalent to the Grail. As its name points out, this sword has a flaw: the baldric, the belt on which it hangs, is made of esparto grass, a material too weak to support it and which does not honour its richness; it's clear that it is not the sword's original belt. Apart from that, it's an enchanted sword: No one can draw it from its scabbard except the man who, as a hero, deserves it. In the scabbard, Galahad and the maiden read the following inscription: "He which shall wield me ought to be braver than any other, if he bears me as truly as I ought to be borne. For the body of him which I ought to hang by, he shall not be ashamed in no place while he is girt with this girdle, nor none be so hard to do away this girdle; for it ought not to be done away but by the hands of a maid, and a maid all the days of her life, both in will and in deed. And if she breaks

282. *Zohar*, Volume V

her virginity she shall die the most villainous death that ever died any woman."[283]

This inventory of Mystic Royalty requirements -bravery, holiness, virginity- foreshadows what will be the subject of my next letter, Blanca: namely, the class of heroism required to be worthy of wielding or girding the sword, of being vested in the Royalty of the Grail. As for the maiden mentioned in the inscription, it's none other than Galahad's young companion, who we see now taking the little chest she got from her castle. Can you guess what's inside?... That's right: the chest contains the true belt, a belt woven in gold, silk, and the maiden's most prized possession, her hair; a belt she made with her own hands, "so beautiful and so perfect -they tell us- it's as if she had spent her entire life making it". She immediately attaches it to the sword, removing the esparto grass belt, a symbol of Matter, destined to be overthrown by the Spirit embodied by the belt of gold, silk, and that third element which personalises the sword: the maiden's hair. Then she proceeds to call the blade it by its true name: "Sword with the Strange Belt", breaking the spell that made it unmovable. Galahad wields the sword and lets the maiden gird it to his belt, and through this gesture, she vests him with Mystic Royalty. But she is also a participant of this Royalty (although this is only implied in the text) given that Galahad and she can only achieve it through each other. Mystic Royalty, Blanca, is that secret that, as I told you in another letter, is locked with two locks, male and female. Do you remember? Galahad and the maiden each hold one of the keys of this secret: only she can break the sword's curse, only he can remove it from its scabbard. It's thanks to their

283. Walter Map, *Quest for the Holy Grail*

mutual collaboration (and, ultimately, their mystic union in the bridal bed) that they will be vested in Unity, in their original Divinity, symbolised by those three sacred objects: the bed, the golden crown, the sword.

Crossed–out note on the margin. The hastily made black marker strikethrough allows us to reconstruct a quick quotation: *"He turned and saw her (reflected in the) mirror"*. If we connect it to the next letter's beginning, it's one of the most enigmatic quotations in these letters.

Galahad is the son of Sir Lancelot du Lac: out of all the Knights of the Round Table, Blanca, I think he would be your favourite because he's innocent like a child, and he loves with the intensity and faithfulness of a child. Lancelot is the prototype of the hero. Although heroism is a state of mind, in the past, it used to be represented by a magnificent appearance; and that's Lancelot from top to bottom, a knight in a shining white armour. The author of *The Childhood of Lancelot* thoroughly analyses his demeanour: he tells us about his tall and broad shoulders, his straight and muscular arms and legs, his arched feet... he only interrupts the panegyric once he gets to the torso, which he notes is perhaps too wide and deep. But immediately afterwards, he adds Queen Guinevere's opinion: she thinks that God made his chest that big so that his heart could fit, simultaneously revealing to us Lancelot's most valuable trait, his kindness, and the love she, Queen Guinevere –King Arthur's earthly (not heavenly) wife– professes for the knight.

Lancelot holds the title of "best knight in the world": where everyone fails, he succeeds. His causes are always just; his conduct, impeccable (only one thing could blemish his record, the adulterous relationship with Queen Guinevere, but even then, he's absolved by the laws of courtly love). He imposes an iron discipline on himself. An austere loner, he lives outside the court, only allowing himself to be seen when he has to perform some heroic deed or rescue some unfortunate soul in trouble, then he vanishes again. Meanwhile, his fame grows unbounded: a fame shrouded in mystery. Every damsel and maiden, around whom the chivalric world turns, want to hold him in their arms; but he will not allow this. Because it's not the love of women to what Lancelot aspires, Blanca, it's the love of *one* woman: his, the one who is destined for him. Objective beauty holds no power over his heart; only his twin soul's subjective beauty can move him. To the point that the only way to make him go to bed with another woman is through trickery: a sorceress casts a spell to make Galahad's future mother appear to him under the shape of his beloved Guinevere.

Lancelot's heroic destiny goes involves Guinevere and is mistaken for her. He is the extreme example of what I was telling you earlier: the confusion, in the hero's heart, of the goal and the means through which that goal is achieved. Reading his adventures, we get the impression that, for him, the Quest for the Grail is more like a pretext for his true Quest, which is the quest for Guinevere. This impression is shared –in a story called *Perlesvaux*– by a hermit to whom Lancelot expresses his chagrin for having succeeded in infiltrating the Grail Castle in vain, that is to say, without the holy cup appearing to him. The hermit explains him why: if he had wished to see the Grail as much as he wished to be with Guinevere, he tells him, there is no doubt he would have seen it. But we can ask ourselves if this is the real reason, Blanca. Because there is no contradiction between erotic love and the love for God. The love for Guinevere and the love for the Grail are complementaries, like the two sides of the same coin. What one loves is always the same thing, only the face changes. This is, my dear, a fundamental postulate of those ancient Muslim sages that abound in these letters, the Sufis. Human love and divine love "are one and the same love – taught us Ruzbihan Baqli of Shiraz, the Persian Love's Faithful–, and it's in the book of human love where one learns the rules of divine love."[284] For Lancelot, the love for Guinevere is the pathway to the love for God; hence, when Guinevere accuses herself of being an obstacle in Lancelot's way, he corrects her: "Lady, you are mistaken. *Know that without you, I would have never achieved the heights at which I find myself*, for I would not have dared to begin my chivalry nor to undertake the deeds others abandoned due to lack of will. But your great beauty (subjective beauty, that is) placed in my soul such honour that I could not find any adventure from which I did not emerge as the victor. For I knew it to be true, *if I did not surpass all others in heroism, I would have never reached you*. And I had to reach you or die: it truly was love, then, that heightened my virtues."[285]

I will now turn to Gawain –or Gauvain–, King Arthur's favourite nephew: Gawain is a consummate womanizer. But one day a messenger appears in Camelot. She is the Grail messenger, Blanca, a recurring supernatural character in Arthurian novels. She addresses the gathered Knights to send them on a dangerous adventure: to rescue a maiden imprisoned at the Orguelleuse[286] Castle. Gawain immediately feels

284. Ruzbehan Baqli Shirazi, *Jasmine of the Lovers*
285. *Lancelot*
286. Proud Castle

that this summon concerns him, that there is a mysterious bond connecting him to the Orguelleuse Castle's prisoner; he feels that his Quest entails the unknown maiden, and so off he goes to rescue her. While he rides, the messenger's words echo in his head: he who liberates this maiden "will conquer a supreme honour... he will be able to rightfully take the Sword with the Strange Belt" (that personalised sword equipped with a belt made from the hero's twin soul's own hair). In other words, he will be vested in the Grail's Royalty. Jean Markale interprets the maiden's importance for Gawain thus: "... he is a natural born heartbreaker and is unable to resist a woman when the occasion presents itself. Thus it is normal that his quest would entail the deliverance of the mysterious maiden, for until then, he has loved women *but not the one woman destined for him*."[287] Chrétien de Troyes, the *Story of the Grail*'s author, died before finishing his novel and, for the remainder of it, there is no more mention of the mysterious maiden (as mysterious as Galahad's companion in Solomon's ship). Unless she is the same maiden that in the last episode of *Quest for the Grail*, and under the name of Duchess Orguelluese of Logres, submits Gawain to tough heroic trials. Wolfram von Eschenbach will resume, a generation later, this unfinished episode and will end it with a wedding. Do you remember those examples of instant recognition that I cited in the first letter? Well, Gawain's encounter with the Duchess Orguelleuse of Logres, while incidental in appearance, dances to the same tune. Our hero finds her in a grove, next to a fountain, falls in love at first sight, and feels that he has found "the joy and sorrow of his heart."[288] Joy, because he finally

287. Jean Markale, *The Grail: The Celtic Origins of the Sacred Icon*, p. 20
288. Wolfram von Eschenbach, *Parzival*

found what he was looking for, his twin soul. Sorrow, because at first she does not recognise him, or pretends not to recognise him. However, he casually confesses to her: "May I die if the truth I speak not, no woman e'er pleased me more–" And Gawain has met hundreds! Then, faced with her contempt: "...mine eyes thus mine heart have brought in danger, for *they* beheld thee, and thy fetters around me wrought. But now, since I be thy captive, I prithee entreat me well."[289] What Gawain's "eyes of the second sight" saw in the Duchess Orgueleuse of Logres, Blanca, cannot be anything other than her subjective beauty, the secret password that gives her away as the counterpart to Gawain's soul and his "private Paradise".

I've saved the protagonist of the *Story of the Grail*, and the entire Grail cycle, for the end: Perceval, whose story I already partially told you in previous letters. He has also found his twin soul, he found it in Blanchefleur (those who know them assure us that "there has never been a knight and a maiden so suited for one another, and it's as if God made them for each other and to be together.")[290] But look, he wasn't able to recognise her. By that time, Perceval didn't even know his own name: he didn't even know himself, so it's not surprising that he failed to recognise his "other self". He spends a short time with her and then leaves. Soon he forgets her. He arrives then at the Grail Castle, but he does not pass the test: standing before his host's suffering, he becomes inhibited and fails to pose the redeeming question that was expected of him. According to Gerbert of Montreuil –one of the writers who continued Chrétien's story– this failure is directly related to his abandonment of Blanchefleur. Afterwards, he

289. *Ibid*
290. Chrétien de Troyes, *Perceval, or Story of the Grail*

wanders aimlessly, lost and in despair, until one morning he is struck by a revelation. What is this revelation? The answer is in my first letter: it's the episode with the ecstatic vision of the three drops of blood on the fresh snow, do you remember? In that instant of clairvoyance, of the opening of the eye of the heart (the ecstasy lasts for several hours, but for him, it feels like a second), Blanchefleur becomes *his* wife; *the* woman, given that for him there is no other anymore. Perceval understands in that magic instant that Blanchefleur is the other half of himself, the half that is missing for him to become *whole*. Because, just as his cousin will reveal to him in Wolfram's version, he is also someone else's half: ""Thou art *Parzival*,' she cried, and thy name it shall mean '*to pierce thro*'..."[291]

That dawn in the snowy meadow, Blanca, Perceval realises that for him, possession of the Grail entails the unification (not the possession, because unification does not imply possessing nor being possessed) with Blanchefleur. However, the effect of this revelation soon fades away; courtly distractions once again plunge Perceval into oblivion. But then comes the Grail messenger and her challenge for the Knights of the Round Table. As with Gawain, the messenger's words are a wake-up call to Perceval's consciousness, so he leaves Camelot to embark on his Quest. Unlike Gawain, though, his Quest will not take him to the prisoner at Orguelleuse Castle, but directly to the Grail Castle. Perceval has a second chance that will allow him to correct the immaturity he displayed. To accomplish that, he must fight, for that is the hero's way. "For he who the Grail would see – notes Wolfram– Sword in hand must he draw anigh it, and swift must

291. Wolfram von Eschenbach, *Parzival,* 466–467

his seeking be!" We must not forget that we are dealing with symbolism here: the fight is an internal one.

In Chrétien's story, Perceval's Quest is interrupted at this point. Others will continue it: Wolfram among them, who will repeatedly suggest that if the Grail is Perceval's goal, then he does not see much difference between the Grail and Blanchefleur (who in the German version is called Kondwiramurs, literally "She who leads to love", and is the Queen of Pelapeire). Perceval confesses that, "for the twain is [his] heart yet yearning"[292]. So, after defeating some knights in battle, he orders them to ride forth to Pelapeire to surrender to the Queen. He adds, "He who in days of yore Faced Kingron for her and Klamidé, for the Grail now sorroweth sore, As he yearneth for her, his lady, and after the twain in thought and deed is he ever striving..."[293] Do you see, Blanca? Love and the Grail are scrambled together in Perceval's thoughts. Same as they would have been in reality, once the hero had accessed the Grail's Royalty after posing the infamous question.

Meanwhile, he must learn how to endure that nostalgia, since that the hero's path (and sometimes Evolution's path as well) is often a lonely one, "And thou, for whose love I am yearning, were it so both with me and thee, That our hearts ever dreamed of parting, nor our love from all doubt were free, It might well be that with another joy and blessing again were mine, But thy love it so fast doth hold me, I may rest on no heart but thine!"[294] He declares that there is no separation possible for his love (he's not referring to physical separation,

292. *Ibid*, Vol I, 609
293. *Ibid*, Vol I, 817-820
294. *Ibid*, Vol II, 889-892

that one is possible, but to the separation of hearts). And he declares this with some degree of sorrow, Blanca, because since at that moment he cannot be with Blanchefleur, a part of him wishes he were free to seek comfort in someone else's arms. The fact is that he's not free (in this sense, the evolutive path has the advantage over the heroic way): he is indissolubly connected to his twin soul. Linked not by a promise, nor by marriage: by a much stronger and secret bond.

TWO PEOPLE RIDING THE SAME HORSE

In another letter, we'll try to unravel the nature of this mysterious bond, so prevalent in ancient literature, which makes twin souls inseparable even when far apart. I can see that you're frowning now because the protagonist of all these stories is always a male. But that's how it is, my love, what can I do? In Grail literature, there are no heroines, only heroes. It's partially an obligation of heroic symbolism. In the *Odyssey*, to quote another example of a heroic journey I suggested, it's the warrior Ulysses who's at sea and living adventures while Penelope patiently awaits at home for his return. But, to a large extent, that's also a characteristic trait of ancient literature. Certainly, there are exceptions to this rule, and it's in traditional oral lore –in your beloved fairy tales– where these exceptions are more common. The example that I'm proposing is a special case because, being a typical sample of popular literature, it has an illustrious background: it finds its origins in the Greek myth of Eros and Psyche, and it was sometimes read by the ancient sages in an esoteric context. The version we'll analyse now was collected by the Brothers Grimm and it's entitled *The Springing, Singing Lark*. Although you know this story like the palm of your hand, I'll summarise it here as if you had never heard it... The title describes a girl's odd request to her father when he offers to bring her a gift upon his return from a trip. It's, as you know, a classic fairy tale introduction: while her sisters ask for jewellery or expensive dresses, the little one is happy with something of no apparent value. The man comes across a lark, but when he tries to catch it, a lion suddenly jumps out and threatens to kill him. To save his own life, he is forced to make a dangerous promise: he promises the lion he will deliver it the first thing that meets him on his return home. He thinks it will be the family dog, but the first one to greet him is the youngest of his daughters. The girl, however, is not afraid and off she goes to fulfil her father's promise. Her valour is rewarded: the lion turns out to be a cursed prince who only returns to his human form at night. They get married and learn to live by night and sleep by day (which I'm also learning how to do, by the way). Then it happens that the wife is invited to her sister's wedding and her husband agrees to accompany her. But only on one condition: he must not be touched by light; if that happens, he warns her, he will turn into a dove for seven years. The wife takes precautions, but the light of a candle infiltrates the sealed chamber through a crack in the door. Thus begins her hero's Quest. For seven years (a symbolic number, remember) she roams the world in search of the dove that was once her husband, but then she loses its trail. She asks the sun, she asks the moon, she asks the Northern wind. The first two only offer her two presents: "Open them when you're in trouble". But thanks to the third one, she finally finds her husband in the Red Sea. He is back in his lion shape and he's fighting a sea dragon. Following the Northern wind's directions, she breaks his curse. Ah, but the dragon then turns out to be a cursed princess who kidnaps the prince and drags him to her palace. Our heroine cries in despair but immediately resumes the Quest. This leads her to the palace where her husband is about to marry the "fake bride". She uses the sun and the moon's gifts as bribes to enter her amnesiac husband's chambers for two consecutive nights. On the first night, she finds him asleep under the effect of a potion made by his illegitimate bride. In the second one, the prince, remembering the murmurs he heard as if in a dream the night before, becomes suspicious of his nightly beverage and spills it, so that when his true bride arrives in his room, he's able to recognise her: "Now my curse is indeed broken! I have lived as though in a dream, for the strange princess had bewitched me to forget you."

The story ends upon the loving couple's return home on the wings of a gryphon. We could think of the "wings of human love" Ruzbihan Baqli of Shiraz talked about, with which the soul travels towards the world of divine love. Ah, by the way, Blanca, there is a significance to this tale's fauna. The gryphon, half-eagle and half-lion, is a guardian of treasures. And the lion –a super animal, like the eagle and the lark– symbolises the divine and spiritual nature of man: the opposite of a dragon, which is an inferior animal that symbolises Matter. The lion-prince fights with a dragon-woman and ends up being kidnapped by her: doesn't it remind you of another princely kidnapping? The protagonist's abduction in the *Song of the Pearl*? Well, let's leave that aside, it's in this story's fauna that we're interested now. It's in the fact that it tells not about the husband's Quest, but the wife's. The fact that its protagonist was a heroine rather than a hero, which, if it wasn't exceptional in popular literature, it was largely so in cultured literature.

We can find a notable exception, my dear, in the Song of Songs, that scholarly poem that nevertheless became enormously popular in the Middle Ages. A poem that was thoroughly commented by Ezra of Girona... The Song reflected not only the joy of the spouses' consummated love; it reflected the previous anxiety of separation and the Quest. And this Quest concerns both husband and wife equally. She seeks to reunite with him with the same zeal with which he seeks to reunite with her. Let's remember the verses in which the wife regrets: "Upon my bed at night ("The night is the suffering, the despair, the darkness of those who are apart", comments Ezra of Girona regarding this verse)...

> Upon my bed at night
> I sought him whom my soul loves;
> I sought him, but found him not;
> I called him, but he gave no answer.
> "I will rise now and go about the city,
> in the streets and in the squares;
> I will seek him whom my soul loves."
> I sought him, but found him not.
> The sentinels found me,
> as they went about in the city.
> "Have you seen him whom my soul loves?"[295]

But, as I said, the Song is the exception: the norm in ancient cultured literature is the protagonist to be a male. In a literary cycle such as the Grail, this has little sense, since it's based on an initiation venture –the Quest– which is by definition a venture for two, an undertaking in which both

295. *Song of Songs*, 3, 1–3

parts are equally involved. Royalty, Blanca, the Unity embodied by the Grail's Royalty, is only accessible *to two*: he cannot become king if she does not become a queen at the same time. One cannot reach this goal on one's own. The Arthurian narrator, though, only follows one half of the heroic duo, and generally omits the heroine's adventure. It's the male who accesses Royalty through the woman –even if one can infer that the same happens the other way around. The woman's mission is to be the hero's initiator, the mediator between the hero and the Grail; her role is almost never the one reality assigns her: the co–protagonist.

One of the few exceptions justifying this "almost", Blanca (I'm jumping from exception to exception: in this case, the anomalies appear to me –as I'm sure they appear to you too– to be more laudable than the norm), is a novel in verse: *Erec and Enide*, a beautiful novel, Chrétien de Troyes' first. Erec and his wife Enide embark on an adventure together: they both achieve Royalty. King Arthur himself invests them in a joint coronation, something quite unusual at the time. Erec and Enide have reached such heights –Royalty, Unity– in the only possible way for them: through each other. To use Ruzbihan's happy metaphor: they soared towards Unity "on the wings of human love". Because just as a bird needs its two wings to fly, my dear, so do Erec and Enide need each other to reach their goal.

In line with this: some sleuth–minded scholars have allowed themselves to pull a verse out of context in which Enide is described in a rather curious way: "With her, you could hunt with a hawk", it reads. As you know, in the Middle Ages the knights practised falconry, hunting for birds using a hawk that would chase its prey. Now, hunting was once a symbol for the Quest. For these detectives, Enide is the hawk with which Erec is chasing his prey. That's why he takes her with him on his adventure (it's charming how Chrétien describes them riding on the back of the same horse). But Erec is also Enide's hawk. This parity is evidenced throughout their adventure, especially at the end, in their joint coronation. It's even reflected in the richness and radiance of the ornaments adorning them during the ceremony. A richness and radiance only comparable to that of the Grail itself, to the point of stunning everyone present, including King Arthur: "At once he ordered two crowns, both of fine solid gold, to be brought forth from his treasure. As soon as he had pronounced this order, the crowns were brought before him, glowing with carbuncles, for there were four of them in each one. The light of the moon is nothing compared to the light the very least of those carbuncles could shed. Because of the light they reflected, all those in the palace were so thoroughly dazzled that for a while they could not see a thing; even the king was dazzled by it, and yet he greatly rejoiced to see them so bright and beautiful."[296]

This supernatural splendour denotes that we are standing before a royalty from out of this world: a Mystic Royalty. Furthermore, Blanca, the comparison with the moonlight may not be coincidental (or it may not appear so to us detectives) given that when Erec and Enide are both happily riding on the back of the same horse at night, Chrétien transfers that joy to the moon's radiance: "...and it gave them much comfort that the moon shone brightly upon them."[297] And now that radiance is eclipsed by their crowns' four carbuncles: "The light of the moon is nothing compared to the light

296. Chrétien de Troyes, *Erec and Enide*
297. *Ibid*

the very least of those carbuncles could shed". Meaning the joy their earthly marriage had brought on them was nothing compared to the one instilled by their heavenly marriage. On the other hand, it's suggested that in the spouse's regalia, the number four associated with the precious stones' luminosity, is repeated, in which we can also observe a symbolism. In numerology, the number four –in association with the One– is a symbol of Totality, of Integrity, just as the circle and the sphere are in geometry: there are four cardinal points, four elements, four seasons, four primary colours... By linking this symbol with another universal symbol of Divinity –the Light, the "great light" shed by the stones– Chrétien is reinforcing the idea that, through each other, Erec and Enide have reached the Divine Unity represented by the Grail, by the *Grail's Royalty*.

A SICK KING AND A BARREN KINGDOM

We can see, Blanca, that the Grail's Royalty is not an earthly and profane royalty: it's celestial, sacred, and transcendent. It's not transient but eternal. It's a symbolic royalty: it symbolises Androgyny, a Divinity that has been lost with the Fall. In the cycle of the Grail, this Mystic Royalty is represented by the Fisher King, a king who, like me, is fond of fishing. "Hey, wait a minute, Mr. Poirot –you'll be saying–, why a fisherman and not a carpenter or a farmer or a merchant, let's say?" Well, because fishing, my dear, is casting the hook into the depths: into the metaphoric "reverse side" of existence. It's like digging the earth or going down a cave in search of a hidden treasure (a common activity among these heroes from the tales, by the way). Or like diving in the sea in pursuit of the "only pearl" like the *Song of the Pearl*'s protagonist... The King of the Grail has also lost that pearl: that's why he became a fisherman, to recover it. And given that the Grail's is a lost or "fallen" Royalty, the Fisher King is shown as being maimed.

The King's disability is the consequence of a "painful blow" delivered with a sword or a spear. In *Sir Perceval of Galles*, when Gawain, standing in front of the Grail, falls into a state of ecstasy, he will have a vision of a king sitting on his throne after being run through with a spear... The loss of Royalty is represented by the King's disability, but by his Kingdom's too. In ancient mentality, a king's fall from grace (and there are plenty of examples of this in fairy tales) is automatically projected on his kingdom. We can recall an example I cited in another letter: when King David's sins led to God turning his back not just on him but on his people too. In the legend of the Grail, the Kingdom becomes barren and desolate. It suffers from the same malady that the ancient sages from primitive societies diagnosed in the lower world. If you can remember what we talked about in the other letter, humankind's first sages believed that, by being so far away from the Origin, the lower world had eroded. Well, the Grail Kingdom is also branded as *terre gaste*, "worn land". Now it's too late for renewal rituals, and intersexual disguises won't be fooling anyone either. At this point, only a heroic deed will finally restore the King's (and his Kingdom's) lost health.

In the present context, Blanca, "health" is equivalent to "Integrity". The King's lost health, which the hero must restore, is what he lost as a consequence of the divorce of the two halves in which all Integrity is based. This agrees with the arguments put forward by the stories; the king or the prince's fall from grace often obeys to a separation from their kingdom or princess, and only upon their reencounter and marriage will the kingdom recover its original fertility and splendour. The Fisher King's loss of his "other half" as a cause for his disability is something that was widely suggested in the different versions of the legend. Thus, in Manessier's, the "painful blow" incapacitated *one of the King's sides*, as if his left side had just left. To stress this idea, Manessier doubles the effect on one of the King's heteronyms –King Goon Desert, introduced as his brother–, who was vertically cut in half with a "painful blow". Apart from that, Blanca, the nature of the Fisher King's wound is revealing: it is a sexual wound. He is wounded "between both muscles", they say as a euphemism for castration. Wolfram, more explicit, informs us that the spear pierced his testicles. Therefore, the ailment afflicting the King is no different from what afflicts his Kingdom: they are both barren, they have lost their fertility. Not their earthly fertility: that is just a symbol of heavenly fertility here, that which in the Origin conceived the Unit, God.

I bet that the wounded Fisher King, and the heroes searching for a cure for his ailments, reminded you of a familiar theme in fairy tales: the sick king whose sons depart in search of a miracle cure. A classic exponent of this theme is a story that I would like to recall here: *The Water of Life*. Again, I will tell it here as if you did not know it: A king falls gravely ill and his three sons go off, in their separate ways, in search of the miraculous Water of Life, which an old man told them to be the only remedy capable of curing their father. The two older brothers, due to their greed and the insensitivity they showed to their neighbours, end up in a quagmire. But the youngest one (the hero is always the youngest one, maybe you can tell me why), because of his selflessness and compassion, reaches an enchanted palace where a princess greets him as her liberator and gives him the Water of Life, which springs from a fountain in the middle of the palace. Then, she asks him to return in a year's time to marry her. This deadline is a probation period in which the hero will ratify the virtue that earned him such honours. It is, in fact, compassion what moves him to rescue his older brothers. Yet, they are still motivated by greed and jealousy, which leads them to swap their brother's Water of Life by brackish water, so that when he gives it to their father to drink, the king's state worsens and they can come in and save the day. Not satisfied with this, they also intend to usurp the enchanted princess. Ah, but the princess has taken the precaution of paving the road to her castle with gold, and she warns the guards to only allow passage to he who walks directly over it. After the deadline passed, the three brothers set forth, one after the other, on the golden road. The two older brothers are dazzled by its magnificence and, in order not to wear it down, they walk along its edge. Only the little one –the hero, who has no interest in gold, who only cares about the princess– treads on the road without even looking. The doors of the palace will only open for him, as will the princess's arms.

See? This story also has a sick king and a hero in search of a cure. The cure, take note, is the Water of Life (*from the Fountain of Life*, a symbol of divine Integrity), and the princess who carries it. A detail which also remits us to the Grail cycle, Blanca, since that, as you're about to see, and as I've hinted at in a previous letter, it's also a maiden of noble lineage who, in the Grail's apparitions, carries the sacred cup –that other exhilarant element, along with the Water of Life. Very well, now, the princess of our story is *the hero's* twin soul, the one who is called upon to restore not the king's, but the hero's health; his Integrity. The wounded King represents, then, the counter figure of the sick hero, who is the appropriate addressee of the Water of Life. This is also noticeable in the Grail cycle, where the Fisher King, in reality, has no identity of his own: he embodies each seeker, each hero who ventures into his castle in pursuit of the Grail. Restoring the Fisher King's, and his Kingdom's, health is equivalent, for the hero, to restoring his own health.

Another revealing fact of the Grail legend is that the "painful blow" that castrated the King, was struck by his own sword, or spear, according to the stories. This sword is the sword of the Spirit, the "Sword with the Strange Belt", the one that bestows Royalty on whoever wields it, and that is equivalent to the Grail. Look at how both objects have, in their earthly manifestation, a defective support: the sword's belt is too fragile, the Grail is held by a maimed King. This defectiveness is a clear sign of its "fallen" condition. Besides, in many of these stories, the sword was broken in half when it struck the "painful blow". When Gawain arrives at the Grail Castle, the trial the King demands from him consists of putting sword's shattered pieces back together. He cannot do it, therefore he is not yet qualified. Only Galahad is up to the task, only he will be able to restore the broken sword: "Thus Galahad takes the pieces of the sword and joins them together: they fit in such perfect manner that there is no man in the world capable of discerning the pieces, or even of realising it was broken."[298]

The restoration of the broken sword, Blanca, is a recurring heroic test in Grail literature. Its symbolism seems clear

---

298. Walter Map, *Quest for the Holy Grail*

to me. The sword represents Integrity and the Spirit. It represents the whole Soul of the Origin, and it's broken into two pieces, which remits us to the Fall, to the primordial One's division into two. The hero's mission consists of restoring that Integrity –the original Unity of his soul– by welding the two halves back together. This test is equivalent to that other one, also very common to these stories, that consists of drawing the immovable sword from its scabbard, or pulling it out from a stone, or snatching it from the supernatural hand that emerges from a lake and holds it over the water. The symbolic value is the same: the restoration of Mystic Royalty, of lost Divinity; a restoration represented by the action of brandishing the sword.

In other occasions, as I said, it's not a sword but a spear. A spear that is not broken but bleeding: a drop of blood continuously flows from the tip down the mast. This spear was used to deliver the "painful blow", and the fact that it's bleeding has, of course, a symbolic significance: it's as if it's crying for vengeance. A cry for vengeance that, according to the scholars, holds its own symbolism; the need for regeneration, the wounded King's urgency for healing. "The King must be avenged" is equivalent to "The King must be healed", "We must recover his original Integrity"... Indeed, the theme of vengeance is repeated throughout the Grail stories, and it's often connected to the following disturbing adventure: In the course of his Quest, the errant knight that comes across a woman standing next to her dead or wounded husband. Sometimes it's her brother whom the woman begs the passing knight to avenge. This revenge often involves obtaining a sword or welding together the two halves of a broken sword. The dead or wounded knight would represent, in our interpretation, the errant knight himself; his wife or sister, the knight's twin soul, who cries for the restitution of her "other half", separated from her as a consequence of the "painful blow" that, symbolically, killed or wounded him.

But getting back to the spear: it accompanies the Grail in a mysterious procession that passes in front of the stunned hero, of each hero that ventures into the Fisher King's Castle. The first one to subject himself to this trial (because that's what this is, Blanca: a heroic trial) is Chrétien's hero, Perceval:

> "...and as they chatted of this and that, a servant entered the hall, carrying his hand at its centre a white lance. He came out of a room, then walked between the fire and those seated on the bed, and everyone saw the white wood, and the white spearhead, and the drop of blood that rolled slowly down from the iron point until it reached the servant's hand. The boy saw that wondrous sight, the night he arrived there, but kept himself from asking what it might mean, for he'd never forgotten –as his master at arms had warned him, over and over. He was not to talk too much. To question his host or his servants might well be vulgar or rude, and so he held his tongue. And then two other servants entered, carrying golden candleholders worked with enamel. They were wonderfully handsome boys, and the candleholders they each clasped in their hands bore at least ten burning candles. A girl entered with them, holding a grail–dish in both her hands. A beautiful girl, elegant, extremely well dressed. And as she walked into the hall, holding this grail, it glowed with so great a light that the candles suddenly seemed to grow dim like the moon and stars when the sun appears in the sky. Then another Girl followed the first one, bearing a silver platter. The grail that led the procession was made of the purest gold, studded with jewels of every kind, the

> richest and most costly found on land or sea. No one could doubt that here were the loveliest jewels on earth. Just as they'd done before, when carrying the lance, the servants passed in front of the knight, then went to another room. And the boy watched them, not daring to ask why or to whom this grail was meant to be served..."[299]

Knowing you, my love, I'm sure that you wouldn't have wasted the occasion to ask the famous question. But who wouldn't have many questions when faced with this phantasmagorical procession? Next, we'll be answering some that occurred to me. But before, let me mention that the configuration of the procession changes from version to version. So, in some stories, it ends with one of the servants carrying a corpse on a stretcher (a macabre detail that I'm afraid will remind you of my granduncle at our wedding reception). A cloth on which the two sword fragments are placed covers the corpse: the hero has the opportunity to revive the dead man through the restoration of the sword. Another variable element is the attitude of the castle's inhabitants. If in Chrétien's story the procession is happening in sepulchral silence, in other versions it passes by drowning in the sound of violent shouts of grief. Regarding the silver dish, in some stories, it's a tray. In the Welsh version, called *Peredur*, it's a tray on which a decapitated head is placed. Let's remember that, according to Elémire Zolla, the head separated from the body signifies the traumatic division of the primordial Androgyne into two parts. Chrétien calls this dish or tray by an Old French word –*tailloir*, "to cut"– which connotes the action of cutting and corresponds to a plate made for that

299. Chrétien de Troyes, *Perceval, or Story of the Grail*

purpose. These three objects –the grail, the spear, the plate– have been given the following symbolism: the grail (the cup, a vaginal symbol) represents the female; the spear (a phallic symbol) represents the male, and they are both separated by the cut –the "painful blow", represented by the plate– that divided the original Androgyne into two halves. The purpose of the procession of these three objects' before the hero would be to remind him of that tragedy and of the need to revert it. Having said that, let's move on to the questions that occurred to me, or more accurately, to certain details of this funeral procession that caught my attention. There are mainly three. The first one refers to a conjunction of colours –red and white– that we have seen before related to Perceval. Back then, it was the red of blood and the white of the snow; now it's also the red of blood, but the white comes from a spear. Although its symbolic value is hidden now, we could attribute one to the previous occasion, where the red and white symbolised Blanchefleur. We can infer, then, my dear, that the bleeding white spear that opens the Grail procession, holds for Perceval this added meaning: it serves as a reminder of his twin soul, whom he forgot. The omission of the saving question that in the first instance he fails to ask symbolises, perhaps, this unfortunate amnesia.

Another remarkable detail, Blanca, is one I mentioned in another letter, which now comes to support, in a way, this one's central thesis: the idea that the male's conquest of the Grail invariably involves the female and vice-versa. I'm referring to the fact that, in its apparitions in the Castle of the Fisher King, the Grail is always carried by a maiden, always the same one, as if they were inseparable. Wolfram calls her "Grail Queen", and makes her answer to the name Repanse de Schoye, "Bringer of Joy"... And, well, the third thing that caught my attention in this strange scene, is the discrepancy between the Grail's magical splendour and the banal context in which that splendour manifests itself. The Grail's situation in the Fisher King's castle seems to correspond to the lame King's and his Kingdom's precarious condition. In the castle, the Grail gives the impression of being like a fish out of water, that this is not its original headquarters, its true "home", that it's there as though in exile.

It turns out that this impression is not baseless, Blanca: the Grail is a holy object that *fell from Heaven*. The legend links it to Adam and Eve's Fall, and Wolfram labels it *lapis exillis* ("exile stone"), a Latin expression in which we can also observe the contraction of *lapis lapsus ex coelis*, "stone fallen from Heaven". I would like to mention another variant of the legend, as well, one that claims the Grail was originally an emerald embedded in Lucifer's (the "light bearer") forehead. When he plunged into the abyss along with the other fallen angels, the precious stone detached from his forehead, and the other angels took it and sculpted it in the shape of a cup. The Grail's true home, Blanca, its original headquarters, from where it fell into this world, is the Hidden Point, represented in Map's book by the "Spiritual Palace", where Galahad and the maiden who accompanied him in the Solomon's ship adventure are buried together. Anyway, my dear, we can recall the Gnostic *Song of the Pearl* and the similarity between those two symbols: the pearl and the Grail. Both represent Unity, the human being's original Integrity; both fell to Earth from their original heavenly headquarters. Now here they are, waiting for the hero who will redeem them.

"WHAT AILS YOU? WHAT DO YOU NEED?"

Even at the risk of you thinking that I acquired the idiotic habit of finishing my letters by refuting impressions you might have gotten from them (because, if I remember correctly, that's how I closed the previous one), I'd like to finish this letter by refuting an impression you might have gotten from it. An impression that would disgust someone like you, someone with a special sensitivity towards the evils of this world and the suffering of people. I mean the possibility that you might be seeing amorous heroism as a "selfishness of two".

Nothing could be further from the truth, my dear. That description is valid for carnal loves, not for spiritual ones: not for heroic loves. After all, selfishness is precisely what the hero banishes from his soul! Remember the fairy tales, the aforementioned *The Water of Life*, for example. Note how selfishness is always punished, and compassion and altruism are always rewarded (usually by the reunion with twin soul). What is certain is that, far from worrying exclusively about their personal Quest, the heroic lover is committed to the fate of the entire Universe. Nothing and no one is foreign to him. Perceval's initiation stages in his pursuit of the Grail are marked by the progressive softening of his hardened heart before the suffering of others. On his way towards the Grail Castle, the Arthurian heroes will not think twice before stopping to help an unfortunate peasant, or before putting themselves in the service of every just cause that crosses their path. They will even stray from the Quest if they receive news that their help is needed somewhere else. Although in reality, that does not divert them, Blanca, it does not delay them or distract them from their Quest. On the contrary:

it's precisely in their altruism, in their unconditional selflessness where the Quest takes place.

Because the Grail Castle has no exact location: it's an enchanted castle. A castle that will only allow itself to be found by the knights who have honoured the ideals of wandering chivalry: namely, to help those in need, to defend the weak against the powerful. The famous question that is expected from the knights who enter the Grail Castle and that will prove to be the cornerstone of their suitability is very simple. According to Wolfram, it's a display of compassion towards the wounded King: "What ails you? What do you need?" The path to God, which is definitely the path to one's self, paradoxically but without fail passes by other people. In such a way that it's not possible to find the Grail if you're wearing blinders, so to speak, ignoring the rest of the world. Look, in Wolfram's *Parzival*, a friendly ambassador bids farewell to the Knights of the Round Table by saying "...and God teach ye to aid me with right goodwill!"[300]

Is there a better wish for a seeker of the Grail? Because empathy, the inclination to feel your neighbour's suffering as your own, is an unequivocal proof that your soul is naked; and a naked soul is an essential requirement for conquering the Grail.

This nakedness has a name: *Love*. True love –altruist, unconditional, gratuitous. Loving the twin soul, but also every other being, Blanca. Loving the whole Universe, because (faithful to its condition as the root of all loves) erotic love, when naked, shows a natural tendency to expand and branch out. It's exclusive only in its specificity, in what is erotic. In what it has of love, it's not exclusive, quite the opposite: it

---

300. Wolfram von Eschenbach, *Parzival*, Vol II, 346

excludes only insofar as it's not genuine, insofar as it is adulterated by Matter and selfishness. In fact, Blanca, the ancient sages would tell you that the love for your twin soul is inseparable from your love for your neighbour. Further still: that it's *precisely* because the true lover loves his twin soul that he also loves his neighbour. And perhaps they would illustrate it with an anecdote like this one sprung to mind now, taken from a thirteenth century poem:

A knight leaves his castle in the middle of a storm at night to meet his lady. But soon after leaving, he overhears a conversation by the side of the road. Two knights, seeking shelter from the storm, talk about how they intend to spend the night at the nearby castle. Upon hearing this, our knight gives up his appointment and turns around to be available to offer shelter when they knock at his door... There. That's it: it's a very short anecdote. But with a lot of substance, no? I just thought that it could have suited your favourite filmmaker, Eric Rohmer, for one of his *Moral Tales*. The chronicler of this short chivalric anecdote, the Genovese troubadour Lanfranc Cigala adds that despite missing his date, the knight does not deserve his lady's reproach. Rather, she should be proud of him, for he sheltered the knights from the storm "*for her love*".

Certainly, I must have remembered this specific story precisely because it takes place during a stormy night. Because it's pouring rain outside, can you hear the thunder? The electricity has been down for an hour. Not just ours, the streetlight outside our window is off too, and I've written the last several pages under a livid candlelight. And I say livid because you have to agree that these blue candles you left me, my dear, while there's no doubt they create quite a lot of ambience, give very little light. So I'll be finishing up. And what better way to do that than with that simile that you used to pose, which fits what we're talking about like a glove. I sharpen my ear and it's as if I can hear you: "If we were on a boat in the middle of the sea and someone fell overboard, wouldn't we rush to sound the alarm and do everything in our power to pull that person back aboard? Well, that should be every human's attitude towards his or her peers. Because we're all aboard the same boat."

How right you are, my dear: we're all aboard the same boat! And for that, the unified twin souls' happiness (the One's happiness) cannot be complete while pain and suffering remain in the Universe –which is the same as saying: while Duality remains split. And it's for that reason that, as the ancient sages assure us, many heroic souls, having completed their cycle of reincarnations, delay the supreme moment of liberation (the reunification with their twin soul, as per our theory) and choose to remain behind to dedicate themselves to helping the other souls in their evolution, either by reincarnating through them, or by secretly guiding them (as you're perhaps doing with me at this very moment) under the invisible form of angels.

Yours

SEVENTH LETTER

TRUE LOVE

(OR NAKED LOVE)

Better to love you and not having you
Than having any woman who would
Take a carnal lover.

Arnaut de Mareuil, twelfth century troubador

Barcelona, November 2nd, 1999

Dear Blanca:

Before I once again delve into the subject at hand, allow me to confirm that I have received your gift and I thank you. It's with intense emotion that I thank you, not only for the gesture and the gift itself, which could not be more to my liking, but because, with it, you have given me one more proof –this time quite unequivocal, I think– that, as exhausting as writing you these letters may be, at least it's not futile. What ineffable joy it was to see you again! For the ancient sages, dreams have always been an occasional communication channel with the Hereafter and the numinous, so it does not surprise me that you used them to show yourself to me. I know you have been trying it for a long time in the oval mirror in the hall, but remember that my sight is not what it used to be. In the dream, however, I could see you clearly. To be honest, I must say that I found you very different. I have no doubt whatsoever that it was you; it does not matter if you are in disguise, I will always recognise you. What I do regret, though, is not having paid enough attention to the plot of the dream. I know there was a plot, things were happening, although I can only remember that there was a library, a blue library like yours, except much older. I was too busy observing you, trying to engrave your new look in my memory... Then I asked myself the following question: How could I thank you? Then, it occurred to me that the only way to give back to you would be by writing. So here I am, in the amber gloom of the dining room, starting a new letter.

You will remember that in the previous one we talked about the "warrior's path", the hero's way. We said that a hero was a person who strived to live "the greatest adventure a knight has ever lived". We talked about how this adventure consisted of hastening the return to the Origin, the return to the Integrity of the soul. According to our theory, to recover its original Integrity, the soul must fuse with its twin into *perfect union*. Now, Blanca, what class of heroism enables this? When we refer to amorous heroism, what kind of exploits are we talking about? Or, putting it in Grail terms, what is the skill, the heroic qualification required to weld the two pieces of the sword, or to pull the sword out of the stone?... To answer these questions, let's take a moment to look at the symbolism of the sword in the stone, as well as the variant in which it's a supernatural hand, an aquatic hand, that challenges the hero to snatch the sword it holds aloft.

The stone, like the waters, symbolises Matter. The sword, as the vanquisher of mortal flesh, is a traditional symbol of the Spirit. If we go back to Greek mythology, Chrysaor's golden sword (according to Paul Diel[301]) was a symbol of supreme

301. Paul Diel, *Symbolism in Greek Mythology*

spiritualisation. There is a reason for the alternative symbol for the Grail being, as we have seen, a sword: a sword in the shape of a Christian cross, which is the shape it adopted in the medieval West. The sword represents Unity, Divinity, and it's embedded in the stone, or submerged in the waters of a lake. The message, then, is obvious: the Spirit is sunken in Matter, the Unit is being held captive by Duality, and we need to rescue it. In Arthurian novels, the sword in the stone appears to the aspiring hero, or, as he walks by a lake, a hand holding a sword surfaces (sometimes, both symbols are combined, and the stone with the embedded sword prodigiously floats on the water). This apparition is informing the hero about the feat to which he aspires: to remove the sword from the stone or water (or both). In other words, to surpass Matter, to sublimate it, and to return to the Unit via the Spirit.

For as long as we are unable to pull out the sword, we remain wounded by it. In an Arthurian story, an errant knight –Nacian– was wounded by the sword. It's the same wound as the Fisher King, Blanca, the same that afflicts every hero of the Quest: only he who obtains the proper qualifications can heal it. And so Nacian is healed by a clergyman who walks over water without getting wet. This ability shares its symbolism with the sword taken from the water: it denotes the overcoming of the *ego*, the sublimation of Matter. Once having reached this level of excellence, the hero does not belong to this world anymore; his heroic mission is complete. Now, he's qualified to wield the sword, to reconquer the Grail; which means that Unity is within reach. In the Grail cycle, only two heroes are shown to be worthy of this achievement: Perceval and Galahad. And Galahad is depicted as a medieval projection of Christ, the quintessential water walker. Just like Christ, Galahad is the Redeemer: his deed redeems the wounded King and his Kingdom. And what is the trait that qualifies him to do so? Well, it's precisely the ability to walk on water without getting wet.

SPIRITUAL NAKEDNESS

We see then, Blanca, what the heroic qualification required to reconquer the Grail, to restore the Origin's heavenly marriage by reuniting (in view of the Spirit's unifying properties) with the twin soul in *perfect union* is. We also see what the aim of the hero is: to spiritualise, sublimate, and elevate himself as much as he can. The ancient sages conceived this objective as a kind of process of distillation or refinement of the soul, a sort of purification or cleansing. Like salvaging a hidden treasure, buried in the deepest confines of one's self. However, above all, they imagined it as a process of *internal stripping.* The Sufi Bayazid Bastami compared it to a snake shedding its old skin. Regarding the understanding the Sufi sages had of this enterprise, Henry Corbin writes, "In short, it is a question of perceiving, of bringing out, the hidden depth of man, his batin, his authentic soul, and of reducing, causing the disappearance of, the apparent, the zahir, the whole apparatus of faculties and powers, and of appearances secreted by those powers, that envelop the soul and turn it from that for which it is made. Ultimately, it is a question of causing the appearance of the soul, of the Stranger or the Oriental hidden under the Occidental disguise of the common condition."[302]

Here, Corbin resorts to a traditional symbolism that sees the earthly East and West as the two poles of the Universe;

302. Henry Corbin, *Avicenna and the Visionary Recital,* p. 155

higher and lower. The idea is that the hero's soul –the Self– should shed all its "clothing", get rid of everything that is superfluous, everything that is foreign, to remain naked, to remain exclusively with what is essential to itself. And what is essential to the soul, Blanca? The Spirit. The Spirit is essential to the soul. The Spirit –as our sages believe– is asexual. Which means that sexual identity, the fact that it's male or female, is circumstantial, it's part of the clothing that conceals the soul. The naked soul, the soul from the Origin, which is that of the Two implicit in the One, has no gender. Therefore, the *essential* complementarity between twin souls (an essentiality that emanates from their divine filiation) is not sexual: it's spiritual, personal; it's not the result of a corporeal circumstance, such as a gender difference, but of a spiritual coincidence: being two halves of the same soul.

Scotus Eriugena, in this regard, opined that "... the human being is superior to sex, given that male and female are not the names of their nature (of the original human nature) but of their division for their transgression."[303] This means, Blanca, that beyond sex there is another complementarity –and, therefore, another attraction– of a spiritual nature, of which we could say that sexual complementarity and attraction are but the fallen transcription. Eriugena invented a paradoxical formula: *spirituales sexus*, "spiritual sex", to describe that other transcendent, personal, and ontological complementarity, the one that our sages considered the essential complementarity of the twin souls, due to the fact they are the two halves of the same Soul. This transcendent complementarity is what unites the two Persons implicit in God. However, since it falls within the scope of *Deus absconditus*, its nature consti-

303. John Scotus Eriugena, *De Divisione Naturae*, II, 534 A

tutes, for us humans, an impenetrable mystery. A mystery of which we can only perceive the tip of the iceberg, the profane transcription: i.e. sexual complementarity.

We mistakenly imagine that this is the original model and we extend it to God, when in reality it's nothing more than the earthly variant of that model. Given the lack of suitable categories to define God in the appropriate terms – the inscrutable God, the *absconditus* God–, we resort to categories that are familiar to us. We anthropomorphise God; we imagine Him in human terms, without thinking that God cannot be compared to man. And thus, we apply human standards to the complementarity between the two Persons implicit in God, we claim it's of a sexual nature; and we conclude that God is a male–female Couple (Mother and Father, Eternal Masculine and Eternal Feminine), or an Androgyne (a word with sexual connotations as well, given that it literally means "man–woman").

Crossed–out note on the margin. The original note took up the entire margin on the page. Only a few loose words and the final fragment of what appears to be a quotation survived the black marker: *.../... in propitious afternoons, lying on the grass .../... playing at recognising the... (shapes?) of the clouds."*

Nevertheless, despite all that, this is an understandable attitude, my love. Because while we cannot know God *as He is*, we still yearn to know Him, and the ancient sages show us that there is a little bit of God in each human being. Moreover, seeing that little bit of Him on each person, Blanca, is an indirect way of seeing God. We cannot look directly at the sun; so what's wrong with seeing it reflected on the water of a pond, for example? Provided we do not forget that what we are seeing is not exactly the sun, but rather its reflection on the water, otherwise we could end up thinking that the sun is wet...

Sexuality is a human category, not a divine one: this emerges from the texts of our sages. Now, Blanca, did we not agree that the essence of the soul was divine, that its humanity was the result of a fall and that it was destined to restore its lost Divinity? So, one way or another, be it by the evolutive path or by the heroic shortcut, the soul is destined to shed its sexual condition. This condition is nothing but a disguise, clothes with which it covered itself when it fell into this world. And to reunite with its twin for the purposes of androgynous restoration, the soul must be naked: because, same as it happens with bodies, only the souls that are completely naked will be able to unite in *perfect union*. If we think about the *symbolon* metaphor: the two parts will not fit each other perfectly as long as there are any residues left in their sectioned corners.

It follows, then, for that matter, that as long as two twin souls are not completely naked, their relationship will not be the rose garden that is expected from a relationship between twin souls. That relationship will be weighed down, even disrupted, by selfishness, which is a centrifugal and disintegrating force. You will remember that, in a previous letter, I mentioned that, according to John Milton, the "incompatibility of natures" is the main cause of divorce. But divorce is not always a sign of incompatibility of natures: couples of twin souls also divorce, and the cause is the selfish clothes that are still in their way. We must strive to throw away those clothes, which are nothing but a wall standing between the harmonious union and the lovers; we must practice, if you allow me the expression, spiritual nudism... What happens is that, just as the clothes we wear are not really a part of our body, they are a supervening attachment, so the clothes of the soul are foreign to it; they were attached as it fell. According to the Genesis, Adam and Eve (who represent every couple of twin souls) walked naked in the Origin, it was after falling that they covered themselves in "skin tunics". "O, how unlike to that first naked glory"[304] writes Milton regarding this famous biblical episode.

Remember the *naf*, the Sufi equivalent of the *ego*: the "carnal soul" or the material component of the soul, inhabited by selfish desires and headquarters of instinct and concupiscence. The Sufi is a hero, and his heroic endeavour consists of detaching himself from his *naf*. That is to say, of releasing all the material ballast of his soul so that, vested in the angels' winged nature, it can soar towards its homeland, from where it's exiled. The Sufi scholars tell us about the merciless war between the hero and his *naf*. They inform us that, occasionally, the hero even visualises his opponent and gives him a physical shape in his imagination: often they give it the shape of a wild animal that is starving due to the fasting to which it's subjected. Since it's a product of the imagination, this beast is often a fantastic beast, Blanca... like a dragon.

How many stories have you read where the hero embarks on a mission to slay or subjugate a dragon? In many ancient cultures, we can find the archetypal image of the hero facing a dragon in single combat. Apollo, Cadmus, Perseus, Siegfried, they are all mythological heroes who have defeated dragons. In Christian tradition, we can find the legendary figures of St. George and the archangel St. Michael, patron

---

304. John Milton, *Paradise Lost*, IX, 1114,1115

saints of medieval knights, who are usually depicted fighting a dragon. For the hero, like in the legend of Tristan for example, what's at stake is often the hand of a princess; in which I believe I recognise the central idea behind our letters, my dear: the idea that the unification with the twin soul is only viable by overcoming the *ego*.

The dragon is the universal image of the hero's antagonist. With its serpentine body, it's a homologue of the devil –shown in the Genesis as having the shape of a serpent. Snakes in general, the serpent and the dragon in particular, are material and animalistic symbols in man, just as birds –specifically the eagle– are symbols of the Spiritual and the Divine. (Medusa, enemy of men, slayer of Perseus, had living snakes in place of hair). The image of an eagle fighting against a serpent or a dragon often appears in universal iconography, and it re–enacts the hero's inner struggle. A struggle heading towards the *undressing*, the stripping of the carnal clothes that covered the soul and concealed its divine essence as it fell into this world.

God, man's conversion into God, is the heroic Quest's ultimate objective. And seeing as Divinity is bipolar, Blanca, seeing as it's structured into two poles, then so the Quest must also be. Therefore, the hero's mission –the struggle against the *ego*, the inner undressing– is a shared mission, a mission for two, comparable to a musical duet. Except that sometimes the two halves of a heroic duo act by themselves and are not even aware of each other; we could say that they are playing their instruments separately, but that by the hand of Destiny, the notes they are playing combine into one single melody. Ancient Jewish sages, under the pretext that the Hebrew word for "life" –*haym*– is a plural form, talk about the life of the soul following the Fall as a "double life": the soul's life, and its twin's life. The old literary theme of the "double" or the "other self" could be referencing the secret life that each individual lives in a foreign body, with an alien awareness. Sometimes, the bipolarity of those lonely lives is not even secret, not only for the protagonists themselves but for everyone around them. And do you know who I'm thinking about right now? Who do you think? Well, I'm thinking about your friend, Sister Clara, and that childhood acquaintance of hers. She told you this story and then you told it to me, do you remember? After she joined the convent, this young man began attending the twelve o'clock mass every Sunday without fail. He went there just to see her, of course, otherwise why would he travel one hour by train and another half-hour on foot to attend a mass in a convent in the middle of nowhere? She confessed to you how excited she would be every Sunday, waiting for his presence in hopeful anticipation, until that platonic idyll became much too evident for everyone -because you cannot hide love- and the mother superior took action.

Crossed–out note on the margin. All I could decipher from the original quotation is this fragment: – "*...the illusory depth of the mirrors*"–, which finds its relevancy at the beginning of this letter.

But we could also recall some famous mystical couples, like St. Francis and St. Clare of Assisi, who on account of being childhood friends -before he embraced the life of an ascetic and she followed in his footsteps–, had to endure gossip and rumours about the nature of their relationship. Or like St. Teresa of Jesus and St. John of the Cross. Or -to name an Eastern couple- Sri Aurobindo and Mirra Alfassa, known by the simple moniker "The Mother" and about whom he declared: "The Mother's consciousness and mine are the same..."[305] I've already told you: the heroic condition is essentially a bipolar condition: there is no hero without a heroine. Because there is no room for the hero's final victory –his coronation and access to Royalty, that is– if it's not shared, if it's not a victory and a coronation *of two*. Thus, the two halves of the heroic couple face the mission of self-spiritualisation, Blanca. Ah, but it's not just the Two that experience an increased spiritualisation, their mutual love becomes more spiritualised as well. Because God's bipolarity *is amorous*. Which means that the heroic Quest for Divinity (although many seekers do not immediately realise this) must follow the path of erotic love.

In fact, for our sages, as we have seen, human love is the touchstone of divine love. Hence, throughout the entire heroic process (and this process may last several lives), the predestined "duo" should coincide if not always, then often. The Two will then come together to play that melody that they rehearsed by themselves. After all, that's why we come into this world: to rehearse, to put our soul to the test in order to polish it, to clean it of impurities. Just like a musician hones his technique during rehearsals. Practice makes perfect. Reincarnations are as vital for the soul as daily physical contact with his instrument is for the musician. We cannot clean the impurities off our soul all the way up from Heaven, just as a musician cannot perfect his technique just by studying musical theory. Theory is the necessary foundation, but it's useless if he does not translate that theory into practice. And that takes time and effort.

---

305. Sri Aurobindo, *On Himself*, p. 361

In the case of a musical duo, perfecting their technique is vital, for the musicians' harmony on stage depends on it. The more refined their individual technique is, the tighter they will sound, and the less dissonant will their performance of that joint melody be, that melody of which each one of them plays half the notes, so to speak. There will come a moment, after many intense rehearsals, when that double melody will sound as if it's being played by one musician only, which is what this is all about. And well, Blanca, the same is applicable to predestined lovers, whose ultimate objective –unification– also depends on the refinement of their souls: the more refined they are, the more refined and true their love will be. And true love is the creator of unification: because if the divorce of the Two was the result of the degeneration of their mutual love, then on what can their new marriage depend if not on the regeneration of their mutual love?

This sounds indisputable to me, my dear: if what caused the Fall was the replacement of spiritual love of the Origin for sexual desire, then the return to the Origin must inevitably involve the reverse movement. That is, certainly, the course of Evolution. In anticipation of a forthcoming letter, I will tell you that the ancient sages devised a symbolic procedure in the interest of shortening this trip. I'm referring to *Alchemy*. "Alchemy is the separation of the impure from the purer substance,"[306] prays a famous definition by Baroque alchemist Martin Ruland. The alchemist purifies solid matter, represented by lead, to liberate its spirit made of gold. Likewise, we twin souls –originally the Two implicit in the One– are called upon to regenerate our mutual love, to free

306. Martinus Rulandus, *A Lexicon of Alchemy*, p. 20

it from material impurities in order to make the gold of our true love shine again.

LOVE COMES OUT FROM THE ATTIC

Such vision of things explains the negative valuation that the ancient sages, in general, made of carnal love. I believe I already cited enough examples in previous letters. Let me just add two more literary testimonies -one from the West and one from the East- taken from two books mentioned in the first letter regarding the subject of predestined love. The first one is from what I consider one of the most beautiful romantic novels: *Julie or the New Heloise*, by the philosopher Jean-Jacques Rousseau. "...my too tender heart needs love -confesses Julie to her beloved-, but my senses have no need for a lover...; I savour the delightful pleasure of loving in all purity. This state makes my life's happiness...; I can scarcely conceive a more blissful one, and the harmony of love and innocence is paradise on earth to me."[307] And later, when she gives in to temptation, she will immediately regret it: "I regret far less having given too much to love than having deprived it of its greatest charm. That blissful enchantment of virtue has vanished away like a dream: our flame has lost that divine ardour which fed it while purifying it; we pursued pleasure, and happiness has fled far from us. Recall to mind those delightful moments when our hearts were all the more united that we respected each other more, when passion drew from its own profusion the strength to control itself... A pure and sacred flame burned our hearts; now, a prey to

307. Jean-Jacques Rousseau, *Julie or the New Heloise*, First Part, Letter IX

the errors of the senses, we are nothing more than vulgar lovers; fortunate at that if jealous love still deigns to preside over pleasures that the bases mortal can enjoy without it."[308]

To be frank, Blanca, I should tell you that the love Rousseau portraits in this novel is an ideal love, a heroic love that even he was not able to put into practice, as we can infer from his memories. The other example is from the classic Chinese novel *The Story of the Stone*. In a passage from that novel, they discuss love in its "natural state", that is to say, naked love, love in its true essence. This love stands in sharp contrast with sexual desire and is attributed to the "immortals", to the human beings that have achieved enlightenment, those who have reached the Higher World and recovered their divine status. To give you some context: this dissertation on love follows a string of deaths: first, it's the matriarch of the Jia clan, then her handmaiden, who takes her own life out of loyalty for her lady. The handmaiden's soul leaves her body and is greeted by a female immortal at the threshold to the other world. She is the one in charge of guiding her to the "Paradise of Love", where she has earned a place, she says, having professed true love during her recently concluded earthly life. Surprised, the handmaiden replies that it was not deliberate, that she does not know what true love really is. So the immortal explains it to her. "People of this world -she begins- confuse love with sexual desire... They do not understand the true meaning of the word *love*. Before pleasure, wrath, sorrow, and joy appear in the human heart, there is the 'natural state' of love. The appearance of those emotions produces passion. The class of love that moves you and I is the natural state of love, a love that is not open to

308. *Ibid*, First Part, Letter XXXII

passion. It is like a flower that remains closed in a bud. Once opened, love is no longer true."[309]

To return love to its "natural state", to its original nakedness. This, Blanca, is the arduous task to which the twin souls are dedicated. For our sages, carnal love is a disguise, a garment covering the Love of the Two as it fell. It's a fallen love and, in this sense, a corrupt and "deviant" love. You know, sexual desire would be to Love what idolatry is to religion: worshipping idols is a deviation from worshipping the one true God; carnal love is a deviation from real love. Because love in on itself, in its pure essence, love in its original nakedness is spiritual. It does not involve the body but the soul. The association of love with the body is accidental and transient; whereas with the soul it is essential and eternal. We have, then, two clearly different types of love, although in reality they are the same love, except one is "naked" and the other is "in disguise". And, from these two different types of love, derive two classes of erotic unions, whose dissimilarity is beautifully highlighted by John Milton in his *Paradise Lost*:

> ...and with eyes
> Of conjugal attraction unreproved,
> And meek surrender, half-embracing leaned
> On our first father; half her swelling breast
> Naked met his, under the flowing gold
> Of her loose tresses hid: he in delight

309. Here the author combines the French translation by Li Tche-Houa and Jacqueline Alézaïs (*op. cit.*, vol. II, p. 1328) and the English one by John Minford (*The story of the Stone*, Penguin Books, vol. V, p. 210)

Both of her beauty, and submissive charms,
Smiled with superior love, as Jupiter
On Juno smiles, when he impregns the clouds
That shed Mayflowers; and pressed her matron lip
With kisses pure...[310]

These are, without a doubt, the early stages of an erotic union, of intercourse ("When he impregns the clouds that shed Mayflowers..."). But a spiritual and divine intercourse, very different from that other one they embarked on immediately after eating the forbidden fruit. Now their mutual "virginal" gaze has turned lascivious:

But that false fruit
Far other operation first displayed,
Carnal desire inflaming; he on Eve
Began to cast lascivious eyes; she him
As wantonly repaid; in lust they burn:
Till Adam thus 'gan Eve to dalliance move.[311]

In general, the ancient sages considered carnal love foreign to the Unit. Therefore, those who intend to return to the One as soon as possible should apply themselves to sublimating sexual desire, distilling their divine essence. Look, in Jewish tradition, there is the figure of the *tzadik*, the "righteous one", the virtuous man, the saint or hero who, once his earthly cycle is complete, finds his place in the intimate sphere of Divinity. In the *Talmud*, God Himself is named the "Righteous of the World" and the "The Righteous One

310. John Milton, *Paradise Lost* IV, 492–512
311. *Ibid*, IX, 1011–1016

Who Lives Eternally". Well, Blanca, the *tzadik* is, first, chaste; he has neutralised sexual instinct. The Kabbalah saw Joseph, the son of Jacob and Rachel, sold as a slave by his own brothers, as the prototype of the "righteous one", because of his chastity as detailed in the Scriptures.[312]

It's true that this, let's call it "idealist", trend of the Kabbalah -which I have described as being more like a mosaic of sometimes contradictory tendencies- contrasts with the stance of many Kabbalists who tried to discover the mystery of God's own sex. But, since I mentioned an episode from the Genesis, my dear, let's take a look at an earlier verse... In Genesis 3: 24 we read that, following Adam and Eve's expulsion from Paradise, Yahweh Elohim stationed an angel armed with a fiery sword at the entrance, entrusting him with the mission of "guarding the path to the Tree of Life". In the nineteenth century, this verse caught the attention of a disciple of Jakob Boehme called Johan Jakob Wirx, who interpreted it in a symbolic context. According to him, it expresses how those who wish to enter Paradise -divine Unity- need to vanquish sexual nature until instinct is annulled. Wriz writes that, with his fiery sword (fire and sword are redundant symbols, for they both have the same purifying character, cleanser of mortal flesh and Matter) with his fiery sword, this symbolic angel "should destroy, root and branch, the animal principle of desire in those who truly aspired to the reintegration of the divine image."[313]

If for Wirz, the human being were (as it is for the exoteric side of religions) a simple creature, a creation of God, you can be sure, Blanca, that he would not have said that. If

---

312. Genesis 39: 7-20
313. Quoted by Julius Evola, *Metaphysics of Sex*, p.212

he believed that man, a combination of animal and angel, was created in this manner by a specific divine will, then he would regard sex in a very different light. But, if we believe, like Wirz, like the ancient sages from the esoteric side of religion, that man is, in essence, a fallen spark of God called upon to restore his lost divinity, then what will bring us closer to that goal? The attributes we share with the animals? Or what we have in common with the angels? Well, that's why "the reintegration of the divine image", which is the image of the Androgyne, the One, presupposes for our sages the sublimation of desire, Blanca; the distillation of its essence.

This essence is true love, the one we metaphorically referred in the previous letter as "ultraviolet love", corresponding to the last stage of the trip towards the centre of erotic love. The heroic lover intends to reach that stage as soon as he can, and for that, he imposes chastity on himself. I know that many people would claim that such imposition is equivalent to renouncing love and its foundations, but that's because today, in general, people believe that there is nothing behind carnal love. Or rather, that sex is behind spiritual love, when in fact it's the opposite. For the ancient sages, sex not only is not the foundation of love (although it is, as we have seen, the evolutive foundation for the return to true love) but it actually masks its essence. By renouncing sex, the heroic lover is pursuing the unmasking of love, the liberation from the obstacles that obstruct true love, which is the radiant love of the pure souls, of the souls free from materiality, the *innocent* souls, as our old friend Swedenborg would say, for whom "marriage love viewed in itself is a state of innocence"...[314]

---

314. Emmanuel Swedenborg, *Heaven and Hell*, 382 a

Talking about the unmasking of love, suddenly –I think I know why– I just thought about Ricky. Do you remember our homosexual, or *gay*, as he preferred to say, neighbour? Of course you remember, you supported him when he decided to reveal his sexual identity back when such a decision was almost a heroic act. Well, I have bad news about Ricky. I mean, maybe they are not bad: I suspect that, from your point of view as a disembodied spirit, him having left this word is actually fantastic news. Indeed, Ricky loved you. He told me you had been like a mother to him. Lately, I tried to be like a father to him, and you will be pleased to know that he faced AIDS and death with the same bravery that he displayed from the moment he decided to remove his mask or, as he liked to say, "come out of the closet"... The point is, if I just thought of Ricky, my dear, that is because to remove the mask of love, we require a similar courage. You know, it's not an easy task, this is not like tearing off one of those monstrous black masks that your brother-in-law collected –I think we would all be spontaneously inclined to do that. No, this is not a repulsive mask, on the contrary: it's an attractive mask, a mask that no one would be inclined to remove at first. Because at first glance, it does not even look like a mask: that's how adjusted to the face it is, how fused it is.

But look, there's something that I would like to stress regarding this mask. If the heroic lover decides to pull it off, he does so in the service of love. This is key, Blanca: it's *for the sake of love* that the hero decides to come out of the closet, to abandon that darkness in which love has remained hidden since the Fall. We should not confuse the heroic hero, then, with someone who renounces sex for any other reason. For organic reasons, for simple lack of appetite or, as in our case, forced by circumstances. We also should not confuse the heroic lover for someone who abstains from sex for purely negative reasons (such as fear of an eventual eternal damnation). Or merely for religious reasons (for love belongs to each person's intimate convictions and it should not be subject to external dictates). But most of all, we should never confuse the heroic hero with those prudish people whose rejection of sex not only does not lead to love, but it extends to it, and even to individuals of the opposite sex who arouse it. To confuse them would be almost sacrilegious.

I quoted above some verses by John Milton. Now, I would like to quote a verse written by another English poet, Ruper Chawner Brooke, an ill-fated poet killed in the First World War. This verse will be useful to illustrate how shedding all materiality from love will give it wings instead of weakening it. Brooke saw in human bodily organs –hands, eyes, ears...–, not the means through which we access the corresponding functions –tact, vision, hearing...–, but precisely the opposite: their limitations. The verse says that when we become pure spirits, we will "feel, who have laid our groping hands away; And see, no longer blinded by our eyes"... And well, Blanca, I think we could say the same thing about sexual organs and the carnal soul of man: when we become pure spirits, we will love; we will truly love, no longer having sexual organs and desires.

Because once again, my love: love is not desire, it's something much nobler and deeper. For our sages, desire is the material and earthly transcription of love, its fallen and falsified recreation, just like tact and vision –the tact and vision enabled by our hands and our eyes– are, for the poet, the fallen recreation of true tact and true vision...

Love and desire: on the surface, two words with the same meaning, synonyms. But something separates them, Blanca, and it's not a trifle. It's like the difference between a hunter and an ornithologist: both are after birds, except one of them has a rifle, the other one has a pair of binoculars. What we are analysing here is a substantial discrepancy between those two words: one of them denotes something spiritual, the other one something material. But there's even a bigger difference, you know? The difference is that in love it's not the self that matters, personal happiness is relegated to the background, it becomes something trivial. *The important thing in love is the other person's happiness.* While in desire, it's the opposite: in desire, it's the other person who exists in function of our personal happiness. To desire someone is a selfish act, to love someone is altruism.

Now, going back to that other substantial difference: if we listen to the ancient sages, the love from the Origin has a spiritual nature, it has no traces of sexuality. Sexuality is associated with Matter, with the body. Therefore, it's incompatible with the subtle nature of the Higher World, with its spiritual and incorporeal nature. Hence Swedenborg observing (since I brought him up above) that "lustful love, a love that withdraws man from Heaven". And then he adds, "this is not easily comprehended by men because there are few who are in genuine marriage love, and those who are not in it know nothing whatever of the interior delight that is in that love, knowing only the delight of lust, and this delight is changed into what is undelightful after living together a short time; while the delight of true marriage love not only endures to old age in the world, but after death becomes the delight of heaven and is there filled with an interior delight that grows more and more perfect to eternity."[315]

315. *Ibid*, 379

We have already seen, Blanca, that according to our sages, the intrusion of sexuality in Love led it to its fall from its original headquarters. It also led to the separation of the multiple Two implicit in the One. Only the sublimation of sex could seal that breach. Hence the heroic hero's necessity of living his love in chastity. At the beginning, this self-imposition entails an active struggle against the *ego*, against the carnal soul, which, in the first stage of his adventure, appears to be an invincible giant. The ogre or the giant (let's think of Morholt the giant, who Tristan faced in single combat) is, like the dragon or the serpent, another form in which the *ego*, selfish love and desire, in particular, is traditionally depicted. If the hero does not shy away, if he perseveres in his fight, his strikes will end up enfeebling and diminishing the giant. The fight will gradually become less fierce until *ego* and desire finally disappear.

Forcing nature like this, Blanca, may seem reckless. Any psychologist would tell you that sexual repression is a source of emotional unbalance. But what about when the negation of sex is accompanied by a parallel affirmation? Because when it comes to our heroes, it's not just a question of draining a well: it's about refilling it with *something else* at the same time. We drain the stagnant waters to make room for living waters. Living waters are the waters of the Spirit, naturally: platonic love. Let's not confuse, then, the heroic lover's struggle for a simple rejection of sex... You know, that struggle could be translated into physiological terms. The ancient sages speak of it like a reversal of trajectory: the trajectory of the essence or vital energy that –known as *chi* to the Chinese sages, *prana* to the Hindus and Buddhists, *pneuma* to the Greeks– brings Matter to life. The energy or *vital elan* –"vital impulse", as the French philosopher Henri Bergson called it–, that in the past cannibalised itself down to the lower abdomen, now ascends, it advances in search of its true roots. Roots that at the same time, Blanca, are summits: the high peaks of the Spirit. As a result of this sublimation of energy, the hero delves into ever more sublime worlds. By breaking free from the empire of the senses and the tyranny of concupiscence, the heroic lover savours *naked love* – with its delicate taste, so different from the crude taste of carnal love – and realises, then, how much of an obstacle to love sex had really been, rather than a stimulus as they once believed.

The ancient sages bring us news of this radiant love –this altruist and selfless love that some called *Agape*–, and believe it to be like a door that leads to Paradise. They also tell us that heroes, the souls of heroes, are younger or older depending on which stage of the adventure they find themselves at (we already said that in this case, old age is preferable to youth). If we abide by Walter Map's story, out of all the legendary heroes of the Quest for the Grail, Galahad has the oldest soul, given that he's already immune to temptation. Galahad and his twin soul –the mysterious maiden that accompanies him to "Solomon's ship"– are more than chaste according to Map, they are *virgins*, and what he means with this word is a virginity that is not the result of forced continence, of the repression of instincts, but a natural disposition of the soul. Closely following Galahad's soul in the ladder of spiritual maturity is the soul of chaste Perceval, who was haunted by temptations, but always knew how to resist them. Then comes Bohort, who succumbed to the voluptuousness of flesh only once in his life...

The Grail cycle, Blanca, is not the only place where chastity is considered an essential attribute of the hero (if not of ordinary mortal people). Our sages, in general, insist on it. Remember, for example, that sentence by H.D. Thoreau that I quoted before: “Chastity is the flowering of man; and what are called Genius, Heroism, Holiness, and the like, are but various fruits which succeed it.”[316] Then we have Paracelsus’ stance on it, which I will repeat here because it’s representative of what most of our sages believe. “Chastity –writes the famous doctor and esoteric– grants a pure heart and the capacity to learn the things of God. God Himself, who ordered things to be thus, gave chastity to men. But if one does not hold power over oneself (meaning, if one has not taken the heroic path), it is better that he should not be alone.”[317] Anyway, my dear, we could vindicate chastity by quoting from eminent Western philosophers such as Immanuel Kant (who considered sexual desire morally problematic from the moment it treats the other person as a means to sexual self-gratification), to Eastern mystics like Sri Swami Sivananda (“Whoever seeks divine realisation with true ardour must observe rigorous chastity.”[318]). Or from poets, like the Renaissance era Ausiàs Marc, who honoured our language with beautiful verses such as this:

> Sí com los sants, sentints la llum divina
> La llum del món conegueren per ficta,
> E menyspreants la glòria mundana,
> Puix major part de glòria sentien,
> Tot enaixí tinc en menyspreu e fàstic
> Aquells desigs qui, complits, amor minva,
> Prenint aquells que de l’esperit mouen,
> Qui no és llassat, ans tot jorn muntiplica.

316. H. D. Thoreau, “Higher Laws”, *Walden*
317. Paracelsus, *Essential Texts*
318. Sri Swami Savananda, *La practique de la meditation*, Paris 1950

(Like the saints who, feeling the divine light, the light of the world they knew to be false, rejected mundane glory, as they felt part of a greater glory, likewise I feel contempt and disgust for those desires that, once fulfilled, result in the impairment of love, and I take those who come from the spirit, which never tires but multiplies every day.)

Now, the following verses, Blanca: "Yet drink not of the muddy stream / Save in extremity extreme, / and when the whole round world contains / No other reservoir but drains. / and never let those lips of thine, / though parched, approach the brackish brine; / Salt chokes the throat; far seemlier then / is thirst endured to honest men", belong to our old friend Ibn Hazm of Cordoba, who imagined spiritual love as pure water; mixed love – a combination of carnal and spiritual love–, as muddy water. And carnal love as brackish water, which rather than quenching thirst, makes it worse: he considers enduring thirst preferable to drinking salt water. Many of his confreres agree; without going any further, we find the ninth century Iraqi poet Ibn al-Rumi, for whom carnal love, the physical embrace, does nothing but exacerbate the lover's thirst: "I embrace her but the yearning of my soul for her remains unquenched; / Is there no drawing nearer than mere embrace? / I kiss her mouth that the pain in my heart may be still, / but the rapture I feel only grows more violent still"[319]... I don't know what you think, my dear, but this impression coincides with my own experience. Even those passionate nights we spent together in our youth felt like too little, as if the water Hazm and Rumi were talking about was slipping through my fingers. I believe that

319. Ibn al-Rumi, in *Les plus beaux textes arabes* by E. Dermenghem

even then I had already vaguely intuited the conclusion they reached: "Nothing, it seems, can cure my heart's thirst except to see our souls mingle"[320]. After trying through carnal union, Rumi understands that the only way to quench his thirst for unification is through a spiritual union, through the souls' embrace. This was a very common observation among the ancient sages, Blanca. We can find an easy explanation if we think about the fundamental discrepancy between love and desire. By their very nature, desire and carnal union are selfish (a selfishness that only subsides to the extent that desire is denatured, grafted with spiritual love); and selfishness, far from uniting, isolates; Selfishness separates.

I believe that, with the appropriate exceptions, we make the following generalisation: The ancient sages believed that carnal union pulled souls apart instead of bringing them together... Yet, my love, there's this contradiction where when one hears about amorous intimacy, one immediately thinks about carnal union. The word *intimacy* itself hints at how false the association of these two ideas is; *intimacy* comes from *intime*, which in Latin means "inside, in the deepest part". From the very beginning of our correspondence, I remarked that everything relating to Matter was, for the ancient sages, merely the epidermis of reality, the superficial cover of things. The true amorous intimacy is the one "within", the one of the souls, of the hearts, the one that exists between two lovers who feel connected even when apart. Like the distance between us during our last New Year's Eve together... Do you remember? You did not want to miss the annual party at Esther and Enrique's. You said that being surrounded by people helped you deceive the sickness and

320. *Ibid*

the pain, which were getting worse. During the party, we became physically distant. But that distance –that while not being great, felt like it in the middle of all those people– was offset by our eyes looking for each other, and when they met, it was as though they silenced the night. So, for a second, the crowded party transformed for us into an intimate dinner by candlelight. A magic moment that your favourite poet defined as the "Privilege of one another's Eyes", except that in her poem ("These Fleshless Lovers met – A Heaven in a Gaze – A Heaven of Heavens – the Privilege Of one another's Eyes"[321]), in Emily Dickinson's poem, that expression alludes to the intimacy between twin souls in Heaven. Whereas we had sparks of such intimacy here on Earth. We were lucky!

Now, I would like to show you two testimonies, provided by the ancient sages, of the strengthening of intimacy resulting from spiritual love. The first one is by a hagiographer, a twelfth century biographer of saints. Jacques de Vitry, the confessor of Beguine, or secular, nun Marie of Oignies, alludes to her union with her husband Juan in these terms: "The more he was separated from her in human affection, the more closely was he bound to her by the ties of spiritual union. Accordingly, our Lord afterwards promised her in a vision, that He would give her back her husband to be her companion in heaven, in reward for what they had given up, inasmuch as through the love of chastity he had renounced all carnal joy."[322] The second may sound familiar to you, for it's a testimony taken from the biography of Gandhi that you have in your library. I did not remember it, so I was surprised

321. Emily Dickinson, "Resurrection" *The Complete Poems of Emily Dickinson*

322. Jacques de Vitry, *Life of B. Mary Oignies*

to discover that, in his youth, Gandhi was dominated by the "bad inclination" (to use a Kabbalist euphemism); he fought against it for years, and it was not until he was thirty seven that he and he his wife, Kasturbai, adopted the chastity they would embrace for the rest of their lives. The Mahatma's conviction was so strong that he even urged newlywed couples to follow his example! Upon his wife's death, when he received a letter of condolence from the British viceroy, he replied with another letter in which, referring to his married life, he said: (Chastity) knit us together as never before. We ceased to be two different entities... The result was that she became truly my better half".[323]

The case is, Blanca, that if I look back, I can see that we could say the same about us. We also fed the dragon of desire for years. I will not say that we were not united back then. But it seems obvious to me that it was different from how we came to be later, when as a result of your illness we had to starve the dragon and (I'm speaking mostly for myself) fight him tooth and nail. It's clear that the union resulting from that fight, that this union now, Blanca, is deeper, *more intimate* than it used to be. I would even say that the feelings are stronger too. Don't ask me why, I only know that today I love you not only in a different way: I also love you more... Look! Maybe the answer is in a passage that jumped out at me from this book I just opened at random. It's also a letter, a fragment of a letter that a Christian saint from the fifth century wrote to a couple who, like us, had transitioned from physical to spiritual love: "He (God) –writes Paulinus of Nola– transforms not only souls but also feelings, changing the transient into the eternal. See how you remain the

323. Louis Fischer, *The Life of Mahatma Ghandi*

married couple you were, yet not coupled as you were. You are yourselves yet not yourselves. Now you know each other, as you know Christ, apart from the flesh."[324]

Or maybe when carnal passion blinded us, it prevented us from truly seeing each other as in a mirror, which is how the ancient sages claim the love between twin souls operates... Yes, have I not told you about it yet? The ancient sages imagined the love between twin souls as a magic mirror: a mirror in which the two faces are the two souls contemplating each other. When Ibn Arabi writes to his beloved Nizam: "It's through my eyes that you see and see yourself", he does it thinking about their mutual reflection in this mirror. A mirror that, similarly to what happens with calm waters, when it's rocked by passions it loses its reflective properties. This reminds me (I'm all over the place, forgive me) of the mythological Narcissus, you know, the young man who drowned when he tried to kiss his own reflection on the quiet water of a fountain. But I'm thinking about a different version of that myth that I learned recently. I'm referring to a version collected by Pausanias, a traveller and geographer of the second century, in the course of his travels through Greece. His version claims that Narcissus was not enamoured with himself, as it's thought, but that it was not his face he was seeing in the reflecting waters. His face evoked an identical one: that of his twin sister who died in adolescence.

Anyway, Blanca, I would remember many other things. Mostly our things, examples of the spiritual communion that lately you and I had laboriously woven. But we cannot run aground, we must proceed with our investigation. It will now focus more on the heroic love of the Middle Ages. This era

---

324. Saint Paulinus of Nola, *Letter to Aper and Amanda*

has been dubbed, and not without reason, "the dark ages". But you will see, my dear, that it was a darkness bespangled with little dots of light, with the shimmery flame of candles...

THE SWORD OF CHASTITY

The Frenchman René Nelli, to whose expertise we have already appealed in another letter, is one of the greatest connoisseurs of medieval Arabic and Occitan erotica. His book *The Troubadours Erotica* is an essential reference to students of courtly love. Courtly love, Blanca, is the Middle Ages' heroic love, a love that was praised and advertised by those poets who composed music for their verses and sang them, the troubadours. In the strictest sense, the troubadours were the Occitan poets who sang in Provencal (a language very close to ours) during the twelfth and thirteenth century, although there were later troubadours from all over Europe, singing in different languages. The troubadour Guiraut Riquier describes his brothers as "men with the God given gift of wisdom, made to bring clarity to the Universe". Many troubadours were professionals who made a living travelling from castle to castle during the warm months. The troubadour's natural audience was the nobility: the ladies and knights of the court, always eager to listen to the new songs composed by the troubadours. Those summertime trips were like the tours of modern day singer–songwriters, except back then there were no airplanes or freeways to shorten the distances. But to compensate for this, there were jongleurs, much more numerous travelling musicians, thanks to whom the troubadours songs could travel quicker than the artists themselves, spreading their music over a wider audience.

I started talking about Occitan troubadours and jongleurs. Before them, there were the Arabic poets and reciters, whose main subject was heroic love as well, pure and naked love. Nelli summarises the conception of erotic love implied by their verses: "Just like the soul is superior to the body, so spiritual love, by nature, is superior to physical love. Arabic chastity, then, cannot resemble in any way Christian continence. It was not a mortification pleasing to God, but the only way to reach the true essence of love... (For the medieval Arabic 'heroes') continence has an esoteric value... it corresponds both to the only love worthy of this name and to a true mystic revelation, leaving the plane of earthly realities way behind. Consequently, for them, chastity was intrinsic to love: love demanded chastity."[325] Talking about the Arabic ideal of chastity, Blanca, is talking about *Udhra love*, which is how courtly love is known in the Arab world. The name comes from a tribe who flourished between the seventh and eighth century in the Southeast of the Arabian Peninsula, in a remote valley in Yemen. The Bedouin tribe of the *Banu Udhra*, the "Sons of Virginity", produced many poets; with the peculiarity that Udhra poetry is monothematic: it deals with one single issue, spiritual love. But, in addition, the Udhra poets practiced what they preached: they became famous for cultivating the type of love they put into verse; a pure and chaste love, so intense (its intensity came from its purity) that it was said they "died of love". The Arabic chronicles of the time tell about Udhras dying of no particular infirmity, but of love towards their lady. Otherwise, my dear, Udhra love verged on mysticism, on religion, to the point that orthodox Muslims denigrated

325. R. Nelli, translated from *L'érotique des troubadours*, p. 56

and accused it of interfering with the worship of the Most High.

Many scholars have pointed out the similarities between Udhra love and the love that moved that legendary couple of lovers whose story we put on hold in the first letter (did you think I had forgotten it?). The love between Tristan and Isolde is also characterised by chastity. "The enjoyment of my body he renounced, and I of his"[326], declares Isolde in Béroul's version. Another reliable example of it, is the famous episode of the naked sword, with which we will pick up the thread of this legend. If I'm not mistaken, we interrupted the story at the point where Tristan and Isolde drank the love potion by mistake (in reality, it was by Destiny's design) and felt its effects. Nevertheless, Tristan resists, keeps his word, and brings Isolde to Cornwall. King Mark marries her. But Tristan and Isolde cannot escape the powers of the potion and, in view of the unsurmountable obstacles their adulterous love would face within the court, they run away together. They find refuge in a small cabin in the woods. In the German version by Gottfried von Strassburg (the version on which Richard Wagner based his famous opera), it's not a cabin but a cave that resembles a temple: the *Minnegrotte* or "Love grotto". This circumstance assumes a peculiar significance, Blanca, if we keep in mind that caves have been seen as the ideal places for initiations ever antiquity; in this case, it's the initiation into love (the altar at the centre of this underground temple is a bridal bed entirely made out of crystal). The initiation into true love, for *Minne* refers to spiritual love: the word was coined by the *minnesänger*, the German "love singers" of the twelfth and thirteenth centu-

326. Beroul, *Romance of Tristan*

ries (Wolfram von Eschenbach and Gottfried von Strassburg among them), to differentiate true love from *liebe*, that is to say, from the current, carnal, and reputedly false love. Well then, the days go by in the woods, happy days for Tristan and Isolde, for they are together. But Isolde's husband is looking for them, he has offered a great reward for their capture. One night, a forest ranger finds the cabin and the sleeping lovers, and he immediately warns King Mark, who comes alone and catches them in bed. And so "In anger, the King raised his sword, / but his anger left him:

> the blow was never to fall on them,
> and it would have been a great sorrow if he had killed them.
> For he saw that she was wearing her tunic,
> that there was a space between them and
> their mouths were not joined.
> And he saw the naked sword between them
> which kept them apart and the trousers that
> Tristan was wearing. 'God, what can this be?'"[327]

Meaning, Blanca, that Tristan and Isolde's love is chaste, it's a spiritual love. This heroic trial –the test of the "sword of chastity", as it's known– is present in much older stories: in Celtic and Nordic love stories, where sometimes what separates the sleeping lovers –a symbol of the purity of their love– is not a naked sword but a cold stone. In yet another retelling of the legend of Tristan, the *minnesinger* Eilhart von Oberg highlights the importance of the naked sword separating the lovers' bodies in bed: "The book tell us that they remained in the woods for over two years without seeing neither villages

---

327. *Ibid*

nor people. During this time, Sir Tristan had one habit and the lady agreed with it: when they were both in bed and had talked enough, he would draw his sword from the scabbard and place it between him and her. The hero did not want to renounce this habit for anything in this world; every time they went to sleep, the sword would be between them. It was a strange proof of the warrior's spirit..."[328]

Let's leave them sleeping now, let's allow their souls to perhaps meet in dreams, and we shall come back to them when they wake up. Meanwhile, if you agree, we can dedicate ourselves to characterising their love, their spiritual love and, by contrast, their carnal love... for which we could make use a photographic metaphor. We could say that if spiritual love is the positive of love, in all the splendour of its colours, then the carnal is love's negative stereotype plate, its inverted projection. They are positive and negative in the primary sense of the words as well, my dear, insofar as spiritual love adds, contributes, and gives: it's eminently altruist; while carnal love subtracts, and seeks to take advantage of the other, it's a selfish love, a "negative" of love. It's a selfish love because in carnal love, it's the *ego* who loves, the "false self", the material component of the soul. The carnal lover chases his own pleasure, the satisfaction of his instincts. The other one is a mere instrument in service of his desires; it's a love based on interest, it offers itself only in exchange for something. And since selfishness entails the desire to possess, the carnal lover is possessive: his ambition is the possession of the other person. This is because he sees the other person as an object, and objects, unlike people, are subject to being possessed.

---

328. Eilhart von Oberge, translated from *Tristán*, v. 4580–4594.

These characteristics are the "photographic negative" of the corresponding qualities of spiritual love. Beginning with the aforementioned and most important of all: altruism. In fact, spiritual love is the love for the other person *for their own good*. For this lover, the loved person is not a mere instrument but an end on itself. Because in this case, Blanca, it's the true Self, the "naked" soul who loves. Besides, it's an unconditional love that expects nothing in return. It does not aspire to possess; the spiritual lover recognises and respects the beloved's independence, her freedom to do whatever it pleases her, even if this is leaving for him someone else. "If that's what will make her happy...", he says, because he puts her happiness before his. And when he thinks of his own happiness, he does not imagine it as a result of possession, but of *identification* with the beloved. Look, in the Gnostic Gospel of Philip there is a beautiful passage that says, "Love never calls something its own, yet it too may possess the same thing. Love never says, "This is mine," or "That is mine," but "All these are yours." Spiritual love is wine and fragrance."[329]

Crossed–out note on the margin. The date remains (9–11–99) and so does the mutilated fragment of a quotation: *...the shimmering flame.*" We know, by what the author writes, that his wife enjoyed the shimmering light from candles.

Do you know to what the spiritual lover aspires, Blanca? To become one with the beloved person. And although down here, in the lower world, that ambition is not feasible, an ersatz union, a *virtual* variant of the *real* communion destined

329. *Gospel of Philip*

to be fulfilled in the Otherworld is. This virtual spiritual communion (about which, God willing, I will talk in the next letter) was considered a precursor of the real *post–mortem* union, and that's why it was the "courtly" or heroic lovers' goal in this world. Of course, my dear, in the Middle Ages –as in any age–, the heroic lovers were a scant minority. The majority were still very far from the evolution level of a Jaufré Rudel, for example, the most famous Occitan troubadour, who after having a taste of carnal love understood that this was only the surface, the shell of love, and set out to reach its centre. Or of a Bernat de Ventadorn, a troubadour who in his songs condemns the love *that re non ama si non pren*, "that does not love if it receives nothing in exchange". Vendadorn contrasts this love with true love and calls it *amor comunau*, "common love", characterising it thus as the main love of his time.

Around the same time, the great Muslim sage Ibn Arabi of Murcia verified that carnal love is "the way in which the majority of people today understands love".[330] This "today", Blanca, refers to the last years of the twelfth century. But could it not be referring to the present days as well? Would this affirmation still be accurate? Not quite, I believe. To me, it seems undeniable that there has been progress since then. Among the evolutive majority, love is no longer conceived, as in the days of Arabi and the troubadours, exclusively in terms of possession, but in the key of identification and spiritual communion. Furthermore, these days, *communion–love* finds its natural framework in marriage. That did not happen in the Middle Ages. In fact, this only began happening rather recently. As late as the nineteenth century, the Roman-

330. Henry Corbin, *L'imagination créatrice dans le soufisme d'Ibn Arabi*, p. 113

tics disparaged their contemporaries' marriage by calling it a concubinage. The thing is that, back then, true love was seen, largely, as leading to adultery. And this was due to an important reason:

We have already seen that the ancient sages discerned in the human heart, or subconscious, two innate metaphysical feelings (both were tightly bound, as I hope to demonstrate). The feeling of God and the feeling of the twin soul. To explain the first one, religion was invented, for the second one, the institution of marriage. In the past, almost everyone in the world was affiliated to a religion and joined in matrimony; but in both cases, this was almost always a formality, empty frames. Just like Christians, let's say, did not generally act in accordance with the teachings of Christ, neither did spouses feel inclined towards what our friend Swedenborg called "true marriage love". Love was still in the early stages, in a rudimentary level of its evolution and, as a result, earthly marriage barely framed anything other than false love.

So much so, that this correlation was reflected in love's ternary classifications, where the lower rank, corresponding to venal, or material love, was also labelled as "conjugal love". In fact, Blanca, earthly love was hardly anything other than a business contract. And an unbalanced contract at that, where the husband had all the rights, and the wife the obligations. Nevertheless, in the days of courtly love (when the subject of true love first emerged), such obligations implicated the *body* and not the soul; the wife was free to seek true love outside of marriage. This as long as she did not go beyond the limits of true love, of course: that is, as long as she abided by chastity.

If the wife owed her body to her husband, courtly love recognised her right to unite with a lover in spirit. The husband *possessed* the wife -her body-, the courtly lover *identified* himself with her. Courtly lovers even invented a new frame for this communion-love, for this socially institutionalised spiritual adultery... but we will leave that for another letter. Anyway, my dear, from those distant days of Jaufré Rudel, Bernat de Ventadorn and Ibn Arabi, love -the love of the evolutive majority, framed by earthly marriage- has slowly been evolving. This means that it has opened room for identification and communion in lieu of possession. This way, earthly marriage and "true marriage love", as Swedenborg would say, ended up converging. True lovers no longer need to find love outside of marriage. Even if this conquest is not universal yet.

"QUI AMA CARN, PERDURA CARN, NO AMA"

Now, let's resume our characterisation of the two contrasting classes of love: spiritual and carnal, the real one and the false one, as per our sages' assessment.

The possessive nature of carnal love (possession-love) entails the lovers' need to be near each other, as you cannot possess from a distance. Unlike spiritual love (communion-love, platonic love), which does not require possession, carnal love does not survive physical separation. And is there a bigger physical separation than the one imposed by death, Blanca? *Qui ama carn, perduda carn, no ama* ("He who loves the flesh, stops loving when the flesh is gone"), versified our great poet, Ausiàs Marc, in the incipient Catalan of the fifteenth century. And he added these next verses that I now make mine:

Even though the woman I love no longer inhabits this world,
the most important part of her remains here in spirit.
And when she lived on this earth as flesh,
I tried to love her soul alone.
I try even harder now that nothing obstructs me...[331]

What obstructed them while she was alive, Blanca, was his lust, given that Ausiàs Marc (to whom we owe one of the most beautiful love poems ever written: *Veles e vents han mos desigs complir...*) experienced in his own flesh the hardships of the heroic battle against the inclinations of the flesh. A predecessor of his, whom I have already mentioned, the troubadour Jaufré Rudel, not only loved his twin soul from a distance, but he had never seen her in his life. In one of his songs, though, Rudel warns us:

Let no man marvel at me
if I love something I will never see
if nothing hurts me more
than that which I have never seen with my eyes
which never lied nor ever spoke truth to me
nor do I know whether she will do it.[332]

These words show us another defining trait of spiritual love: *exclusivity*, fidelity towards one single loved person. It stands in stark contrast with carnal love, which is of a promiscuous nature. Tristan and Isolde, the courtly lovers, Jaufré Rudel and the troubadours who, like him, honoured the

---

331. Ausiàs Marc, *Poems*, XCIV
332. J. Rudel, *No sap chantar qui so non di (He can't sing, he who doesn't utter a sound)*, II

ideal love advocated in their songs, the Udhra poets, the knights of the Grail... in short, by accelerating Evolution, the heroic lovers are not only spiritualising their love: they are *personalising* it as well, they are focusing it on one specific and unique person. A person that, as expressly designed by Destiny (by work and grace of "necessary chance"), happens to coincide with their twin soul. The reason for this exclusivism (which I have already pointed out in another letter), is that the course of Evolution, and of love as well, is that of a progressive personalisation.

And it's precisely at the Evolutionary stage where love incorporates the spiritual and personal factor, Blanca, when the concept of twin souls, and the amorous theory it implies, begins to take on a greater significance. Because, up until that moment, nothing in the behaviour of lovers had induced such concept and theory. For the first time, erotic love begins to reveal itself as a spiritual and personalised search. For the first time, it's no longer the body alone (the satisfaction of instincts) pushing man to search for someone. Now the soul is also seeking company. And this company can only be provided by another soul. Not just any soul, but a kindred soul, a soul that makes if feel at home. Little by little, the search stops being indiscriminate and it personalises. It no longer searches blindly, but increasingly searches for someone in specific. This happens on a subconscious level, of course; but the subconscious motivations are the strongest ones, Blanca. In short, for the first time we get a glimpse of the true nature of the search for love, and we verify that –just as the ancient sages intuited– it involves the concept of spiritual kinship of the souls.

Do you remember when in another letter we cited *De Amore* by Andreas Capellanus? Well, that twelfth century treatise includes the adaptation of a much older amorous code: the *Regulae Amoris*, the "Laws of Love", and among its precepts, there are two devoted to amorous fidelity: *No one can have two loves at the same time. The true lover does not desire other kisses other than his beloved's.* Ibn Hazm also proclaims in his *The Ring of the Dove* that *there is no room in the heart for two loved ones* (an expert opinion, if we take into account that it comes from someone who was raised in a harem). Troubadours and poets took upon themselves to disseminate this fundamental law of true love: exclusivity. Thus, Arnaut de Maruelh sings to his lady and assures her that "[his] heart will never turn to another, even if he so desires", because "Love does not allow him to love another one". And in that courtly novel that I mentioned above, the *Romance of the Rose* by Guillaume de Lorris, we can read, "So that you may be a loyal lover, I want and order you to place all of your heart in one single place, so that you are not split but whole and without deception, for I do not like divisions. He who has his heart in several places at the same time will always bear the brunt."

Often, Blanca, it's the carnal lover who has his heart in many places at the same time, and although he may have a wife (or a husband if it's a woman: although let's see this through the male perspective, if you don't mind), he will be unfaithful to her at the first chance he has. Besides, the woman with whom he got married is not *unique*, she's not irreplaceable. It does not matter if he sensed his twin soul in her: he married her as he could have married anyone else and, if she were to disappear, he would find a replacement in no time. The reason is that carnal love does not have a specific woman as its object: its object is women in general; it's not a personalised love, it's a generic love. Whereas, on the contrary, spiritual love is inherently exclusive; it focuses on one single person. The spiritual lover has recognised his twin soul in her heart (although, as we know, this recognition may be fallible) and he no longer sees any other woman as the object of his love. His love is exclusive and irreplaceable.

Exclusivity, altruism, and gratuity: Spiritual love flows, Blanca, along these channels. But keep in mind that we are characterising it in abstract, in its chemically pure state, which is not how spiritual love usually presents itself in the reality of our world –where it appears sparingly, blended with carnal love–, and that every one of its attributes becomes subtler... Speaking of which: do you remember that drawing by the Italian Love's Faithful Francesco da Barbarino I showed you once? It depicted twelve men and women symmetrically distributed in couples, standing on both sides of a central androgynous couple. These couples formed the different rungs of a sort of amorous hierarchy. Well, it turns out that in that drawing there were a couple of details that you may have overlooked, my dear, but that an emulation of Hércule Poirot such as me would never allow to go by unnoticed. First, I'm referring to the fact that the divorced couples of the lower and material rungs appear to have been struck down by a shower of Cupid arrows, while Francesco da Barberino shows us the couple that is closest to the centre as having been pierced by one single arrow. Doesn't it sound probable that what he meant by this was that the love of the inferior rungs is promiscuous by nature but that, as it ascends to the Centre, love becomes increasingly exclusive and begins to focus on one single individual? Let's say that, in those higher rungs, Cupid removes the blindfold with which (to justify the indiscriminate character of love in the first stages of its trip to the Centre) the classic artists usually depicted him. The more unitary and spiritual couples of the higher rungs, Blanca, including the central Androgyne (and that's the other significant detail I find in this drawing) are holding roses in their hands as a sign of victory. The victory –it appears to me– of realisation over disintegration, of Order over Chaos, of love over sex.

"THERE IS NO ONE MORE LOVED THAN MY BELOVED"

The "hero" tends towards spiritual love, Blanca, and, *for that reason*, towards exclusive love. He is not looking for a companion but for *his* companion, the one that is destined to him. We could remit to every literary character that has been parading through these letters. We would cite Tristan and Isolde, Bao-yu and Dai-yu, Malivert and Lavinia... We could remit to the Song of Songs ("Sixty queens there may be, and eighty concubines, and virgins beyond number; but my dove, my perfect one, is unique." Song 6: 8–9), the courtly lovers and the heroes from the Arthurian novels, each one of them obsessed with his "unique maiden". But do you know who I think embodies the paradigm of exclusive love? The poets I mentioned a few pages back. The Udhra poets.

In antiquity, it was customary to add the name of one's hometown to their proper name. We saw it regarding the Alexandrian sages: the place of birth identified the person. But the Udhra poets did not follow that tradition. Following their name, they added not the name of their hometown, but the name of their beloved. They considered that she identified them more thoroughly than their native town, and, thus, called themselves Jamil Buthayna, Addah Rawda, Kutayur Azza... It was also a way of proclaiming Buthayna, Rawda, and Azza's condition of "the only woman". It's said that Jamil, the most famous of all Udhra poets, was wanted by seven noble ladies, and that he brought them all together and composed a love poem in front of them dedicated to Buthayna. She was his "only woman". That exclusivity, Blanca, is what the Quran attributes to God in *Shahada*, the profession of Muslim faith: "There is no God other than God"; which led Jamil to verge on sacrilege when he proclaimed, "There is no beloved other than my beloved". This highlights that aspect of Udhra idiosyncrasy that I commented before: the blurry line that separates the worship of a "one and only God" from the worship of a "one and only woman", the twin soul.

Such ambiguity manifests itself particularly in the tendency to sacralise the loved one. When he prays, Jamil thinks of Buthayna: "Wanting to pray, I weep when I remember her." The same worship confusion happened in the hearts of those who sought the Grail, as well as in the heart of Occitan troubadours. That happened, for example, in the heart of Guilhem de Cabestanh, a troubadour who confessed to his lady: "Often, when I pray, I see you in front of me." (The heart of Guilhem de Cabestanh, by the way, is featured in a gruesome legend according to which, after the troubadour was murdered by his beloved's jealous husband, his heart was ripped out and she was forced to eat it. Afterwards, she refused to eat ever again and ended up starving to death.) This is not about a mental distraction: it's not about an unrelated thought interfering with the prayer; it's that, in the mind of the praying lover, this thought and the object of his prayer are akin, they are so indissoluble that they can be mistaken for each other. This confusion, so common to the heroic lovers, can be explained by the circumstance I pointed out in the previous letter, my dear, and it's that for Jamil, Buthayna is (and vice-versa, of course) the stairway, the only stairway that will lead him to God, to the reestablishment of his original Divinity. In some way, he realised this, hence Buthayna and God being so inextricably connected in his heart. So much so, that when he prays, it's her he sees in his mind.

The same thing happened to Majnun and his beloved Layla. You remember the "love Madman" I told you about in my first letter? In one of those passionate poems that generations of Arabic poets attributed to him, Majnun confesses, "each time I pray, I turn towards her, as if the Kaaba stood behind me". As you know, the Kaaba in the holy city of Mecca is the place towards which Muslims turn when they pray: that is their *Qiblah*, the direction of their prayers. But, metaphorically, the *Qiblah* also references the object of their worship. Well, a worthy successor of the Udhra poets –the Lebanese Kahlil Gibran– dared to propose that, apart from the *Qiblah* common to every man, apart from God, there is a *Qiblah* particular to each person, and that *Qiblah* is their twin soul. "Each heart has its own *Qiblah*, each heart has a particular direction towards which it turns",[333] he writes. Perhaps it's not that easy to appreciate it in the two books by this modern-day poet of "ancient perspective" treasured by your library, my dear, but a reader of Gibran's romantic short stories (those stories were published early in his career in Arabic newspapers and magazines, but we have no reason to believe that the passing of time changed his opinion)

---

333. Kahlil Gibran, translated from *Cartes d' amor*, pp. 135–136

will verify the author's belief in the ancient doctrine of twin souls.

One of the stories, for example, talks about a peasant's love for the daughter of a powerful emir, how she recognises him as her predestined companion: "I saw you, sweetheart, in my dreams; I looked upon your face in my loneliness. You are the lost consort of my soul and the other better half from which I was separated when I was ordered to come into this world."[334] Here, it's a dream that puts the soul on the trail of its twin. In an Indian version of the legend of Majnun and Layla, Destiny takes an even more beautiful and mysterious path. The soul finds the trail to its twin through a loose word in a recitation of the Quran: Majnun feels engaged by that word –*layl*–, he hears the call of Destiny in it, and so he goes off in search of a woman named *Layla*... In another one of Gibran's romantic stories, someone does the same thing I am doing right now, Blanca: writing to his beloved. And he starts the same way I could have started this letter as well: by apologising for "addressing you as *you*, for you are my other half which I lost when we let go of the hand of God at the same time."[335] This moment –the forced descent into this world to which the princess from the first story also alluded– is the Fall of the soul (of the twin souls) from its higher home in God. Gibran himself would describe that home as the "infinite space" where the soul and its twin "were love itself that dwells in the heart (meaning, in the most intimate) of the white silence."[336] And indeed, this image of the White Silence in reference to Divinity, is used by other ancient sag-

334. Kahlil Gibran, *In a Year Not Registered in History*
335. Kahlil Gibran, translated from *Palabras de amor*
336. Kahlil Gibran, *Lazarus and his beloved*

es. Why silence? Because words are as bridges aimed at shortening the distance between the separated Two and the fragmented Multiple, but when the distance is null, no words are needed and silence prevails. And white, because white encompasses every colour, like the rainbow, and so it's the colour of Totality and the Divine.

Crossed–out note on the margin. This time, the black marker did its job efficiently, only leaving out the name of a country –*Switzerland*–, which also appears in other quotations.

In his stories, Gibran portraits predestined loves, never circumstantial loves. "Love arising from circumstances -he opines- is similar to stagnant waters"; meaning, it rots over time. If we believe in an essential Self underneath the acquired self, Blanca, then why not also believing, correspondingly, in the existence of an essential love beyond circumstances? Circumstantial loves can be innumerable, as innumerable as the circumstances that foster them. Essential love, however, is unique and exclusive; it tends to focus on the same person, the same soul, life after life. As everything that is created, circumstantial loves have an ephemeral life; whereas, essential love is uncreated and therefore it's eternal. Its waters do not stagnate; they are constantly renewed, like the waters of a mountain brook. We could say that the twin souls' essential love reincarnates with them. Naturally, it reincarnates each time in the middle of a different set of circumstances. And not every twin soul has the degree of evolution necessary to elevate their love above unfavourable circumstances and make each new life together a beautiful love story. Evolutive underdevelopment is already the main obstacle to the blossoming of essential love. However, that love will never stop giving itself new opportunities to grow, for it's destined to triumph in the long run.

A MODERN FAIRY TALE

There is a French writer from around the same time as Gibran that you know very well, my love, because not only was he one of the first tenants of your library (after Josep Pla), he is also among the ones who take the most space. There, we have *Night Flight*, *Southern Mail*, *Wind, Sand and Stars*, *Flight to Arras*, which are all titles by Antoine de Saint-Exupérie. And, above all, the one that I will not hesitate to declare your most beloved book, *The Little Prince*, of which I now want to talk to you... More specifically, I want to talk to you about one of its secondary characters, although perhaps you will agree with me in that, in a sense, it's the book's central character. I want to talk to you about the rose that was growing in the Little Prince's tiny planet, who he had to leave behind when he came down to Earth. He, who loved this rose more than anything in the Universe, did not know that it was just a rose like so many others. He supposed that it was the only specimen of an unknown flower species, that there was no other like it in the Universe. That is why he is greatly disappointed when he discovers gardens on Earth filled with roses like his: "I thought I was lucky to have one flower, but all I have is an ordinary rose". But then he comes across the most peculiar sage in our letters, Blanca: a fox. And what does this wise fox teach him? That, despite the countless roses, his is certainly unique. And the Little Prince quickly learns his lesson: "Of course, any ordinary person walking past my rose would think she was just like you –he says to the garden roses–. But she is much more important than all of you put together... because she's my rose."

It's *his* rose, Blanca. That's what makes it different from the others, what makes it unique and so important to him. In the kingdom from where the child known as Little Prince comes (because let's not forget it, my dear: the Little Prince is a child, and it could not be otherwise), it's as if each human being inhabited his or her own little planet. However, they are not alone on that planet: a rose is growing there. That rose is no different from any other, from any of the roses growing on other planets. But at the same time, it's a unique rose. It's unique for each inhabitant of each planet, who could single it out from a million other roses. Of course that only the owner of the rose is capable of seeing the difference: for "an ordinary person", it's just a normal rose like so many others; its beauty is common to every rose. Nevertheless, for the inhabitant of each planet, the beauty of his rose is unparalleled in the Universe.

I'm sure you noticed, Blanca, that the message I tried to convey in my first letter is implied here. The idea that, beyond objective beauty, there is another subjective or "coded" beauty that is like a sign of Destiny, a sort of secret key that opens the door to the recognition of the twin soul... Except that to perceive this other beauty, my dear, one must be capable of looking beyond appearances. This is what the Little Prince had forgotten. And what he will remember when, after speaking with the garden roses, he goes back to the wise fox, who had promised to tell him its last secret. Its last secret is the most important of all: "You only see clearly with your heart. The most important things are invisible to the eyes." In other words, if one wants to recognise his rose among the millions of roses in the Universe, one should learn how to look with the inner eyes of the soul. This will enable him to decipher the subjective beauty of his rose, to recognise it, to perceive in it that which makes it different and unique among its species in the Universe.

The Little Prince has learned all the lessons he came down to Earth to learn. Now he is ready to return to his kingdom. However, those lessons suit everyone, Blanca. Each one of us has a unique rose that is destined for us, but if we do not learn to look with the heart, every rose will look the same. That's what happens to the majority of people, says the Little Prince, they "grow five thousand roses in one garden... yet they don't find what they're looking for... And yet what they're looking for could be found in a single rose, or a little water... But eyes are blind. You have to look with the heart"... To me, this sounds like a clear reference to men and women who look for satisfaction in circumstantial loves –which can be innumerable, as we said– rather than looking for it in *essential love*, which is the love of the twin souls. They search with their senses and not with their heart, and they go around tasting from each flower as if they were bees. They do not know that they will only find true satisfaction in a unique rose: their rose, the one that is destined for them.

Here you have it, then, Blanca, the message that your humble detective believes he found in the relationship between the Little Prince and his rose. A relationship strangely similar, if you can remember, to that other one embraced by the protagonist of *The Story of the Stone* before descending upon our world: in that story, the love of the Origin was also depicted in terms of selfless care for a flower. Finally, to finish with this book, there is a fact that maybe you don't know, that its author revealed a few days before dying. As you know, Antoine de Saint-Exupéry died when his plane crashed in the Mediterranean Sea while on an Allied mission towards the end of the Second World War. His remains were not found, but about a year ago I woke up to the news that some fishermen in Marseille had caught on their nets an identification bracelet that had belonged to the author of *The Little Prince*. And look, the news article included a detail: there was a name engraved on the inside of the bracelet. It was his wife's name, which, according to the author, Blanca, was also the name of the rose: the person he had in mind when he was writing about the rose.

THE PERFECT CONVERSATION

With Gibran and Saint-Exupéry, we have made a double incursion into the twentieth century. Now, my dear, let's continue with the medieval testimonies. With them, we will wrap up the subject of exclusivity as the hallmark of true love, and its heroic consequence: the "worship" of the *unique* man or woman. A subject at the centre of that legend that had such strong resonance in the imagination of medieval people: Tristan and Isolde...

A few pages back, we left the lovers asleep in the *Minnegrotte*, the "Love grotto", at the mercy of King Mark, who was about to cut them down with his sword. But something was holding him back: the sight of the naked sword between them. In Gottfried von Strassburg's version, Mark even has the courtesy of taking some leaves and herbs to cover a crack in the wall through which a sunbeam was falling on Isolde's face. In the versions by Béroul and Eilhart von Oberg, Mark only swaps Tristan's sword for his own as a warning. When Tristan and Isolde wake up, they find the King's sword between them and realise there is no escape. She goes back to her husband and he flees across the Channel, to Brittany. There, he tries to avoid the effects of the potion by marrying another woman (the false bride from the fairy tales). But look at this: he chooses another Isolde, another woman with the same name. The legend gives them a nickname so we can tell them apart: the original is Isolde the Fair, the substitute (because that's what she is, Blanca: a substitute, an ersatz Isolde) is Isolde of the White Hands. Nevertheless, the marriage will never be consummated. On the wedding night, the ring that Isolde the Fair had given Tristan as a proof of her exclusive love, will come off his finger. It's the last straw for his nostalgia. The true love he professes for Isolde eclipses all carnal desire and so he comes up with an excuse not to consummate the marriage: he says an old wound prevents him from doing it. Then, months go by. The two lovers despair because of their separation, and one day he ventures to visit her in secret. They spend the night together and in the morning, they bid farewell, certain they will never see each other again: "Friend, take me in your arms to that happy country you told me, from whence no one ever returns... Yes, we will go together to the land of the living. Have we not drank all the misery already? All the joy? The hour is upon us: Isolde, will you come when I call you?... You know I will"[337], she replies. And again they part.

During an adventure, as he rescues Kahedin, his brother-in-law, Tristan is once again wounded by a poisonous

337. Béroul, translated from *Tristán e Iseo*, Edición de Roberto Ruiz Capellán, Cátedra, 1985

spear (it reminds us of another spear, Blanca: the one that wounded the Grail King, a symbol of the twin souls' tragic separation). He knows that seeing Isolde is the only thing that will cure him, so he sends Kahedin to find her, taking his ring as a sign of recognition. The wound worsens, but Tristan drags himself to the beach every day, hoping to see the convened signal: a white sail. While all this is happening, the other Isolde discovers the truth about her unfortunate marriage and, full of spite, lies about the colour of Kahedin's sail (it's black, she tells him), which can already be seen in the distance. Isolde is the first one to disembark, but it's too late: his hope having been shattered, Tristan dies with her name on his lips. Isolde collapses over his dead body, keeping the promise she made him when they parted: of joining him in the Otherworld –which for them is not the kingdom of death, Blanca, but rather the "land of the living". The two will be buried side by side. King Mark, filled with regret, orders a rosebush to be planted on her tomb and a vine on his. And so, as the foliage of both plants grows, they become inextricably intertwined: a symbol of the eternal union of their souls in Paradise.

The legend of Tristan and Isolde has its roots in Celtic lore and presents many parallels with other stories of the same origin. Love stories such as Baile and Aillinn's, whose tragic ending reminds us of *Tristan*'s: here, the heroes also fail to show up on time to their meeting "as it was foretold by druids and good prophets for them, that they would not meet in life, and that they would meet after their deaths, and that they would not part for ever after."[338] There are just as many similarities and parallels with the Udhra love sto-

338. Bailé the Sweet-Spoken, son of Buan

ries, Blanca. Consider, for example, the story of Urwa Afra, which, of course, fits the universal pattern of love stories that I highlighted in my first letter, if you can remember, and of which we will see more examples in the next one. Urwa is an orphan who, ever since he was a small child, has lived with his uncle and his cousin, Afra, with whom he was raised. The cousins are in love with each other, but when Afra reaches the age of getting married, her father chooses another husband. When he tries to win her back, all Urwa manages to accomplish is to be banished. Unable to bear the separation, he dies of love, and Afra, when she finds out about this, meets the same fate. The foliage of two bushes, intertwining into one only, sprout from the grave where they are buried.

The subject of death out of love, so cultivated by the Udhra poets, is also one of the main subjects of troubadour songs. "I cannot do anything else but die –cries Jaufré Rudel– unless I have some relief in short."[339] Rudel is being killed by nostalgia for a woman he has never seen. But he ends up putting a face to this woman: she is the Countess of Tripoli, whom he recognises as his twin soul on account of the stories he hears from travellers returning from the Holy Land (Tripoli was one of the areas conquered by the Crusaders). He even becomes a Crusader himself just so he can go see her. However, during the trip, he falls ill and arrives at Tripoli on the verge of death. When the Countess learns of his presence, she rushes to be at his side, and so he dies in her arms, thanking God for allowing him to see her... This, Blanca, might very well be the most beautiful love story ever told. The most moving story chronicled by troubadour literature, which, as I was saying, has death

---

339. J. Rudel, *Pro ai del chan essenhadors (I have good singing mentors)*, III

out of love as one of its main themes. Although this death was metaphorical, the cases of actual death are considerable (hasn't modern science documented the eventual connection between particular states of mind with somatic illnesses?) What kills the courtly lover is the nostalgia caused by the distance separating him from his beloved, or his heartbreak; but, paradoxically, sometimes it's the excess of joy from his love for her. *Colps de joi me fer, que m'ausi*, "I feel a joy–blow that kills me"[340], sings Rudel...

There is another particularity of courtly love, of true love in general, Blanca, that comes to the fore here, and it's the strange combination of sorrow and joy it arouses. Sorrow, due to either heartbreak or the absence of love or because of the current impossibility of joining her in *perfect union*. Joy, because the existence of his beloved alone is enough reason to rejoice: The famous *joi d'amors*, the troubadour's "joy of loving". The *joi d'amors* is the emotion of being in love multiplied by infinity. A boundless euphoria that makes the lover feel as though he is in Paradise, as though he is the happiest being on Earth. The troubadour Arnaut de Maruelh, to convey the *joi d'amors* a mere glimpse of his beloved arises in him, resorts to a curious metaphor: he says her body is *rizen*, her body "smiles to him". It smiles at him alone, causing him to laugh, which in troubadour poetry is an expression for a feeling of endless joy. But, my dear, it's an intimate joy, a joy of the soul, a delight from out of this world that has nothing to do with physical pleasure. "The *joi* belongs to the domain of pure love"[341], confirms R. Nelli.

---

340. J. Rudel, *No sap chantar qui so non di (He can't sing, he who doesn't utter a sound)*, II

341. *Op. cit.*, p. 169

Perhaps you will laugh and call me silly, but I would say your body smiled at me that rainy afternoon on the tram, when I met (recognised) you, and, in a way, that feeling has never left me since. Ah, but unfortunately these last few years I have been much too familiar with the other side of that coin: the sorrow of distance, of separation, worsened by the uncertainty of our reencounter. Because I will tell you, Blanca, tormented by the idea of never seeing you again, for some time I was the unhappiest man on Earth. I had that questionable honour. I could not conceive a sorrow greater than mine. That state of mind prevented me from writing to you as I am doing now. Now that I have not the certainty, but the somewhat justified hope, which is no different from what Jaufré Rudel expressed as he thought of the Countess of Tripoli: the hope that one day I will be with you again in what, in his most famous song, Rudel calls "the faraway lodge":

> It will certainly feel like joy when I ask her,
> for the love of god, to be hosted;
> and, if she likes it, I shall lodge
> near her, although I come from far away.
> Conversation is so pleasant
> when the faraway lover is so close
> that he would long to be welcome with kind intentions.[342]

In these verses loaded with symbolism, Rudel exposes his idea of *perfect union*, of the heavenly marriage he one day hopes to enjoy in Paradise with the Countess of Tripoli. He

342. J. Rudel, *Lanquan li jorn son lonc e may, (During May, when the days are long,)*, IV

conceives this union as a spiritual intercourse, rather than physical. And look, the best image of spiritual intercourse he can think of is a conversation, an intimate and "pleasant" conversation between his soul and its twin. A conversation like the one you and I had in the hospital on our last night... But I was going to tell you about Rudel's "faraway lodge", where distance will turn to closeness on account of the union with his beloved. That is one of the countless words the troubadours coined to describe Paradise. For that "place" that is not really a place for it's outside Space (and Time), but a state, a *state of love*. In Rudel's songs, that "place" is embodied by an adverb: *there*, which the troubadour contrasts with the lower world, *here*, and that –in line with so many ancient sages– is represented under the shape of a chamber or a bridal bed where the twin souls lie together in *perfect union*. "*There* is my being, which has no up or down, and sleeping under the bedspread with her, *there* it is, my spirit." It has no up or down, my dear, because the original being of the soul, the being of the soul over *there*, is an infinite being. Rudel dreams of that "place" every night: "I never fell asleep so placidly that my spirit wasn't *there*..." And he longs for it during the day too: "My desire follows its course, at night and in the light of the day, towards *there*, seeking help; But it comes back slowly, and talks to me slowly: "My friend", she says, "some jealous louts have started such a brawl that it'll be hard to part it so that we can both be satisfied"[343]

In the cryptic language employed by Rudel, the "jealous louts" are the *ego*, the material and selfish temptations that, with their "brawl", they hinder the hero and his lady's intimate will to go back over *there*. However, they calm down the

---

343. J. Rudel, *Pro ai del chan essenhadors (I have good singing mentors)*, VI

brawl, because the love between Jaufre Rudel and the Countess of Tripoli is spiritual, it's a love between souls. Theirs is a love that goes deep, it's not merely external... And this is precisely where we can find another substantial discrepancy between spiritual love and the carnal one, Blanca; the former is essential love, love for the soul, for the *person*, while the latter is superficial, it's a love for the outward appearance. To this second love, the word love might even be too much. For our sages, carnal love is not actually *love*; it's an impostor, a tinpot love, to use an expression you often used. A substitute, a parody. It's not authentic jewellery: it's costume jewellery. The medieval troubadours called it *fals'amors*, "false love". On the other hand, they considered spiritual love to be true love, and they had many names for it. In a clear demonstration that a society's worries are reflected in its vocabulary, they called it *fins'amors*, "pure love"; *bon'amors*, "good love"; *amor corau*, "love of the heart"; *verai'amors*, "true love"... And between those two, stands mixed love, for which a heroic lover such as Ibn Hazn will not settle:

> Yet between the twain
> Is distinction plain,
> And the man of sense
> Notes their difference.
>
> Silver fused with gold
> Readily is sold
> "Pure, without alloy"
> To the foolish boy.[344]

---

344. Ibn Hazm, *op. cit*

There are many degrees of mixed love, depending on the blend's proportion. If it's more inclined towards the Spirit (this is the love where the body's emotion is in service of the soul), the ancient sages framed it as true love. Whereas, when the predominant component was carnal love, they classified it as false love. Using a metaphor we used before: if the scales of love are mainly tipping to the left –the material side–, then we are talking about a false lover; if the scales are tipping towards the side of the Spirit, then it's a true lover. Even with this generous point of view, my love, true lovers are still in the minority.

TAKING THE BAIT

Well. We have listed the defining characteristics, as per the ancient sages, of false and true love. What we could do now to illustrate this, is putting a face to those two types of love. Let's consider first the case of a false lover: let's call him Sergio. Let's be chivalrous, though; first let me introduce you the woman with whom Sergio is enamoured. In light of your fondness for Proust, I will borrow his pen: "...a young woman, by no means beautiful but of a curious type, in a close-fitting mob-cap not unlike a 'billy-cock' hat, trimmed with a ribbon of cherry-coloured silk..."[345] We will call her Silvia. Like with every human being, there is something substantial in Silvia, something essential, something that is "what she is": that is to say, *she herself*, her true Self, her soul. Then there is also something in Silvia that is an accessory, an add-on and therefore foreign to her, as foreign as the little hat she is wearing. The

345. Marcel Proust, *In Search of Lost Time*

substantial in Silvia is her *person*, her spiritual essence. Her personal information is circumstantial: details such as her name, age, marital status, profession, and etcetera. But, look, according to the ancient sages, Silvia's body (and by extension her physical appearance) and carnal soul or *ego*, are also ancillary attributes. But apart from all this, Blanca, there is a fundamental element in Silvia that is responsible for attracting Sergio's love. I'm referring to her sexual condition, of course; her feminine nature. Now, where would you fit this element? In Silvia's substantial part, meaning her spiritual soul, or in the carnal one? In what she *is* or in what she *has*?

Our sages will notoriously choose the second one. For them, the sexual condition is part of the *ego*, part of the soul's "clothing". So, when they read in the Genesis that, upon being banished from Paradise, the man and his wife were dressed by God in "skin tunics", many considered this expression included the sexual organs. For our sages, Blanca, the soul in on itself, the naked soul buried underneath the *ego*, lacks a gender; that is because the Spirit is sexless, and the naked soul is spiritual. The soul from the Origin was sexless because it was spiritual, *but also because it was whole*, because it's two integrated halves (I remind you that sex is division, separation). When it fell, the naked soul from the Origin covered itself with those material garments –the *ego*– of which sexuality is a fundamental component. Sexuality is linked to the Fall, to the divorce of the Two. When the Two of us were married within the One, our complementarity –and, by extension, our mutual love– was a result not of sex, but of the fact that we are the *two halves of the same soul*. Therefore, ours, Blanca, was a spiritual and personal complementarity, of which the current sexual complementarity is but a disguised version, a simulation.

And well, now that we did the honours with Silvia, let's move on to Sergio. Unfortunately, I should start by saying that Sergio does not really love Silvia. I mean, he does not love what is substantial in Silvia, her true Self. Just as it's not Sergio's true Self who's in love, but *the male* within Sergio, his *ego*, the carnal casing around his soul. It's a superficial and hollow infatuation, an infatuation that stops at the outskirts of love without ever penetrating its essence. Because, I repeat: sexual condition, as our sages so emphatically remind us, is ancillary to the individual; it's not part of the soul in the strictest sense, rather it's like its clothing, so to speak. Think about it: would it not be ridiculous to love someone for how they dress? (Can you imagine? "Oh, what a beautifully cut suit, such an elegant hat!... I'm in love.") Well, it makes as much sense as loving someone exclusively for their sexual condition. Sure enough, this is (as I told you on another occasion, this may be due to the concurrence of a similar degree of objective beauty in the lovers, that acts like a catalyst for the subjective one) a *sine qua non* requirement for erotic love. But it should not be the only requirement nor the main one.

In this lower world, the act of falling in love has, by necessity, a sexual foundation. There is no doubt about it: two people, to fall in love, need to feel sexually attracted to each other. However, this should not be enough, Blanca, they should not settle for this. The ideal, the ancient sages tell us, would be for the attraction to soak through to the deepest level. Sexual attraction should be nothing more than a pretext to fall in love; the bait that makes us bite the hook of love, which is a profound attraction. That attraction can be harder to find than the other one; it may not be instantaneous, it may be delayed. That is why it's convenient, Blanca, that in long relationships such as ours, sexual attraction should subside over the years. This remission is an opportunity for love; it's a chance for love to mature, to move beyond the bait. Many people let that opportunity pass them by: they spend their lives eating the bait without ever biting the hook, and hey even brag about it, the fools. Like Sergio, for whom sexual attraction is not a mere pretext, but the very reason for his love for Silvia.

And more, Blanca: for Sergio, the pretext is Silvia. She is merely a hanger where he hangs the garments of the feminine sexual condition, which is what he really fell in love for. Deep down, any hanger would do for Sergio; any person would do as long as it fulfilled the essential requirement, which is being a female. By loving the female more than the person, by loving *something* (a sexual garment) rather than *someone* (a naked soul), Sergio is loving not Silvia, but the generic and impersonal woman within her; the woman of which Silvia is but one of its innumerable avatars, one of its infinite replicas. Sergio loves women exclusively for their gender; he loves women in general. The realisation of this generic love in Silvia, or any other, has no greater importance for him. His love is eminently indiscriminate and promiscuous, from the moment he is loving something –the feminine condition– which is not exclusive to Silvia, it's common to all women. Naturally, Sergio will have his preferences, but those preferences will be secondary and will be bound to the sexual condition: they will be preferences in "clothing". He will be more attracted to a certain type, he will like tall or short women, blonde or brunette, and he'll focus more on breasts rather than legs. In short: he will be attracted to a *female* –not a *person*– over another.

And this is what makes him a false lover. Let's consider now the opposite experience: the experience of a true lover.

Let's imagine... But no, this time we can take an example from real life. And I already have one in mind. A British writer from the first half of this century who suffered a loss as profound as mine... Let's take the case of Clive S. Lewis.

I will begin by saying that, if we listen to the bountiful testimonies, he was, above anything else, a kind person. And so, Blanca, we once again see kindness appear as an evolutive trait tightly bound to true love. A successful author in his time, C.S. Lewis remains today a widely read writer, especially his science fiction novels and his stories for children. But on an academic level as well, with his eminent essays precisely about courtly literature, a subject he taught at Oxford and Cambridge from a very young age. He also wrote dissertations on religious subjects, for he was a committed born-again Christian. What interests us here, though, is his personal circumstances... Professor Lewis was about to enter his twilight years and he remained a bachelor. His marital condition did not seem to be under any kind of immediate threat, when suddenly he found himself "surprised by Joy", to use a private joke his friends so often made. This is because he had chosen the title *Surprised by Joy* for the book in which he described his conversion into Christianity, and now that title appeared to be premonitory since he ended up falling in love with a woman named Joy. Who was this woman? First, let's get the least important fact out of the way: she was not a beautiful woman. Lewis would complain that photographs do not do her justice. But that's because the beauty he perceived in Joy, my dear, cannot be captured by cameras. And this is where I would tell you about each individual's subjective beauty, if I had not done enough of that in the previous letters. Joy Davidman was a writer, an American poet. This is what is important: they had interests in common, they shared a special sensibility towards literature. Maybe they even read together after dinner, as we used to do...

But it was not Lewis' literary works that inspired Joy in a moment of existential crisis, it was his religious thought. It drove her to write to him and, later, to travel to London to meet him. She soon became his collaborator, his intimate friend and confidant. For a very long time, they resisted calling the profound love that had formed between them by its name. They only opened their eyes when she was diagnosed with a serious disease that threatened to separate them. That disease, though, would end up following through with its threat, which had an apparently unthinkable impact for a man of such solid religious beliefs such as Lewis. The loss of Joy led him to question what, up until then, had been his greatest convictions: namely, the kindness of God, and even His very existence. In a desperate attempt to exorcise his pain and rage, he began to write a kind of war journal of his inner struggle with God. From that struggle, his faith would ultimately come out stronger; but that is when Lewis found himself face to face with that most crucial and harrowing theological problem we mentioned before, Blanca: the absence of God. Published under the title A *grief observed*, that notebook would serve, years later, as the basis for a British film that I might have seen a dozen times.[346] There is no doubt that I am quite sensitive to the plot, but also to the main actress' strange resemblance to you...

Now let's get to the subject for which I broached mister Lewis.

I already said he was a respected essayist. In a monograph he wrote about love, he said the following about the man

346. The film is *Shadowlands*, from 1994, by Richard Attenborough

who is truly in love: "A man in this state really hasn't leisure to think of sex. He is too busy thinking of a person. The fact that she is a woman is far less important than the fact that *she is herself*."[347] With these words, Lewis proves that he knows the secret of true love, Blanca, that secret allegorised in the ancient Greek myth of Eros and Psyche; when Eros is imprisoned by her own virtue –true Love–, he is focused not on the body but on the soul (psyche). Lewis knows that, in true love, sexual attraction is like a backdrop: it frames the personal; it gives it a necessary pretext, but the most prominent role clearly falls on the personal level. To the point that a strictly sexual attraction can even pass unnoticed by the lover; it's present, of course, but it's as if implicit in personal attraction. It's the consequence of having displaced the centre of gravity of love from the material plate to the spiritual plate of the scales. Or in what we could describe as "the relay race of love", the consequence of having transferred the baton from the hands of the flesh to those of the Spirit.

So then, the attraction Lewis felt for Joy was *also* sexual, but *not mainly* sexual: it was, above all, a *personal* attraction. He felt attracted to Joy's *person*, to her spiritual Self. This *person* is unique; hence exclusivity being a fundamental component of true love. The love Lewis felt for Joy is exclusive because its object is not the woman in Joy, but the Joy in the woman. There is an infinite number of women, but there is only one Joy Davidman. Putting it another way: the man who falls in love with a *person* rather than a woman –the man for whom what is relevant is not so much that his beloved is a woman but that she is *herself*–, will not settle for just any woman, he will only be satisfied by the woman he loves. Furthermore, by

347. C.S. Lewis, *The Four Loves*, italics by the author.

not being linked to an appearance, to external and corporeal attributes, that love will not decline over the years. It will transform, certainly, but the feeling will remain unchanged. We can say it with the sublime words of Shakespeare: "Love is not love which alters when it alteration finds..."[348]

Well, this letter is already too long and I will conclude it now. To wrap it up, I would like to tell you an episode of *Tristan* that I left out before (it was not the only one; I have no intention of making an exhaustive retelling of *Tristan*). The wedding of Isolde and King Mark has just been celebrated. But Tristan intends to prevent the marriage from being consummated and, with the assistance of Isolde's handmaiden –who wishes to atone for her guilt in the episode of the magic concoction– he devises a plan. On the wedding night, under the cover of darkness, the handmaiden takes her lady's place in the bridal bed. And look: King Mark cannot tell the difference. The German version by the *minnesinger* Gottfried von Strassburg explains it by saying that, for Mark, "one woman was the same as the other one", implying that the deception would not have been possible if indeed he was a true lover; that Tristan would have certainly noticed the difference. For the simple reason, Blanca, that Tristan does not see women –does not see Isolde– exclusively or preferably from a sexual perspective. For Tristan, one woman is not like the other one.

Yours

---

348. Shakespeare, *Sonnet CXVI*

EIGHTH LETTER

SPIRITUAL MARRIAGE

(OR THE EXCHANGE OF HEARTS)

Come, bring a knife and cleave apart
This solitude within my heart,
Then lay my love within the tear,
And stitch it up with tender care.

And with the morn I pray she shall
Look for no other place to dwell,
But fondly keep this little room
Her own, until the Day of Doom.

Ibn Hazm, *The Ring of the Dove*

Barcelona, November 21st, 1999

Dear Blanca,

I've just said goodbye to Esther and Enrique, who dropped by to see me this afternoon. No, they did not send you their regards, but that's because they don't know we've been in touch, you know how much they care for you. I, of course, am reluctant to entrust them this secret. They would not understand. Naturally, they know about my late fondness for studying: I cannot hide the piles of books and papers every time they come over. (On those occasions, I confess that I must resist the temptation to lower the lights and ask them to leaf through the pages of the blue books.[349]) They know I'm writing something, they just don't know what that something is. I tell them it's a spy novel, I even improvised the plot, imagine that: a dumb story about a spy with a split personality disorder. But you know Esther and Enrique, they're too smart, I very much doubt they believed me. Be it as it may, I don't think they suspect I'm writing to you letters such as this one, the eighth one, which I now begin.

In the previous letter, we saw the peculiarities of pure, true, and naked love, stripped of impurities, stripped of everything that is not itself. The achievement of that love is –if our theory is on the right track– the goal towards which every twin soul in this world progresses. We will take as much time as it takes, as many lives as we need; the trend is inexorable, no one can avoid it. Can the mountain brook, by any chance, however twisted and fractured it may be, escape the pull towards the valley? The "valley" of twin souls, their secret purpose, is to unmask the highest essence of love. To bring that hidden love to light: spiritual and true love, the love from before the Fall, hidden underneath the debris of Matter. It's a process of debris removal, then: a process of cutting and polishing, similar to what a jeweller does to a rough diamond. It's a remembrance as well: rescuing Love from the clutches of oblivion.

Those clutches, Blanca, let's be clear, are the clutches of sex... Why is it that every time I broach this subject, it's like I can hear a cough in the background? Is it a sign of dissent? If so, I think you are exaggerating. I mean, have I, at any point, said sex is something perverse? Sex is connatural to human

349. Third and final allusion supporting the theory presented in the preface.

beings; it's the form of love in this world... What happens, my dear, is that if we listen to the ancient sages, the human condition is not the final condition of man, neither is this world his true home. We are pilgrims, passers–by on our way to the other world. And our love travels with us. Isn't it natural, then, that it changes and evolves along with us, that it adapts to the conditions of that new world towards which we march? Such adaptation consists of a process of progressive spiritualisation. Because the conditions of our destination world are encapsulated in the Spirit.

Let's clarify this, then: sex is the form adopted by love as it waits for true love. If we look closely, though, those two things are not that different: it's always amorous complementarity that is at stake. Because, just as the lower world is the fallen reflection of the higher world, according to the Kabbalah and other esoteric traditions, so is sexuality, my love, nothing more than *the reflection* of a higher complementarity. As such, it duplicates, like a mirror, the delights of that higher complementarity. But it's only a reflection. Earthly delights are sweet and lovely, but ah... heavenly delights are even better! Remember that verse by St. Paul: "For now we see in a mirror, dimly, but then we will see face to face." (I Corinthians 13:12) The picture quality in the mirror is quite far from that of the real object; the image is incomparably poorer next to the object. When Hieronymus Bosch portrays Paradise as a garden of amorous delights, he is not thinking about earthly delights, but in other incomparably greater ones...

The ancient sages tell us about the superiority of spiritual joys compared to physical ones. The erotic delights of Paradise, they assure us, are more splendid, more vivid than the ones down here. These are but the material translation of those. And we already know that part of the strength of the original is always lost in translation. “Take all the voluptuousness of the Earth,” exclaimed the fourteenth century Flemish mystic Jan van Ruysbroeck, “merged into one and project it whole onto one man: all this will be nothing compared to the joy of which I speak!”[350]

Finally, take this other account. An angelic testimony taken from *Conjugal Love*, our friend Swedenborg’s book, in particular from that famous chapter titled *Marriages in Heaven*. The Swedish mystic refers to a conversation he overheard in the spiritual world between three newcomers –three dead young men who were still shaken by the lust for sex– and some angels. “We have heard, in the world from whence we have departed, –the young men point out on account of that evangelical command that, apparently, denies marriage in Heaven– that in Heaven they are not given in marriage, because they are angels. Is there then the love of the sex?” The angels reply: “Your love of the sex is not there, but the angelic love of the sex which is chaste, free from all allurement of lust.” “O, how dry is the joy of heaven! –the young men protest– Then there is no love of the sex in Heaven. What is a chaste love of the sex but the love emptied of the essence of its life?” And then comes the answer, the testimony I wanted you to read: “You do not know at all what the chaste love of the sex is, because you are not yet chaste. That love is the very delight of the mind, and thence of the heart.../... the delights of the chaste love of the sex that are too interior and too rich in pleasantness to be described by words.”[351]

---

350. Jan van Ruysbroeck, translated from *Obras escogidas* (quoted by Roland Barthes, *Fragmentos de un discurso amoroso*, p. 217)
351. Emmanuel Swedenborg, *Conjugal Love*, 58–59

And you can see, Blanca, here on Earth, we tend to think like those young men: that the joys of love are corporeal, that that are no other erotic delights outside those of the senses. For the ancient sages, this conception is a result of ignorance. According to them, what we ignore (and this is what Buddhism refers to when it cites ignorance among the three causes of the soul's permanence in exile) is that the material aspects of existence are only the sign and appearance of true reality, which is spiritual in nature. This postulate –known in Philosophy as *theory of Forms* or, in its Platonic formulation, *of Ideas*– supports the entire argument of my letters, Blanca. It's an extremely daring argument that contradicts the natural human perception of things (this room, for example, at first glance appears to be much more real than your invisible presence in it). But I don't need to remind you that we are not interested in the perception of the majority here, but that of a small minority of men and women who are more evolved than the rest of us, and from whose privileged position things are not what they appear to be.

Plato illustrates his theory of Ideas through the following parable: Some men are held captive deep inside a cave. They have been fettered there since they were born, facing the wall without ever being able to turn towards the entrance. They have never seen the light directly and neither have they directly seen any object. All they can see are *shadows* of objects. That is because, at the entrance of the cave, other men carry objects in front of the light of a fire, and the flames project their shadows on the wall. And since their entire experience of reality is reduced to that, the captive men believe the shadows to be the objects themselves... With this parable, Plato points towards the fact that the lower world is deceitful: its appearance of reality leads us to confuse the material reflection or shadow with the thing itself. The thing itself is spiritual, Blanca; and this applies to the joys of the amorous union; it applies to the amorous union itself; it also applies to the complementarity that supports that union.

Since that, for the ancient sages, sexual complementarity is the pale reflection, the shadow of the original complementarity, which is based on spiritual kinship: on the fact that the two lovers are the two halves of the same soul. This spiritual and personal complementarity, Blanca, is the "reverse side" of love, it's the key to the true Love, the only love worthy of that name. The key to the Love of the Origin, which spilt, upon falling, over the crude language we speak in this world, the language of Matter. The result is carnal love, although calling it "love" would be giving it too much credit, a more appropriate word would be "lust" (*lust in the robes of love*[352], as the seventeenth century English mystic poet Henry Vaughan defined it). Returning love back to its original language, the language of the Spirit, of the *person*: this, my dear, is the arduous task to which the Universe is committed.

"D'AMOR MOU CASTITATZ"

We have just concluded that sexuality is the reflection of Love. Now, to stress this idea, we will reverse it and ask ourselves what is Love in relation to sex. If we are feeling poetic (and sometimes you did), we might say pretty things such as, "Love is the pearl hidden in the shell of lust". Then, it's a matter of exhuming that pearl. Up until now, we have only

---

352. Henry Vaughan, *Idle Verse*

succeeded in opening the shell halfway, but we can already glimpse the glow through the crack. If we say it's like an aromatic liquor (and I'm thinking of that cherry flavoured one you liked so much), we will imagine the distillation process, the extraction of the "spirit" from the must. If it's like a diamond, then we will think about the long process of crystallisation that converts black carbon into a precious stone; or in the following process of cutting and polishing undertaken by the jewellery maker: So does the Universe, through Evolution, cleanses Love of all its contingencies, of everything that is superfluous, of everything that is foreign.

But the cutting and polishing, the crystallization, the distillation, the exhumation of Love (you can pick your favourite metaphor), is a naturally slow work, a work that can take millennia. And the "heroes" are not willing to wait that long. So, they strive to complete that operation on a tighter schedule, in one life only, if possible... I want to describe to you now the heroic process of the distillation of Love (I have allowed myself to choose for you: talking about the wine country and the spirit of wine, it seemed to me like the most suitable metaphor), such as it was conceived and practiced in the South of modern-day France, in Occitania, during the twelfth and thirteenth centuries. "We cannot overstate -writes R. Nelli- the importance of the necessity of purifying everything that animated the twelfth and thirteenth centuries and which should lead to isolating love, to liberating it from every practical, utilitarian, and moral worries."[353] Nelli himself would define this liberation as the "evolution of love towards its pure essence"[354].

---

353. R. Nelli, translated from *op cit.* p. 323
354. *Ibid*, p. 219

Although, "evolution" is not the word here, my dear. What happened in those centuries in the Christian West (within small circles, of course) was an authentic love *revolution*. This revolution would have already happened in the East, in the rich Islamic civilization of the eighth and ninth centuries. The Udhra poets laid down its foundations, hence it being known among the Arabic people as *Udhra love*. In the West, they called it *courtly love* because it originated in the noble courts: first in the Eastern (in the luxurious courts of the *One Thousand and One Nights*, the courts of Baghdad, Damascus, Istanbul, Cairo, Alexandria, in Cordoba and Granada, in the Indian courts of Bengal...), and then in the West. Said revolution, which places erotic love at the centre of existence, was fostered by a discovery of a religious nature: the aforementioned discovery, by the Love's Faithful, of human love as the stairway to God. A discovery that was quickly disseminated by the poets, often in songs, as is the paradigmatic case of the Occitan troubadours.

"I shall be saved through her", sings Guilhem de Peitieu, one of the first troubadours. And Uc de Saint–Circ offered his lady his own life as a tribute "while you allow me to ascend Heaven through you". The longing troubadours claim to feel for a "great love", the love of a lady, adjoins the longing for God, Blanca: it's –we have seen it already– a particularity of heroic love. Besides, the border is blurred. It has been said that *courtly love* constituted a religion, a love religion of which the knight was a believer and where the face of God had been replaced by that of his lady. We have a beautiful and late example of this in "Paradise" from the *Divine Comedy*, where, in the eyes of Love Faithful's Dante Alighieri, the Sun of Christ is eclipsed by the sun of his beloved Beatrice. Although we can also think that for the heroic lover, the lady is indissoluble from God, and God from the lady. We can see both aspirations as supporting each other. In any case, it was not the physical lady they yearned for, but her heart, her soul, thus in courtly language, as we have seen, *amor corau*, "love of the heart", was synonymous with "spiritual love", "pure love" or *fin'amors*. Because, to access Heaven through the Lady, Blanca, to go up this stairway to God which, to man, is the Woman, and to the woman is Man, human love should break free from the chains that bound it to Earth. It should sublimate itself, purify itself, and liberate itself from all material barriers. In short, it should cease to be human and become divine instead, a demand that gave rise to the courtly ambition par excellence: the ambition for refining love, for distilling its divine essence imprisoned by Matter.

Crossed–out note on the margin. Although clipped, the quotation has survived: *26–11–99 "I recommend you hypnosis –he blurted out .../... Have you ever heard (of Sigmund) Freud?... of taking his patients back to previous states in their lives?"* This quote is the first of what could be interpreted as a series of connected quotations.

To become true lovers –*amadors coraus*, "lovers of the heart"–, the courtly knights dedicated themselves to shedding their love of all carnality, of all its material clothing. It was a long ascesis, at the end of which the lady (who during these early stages has a higher place in the hierarchy than her lover) puts her "vassal's" love to the test. "My lady tries me –sings the troubadour– and tests me to know how I love her". And she would do this through a kind of ritual, the *assag*. The lady would receive the lover in her room, she would undress before him, allow him to hold her, kiss her, caress her, and even lie down next to her. They would lie down in bed (as it's written in a text) "*nudus cum nudus*", naked with naked, but always leaving out intercourse because, to pass the test, the lover should sublimate his sexual instinct, therefore proving that it was not her body what he desired, but her "heart", her person, her soul.

The *assag* was also a heroic test for the lady, who likewise had to show the purity of her love for her beloved. The belief behind this ritual, Blanca, is summarised by the famous troubadour motto: *D'amor mou castitatz*, "From love comes chastity". Meaning that true love is chaste by nature: a true lover does not need to strive to remain chaste before his beloved, even if she is naked. Which makes me think (forgive me for the digression: it's related to a blue book I've been re–reading these past few days) about a comment that the narrator of *Sentimental Education*, Gustave Flaubert, makes regarding Frederick, its protagonist, "One thing caused astonishment to himself, that he felt in no way jealous of Arnoux (his beloved's earthly husband); and he could not picture her in his imagination undressed, so natural did her modesty appear, and so far did her sex recede into a mysterious background." There is another line in this wonderful novel, by the way, that I cannot resist transcribing here, Blanca, because it illustrates the amorous recognition, the central motif of our letters: "She smiled, every now and then, letting her eyes rest on him for a minute. Then he felt her glances penetrating his soul like those great rays of sunlight which descend into the depths of the water. He loved her without mental reservation, without any hope of his love being returned, unconditionally; and in those silent transports, *which were like outbursts of gratitude*, he would fain have covered her forehead with a rain of kisses."

Going back to the medieval *assag*: after overcoming it, the hierarchical difference between them is revoked. They ceased to be lady and vassal to become equals in love. This step was indispensable because equality between lovers, reciprocity, is essential to Love. If in *courtly love* there was a long preamble of inequality, of the knight's submission to his lady, it was only to compensate for an opposite inequality: the inferiority that befell the feminine sex in medieval society. Once on equal footing, the true lovers were in a position to reach the summit of *courtly love*. This last stage of the Evolution of Love (this final landing on the stairway to God) was known to the amorous medieval court by an enigmatic name: they called it "the exchange of hearts".

What is this exchange of hearts thing? Ugh! I would be happy to change the subject and talk about, I don't know, the great time we had that day we got lost in Montseny, do you remember? Oh, no, that's not true: it was in Montnegre. You were keen to test your sense of direction and so we were this close to ending up in the bottom of the sea. But don't worry, I will constrain myself to answer you. Although I must humbly recognise that I will not take this path as confidently as I took others, and that sometimes I feel almost as lost as we were that day on the mountain. For the time being, I will put it like this: the exchange of hearts is the result, in this life, of the "true conjugal love" about which Swedenborg wrote, which "is a chaste love, and has nothing in common with unchaste love. It is with one and only one of the opposite sex, all others being removed; for it is a love of the spirit."[355] And, given that this "true conjugal love" is the conjugal love from Heaven, Blanca, the resulting exchange of hearts is the

---

355. Emmanuel Swedenborg, *op. cit.* p. 59

lead up to the Heavenly *post–mortem* marriage. It's already in itself a marriage, a spiritual union so powerful, according to Rene Nelli, that "it was interpreted as the result of a union prior to the lovers' appearance in this world."[356]

There is a third category of marriage, then, between the heavenly and the earthly one. Three categories we could succinctly characterise in the following manner: Earthly marriage is a *formal* union; the spiritual one, as we will call it, is a *virtual* union (I'll justify this adjective in a moment); and heavenly marriage is a *real* union. Out of these three, only earthly marriage can be contracted by two souls who are not twins. The spiritual one requires the souls to be twins. It requires that they should have already been married to each other before, in the Origin, for it's an *effective* union, Blanca, and only that which was united in its origin can unite in this way. Only a common origin will determine a common destiny. Only the two halves of the same *symbolon* will match and come together to open the door for an effective union between them. Two different halves may juxtapose, they may stand next to each other, but will never get to unite, they will never get to form one thing only, just as an old alchemy treatise warns: "Know ye, further, that unless ye rule the Nature of Truth, and harmonise well together its complexions and compositions, the consanguineous with the consanguineous, and the first with the first, ye act improperly and effect nothing."[357] It's also what –if you remember the meaning of the expression "predestined enemies"– Chinese wisdom teaches us with this old proverb: *In this lower world, there is no union but that of lovers who were born enemies.*

---

356. R. Nelli, *op cit*, p. 53
357. *Turba Philosophorum*, p. 32

A MAGICAL BRIDGE

Now, what does spiritual marriage, the final stage of human love, consist of? (The next stage, heavenly marriage, is already divine love). I will try to explain it even if, as I warned you, it might sound confusing. Let's take, for now, that metaphor we used before: the metaphor of the weighing scales. When a couple of twin souls moves their mutual love from the left plate to the right plate (meaning, from the sexual act to God), they establish a strong secret connection between each other. Physical distance is not an obstacle because it's not a material connection. Their love involves their inner and spiritual life in a profound manner, where closeness or distance do not obey physical parameters. So, one can stand at the antipodean of where the other one is, and still their connection will remain. That is what the troubadour Peyrol expresses in this song:

> Where my lady is, it does not matter,
> My heart will always be hers
> For pure love joins and chains together,
> Even under different skies,
> Two hearts burning for each other.[358]

As the couple delves deeper into *pure love* –the highest degree of love's tripartite classifications–, the secret connection between them sharpens. So much so, Blanca, that the first degree of love was also baptised by the ancient sages with the name *communion–love* or *bond–love*. This secret connection ends up becoming a kind of bridge across which lovers

358. R. Nelli, *op cit* p. 221

"exchange their hearts": or rather, get married in the Spirit. The nature of this bridge is mysterious; the ancient sages' explanations are not clear at all, they are magical explanations. Even with all that, we can attempt an approximation based on that notion I put forth in another letter: the notion of erotic love as a *ménage à trois*, as a love triangle. Erotic love – we said back then– is supported by three pillars. Those three characters are the twin souls and God above them. Or, more accurately, the twin souls and their particular *Name of God* above, "the Name that each of them (that each couple of twin souls) bears as their secret nostalgia"[359] beautifully put by Henry Corbin, who also tells us that in some hermetic texts, instead of the Name, they talk about the "Perfect Nature" of the soul, and that such Perfect Nature is conceived as a "way of being *syzygic*", from *Syzygia*, "union of two".

This third character, Blanca, is none other than the personification of the Original and future Unity of each couple of twin souls. And it's, contrary to appearances, the true protagonist of the amorous drama. Except that, on the first part of this drama (while the scales remain tipped to the side of Matter), the protagonist is only a potential: it's only there in a latent and potential form, it's a "could be" that still is not. We could think of the role a crucial character would play in a mystery novel, decisive for the clarification of the facts and resolution of the plot, and yet this character remains in the shadows and does not appear until halfway through the book. That is when, well into love, or rather while the twin souls begin to penetrate the "shell" of love, while they begin their approach to what Vladimir Solovyov called their

359. Henry Corbin, *Alone with the Alone, Creative imagination in the Sufism of Ibn Arabi*, p. 129

“internal meaning”, when this hidden protagonist –the original Unity of twin souls– begins to become explicit, to activate itself. Jorge Luis Borges, whom I admire, wrote this line somewhere, which we could apply here: “It was as if a third more complex speaker had joined the conversation”.

Crossed–out note on the margin. The brief preserved fragment: *(under the effects of) hypnosis, young Marcus went back to...,* is enough to verify that the message carried by this quotation is in line with the subject of the previous quotation (they probably have the same source). This allows us to conjecture: If the author saw these quotes as messages from his deceased wife, would he have felt compelled to visit a hypnotist?

Every human being, my dear, can be defined by one of the corners of a love triangle. Every human being has, then, two very intimate referents. One is a peer, another human being like him: his twin soul. Their intimacy coming from them having integrated a Unit in the past. The other referent –God– is infinitely superior to the human; however, it's just as intimate and close to him as the first one: because God is the Unit the twin souls integrated in the past. It's only in the advanced stages of Evolution that it becomes clear that these two intimate referents of every human being need and support each other. To the point that, in a spiritual advanced human being, it's not uncommon that they even get confused with one another. And this would explain that curious reversal of concepts incurred, on one hand, by contemplative mystics, and on the other by heroic lovers such as courtly knights. I'm referring, Blanca, to the apparent contradiction that surrounds the act of loving

God with the love destined for the twin soul –that is, with erotic love–, and the twin soul with the love reserved for God: meaning, worship–love.

Because, effectively, if we examine this feeling of *worshipping* the twin soul (of which the amorous stereotype "I adore you" is a profane reminiscence), we will see that it's characteristic of the spiritual marriage and, therefore, of amorous heroism. This is because that, in spiritual marriage, each "spouse" refers to the other one in that third sacred corner above them. But not just the other one, Blanca: each spouse cannot help but refer to himself, to think of himself in God. Because God is the true identity, the secret and momentarily suspended identity of the soul and its twin. Of the two of them, but especially of both of them together, of both of them as a couple. In this last stage of the voyage to the centre of love, the twin soul "exists in God and possesses, in this sense, an infinite significance", writes V. Solovyov. And he continues:

> It must be understood that this transcendental relation to one's other, this mental transference of it into the sphere of the Divine, presupposes the same relation to oneself in the sphere of the absolute. I can only acknowledge the absolute significance of a given person, or believe in him (without which true love is impossible) by affirming in God, and consequently by belief in God Himself, and in myself, as possessing in God the centre and root of my own existence. This triune faith is already a certain internal act, and by this act is laid the first basis of a true union of the man with his other and the restoration in it (or in them) of the image of the triune God... The individual union between oneself and another in this relation is the first step towards a real union. In itself this

step is small, but without it nothing more advanced or greater is possible.[360]

This "triune faith", Blanca, is the mystery of the Trinity, which is the supreme mystery, the mystery of Divinity, of which the Christian Trinity would not be but a distorted variant. We could resort to a theatrical image to outline it. We would say that there are three Persons in God, and those three Persons are the One on the proscenium and the Two on the wings. There was a time when human beings were part of that sacred drama. But we fell: the One made Itself scarce when the Two burst onto the stage. Now, it's about restoring God's corresponding lead role in the human amorous drama; leading the Two (the twin souls) back to the side of the stage, leaving the proscenium to the Unit. In short, my love, it's about reediting the trinity mystery in ourselves, the mystery of which spiritual marriage is but the entrance hall.

The interpretations of spiritual marriage offered by the ancient sages are, as I was saying, of a magical nature. First, we have the medieval concept of the "exchange of hearts". As far as I can understand it, the souls of the predestined lovers, arriving at the highest rung of love –*pure love*, naked love–, become pervious to one another, they intertwine, and they amalgamate. This is a gradual process consisting of the lover's interiorisation of the beloved. And it's not a matter of the lover having the beloved constantly on his mind, Blanca: it's not a purely mental interiorisation, it's also emotional. If we are to believe the ancient sages, this is not merely a subjective thing: we are not talking about a mere feeling, but something endowed with a kind of virtual or magical reality.

360. V. Solovyov, *The Meaning of Love*, p. 88–89

In virtue of that mutual interiorisation, a double heart, an androgynous soul, appears in the lovers' chest. "Beautiful lady –sings the troubadour–, you have two hearts, mine and yours."[361] This way, the two of them become one individual in two bodies (in light of certain Buddhist investigations, this osmosis would not be as unthinkable as it may appear), always in each other's company no matter how physically apart they may be.

The "exchange of hearts" is a medieval interpretation. The Middle Ages were followed by the Renaissance, a fertile time for dissertations about love, especially the sixteenth century Italian Renaissance. The bibliography of Love in the *Cinquecento* is impressive: *Lezzioni Sopra l'Amore, Della Infinità di Amore, Dialoghi d'Amore, Conclusioni Amorose, I Tre Libri d'Amore, Sopra lo Amore, Libro di Natura d'Amore, Lo Specchio d'Amore*, the list goes on. Never, and nowhere, have we seen such concentration of detectives investigating the same subject at the same time! And well, my dear, do you know what is the most agreed upon conclusions these illustrious "colleagues" of ours reached? It's that in the highest degree of love, the lovers' souls perform this sort of miracle, "they unite in all their parts, combining and intertwining"[362], "they transform into one another"[363], "they become one soul in two bodies"[364]. Now then, if being *one in two* is a union, this

361. Folquet de Romans, *Domna, ieu pren comjat de vos*
362. G. Betussi, *Il Raverta*, in G. Zonta, *Trattati d'Amore del Cinquecento*, p. 34
363. F. Sansovino, *Ragionamento nel quale brevemente s'insegna a'Giovani Uomini la Bella Arte d'Amore*, in G. Zonta, *Trattati d'Amore del Cinquecento*, p. 180
364. B. Gottifredi, *Lo Specchio d'Amore*, in G. Zonta, *Trattati d'Amore del Cinquecento*, p. 297

union is still virtual, similar to an image on a mirror; it's only real in the magical plane, in the imaginal plane or world, which is how H. Corbin translates what the Muslim sages from ancient Persia called the middle world; *âlam al–mitâl*. The imaginal (not imaginary) world is, according to Corbin, "where the phenomenology of the spirit takes place"[365]: visions, ecstasy, lucid dreams, mystical initiations... and, of course, spiritual marriages too. Ah, but even in the middle world, Blanca, being *one in two* does not form the perfect union yet; this is only accessible from Heaven, and it consists exactly of the inverse condition: being *two in one*. The *one in two*, however, was considered the step immediately before the *two in one*; the virtual union, the entrance hall to the real union.

Yes, it's all very strange, my dear. Maybe an example will help clarify things for you. An example taken from an epistolary love as, in a way, ours is for now... In the previous letter, I told you about the *Qiblah*, the direction towards which Muslims pray. And I told you that the Lebanese poet and artist based in the United States, Khalil Gibran (represented in your library by two books, two mystic poems: *The Prophet* and *The Wanderer*), declared his faith in the existence of a *Qiblah* specific to each human being, alluding to the twin soul. Well, in a letter dated from the early 1920's in New York, Gibran wrote, "For years, I've had the feeling of having discovered the direction towards which my heart turns."[366] This confession, Blanca, is also a declaration of love, because Gibran's own *Qiblah*, the woman in whom Gibran believed he had recognised his twin soul, was precisely the recipient

365. Henri Corbin, *Spiritual Body and Celestial Earth*
366. Khalil Gibran, *Love Letters*

of that letter, one of many exchanged by the Lebanese writer and his compatriot based in Cairo, May Ziadah, another great figure of Arabic literature. Well then, around the same time, in a letter addressed to May, Gibran makes an assessment of his day, and writes, "Ours has been feverishly hectic day, from nine o'clock in the morning until now we have not stopped saying goodbye to people, and we have to come back and say hello to the newcomers, but all this time I have been watching my companion, minute by minute..." Surely, you will think May had travelled to New York to spend that day with her beloved. But no. In fact, Blanca, Gibran and May never met in person. What's happening, then? Something very strange is happening: through their letters, Gibran interiorised May to the point that, somehow, she lives inside him; or better yet, that he is also her. "I have praised God –he continues– and thanked him for the day and its length because, today, May has spoken through my tongue, she held my hand and, thus I held other people's hands. The whole day, I have seen through her eyes, discovering kindness on everyone's face, and I have listened through her ears, feeling the sweetness of their voices."[367]

Although they lived in such distant cities, Gibran and May were never apart. Because, as she wrote in another letter, "you live in me and I live in you".

THE VEIL OF ISIS

I just wrote that Gibran and May never met in person. Of course, back then, New York and Cairo were much farther

367. *Ibid*

apart, in travel days, than they are today. But, don't they say lovers would travel to the end of the world to be together? Let alone to meet in person rather than just by mail and photographs! But let's not rush to judgement. This apparent lack of interest for personal contact, Blanca, fits what appears to be a paradoxical peculiarity of the "exchange of hearts". And it's that, once it's consummated, the perception of the beloved through physical senses ceases to be indispensable. It can even become superfluous because he or she lives in the heart of their lover: there, they can summon up the other one every time they want, be it in dreams or daydreams, in meditation or in awake fantasy. "My lady – sings the troubadour–, I contemplate you without a veil on my heart."[368]

This veil without which the troubadour contemplates his lady in his heart, my love, is the veil of human condition. Because the soul of the beloved is not transferred to the lover's in one piece: during the process of interiorisation, the soul is sieved, it goes through a sifter. The lover winnows, in his heart, the divine grain of his beloved, her essential Self, separating it from the human chaff, her acquired Self. As he interiorises her, he transfigures his beloved, stripping her of her mortal condition: *he deifies her*. V. Solovyov expressed it by saying that he referenced her in God, do you remember? The reason for this operation is that, in these last stages of Evolution, human love has already mostly transformed into divine love, into a purely spiritual love, and divine love naturally tends to project itself onto a spiritual being. The thing is, Blanca, that by working in this fashion, by transfiguring

---

368. Raimbaut d'Orange. Quoted by R. Nelli, *op. cit.*, p. 197 (Italics by the autor of the letter)

the virtual beloved who lives in his heart into a goddess, the lover is anticipating what was bound to happen in reality: that is, the conversion of both twin souls into what God is, in virtue of their mutual unification.

Just a moment ago, we alluded to dreams as one of the ways to evoke the loved one in the last stage of the Evolution of love. Now, we will take up that allusion to discuss a famous dream from Literature. Famous, most of all, among the sages from the hidden or "reverse" side of wisdom, to whom it became a cult text. This book is another exponent of the exuberance of Italian Renaissance for what it did to romance literature. Following the practice of so many ancient sages, the author omitted his name. But, if we put the first letter of each chapter side by side, we can read a sentence in Latin: "Poliam frater Franciscus Columna peramavit", "Brother Francesco Colonna loved Polia". And the scholars have located in a convent in fifteenth century Venice, a Dominican friar with that name who had been married to a Hippolyta. Maybe grief led him to take holy orders and write this enigmatic book filled with symbolism: the *Dream of Poliphilo.*

But that is only an abbreviation. The real title –*Hypnerotomachia Poliphili,"Polipho's Strife of Love in a Dream"*– is descriptive, for it's the story of a struggle, of a heroic lover's arduous walk in dreams towards heavenly marriage. Note, Blanca, the main character's name: *Poliphilo* means "he who loves Polia". So, just as we have seen the Udhra lovers do, this hero of the Renaissance identifies himself through a reference to his beloved. In the dense and pedantic style that characterises him (and which I very much doubt you would enjoy), Brother Colonna writes: "Love, which moves all things that are similar", took care of "calling and conciliating them opportunely"[369] on Earth. However (as in our case, my dear, and for the same reason), this conciliation did not last as long as they would have hoped. Now, the entire purpose of his dreamed trip to Heaven is focused on making sure that they are "both strongly united with one single bond."[370]

> **Crossed–out note on the margin. There is a quotation hacked to bits here: *.../...; she... of cotton...; her husband, levitates.../... (Shoes) with a buckle.../... touched him with a three–pointed–hat"*. Another reference to the eighteenth century, to which corresponds the clothing described.**

Poliphilo dreams himself lost in the thicket of a forest, overcome by a thirst (carnal appetite) that burns his throat. Finally, he finds a fountain and he prepares to drink. But that's when he hears a divine song: a song "The sweetness whereof so greatly delighted me, as thereby I was ravished of my remembrance, and my understanding so taken from me, as I let fall my desired water through the loosened joints of my feeble hands."[371] Then he escapes the onslaught of a furious dragon and finds the exit of an underground labyrinth (the dragon and labyrinth of passions). Having overcome all these trials, his beloved comes out to meet him. At first, he struggles to recognise her, because this dream Polia is a heavenly and divine Polia: "O, Highest Jupiter, here is a trace of your divine image", he says upon seeing her. However, "only her lovely face and her gracious presence moved through my

369. Francesco Colonna, *Dream of Poliphilo*
370. *Ibid*
371. *Ibid*

eyes towards within my most intimate self, *my memory, which remembered her, awoke.*" Later, on the way to the island where Venus, the goddess of Love, officiates heavenly marriages, he is once again assailed by doubt. But look: he is always faithful to his earthly love. Even when desperately in love with this dreamed goddess, he appears to be willing to renounce her if she turns out not to be his dear Polia, and he only agrees to marry her once her identity is confirmed.

For this reason, Blanca, the dreamer Poliphilo is the perfect example of someone who avoided that common mistake among the heroic lovers, namely: that, once the deification of the beloved has been fulfilled within the lover, the perception of her still human reality by the senses becomes not just dispensable and superfluous, it becomes counterproductive. "I suffer not that we should meet –Ibn Hazm tells his beloved–, intending rather that we keep, our rendezvous, when I'm asleep. For if I slumber, then my soul shall have thee only, have thee whole; no body gross shall come between our spirits, subtle and unseen. This spiritual unity more sweet a thousand fold shall be, more fine, more tender, and more fresh than the hot intercourse of flesh."[372] Just like Poliphilo, Ibn Hazm cherishes the heavenly marriage in dreams. But he does not care about his flesh and blood lover. Majnun too, having reached the last stage of his love, shuns the physical Layla, who distracts him from the contemplating the "veil-less" Layla, the purely spiritual Layla he houses in his soul. This is the image of the true Layla, who does not even answer to that name since the name "Layla" is yet another veil: it's the name of her acquired self. Our friend, the Görlitz

372. Ibn Hazm, *The Ring of the Dove*

cobbler, would say that her true name is Sophia, the divine Virgin, the true object of every man's love.

This true object of his love is revealed to him in the last stage of its evolution. That is when, dazzled by such revelation, Majnun (and Ibn Hazm and Boheme and so many others) incurs in the mistake of dissociating Sophia from Layla, losing sight of the fact that, in the end, these are two names for the same person. At the root of this mistake, Blanca, is, without a doubt, the great servitude of platonic love, which by its very nature tends towards the eternal and immutable and avoids the precarious and volatile. The "angelic hypothesis" could obey this mistake if we are debating the lost half of the soul. (But let's not do that. I don't want to disqualify any of its four hypothesis: they are all worthy of consideration, they are all possible.) This mistake is in line with that spurious advice that some intellectuals like to impart, an advice I had to hear coming from don Ignacio, my old Latin teacher: "If one day you come across your other half –he told us once, commenting on a text–, no matter what, do not make the mistake of marrying her." He had the idea that everyday life, that daily co–living, by domesticating love, takes away from its mystery, therefore killing it. I ask myself: what would he say of our fifty years of happy marriage? A clear refutation of his idea!

Would you like a fairy tale? You might not be familiar with it. Ah, but don't be surprised, it's not a very famous story. Its author, the German Romantic Novalis, includes it in *The Disciples at Sais*, as a kind of synthesis or distillation of that unfinished novel, and it's a very meaty story. It's about two children with very tacky names, Hyacinth and Rosebud, two children who tenderly love each other and live in neighbouring houses, which results in them being raised together.

They grow up, and one day Hyacinth is visited by an old wise man who tells him about The Hereafter; where, he says, a great enigma resides. That enigma, my dear, consists of a "mysterious chamber" (the Bridal Chamber) where a "veiled virgin" awaits for Hyacinth. The virgin's veil is the nuptial veil, and it's the veil of the Egyptian goddess Isis (a goddess who captivated the ancient sages from before the turn of the last century.) In short, Hyacinth becomes obsessed with this goddess. As a consequence, he increasingly neglects Rosebud, whom he ends up abandoning to go off in search of Isis, determined to marry her. Towards the end of his trip, which is long and filled with hardships (This trip is none other than the heroic journey whose itinerary we are outlining in these letters: the journey of love towards its "internal meaning"), Hyacinth leaves Earth behind and ascends to the residence of the gods. As he walks across heavenly fields, he transfigures into a god himself. And finally, he arrives at his destination. He arrives at the "mansion of eternal centuries, the Sancta Sanctorum", where the old wise man's message is confirmed. There, the one who is promised to him, the "celestial virgin" for whom he yearned, the goddess Isis, awaits him. Hyacinth approaches her throne, anxious to marry her, to unite with her through the traditional symbol of *perfect union*: the kiss. He lifts her veil and... who do you think is standing before him? A familiar face, Blanca: Rosebud.

"A kiss reveals the enigma, sweetly solves the riddle."[373] With these words, Novalis concluded his notes for this sketched story which, although I don't know if you enjoyed, will be useful to understand the misguided attitude we were talking about, the one sometimes adopted by heroic lovers

---

373. Included in Novalis, *Disciples at Sais*

towards the end of their Quest. The love of Hyacinth for Rosebud has transformed: it's not a human but a divine love. But she remains being made of flesh and blood. Hyacinth, then, deems Rosebud, human Rosebud, to be unworthy of his love. She becomes too little for him, so to speak, and so he seeks someone more suitable for his love: a divine beloved. When he finally finds her, he realises the error of his ways: he discovers that the divine beloved he was after is none other than his transfigured human beloved, his human lover having ascended to the category of goddess.

This devaluation of the human loved one –who is considered to be incompatible with the divine Loved One– and the following attitude of detachment towards him or her, frequently happens in the "front" side of religions, Blanca, no so much on the "reverse" side. Contemplative saints and ascetics often consider the love for God and human love as a quandary. But I have already told you: it's a false quandary. Incurring in this mistake is forgetting that God is the third element, the upper corner of an eternal love triangle. When at the end their evolutionary journey, those saints and ascetics (who presumably were heroic lovers in past lives), manage to see the face of God (in numerous spiritual traditions, this Face remains hidden by a veil like the goddess Isis, a veil that will only be lifted on the soul's Judgement Day), upon revealing the face of God, I say, they will stand before the same surprise as Novalis' Hyacinth and Francesco Colonna's Poliphilo: they will discover that God has a familiar face.

Because God has a Face –*a Name*– specific to each soul and for each couple of twin souls, Blanca. Do you recognise these verses? "The 'Life that is to be,' to me / A Residence too plain / Unless in my Redeemer's Face / I recognize your own—"[374] Of course you do: I took them from one of the most lovingly handled tomes in your library. I'm referring, of course, to the *Poems* by the nineteenth century American poet, Emily Dickinson, who –along with her English contemporary Elizabeth Barrett Browning– is your most cherished poet. Their verses in bilingual editions (one with an indigo blue cover, the other with a livid sky blue cover) stayed on your bedside table after you left. At night, you used to read a poem by each one of them before you slept, even though we went to bed late, quite late sometimes, after having gone out to the cinema or to a restaurant. And even if on these occasions you chose a short poem, there were nights where sleep still got the better of you, and so it was I, who always had more trouble sleeping than you, who was in charge of very carefully, lest I woke you up, taking the book from your chest, tucking you in, and turning off the light... never without stopping for a few moments to look at you, because looking at you while you slept was a delight.

Yes, forgive me, I'm rambling on again. Let's examine the verses: "The 'Life that is to be,' to me / A Residence too plain / Unless in my Redeemer's Face / I recognize your own—" Influenced by Christian theologians, Emily Dickinson conceived of a "Future Life", meaning eternal life in Paradise, as the blessed ones' perpetual contemplation of the Face of God –a Face like Christ the Redeemer's, for Christians. But look, in this Face, she hoped to recognised her earthly lover: a man whose identity she hides behind an alias in her poems; someone whom, according to her biographers, she knew in her youth and then lost in unknown circumstances. The hope of reuniting in Heaven with her secret lover

374. Emily Dickinson, *Because that you are going*

and of consummating There the marriage that on Earth they had been denied, was apparently the greatest incentive in her lonely life. Many of her poems seem to demonstrate this..., such as the one that says: "Sufficient troth, that we shall rise – Deposed – at length, the Grave – To that new Marriage, Justified – through Calvaries of Love–"[375]

This "new Marriage" that awaits the poet and her twin soul after the Resurrection (another Christian echo), is the heavenly marriage, my dear. That of which, in this world, the spiritual one, we were saying (thus picking up the thread of my letter), is the entrance hall... Spiritual marriage is the highest degree of union to which two twin souls can aspire while they remain embodied. For even if every other obstruction (the *ego*) has been toppled, the physical body still rises as the last obstacle on the way to true union. Twin souls married "by the Spirit" should, then, wait until death to get married "by Heaven", to *truly* unite as is their intimate desire. Until then, and despite that subtle bridge, that magical bridge stretching between them, they will remain *two*. Only death can abolish that last obstacle and thus truly convert the two into one only. It's what, in so many legends of heroic love, is symbolised by two intertwined branches hanging over the lovers' tombs.

Crossed–out note on the margin. We can scarcely discern the words: *white throne of God*. The recent mention of Elizabeth Barrett Browning has allowed me to identify them: they belong to a verse from one of the *Sonnets from the Portuguese* by the English poet. The complete verse reads: *"To the white throne of God, I*

375. Emily Dickinson, *There came a day at Summer's full*

***turned at last*", and it continues: "*And there, instead, saw thee*". It is one of the few cases where the quotation on the margin seems to be related to the context of the letter.**

THE CHURCH OF LOVE

Above, when I alluded to the contemplative saints and ascetics that presumably would have been heroic lovers in past lives, something crossed my mind –like a possible image from those earlier lives– the spiritual marriages between the first Christians. What happens is that sources of ancient historiography, Blanca, tell us that, in the early centuries of Christianity, there were plenty of marriages based not on procreation, as orthodoxy demanded, but on the spouses' spiritual bond. And that was a bond that found its strength in chastity. There were many Christian marriages, back then, who saw the virginal union of Joseph and Mary as a role model. It was believed that such chaste unions, by propitiating the mutual sanctification of the couple, paved the way to the Resurrection; but also to the future reunification of the spouses by consolidating the spiritual bond that united them. There is even evidence of these couples eventually forming fairly numerous monastic communities, such as the one founded towards the end of the fourth century around Naples by St Paulinus of Nola and his wife Therasia.

Like many other pious couples, Paulinus and Therasia honoured the altruist qualities of true love, dedicating their lives to supporting the underprivileged and caring for the ill. The fact that they were married did not prevent Paulinus from being ordained priest and even becoming a bishop.

Many clerics and hermits from the early centuries adopted *syneisactism*, which is the Greek word that describes this ascetic lifestyle, characterised by the chaste cohabitation of two ascetics of the opposite sex. In many cases, such couples shared a bed: *syneisactism* implied, then, a heroic test comparable to the medieval *assag*. But what was its purpose? According to some sources, it was to define –based on the evangelical devaluation of earthly marriage as it was formulated in Matthew 22:30, Mark 12:25 and Lucas 20:30–36– a new model of marriage founded on the couple's spiritual communion. As much as syneisactism was declared heretical in the year 325 by the Council of Nicea, in fact, it endured until the sixth century and, in some isolated Christian regions like Ireland, until much later.

Although it's with disdain that orthodox sources describe these clerics and ascetics as *agapeti*, "male beloveds", and their virgin companions as *agapetae*, "female beloveds" ("virgin", back then, being a word for nun, for the woman who followed the religious path), it's the denomination that best fits them, my dear, since *Agape* –spiritual love, divine love– is precisely the class of love that these ascetic couples professed. However, one of the pretexts cited by the orthodoxy to condemn such unions was their scepticism regarding their chastity. Athanasius, Father of the Church, mentions the case of a cleric called Leontius who, to refute that argument, did not hesitate to castrate himself, thus proving that his love for Eustolia had no trace of lust. Other even more striking cases –as they involve miracles– are these two, chronicled by Gregory of Tours, that exemplify those legends of heroic love I mentioned a moment ago, destined to culminate in death:

The coffin of a third century bishop called Riticius (whom Gregory says was bound to his wife "by the embrace of spiritual love") put up a resistance as they tried to bury it in its grave. Until someone remembered that, on her deathbed, Riticius had promised his wife they would be placed in the same tomb, so that "as the love of a single chastity preserved them in one bed, it would maintain them on the fellowship of the same grave."[376] The confessor saints Injuriosus and Scholastica too –Gregory continues– slept on the same bed "with laudable chastity" and were also rewarded with eternal union. In fact, when she died, it did not take long for him to follow her, but again they failed to bury them together, so again a miracle took place: "When morning dawned and the people came to visit the place, they found the two tombs side by side, although they had left them far apart. This shows that when heaven unites two people the monument that covers their buried corpses cannot keep them apart. Even up to today, the inhabitants of the place have chosen to call them 'the Two Lovers'."[377]

These two examples, my dear, clearly show us the vocation for eternity of these chaste unions. As the main Christian supporter of spiritual marriage suggests –as Saint Augustine suggests in *De nuptiis et concupiscentia* and *De bono coniugalis* –, the divisive nature of sex stands in stark contrast with the unifying and indissoluble properties of spiritual love.

In primitive Christianity, there were still no proper nuptial rites as such: marriage was a private act that only required the consent of the contracting parties. But, as we have seen in another letter, Blanca (do you remember the "Chrism in the Bridal Chamber"?), some Christians of the time indeed practised a nuptial rite: except this rite was not conceived to

376. Gregory of Tours, *Gloria confessorum* c.74
377. Gregory of Tours, *Libri Historiarum* X, 1.47

formalise earthly marriages but spiritual ones... There is a curious fact that will be of interest to you. Although where you are, you have no use for our calendar, surely you remember the 14th of February. This fountain pen that I am using to write to you now was your gift to me on this most celebrated day in Western culture: St. Valentine's Day, the solemn Lovers Day. Now, did you know that up until well into the nineteenth century the celebration of these festivities included rituals of a nuptial character? In virtue of such rituals, men and women –called *valentines* and *valentinas*, and coupled through a raffle– were united by a spiritual bond that did not interfere with "earthly" marriages and that forced each couple to remain mutually faithful until next year's festivities. Even if the origin of such rituals is uncertain, some scholars opine that they could be reminiscences of spiritual marriages celebrated in Valentinian Gnostic communities of the second century. That is where St. Valentine's Day would have gotten its name, not from the Roman saint and martyr (such claim would have been an attempt by the Church to appropriate the holiday), but from a Gnostic master.

And since I brought up the most notable of all Gnostic masters, my dear, Valentine held the ancient conception of Duality as the underlying principle of the totality of the Universe. Accordingly, he bestowed a great importance on the amorous relationship between men and women. This relationship was destined to culminate in Heaven, on a heavenly marriage. But such culmination entailed a previous marriage of a spiritual nature here on Earth. In a Valentinian Gnostic text, possibly written by Valentine himself, we can read: "Any man who is in this world and has not loved a woman in such a way that he becomes one with her, will not reach the Truth." For the Gnostics, Truth and Divinity were synonyms. The formula "any man who is in this world" is not gratuitous. Valentine distinguished between the men "of the world" and those "who are in the world". That is to say, between those whose soul is still composed by a material component –therefore still belonging to the physical world–, and those others who, having shed all Matter from their soul, are already foreign to our world: they are not *of* this world, they merely *are* in it. This achievement, though –the undressing of the soul–, is not enough, they tell us: as well as loving a woman (their twin soul), he who seeks the Truth must also love her "in such a way that he becomes one with her". We have already seen how to become one with our twin soul, how to achieve an effective union with her; it's by spiritualising and undressing their love. That is why Valentine –or his disciple– added this second part to his note: "But he who *is* of the world and comes together with a woman, will not reach the Truth, for he practised sex for concupiscence only."

The Gnostic marriage ritual was not the only ceremony that formalised spiritual marriage in the past. There is evidence of the existence of spiritual marriages formalised by rituals all over the world, all throughout time. Such rituals ranged from simple oath exchanges, like an incision on a fingertip to make a small blood exchange, to solemn ceremonies. In the previous letter, I mentioned a medieval model: one devised by courtly lovers who were after a new framework for their love. Said ritual included witnesses and a solemn ceremony with a protocol and a pre-established formula. In a chanson de geste[378] from the twelfth century –although it's anachronistically set three centuries before–

378. Song of heroic deeds

entitled *Girart de Roussillon*, we can find a fine example of this model:

Two courtly lovers, Gerart de Roussillon and Elisenda of Byzantium, are betrothed to each other. They have a commitment of love, which is something exceptional for the time. A more commonplace marriage, one of convenience, has been arranged between Charles the Bald (the French king who welcomed our friend Scotus Eriugena into his court) and the other daughter of the Byzantine emperor, Bertha. Charles and Bertha have never seen one another in person and, when this happens, the king is less impressed by Bertha's beauty (there is no doubt he is only moved by objective beauty) than he is by her sister's. He immediately decides to change his plans: Charles will marry Elisenda and Gerart will marry Bertha. Gerart and Elisenda do not complain, but this should not surprise you, my dear: remember that back then, earthly marriage had little to do with love, true love had to go build its nest elsewhere. And this nest could be built in this new type of marriage I was telling you about. Their respective "spouses" could attend the wedding since a spiritual marriage was not considered to interfere with an earthly one: both types involved different aspects of the person. During the ceremony, Elisenda addresses the witnesses with these words: "Hear me, Count Berthold and Count Jarvis. And thou, dear sister, be my confidant. And thou above all, Jesus Redeemer. I take thee as witnesses and guarantors that with this ring, I forever give my love to Duke Gerart. With my kiss, I shall give him the golden flower (another ancient symbol of Unity), for I love him more than my father and my husband. Upon leaving his side, I can only cry." Then comes the narrator's colophon: "...the love of Gerart and Elisenda lasted forever, pure of all bad thought, and there was nothing else between them other than goodwill and hidden understanding."

Bertha and Charles' tolerant attitude towards their "earthly" spouses' spiritual wedding, doesn't it remind you of King Mark's reaction to the sight of the naked sword between Tristan and Isolde? According to Eilhart von Oberg's version of *Tristan*: "He saw the sword between them, he examined it and, raising his hand with great care –for they were asleep–, he took Tristan's weapon. And while he took it from between these two beings of the highest worth, he drew his sword from its scabbard: and, without harming them, he sheathed Tristan's sword and placed his own where the other one was before."[379] Through this act, Mark is leaving them a message: he is communicating that he was there, that he could have killed them, but he abstained from doing so once he discovered that their love is chaste. Mark recognises the "highest worth" of the two lovers. Now: from the moment these two escape together, their spiritual marriage clashed with Mark and Isolde's earthly marriage. Because of that, the king takes a further significant action after replacing the sword: he leaves his glove, representing his hand, on his sleeping wife. With this, he is reminding Tristan that his right to Isolde ends at spiritual communion; her possession belongs to him, the earthly husband. Tristan understands this, and so he, in agreement with her, delivers Isolde to her husband and then flees into exile.

In *Tristan*, the spiritual spouses go to bed together but with a sword lying between them. This Cathar tradition, surely taken from the first Christians, mandated that the spiritual spouses should share a bed, although dressed and without

379. Eilhart von Oberg, *Tristán*, vv. 4626–4636

touching each other. "Even those wiser than me are wrong because I well know for sure that a perfect love doesn't betray anyone. I'd better go to bed dressed than naked under the covers."[380] These words come not from a Cathar per se, Blanca, but from a troubadour. In Occitania, the revolution of love disseminated by the troubadours had Catharism has an ideological background. Same as their Gnostic ancestors, the Cathar believed in the necessity of the human soul to let go of the material contingencies that weight it down in order to escape its exile in this world and return to its origin in God. This ideal of purification justifies the name "Cathar" – from the Greek *katharós*, "pure" – by which the common folk knew them. They called themselves *bonshommes*, "good men", or simply "Christians", and divided themselves into "Cathar Perfect" and "Believers". The strict rules, by which the former lived, were more flexible to the latter. We could say the Cathar Perfects –and these could both be men or women, for Cathar society was egalitarian– had chosen the heroic path, while the Believers would come to be the representatives of the evolutionary and majority path, the one that slowly progresses (reincarnation was also a Cathar belief) in the course of a long succession of lives.

Chastity was at the centre of the Cathar ideal life. Chastity not in the negative sense of mortification of the flesh, but in the positive sense of potentiation of the Spirit: since that for the Cathar too, my dear, chaste and spiritual love was a stairway to God. They rejected the earthly marriage, in their time based exclusively on practical and materialistic criteria, and, in the manner of the early Christians, they advocated for a new form of matrimony of which the foundation was

380. J. Rudell, *Belhs m'es l'estius e'l temps floritz*, V

the spiritual love between the spouses. Of course, not all believers –counting many noblemen among them– could escape the social constraints that compelled them to contract marriages of convenience. But it's known, Blanca, that during the bloody crusade instigated against them by the Pope, there were many Cathar ladies and knights who, abandoning their earthly spouses, fled with their platonic lovers, who they considered to be their true spouses. It's recorded in the archives of the Inquisition that in the fort of Montsegur, the last bastion of the Cathar resistance, there were hardly any "legitimate" wives: the knights lived there with their *amasiae uxores*, with their "friend wives". Although, in their quality of simple believers, sex was not off–limits, it appears that most of these couples avoided it voluntarily, abiding by the same high idea of love that led them to escape together. Yes, Blanca, and there is enough evidence to think that many of these couples were married by the Cather Perfects, by the ministers of the "Church of Love", which was how the Cathar Church became known, thus putting this new form of marriage they conjured into practice: a marriage based on spiritual love, willing mutual consent, and reciprocal fidelity.

I have just alluded to the crusade that, in the thirteenth century, put a violent end to Catharism and the blossoming Occitan civilisation that supported it. What happened, Blanca, was that the Cathar accused of heresy; which means they had their own way of understanding and living Christianity. A similar way to the Gnostics', and much closer to the original Christianity (just consider how far the idea of a crusade is from the teachings of Christ) than the official Christianity of the time. It's been around three years since I read everything that I could find about the Cathar, but their story still impresses me, it echoes in my imagination like on the first day. (By the way, during those readings, I noticed a detail that I'm sure will interest you: I learned that the Cathar had a favourite colour, and that colour was blue: the Cathar Perfects dressed in dark blue tunics and although during the crusade they dressed in more regular clothing, their preference for blue continued to denounce them). After inquiring about their tragedy, I felt the impulse that every good detective feels and I wanted to examine the scene where it all happened, and so I convinced Sebas (you know, our neighbour from the fourth floor, the one with the hammock in the living room) to accompany me on a cultural trip across Occitan and Provence. I will never forget that misty dawn when I went up to the eagle's nest on a cliff that is the castle of Montsegur. The emotion that seized me among its ruins when I thought about the bravery of those heroes, of those "martyrs of pure Christian blood" as they have been called, who (again imitating the first Christians) preferred to die rather than retracting their beliefs. With a heavy heart, I imagined their last days under siege, those fateful days where stones were raining down from the sky while the women rushed to help the wounded, and the Cathar Perfects imparted the *consolomentum*, the Cathar sacrament, to guide the dying across the gates of Eternity. While I was walking down to the road, where Sebas was waiting for me, I could not hold back the tears as I thought about all those couples of spiritual spouses who were burned at the foot of that hill, in a gigantic nocturnal pyre.

But, what do you think were those beliefs they died for? The core of Cathar doctrine, Blanca (and of Manichaen and Gnostic if that's where we are going), makes a reference to the existence in this Universe of two elemental principles or substances in a perpetual struggle. The Cathar were sensitive to the imperfection and suffering that the split Duality of this world entails, and they could not admit that God was responsible for or consented to it. Not the merciful God, the God of Love in whom they believed. Therefore, they conjectured the existence of another God independent from the true One; an evil God who would have created this imperfect world filled with suffering. They did not think (or maybe they did not find it plausible) that this bastard God whom they blamed for the split Duality and all the suffering, could be nothing but a fallen portion of the true God, and that this fallen portion could be the human being. There is no need to resort to an evil God with similar powers to the real One to explain the existence of Evil in the world, my dear. We only have to remember that Evil is inherent to split Duality and to the Matter the world and man have been made of since the Fall. And it's also not like God allows the presence of Evil or not. Evil is a moral aspect of Matter, it's consubstantial to it in the same way that humidity and the property of making things wet are connatural to water. Just like it's not up to God to make water dry, neither is it up to Him –to the One God, to the kind and true God– to conjure the Evil of this world.

What happens is that, for the Cathar, Matter –and Evil and suffering along with it– did not appear because of the Fall. Matter already existed and it yearned to drag the spiritual angels away from Heaven and trap them in its bosom. These angels were dual angels: two joined in one. And so Matter, personified by the Devil, sneaked into Heaven, into the celestial Paradise of the Origin, under a tempting sexual form and seduced a number of those androgynous angels, who from that moment onwards split into their two natures. They fell onto the physical world, where the Devil had their material bodies ready to imprison them. And that was how, Blanca, according to the Cathar cosmogony, the androgynous angels of the Origin lost their androgyny and its inherent spiritual love. The spiritual and profound knowledge that those multiple couples of twin angels had of one another were swapped for carnal knowledge. That is the involution the Cathar strove to revert through their ideal of chaste love.

UNDER THE SIGN OF *GEMINI*

While the ancient sages described the effects of spiritual communion or identification –that subtle and mysterious bridge which is the substance of spiritual marriage– as *magical*, today we would call them *paranormal*. I'm mostly thinking, Blanca, of a phenomenon that features heavily in courtly literature: the telepathic communication between spiritual spouses. Or rather, a psychic synchronicity that allows them to have feelings and emotions in unison, to have their thoughts and mental states coincide. As if their souls were porous. As if what happened to one of them were transferred to the other through some sort of spiritual consonance. This consonance can even be seen in their bodies. In fact, a similar demeanour, a similar repertoire of postures, gestures, and facial expressions, can often make the spouses look like twins. And it's curious, my dear, because it's well known that such psychic synchronicity exists between twins. Which brings us to another matter (because our subject is like a basket of cherries; when we take one, it's always linked to another), to another clue in our inquisitive path; a clue that detectives such as you and I cannot help but follow.

In another letter, I pointed out the parallels between biological and spiritual twins. On the surface, the apparent identity of biological twins corresponds to the essential identity or complementarity of spiritual twins. But beyond this, Blanca, we should also consider the similarity of vicissitudes. Two twin brothers, in the early stages of their gestation, are so unified that they make one compact whole; only then, as they come into this world, do they dissociate. Each couple of twin souls also formed a whole in the Origin, and it was only upon falling that the whole split into two halves. Perhaps such concordance explains the fascination biological twins have always held for human beings. (I remember how you always stared at those double prams we would see on the street.) But do you know who found this concordance especially noteworthy? The ancient sages. They saw biological twins as some sort of metaphor, like Nature's imitation of spiritual twins.

Crossed–out note on the margin. The quotation, chopped and headed by the date (*8–12–99*), is easily recognizable. It is from Ovid's *Metamorphosis*, even though it is quoting it indirectly. In the first chapter of *The Snow Leopard* by Peter Matthiessen (catalogued in another letter as being one of the blue books), there is an epigraph with the famous Ovid quote: "*When all the other animals, downcast looked upon the earth, he [Prometheus] gave a face raised on high to man, and commanded him to see the sky and raise his high eyes to the stars.*"

Maybe you are asking yourself how the ancient sages explained the most disturbing version of the phenomenon of biological twins, identical twins. For sure, they could not cite a modern scientific argument and say they shared the same genes. But, although they could have done it, my dear, that explanation would not have been enough. For them, genes would have only explained such identity up to a point. We have already said in a previous letter that genes could explain the "front side" of the human being, but not his "reverse side", not his soul. Neither did they turn to the theory of twin souls, as one might expect: for the ancient sages, identical twin souls are not the two halves of the same soul: they are more like one single "half soul", repeated by a whim of Nature (which would explain, beyond genetics, certain major affinities existing between identical twins). In any case, it seems logical to think that it all depends on at what point of embryo development incarnation takes place: if it's before the fertilised egg splits, then the result will effectively be one duplicated single individual; but if incarnation occurs after the split, then we are talking about two individuals. Anyway, Blanca, the twins our sages used as a metaphor were not the identical, same–sex ones, but the fraternal twins of the opposite sex. In fact, traditionally, this is how they imagined twin souls. And the best example of this can be found in a very widespread literary genre from way back in ancient times, which always had twins, a boy and a girl, as main characters. This type of stories was called "idyllic love stories".

Every story in this genre follows the same pattern, the cosmic drama we have been discussing here. They are metaphors for the Fall, the split of the primordial "double being" into two halves; the following Quest for the restoration of the original Unity. You will see that these stories have the naive aftertaste of fairy tales. And the fact that the main couple is not an adult couple, always a couple of children, is significant. We have already talked about children in these letters. But there is still something else I would like to say...

The ancient sages' opinion of children, my love, was not very different from yours. And I remember very well suddenly discovering what this was after something you said. It was a short time after we met. We had just left the cinema, one Sunday, and we were eating bread and cheese on a bench in Parc Ciutadella as we watched nearby children play. Then, you just dropped this *boutade*, this riddle: "The world is like this cheese: it's riddled with eyes". And then you specified: "the eyes of Heaven". With time, I got used to this kind of disorienting quips coming from you. But at that point I was not used to it yet, and for a moment, I confess, I thought I had fallen madly in love with a madwoman. It took me a minute to solve the riddle, to understand that you were not exactly referring to the Planet Earth, but rather to its human dimension. And that those eyes of Heaven that according to you constellated the world as if it were a Swiss cheese, were the millions of children who flocked all over it. I understood then that you liked children; I was also startled when I realised that, for you, a child was something like a pocket of air in a dense, oxygen-less world. Which is not so outlandish after all, my love, if one thinks -like Novalis wrote- that a child is "a spirit here, playing fresh from the infinite fountain" (or rather, from the period in-between lives, where the *ego* or carnal soul is kept in suspense) and, as such, "is just entering on a course so critical, the impress of a wondrous world, which no earthly currents have yet obliterated".[381]

Like you, Blanca, the ancient sages detected that angelic and heavenly thing children have. That is why they believed

381. Novalis, *Henry of Ofterdingen*

their way of being was the closest to that of the naked soul. "The state of little children surpasses the state of all others – notes Swedenborg in *Heaven and Hell*– in that they are in innocence."[382] And Novalis, who loved children, portrayed the ancient sages learning from "child-lovers", from their innocent love, the spark –he says– of the Golden Age[383]... We all carry a child inside, they say; and it's true, my dear: that child is our true Self. Who should be stripped off his "adult" clothes, for as the greatest sage warned us: "...unless you change and become like children, you will never enter the Kingdom of Heaven" (Matthew 18, 3). An idea reiterated by the Gnostic Gospel of Thomas, according to which "Jesus said: 'When you disrobe without being ashamed and take up your garments and place them under your feet like little children and tread on them, then will you see the son of the living one, and you will not be afraid.'"[384] Only those who become pure like children will be allowed to see "the face of the Father", the face of Unity: "Take care that you do not despise one of these little ones; for, I tell you, in heaven their angels continually see the face of my Father in Heaven" (Matthew 18, 10). It's not by accident, Blanca, that in the Gnostic Gospels, Jesus sometimes appears to his disciples in the shape of a child.

All these reflections remind me of that famous saying by Picasso that you sometimes quoted, "It took me four years to paint like Raphael, but a lifetime to paint like a child". For the ancient sages, as I'm telling you, there is nothing in this world as close to the purity of the soul and the genuine happiness of Paradise as the innocence (except that in Paradise this

382. Emmanuel Swedenborg, *Heaven and Hell*, 330
383. Novalis, *Disciples at Sais*
384. *Gospel of Thomas*, 37

innocence is conscious) and happiness of children. Hence them frequently imagining the "double being" of Paradise, the Androgyne, looking like a child: like an androgynous child or –as in idyllic love stories– like a couple of twin children. If this image is universal, that is because it's rooted in the human subconscious, where the nostalgia for Perfection lives, the nostalgia for the Integrity of man: any form of expressing that nostalgia entails, among other symbols, the "double child". It's a common image in Alchemy, for example. It can even be found in the Zodiac, in the *Gemini* sign, the "Twins", represented by a couple of children... But I was going to tell you about idyllic love stories; in particular, the ones produced in medieval Europe, studied in detail by Myrrha Lot–Borodine in her essay *The idyllic novel in the Middle Ages.*

TWO BEAUTIFUL CHILDREN WHO LOVE EACH OTHER

The beginning of these stories, oftentimes written in verse, is the happy childhood of two twins, a boy and a girl, who love each other with the intense and innocent love typical of their age. In Lot–Borodine's description, it's "the painting of an ingenuous love that is born and develops in two young hearts; the story of the courtship of children who laugh and hold hands from a tender age. This is an idyllic subject that evokes in us the dream of the Golden Age, the nostalgia for the lost Paradise where innocence reigns and desire does not stain."[385] This childhood in common, Blanca, symbolises the

385. Myrrha Lot–Borodine, translated from *Le roman idyllique au moyen age*, Slatkine Reprints, Ginebra, pág. 3

androgynous Unity from the Origin, the paradisiacal state of the twin souls before the Fall, when they still had not separated from God, from the Unit; in short, when the two twins were still one *double thing* only.

As it befits the "double being" from Paradise, the two children are of a radiant beauty. Pyramus and Thisbe (not the characters from the Ovid story, but the ones from the medieval Norman story) are endowed with the beauty of sacred Royalty: "No king or queen had such beautiful offspring."[386] In order to avoid the delicate subject of incest, the authors –usually anonymous– of these stories avoided specifically categorising these two children as twin brother and sister. But both their physical appearance and their personal circumstances leave no room for doubt. Physically, they could be said to be the male and female version of the same child. In *Guillaume and Aelis*, we can read, "No one could choose between Guillaume and Aelis; even searching everywhere, no one could find two so alike in face or mouth or eyes. They looked like brother and sister."[387]

As for their personal circumstances, the two were born at the same time (Floris and Blanchefleur are "conceived on the same night and born on the same day") and they are inseparable growing up (Pyramus and Thisbe "did everything together: they played together, slept on the same bed together, ate together"). To justify this common childhood, the authors resorted to artifices, such as placing the children's corresponding families in adjoining houses, or, more frequently, making one of the children adopted. In *Galeran of*

386. *Pyrame et Thisbé*, quoted by M. Lot–Borodine, *op. cit.*
387. *L'escoufle ou Guillaume et Aélis*, v. 1942–1947, citado por M. Lot–Borodine, *op. cit.*

Brittany, Galeran and Fresne grow up together in an abbey: he is the son of the Count of Brittany, and she is an orphan found underneath an ash tree[388]. In *Floris and Blanchefleur*, the slave in service of the son of the king has a daughter of the same age, which justifies them growing up together. In *William of Palerne*, the emperor of Rome finds a boy in the woods and takes him in to serve as his daughter's page. In *Guillaume and Aelis*, the same high-ranking personage and his constable father a boy and girl respectively, and the children grow up together...

The paradisiacal state in which these couples of children live consists of being intimately united. That is what Paradise is, my love: Unity, the *perfect union* of the Two. This paradisiacal state was often framed as an idyllic garden (the Arabic word for "paradise", *aljanna*, means garden, the word "paradise" itself comes from the Persian *faradis*, "gardens"). Or an island too, as we will see: islands and gardens have traditionally been considered the ideal backdrop for the lovers' happiness in the Hereafter. In the Middle Ages and the Renaissance, pictorial and literary representations of the "Garden of Love" abound; a green cloister presided by a central fountain, around which the lovers are relaxing. They are the "Elysian Fields" in miniature, the Golden Age of Classic mythology, where the pure souls –sometimes depicted as children– join in couples and enjoy the peaceful pleasures of Paradise. Pleasures in which love plays a fundamental part, Blanca, because the Golden Age was, for the ancient sages, synonymous with the Age of Venus. Milton, in his *Paradise Lost*, portrays the mystic Garden of Eden, a model for the "Garden of Love" and setting for the pure and innocent

388. N.t. Fresne is French for ash tree.

love of the primordial couple (of the "double being" from the Origin) with these verses:

> So passed they naked on, nor shunned the sight
> Of God or Angel; for they thought no ill:
> So hand in hand they passed, the loveliest pair,
> That ever since in love's embraces met;
> Adam the goodliest man of men since born
> His sons, the fairest of her daughters Eve.
> Under a tuft of shade that on a green
> Stood whispering soft, by a fresh fountain side
> They sat them down...
> .../...
> Nor gentle purpose, nor endearing smiles
> Wanted, nor youthful dalliance, as beseems
> Fair couple, linked in happy nuptial league.[389]

It's a very similar description to the ones the authors of idyllic love stories make of their twin protagonists' childhood. In another passage, Milton will compare Adam and Eve in Paradise to "two gentle fawns at play"[390]. His intention is the same as the anonymous medieval author of *Aucassin and Nicolette,* when he presents us his twins as "two beautiful children who love each other". The same that drove the author of *Floris and Blanchefleur* (and Novalis, with his *Hyacinth and Rosebud*) to give his characters floral names... You can see me grimacing, Blanca, but pay no mind: you know this kind of maudlin images (otherwise so common in fairy tales) have never been to my liking. Although that will not stop me from

389. John Milton, *Paradise Lost,* iv, 319–339
390. *Ibid,* iv, 404

praising their intention, which is to portray the paradisiacal innocence and purity of the primordial couple; and most of all, the purity of their love, a love unsullied by materiality.

The Paradise of the two children, we were saying, consists of being together; it's a state of intimate communion with the twin soul. That Paradise fades away, then –the Fall happens– on the day their parents decide to separate them. From then on, the heroic odyssey, the strife to reunite with the lost half begins. In the medieval story of *Aucassin and Nicolette*, the search for the twin brother is depicted through that ancient symbol of the Quest: the hunt. Aucassin and Nicolette live with the burden of their traumatic separation. Nicolette comes across some shepherds and leaves them with a message for her "brother and friend": "So God help you, fair children, tell him that there is a beast in this forest, and that he is to come and hunt it. And if he can catch it, he would not give one limb of it for a hundred marks of gold, – no, not for five hundred, nor for any wealth. The beast has such medicine that Aucassin will be cured of his wound."[391]

This is not the first memento we come across in these letters. Remember the talking letter that descended over the captive prince from the *Song of the Pearl*. And the knights of King Arthur whom an unaware Perceval finds in the forest. Now it's this hunting message that the shepherds pass on to the desperate Aucassin, who understands its meaning. He understands that the hunting trophy he is being urged to acquire is a reference to his twin sister Nicolette: only she can cure "his wound". Evidently, Blanca, his wound is being apart from her, from his other half, and it's symbolised in a curious manner: Aucassin's shoulder –they tell us– is

391. *Aucassin et Nicolette*, quoted by M. Lot-Borodine, *op. cit.*, p. 125

"broken in two". When they finally find each other after a long search, Nicolette will cure his broken shoulder: "She felt him about, and found that he had his shoulder out of place. She plied it so deftly with her white hands, and pulled it, (as God willed, who loveth lovers), so that it came again into place. And then she took flowers and fresh grass and green leaves, and bound them on with the lappet of her smock, and he was quite healed."[392]

As is also the case with fairy tales, Blanca, the end of idyllic love stories is invariably happy. After many trials and tribulations, the children always end up reuniting, restoring their paradisiacal original Unit. Because, my dear, that is the ineluctable destiny of the twin souls, whose epic tales of idyllic love are novelised. Another example is the aforementioned *Floris and Blanchefleur*: During a raid, a pagan king imprisons a young Christian maiden; the young maiden is pregnant, and the king puts her at the service of his wife, the queen, who is also pregnant. The two women, who "conceived on the same night", also give birth on the same day: the Queen to Floris; the slave to Blanchefleur. Strangely, Floris and Blanchefleur "look like brother and sister" and they do everything together, including activities that are normally forbidden to the offspring of slaves, such as attending school, for which the king finds himself forced to grant a special permit to Blanchefleur, as Floris declares that he cannot learn anything without her.

Parallel to the two children's mutual affection, which only grows over the years, the king becomes increasingly worried, until he finally decides to cut that inconvenient bond. The queen intercedes and prevents the king from having

392. *Aucassin et Nicolette*, quoted by M. Lot-Borodine, *op. cit.*, p. 126

Blanchefleur murdered, but their separation has been set. The king devises a scheme: telling him his teacher is ill, he sends Florius to an aunt's house to continue his studies. But since Floris refuses to go anywhere without Blanchefleur, he promises him that Blanchefleur will be joining him in a few days. Everyone at the court is confident that, away from Blanchefleur, Floris will end up forgetting her; but all he can think about is his "far–away friend". Continuing with his plan, the king sells the young girl to some merchants, who resell her to the sultan of Babylon. Then he orders Floris to return home, gives him the news of his friend's death, and takes him to her tomb: a sepulchre made of marble and crystal he purposely had made.

Floris attempts to commit suicide right there and then, in front of the false tomb, but their remorseful parents confess the truth. And at that very moment, Floris begins his Quest: which undoubtedly is the quest for the twin soul, Blanca, but at the same time, it's the quest for Unity, the quest for God. His extraordinary similarity to Blanchefleur makes things easier for him, because during his travels he comes across people who remember seeing a girl who looked identical to him. Thanks to those directions, he finally reaches Babylon. He stays at an inn run by a couple, who also recognise him as the twin brother of a former guest: "And when I saw him, I truly thought I was seeing fair Blanchefleur. I believe that she is his twin sister. This boy has the same face and the same heart has her."[393]

With their help, he manages to gain access to the sultan's fortress and secretly reunite with Blanchefleur in the "tower of virgins", where she is held captive. Upon seeing each

393. *Floíre et Blancheflor*, vv, *op. cit.*

other again after so long, they "cry of sorrow and love, falling into each other's arms, and they kiss, and forget everything else."[394] This scene is known as the *recognition scene*, Blanca, because although a long time has passed and they are both very different, and despite him being in disguise and she dressed in Muslim clothing, they still recognise each other. (This test of whether a disguise can prevent twins from recognising each other is another commonplace of idyllic love stories.) For a few days, the two lovers enjoy their early honeymoon at the tower. But then the sultan catches them in bed. He sentences them to death..., but of course, moved by their story, he sets them free.

This is the story of *Floris and Blanchefleur*, an eminently symbolic story imagined by an anonymous twelfth century poet. And the key to this symbolism, my dear, is the epic poem, the twin souls' adventure. Fifteen centuries before – in the third century before Christ– *Daphnis and Chloe* was composed in Greece, the first known idyllic love story. Other Greek models will follow it, such as the one from where the medieval main characters from the Norman story I mentioned earlier took their names: *Pyramus and Thisbe*. But the place where idyllic love stories were more widespread was in the East. We can find great examples of it in the *One Thousand and One Nights*. Let me remind you of the moving beginning of one of those stories: the one that has prince Daw' al-Makan and his twin sister Nuzhat for main characters.

The two children are the offspring of the king of Iraq. They live in Baghdad, a crucial city in the *Nights*. One day, the sight of a pilgrim caravan awakes in them the desire to visit the Holy Places. Their father forbids them to go, but they

394. *Ibid*

collect some money and furtively join the caravan. They travel incognito to Mecca, then to Jerusalem, where the prince falls ill. His sister takes care of him in a rented room at an inn... And at this point, Blanca, I would like to make a brief interruption to remind you of a parallel episode from our lives: when, many years ago, we were coming back to Barcelona, and a sudden new outbreak of your illness forced us to stay overnight at Granollers. We were becoming accustomed to this kind of emergencies that confined you to a hospital bed for a few nights. But that time, you didn't let me call an ambulance. You had been taken with the old-fashioned atmosphere of our hostel – Hostel Europa, of which we ended up becoming regular guests– and you preferred to stay in bed there. For three days and nights, until the crisis abated and we were able to continue our trip, I was your nurse as well as your husband –dual roles that from that moment onwards I would assume naturally. But, getting back to the story, poor princess Nuzhat did not have it so easy. Because, as the days passed, her brother's illness only becomes worse. Soon, they run out of money and the princess is forced to go out looking for means of support. She intends to get a job as a maid for a wealthy family but, as they say, when it rains it pours: Nuzhat is kidnapped. Increasingly worried by her absence, her brother sets out looking for her. But he is very weak, he can barely walk or talk. Passers-by on the street think he is dead. And that's what would have happened if it were not for the charitable soul of a street sweeper who takes pity on him. From that moment on, their lives take different paths for a very long time, before, after many adventures, Destiny brings them together again. The prince will summarise their nostalgia in a few verses that work as an illustrative example of that literary comparison: that of Paradise with the union of twin souls, and Hell as their separation: "So close yesterday, so far apart today! Where are you, Eden? O, eternal Paradise! Without realising, I traded hills and sweet rivers for heavy chains and the pus drenched wastelands of Hell!"

If we are talking about the proliferation of idyllic love stories in the Ancient East, we should make a special mention of Persia. Persian literature is rich in love stories featuring couples of androgynous children who, having grown up together, are traumatically separated, and then spend the rest of their lives looking for each other, until finally they reunite and get married. These couples tend to be brothers and sisters, or cousins. Some titles are *Gushtasp and Ketayuna*, *Mihr and Mushtari*, *Warqah and Gulshah*, *Houmay and Houmayoun*... But among all these, perhaps the most famous one –thanks to a celebrated Arabic version by the Sufi poet Jami– is a text originally written in Greek amidst the Hermetic circles of Alexandria: the story of *Salaman and Absal*, which goes a little something like this:

A king entrusts his son to the care of a young nursemaid (in other versions, Salaman and Absal are brother and sister). Salaman grows up very close to Absal. With each passing year, it becomes increasingly clear that they are in love with each other. But the king is not willing to allow such matrimony and thus decides to separate them. First, he tries to accomplish this through subtle means, but he fails. Then he decides to kill the young woman. But Salaman is one step ahead of him and he flees with his beloved. He flees, we are told, "beyond the Western sea". This escape, Blanca, in reality, is an exile: remember that in the ancient sages' symbolic geography, the West stands for the lower world. The king resorts, then, to his magical arts and he puts a spell on the lovers so that it becomes impossible for them to consummate their union, which substantiates the essence of the Exile: the loss of the *Tawhid*, the privileged state of *perfect union*, of non–separation or non–Duality. Unable to unite as before, the young lovers opt for suicide, and so they hold hands and cast themselves into the sea. But the king, who is spying on them through a crystal ball, summons the spirits of the water to save his son. However, Absal's death makes this rescue effectively useless, as Salaman's grief was so powerful it was on the verge of killing him. His father takes him to a sage who, mysteriously, assures him: "A few days will suffice me to cure him and to make Absal his companion for eternity." Salaman agrees to spend forty days in invocations in a cave, just as the sage prescribes (caves, as I told you, were considered to be the ideal place for initiations). He also accepts the conditions he is imposed to recover his beloved, the main condition being that he must not love another woman. He must also dress like Absal, in what we can observe an exponent of that ancient practice we mentioned in another letter: the practice of dressing in the clothes of the opposite sex, often those of the spouse herself, with the purpose of symbolically restoring the individual to his lost half.

Salaman, then, enters the initiation cave. Following the sage's directions, he progressively interiorises Absal. With each passing day, he sees her more beautiful in his heart, until, at the end of the symbolic forty days, it appears to him that it's not Absal who he sees. In her place, he sees a divine Figure, a feminine Figure of extraordinary beauty: the goddess Venus – "Sophia", Jakob Boehme would call her. Salaman, then, turns his back on Absal (just as we have seen young Hyacinth do with Rosebud) and can only think of this goddess: "O Sage! I no longer wish for Absal. In this Figure I have found a sign that has made me averse to the company of Absal. I desire nothing but this Figure." But the sage reminds him of his commitment to not love another woman: "Now we are nearing the moment when the return of Absal, who shall be restored to you, will signify the fulfilment of our prayers"[395], he tells him.

At the end, Blanca, his twin soul is indeed returned to him, and in such a way that nothing will be able to separate them ever again. However, the ending to this story is confusing. First, we should infer that, at the supreme moment, Venus and Absal represent each other. That would be the most plausible ending for us: Salaman ends up recognising the familiar face of Absal in the goddess. But what is certain is that Absal seems to become an allegorical figure at the end; that should not surprise us, my dear, if we take into account that this idyllic story comes to us as a thoroughly reworked version. In its original version, it probably did not stray much from the classic scheme: that is to say, the story of a boy and a girl who, after a happy childhood together, are separated and then frantically search for each other until they reunite. There must have been successive versions of this story that, working over this simple plot, weaved increasingly more complex ideas. It's like in the "broken telephone", that children's game consisting of whispering the same message along a human chain, you know? I'm sure you played it when you were little. The fun of this game is in something almost inevitable: when the message arrives at the last person of the chain, it will be practically unrecognisable. I suspect that what happens with symbolic stories like *Salaman and Absal* is something along those lines: the original symbolism fades away with each new retelling.

---

395. Quoted by Henry Corbin, *Avicenna and the Visionary Recital*, 216

Because the original symbolism of these stories, Blanca, is like a secret cypher in which they are written. That cypher comes from intuition, and intuition is exactly what is needed to decipher the hidden meaning of the story. When we try to do it, as we customarily do, by means of reason, the hidden meaning comes out false. In fact, I find that this principle can be applied to every sphere of existence. Haven't you noticed that, at a certain point, the more we analyse a problem, the more unsolvable it becomes? That oftentimes, when we stop rationalising over a problem, the solution emerges by itself? In addition, contrary to the assumption that profound meanings are by definition obscure, the solution always turns out to be the simplest... If we were to untangle the deep significance of idyllic love stories from reason (from reason placed in the service of faith, as it's commonly said in these cases), we could arrive, in accordance with our personal beliefs, to a wide range of conclusions, each one more convoluted than the one before. But look: in here, reason is unreasonable, if you forgive me the easy wordplay. To unravel the hidden meaning of idyllic love stories, we must employ intuition. This hidden meaning, judging by my own intuition, is quite clearly the cosmic drama of the twin souls: their fall from Unity and their struggle to return to It.

This struggle, when it's deliberate, is a heroic struggle, Blanca: the idyllic love stories are also stories of heroic love. We will stop now (and this will be the final argument of this letter) to consider a heroic love story from the eighteenth century. A famous story, admired all over the world, although not for the story itself, but for its music. It's a musical story, an opera. But an opera that feels like a fairy tale. And with this, you must know which opera I'm talking about, right? I'm talking about *The Magic Flute*, of course; or, as it could very well be titled, if it followed the pattern of other idyllic love stories: *Tamino and Pamina*, the names of the main couple.

TAMINO AND PAMINA

Well, you already know this opera by Mozart, I don't intend to introduce you to it here. But there may be a few things about its libretto that will be new to you. First, did you know that it's inspired in the postulates of the Freemasonry, a secret society that was partly a repository for ancient knowledge, and of which Mozart allegedly was a member? More importantly, did you know that the love story it tells is of a heroic or initiatory character? Tamino and Pamina form the heroic couple. However, as you know, this couple finds its comical and charming counterpoint in Papageno and Papagena, a caricature of the twin souls who go along with the majority or evolutive path. Both couples, Blanca, are couples of twin souls, as the nigh identical root of their names gives away: only the gender varies, which constitutes a clear sign of kindship, of them sharing one single soul.

Can you hear the music? Can you hear Mozart's delightful music that is playing now, quietly given the untimely hour, in our record player? Indeed, talking about the *Magic Flute* without mentioning such beautiful music sounds absurd, no? But let's make an exception this one time, since what we are interested in now is not Mozart's music, but the opera's libretto. This is because every single subject we have been discussing in these letters is in there, Blanca. Starting with their *leitmotiv*, to use an opera term, summarised here in Papageno and Papagena's duet: "[Love's] higher purpose is our guide, and nothing is nobler than wife and man. Man and wife, and wife and man attain divinity."

This *leitmotiv* concurs with the theme of love predestination. Sarastro, the supreme priest, announces to the assembly that "Sweet, virtuous, young Pamina is destined by the gods to this handsome prince", referring to Tamino. Papageno, on the other hand, is approached by a priest: "And if Sarastro had a young lady who looked exactly like you, both in looks and in how she dressed, destined for you?", in a clear allusion to his twin soul. Then we have the theme of recognition. Tamino and Pamina recognise each other as soon as they set eyes on one another: "–It is he! –It is her! –I can hardly believe it! –I'm not dreaming! –I shall embrace him/her!" Papageno does not recognise Papagena the first time he sees her but, in his defence, she is in disguise as an "ugly old woman", which touches upon another main theme in our letters: subjective beauty, the need to look with the eyes of the heart rather than the physical eyes, if we want to recognise our twin soul. And it touches upon this subject the same way heroic love stories and fairy tales usually do it: with the disguise test.

In this opera, we also have –in the same broad strokes as fairy tales– the contrast between lower carnal love, personified by Pamina's lascivious jailer, Monostatos, and the high, spiritual love of Tamino. You will remember that he has a portrait of his twin soul in his possession: the one some fairies gave him; based on that *symbolon*, he will recognise Pamina as soon as he sees her. At this point, Blanca, maybe a small gallery of female portraits will parade across your memory. The portrait king Duyshanta painted of his secret wife. The portrait of Badr-ul-Jamal that prince Saif-ul-Malook discovered sewn in the lining of a tunic King Solomon gave him. Or another I did not mention in these letters, but that you and I read about in the *One Thousand and One Nights*. I mean the image prince Ibrahim-ben-Alkhassib finds as he is leafing through a book. He abandons everything to set off in search of the woman in the portrait, Jamila, who is waiting for him because she too fell in love with him in a similar manner. Ah, and maybe you have Portrait *of Jennie* fresher in your mind as I have on mine: in that delightful film by William Dieterl, an artist paints a portrait of a woman who only existed in his mind or perhaps in an impossible past too...

I bet, my dear, all those portrait owners subscribed to the words of Tamino at the beginning of *The Magic Flute*, when, concerning the portrait of Pamina some fairies had just given him, he says to himself: "I feel as if this angelic picture were filling my heart with a new emotion. This something I cannot name, but I feel it burning here. Can this sensation be love? Yes, yes! This can only be love. Oh, if only I might find her! If only she stood before me! I would -would warmly - chastely - what would I do? I would, in ecstasy, press her to my ardent heart, and she would be mine forever!" Meaning, Blanca, the ultimate aim of Tamino's Quest is to become one with Pamina, to merge with his twin soul for all Eternity. But he is also aware that, to accomplish this, he must love her with a pure heart. "*Warmly* - chastely," he says as if to point out that pure love is not at odds with the heat of passion -except that it's a different kind of passion, different from the sexual one. Which remits us to another central idea in our letters: the need for the purification of the individual as a requirement for the final reunification of the twin souls.

It's also one of the core ideas in *The Magic Flute*. Indeed, in accordance with the conventions of fairy tales, Tamino and Papageno must pass a series of tests if they want to reunite with their respective spouses. These tests consist of an ascesis, a process of internal undressing. "For first they must be purified", claims Sarastro. It's a process that demands great sacrifices: "The path you will walk is harsh and dangerous, but with the help of the gods you shall emerge the victor". Tamino is a hero, and as such, he steadfastly advances along this tortuous road. When Sarastro asks him whether he will submit to all the tests, he answers "Yes, to all of them" without hesitating and, always with Pamina in mind, he overcomes them all one by one. Papageno follows him but lacks conviction: "If the gods have destined a Papagena for me, why should they offer her wrapped in so many dangers?" he complains. He is constantly on the verge of throwing in the towel and renouncing his goal: "This trip, so long that it feels like an eternity, makes me even lose the desire to find love." Just like Tamino, he wanted to reunite with his twin soul as soon as possible; but he is not willing to face the sacrifices of the heroic path. He knows that he is not the only one in this position, that the path he is walking is the path where the majority trudges along: "There are many people like me. What I would like now is a good glass of wine, which sounds so much better now than all those other great delights." And although he reluctantly takes the tests, he fails over and over again, distancing himself from his twin soul: "Move away, young lady –a priest admonishes Papagena–, for he is not worthy of you yet". Papageno's ridiculous portrayal –a personification of the evolutive path– clearly exemplifies the ancient sages' partiality for the heroic path, which is Tamino's path.

Pamino's soul is engaged in a battle: as he overcomes the trials, the Spirit, represented by the light of day, is gaining ground against Matter in him, symbolised by the darkness of the night ("The dark night retreats from the light of the sun!"). Because what Mozart is dramatising in this opera, my dear, is the mythological battle between the traditional icons of Spirit and Matter: light and darkness. It's a story that many considered simplistic, a story of good versus evil, like fairy tales and so many other stories throughout the centuries (pirate stories, cowboys and Indians, swashbucklers, heroes and ruffians...) that caught the imagination of people, children in particular, because they are in tune with a simple truth which, deep down, we all vaguely feel.

Representing Matter –darkness, the split Duality–, we have the Queen of the Night and her acolytes; as well as the henchman Monostatos, who is depicted with diabolical traits, and whose name is significant, for it connotes unilaterality. (In consonance with other devils from literature and mythology, Monostatos is a lonely being, lacking a twin soul: "Every creature feels the joy of love, and bill and coo and hug and kiss – but I must forego love" he cries.) On the other corner we have, representing the Spirit –Light and Unity–, the supreme priest Sarastro and the priests of the Temple. They already are initiates and have reached the end of the laborious path along which now walks Tamino, who "aspires –says Sarastro– to accomplish a goal that all of them accomplished through blood, sweat and tears. In short: this young man wants to lift the night veil that covers him and in holiness see the great Light".

The "night veil that covers him", Blanca, is the *ego*, the material lining of his soul; the Light is the light of the Spirit, the light of the One. The battle fought between Sarastro and the Queen of the Night is the exteriorisation of the hero's inner struggle: the struggle against the dragon of the *ego*. The priest announces, "He who travels these laborious paths *will be purified* by fire, water, air and earth. If he overcomes his fear of death, he will raise himself from earth, soar heavenwards! In the light of this higher level he can dedicate himself wholly to Isis's mysteries." In the mythological context of this opera, Blanca (which is the mythological context of Freemasonry), God is embodied by the divine Spouses of ancient Egypt, Isis and Osiris. "Dedicate himself wholly to Isis' mysteries" is equivalent, then, to reaching Divinity, symbolised here also by Royalty (the royal status is a higher symbolic level among the Freemasons): "Prince, heretofore your conduct has been valorous and patient; but there are still two very dangerous stretches of road to go. If your heart beats for Pamina with the same ardour *and you wish to one day rule as a wise sovereign*, then may the gods be with you on your way."

After the individual tests comes a joint test: Pamina reunites with the Tamino so that they may face together the last stage of their journey. What is being tested now is the purity of their love. Similarly, to the courtly heroes, who had to stand unaffected before the sight of their naked lady, Tamino and Pamina must remain impassive as they cross the territory of desire, of carnal love, symbolised by a wall of fire. The stage directions says, "Tamino and Pamina are seen making their way. Tamino plays on

his flute. As soon as they have emerged from the fire they embrace one another." Thanks to the sweet sounds of the titular flute that symbolises the pure love of the true lovers. "We passed through the glowing fire and bravely faced the danger." But there is a second part to this test, consisting of an extension of water the lovers must also cross. Walking on water without getting wet is –as we have seen, Blanca– a sign of overcoming the *ego*, of sublimation of Matter; and it's only within reach to heroes who have transcended the human condition.

The opened gates of the Temple await them at the end of the trial (the Temple represents Divinity, Unity, Mystic Royalty). "Suddenly, the scenery is brightly lit, -'Ye Gods, what a joyful moment! -celebrate the victorious lovers- The joy of Isis is accorded to us!'" And the priests in unison: "Victory, victory, victory, o noble pair, You have overcome the danger! Isis's rites are now yours! Come, come, enter the Temple!" Before this, three children who had come down from Heaven on a flying machine (three angels) had prophesied: "The sun, the splendid herald of the morn, will soon set off upon his golden course .../... and mortals be like Gods." Now the prophecy has been fulfilled: Tamino and Pamina have gone up from the rung of men to that of divine dignity. "What joy to meet again and enter the temple happily, hand in hand!... and death is worthy and will be made initiate!" This also fulfils Tamino's greatest desire, expressed at the beginning over the portrait of his twin soul: "I would, in ecstasy, press her to my ardent heart, and she would be mine forever!" At the end, Blanca, we have the final victory of the forces of Light (Sarastro and the priests of the Temple) over the forces of Darkness (the Queen of the Night and her acolytes). And Papageno? He gets married too, with Papagena, of course. But this marriage is not like Tamino and Pamina's: it's not a heavenly marriage but an earthly one. It does not bear Divinity, only a healthy brood of little Papagenos and little Papagenas who are their parents' delight (as they would have been of ours, am I right, Blanca?). But they are not sublime and ineffable delights, the kind enjoyed by Tamino and Pamina, whose solemn joint coronation concludes *The Magic Flute*. And thus concludes this letter as well.

Yours

NINTH LETTER

THE TWINS

(OR THE "DOUBLE THING")

By the name of Luna Philosophers
understand not the vulgar Moon
...
and offer sister to brother in firm union,
that from thence he may receive Sol's noble Son.

Jean d'Espagnet, sixteenth century alchemist,
The secret work of Hermetic philosophy

Barcelona, 29th of December, 1999

Dear Blanca,

Would you like to know where I spent my Christmas Eve? Well, in Arenys, where else? I was with Inés, Marcel and all my cousins. Then, as always, I spent Saint Stephen's day at Esther and Enrique's. This year, in addition to the usual guests, the Dalmau were there; and Patricia and her husband too, who made us laugh our heads off with countless anecdotes from his travels; and a Peruvian couple you don't know but with whom I'm sure you would have been good friends. I was the only one there without a partner, but don't think that upset me. This would not have even happened in other years, because Esther would invite a single friend of hers. They gave up a long time ago, but Esther and Enrique were dead set on helping me rebuild my life, as they called it.

With the best intentions, they would introduce me to their friends, usually divorced women, and the four of us would go out at night. We would go out to the cinema, or the theatre and a restaurant. However, I could never move past those first dates. It's not like they were not great women, not at all; I'm sure I could have rebuilt my life with any of them.

Except I'm not interested in rebuilding my life. I explained it to Esther and Enrique, and it seems like they finally understood.

On the other hand, I suspect they did not like me very much either. Among other things, because all I did was talk about you. Ah, and speaking of these nights out: on one occasion, the four of us (I cannot remember which friend it was that time) went to a staging of the *Nutcracker* at the Liceo. And well, you can picture it, I was assaulted by the memories of all those times you were there sitting by my side on those very same stands. At the end of the first act, I could not take it anymore, I had to tell them I was feeling indisposed and I left... What am I waiting for to get to the matter at hand? Don't be impatient, my dear, let me do this. Can't you see I'm setting up the introduction for the first subject of this letter? Because if we closed the previous one with an opera by Mozart, then we will begin this one with the first act of another famous opera. Or, more accurately, a "musical drama", which is how Richard Wagner liked to categorise his works.

Crossed–out note on the margin. Under the quick pen marker lines, we can still read enough (knowledgeable as we are of the author and his wife's fondness for this novel) to identify the quotation –in the original French– as belonging to Thomas Mann's *The Magic Mountain*,

"Mais quant à ce que je t'ai reconnue et que j'ai reconnu mon amour pour toi, –oui, c'est vrai, je t'ai déjà connue, anciennement, toi et tes yeux merveilleusement obliques et ta bouche et ta voix, avec laquelle tu parles".

I know, I know, who you really love is Puccini. And more, I would say Wagner makes you a little uneasy, am I right? Because the Nazis liked his music. But let's be sensible. How was that Wagner's fault? Especially if we consider that his operas exalt compassion as a supreme value, and you don't need me to tell you that the Nazis thought very little of such quality. In any case, whether you like it or not, the music that has accompanied us throughout these eight letters is not Puccini's, it's Wagner's.

Oh, yes, my dear. Had you sharpened your ears when we were talking about Tristan and Isolde, and you would have certainly heard the famous chord from his homonymous opera playing in the background (an opera that Wagner composed under the influence of his encounter with Mathilde Wesendonck, the woman in whom he believed to have recognised his twin soul). And, in the first letter, when Shankuntala is crying over her true husband's memory loss, didn't it sound to you like there was this muffled music playing? It was a scene from *Twilight of the Gods*, in which the hero Siegfried, under a spell, not recognising his wife Brunnhilde, marries another woman. And when we were discussing the Holy Grail, if you tried a little bit harder, you would have heard the notes and verses of the *Lohengrin*, or of the *Parsifal*, based on the book by Wolfram von Eschenbach. Even when we were talking about the troubadours, the music playing was not by them: it was his *Tannhäuser*, a drama composed around the legend of a *minnesinger*, a German troubadour from the thirteenth century who finds redemption for his dark past in the pure love of a lady. And there is more, my dear: Wagner is still with us. But, in case that are still any doubts, I'll get up and push play on *The Valkyrie*, which is the opera, pardon me, the musical drama I'll be talking about now.

The second part of the famous tetralogy, *The Ring of the Nibelung*, *The Valkyrie* revolves around a couple of twin brothers from Nordic mythology. The hero, Siegmund, is a knight-errant whose life is sadly marked by the separation from his sister Sieglinde, abducted as a child and of whom nothing is known... And at this point, Blanca, I could tell you about a strange childish fantasy that many psychologists and psychoanalysts observe in their consultations, which is the fantasy many children have of having been born with a twin brother whose existence, or death at birth, has been hidden from them. But I will not go into this "imaginary twin" fantasy, as it's known, because the curtain has just gone up and... look! Young Siegmund is running through the woods after being wounded in a fight.

Bleeding and unarmed, he arrives at a hunter's cabin. The hunter is away, but his wife takes him in. Wagner's music emphasises the singularity of this meeting, for although it is the first time they see each other, Siegmund and the hunter's wife seem to recognise one another. Obviously, in reality, it is not the first time, and they can feel it as their eyes meet. This feeling will later be confirmed, when their respective pasts become known and turn out to coincide. They will recognise each other, then, as the twin brother and sister who were traumatically separated at childhood, and, in a famous operatic dialogue (as famous as that other from *Tristan and Isolde* where both end up merging their names and singing the unification of their souls, and their victory over Time and Space and human bondage) they declare their love for each other.

Of course, there are many other vicissitudes, but that is the main focus of the story. A story in which Wagner, versed in medieval symbolism, suggests the "sword test". Do you remember the sword in the stone, the unmovable sword that defiantly stands before the heroes of the Grail? You will also remember the fact that pulling the sword from the stone symbolised, as we said, the reintegration of the primordial Unity of the Two: the restoration of their Divinity, of their Mystic Royalty. Well, this is when Sieglend, after revealing that the hunter is one of her kidnappers and that she was forcibly married, describes a strange episode. She says that a mysterious old man crashed her wedding reception and... (you will laugh, my dear, by as I was picturing this, I could not help but think about the scene my granduncle made at our reception) and, drawing his sword, he plunged it to the hilt on a tree, declaring that only he who is able to remove it will be worthy of Sieglinde. Since then, many have tried but all of them failed, until it gets to Siegmund's turn. The sword gives in to his hand, because Siegmund is Sieglinde's twin soul, therefore he is the only one capable of attaining a *perfect union* with her.

Like other modern creators (like Thomas Mann, for example, whose novel *The Blood of the Volsungs* adapts the myth of Siegmund and Sieglinde to the twentieth century), Wagner shares with the ancient sages the fascination for twins, for the theme of twins of the opposite sex who are in love with each other. There is nothing scandalous in this theme, my dear, because biological kinship remits to spiritual kinship: the incestuous love between brother and sister is metaphorical, it represents the mutual love between twin souls; in any case, it's a spiritual love. This metaphor –often subconscious– has a strong presence in universal Literature. In the previous letter, I cited some medieval examples. Ow, though, let's take a look at other eras. Let's begin with a masterpiece by one of the greatest and most elegant writers, according to the critics, of this nearly finished century of ours. I'm referring to Robert Musil and his monumental unfinished novel, *The Man Without Qualities*.

The protagonist has a sister from whom he was separated in their youth, and whom he barely remembers. Many years later, on occasion of their father's death, Ulrich and Agathe meet again, and their first impression is of astonishment over their physical resemblance, "[Ulrich] felt as if it were his own self that had entered through a door and was coming to meet him, though it was a more beautiful self." In a simile you will enjoy, Ulrich will later compare their two faces to two identical drawings made with different techniques: she is a pastel while he is a woodcut. In that moment of reunion, this similarity is highlighted by a detail, an extraordinary coincidence; they are both wearing square–patterned clothes. "I had no idea we were twins!" says Agathe upon seeing her brother after all those years. Technically, Blanca, Ulrich and Agathe are not twins. But they will not hesitate in attributing themselves such condition at the sight of their extraordinary resemblance:

> "So we declare ourselves to be twins," he agreed. "Symmetrical creatures of a whim of nature, henceforth we shall be the same age, the same height, with the same hair, walking the highways and byways of the world in identical striped clothes with the same bow tied under our chins. But I warn you that

> people will turn around and look after us, half touched and half scornful, as always happens when something reminds them of the mysteries of their own beginnings." – "Why can't we dress for contrast?" Agathe said lightly. "One in yellow when the other is in blue, or red alongside green, and we can dye our hair violet or purple, and I can affect a hump and you a paunch: yet we'd still be twins!" But the joke had gone stale, the pretext worn out, and they fell silent for a while. "Do you realize," Ulrich then said suddenly, "that this is something very serious we're talking about?"[396]

However, Blanca, physical resemblance is the least important; it's only a sign of a deeper complementarity. Soon, Ulrich and Agathe also become aware of this, of something "secret and indeterminate that brings them together". Straight away, they recognise one another as each other's double, as each other's *secret, other self*. According to Musil, this recognition is at the root of all the great amorous passions, "...great reckless passions all have something to do with the fact that everyone thinks it's his own secret self peering out at him from behind the curtains of a stranger's eyes." Agathe will compare her brother and hers spiritual duplication –the recognition of herself in a different *other self*– with the collision of one's breath against a veil, which returns that breath as if it were someone else's... This essential identity is not only visible in their similar appearance: it manifests itself, most of all, in a strong spiritual understanding. "When you said something, for me it was as though it had been said in my own voice; when something in your voice changed, it would also change in my thoughts, and

396. Robert Musil, *The Without Qualities, Vol 3*

when you felt something, I am sure that its effects would be felt in my heart."

That feeling of being one individual in two bodies, leads Ulrich to come up with a formula to describe themselves: "unseparated but not united". Fascinated by that ineffable feeling, they abandon their mundane duties and move in together. In this voluntary retreat, they focus on thoroughly living their "mystic love", as they label it. A love that Ulrich connects to a distant past (Ulrich calls it "the Millennium") in which his intuition sees "two inseparable twins". What are Ulrich and Agathe looking for in each other? They seek to abolish their Duality, to restore their original Unity, their Integrity: "They were both searching, as in dreams, for a common interior way and, often, they believed themselves to be, by virtue of that feeling, almost one single body, pregnant with a strange blessing and yet painfully nailed to the cross of Duality." Because they are virtually united, Blanca, Ulrich and Agathe continue to be two. Only the real union saved for the Afterlife will abolish that painful Duality to which we are nailed, says Musil, as if it were a cross. (And at this point we can remember Jakob Boehme, when he compared the tragedy resultant of the primordial Androgyne's split to the crucifixion of Christ.)

That is to say, their spiritual marriage is not enough. They were not satisfied with being one single individual in two bodies, they wished to take the next step, the *two in one*; they can feel that is where Paradise lies. They seek to fulfil "their passion for being one, a passion that dominated them in a multitude of ways, as they spread, like jealousy of the spirit, until the unattainable, the past and the possible." In short, Blanca, Ulrich and Agathe aspire to cease being Ulrich and Agathe to become Ulrich–Agathe, one of the innumerable

Faces of the Androgyne, one of the innumerable Names of God.

Such aspiration also fuels the love between the couples of twins that inhabit the novels of a contemporary of Musil: the British writer Rose Macaulay. Compared to Musil's, hers is a lesser work, but mystic intuition does not distinguish between great or minor geniuses; and Rose Macaulay was assisted by the intuition of biological twins as a metaphor, as a symbol of spiritual kinship. From the numerous twins in Macaulay's work, we will pick two representative couples: Lucy and Peter from *Lee Shore*, and Joanna and Tudor from the *Valley Captives*.

What happened with Lucy and Peter was the opposite of what happened to Ulrich and Agathe: these were brother and sister without being twins; Lucy and Peter are twins without being brother and sister. What a paradox, isn't it? And it's that sometimes Macaulay gives her twins the same nuance ancient writers gave theirs, which is making them *cousins*. Their kinship, however, leaves no room for doubts. First, to themselves: Peter is aware that Lucy and he "have always been different from most cousins... more like brother and sister". "I know –she admits– It's not only looking and laughing and words; we think alike too." Then, to everyone around them, "Absurdly like Peter [Lucy] was... Then Peter came in... After all, Rhoda didn't see now that they were so alike...But when one had said all this, there was something... something inner, essential, indefinable, of the spirit, that was not of like substance but the same. So it is sometimes with twins."

That's how it was with Ulrich and Agathe too: their outer similarity was the reflection of their inner affinity. But have you noticed how Rhoda describes the nature of that essential affinity? It's not a "like substance", she says, "it's the same". That is to say, Lucy and Peter share the same spiritual substance, the same soul, of which they are its two halves. "I was only half a person without you", she will confess to him after a long absence... As every lover, the twins from Macaulay's novels show the pain of separation. But it's a relative separation, Blanca, more physical than spiritual. Thus, Joanna and Tudor spend a long time away from each other; and however, "in a way, Joanna was very close to him... They were as close as when they shared a childhood and were united in a mutual alliance for self-defence and mutual camaraderie for adventure." Joanna and Tudor have attained a spiritual marriage, a virtual unity. A union that transcends death, as it's suggested by their blood mixing when Joanna leans over Tudor's corpse, who died saving his sister's life, who in turn "had always loved him more than herself".

The pain that comes over Peter when Lucy gets engaged to another man, shows him to what point "she was rooted in the very fibre of his being; it wasn't so much that he consciously loved her as that she was *his other self*." In a desperate attempt to forget her, Peter marries another woman, Rhoda. But Peter and Lucy's marriages are doomed to fail, Blanca (just like Tristan and Isolde of the White Hands' marriage, and Isolde the Fair and king Mark's). Because they are already married to each other – as it's attested by the fact that between them there's no need for words, "For always they had leaped to one another's thoughts and emotions and desires." Rhoda quickly realises this. That's when she recognises there is something essentially identical between the brother and sister, and understands that, in a profound sense, she is a stranger for her husband.

ROMANTIC LOVES

We have cited Robert Musil and Rose Macaulay. It would not be difficult to find other examples, though. Examples of modern writers that, supported more or less consciously by the same intuition, made twins of the opposite sex the main characters of their love stories. However, I propose that we go further back in time. Specifically to the last decades of the eighteenth century and the first of the nineteenth, a time when –as a reaction to the mechanistic understanding of things typical of the Age of Reason– one of History's most influential artistic and spiritual movements blossomed in Europe. And this is a movement of great interest for our investigation, Blanca: Romanticism.

It's true that, in general, the lives of Romantic poets were far from being exemplary. Such is the case with Lord Byron, who probably had the biggest *ego* in the history of Literature. But there's no reason to focus on their lives, let's focus on their work. And since Lord Byron's name came up first, let's take his poem *Manfred*, which broaches the subject at hand: the incestuous love between two twins of the opposite sex. Same as in the Macaulay's novel I mentioned above, one of the two has involuntarily caused the other one's death; this keeps him mired in pain, cloistered in a tower of his castle in the Alps. Let's consider these verses:

> Count Manfred was, as now, within his tower,—
> How occupied, we knew not, but with him
> The sole companion of his wanderings
> And watchings—her, whom of all earthly things

That lived, the only thing he seem'd to love,—
As he indeed, by blood was bound to do...[397]

It's one of Manfred's servants, who's speaking retrospectively. Note, Blanca, this last, enigmatic verse: *As he indeed, by blood was bound to do.* Meaning that, by blood, his lord was destined to love his twin sister Astarte above all other earthly things. Let's examine the words "by blood". To understand it, we must keep in mind that back then, blood enjoyed a magical and sacred prestige: if the heart was the headquarters of the soul, then the soul was distributed across the entire organism -bringing it to life- through the veins. Blood was a magical substance that carried the individual's soul, hence one of the rites that formalised spiritual matrimonies in the past being the mixing of bloods (hence the symbolism of the posthumous mixing of bloods between Joanna and Tudor in *The Valley Captives*). What does it mean then, metaphorically speaking, that, by virtue of being twins, the same blood circulates in Manfred and Astarte's veins?

You said it yourself: they both share the same soul. Manfred and Astarte are two halves of the same soul, Blanca: that's why they can be said to be destined to love each other above all other earthly things. Further down in this letter, I will tell you about Alchemy. One of its most famous treatises, *The Turba Philosophorum*, instructs its adherents, warning them that "Know ye, further, that unless ye rule the Nature of Truth, and harmonize well together its complexions and compositions, the *consanguineous with the consanguineous*, and the first with the first, ye act improperly and effect

397. Lord Byron, *Manfred*, Act III, scene 3, 49–54

nothing."[398] Note that, same as with Macaulay's twins, we are not talking about a similar substance, but the *same substance.* This "sameness" -symbolised here by consanguinity- makes incestuous love between twins the ideal metaphor for love between twin souls. It expresses the foundation of this love, which is a shared essence; the fact that twin souls are made of the same spiritual substance, just as the two halves of a *symbolon* are made of the same piece of wood.

Manfred and Astarte are the two halves of the same *symbolon*: and as such, their love is in no way coincidental, it's not a mere circumstantial love, it's an essential and necessary love. A predestined love, Blanca. And just as a common essence presupposes a common origin, then by definition it presupposes a common destination as well. Of course, in absolute terms, we all share the same essence; we have then the same origin and the same destination: we all come from God and we are all destined to return to Him. That we are all brothers is an assertion that belongs to the common spiritual heritage of every religion; no one is a foreigner to anyone because the same "blood", the same divine essence, flows through everyone's veins (through the veins of the Universe). Nevertheless, within this universal brotherhood, within this great family, there are degrees of kinship; and the closest kinship is what binds each one of us to our *other self*, each *I* to its particular and exclusive *you*: each soul to its twin.

Crossed–out note on the margin. The marker pen went too fast here, the author failing his attempt to erase the note: *("At the) Clock Tower the robots began their dance...; she (appeared) to snap out of her fascination.*

398. *The Turba* Philosophorum, p. 32

***(Happy) New Year my love – she whispered."* The Clock Tower, with its dancing mechanical figurines, is an icon of the Swiss town of Bern. Although the date has been crossed out, it is an easy guess: 31–12–99.**

It's in this relative sense that we can talk about the different origins –and destinations– of souls, Blanca. That we can talk about "foreigners" in relation to oneself, as we have seen Rhoda do as she considered what she was to her husband, and as it's insinuated too (to quote an example from the blue library) by Catherine from *Wuthering Heights*, when she describes the different types of affection that connect her to her husband and her adoptive brother. Maybe you remember the passage, "...It would degrade me to marry Heathcliff, now; and that, not because he's handsome, Nelly, but because he's more myself than I am. *Whatever our souls are made of, his and mine are the same*, and Linton's (her husband) is as different as a moonbeam from lightning, or frost from fire."... But let's go back to Byron. As is characteristic of Romantic loves, Manfred's love for her twin sister is moving for its intensity, for its exclusivity, and for its "nudity". And also for the extreme idealisation of the beloved, who her brother's love converts into an angel, a virgin or a goddess. When he recalls their likeness, Manfred always confers her a greater perfection: she is identical to him, except more perfect:

> She was like me in lineaments—her eyes,
> Her hair, her features, all, to the very tone
> Even of her voice, they said were like to mine;
> But soften'd all, and temper'd into beauty;
> She had the same lone thoughts and wanderings,
> The quest of hidden knowledge, and a mind

To comprehend the universe; nor these
Alone, but with them gentler powers than mine,
Pity, and smiles, and tears—which I had not;
And tenderness—but that I had for her;
Humility—and that I never had.
Her faults were mine—her virtues were her own—[399]

We can say of Manfred and Astarte the same that, in another one of his poems –*Sardanapalus*– Byron will say of his main couple: that both find themselves connected to each other by "some unknown influence". Except it's not unknown to us, Blanca: that influence is their spiritual kinship. It's the influence that (just as with Brunnhilde, who throws herself into Siegfried's funeral pyre, or with the little lead soldier from Andersen's story, who jumps into the fireplace where the paper doll is burning) will urge Myrrah, Sardanapalus' beloved, to decide to die with him when, to avoid being captured by his enemies, Sardanapalus has a funeral pyre built so he can self-immolate:

- My Myrrha ! Dost thou truly follow me, freely and fearlessly?
- And dost thou think a Greek girl dare not do for love that which an Indian widow braves for custom?
- Then we but await the signal.
- It is long in sounding.
- Now, farewell; one last embrace.
- Embrace, but not the last; there is one more.
- True, the commingling fire will mix our ashes.
- And pure as is my love to thee shall they.

399. Lord Byron, *Manfred*, Act II, scene 2, 112-123

The purity of their love guarantees their reunification after death. But there is that previous requirement, Blanca: spiritual kinship, or rather, a common origin. A common destination is the inevitable consequence of the lovers' common origin. This subject is repeated again and again in Romantic literature. Let's take *The Devotion of the Cross* as a model, an amorous drama by an early precursor of literary Romanticism, the Spanish playwright Pedro Calderón de la Barca. Based on a mystic legend from ancient Spain, this drama also features a couple of twins as its main characters. Julia and Eusebio's birth was a miracle; they were born at the foot of a cross on a mountain. The sign of their predestined love is, then, in this case, a divine symbol, the Christian cross. It seems remarkable to me: it shows, perhaps, that Calderón intuited the divine and heavenly root of love predestination. Julia and Eusebio's childhood together is taken away from them. At this point, their story takes a different path than most twin stories: they are separated at birth. But, in their youth, they reunite and fall deeply in love for each other. They fall in love without suspecting their common origin, Blanca, since their kinship is a secret to them. It does not manifest itself in physical likeness, as to suggest that it's their souls, and not their bodies, who are twins. This is also the case, by the way, of a celebrated epic Renaissance poem: *Orlando furioso* by Ariosto. In *Orlando furioso*, a voice from Heaven finally reveals to Marphisa and Ruggiero that they are twins. In *The Devotion of the Cross*, it's an identical birthmark. –"...a cross of blood and fire"– they both discover on their chest. We could say that is their *symbolon*, their love countersign.

In spite of that, Blanca, this predestined love turns out to be inviable, and again due to the opposition of family. As in so many Romantic stories, only death can bring these lovers together. Eusebio will die at the hands of his father, Julia, embracing the cross at her brother's tomb. But look, this cross will perform a miracle, which will be the opposite replica of the miracle at the beginning of the story, which brought both siblings into this world. Back then, it was a cross, a votive cross on a mountain that cast them onto Earth; now it's this funereal cross that will pull them both up to Heaven. Their destiny is thus fulfilled, the destiny of the twin souls, which is to unite in God (embodied here by the Christian cross), in whom, through that same unifying act, both must transform.

The English Romantic William Blake, painter, engraver and mystic poet, also imagined the twin souls' final reunion in God. Blake has many points in common with that other famous mystic, Swedenborg, by whom he was influenced. Their most remarkable common trait is their visionary gift, although, in this aspect, Blake was more precocious than our friend Swedenborg, since his visions seem to date back to his early childhood (he saw some angels perched on a tree while he was strolling around London with his father, who severely admonished him for telling lies!). These visions accompanied him throughout his entire life. They greatly inspired his work, Blanca, as the following anecdote, told by one of his disciples, will attest: this disciple was going through a time of creative crisis and, one day, visiting Blake's house, he started to complain about it. Blake patiently listened to him, and then he turned to his wife Katherine and said, "The same thing happens to us, does it not, Kate? For weeks on end, the visions abandon us. What do we do then?". "We get on our knees, and we pray", she answered.

This anecdote illustrates more than the importance of the visionary element in Blake's work, more than the importance of religion in his life. It illustrates the ascendant, in his work as in his life, of his wife Katherine, and the high level of spiritual communion they attained (to the point of him speaking of his visions as though they had appeared to the both of them). There are plenty accounts of this in his poetry; particularly in verses concerning two characters from his poetic universe: the spouses Enitharmon and Los, stand–ins for Blake and Katherine themselves, as we can infer by their characterisation. In fact, Blake's characters often personify faculties or properties of the soul, and as such, in this role distribution, Los corresponds to Poetry, Enitharnon to "Spiritual Beauty". In addition, Los –the Poet– illustrates his poems with drawings that are then coloured by Enitharnon, a process also followed by Blake and his wife. If you still have any doubts, I can tell you that scholiasts have highlighted how "Enitharmon" is composed from the last two syllables of the word "Katherine".

Enitharmon is described as Los' sister and wife, his split half: "*his parted soul*". Enitharmon and Los are merely a couple of mortal spouses now but, before the Fall, the integrated a heavenly marriage, an androgynous being of a spiritual nature called Urthona. Urthona is only one of its names; in Blake's strange and beautiful poetic universe (which is, at the same time, a mythological universe), the original Androgyne corresponding to each couple of "*parted souls*" receives a different name, which evokes the Sufi notion of the infinite Names of God. But let's move on to the general subject of Blake's work, a vast and complex subject which here we can only outline.

For Blake, the Man of the Origin was no different from God, the "Eternal One" as he called Him. That "divine Man" was androgynous: two complementary halves existed in Him in intimate union. And this union was so tight, Blanca, so compact, so *perfect*, that it could not be said to have two wills but a single one: the Will of the "eternal Man", resulting of that *perfect union*. The basis for that balance, for that complete Unit, consisted of the two divine halves' rejection of their separate individuality, that is, their *ego*. Both sacrificed their individual will to that higher common Will that was their "*real Self*". But selfishness, which Blake personified in the figure of the Devil, interfered with that idyllic state of affairs. Each half of the "eternal Man" began to exert their own will, leading to the disappearance of the common Will, which was the Divine Will. As a result, the two halves separated from one another, thus becoming shadows or spectres of Themselves. In "shadows" or "spectres" –I'm using Blake's terminology– of their "real Self", which was the now fallen "eternal Man". In this event, Blake sees a tragedy of cosmic proportions. Because the "eternal Man", my love, was the cosmic Man: it encompassed all reality inside him. (You once told me about the "cosmic conscience", the ecstatic feeling some people felt of being one with the Universe; of engaging in introspection, let's say, when they look up to the sky. Well, then, this feeling would be but the pale trace of the Cosmic Man we all were in the Origin.)

The characters from Blake's poetic–mythological universe are the half souls, the "parted souls" resulting from the "eternal Man's" collapse (since while the "eternal Man" was one, the split halves are innumerable). Characters such as Urizen, who, astonished, contemplates Ahania, his split half, for the first time. He beholds "Her shadowy form now Separate he shudder & was silent... Two wills they had two intellects & not as in times of old."[400] Or likewise, the afore-

400. William Blake, *The Four Zoas*, Night the second, E, 320; K, 285.

mentioned Los, stand-in for the poet himself, who after the Fall laments: "What shall I do! or how exist, divided from Enitharmon?"[401], and reminisces with his wife and sister about those happy times "where thou & I in undivided Essence walkd about Imbodied. Thou my garden of delight & I the spirit in the garden Mutual there we dwelt in one anothers joy revolving..."[402] The poet Los lives in yearning for the day when they once again will "reunite in those mild fields of happy Eternity"[403].

The plot weaving all those characters together is intricate, but it can be summed up by their heroic struggle to recover their lost Unity through the unification with their other self. This struggle involves the abolishment of selfish will: that is to say, stripping their "*false garments*", as Blake calls the *ego*. Which entails the sublimation of sexual identity, Blanca, since, for Blake too, the Fall happened following the degradation of love into sexual desire. For Blake, sexuality is consubstantial to the fallen state. The redemption of such state demands, then, the restoration of the original "nudity" to desire: meaning, to delve into the mutual love between twin souls down to its very root. "Why a little curtain of flesh -one of these "parted souls" asks- on the bed of our desire?"[404]

That is the core of Blake's work. This work forms a coherent whole, but it's dense and abstruse and, in this sense, very different from his Romantic coreligionists. Very different, for example, from the work of René de Chateaubriand,

401. William Blake, *Jerusalem* 12: E, 155; K, 631.
402. William Blake, *The Four Zoas* VIIa; E, 359; K, 327
403. *Ibid*, E, 359; K, 326
404. William Blake, *The Book of Thel*, 4: 20

author of a novel – *René* – that tells the story of a young man who is secretly in love with his sister. She is "the only person in the world that I loved, that all my feelings were compounded in her with the sweetness of childhood memories." Again, Blanca, we see childhood become (a common childhood, a childhood where we "often fell asleep together") a heavenly referent for the two siblings. And I say for the two of them because it's a reciprocal love. But also a secret love that must not be revealed; a love riddled with feelings of guilt that, at the end, will compel the sister to take her vows in a convent. René attends the ceremony: she had asked him to come in a letter where she allows herself to be carried away by the nostalgia for their happy childhood days, "At night, in the depths of my cell, I will hear the murmur of the waves bathing the convent walls; I will think of the walks I took with you in the woods, when we thought to discover the sounds of the sea in the agitation of the pine trees' summits. Kind companion of my childhood, shall I see you no more? Scarcely older than you I rocked you in your cradle; we often fell asleep together. Oh, if only the one grave would reunite us some day!"

Let's take a look now at another great English Romantic poet. Probably (although that is a matter of taste) the greatest of them all: Percy B. Shelley, who, as he confessed, dreamt of a "veiled maid" whose voice "was like the voice of my own soul"[405]. To express this dream, Shelley also made use of the metaphor of incestuous love between siblings. Siblings are (no matter how much his editor censored this kinship by turning them into stepbrother and sister) the protagonists of his famous poem *Laon and Cythna*. Laon describes Cythna

405. Percy B. Shelley, *Alastor*, 151–153

as "a second self, far dearer and more fair." They both need to be together at all times; they are incapable of thinking of themselves as autonomous individuals: the individual is the conjunction of the two. When he looks in the mirror, Laon (as it happened with Pausanias' Narcissus, as I told you) he does not see Laon, he sees Cythna. To such degree that when she is away, he loses the referent of his own identity and, consequently, becomes sick and loses his balance.

The two siblings' self-confessed goal is to "blend two restless frames in one reposing soul". In short, they seek Androgyny, Unity, which for Shelley was the same as Divinity and eternal rest. By being committed to the cause of Liberty, Shelley's personal goal blends with a political goal: Laon and Cythna participate in the conspiracy to topple a tyrant. But this, Blanca, can also be seen as an allegory for the personal goal. In the dangerous adventures in which their political commitments involve them, we can see a parallel with the medieval heroes' Quest; the tyranny against which they are fighting could be seen as a metaphor for that other cosmological tyranny: the tyranny of Matter, of split Duality. The legitimate order that, along with the Freedom such order entails, Laon and Cythna fight to restore would be, metaphorically speaking, Androgyny... Halfway through the poem, the two siblings dramatise, through a matrimonial rite, the achievement of this yearned for goal. But Shelley knows that only death will open the door to the real achievement, because at the end of the poem he seems to emulate Byron's *Sardanapalus*: Laon is captured and sentenced to be burned to death, and Cythna joins him voluntarily. They burn in the pyre, but also –as Shelley says– in the fire of their mutual love. By bringing them together in the merging fire, the tyrant accomplishes the exact opposite of what he wanted, since Laon and

Cythna's death supposes their triumph, the triumph of their predestined love over the tyranny of Matter and split Duality. Like the Phoenix, Laon and Cythna rise from their ashes transformed into Laon–Cythna, another one of the divine Androgyne's innumerable Names.

Shelley was very close friends with Bryon and, like him, led a hectic life. The girl he married when he was a young man committed suicide by throwing herself into a lake when he left her for another woman. This other woman would be remembered –by the name of Mary W. Shelley– as the creator of a literary character that unsettled many generations of readers and spectators: Frankenstein's monster. After getting married, the couple travelled to Italy, where their love cooled, and where –shortly before drowning, like his first wife– the poet seemed to come across the "veiled maid" of his dreams. This woman in whom Shelley believed to have recognised the voice that was "like the voice of [his] own soul" (although, as we know, recognition is fallible, and so this familiar voice could very well have been Mary W. Shelley's voice, or his first wife's) was called Emilia Viviani and was a young aspiring writer. In an autobiographical poem with an almost unpronounceable title: *Epipsychidion*, Shelley writes, "I knew it was the Vision veiled from me So many years – that it was Emily."[406] The preface for this poem includes a text by Emilia Viviani, taken from a short treatise of hers –*True Love*– in which the young lady displays a complete understanding of the ideal of love of her mentor and lover, an ideal supported by two pillars. The first one, the human need for restoring the original Androgyne, the "double being" that each person integrated in the Origin, when

406. Percy B. Shellley, *Epipsychidion*,

they were *perfectly united* to their "second self". The second one, the power of refined love as the only power capable of answering that spiritual need for merging two "identical but different beings in a happy ending". In those verses, Shelley addresses Emilia as though she is his wife and sister, the "sister of my heart". "I'm not thine –he tells her–, I am a part of thee."[407] And he traces a parallel with a musical composition: "We — are we not formed, as notes of music are. For one another, though dissimilar."[408] By imagining Paradise, by imagining the state resulting from the final reunification with Emily after death, Shelley evokes an idyllic life on a desert island: there, they would be "conscious, inseparable, One."[409] There, "to love and live, [would] be one"[410]

> The fountains of our deepest life, shall be;
> Confused in passion's golden purity,
> As mountain-springs under the morning Sun.
> We shall become the same, we shall be one
> Spirit within two frames, oh I wherefore two?
> One passion in twin-hearts...[411]

There is another philosophical poem by Shelley –*Prometheus Unbound*– in which the theme of two twin souls yearning for reunification takes a prominent position. Except that, in this case, the characters are not beings of flesh and blood: they are –like Blake's characters– mythological beings. Prometheus wistfully reminisces about the old days,

407. *Ibid*
408. *Ibid*
409. *Ibid*
410. *Ibid*
411. *Ibid*

when he "wandered once with Asia, drinking life from her loved eyes". The word "life" here should be understood not in a biological sense, Blanca, but in the symbolic sense the ancient sages assigned to it when they talked, for example, about the Fountain or Tree of Life. That is to say, *eternal life*, Life as a synonym for Immortality, Divinity, Unity. In the old days, then –in the Origin, when the Two were One–, Prometheus and Asia were reciprocally infused in the One: because the One was the fruit of their union.

That paradisiacal state of affairs, though, belongs now to the past. Prometheus and Asia are currently separated, they no longer drink *eternal life* from each other's eyes. But they long for those days and can think of nothing else but reunification. A reunification that will not come from a sexual union, but from a spiritual one. From the union of the souls, Blanca, since Shelley –as so many other Romantic poets– distrusted sexual love, which he considered selfish and therefore false. He despised the *ego* ("that burr that gets stuck to one; I have not been able to pull it out yet") and he was dedicated to the task of stripping it away from his soul. A task he had in common, as we have seen, with all the heroic lovers throughout time.

And that's it. With Shelley, we will close the chapter dedicated to Romanticism (although we will reopen it in the next letter). Now, my dear, prepare yourself to take a great leap backwards in time.

PRIMITIVE TWINS

Figurines depicting Siamese twins have been dated back to the Neolithic and the Bronze Age. This confirms a well-known fact; that along with androgynous beings, couples of twins abound in primitive societies' "creation myths". Not only the creator God, but the first created men as well –the mythic ancestors of humanity– are a couple of twins of the opposite sex (or rather an Androgyne). In another letter, I mentioned these mythical ancestors, which are not like the historical men that descended from them. These first created men, equivalent to the Bible's Adam and Eve, inhabit the unhistorical time of the Origin, and display Divinity's specific characteristic: Androgyny, being Twins, reason for which they were worshiped as gods.

They were considered gods, Blanca, and yet they were not identified with supreme Divinity. How can this be explained? Easily, if we think that, in primitive times, while Androgyny was considered to be a monopoly of the Divine, the Divine was not supposed to be a monopoly of one single God. They did not see the Divine as something unitary, concentrated on one supreme God, but rather as a characteristic that the supreme God shared, in different degrees, with a large cohort of subordinate gods, of minor gods, our mythic ancestors among them. In the early days of humanity, we still had not arrived at the ancient sages' intuition that there is only *one* divine being. Neither had we intuited its logical consequence: that the mythic androgynous –and therefore divine– ancestor of humanity, is none other than God Himself, the Only One... Let's take a look at some examples of mythic ancestors characterised by their Twin kinship.

Indo-European mythology mentions the story of Yama (literally "twin"), a deity that, at the dawn of time, descended to the rank of man accompanied by Yami, his twin sister and wife. The myth claims that historic human beings are the descendants of this couple of divine twins, known in Iranian mythology by Yima and Yimak. But this is not the only Iranian myth concerning the creation of man that involves a couple of twins, Blanca: there is also the myth of Mahryag and Mahryanag, where the creation of man is described in several stages, in which we can observe the downwards progression of the Fall. The protagonist of this myth is Gayomart, the essential Man, created as a high-ranking god, as he was a "double being", an androgynous being. But the demon Ahriman managed to sneak death into him, and thus Gayomart, who had been created as an immortal, became mortal, meaning, a man.

So then, when the time came, he died. But that's when his soul was rescued by Spenta Armaiti, the Archangel of the Earth, who kept it in her bosom for forty years, "at the end of which time an extraordinary plant germinated from the 'soil'; this plant formed the first human couple, Mahryag-Mahryanag, two beings so like one another, so closely united with each other, that the male could not be distinguished from the female, much less isolated."[412] The male and the female were then implicit in the first human being, who thus preserved the Androgyny of Divinity. But this privileged situation could not last from the moment the demon Ahriman sneaked into Gayomart, the precursor of Mahryag-Mahryanag, the mortal and human condition. (Are you following me?) So that, after some time struggling between his original and divine condition and the human condition forced upon him, Mahryag-Mahryanag saw the latter triumph. His internal Duality became explicit: Mahryag-Mahryanag split into Mahryag and Mahryanag, two separated twins. And, in tandem, the male and the female became different from each

412. Henry Corbin, *Spiritual Body and Celestial Earth*, p. 47

other, they became explicit. And that is, Blanca, according to this intricate Iranian myth, the origin of sex. The sexual union between Mahryag and Mahryanag emanates the historical and fallen humanity, the humanity of today, whose individuals are characterised by being half halves.

In the African continent, we can also find twin kinship linked to the myths of creation. You will remember that in another letter we talked about Nummu, the mythic ancestor of the Dogon people in West Africa. Up until the 40's, in this century, the Dogon creation myth remained a mystery to foreigners. Now we know that Nummu was created by the supreme God Amma as an Androgyne integrated by a couple of twins of the opposite sex. This "double being" divined that the human beings who succeeded him would not be as lucky: lucky to be born, like him, with two souls rather than a single one; lucky to be born twined, as a couple. They would be born alone and, therefore, they would be unbalanced: they would be like half halves; they would not be whole. Nummu, then, decided to do something about it, and so he took advantage of his magical knowledge. As humans were born, he made them lie down on a drawing depicting a double man, a man and a woman united into one single being. This way, he granted each one their missing soul. Since that among the Dogon, Blanca –but also among other African peoples–, Integrity, Unity, is the union of Two, while individuality is an imperfection, an ontological anomaly that must be corrected to the extent possible. How? Through matrimony. But also in a symbolic manner, through rituals.

A VACANCY IN BED

Anyway, Blanca, as I hope to have sufficiently demonstrated at this stage, the belief in the essential duality of the soul –the belief that the balanced and health state of the human being is, let's say, to be in possession of two souls –is not exclusive to primitive societies. Neither is it restricted to the ancient sages: more than a few modern sages share it. Modern sages of an "ancient perspective", as Henry Corbin, who thought, "the true way of being of the soul is not in solitude but as a being-in-Duality"[413]. Or C. G. Jung, father of "depth psychology"... Depths into which we will now delve. And we will do so hand in hand with Jung, in accordance with his findings; but without ever renouncing our own point of view, the one brought to us by the theory of twin souls. We may even feel encouraged to do it by Jung himself, when he wrote, "But I do not imagine for a moment that the psychological interpretation of a mystery must necessarily be the last word."[414] And the thing is that although Jung's field of study was the *psyche*, Blanca, for him this concept transcended the narrow definition most of his colleagues attributed it. Same as for the ancient Greeks who coined the term, for Jung the *psyche* was, strictly speaking, the *soul*; it was directly related, then, to the scope of the Sacred and the Metaphysical.

Through his medical practice as a psychologist, Jung's mystic intuition uncovers in the human soul what we could pretentiously call a "sexual structured duality", or a "structural androgyny". That is to say, two aspects of the opposite sex. This duality of the soul corresponds to another double

---

413. Henry Corbin, translated from *El Hombre y su Angel*, p. 63
414. C.G. Jung, *Mysterium Coniunctonis*, p. 173

aspect that his mentor Sigmund Freud had discovered in the *psyche*: the conscious/unconscious duality. Which means, Blanca, that in this sense, the human soul is unbalanced: one of its two sides is "filled" with consciousness while the other one is "empty"... Let's employ a metaphor. A metaphor that evokes that image to which we referred in another letter: the "bridal bed" from esoteric tradition. Let's say that the human being's current soul, an individual soul, is resting on a double bed, a couple's bed. Just like the bed, the soul has two sides. But only one is occupied, only one is conscious. However, we can suppose that the empty side of the bed was not originally vacant, in its origin, both sides were occupied...

In the debate over the fate of the lost half of the soul, Jung supports the "psychological hypothesis": the loss half is a inhibited half, unconscious; so it's a question of making it blossom, placing it under the spotlight of consciousness; and this is achieved through a psychic process he calls "individuation". Despite all this, Blanca, from our privileged watchtower, which is the theory of the twin souls, we can conjecture that the vacant half of the soul is but the "emptiness" left by its twin, by its other self, upon separating from it following the Fall. In fact, another one of Jung's findings seemed to support this hypothesis. Well, if the half soul that holds our identity is the "occupied" half, Jung tells us that the "vacant" half has, in its unconscious way, its own identity as well. For the moment, it has a sexual identity: it's of the conscious self's opposite sex; it's man or woman. But not only that, Blanca: it's also *a specific type* of man or woman, a different type in each individual.

Jung stops here. But there is nothing preventing us from going farther. We can conjecture: and what if it was not just a specific type of man or woman? What if, in reality, it was a specific man or woman? Because if the bed's vacancy, if that sort of "emptiness" of consciousness, has an identity, then from the point of view of our theory that is very telling: it denotes that the empty side of the bed was once occupied. You will agree with me, Blanca, that the solitude of someone who has always been alone is not the same as the solitude of someone (like me) who once had company. In both cases, there is an empty space on the bed. Ah, but how different that empty space is! On the bed of the person who has always been alone, that vacancy has no face, while on the bed that was once shared, the vacancy has a face, an identity... I repeat the experiment every night: I slide my hand towards your side of the bed, and what do I find? A hollow. In other words, in reality, that empty space is *an absence*, Blanca: *your* absence. That face, that identity is like the "ghost" of someone who is absent, someone with whom we shared our bed for years before they left us, but someone whose memory remains latent, whose perfume still permeates the sheets.

(At least in my case, this last part is not a metaphor. Right now I can smell, I believe I can smell, your perfume. But only while I'm writing to you, and so, foreseeing the end of these letters, I would like to reiterate my old question: your perfume, what was it called? I keep your childhood smells like a treasure, your fragrancy collection that you patiently gathered throughout the years: incense, rose water, fennel, the lavender your mother put in little envelopes between your clothes, homemade soap, the colognes and perfumes, boxwood, varnish, printer ink, essence of jasmine, your grandfather's pipe tobacco...; the entire odoriferous museum of your youth, with their carefully labelled little bottles. But, silly me, I did not have the basic foresight of keeping a bottle of your perfume. In search of that fragrance, I scoured every perfume shop in town in vain. Once, in the middle of the human tide of the Ramblas, I smelled it for a moment. I was about to shout, "Stop! Nobody move!", just like a robber, can you imagine that?)

I was telling you that perfume, or that concavity in bed, is like the "ghost" of an absent person. Well, Jung calls this ghost of a woman present in the soul of every man *anima*; *animus* is the ghost of a man present in every woman. In light of the theory of the twin souls, the *anima* or the *animus* would be the reminiscence, the remains left in the soul by the spouse from the Origin as a result of its departure. (Although our spouse had no sexual nature in the Origin, its "ghost" does: the conscious self will inevitably sexualise it, because he or she is sexualised, and in this world, erotic love operates under a sexual key.) This "ghost" can appear in our dreams, Blanca; the expression "the woman –or the man– of my dreams" would be an allusion to it. Because dreams, my dear (as you may very well know; it has not been long since you slipped into one of mine), are not necessarily the usual banal and inconsequential dreams that serve as an outlet for the worries of waking life. When one pays close attention, dreams can become windows with a view to the backyard of reality, of hidden reality... In his medical practice as a psychologist, Jung often came across patients whose dreams where populated by such "ghost": the *anima* or the *animus*. But don't worry, I will not use one of Jung's clinical cases as an example. The example will be provided by a tenant from your library...

Two years after the death of Samuel L. Clemens, better known by the pen name Mark Twin, an already a world famous writer, a brief essay he had written a few years prior came to light and surprised his friends and family and everyone else. He titled it My *Platonic Sweetheart*, and, in it, he talked about what he believed to be a recurrent subject of his dreams: a girl, always the same one despite the changes in her appearance, whom he called "*my Dreamland sweetheart*". Although that epithet may probably remind you of the secret fairy kingdom, my dear, for Twain the Dreamland is the world in which you live now: the spirit world, where souls go after their bodies die, but also where they sometimes go during sleep. He considered that world much realer than the one down here, where "we go about awake and clothed with our artificial selves", he wrote. That superior reality of the Other World manifests itself (and his description agrees, to an astonishing degree, with those by astral explorers such as our friend Swedenborg) through the extraordinary vivacity of the colours and definition of shapes, next to which the earthly colours are dim and the shapes blurred.

Twain dreamt about his "Dreamland sweetheart" for the first time when he was nineteen years old, and he kept sporadically dreaming about her from then on –around once every two years, he said. Sometimes, the duration of the dream allowed him to enjoy such sweet company, but usually they were more like fleeting glimpses: "Mainly these were glimpses, but she was always immediately recognizable, notwithstanding she was so given to repairing herself and getting up doubtful improvements in her hair and eyes." Twain claimed he did not know this girl in his waking life; but in Dreamland, they were old friends, although they knew each other there by different names. In that first dream, for example, she called him George and he called her Alice, and those were the names by which they knew each other in some other time, as it felt natural to them to be addressed by them. She was fifteen years old, he was seventeen, and that's how it was throughout the entire series of dreams, where time does not pass. Another constant was the class of love they both professed, a love that "was not the affection of brother and sister--it was closer than that, more clinging, more endearing, more reverent; and it was not the love of sweethearts, for there was no fire in it. It was somewhere between the two, and was finer than either, and more exquisite, more profoundly contenting."[415] (We would be hard pressed to find a better definition of the type of love between twin souls.)

A variable in these dreams, however, is the space-time framework in which they take place. The one in ancient Athens is particularly remarkable, "a city which I had not then seen, but I recognized the Parthenon from the pictures, although it had a fresh look and was in perfect repair." He walks by it on his way to a palatial mansion of red terra cotta, where he meets his beloved, who is dressed in a Greek costume and is sitting on an ivory settee doing crochet work. While they have a friendly conversation, several Greeks of a majestic demeanour enter the room having a heated discussion, they greet them courteously as the pass by them. Among them, the dreamer recognises Socrates...

Although some of these dreams end abruptly with the girl's death, Twain observes that the tragedy has no impact on their next encounter, as if they were accustomed -he conjectures- to death and rebirth, thus knowing, by their own experience, that death is not forever, so there is nothing to worry about. To conclude his essay, Twain confesses that this recurring dream had been one of the most beautiful and pleasant experiences of his life. But there is a detail he omits,

---

415. Mark Twain, *My Platonic Sweetheart*

Blanca, a detail his biographers revealed and that I'm sure will be of your interest...

We have reasons to believe that, a few years after meeting his twin soul in dreams, he met her in real life as well. He was twenty years old and she was fourteen; he was a pilot of one of those steamboats that ploughed through the Mississippi; she was travelling on another boat, and they met on a dock in New Orleans. Twain himself describes the encounter in his posthumous *Autobiography*: he says it did not take him even a second to recognise Laura Wright as his "instantly elected sweetheart". They only spent a few hours together, during which they merely chatted and strolled. But as they said goodbye, she gave him a golden ring, and he went back home determined to ask for her hand in marriage in two years' time, when she would be sixteen. Unfortunately, they were not allowed to marry. But all their lives, they kept an indelible memory of those hours they spent together, and a profound mutual affection that only recently the literary detectives are bringing to light. What happens, Blanca, is that those inquiries are revealing that the mysterious girl that inhabited Mark Twain's dreams may have been the same girl that inhabited his waking fantasies ever since that day on the dock, when they were young and he was a steamboat pilot on the Mississippi, and she gave him a golden ring as a loving gift.

Maybe the separation from his twin soul in this life only managed to reinforce the unconscious feeling of loss caused by their original traumatic split, of which that recurring dream would be a compensatory mechanism. Because what Mark Twain calls "my Dreamland sweetheart", my dear, is possibly no different from the mysterious maiden who carried the Grail in the castle of the Fisher King, and who also appeared as if in a dream. It was his *anima*. That is –in light of our theory–, the "ghost" of his absent twin soul. A ghost summoned by his nostalgia.

Crossed–out note on the margin. The marker pen, in a rush, instead of striking through, highlighted the only word on this note: *polyhedron*. As I have done in previous crossed–out notes, where I speculated about the meaning of the quotations, I wanted to sound out this word's possible link with the question the author recently posed his wife, and I have discovered a perfume called *Polyédre* that has not been manufactured for a few years now. But, contrary to the author's presumption (read the ending of the first letter), linden blossom is not part of that perfume's composition.

The *anima*, then, would be something like the ghost that inhabited the mind of a man who was abandoned by a woman with whom he had been very happy. That ghost can impregnate not only his dreams: in a subconscious manner, it will also impregnate his waking hours. To the point that his amorous relationships will be impacted by the nostalgia for that woman: involuntarily, he will tend to fall in love with women that in some way remind him of her. And now I just thought of a film that will help us illustrate this, a film by Alfred Hitchcock that we saw when it came out and then watched again many times on television, Blanca. I'm talking about *Vertigo*. You will remember that the character played by Kim Novak dies, and for her lover, James Stewart, her image becomes something like an icon of the feminine. Like a composite picture he carries in secret, hidden in the most intimate depths of his heart, in his subconscious. Which reminds me (I'm hopping from one example to another, please forgive me) of a sentence in Gustave Flaubert's *Sentimental Educational*, that turquoise blue book, "He related to her (to Madame Arnoux) how melancholy broodings had haunted him at college, and how *a woman's face shone brightly in the cloudland of his imagination*, so that, when he first laid eyes upon her, he felt that her features were familiar to him."[416]

See, Blanca? Frederick also treasures in his heart a composite portrait of his twin soul. We can presume that, before meeting Madame Arnoux, the first thing Frederick did when he met a woman was to unconsciously measure her against that portrait. And that's what happens to James Stewart. The unconscious portrait of Kim Novak is equivalent to the crystal shoe the prince from the story tries on every woman he encounters. Naturally, Stewart's subconscious must abstract itself from the human condition of these women to appreciate their eventual resemblance to the portrait. So just like Cinderella's shoe is splendid (and so, for that reason, the prince must not take into account her impoverished appearance to recognise her), the portrait is of a goddess. In case you haven't noticed, the portrait is the same (although the portrayed person is different) that the enraptured prince Tamino contemplated at the beginning of *The Magic Flute*, and over which he formulated the ultimate objective of his heroic Quest: "I feel as if this angelic picture were filling my heart with a new emotion. This something I cannot name, but I feel it burning here. Can this sensation be love? Yes, yes! This can only be love. Oh, if only I might find her! If only she stood before me! I would –would warmly – chastely – what would I do? I would, in ecstasy, press her to my ardent heart, and she would be mine forever!"

416. Gustave Flaubert, *Sentimental Education*, p. 359

The divine image James Stewart secretly carries in his heart, Blanca, is none other than *his* Sophia, the true object of every man's love, according to Jakob Boehme. When Stewart abstracts a woman's human condition, and his subconscious recognises in her *his* Sophia, he will become irresistibly attracted to that woman. And we would not be able to tell why that woman attracts him with such power if we did not know the beautiful love story in his past: we would ignore that, among every woman, James Stewart is looking for one in particular; Kim Novak, the woman in the portrait, the owner of the crystal shoe.

So it goes with the human soul: we are not looking blindly for a spouse; even without being aware of it, we are following the trail of our twin soul. To recognise it, we each have half of a *symbolon*, its composite portrait, let's say: the *anima* or *animus*. The soul –which in its eternal quality knows how to abstract temporary attributes–, is attracted by the souls that have a certain resemblance to that portrait. In addition, since each one has its particular *anima* or *animus*, each one has its own ideal spouse. That ordinary phrase: *He/she is not my type*, would turn out to mean: "He/she does not resemble the portrait I keep in my soul". It's only when it indeed resembles the portrait, Blanca, that we risk erroneously recognising our twin soul. But when the resemblance is total, when we come across not just a similar soul, *but the original person in the portrait*, then the heart will not fool us. And that encounter is in reality an appointment: it's inscribed in what Jung calls *synchronicity*, which is the coincidence produced when a psychic incident –an inner image of a woman– agrees with an objective incident in the outer reality –a flesh and blood woman we might see on the street or, say, on a yellow tram like those that ran in Barcelona years ago.

THE GREAT WORK

C.G. Jung discerned a very close link between his discovery of the soul's sexual polarity and an ancient technique or art with a high symbolic content, which the Arabs, borrowing a Greek word, baptised as Alchemy.

There were alchemists, before anywhere else, in China, in Syria, and in Egypt; and only then –from the Middle Ages to the Baroque– practically in every European city. But I know, my love, that in your specific case, saying Alchemy is like evoking Prague's Golden Lane, that narrow street of little brightly coloured houses that you thought looked like doll houses, where legend says that King Rudolf II kept a cohort of alchemists working hard in search of the Philosopher's Stone... But is that what Alchemy is really about? The search for a stone? Obviously not, Blanca. It's the same as with the Grail: the physical object is a symbol for something higher. One of Jung's books –one of the most exhaustive on the subject–, as its title highlights, is about Alchemy. It's titled, in Latin, *Mysterium Coniuctionis*, that is to say, the "Mystery of *Coniuctio*", of the Conjunction, of the Union, of the Marriage. Every work was striving towards that goal. Naturally, you will be intrigued to know who the spouses were. I will tell you: they were the two separated halves of the human soul. And they gave birth to a son –the "Real Son", the "Son of Wisdom" or the "Philosopher's Son" – whom we know very well, my dear, as it's the Androgyne, also known to the alchemists by a Latin word that, appropriately, is the result of the conjunction of two others: *Rebis*, *Res+bis*, the "Double Thing".

In the alchemy texts, this *Rebis* is often embodied by the figure of a child: the "Divine Child" or the "Perfect Child" or "Hermaphrodite Child" (a child with both sexes), also called "Eternal Child" or *Infans Noster* ("Our Infant"), or Sun-and-Moon Child. "...the perfect state melts sponsu and sponsa into one figure, the sun-and-moon child"[417] writes Jung, who despite having interpreted the alchemical work from a psychological point of view, left the door open for interpretations of a different nature. In fact, he seems to go much further than such point of view when, near the end of his life, he claimed, "Somewhere, sometime, there was a Queen, a King, a Palace; a Loved Man and a Loved Woman, a long time ago, over the Sea, on an Island... It is Love, it is the Mystical Flower of the Soul, it is the Centre, it is the Self"[418]... But you are asking yourself, what island is this? This Island, my dear, is not a physical island; it's an ancestral symbol of Paradise, of the Hidden Point, which is, in fact, a kind of central paradisiacal island, an island of Unity in the middle of a tempestuous ocean of divorced Dualities. This is the island where Shelley imagined his eternal life resulting from his *perfect union* with Emilia Viviani taking place. It's the island of Ithaca, home of Ulysses and Penelope, as well as the Ionian island of Kythira, fief of the goddess of Love, Venus, where Brother Colonna placed the heavenly marriage of the dreamer Poliphilo. And it's also the island of Avalon from Celtic tradition. But, in the West, it's above all the secret "Fortunate Islands" that classic authors tell us about. And, in the East, the Island of the Jewel: a round and golden island with pulverised jewels covering its beaches in the place of sand (the beaches of Kythira imagined by Broth-

---

417. C.G. Jung, *Mysterium Coniunctonis*, p. 434

418. Jung, in conversation with Miguel Serrano, *El círculo hermético*, p. 99

er Colonna shined for the same reason) and where at the centre of which a golden palace stands.

To tackle the origins of Alchemy, Blanca, which is what I intend to do now, we should start by remitting to a previous letter. The one where we talked about primitive peoples and of how they felt the need to repair somehow the cosmic catastrophe that, in time immemorial, had ripped man away from the One, away from divine Integrity. If you remember, we mentioned then some of the symbolic procedures they idealised to accomplish said repair. Very well, now we can add this next procedure to our list: Alchemy. Its origin is then, as you can see, quite remote; it's linked to the discovery of the manipulation of metals: the appearance and development of smithery, a trade associated with the shaman, as both deal with fire –one with the forge, the other one with the Spirit (the alchemists would be dubbed the "the philosophers of Fire"). It's possible that the shamans that came before the first alchemists vaguely intuited that the Universe, headed by the human being, evolved. That it was moving somewhere, and that the destination of the Universe was none other than its own essence. This movement was a path of improvement, which for them was equivalent to a path of androgenisation, meaning, a search for Integrity. And they transferred this intuition to the field of metals. They discovered that, other than practical uses, metals could also have a symbolic use: they could represent man and his path of improvement. Among the metals, there were noble and perfect metals, such as gold; and vile and imperfect metals, such as lead. They saw lead as the image of the current man, imperfect due to his unilaterality, due to only having "one soul". While gold, the so-called "underground sun", appeared to them as the perfection of the original Androgyne. At the same time, they projected onto the middle metals the different phases of this path of improvement, since lead was destined –they imagined– to become gold through a slow natural process of maturation.

But take note, Blanca: these shamans/blacksmiths did not just vaguely intuited the path of the majority, the evolutive path back to the Origin. They also intuited –more importantly– the heroic path. They divined that such growth and refinement process, which in normal conditions could take tens of thousands of years, could be artificially accelerated. And, urged by the nostalgia for that lost bliss, they conceived a technique of metal manipulation that would allow them to accelerate –through fire– the natural process of lead's conversion into gold. That is to say, the natural conversion of man into God, through the Spirit. With the passing of the centuries, this technique or this art would lead to Alchemy, whose beginnings the Western ancient sages place in the Pharaoh's Egypt. They learned about it through the Arabs, and these through the Alexandrian alchemists from the first centuries of our era (but Alchemy blossomed in the Far East too). I told you already about Egypt's Hermes Trismegistus, considered to be the inventor of writing, the patron of libraries and hidden knowledge. These sages also placed Alchemy under his authority, thus making it the Magisterium or Art of Hermes, while everything relative to the Great Work –as alchemical work became known– adopted the cognomen "hermetic".

Alchemy is an eminently symbolic art. "Our gold is not ordinary gold", the alchemist warns. In fact, Blanca, their gold is called "live Gold" or "Philosopher's Gold", equivalent to the *Rabis*. The most precious of metals always held a symbolic value to the ancient sages. I will quickly mention that, for Ibn Arabi, gold was a symbol of the soul's innocence in the Origin. If we look back, we have seen gold repeatedly appear throughout these letters. For example, concerning the Origin or the primordial age of the world, described by classic tradition as the "Golden Age". The two cherubs on the Arc of the Covenant were cast in gold, as was the Grail cup and the crown of Solomon that vested Mystical Royalty. The sword of Chrysaor from Greek mythology, symbol of supreme spiritualisation, was a golden sword, and the cups and bowls the virgins of the Grail Kingdom served the blessed knights were also made of gold. The courtly lovers Gerart of Roussillon and Elisenda of Byzantium sealed their spiritual wedding with a kiss and a *golden* flower. And, finally, you are aware that the symbolism of this metal is often repeated in fairy tales. This symbolism derives from that of Light, my dear, since gold evoked crystallised light: it denoted, then, Divinity and the Spirit.

The transmutation of lead into gold... or, more accurately, the restoration of lead's true essence, which for alchemists was gold, entailed the reconversion of Matter into Spirit (which, by the way, is also what motivated those other alchemists, the Gothic builders, who were determined to liberate the walls of their weight and build them out of glass, thus converting stone into light, a winged substance). But the conversion of lead into gold, my love, included at the same time the transmutation of the split Two –man and woman– into the One or the divine Androgyne, a transmutation through which man would be reborn into Eternity. The architect of this miracle was the famous Stone of the sages, the "Philosopher's Stone"; eagerly sought by philosophers and adepts, two denominations the alchemists bestowed upon themselves. This mysterious Stone, as I told you, was eminently symbolic. It's true that the alchemists conducted operations in their laboratories; but the pretence of discovering an artificial stone that would transform metals was only a pretext. The operations' true nature was about projecting the human being's most intimate nostalgias and desires, particularly his nostalgia for Unity, the desire to join his two split souls. Jung explains that the adept (from the Latin *adeptus*, "he who has obtained"), "even when he spoke of the union of 'natures', or of an 'amalgam' of iron and copper, or of a compound of sulphur and mercury, he meant it at the same time as a symbol: iron was Mars (the male) and copper was Venus (the female), and their fusion was at the same time a love-affair."[419]

A HERMETIC LOVE-AFFAIR

In the symbolic art or technique that is Alchemy, my dear, we once again find the entire catalogue of motifs that appear throughout our letters. We have the motif of the purification or undressing of the soul. Because, as Jung points out: "gold comes into being only through the liberation of the divine soul or *pneuma* from the chains of the 'flesh'."[420] I have already mentioned that gold symbolised the original state of innocence of the soul. And since a few monks and nuns (such as your friend Sister Clara) have already paraded through these letters, and will perhaps continue to parade, let me also quickly tell you that when I walk by the lattice-work of a monastery or convent, I cannot help but think it's a secret alchemy laboratory where a team of alchemists

419. C.G. Jung, *Mysterium Coniunctonis*, p. 457
420. C.G. Jung, *Mysterium Coniunctonis*, p. 262

works hard to transform Spirit into Matter. Except that in principle, Blanca, they do it without the assistance of their "mystic sister", which is what alchemists called their twin soul... John Pordage, an English alchemist and theologian from the seventeenth century, could indeed count with the invaluable collaboration of his sister *in Spirit*, whom he lectured in a letter: "Mars, or the husband, must become a godly man, otherwise the purely Venus will take him neither into the conjugal nor into the sacred marriage bed. Venus must become a pure virgin, a virginal wife, otherwise the wrathful jealous Mars in his wrath-fire will not wed with her or live with her in union."[421]

Another exponent of the same is the following quote by a sixteenth century French alchemist, Jean d'Espagnet:

> Now that the progeny may be born more vigorous and active, let both the combatants be cleansed from every ill and spot, before they are united in marriage. Let nothing superfluous cleave unto them, because from pure seed comes a purified generation, and so the chaste wedlock of Sol and Luna shall be finished when they shall enter into combination, and be conjoined, and Luna shall receive a soul from her husband by this union; from this conjunction a most potent King shall arise, whose father will be Sol and his mother Luna.[422]

The alchemy texts expound on the undressing of the soul, Blanca..., but also on its inherent difficulties. Thus, in the anonymous treatise *Aquarium Sapientum*, we can read, "Man

---

421. John Pordage, quoted by C.G. Jung in *The Psychology of the Transference*, p. 136
422. Jean d'Espagnet, *The Secret Work of the Hermetic Philosophy*, 27

is placed by God in the furnace of tribulation, and, like the hermetic compound, is greatly afflicted by all kinds of hardships, various calamities and anxieties, until the old Adam and the flesh die, and rises again as a truly new man." But do you know what the alchemy texts talked about, most of all? They talked about the mutual love of the Two... And I saw this clearly in one of the first texts I read on Alchemy (on one of the first things I ever read on esoteric subjects, in fact). I still remember the joy I felt when I read in that first work – *La Vie quotidienne des alchimistes au Moyen Âge*423, by Serge Hutin – the following passage, "Through the union with his predestined companion, the alchemists regains the celestial androgynous state he lost following the original sin. He would be able recover Adam's immortality."[424] This passage set the detective in me on the trail of true Alchemy, Blanca, which is the Alchemy of feeling. Or at least it was so for a good number of alchemists, since we can also find among them a great variety of opinions regarding the lost half of the soul. (The *Coniuctio*, or –such as it was defined in the *Turba philosophorum*– the mystery of the union of the "two natures" of the human soul, has been frequently interpreted under the light of the "angelic hypothesis".) In any case, for our sages, the genuine element of Alchemy is erotic love. It's understandable, then, how important for the adept his *soror mystica*, his mystic sister was; a denomination that remits us, certainly, to other recurring motifs not only in our letters but also in Alchemy, in which the *Coniuctio* was often depicted as an incestuous union between a brother and a sister.

---

423. The daily life of alchemists in the Middle Ages
424. Serge Hutin, translated from *La vida cotidiana de los alquimistas en la Edad Media*, p. 148

The adept and his mystic sister: the architects of the Great Work. According to texts and prints, both collaborated closely on the works. In a textless book, consisting mainly of illustrations: in the *Mutus Liber* or "Mute Book" we can observe them hand in hand, working together to prepare the hermetic compound, heating up the furnace, stirring and watching the pot, operating the bellows to kindle the fire... It could not be in any other way, Blanca, seeing that in those alchemy works, the alchemist and his companion projected the heroic process of an amorous nature in which their souls were immersed. A process that the goal was the restoration of the androgynous Unit they originally integrated. "How good it is for two to inhabit one!", reads the *Aurora Consurgens*, one of the most notable medieval alchemy treatises. But I will refer to this text later. What I want to do now, is to trace the profile of an alchemist about whom you and I learned on our first trip to Paris. Yes, yes, don't you remember that little restaurant on the *rue de Montmorency* where we had dinner one night? It was called *Nicolás Flamel*, in honour of the building's old owner, the alchemist sage we will be talking about next.

Nicolás Flamel found what all his brothers were looking for but few obtained; the famous Philosopher's Stone. At least that's what he says in his *The Book of Hierogliphic Figures*, a book he redacted as a sort of guide to decipher the allegorical figures from the different phases of the Great Work, which he had painted on the arch of the Holy Innocent's Cemetery in Paris. The numerous biographical elements in it, added to an exhaustive investigation performed towards the end of the nineteenth century[425], allows us now to piece

425. Cf. Albert Poisson, *Nicolas Flamel, sa vie, ses fondations, ses oeuvres*, París, Biblioteca Chacornac, 1893

together his story. A story blending fact and legend that begins in Pontoise, near Paris, where he was born in 1330 in the bosom of a lower bourgeois family. He starts working very young as a scribe. Today there is no such trade anymore, Blanca, but at a time when most people were illiterate and the invention of the printing press was still one century away, you can see how it was a prosperous profession. At twenty years old, he marries Perrenella, a determining event in his life, as attested by the fact that she almost always appears alongside him in his surviving iconographic images.

Those images reproduce the original bas-reliefs carved in some tympanum of the numerous churches, hospitals and shelters funded by the alchemist throughout his life. In the portico of the Saint-Jacques-la-Boucherie Church, for example (to which his office was attached), a carver carved a relief of the happy couple praying at the feet of the Virgin. Because the hermetic laboratory included a small chapel, Blanca: the alchemists were pious people. In this sense, they stood out from the so-called *blowers*, the much more numerous spurious alchemists, whose search was material, who pursued only ordinary gold or the indefinite extension of life.

With time, Flamel expanded his little business of buying and selling books. And that's when, one day, a student walks into his office, intent on selling what he describes to us as "a gilded book, very old and large" and "the cover of it was of brass, well bound, all engraved with letters, or strange figures". He purchases the book on the spot, for it was not the first time he saw it: a few years before, an angel had showed it to him in his dreams. The first page was headed, in great and golden capital letters, by the following high-flown words: "Abraham the Jew, Prince, Priest, Levite, Astrologer, and

Philosopher, to the Nation of the Jews, by the Wrath of God dispersed among the Gauls, sendeth Health." This was followed by twenty-one leafs divided into folds of seven, and the leafs were made not of paper nor parchment, Blanca, but of rinds of tender young trees -therefore the book probably emitted one of those peculiar smells you liked so much... Although it was written in French, the text was riddled with strange characters, indecipherable to Flamel, who believed them to be letters from an ancient alphabet. Additionally, the last page of each fold contained symbolic images. For example, a rod with two intertwined serpents, known as "caduceus" or "staff of Hermes", the origin of which dates back to a hermetic legend that tells the story of how the Greek god Hermes found two serpents fighting and, with one touch of his golden staff, made them entwine around it and copulate instead of fighting. The staff of Hermes represents the reconciliation of opposites and is a symbol the Androgyne carries as a sceptre in alchemist treatises.

A first reading of the *Book of Abraham the Jew* shows Flamel that it is indeed an alchemy text, with the relevant experiments thoroughly recorded; and he enthusiastically applies himself to those works. But, no matter how scrupulously he follows the instructions, he fails to conclude them with any success. Suspecting he was working with the wrong raw material, he consults several scholars, but none is able to enlighten him. When almost all hope was lost, he commended himself to St. James, patron of Christian alchemists, and sets off on the St. James' Road, as I did not so long ago, towards Santiago de Compostela. He explains in his book that, apart from the pious purpose, he believed he could find in Spain a sage who could provide him with the key for the correct execution of the Great Work. And this is where the long awaited encounter took place. It happened on his way back, in a village in Leon, where Flamel befriends an old converted Jewish man (who knows, maybe he was an old disciple of Moses of Leon, the possible author of the Zohar!). Master Cánches, possibly Sánchez, proves to be familiar with the illustrations in the book, of which he owns a copy. He accepts Flamel's invitation to accompany him back to Paris, but he dies on the way. However, before passing, he tells the alchemist the key he was looking for. Faithful to the adept code of secrecy, Flamel does not specify what that key is, Blanca. But maybe we can infer it if we take a close look to an apparently trivial detail...

> Finally, I found that which I desired... knowing the preparation of the first Agents, and after following my Book according to the letter, I could not have missed it, though I would. Then, the first time that I made projection was upon Mercury, whereof I turned half-a-pound, or thereabouts, into pure Silver, better than that of the Mine, as I myself assayed, and made others assay many times. This was upon a Monday, the 17th of January, about noon, in my house, Perrenella only being present, in the year of the restoring of mankind, 1382. And afterwards, following always my Book, from word to word, I made projection of the Red Stone upon the like quantity of Mercury, in the presence likewise of Perrenella only, in the same house, the five and twentieth day of April following, the same year, about five o'clock in the evening; which I transmuted truly into almost as much pure Gold, better assuredly than common Gold, more soft and more pliable. I may speak it with truth, I have made it three times, with the help of Perrenella, who understood it as well as I, because she helped in my operations, and without doubt, if she would

have enterprised to have done it alone, she had attained to the end and perfection thereof.

Did you notice? Three times, he names his wife. She is present and she helps him with the operations, which contrasts with the description of his work before the pilgrimage to Compostela, when Flamel apparently worked alone (at the beginning, he hides from his wife the discovery of the book that will deeply affect their existence). This leads me to suspect, Blanca, that the key the alchemist had ignored at first, the fundamental ingredient missing from his mixture, was not mercury nor sulphur nor arsenic nor antimony... It was an ingredient that is quite tricky to find, but which fortunately had always been within his reach. It was his twin soul, Perrenella, "whom [he] loved –he tells us– as [himself]".

As I said, *Coniuctio* –the Conjunction, Union, Marriage– was the goal towards which every work was headed. Certainly, my dear, the *Coniuctio* attained by the most devoted couples of alchemists, did not go beyond a virtual union, an exchange of hearts. To take the next step, the real union, they would have to wait for death. "All there is left now is to wait for death, so Rebecca and I may begin our heavenly and eternal life", declares the alchemist Thomas Vaughan after the death of his wife and mystic sister. Nevertheless, what the texts are unequivocally referring to, is the real *Coniuctio*, heavenly marriage. That *Coniuctio* was sometimes figured as a chemical marriage in which the spouses were sulphur and mercury. Sometimes, as a planetary marriage or conjunction: then, the spouses were the Sun and the Moon. On other occasions still, they were depicted as a royal matrimony, a king and a queen. But regardless of whether their marriage was chemical, planetary, or real, Blanca, the true spouses were none other than the two split halves of the human soul: for us, the soul and its twin.

THE CONIUCTIO

Some alchemy texts from the Renaissance and the Baroque make veiled allusions to a secret ceremonial ritual performed by the adept and his mystic sister. According to scholars, it would be a kind of nuptial rite analogous to those practices by the Gnostics centuries before. This ceremony is also hinted at in the illustrations that accompany the text; like this engraving I'm showing you here that illustrates a Kabbalah and an Alchemy book (two intertwined subjects by then) published in Hapsburg in 1615.[426]

The mountain you are seeing is symbolic: it represents the "Mountain of the adept". A transversal cut of the mountain reveals a hidden temple, where the adept and his mystic sister celebrate a kind of nuptial rite. Behind them, we can see the alchemist's furnace or athanor, where they operated the Great Work. The temple is crowned by the Phoenix, an androgynous symbol of immortality, and can be accessed by climbing seven steps, each representing a stage of alchemical realisation. Now pay attention at those other couples who, also holding ritual objects, occupy the two sides of the mountain. Note that –unlike the central couple inside, who appear together– those other peripheral and outer couples are split: their two halves occupy opposite sides, and the higher they

426. Steffan Michelspacher, *Kabbalah, Mirror of Art and Nature in Alchemy*

are on the mountain, the shorter the distance between the adept and his mystic sister. The small figure standing on a pedestal is a little harder to discern precisely, but the caduceus or staff of Hermes it holds give it away: it's the Androgyne, the alchemists' totem.

Doesn't this illustration of the "Mountain of the adept", my dear, remind you of the other one we examined a few letters ago: by the Love's Faithful Francesco de Barberino? It's not unreasonable to confer it the same symbolism. It represents, then, the gradual ascension of couples of twin souls from their current split state to their primordial Unity. An ascension accelerated by the alchemical Work.

Crossed–out note on the margin. The black marker barely touched this short quotation: *el pas dels núvols blancs sobre el blau tendre* (the passing of white clouds over the tender blue). Thanks to that and to Josef Pla being mentioned in another letters, I was able to identify the source book: *Les hores* by Josef Pla.

In the *Coniuctio,* in heavenly marriage, the Two disappear only to subsequently reappear transformed into the One. This figures in the treatises for the death of the Two. At the time of the *Coniuctio*, the Two die and are buried together, before resuscitating in the form of the Androgyne or the One. Although it was the union of the souls, Blanca, the *Coniuctio* was often symbolised by the union of the bodies: "...and the fiery King –writes Basil Valentine, although that was not his real name, because most alchemists hid their true identity behind that pseudonym– and the fiery king will be seized with great love towards the Queen, and will take his fill of delight in embracing her, until they both vanish and coalesce into one body."[427] But the sexual imagery does not take away from the spiritual nature of the *Coniuctio*. The bridal chamber is a "Chaste Chamber"[428]. Only in chastity can the Two die as a Duality (as a split Duality) and be reborn as One (as an integrated Duality). Let's analyse this passage from *Aurora Consurgens*: "Therefore, will I arise and go into the city, seeking through the streets and broad ways, 'a chaste virgin to espouse'... that she may roll back the stone from the door of my sepulchre and give me wings like a dove, and I will fly with her into heaven and then say 'I live forever,' and will rest in her."[429]

The chaste adept seeks to marry a "chaste virgin"; only such marriage will lead to the *perfect union*, to the union capable of "rolling back the stone of his sepulchre": meaning, of resurrecting the One. This unification is symbolised by the flight of the soul and its twin into "heaven" – into Paradise, into the One–, a flight for which they provided each other with wings. Only the union with the "chaste virgin" can make the adept be reborn into *eternal life* ("I live forever"), conceived as an eternal rest that the twin souls united in the One confer each other. In the same text, the wife defines herself in relation to her spouse in the following manner, "I am the crown wherewith my beloved is crowned."[430] What this means, is that through their heavenly marriage, she will infuse him with Royalty, and vice-versa. Royalty, Blanca, is, as we know, an ancient symbol of Unity, of Divinity; and it's remarkable that in antiquity and in different cultures all

---

427. Basil Valentine, *The Twelve Keys*, Sixth key
428. Sir George Ripley, *Cantilena, George Ripley's Song*, XV
429. *Aurora Consurgens*, Parable XII
430. *Ibid*, p. 141

around the world, marriage was linked to Royalty. A classical marital rite is the double coronation of the newlyweds. Even today, in the Greek marriage rite, the bride and groom touch each other with crowns. In Jewish weddings too, the newlyweds were honoured as a king and queen, as it can be observed in the Song of Songs: "Go out, O daughters of Zion, and look upon King Solomon, with the crown with which his mother crowned him on the day of his wedding, on the day of the gladness of his heart." (Song 3:11).

And speaking of the Song of Songs, Blanca, we have already seen that, according to the esoteric interpretation, the spouses from the Song find themselves on a heroic Quest for Unity through each other. That is why the alchemy texts often use King Solomon and the Queen of Sheba (as well as Adam and Eve) as the prototype of a couple of twin souls. Thus, in *Regulae et canones* by Penotus, we can read, "Give her a husband that is fitting for her! She is the Queen of Sheba", which essentially means: Give her a husband that is fitting for her like the other half of a *symbolon*. The ideal husband for the Queen of Sheba is King Solomon, who is a foreigner to her from a nationality point of view, but not in a spiritual sense. To marry him, she embarked on a long journey (her story is the opposite of Jaufré Rudel: in her case it's the woman who falls in love with a man she has never seen, and who then departs in search of her "faraway lover"). "For she the Queen of Sheba came from the uttermost parts of the earth to hear the wisdom of Solomon... has given herself to Solomon, and not to any other who is a foreigner..."[431] When it comes to erotic love, everyone in the world but King Solomon is a foreigner to the Queen of Sheba. She can feel

431. Penotus, *Regulae et canones*

it, and so she does not want to join anyone else in matrimony. The *Arca Arcanica* by Johanes Grasseus insists on this point: "She of the white veil (a bridal veil) is the chaste and rich Queen of Sheba, who wished to give herself to no one but King Solomon. No human heart is capable of fully understanding this."

Let's now take a look at a famous medieval alchemical treatise, the *Rosarium Philosophorum*, where the different stages of the Great Work are depicted in a series of illustrations. In the first one, we see the main couple dressed in royal regalia. They are destined to one another, as it's suggested by the each one of them holding a flowery branch, and a dove coming from above, holding another branch in its beak. The dove is shown with the text "the unifying Spirit". It represents God, then –and as such, Blanca, we once again see predestined love being ascribed a divine and heavenly filiation. The second illustration shows the same king and queen, although now they are naked. They have undressed their souls; therefore, their union is now possible. When the king asks the queen in marriage, she accepts. In the next image, we can see them in full copulation, in *Coniuctio*. To show that the nature of the intercourse is spiritual, the illustrator has drawn wings on the spouses. Finally, they both appear inside a tomb: their marriage also meant their death. However, that is not the end. From their dead bodies, a naked child ascends to Heaven: that is the fruit of their *Coniuctio*, the "Royal Son" or Hermaphrodite Infant, a symbol of the unified Two. Symbol of the One, of God.

Sometimes, Blanca, the alchemy texts involve a most curious symbolic fauna. Look at this example: "...the infant hermaphrodite, who is infected in his very cradle with the bite of the rabid Corascene dog, whereby he is maddened... Yet in the grove of Diana, there is a pair of doves, which assuage his raving madness... When the moon is at the full give him (the Corascene dog) wings and he will fly away as an eagle, leaving Diana's birds dead behind him"... No, it's not a joke, it's a real example: it comes from the *Introitus apertus* treatise, by the seventeenth century alchemist Eirenaeus Philalethes. Obscureness is typical of alchemy texts, it was a method employed by the authors to keep their knowledge away from the non-initiated. I would not understand a word, my dear, if it were not for scholars such as Jung, who, analysing this passage, clarified that "these doves form a pair – a love pair"[432]. Or if I did not remember that doves or turtledoves are an ancient symbol of conjugal love and chastity and (because doves mate for life, and if one dies the other one will never seek another mate) faithfulness beyond death. Or if I did not know –also because of Jung– that the texts usually pair the Corascene dog with the dog from Armenia, often depicting them in a reciprocal and poisonous bite, symbolising the dark side of love, meaning lust. From all this, Blanca, we can infer that the two doves are the twin souls before the Fall; and the two dogs are the same souls having fallen and been possessed by passions, by earthly trepidations, and in need of rising again, of transforming back into birds... And well, with this set of keys, we can venture to deconstruct the passage, to untangle its dense symbolism, which, if I'm not mistaken, would be this: The Hermaphrodite Infant from the Origin is "infected", that is to say, is sick, fallen. This infection is the split Duality: its two souls –the two doves– are divided, which causes him pain, it drives him mad with pain. The rabid dog that caused the infection with its bite,

432. C.G. Jung, *Mysterium Coniunctonis*, p. 157

embodies lust, the material and selfish love that infiltrated the One. The pain the Hermaphrodite Infant suffers can only be appeased when the infection –when the division of his Duality– remits: which can be achieved by the caresses of the doves. Such caresses represent the mutual spiritual love of the two birds, whom, upon virtually uniting, mitigate its separation and the pain of the split with it. The secret lies in "giving the Corascene dog wings"; meaning, in sublimating lust, in spiritualising love. With the real union, with the *Coniuctio*, separation and pain disappear. The two doves become an eagle and give birth to the One, thus curing the Hermaphrodite Infant's infection.

Note, Blanca, how the eagle –symbol of the Spirit and the Divine– does not take flight without leaving the two dead doves behind. The death of the Two is an essential requirement for their joint resurrection as the One. To germinate, the seed must die. But I insist, death here is a metaphor. What happens to the Two on their reunification, is not death, strictly speaking: it's an occultation, a move into the background, it's surrendering the stage to the One, an exit stage left to move forward behind the scenes. Anyone who has ever worked in theatre, as you did when you were young (although it was only the amateur theatre of your neighbourhood's Catholic Circle), knows that without all the hard work behind the scenes, nothing happens on stage... So, the Two survive, they remain present in the One. Except now, it's in an implicit way.

I don't want to bore you. I will finish now. It's late already, my eyes are closing, and I have told you practically everything I wanted to tell you in this letter. Too succinctly, I'm afraid, for how vast the subject of Alchemy is. In any case, Blanca, I'm confident that I have said enough for this purpose: to make you see that the Great Work is nothing but a symbolic representation of the process every man is destined to culminate sooner or later: his ascension to the divine rank. That this process entails the reintegration of the lost half of the soul. That is to say: if our theory is correct, it entails the mutual coming together of twin souls culminating in their final reunification. The "Double Thing", the *Rebis*, which is what the alchemists called that culmination, depended on obtaining a rare element: the Philosopher's Stone, which –in case you haven't guessed, my dear– is a veiled symbolic allusion to *pure love*. But while they remained incarnate, the *Rebis* was not within reach for alchemists other than in a *virtual* way. And so, as they waited for death, which one is not allowed to anticipate, the culmination of the *real* was only possible on the symbolic plane. Hence the zeal with which the adept and his mystic sister blended sulphur and mercury in pursuit of the "live Gold", in pursuit of the *perfect union*.

Yours

TENTH LETTER

HEAVENLY MARRIAGE

(OR MYSTIC UNION)

...and I believe that if our loves were
perfectly accomplished, and each one
returning to his primeval nature
had his original true love,
then our race would be happy.

Plato, *Symposium*

Barcelona, January 23rd, 2000

Dear Blanca,

Did you receive my last letter on time? What I have yet to say concerning twin souls will fit, I believe, in this letter that I'm writing to you now, which will be the last one. The last instalment of this sort of hope bulletin –hope that one day we will be together again– of which you and I are the only subscribers. In this letter, which is the tenth one if I'm not mistaken, on this final stretch I will be talking about the heavenly marriage and the flashes of it the contemplatives obtained. I will tell you about the essentially religious nature of love, and about the cosmic game between and the self and the you, about which C.J. Jung writes, "Wholeness is a combination of I and You, and these show themselves to be part of a transcendent unity whose nature can only be grasped symbolically, as in the symbols of the rotundum, the rose, the wheel, or the coniuctio Solis et Lunae."[433] The transcendent unity he is referring to is God, the One: I will also tell you about Him, Blanca... But first, I feel like telling you a story that I was fortunate to witness *in situ*, an insignificant story, although at the time it had a strange significance for me.

Do you remember that I told you about how, many years ago, Sebas and I travelled to Provence to visit the site where the Cathar events took place? Well, before I left, I visited a friend of mine who is a bookseller, the same one who has been providing me with most of the books I need for my investigative work (the other great provider has been "chance"). I paid him for the last batch of books, which were on Alchemy, and I told him about my upcoming trip. He, then, asked me if I would like to meet "a living alchemist". The question, as you very well understand, surprised me. Immediately, I thought about the elixir of eternal life that so many alchemists went to great lengths to obtain, according to what I had read. But I also knew that such elixir was symbolic, like the Philosopher's Stone, and that the "eternal life" it granted did not refer to life on earth, but to everlasting divine life, meaning that someone claiming to have extended their life from the time of the alchemists to our days, could only be a "blower", a fraud.

My friend quickly clarified: he did not mean an ancient alchemist; he meant a modern one. "I didn't know there was still alchemists these days", I said. After confirming that yes, some still remained, he searched in his filing cabinet and wrote down a name on a piece of paper, some directions in French, and the name of a small village in

---

433. C.G. Jung, *The Psychology of Transference*, p. 83

Provence. Sebas, bless his heart of gold, agreed to take a break from the Cathar, to dedicate a day of our trip to those other "seekers", the alchemists. And so it was, that on a cold autumn afternoon (night was falling and the sky adorned itself with that cobalt blue you liked so much) we parked our car in front of a stony façade festooned with a climbing vine. The vine was covering the windows, which told us the house was abandoned. The owner of the hostel confirmed this, and gave us an update on the information the bookseller provided me: the "living alchemist" was neither alive nor an alchemist, according to recent investigations. I noted this last part called for a more elaborate clarification, so he led us to a small and comfortable room, constellated by hunting trophies, where we sunk into two armchairs by the fireplace, and listened to the following story (his retelling was somewhat clumsy, so I will try to give it a more literary varnish):

Our protagonist –who was said to be driven by an unfortunate love– moved to the capital when he was very young. Intellectually awake, he combined work with his studies, obtained a degree in Chemistry, and devoted himself to research. But he strayed from orthodox science towards pseudo–science, towards Alchemy. He wrote several scholarly books on the subject, which allowed him to mingle with renowned intellectuals and artists, and garnered the increased attention of the press. That proved to be his downfall: an article in a tabloid newspaper uncovered his fortune of unclear origin, insinuating he had discovered the Philosopher's Stone (later, it came out that what gave him away was not his luxurious lifestyle, which was not luxurious at all, but his reckless charity work). He claimed his money came from a big lottery prize, but the public went with the magical version. Feeling that unwanted fame, he returned to his hometown, but fame, relentless, caught up with him, turning his house –the ancient abandoned mansion we found outside the village– into a pilgrimage site for followers of the occult sciences.

Years later, when he died (which already disappointed many people), his house was meticulously inventoried by notarial order. While the civil servants were doing their job, a crowd of curious people was gathering outside waiting for news. Or rather, waiting for *the* news: the discovery of a secret chamber equipped with distillers, glass retorts, flasks, test tubes, crucibles, and in a box or a safe, a stone: a glowing blue stone of an unknown alloy. Ah, but instead of all that, what did they find? The receipt for a winning lottery ticket from several decades ago, as well as proof of many profitable stock investments made since then. But what finally put an end to the esoteric fame of our alchemist, Blanca, was the discovery of a notebook with reflections and thoughts that projected an image incompatible with the alchemical achievement that until then he had supposedly attained: they projected the image of a tormented man, a man given to distress and melancholy.

And on that very night, by a stroke of luck, I had access to that notebook. It's true that it's the diary of an unhappy man, a man who felt like he was stuck, as he wrote, on "the sorrowful side of life". Because in his perspective, you know, humankind could be divided into two categories: happy humankind, and sorrowful humankind. But let me transcribe the fragment where he explains it. It says, "If I was the only unfortunate human being on Earth, certainly I would rebel against my own misfortune. But as it happens, I look around and see millions of human beings as unfortunate as I am, or worse. I understand then, that life is like a coin with two sides, the side of happiness, and the side of misfortune. When a person is born, the coin is tossed into the air, and the question is not on which side of life the coin falls, but to what the dark side owes its existence. But from the moment it exists, from the moment I look around and see the crowd, I cannot think of any reason why I should have had better luck. Am I, by any chance, better than them?..."

Moved by these words, on the following morning, before continuing our trip, I went to the cemetery outside the village to leave some flowers on his grave. But there was a surprise there: on his tombstone, in addition to his name, was the name of a woman. And when I read the dates and realised how short her life was, all that sorrow that I did not understand started to make sense, and I saw, as though in a film, the scythe of death cutting down a young love, a love in which the surviving half remained trapped, as an insect fossilised in amber. Embarrassingly, I was tempted to crawl around the grave, looking for two intertwined branches. Finally, I had the conviction that I was standing before the tomb of a true alchemist..., an alchemist that, if he did not find the Stone, at least he knew where to look...

ONE PHOENIX, ONE TURTLE, AND ONE PHOENIX–AND–TURTLE

There is a poem by William Shakespeare that deals with the souls' ascension to Divinity, the return of the multiple Two to the single One. It's a poem rich in alchemical symbolism, Blanca. We will take some stanzas from it and, with the help of the poets Robert Marteau and Jonathan Boulting[434], we will untangle their dense symbolism... Similarly to an alchemical fragment I cited before, the protagonists are a couple of birds. Shakespeare called it *The phoenix and turtle*. Note how he uses only one definite article for the two birds: he does not write "the phoenix and the turtle", he writes "the phoenix and turtle" (this is the kind of detail that does not go by unnoticed to a good detective). It's not a grammatical error, my dear, it's deliberate: it directly states the poem's theme, which is the alchemical transformation, the conversion of the two birds, phoenix and turtledove, into one single androgynous bird.

This "phoenix-and-turtle" is equivalent to "man-and-woman", to the Androgyne of the ancient sages. Why did Shakespeare choose two birds to represent twin souls? And why a dove and a turtledove specifically? The depiction of the soul as a bird was normal in antiquity: by being of a spiritual nature, the soul was considered a light and flying substance, like birds. As for those two species in particular, there is something that the phoenix and the turtledove have in common, apart from wings: they are two traditional symbols of conjugal bliss and androgynous union. Unlike the turtledove, the phoenix is a mythological bird; it's possible that Shakespeare chose it for its famous peculiarity: the ability of rising again from its ashes. Which is exactly what happens to this couple of birds: they rise again from the ashes of their Duality converted into the One.

The first stanza reads:

434. The notes were published by these poets on POESIE magazine, and later included on an edition of William Shakespeare's *The Phoenix and Turtle* by Nicole d'Amonville Alegría.

Let the bird of loudest lay,
On the sole Arabian tree,
Herald sad and trumpet be,
To whose sound chaste wings obey.

"The bird of loudest lay" is the rooster (Shakespeare gives it an Eastern touch by placing it perched on a palm tree, "on the sole Arabian tree"). When it crows, only the chaste birds may rise and fold their wings (those who during the night threw themselves to the pleasures of the flesh cannot rise that early in morning). In this veiled way, he is implying whom the poem is addressing. Meaning, he is warning us from the outset that the alchemical transmutation at stake is only within reach of those couples of twin souls that have purified their love, those who have cleansed it, to the extent possible, of contingencies. Those are the heroic lovers and this poem is for them.

Now we will skip three stanzas describing the operations and go straight to the decisive moment, the moment of *Coniuctio:*

And thou, treble-dated crow,
That thy sable gender mak'st
With the breath thou giv'st and tak'st,
'Mongst our mourners shalt thou go.

Shakespeare places the amorous copulation of the two birds under the auspice of another bird, the crow. With this, he is hinting at the spiritual nature of the *Coniuctio*, Blanca, since there was the superstition, alluded to in these verses, that the crow conceives and gives birth through its beak: there is no sexual exchange between male and female, but

–as in a kiss– the exchange of breaths and vital spirits. The crow is part of a funeral procession; it's one of the mourners. But, who died? Our protagonists did: the phoenix and the turtledove have died. But they have died in Duality only to be reborn converted into a "mutual flame":

> Here the anthem doth commence:
> Love and constancy is dead;
> Phoenix and the turtle fled
> In a mutual flame from hence.

R. Marteau comments this stanza thus: The phoenix and the turtle "escape, disappear, spouses in the consummation they arouse in each other". This consummation is the consummation of Unity, of Royalty. They crown each other as Kings. They are each other's means to ascend to Divinity, which they can only reach together. It's inevitable, then, Blanca, that in some way they see one another as the symbol (let's say) of Divinity, of the One/Whole. Hence J. Boulting's observation, "The phoenix is the turtle's Whole", which also works the other way around... This reminds me of a verse by a contemporary of Shakespeare, by my favourite poet (you will be surprised to know that I know some of his poems by heart), a verse by John Donne that says: "so we shall be one, and one another's All"[435].

In the next stanza, Shakespeare describes the proper nature of Divinity, consisting of being "two in one":

> So they lov'd, as love in twain
> Had the essence but in one;

435. John Donne, *"Lover's Infiniteness"*, *Songs and Sonnets*

Two distincts, division none:
Number there in love was slain.

The essence of the Two is the One, my love, and this essence is the fruit of their love. They are Two in love, One in the fruit it bears. In the fruit (in the explicit, that is) there is no distinction between the phoenix and the turtledove. However, in love (in the implicit) they remain two, different from one another. We could interpret the last verse in the following manner: by coming together, the two twin souls cancel each other out, that is to say, they annul their Duality, their division. In other words, they become zero. "This stanza is dedicated to the two in one –Boulting explains–. One in two and two in one are none," they are zero, and zero, he adds, symbolises "the annihilation of the lover in the beloved and of the beloved in the lover". In the explicit, that "number in love" (the Two) dies as a Duality, the number transforms into an infinity, into zero.

The following stanzas describe the mystery of the "two in one", which is the supreme mystery, the mystery of Divinity:

Hearts remote, yet not asunder;
Distance, and no space was seen
'Twixt the turtle and his queen;
But in them it were a wonder.

Between the phoenix and the turtle there is distance, but at the same time, there is no space. Meaning, Blanca, that the Two are One at the same time. Marteau stresses that what inextricably joins the Two is precisely what distinguishes them: difference, otherness.

So between them love did shine,
That the turtle saw his right
Flaming in the phoenix' sight:
Either was the other's mine.
Property was thus appall'd,
That the self was not the same;
Single nature's double name
Neither two nor one was call'd.

Both are aware they are each other's inseparable half. The other one is part of the self, the other one is *another self*. Property, then –what is mine as opposed to what is yours–, loses its meaning. "That the self was not the same". This here, my dear, is the essence of spiritual twin kinship: the fact that part of the self is outside the self, in another person who is the *other self*. Marteau comments: "Mine and yours are abolished. The two opposites are merged and confused without losing their difference. *The self* (the I) that was no longer seen as one's own, identifies now with the self that is no longer mine, being yours, while yours is mine: a miracle performed by love. It's the double Unit, the *Tai Kih* composed by the *yin* and *yang*, combined although separate"... Look, Blanca, at how, to point out the coexistence of Unity and Duality in God, Shakespeare alludes, in the penultimate verse, to the ability each thing has to be called by different names, just like Ibn Arabi had done to refer to divine Unity and Multiplicity.

The next two stanzas narrate the surrender of reason to the power of love, a power capable of doing what reason considers impossible: making the One be simultaneously Two.

Reason, in itself confounded,
Saw division grow together;
To themselves yet either-neither,
Simple were so well compounded
That it cried how true a twain
Seemeth this concordant one!
Love hath reason, reason none
If what parts can so remain.

The heavenly marriage of the phoenix and the turtledove meant their death. The death of split Duality. Their death as separate birds. But it has also meant their rebirth in Unity, their rebirth as one single bird. The phoenix and the turtle are dead, long live the Phoenix-and-Turtle!

Death is now the phoenix' nest;
And the turtle's loyal breast
To eternity doth rest,
Leaving no posterity:--
'Twas not their infirmity,
It was married chastity.

The chastity of their marriage is evidenced by the fact that, despite not being sterile, they left no descendants. Although this is not entirely accurate, Blanca, because they did have one son, except that this son -the alchemists' "Royal Son" - is themselves... themselves united in *perfect union*. As Marteau points out: both "are really their own posterity. In their union, they are their own royal progeny". Their marriage ("a marriage between two chastities" as Boulting defines it) has borne fruit not in the lower but in the higher plane. It has given birth to the Phoenix-and-Turtle, one of the innumerable names of God.

A KNOT OF REAL LOVE

To this urn let those repair
That are either true or fair;
For these dead birds sigh a prayer.

The poem, *The Phoenix and Turtle*, ends with this tercet. A poem that, as we know, was inspired by a love-affair Shakespeare had witnessed and admired: the relationship that united Queen Elizabeth I of England to the Count of Leicester, Robert Dudley. Surely, you know that Elizabeth I is known as "The Virgin Queen" because she never married. Ah, but that does not mean she was a stranger to love. In fact, it appears that she knew love in its purest form: it was a love of this kind –according to the poets of the time, such as Shakespeare, who praised her– that had united her to the Count of Leicester since childhood. As it happened, they were both born on the same day, at the same time, as though they were the main characters of an idyllic love story. If you allow me this bit of gossip: when the Queen died, they discovered she kept in her jewellery box, as if it were a precious item, the last letter the Count wrote to her before he died; and, in her coffer, she had his miniature wrapped in a piece of paper where she had scribbled: "*My lord's picture*".

The affair between Elizabeth I and the Count of Leicester, albeit exceptional, is not the only instance of chaste love between people of high birth. There several examples of this type of exception in medieval hagiography. The ecclesiastic hierarchy of the time looked down at such unions, as they considered virginity in marriage a dangerous anomaly. To cite some examples, we have the case of the German emperor Henry II and Cunigunde of Luxembourg, of whom an apocalyptic treatise from the thirteenth century sings the highest praises and proclaims, "The glorious rulers of the earth, loved each other in life not in a carnal way, but spiritually, so that in death they were not separated nor divided by burial."[436] Another princely couple, Salome of Greater Poland and Konrad of Hungary, knew each other from a tender age: ever since, having been promised in marriage by their parents, Salome moved to the court of her future husband, with whom, a few years later, she would take solemn votes of celibacy. The spiritual marriages (or "white weddings", as they have been called) of Alfonso II of Asturias and Berta, of Edward the Confessor and Edith, of Boleslaw V the Chaste of Poland and Kinga of Hungary, are other regal exponents. But, in my opinion, Blanca, the most beautiful example is the marriage of Dauphine and Elzear of Sabran, who were not of as noble lineage. We will stop to focus on them for a moment.

Although there is no doubt it was Destiny, at the dawn of the fourteenth century, that united this noble Provencal couple here on Earth, Destiny used their parents to implement its plans. They arranged the young couple's wedding behind their backs. We have the testimony (I hope you don't accuse me of indiscretion) of their wedding night: Dauphine lauds the merits of chastity between spouses and cites examples taken from the lives of holy men and women. He is filled with lust, but he respects Dauphine's will and the marriage is not consummated. She is aware her method is working, so

436. "Ein Elogium Joachims von Fiore auf Kaiser Heinrich II und seine Gemahlin, die heilige Kunigunde", *Liber Floridus, mitellateinishche Studien: Paul Lehmann*. Quoted by Dyan Elliot in *Spiritual Marriage, sexual abstinence in medieval wedlock*, Princeton University Press

every night she repeats it. These stories of spiritual love that, like Scheherazade, she tells him every night before going to bed make an impression on young Elzear, who accepts postponing consummation indefinitely. But Dauphine aspires to a definite renunciation, and that's why she resorts to a clever ruse: taking advantage of an illness that temporarily confines her to bed, she sends for her husband and tells him she is certain she will die unless he agrees to sacrifice himself for her. The chroniclers imply Elzear played into her hands because he truly loved her and was determined to lead a chaste life. For some time, he would still fight fiercely against instinct, until he revealed a mystic temperament that eliminated all sexual desire from him. But Dauphine and Elzear's amorous heroism would be evidenced by other trials. Eager for heirs, his parents subjected the couple to all sorts of schemes: they stationed spies in their bedroom, they mixed aphrodisiac potions in their beverages, they surrounded them with a libidinous environment, and they even tried to poison their daughter-in-law. But what happened, my dear, is that all those trials and tribulations only strengthened Dauphine and Elzear's spiritual love. What emerges from the chronicles is that they were such a united and attuned couple (precisely because of the spiritual nature of their love), that the pretension of the hagiographers of this type of couples seems entirely justified, namely that such unions cannot but endure beyond death. And that, Blanca, is in virtue of their pure love... When Dauphine is incapable of understanding the elation with which an acquaintance of her accepts his wife's death, and the ease with which he rebuilds his life, Elzear explains: "Between husbands and wives who love the world, it often happens that the carnal love which is between them fails like the flesh. But between me and you, there is a spiritual and pure love and such love, just like the spirit, will last forever and not fail."[437]

You see, then, Blanca, that spiritual love was seen as a guarantee that the union of the twin souls would live on in the Afterlife. This final reunification of the twin souls is one of poetry's favourite subjects. Because the main theme of poetry has always been, universally, erotic love. And what is the natural outcome of erotic love? Due to the fact that everything tends to its fulfilment, to its perfection, and because the perfection of love consists of the effective union of the lovers, and due to the fact that this union is only viable between twin souls (because a common origin determines a common destination), the natural outcome of erotic love is none other than heavenly marriage. Thus, that is a key subject of poetry, *The Phoenix and Turtle* being a sublime example of it. But not just in poetry: in art in general. The subject of the final reunification of the twin souls has been widely studied by visual artists. And you would have a lot to say about this, my dear, much more than I do, because visual arts are you speciality. I will just show you one example: this engraving from the Renaissance that I have before me.

It shows, as you can see, a naked, androgynous individual. Like many other graphic representations of the Androgyne, it shows a certain resemblance to the letter Y. This letter is, because of its peculiar shape, another ancient symbol of the divine bi-Unity or the "two in one" (in some alchemist engravings, we can see the Androgyne holding a Y on his hand). In our engraving, the common torso diverges into two heads of the opposite sex that come together in a passionate kiss.

437. *Vie... Dauphine* 8.2, p.178. Quoted by Dyan Elliot in *Spiritual Marriage, sexual abstinence in medieval wedlock*, Princeton University Press

Over the half-male, half-female chest, their two upper limbs are crossed, as if in a self-hug, and a knot in the shape of a cross weaves over this "two in one" from their heads to their feet. Underneath them, roots have sprouted, and the crown of a tree expands over them. Elémire Zolla clarifies us on the symbolism of the knot and the tree: "The man and the woman are united by a true-love-knot and become one with the Tree of Life."[438] The illustration is titled *Matrimonii Typus*, "Symbol of matrimony"[439]. Obviously, Blanca, this is not an everyday marriage, it's not even an exceptional marriage such as Dauphine and Elzear's. It's not an earthly nor a spiritual marriage, but a heavenly marriage, a *perfect union*. The fact that it's identified with the Tree of Life -symbol of the Centre, of Unity- proves it: it denotes that, through their mutual unification, the two spouses have joined the ranks of Divinity.

THE BLUE FLOWER

Now, my dear, if you don't mind, we will fill a gap, one of many gaps, in my previous letter. Because, when I talked about Romanticism, I skipped some notable representatives of this movement: the German Romantics. I have the excuse that it was a deliberate omission; I was saving them for this letter, since these poets and philosophers had a great influence on the subject that we are dealing with here: the

---

438. Elemire Zolla, *L'Androgyne alchimique*, included in *L'Androgyne*, Cahiers de l'Hermetisme, p. 132

439. Barthélemy Aneau, "Matrimonii Typus", *Picta Poesis ut Pictura Poesis Erit*, Lyon, 1552, p. 14.

final reunification of the predestined lovers. A subject that, as usual, derived from the belief in the original Androgyny of the human being.

"Poets and philosophers", I just wrote. Johann Wilhelm Ritter would fit into the latter category, although he had a great ascendency over the former. He was also a doctor and a scientist, one of the so-called "Romantic physicists". For these sages, science and spirituality were not at odds with each other. Ritter discovered, among other things, the physical phenomenon we referenced in these letters to describe love in the last stage of its journey to the Centre: ultraviolet rays. For our purpose, we only need one sentence from his extensive philosophical writings, because it synthesises his idea of the human being, which is the idea of an originally androgynous being destined to re-establish his original condition. At the end of times, he says "man and woman will completely dissolve in radiance, they will emanate but a single light, and the radiance will form itself into a body, into a body without sex, and therefore immortal."[440] (Note the connection that is established between lack of sex and immortality, and how it agrees with the ancient notion that the appearance of sex was the triggering factor of the Fall, and therefore the responsible for man's mortal condition.)

According to Franz Xaver von Baader -another Romantic philosopher who, like Ritter, was a mentor to poets- , "the difference between sexes is a developmental disease, inherent to the condition of mortal individuals."[441] Baader professed

440. J. W. Ritter, *Fragmente aus dem Nachlass eines jungen Physikers* (quoted by Albert Béguin, *El alma romántica y el sueño*)

441. Franz. v. Baader, *Sämmtliche Werke* (quoted by Albert Béguin, *El alma romántica y el sueño*, p. 105)

the ancient belief that the divine Man from the Origin was an asexual Androgyne. And he subscribed to the theory that every man is called upon to restore his original Androgyny by merging with his other half, who split from him following the Fall. A trained doctor, he even saw, in human anatomy, traces of the soul's predestination to reunify with its other half; the human thorax and arms appeared to him purposely made to embrace a peer: "In this gesture, man desires to re-integrate the woman in his body, to put her back where the rib was torn off as a result of his fall."[442] But we must not confuse an embrace with copulation, he warns us. The part of the human body that operates the arm is the upper part, meaning, the area of the heart, the symbolic headquarters of the soul, while in sexual intercourse, the ruling region is the lower body, the lower abdomen, the symbolic headquarters of passions, of the corporeal, of the *ego*. Baader opines that sexual copulation, "taken by itself in the abstract, is so little an act of union and love (or marriage) that it expresses rather the opposite, the greatest mutual reinforcement of selfishness (or nonlove), which ends nor in union but in indifference and in the separation of two despiritualised poles and indeed in the reciprocal loss of the one within the other and even in the torpidity which is the brother of death, for it is an animal act that can only be exorcised through embracing, that is, through love."[443]

For Baader, Blanca, sexual desire carries an implicit "inner hatred", as it's shown by the fact that, when one truly loves, this desire fades away until it disappears. In general,

442. Quoted by Jean Libis, *Le mythe de l'androgyne*, p. 149

443. Franz von Baader, *Gesammelte Werke*, vol.VII, p. 236. (Quoted by Julius Evola, *La métaphysique du sexe*)

my dear, the Romantics of the eighteenth and nineteenth centuries identified themselves with the ancient sages' sacred conception of love. In other words, they shared with the ancient sages the ternary notion of love, according to which love is not a matter of two but of three, Divinity being the third vertex towards which the other two unknowingly converge. There is another German Romantic scholar, Friedrich Schlegel, who, in line with his fellow believers, maintained that the human being is a fallen portion of the divine One, that he is destined to return to his high Origin, and that such return entails, by necessity, the reunification with the complementary half of his soul. It's the thesis of his novel *Lucinda*. In it, we see Julius, the male protagonist, address his beloved in the following terms:

> Marriage is the everlasting unity and alliance of our spirits, not only for what we call this world and the other world, but for the one, true, indivisible, nameless, endless world of our entire being, so long as we live.
>
> .../...
>
> The time is coming when we two shall behold in one spirit that we are blossoms of one plant, or petals of one flower. We shall then know with a smile that what we now call merely hope was really memory.
>
> Do you know how the first seed of this idea germinated in my soul before you, and took root in yours? Thus does the religion of love weave our love ever and ever more closely and firmly together, just as a child, like an echo, doubles the happiness of its gentle parents. Nothing can part us; and certainly any separation would only draw me more powerfully to you.
>
> .../...

How could separation separate us, when presence itself is to us, as it were, too present?[444]

In this passage, Blanca, I wanted, first, to call your attention to the implicit allusion to the theory of the twin souls as a foundation to what Schlegel calls "the religion of love". Since that, in fact, what confers erotic love its essential and sacred character is the idea carried by the theory of twin souls: the idea that love is, in its origin, the reciprocal feeling between two Persons, between multiple two Persons that are behind the divine Unity. Furthermore, my dear, for Schlegel love is also, in its history, the *Bildungselement*, the "formative element" of the Universe, envisaged by God to transform chaos into order through the reunification of all opposites. Now then, let's be clear: by the time he wrote *Lucinda*, Schlegel did not see (as he did in his youth) in the antidote to chaos that Eros was for him, a necessary secret tendency towards the spirit: *Lucinda* was a controversial book in its time because of its shameless sensuality, which went against the Romantic ideal.

As you can see, Blanca, the Romantic thought is not monolithic; within its fundamental affinity exist several different opinions. F. Schlegel did not accept the progressive ascension of love from sensuality to spirituality: for him, true love entailed both planes; love was only true insofar as it was predestined, insofar as both lovers were twin souls. The "Romantic physicist" Gotthilf H. von Schubert, on the other hand, did not share a negative conception of the Fall with most Romantics. He saw it more like a voluntary and

444. *El entusiamo y la quietud. Antología del romanticismo alemán*, edited by Antoni Marí, pp. 132–134

necessary descent: "An eternal law requires the One to divide incessantly into two poles, so that these, upon loving each other, can recreate a superior Unity. And when the poles separate, the nostalgia for the union is reborn in them: such is the voice of the great universal ascension for Love". And so, Blanca, we could continue enumerating discrepancies. However, underneath the different variations, the same melody is always playing. A melody that talks about the original divine androgyny of the human beings, and about their future restoration through a predestined love: the love towards "the other pole of one's self", in Gotthilf H. von Schubert's own terminology. In his passage I transcribed above, this melody is easily recognisable.

And so it is in this sentence by Schlegel: "Only in the answer of its corresponding You, can each self fully feel its infinite unity"[445]; a unity he sees as the "original harmony" of those two souls, each of them being, for the other, "the eternal and only beloved". We can also hear this persistent melody when we read about "the only true and eternal love" in *Lucinda*; or when we read, in his notes for the planned sequel of his novel, that Julius and Lucinda loved each other "because they had always loved each other", ever since eternity; they had loved each other even before they met in this life: "Because she already loved me before she met me. She has to love me: she is compelled to it by nature..."[446] But in my opinion, the Romantic who most echoed this ancient melody, Blanca, was Friedrich Hölderlin.

A lone Romantic poet, Hölderlin had a difficult life: he was hounded by financial problems, misunderstood by his

445. Friedrich Schlegel, *Literary Notebooks* 1481
446. *Kritische Ausgabe* V, 31–32

contemporaries, and, towards the middle of his life, he suffered from a mental illness that prevented him from living a normal life. But all these tribulations were eclipsed by the joy he felt when he met Susette Gontard, the companion soul he had been seeing in dreams ever since he was a child, and with whom he would be united by a love he would describe as "sacred and eternal"[447]. Recognition was instantaneous and reciprocal ("Is it you, is it really you?!"[448]). Their encounter was a typical case of synchronicity. The same circumstances of their meeting were predicted, with astonishing precision, in the first drafts of his novel *Hyperion*. Hölderlin would see his female protagonist embodied in this woman, who was of a sensitivity so close to his, as we can read in the beautiful letters that she wrote him after their forced separation. Their romance –one of the most beautiful of all Romanticism– would endure in those letters and furtive encounters (Susette was a married woman) until her premature death.

The subject of the predestination of love permeates *Hyperion* from start to finish. "Before we both knew it, we already belonged to each other"[449], declares the male protagonist, who intuits he and his beloved Diotima shared a previous life together in Paradise: "Then [my heart] told me how the spirit of Hyperion had played with his sweet Diotima at the gates of Elysium, in a divine childhood, before coming down to Earth."[450] Doesn't this divine childhood remind you of the idyllic novels and the alchemists' "divine Child"? This childhood together in Paradise is a symbol of the lovers' com-

447. F. Hölderlin, *Hyperion*, p. 139
448. *Ibid.*, p. 150
449. *Ibid.*, p. 91
450. *Ibid.*, p.102

mon origin and, for Hölderlin, it's a guarantee of their reencounter in successive lives. "It's impossible –he tells us– that we lose one another. I will search the stars for millennia, I will take on all forms, I will learn all languages of life to find you again. But I think that what is alike soon finds each other."[451] "What is alike": meaning, what is twin, that which is made –as an analogy for the two halves of a *symbolon*– out of the same piece of wood. (I'm sure you remember that this notion of similarity, so widespread among the ancient sages, supported the Swedenborgian anthropology.)

Hölderlin is not only a notable name in German idealism and poetry, Blanca. Among the great names of literature and thought, his stands as one of the most admirable from the point of view of personal integrity. Few lived in accordance with their high principles as he did. "Living in purity of heart is the greatest / wise men ever discovered / and the wisest men ever practiced", he wrote; and it appears he was among the wisest.

The German Romantic movement was even more numerous than the English one. It's one of those curious cases that happen in History from time to time, when in a minute space-time breadth (in this case, the German region of Saxony at the end of the eighteenth century) converge a surprising number of geniuses. Fichte, Kleist, Hoffman, Clemens and Bettina Brentano, Jean-Paul, Tieck, Arnim, Schleirmacher, are just a few of the great poets and thinkers of that distinguished group. It's impossible to list them all, Blanca, so let's focus on one that encapsulates their essence, the prototype of the Romantic poet and, perhaps, along with Hölderlin, the highest and most profound of all. I talking about

451. *Ibid.*, p. 166

Friedrich Leopold von Hardenberg, the very same man who has appeared in these letters under his literary pseudonym: Novalis.

There is one thing you and Novalis have in common, my love; maybe more, but at least one. I don't mean great essences, such as a moral attitude before the world; or even a character trait, although you probably share some as well. I mean the little detail that you both prefer the colour blue to any other. I'm not aware of whether Novalis bound the books of his library in any specific colour; but if he did, I bet his would be, like yours, a blue library. The books he wrote are filled with that colour, a colour that was for him the icon of the Spirit and the Higher World. "Everything is blue in my book", he writes concerning *Henry of Ofterdingen*, his masterpiece, the novel he will be working on for the last years of his life and that he will never finish. In *Henry of Ofterdingen*, it's a blue Flower that embodies the yearned goal of the protagonist –the medieval *minnesinger* of the same name–, a Flower seen in a childhood dream:

> A sweeter slumber now overcame him. He dreamed of many strange events, and a new vision appeared to him. He dreamed that he was sitting on the soft turf by the margin of a fountain, whose waters flowed into the air, and seemed to vanish in it. Dark blue rocks with various colored veins rose in the distance. The daylight around him was milder and clearer than usual; the sky was of a sombre blue, and free from clouds. But what most attracted his notice, was a tall, light–blue flower, which stood nearest the fountain, and touched it with its broad, glossy leaves. Around it grew numberless flowers of varied hue, filling the air with the richest perfume. But he saw the blue flower alone, and gazed long upon it with inexpressible

tenderness. He at length was about to approach it, when it began to move, and change its form. The leaves increased their beauty, adorning the growing stem. The flower bended towards him, and revealed among its leaves a blue, outspread collar, within which hovered a tender face. His delightful astonishment was increasing with this singular change, when suddenly his mother's voice awoke him, and he found himself in his parents' room, already gilded by the morning sun.[452]

The English Romantic S. T. Coleridge imagined a fable that sounded, if the story of the Blue Flower stopped at this point, like its corollary. He imagined a dreamer that, as a souvenir from his dreamed stay in Heaven, received a flower and, when he woke up, he found the flower in his hand. The Blue Flower dreamt by Novalis would become an emblematic image of the Romantic spirit, Blanca. But we do not t owe that imagery to Novalis, it's much more ancient: it's one of the symbols of Nature traditionally associated to the Androgyne. Some alchemy texts mention the "sapphire blue flower of the Hermaphrodite". In painting, the Blue Flower (the colour is not incidental for you) is usually an iris; or a yarrow, a flower with blue petals that, by the way, in other languages has a name curiously related to our subject: *amor perfeito*, "perfect love" in Portuguese; and, in Provencal, *mount au ciel*, "ascent to heaven". But getting back to Novalis, his life, like his book, was unfinished; the Romantic's disease, tuberculosis, took it away from him before his twenty–ninth birthday. But it was an intense life, richer than most. Not rich like in the manner of Lord Byron's: rich in true wealth, which is internal to one, as Novalis knew, writing

452. Novalis, *Henry of Ofterdinger*

in a famous paragraph: "We dream of travelling through the Universe –but is not the Universe within ourselves? The depths of our spirit are unknown to us –the mysterious way leads inwards. Eternity with its worlds –the past and future– is in ourselves or nowhere. The external world is the world of shadows –it throws its shadows into the realm of light. At present, this realm certainly seems to us so dark inside, lonely, shapeless. But how entirely different it will seem to us –when this gloom is past, and the body of shadows has moved away."[453]

Crossed–out note on the margin. A painstaking salvaging work allowed me to decipher only the beginning of a large annotation: "*The portrait that Thomas Gainsborough…*" The rest has been lost under the black ink of the marker pen. I will only remind the reader that Thomas Gainsborough was a famous painter from that century that is beginning to become an obsession in these letters.

There is a central concept around which revolves everything that came out of Novalis' pen: his novels, his stories, his *Spiritual Songs*, his poems. And that central concept, Blanca –which in reality is common to every Romantic–, is erotic love. Love is "the eternal mystery", he proclaims in *Ofterdingen*. And the characters in his work, seekers like the heroes of the Grail, had great loves, which will be decisive for the achievement of their transcendent goal. Thus, Matilda, Henry of Ofterdingen's girlfriend, will appear to him as the key for the mystery of the long sought Blue Flower. He

453. Novalis, *Philosophical Writings*, p. 25

will recognise in Matilda the face of the woman (the shadow of that heavenly face) he saw as a child in the petals of the dreamt flower. "It seems to me that I knew thee long, long ago", she tells him when they first meet. And when she expresses her fear that his love will fade away with her beauty: "That which draws me so inseparably to thee, that has awakened in me such everlasting desire, is not of this world. Couldst thou but see how thou appearest to me, what a wonderful form penetrates thy shape, and everywhere is raying towards me, thou wouldst not fear age. Thy earthly shape is but a shadow of this form... The earthly faculties strive and swell that they may incarnate it; but nature is yet unripe; the form is only an eternal archetype, a fragment of the unknown holy world."

Matilda dies shortly after their wedding (old literature is filled with widowers, I'm sure you noticed). But before she dies, she gives birth to a boy, Astralis. The son of Henry and Matilda is not like those you and I could never have, my dear: he is a strange creature, an Androgyne that has "conquered death". This divine child –the embodiment of the Blue Flower and herald of the age of Love that, according to Novalis, awaits humanity in the future– is none other than the alchemists' "Divine Child". He is not the fruit of his parents' sexual copulation, but of their chaste embrace, the result of the fusion of two souls into a single one: "Matilda and Henry were alone united, into one form... new–born I rose"... But it was not just his characters, Blanca: Novalis himself had a great love in his life. He loved Sophie. No, I'm not talking about Boehme's "divine Virgin" now: Novalis' Sophie was a flesh and blood girl, although our poet, a fervent reader of the Görlitz cobbler, will be shocked by the coincidence and will use it in his mystic speculations. Unlike

Boehme's, Novalis' Sophie was not even beautiful: according to his friends, only he could see her charm (which takes us back to the first subject of our letters: subjective beauty, the beauty reserved for the eyes of the twin soul). But the joy of this homecoming, which is what his relationship with this girl meant for Novalis, did not last long: she passed away after only three years. From the grief over this loss, but also from the hope of one day seeing her again, came what has been considered the masterpiece of Romantic poetry: the *Hymnen an die Nacht*, the "Hymns to the Night".

I know, my love, that the night fascinates you. While you were alive, sometimes I woke up and you were not there. I would find you leaning on the balcony, contemplating the night, taking in its aromas... The night also fascinated the Romantics. However, they related it to something that I imagine did not even cross your mind in those nights on the balcony. They related it to death. For them, though, death was not as terrible as it was for you (wasn't it?) until you tried it for yourself. For the Romantics (and for you too now, I'm sure), death was a gateway to a more complete existence; the access gate to the divine Unity substantiated by the union with the twin soul. Because, you know, the Romantics shared the ancient intuition that the unification with our other self, with our other half, can only be achieved after death. That is the message behind so many Romantic stories of *liebestod*, of "love–death", love stories where the bridal bed is the shared grave. Among Novalis' philosophical thoughts, there is the famous "A union that is arranged for death, is a marriage that will give us a companion for the Night. Death is where the love is sweeter. For he who loves, death is a wedding night, a secret of sweet mysteries". Novalis assumes that he and Sophie have a heavenly marriage reserved for after death. "Our engagement was not for this world", he writes in his diary. But he knows that such matrimony can only happen once their souls have fully undressed and matured. That is why, in *Hymns for the Night*, he urges Sophie to "consume with spirit-fire my body, that I, turned to finer air, may mingle more closely with thee, and then our bridal night endure forever."

But for Novalis, this mystic and luminous conception of death was not a spontaneous acceptance following the death of his beloved. With a hypersensitive temperament such as his, the tears and grief soon reached the point of paroxysm. And this is when, Blanca, a famous event in his biography took place, the incident that allowed him to look at the "reverse side of the tapestry" of existence, and that transformed his outlook on death. Maybe it will give you chills, since it happened in a cemetery. You know how much the Romantics liked those kind of places. But Novalis had a good reason to visit Grünigen cemetery every afternoon: Sophie was buried there. And in one those afternoons, he sat by the tomb of his beloved when... It's better if he tells you himself, since we have his account, recorded in his diary, in some of his letters and, most of all, in *Hymns for the Night*:

> Once when I was shedding bitter tears, when, dissolved in pain, my hope was melting away, and I stood alone by the barren mound which in its narrow dark bosom hid the vanished form of my life -- lonely as never yet was lonely man, driven by anxiety unspeakable -- powerless, and no longer anything but a conscious misery. -- As there I looked about me for help, unable to go on or to turn back, and clung to the fleeting, extinguished life with an endless longing: -- then, out of the blue distances -- from the hills of my ancient bliss, came a shiver of

> twilight -- and at once snapt the bond of birth -- the chains of the Light. Away fled the glory of the world, and with it my mourning -- the sadness flowed together into a new, unfathomable world -- Thou, Night-inspiration, heavenly Slumber, didst come upon me -- the region gently upheaved itself; over it hovered my unbound, newborn spirit. The mound became a cloud of dust -- and through the cloud I saw the glorified face of my beloved. In her eyes eternity reposed -- I laid hold of her hands, and the tears became a sparkling bond that could not be broken. Into the distance swept by, like a tempest, thousands of years. On her neck I welcomed the new life with ecstatic tears. It was the first, the only dream -- and just since then I have held fast an eternal, unchangeable faith in the heaven of the Night, and its Light, the Beloved.[454]

I don't need to tell you how much this passage moves me! Novalis would never be lonely again. At least, from that moment, he knew that his loneliness was fictitious, that in reality he and Sophie would never be apart. He understands that, as they waited for death and their heavenly marriage, he and his beloved contracted an early matrimony. A secret bond that united them. And this bond is sacred: "What I feel for Sophie is religion, not love -he wrote in his personal diary-. An absolute love, independent of the heart and founded on faith, is religion. By absolute will, love can become religion." Through his character, Henry of Ofterdingen, he asked the question: "What is religion but an infinite harmony, an eternal unison of loving hearts?"...

---

454. Novalis, *Hymns for the Night*

I could give you more examples. There is a famous one by John Keats, who, in his letters to Fanny, declared, "My Creed is Love and you are its only tenet". Many examples of Romantic quotations coincide with the insistent message of ancient wisdom: the essentially sacred nature of erotic love. Because love, my dear (I hope I have made it clear by this point), is love in itself, it's not a trivial subject as it may appear at first sight. It's not a mere fever or inebriation of the senses. That is the husk, the shell that covered love as it fell into this world. Break the shell, the ancient sages tell us, and you will get the grain. Take a look at the other side of the tapestry and you will see that, in its essence, erotic love is something much more intimate and mysterious; it connects to religion, to the sacred, it's an affluent of the Divine... This has never been a secret for heroic lovers. Even without ever reaching the point of heroism, true lovers can feel it... we can feel it, Blanca, that our love has a tight bond with the ultimate truths, with divine Infinitude. Our love takes us (does it not?) to peaks of joy that we thought were reserved to God; which makes us feel what Friedrich Schlegel called "the irony of love", that "emerges from the feeling of finitude, of our own limitation and the apparent contradiction of this feeling *with the idea of infinitude that every true love entails.*"[455]

And why is love, in essence, sacred? We said it before: love is essentially sacred because it's of divine filiation. Because, in its origin, it's what united the *Syzygia*, what unified the multiple Couple implicit in God; therefore, it's what conceives

455. F. Schlegel, *Kritische Ausgabe*. Quoted by Daniel Inerarity, *Hegel y el romanticismo*, p. 96 (italics by the author of the letter)

Him. Essential love is one hundred percent spiritual, my dear, otherwise it would not be a unifying element. When love is pure and naked, it becomes a centripetal force, a cohesive force that attracts inwards, towards the Centre, towards the One. Likewise, then, an opposite force was responsible for the Fall. A force that infiltrated the highest Love of the Origin and centrifuged the One, disintegrating it into the multiple Twos that implicitly integrated it; Twos that were expelled from the Centre, ending up in exile, then, in the outer circle of the cosmic mandala. Certainly, love became desensitised after that. Even so, Blanca, love stands (to use Schlegel's expression) in the *Bildungselement*, as the formative element that shapes the Universe, that leads it, little by little, to its future realisation. Love holds the seed to restore the original unitary form of the Universe. That is why it's sacred.

The idea of the Fall and the return to the Origin through cosmic Evolution, is one of the main ideas of Romanticism. The goal is Unity of opposites, embodied by the twin souls. But, as I have said, not every Romantic thinker agrees on how to restore the lost Unity. For some of them, the amorous dialectic between opposites is in itself the driving force leading to the unifying synthesis. Others subscribe to the opinion of most ancient sages, condensed in this sentence from the *Rosarium Philosophorum*, the famous alchemical text: "It's the Spirit that brings together". In other words, for the Romantics, the cosmic Evolution entails the decantation of the love between twin souls towards the Spirit.

In one of his aphorisms, Novalis suggests a rather beautiful metaphor: he says that perhaps sex is to love what sleep is to wakefulness, staying awake being preferable to being asleep. Let's imagine, then, that love is soundly asleep, and the conscious is slowly making way through its dream, first pulling it into a light sleep –the current state of love, where the oneiric and the real mix– and finally waking it up. Or –since we are among books– let's suppose that the love between twin souls is a book, a blue book if you want. That book was originally written in the language of the Spirit, the language of God, which makes it a sacred book. Well, then if our sages are not mistaken, the Fall meant the enunciation of that book in the dialect of Matter, of sexuality. The appearance of sex supposed then the profanation of love, its conversion into something profane. Now, it's a matter of restoring the book back to its vernacular language, of rewriting it in the language of the Spirit based on the fallen translation.

A classic metaphor to picture the evolution of love between twin souls Blanca, is the hidden treasure, or the precious stone buried deep underground. This stone is like the black stone of Kaaba: a sacred stone, and our mission is to unearth it. As we make progress on that difficult task, we will begin to glimpse (we have already begun) the sacred and divine flashes the stone radiates. The deeper we dig into our mutual love, the more we undress the love between twin souls, the more palpable its sacred nature will be. There will come a time (because there will come the day the stone will be completely uncovered) when the very embodiment of the sacred, when God Himself will stand between us. In one of his numerous essays about the evolution of love, Teilhard de Chardin draws the roadmap: "Man and woman, appointed by life to promote the highest degree possible of spiritualisation of the Earth, should abandon, to attain it, the way that until now has been the only rule of beings... Not keeping from their mutual attraction more than what makes them rise as they come together, they will pull each other forwards. Not an immediate contact, but convergence up above. The instant of total surrender will coincide then with the divine reencounter"... This instant of divine reencounter, Blanca, is, if you can remember, the moment that Solovyov said the twin souls mutually referred each and themselves in God. The moment in which Unity would be re-established between them; first in a virtual way, while they remain incarnate; and then in a real way, after their death. That moment will come, my love. Our mutual love will bring us together again; it will unify us in a *perfect* way, as it did before in the Origin.

The fact that erotic love buries its roots in Divinity itself, does not just make *eros* something sacred: it also makes religion something tightly close to eroticism. The proof of this reciprocal bond is that those who delve deep into one of those fields will inevitably find themselves in the other, as the class of words employed by both evidences it. Heroic lovers use religious terms to refer to their beloved; the contemplative mystics use erotic terms to refer to God. Most of all, I'm thinking about the religious term of *adoration* and the erotic term of *union*: heroic lovers adore their maiden, the contemplatives believe they unite with God. We have already seen some examples of the former here in these letters, so I will confine myself now to the latter, that is, to the unifying character of the contemplative's ultimate experience.

Precisely due to its unifying character, this experience is known in the West by the Latin words *unio mystica*, "mystical union". I'm not telling you anything new when I say that the descriptions of *unio mystica* the contemplatives give are almost always in terms of marriage, of amorous copulation. In fact, my dear, if an unsuspecting reader were to go over contemplative literature, he could come out with the wrong impression: it could appear to him that he was browsing the records of a call house. That is how many references he would find to love, lovers, to the union with a beloved, and to the ineffable delights resulting of that union. Except it's not about carnal eroticism, but a different, more elevated, more genuine kind of eroticism: the delights derived from the *unio mystica* are not (despite how much they lend themselves to that metaphor) sensual, they are the delights of the Spirit. But let's take a look at some examples.

The thirteenth century Beguine Hadewijch of Antwerp described the peak of her ecstatic experience in erotically charged verses:

> Calm reigns at last,
> When the loved one receives from her Beloved
> The kisses that truly pertain to love.
> The loved soul in every way,
> Love drinks in these kisses and tastes them to the end.
> As soon as Love thus touches the soul,
> She eats its flesh and drinks its blood
> Love that thus dissolves the loved soul
> Sweetly leads them both
> To the indivisible kiss–
> That same kiss which fully unites
> The Three Persons in one sole Being.[456]

In the eighth century, the Muslim contemplative Rabia of Basra talked about her "heavenly marriage" with Allah, "which had made her and Him One". Centuries later, St. Teresa of Jesus would use similar terms to celebrate her "mystic marriage" with Christ. Although St. Teresa refers to Christ as "my bridegroom", sometimes her bridegroom turns out

---

456. Georg Feuerstein, *Sacred Sexuality*

to be an angel. "Not a tall, but a short and handsome" angel, who, in a common metaphor among the contemplatives, pierces her heart with a spear or arrows: "In his hands I saw a long golden spear and at the end of the iron tip I seemed to see a point of fire. With this, he seemed to pierce my heart several times so that it penetrated to my entrails. When he drew it out, I thought he was drawing them out with it and he left me completely afire with a great love for God. The pain was so sharp that it made me utter several moans; and so excessive was the sweetness caused me by this intense pain that one can never wish to lose it..."[457]

It's clear, Blanca, that St. Teresa is describing here an amorous copulation. And, although it was of a spiritual nature, this is not what, in her opinion, was to be expected from a union with God: and this is how St. Teresa comes to mistrust her own mystic experiences. And the same happens to her great friend and collaborator St. John of the Cross. The contemplative verses by this Castilian saint are also unequivocally erotic:

> Upon a darkened night
> on fire with all love's longing
> – O joyful flight! –
> I left, none noticing,
> my house, in silence, resting.
>
> ...
>
> In the joy of night,
> in secret so none saw me,
> no object in my sight

457. Georges Bataille, *Erotism*, p. 224

no other light to guide me,
but what burned here inside me.

Which solely was my guide,
more surely than noon-glow,
to where he does abide,
one whom I deeply know,
a place where none did show.

O night, my guide!
O night, far kinder than the dawn!
O night that tied
the lover to the loved,
the loved in the lover there transformed![458]

These are the famous verses of *The Dark Night* (the Romantics were not the only ones fascinated by the night). The following verses are also by John of the Cross, but from his *Spiritual Canticle*, which is a poem directly inspired by the Song of Songs:

Let us rejoice, Beloved,
and let us go forth to behold ourselves in your beauty,
to the mountain and to the hill,
to where the pure water flows,
and further, deep into the thicket.

And then we will go on
to the high caverns in the rock
that are so well concealed;

---

458. John of the Cross, *Dark Night*

there we shall enter
and taste the fresh juice of the pomegranates.[459]

Aren't all these metaphors quite explicit? Especially the last one, considering the pomegranate is an ancient erotic symbol (in the Song, the spouses get together in a pomegranate orchard). However, you see, the author will confess to be unsure if the mystic experiences that inspired them came from God or the devil. Whereas other contemplatives have no problem in accepting the erotic nature of their experiences. Hadewijch of Antwerp instructs a disciple: "And may He submerge you in Him, where the abyss of his wisdom is, he will teach you what He is (for Hadewijch, He is Love: "In the fruition you will experience that I am, I, Love", as we can read in her *Visions*), and with what wondrous sweetness the loved one and the Beloved dwell one in the other, and how they penetrate each other in such a way that neither of the two distinguishes himself from the other. But they abide in one another in fruition, mouth in mouth, heart in heart, body in body, and soul in soul, while one sweet divine nature flows through them both and, being in each other, they are both one and they remain completely one -- yes, and remain so forever.[460]

Crossed–out note on the margin. *...to start a new (life?) together"*. This is all I could salvage from the original note, which was much longer.

A modern day contemplative, the Nicaraguan poet Ernesto Cardenal, is also no stranger to experiencing Divinity in

459. John of the Cross, *Spiritual Canticle*
460. Hadewijch of Antwerp, *Letter IX*

erotic terms. He describes his *unio mystica* with God like a lover going over an erotic date. Except in this case, it's not a carnal erotism: "there is an erotism without the senses, for very few people, in which I am an expert"[461], he notes. Except this date takes place "in an infinite place and on an eternal date, but as real as saying meet me tonight at eight"[462]...

> I close my eyes and you draw closer
> In the night of nothing
> How well I know your taste
> And you mine.
> ...
> Silent caress
> In the night of nothing.[463]

Through his contemplative practice, Cardenal searches for "a lover in the Universe"[464]. Aware that "we have been created for nuptials"[465], he searches for his spouse. And he finds him -he believes he finds him- in God.

> If they could hear what I say to you at times
> They'd be scandalised. Really, what blasphemies!
> But you understand my reasons.
> And besides, I'm teasing.
> And they're things that people in love say to each other in bed.
> ...

461. Ernesto Cardenal, *Telescope in the Dark Night*
462. Ernesto Cardenal, *Cosmic Canticle*
463. *Ibid*
464. *Ibid*
465. Ernesto Cardenal, *To Live is to Love*

Beloved, let's make love.
I don't know what they mean by "giving glory to God."
Love yes.
To me glory is having God in my bed or in the hammock.
Let's give pleasure to each other.
The stone curlews are in flight.
Let's give pleasure to each other, beloved.[466]

Anyway, there is no need to add more examples. These few are enough to support the postulate that, when we delve deep into religion, sometimes we might find ourselves unexpectedly face to face with eroticism. So much so, Blanca, that, in the East, the expression "Love's Faithful", or another equivalent one, could be applied to the contemplative mystics, such as those I had the pleasure of citing here.

THE SEVENTH PALACE

We come now, my dear, to what is probably the most controversial part of these letters. Because the contemplative interprets that the Beloved to whom he or she is uniting in the *unio mystica* is God: but that, I dare say, is not at all certain. Three things seem certain to me about the *unio mystica*. The first one is that, by way of ecstasy, (*ekstasis* is the Greek word that connotes displacement outside oneself) the soul moves back towards the Hidden Point, which is where the union takes place. The second one is that the *unio mystica* is equivalent to a momentary experience of Divinity. "Becoming God in God" or "coming to be what God is" are two expressions

466. Ernesto Cardenal, *Telescope in the Dark Night*

used by the contemplatives to describe their experience. And the third certain thing is that this experience has a nuptial and erotic character, it's an intimate loving relationship with one "other". If, equipped with these three convictions, we begin to build the puzzle of *unio mystica*, and we do it in light of the theory of twin souls, we can only differ from the interpretation the contemplative mystics make of their experiences. And you will ask me: "who better than them to interpret it?" But allow me: the subject of an experience is not necessarily its most faithful exegete; in the field of interpretation, subjectivity can be deceitful.

If we are consistent with our theory (and at this point, I believe we have that obligation), the *unio mystica* would not be about the soul's marriage with God, but, based on what we have seen in our letters, with its original spouse, whose union with the soul formed God in the Origin: in other words, with its twin soul. It would be, then, the soul's recreation of the original birth of God. Certainly, said recreation would obey the reunification of the soul not with its original spouse, not with its twin, who is absent from that experience, but with the recalled image of its twin, with its *anima* or *animus*. The *unio mystica* of the contemplative would be nothing but the remembrance, and at the same time the prefiguration, the anticipation, thanks to a momentary access to the Hidden Point, of the heavenly marriage. In the Hidden Point, the contemplative would get married to the image (that image is imprinted into his subconscious) of his or her twin soul. His or her twin soul such as it was before the Fall, such as it was before they came apart, when the two were still covered in Divinity. In the terminology of Boehme and his disciples, the soul would get married to the memory of Sophia (or her male equivalent), a memory that would become brighter and conscious in the Hidden Point.

What do you think? Do you think, like me, that all this is possible? Look, Blanca. The ancient sages teach us that Unity is only accessible through Duality. That is to say, according to our theory, through one another; and not just any other, but the other that is predestined to us: our specific and exclusive other. Among the contemplatives, however, prevails the belief that the path to Unity is a lonely path. So much so, that Hadewijch of Antwerp herself –who, as we have seen, naturally accepted the erotic character of her unifying experience– was disturbed to realise this experience was shared with another human soul (in her case, with the soul of St. Augustine of Hippo, to whom she felt particularly connected); when she discovered that, contrary to what she believed, God was not her spouse in the *unio mystica*, but the fruit of her union with another soul (with the *image* of another soul) like hers. Hadewijch's retelling of this revelation is filled with symbolism. She wrote that on Christmas night, lying in bed, she was hurled into "a very deep whirlpool, wide and exceedingly dark" where eagles flew. Those eagles (which, as we know, symbolise the Spirit) are personifications: "one was St. Augustine, the other was myself". "Then I saw coming as it were a bird, namely the one called Phoenix" and who swallowed them both. She clarifies that "the Phoenix that swallowed the eagles was he Unity in which the Trinity dwells, wherein both of us were are lost". "When afterwards I returned to myself, –she continues–...

> ... I reflected on this union on this union with Saint Augustine to which I had attained. I was not contented with what my dearly Beloved (God) had just permitted, in spite of my

consent and emotional attraction; it weighed on me now that this union with Saint Augustine had made so perfectly happy, whereas previously I had possessed union far from saints and men, with God alone... And as I thought about this attitude, I asked my Beloved to deliver me from it. For I wished to remain in his deepest abyss, alone in fruition... But I well know that whatever was in him is, in highest measure, eternal glory and perfect enjoyment, but I likewise wished to remain in him alone. I understood this when I asked for it, and so great'-desired it, and suffered so much; I remained free. *No doubt I continued to belong to God alone, while being united in Love to this creature (Saint Augustine).*[467]

As you can see, Hadewijch is disturbed by the happiness brought to her by her mystic union with St. Augustine -her dearest Saint. The idea that God is the natural spouse of the soul is so ingrained in her, that she struggles to accept the fact that her access to Him -to Unity- requires a mystic union with another creature like her, even feeling fully realised in that union. Hadewijch wants something that, if we listen to our sages, Blanca, is equivalent to wanting to be a mother without the assistance of a father. She asks God to deliver her from that intermediation, which for her is an imperfection, and her prayer is heard. But not in the way she was hoping for: God frees her not from the intermediation, but from her reluctance in accepting it: "*No doubt I continued to belong to God alone, while being united in Love to this creature.*"

Hadewijch's story exemplifies this common prejudice among the contemplative mystics: the incompatibility

467. Quoted by Georgette Epiney-Burgard and Emilie Zum Brunn, *op. cit.*, p. 159

between loving God and the erotic love for another human being (which can only be understood from an erotic conception of the love for God). Rather than showing you another example, I would prefer citing an exception that confirms the rule. The thirteenth century monk Jordan of Saxony –Master General of the Dominicans for fifteen years– and the Bolognese nun Diana d'Andalo never felt like their mutual love interfered with their love for God, as it's proven by their surviving letters. Letters such as the one in which he writes: "O Diana! What a wretched state of affairs this is, which we have to endure! Our love for each other here is never free from pain and anxiety. You are upset and hurt because your presence is so rarely granted me. I wish we could be brought into the fortified city (the celestial Jerusalem: one of the medieval names for Paradise), the city of the Lords of Hosts... where we shall no longer be stranded from Him or from each other."[468]

The modern–day scholars of ancient wisdom have emphasized that this idea, so widespread among contemplatives, that the path to God is a lonely path and not a shared path, a path for two, contrasts sharply with the teachings of the ancient sages. Thus, Mario Satz insists on the necessity for the "participation of the other sex (or rather, the other self) for the correct attainment of enlightenment, or for the reabsorption into the indivisible One." "Every asceticism is temporary –he adds–. As the Song of Songs insinuates, only when the male truly dialogues with the female, is it possible to totalise and make effective the power contained in the Tree." The Tree, obviously, is the Tree of Life. Another

---

468. Jordan of Saxony, Letter 13, quoted by Colleen McDannell, Bernhard Lang, *Heaven: A History*, p. 97

example: Antoine Faivre, in a magnificent study on Western exotericism, writes, "the ascetics are often mistaken in their representation of the love of God, of the Creator, in contrast with the love between creatures... true religion expressly orders us to love creatures *in* the Creator, wherein... they find their unity and completion."[469] In this passage, Faivre is glossing the opinion of Franz von Baader, a German Romantic we mentioned a few pages back. Note, Blanca, that he references God, the Creature, as the place –a mystical place rather than a place in space– where creatures love each other, and where (precisely by loving each other, I add) they find their Unity and completion. It refers, then, to the place where the heavenly marriage occurs, both the real and the prefigured one. This place, my dear, is the "infinite place" where Ernesto Cardenal situated his amorous encounter with his heavenly spouse. It's the Kabbalists Hidden Point, also known in the *Zohar* as the "Seventh Palace", the Palace of Unity, in which Simeon bar Yochai –the protagonist of the *Zohar*– entered in the course of his last ecstatic vision. It happened like this:

The "Holy Lamp", as his disciples called Simeon bar Yochai, was imparting his teachings, shedding light on the mysteries of existence, when suddenly he went quiet, closed his eyes and lied there as if he were dead. The eager disciples waited, knowing that "his soul had left his body and was exploring the higher regions". After some time, he came to, his face showing the profound delights he experienced. "I know –he told them– that my face reflects delight, but the delight you see in it is only an infinitesimal reflection of the joy that came to me." And he began telling them what he

469. Antoine Faivre, *Access to Western Esotericism*, p. 235

saw... What he saw, Blanca, were the seventh Heavens with their corresponding "circles" (remember the cosmic mandala) or "palaces". He described these palaces one by one, until he got to the Seventh one, where God's throne is, and where -through the *unio mystica*- he was temporarily allowed to incorporate the inner dynamic of Divinity: the Two implicit in the One. "And I came to the Seventh Palace, which is the most hidden of all. It has neither form nor image, nor can it in any way be presented to the imagination... Here in the most mysterious recess is the Holy of Holies, towards which all souls are striving... In this palace are to be found all the joys, both the known ones and those that are beyond the imagination of man. Here takes place... the union of the male with the female"[470].

Real or prefigured, the heavenly marriage -the "mystic union" of the Two- is only possible here: in the Seventh Palace or Hidden Point, headquarters of the Unit, of Divinity, also known in the Kabbalah and other esoteric schools of thought as the Bridal Bed or Chamber, precisely because it is the only "place" where the heavenly matrimony can be consummated.

THE MAGIC MIRROR

The "mystic union", then, does not consist of the marriage of the soul *with* God, but *in* God... God is the "locale" where the heavenly marriage of the twin souls takes place, Blanca. But it's also the mysterious fruit of that marriage. Because -as we know- that is what Divinity is: the result of a wedding.

---

470. *Zohar*

And given that, in those nuptials, each human soul was originally one of the two spouses, in what other way could the soul experience God other than in marriage, other than erotically? Isn't it natural that, upon temporarily returning to its origin in God, the soul goes back to its original role and function: the role and function of *spouse*? Decidedly, my love, this role and function belongs to the souls; the twin souls; I very much doubt that God plays the role of a spouse. A spouse is the half of a *Syzygia*, the half of a couple, of a matrimony; and God is not the half of anything; God is in Himself a Whole, an entire being –that is precisely of what his divine nature consists, as we have seen. God is the *Syzygia*, the couple, the matrimony. He is the Androgyne, He is the being in whom Integrity is verified, the condition of the "two in one". He is not one of the Two, but the One, the result of the *perfect union* of the Two.

And if God is not the natural spouse of the soul, my dear, then neither is He the natural recipient of erotic love... Don't get me wrong: I'm not saying that we should not love God; I'm saying that we must love Him with the kind of love that corresponds Him. The human being has different amorous partners, and each one of those partners demands a specific kind of love. The love demanded by sons and daughters is different from the love demanded by parents; conjugal love is different from the love for one's neighbour; friendship is different from fraternal love... God also demands from the human being a specific kind of love. A kind of love that, in my humble opinion, is not *eros* –which has another partner, another recipient–, but a love we could call *adoration or worship–love*: a similar love to filial, except infinitely amplified.

As any specific kind of love, erotic love differs from all others. But, according to the ancient sages, it has a close similarity with another type of love: friendship. Like with friendship, parity is an absolute condition of erotic love. We have seen in another letter that, in order for an amorous union to exist (virtual or real, it's the same), the lovers must be on equal footing: only two symmetrical realities can come together in love. Now then, Blanca, it's obvious that God and the soul are not on the same level. And they cannot be levelled, like when the courtly maiden levelled with her knight –do you remember?– by getting off the imaginary pedestal he had put her on. God cannot come down from His pedestal, and neither can the soul climb on it. Not by itself: to do it, it must first heavenly marry its natural spouse, its twin.

> **Last crossed–out note on the margin of the manuscript. This note: *The proof, in the form of love letters, came from (the back of) a drawer of…*, dated from the 1–2–00, is the inspiration for the title of this collection of letters.**

"The soul's natural spouse" is the same as saying "the soul's natural *you*", its particular and specific *you*. This *you*, Blanca, is the soul's *other self*, say, a you in the second person. That is, a *self* in a sense foreign to me, a *self* outside of myself, as one's reflection in the mirror. Thus we come, my dear, to the metaphor of the mirror, which is one of the most used by the ancient sages to explain the intimate bond that joins twin souls, that joins the *self* and the *you* (and also each couple of twin souls and God). In this metaphor, love would be the mirror; the *self* and the *you*, its two faces, the one that is in front of the mirror, and the one behind in the mirror, the one that contemplates and the one that is contemplated. Except there is no discrepancy whatsoever here between both their natures, since this mirror is like a mirror from a fairy tale, Blanca: it's a magic mirror. A mirror in which –as Ibn Arabi beautifully observes– each face regards sees itself through the eyes of the other (except that, to return a reflection, the soul must be clean, free from the passions that tarnish it).

Now: the mirrored game of the *self* and the *you* is a game of reflections. The *you*, reflection of the *self*; the *self*, reflection of the *you*. Deep down, the *self* and *you* do not exist by themselves, my love: they are given their existence, their existence is reflected. They mutually reflect each other, but they are both the reflection of a higher reality. This higher reality, which is what exists by itself, is God, the One/All that, by contemplating Himself in this magic mirror (a superior mirror to the ones in fairy tales), grants the reflection its very existence: the *self* and the *you*. In the Universe's game of mirrors, only God exists by Himself. Only the Unit exists, everything else is His reflection. Everything else –Duality and Multiplicity, which go hand in hand– is behind the mirror; behind the mirror that reflects not the essential Unity of God, but His internal Duality and Multiplicity.

It follows, Blanca, that the Two only exist by themselves when they are united in *perfect union*: that is, *while they are One*. That is why I was telling you in another letter that we should not worry about the destiny of the Two, about their overlap in the One. If they sacrifice themselves for the sake of the One, that is because the Unity is their raison d'être, their intimate vocation. It's because in the Unit is where the Two find their plenitude and true existence. That which *is* not by itself, but is the reflection of something else, loves and aspires with all its strength to become that other thing, which is its *true identity*. Look, my friend Ariel taught me an old Jewish saying. At first, it sounds like a riddle: "*If I am I because you are you, and if you are you because I am I, then I am not I and you are not you.*" Although it could equally refer to the necessity that, to identify as such, the human being needs his peers, Ariel cited it to me in relation to the magic mirror of the twin souls: the peculiar reciprocal dependency between two faces, one reflecting the other, and both reflecting God. If by you being the other half of myself –it says–, I need you to be me, and if by me being your other half, you need me to be you, then the two of us are, in reality, a Third one above us: the two of us are the result of the *perfect union* of our two halves.

What does it matter, Blanca, if you and I disappear in that *perfect union*? If we disappear in the literal sense of the verb, if we cease to be apparent, if we become invisible. What does it matter if we become implicit in our Unity, if it turns out that this Unity is our true identity, what we really are... I just remembered an episode from your childhood (I almost remember your childhood, what you told me of your childhood, better than my own). Your father had given you some silkworms that you kept in a shoebox lined with glossy paper. You fed them leafs from the mulberry in your garden and watched them grow every day, until something unexpected happened. The silkworms, which you had named, spun a cocoon around themselves and disappeared from your sight. Your father did not want to spoil you the mystery: soon you would find out for yourself, he told you. And indeed, after a couple of weeks, the cocoons cracked and from them emerged butterflies! You were quite surprised. But if I'm not mistaken, it was not a sad surprise, you were not disappointed; rather, you were marvelled and happy for your silkworms. You were happy that, in some way you could not explain, they had managed to free themselves from the grey existence at ground level to which they appeared to be doomed. From the innocence of your youth, you intuited the truth... The truth, my love, is that the metamorphosis through which the butterflies come to be does not mean the silkworm's defeat. Since that it's in the winged nature of the butterfly that the silkworms become fully realised. Far from being something alien to the silkworm, the butterfly is its essential identity, its secret identity. And, therefore, its intimate vocation.

But let's go back to the game between the *self* and the *you* and why God is not –and cannot be, in my most modest opinion– the *you* of the soul. Let's replace the metaphor of the mirror with another classic metaphor for the Duality entailed by the Unit: the metaphor of the coin. Let's consider the unlikely assumption that the head of a coin was capable of erotic love. Don't you think that the natural recipient of that love would never be the whole coin, but rather its other side? Well then, in this metaphor, God is not the other side of the coin: He is the whole coin, the *perfect union* of the obverse and reverse. God is not, in relation to the *self*, the *you*, but the *He*: the third fruit of their *perfect union*. (Interestingly, Ibn Arabi had a vision of God in the form of the word *Hû*, "He", and God, in his most recondite intimacy, is sometimes referred to as "the He" in the Kabbalah.) God is not an obverse or a reverse, He is not a man or a woman; He is not a half –it would be a blasphemy to say so–, He is one whole being: He is the Androgyne, he is *He*... The *He*, that is also a *self*, the supreme *Self*, but a *self* that does not need the *you*, because he encompasses it. God is enough for Himself, He does not need to come together with another being to become whole. It's the human soul that the needs another one to be whole. And not just any other one, but its reverse side, that with whom it integrates the whole coin in the Origin. (The coin is unique: there are infinite obverses, infinite reverses, but only one single whole coin.)

...AND THE FLOWER WAS STILL IN HIS HAND

So, if we are consistent with our theory, the contemplatives were mistaken when they saw God as the natural recipient of erotic love, the *partenaire* of the soul, we could say. This confusion is understandable, though. For the same reason that we understood how the heroic lovers could confuse their beloved with God. Both tendencies are symmetrical: in this case, the Whole is mistaken for the part, in the other it's the part that is mistaken for the Whole. At this last stage of the journey to the centre of love, it's not easy to make distinctions such as what Christ proposed: "Render unto Caesar the things that are Caesar's, render unto God the things that are God's". It's not easy to draw the line between the love that is God's and the love that is the twin soul's. We can find clear exponents of this difficulty in the work of many poets. Here you have, without going any further, that great poet of the Baroque of whom I have already given full reference in these letters: John Donne, a poet that certainly deserved a prominent spot in your blue library. Donne –I think I may already have said this here– started as a libertine in matters of love. It was partly that bad reputation that motivated Anne More's father to reject him as a son–in–law. This flippant and cynical attitude towards love, can be observed in the first poems of his famous *Songs and Sonnets*. But look the scholiasts can discern in the life of Donne the same before-and-after they discern in his life: before and after his encounter with Anne More. It's in this second period, with a gradually increasing force, that a transcendent idea of love emerges from his work. And also when the poet begins his religious output, his *Holy Sonnets* more notably, in which he turns to God and, without ever renouncing love (for we can see the figure of Anne More as the golden thread that runs through these poems), rejects his libertine past.

You know, Blanca, when I read John Donne, especially his *Songs and Sonnets* (poems such as "Lovers' Infiniteness", "The Good-Morrow", "The Ecstasy"), for a few moments I get the impression that he and his wife are those lovers from Plato's *Symposium* who spend their entire lives together in mutual company, and who would not hesitate, if given the chance, to merge and become two beings in one. Donne proclaims this longing, omnipresent in the book, through different metaphors. Thus, in "The Canonization", he compares himself and his beloved –in a distinctly alchemical image– to the Phoenix, destined to reemerge from its ashes: "The phoenix riddle hath more wit / By us; we two being one, are it; / So, to one neutral thing both sexes fit. / We die and rise the same, and prove / Mysterious by this love." The one neutral thing both sexes fit after the final reunification in Paradise, is none other than Unity in God, which is neutral, for it belongs to a third gender, the androgynous gender, which is both male and female at the same time; meaning it's neither male nor female, since those are the genders of split Duality.

Anyway, Blanca, with John Donne, with my favourite poet, we are almost reaching the end of this letter. And with it, the end of this strange correspondence. Strange... because I had no need to send it for you to receive it –at least, that has always been my impression. Regarding these letters, I can only say that, if they were to fall on hands other than yours –your now ethereal hands–, they would attract, apart from other justifiable reproaches, accusations of naivety. The visions of the "reverse side" of existence always raise that kind of criticism. They are labelled as wishful thinking and compared to dreams, where wishes pretend to come true. "One is free to dream, if it makes one happy –state those who do not believe in the 'reverse side'–. But sooner or later, they will wake up, and then their disappointment will be great"... Maybe we are dreaming, my dear, my dear, yes. But who can say with absolute certainty that, when we wake up, it won't happen the same thing that happened to the Romantic character who, in a dream, received a flower as a gift from Heaven... and when he woke up, the flower was still in his hand.

Anyway, Blanca: I have presented you with a theory. I'm well aware this theory cannot be proved true or false: it's a conjecture. But, at the end of the day, aren't philosophical systems conjectures too? Or the theological foundations of religions? When faced with the great questions about existence, there are no right answers for the human being. No matter how much intuition assists us (the *Imaginatio vera*, as the alchemists said: the "true Imagination", the one that does not invent, it discovers), when we are talking about the ultimate realities, we are not on steady ground: we are moving over quicksand, we are entering the fragile territory of conjectures. But won't this dearth of certainties set us back? Won't it makes us refuse to personally look behind the tapestry, or to take an interest in what others have seen (or believe to have seen) on the other side? Absolutely not. It's in the nature of the human being to conjecture about the meaning of his or her existence. And what's most important, Blanca:

to have faith in that conjecture, to make it *his* or *her* truth; because –as the great Danish philosopher Soren Kierkegaard pointed out– ultimately, the essential questions of existence must be approached through faith... You will have noticed, my dear, that this conjecture of mine places you and me, the twin souls, at the very centre of the complex web of the Universe. To be honest, that conclusion overwhelms me, it's too much for me. My intention when I started investigating the ancient wisdom was much more modest. What I was searching for –and what I discovered, thank God– was a glimpse of hope that someday I would see you again; nothing more –and nothing less– than that. Everything else came as an extra, following that aspiration. But don't novelists say that sometimes that is what happens with their novels as well? That they get out of hand and go way beyond their initial projects, taking paths that surprise even them?

If we think about it, in my case, there is nothing strange about it, my love, because my conjecture (and that's where it gets its worth) is not really mine. In the sense that it's supported by other conjectures devised throughout the centuries by wise people (which certainly I am not). People who made an effort to look at the "reverse side of the tapestry" of existence.... It's on those eminent conjectures, then, that our hopes are hanging, Blanca –I believe I can speak for you too. A hope that is no different from John Donne and his wife's, or from the Platonic lovers': you and I too wish, above all, to become two beings in one... Ah, but meanwhile? Meanwhile, this hope should not become unbearable. Not even now, when we are physically apart. Because our separation does not go beyond that, it's only physical. In a mysterious way, you remain here by my side. Isn't that how you had access to these letters? We have seen that that the ancient sages insisted on this paradox: closeness in distance, presence in absence due to a secret harmony, a virtual union. Of course, such union is only viable between true lovers, between lovers whose love is pure and naked. But hasn't ours been like that for a long time? Even long before your departure? When it's not based on material criteria, love keeps lovers together even in the distance. John Donne knew that; that is why, before leaving on a long journey, he wrote Anne a heartfelt poem to comfort her, in which he claimed what many sages before him had already observed: true love is absence-proof. I quote it from memory:

Dull sublunary lovers' love
    —Whose soul is sense—cannot admit
Of absence, 'cause it doth remove
    The thing which elemented it.

But we by a love so much refined,
    That ourselves know not what it is,
Inter-assurèd of the mind,
    Care less, eyes, lips and hands to miss.

Our two souls therefore, which are one,
    Though I must go, endure not yet
A breach, but an expansion,
    Like gold to aery thinness beat.

If they be two, they are two so
    As stiff twin compasses are two ;
Thy soul, the fix'd foot, makes no show
    To move, but doth, if th' other do.

And though it in the centre sit,
Yet, when the other far doth roam,
It leans, and hearkens after it,
And grows erect, as that comes home.

Such wilt thou be to me, who must,
Like th' other foot, obliquely run ;
Thy firmness makes my circle just,
And makes me end where I begun.[471]

Perhaps in the sewing workshop where you worked when you were young, you used a wooden compass, one of those with a chalk tip tailors use to mark their patterns. Well, look: the compass was also widely used by the ancient sages. Except it was a metaphorical compass. They used it to evoke the heavenly marriage or the Androgyne, although Donne uses it here somewhat differently: his compass evokes the spiritual marriage that binds him to Anne. You and I are –he says– like the two arms of the compass; we are inextricably connected; so, regardless of how far apart we may be, we are still together, we are still united by the same vertex. The compass' vertex represents God, same as the complete circle drawn by its two arms together. This circle, my love, is what every heroic lover throughout time has aspired to draw. And they know they cannot do it by themselves. It requires the collaboration of the other arm of the compass, of the other intimate referent of the soul. The collaboration of *their twin*.

Always yours

471. John Donne, A Valediction Forbiding Mourning, *Songs and Sonnets*

EPILOGUE

In the *Announcement* at the head of this correspondence, I alluded to a final and mysterious journey on which the author would have embarked, and I did not mean his death soon after. Maybe the reader searched in vain for the testimony of this trip in the letters. If that is the case, I owe you an apology. I should have warned you: such testimony cannot be found in the letters. It all starts with a leaflet written in French that I found lost in the middle of one of the volumes that belonged to the author, where I had also found his manuscript. Printed around February of the year 2000 in a small Swiss town, it was a simple programme of events. They were the rather lean events that commemorated the tercentenary of the birth of a man of letters of local fame. Like with the crossed-out notes on the margin, I did not pay much attention to it at first. It was not until recently, when I started investigating it, that I realised said ephemeris remitted precisely to the eighteenth century, a recurring century in the redacted notes. That is also when I noticed that the name of the honouree coincided with a name mentioned in one of the letters. Intrigued by these coincidences, I took a few days off from work and travelled to an Alpine Swiss canton (a recurring place in the notes), where I gathered information about Zacharie Abecassis, a school teacher, cultural organiser and enlightened writer of Jewish ancestry (author of a short treatise with a Kabbalistic touch: *Du Plaisir dans la contemplation des nuages*, "On the pleasure of contemplating clouds"), whose dim memory those tributes ten years ago apparently were not able to rekindle. Thanks to the kindness of the current owner, I managed to visit the house where "maître Abecassis" had lived together with his wife and their son. I did not know what I was looking for until, as I was saying goodbye, she suggested in French: "Perhaps you would like to see his books too". And she said she remembered a fellow countryman of mine that also visited the house, years ago, and had been very interested in seeing them.

The reader can imagine the jolt I felt when I heard those words! Immediately, I subjected her to a barrage of questions. She could not tell me the man's name, but she did vaguely describe him to me. As for the books, the good woman was referring to the library of Master Abecassis: a valuable collection with over one hundred tomes collected by him and his wife Sara throughout forty years of happy marriage and shared passion for Literature. The library was not at the house. The deceased David Abecassis, the last descendant of Zacharie and Sara, had sold it to a bibliophile in Bern halfway through the last century. I took the first train to this city and showed up at the bibliophile's house, as the author of this manuscript must have done, although with the passing of the years, my elderly host did not remember him. After a few minutes of friendly conversation, he led me to a small office with the walls lined with books. It was the personal library of the Abecassis couple, composed mostly of novels from the seventeenth and eighteenth centuries, as well as poetry collections, some of them even older, as I could see during the course of that afternoon. There was also a selection of Hebrew writings. But what shook me the most when I walked in, what made me feel the ineffable breath of mystery (as I am sure the author of these letters felt), was not the content of those centenarian books, but what enclosed them. The fact that they were all neatly bound in hardcovers of different shades of blue.

Xavier Pérez i Pons
Puigcerdá, August 9th, 2011

TABLE OF ILLUSTRATIONS

Cover: Edward Burne-Jones, *With the Wind* (Paolo and Francesca Dante's vision), *The Flower Book*, around 1885

Cover of the first letter: Bartolo di Fredi, *The creation of Eve*, fourteenth century

Cover of the second letter: Illustration of the Michael Cochem manuscript, around 1530, (Vadiana de San Gallen Library)

Cover of the third letter: *Androgynous Shiva*, nineteenth century (Ajit Mookerjee Collection)

Cover of the fourth letter: *Humana Origo et Finis* ("Origin and End of the human being"), Barthélemy Aneau, *Picta Poesis ut Pictura Poesis Erit*, Lyon, 1552 (British Library, London)

Cover of the fifth letter: *Hermes and Aphrodite*, Michael Maier, *Atalanta fugiens*, 1617

Cover of the sixth letter: *Androgyne with Goats' Heads*, Codex germanicus Monacensis, Germany, 15th century (Bayerisches Staatsbibliothek, Monaco)

Cover of the seventh letter: Illustration of the manuscript of Salomon Trismosin *Splendor solis*, Germany, sixteenth century

Cover of the eighth letter: Miniature from the thirteenth century (Archive Album)

Cover of the ninth letter: *Siamese Hermaphrodite Twins*, Caspar Bauhin, *De Hermaphroditum monstrosorumque*, 1600 (British Library, London)

Cover of the tenth letter: *Matrimonii Typus* ("Symbol of Matrimony"), Barthélemy Aneau, *Picta Poesis ut Pictura Poesis Erit*, Lyon, 1552 (British Library, London)

Printed in Great Britain
by Amazon

28373071R00418